हिंदू राजतरंगिणी

ENGLISH EDITION

Prof. Ratnakar Narale

PUSTAK BHARATI
TORONTO, CANADA

Author : Dr. Ratnakar Narale, Ph.D (IIT), Ph.D. (Kalidas Sanskrit Univ.)
Prof. Hindi, Ryerson University, Toronto
email : books.india.books@gmail.com

Title : Hindu RajTarangini, English Edition

Since last thousand years before the Indian Independence and about 70 years after the Independence, history of Divine Hindu Culture and its wonderful History has been suppressed, hideden, falsified, tainted, ignored, misrepresented, misinterpreted, discredited, disgraced and kept unpublished as well as away from the eyes and minds of the school and college students. However, now the time has come to stand up and write our own History and Culrute ourselves as it is as a sacred duty and to educate our boys and girls in the schools and colleges. It is hoped that the storehouse of knowledge in this book will enrich our children and adults alike and inspire the research scholars to take it further.

Published by :
Pustak Bharati, Toronto Canada
books.india.books@gmail.com

Web : www.books-india.com
email : books.india.books@gmail.com

For :
Books India, Toronto, Canada

ISBN 978-1-989416-21-1

Copyright ©2021
ISBN 978-1-989416-21-1

© All rights reserved. No part of this book may be copied, reproduced or utilised in any manner or by any means, computerised, e-mail, scanning, photocopying or by recording in any information storage and retrieval system, without the permission in writing from the author.

INDIA AT THE CENTER OF THE EARTH

वामे च दक्षिणे यस्या रत्नाकरोऽस्ति पादयो: ।
हिमाद्रिर्मुकुटो शुभ्रो वन्दे भारतमातरम् ॥
शरणोऽस्मि गिरे तुभ्यं नतशीर्ष: कृताञ्जलि: ।
त्वत्त: प्राप्तुं दिशं मार्गं रत्नाकर: पदे पदे ॥

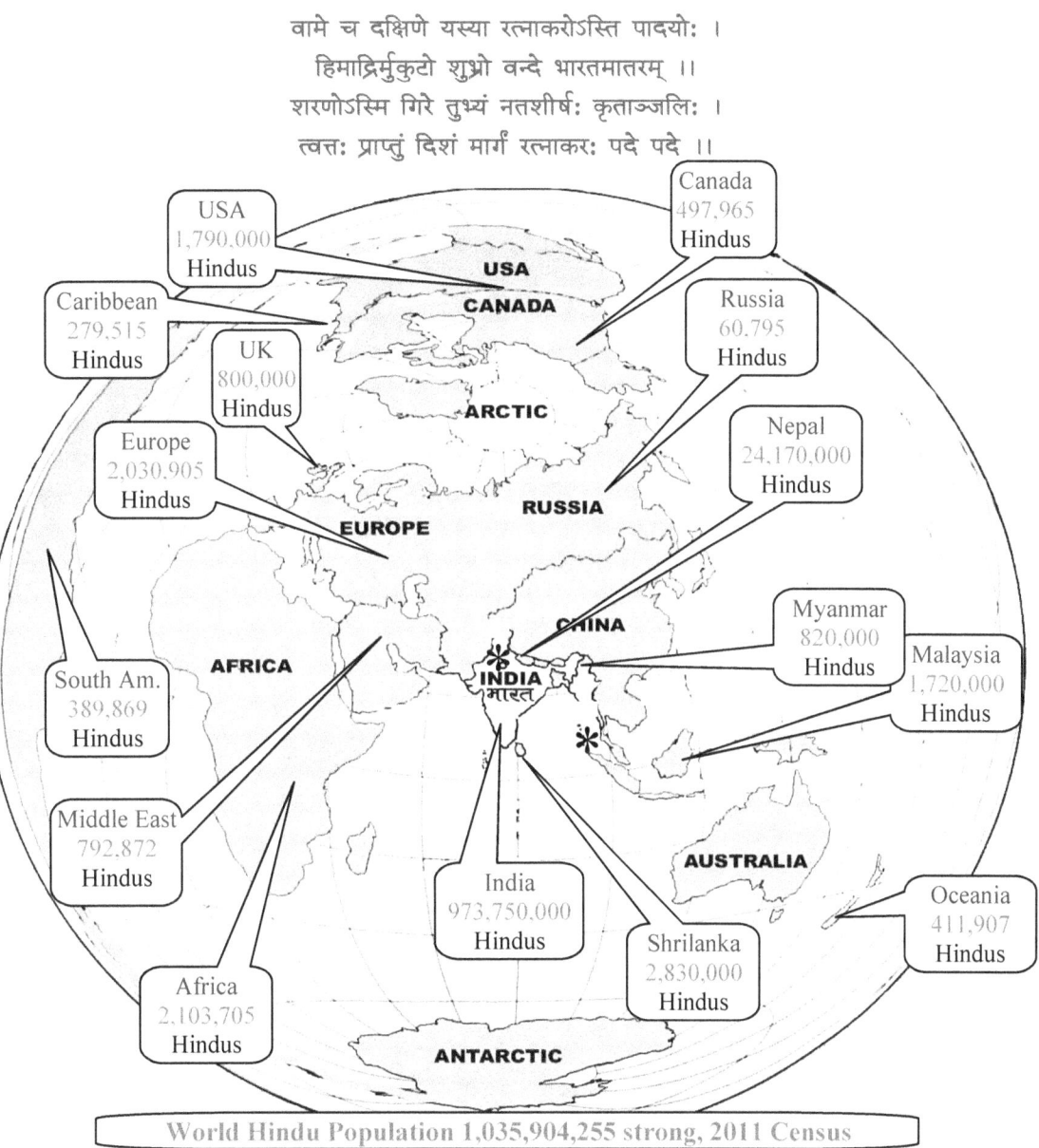

World Hindu Population 1,035,904,255 strong, 2011 Census

On the left and the right side, As well as at your feet,
There is an ocean and the Himalaya is your crown,
I pray to you at every step, With my folded hands,
I bow my head humbly at your feet, O Mother India!

Alphabetical Index of the Hindu Dynasties

Dynasty Number	
1.	Atri Dynasty (**Ancient** Time)
2.	Ahom Dynasty, Kamarup, Asaam (355-1826)
3.	Ajamidh Dynasty (**Ancient** Time)
4.	Angre Dynasty, Kulaba, Maharashtra (1680-1844)
5.	Avanti Bai, Queen of Ramgadh (1831-1858)
6.	Bana Dynasty, Vanapuram (720-900)
7.	Bharat Dynasty (**Ancient**)
8.	Bhati Raval Dynasty, Jaisalmer, Rajastan (731-1948)
9.	Bhosle Dynasty, Satara (1594-1848)
10.	Bhosle Dynasty, Kolhapur (1689-1940)
11.	Bhosle Dynasty, Tanjavar (1675-1855)
12.	Bhosle Dynasty, Nagpur (1675-1855)
13.	BHUTAN, Wangchuk Dynasty (1907-1948)
14.	SIKKIM, Namgyal Dynasty, Gangtok (1642-1948)
15.	Brihadrith Dynasty, Magadh (**Ancient** Time)
16.	BURMA (Mynmar), Hindu Dynasties (50-1828)
17.	Chach Dynasty, Alor, Sindh (631-712)
18.	Chalukya Dynasty (West), Badami (525-753)
19.	Chalukya Dynasty (West), Kalyani (696-1189)
20.	Chalukya Dynasty, Lat, Gujrat (590-750)
21.	Chalukya Dynasty, Kathiawad, Saurashtra (750-900)
22.	Chalukya (East) Dynasty, Vengi (440-1070)
23.	Chandela Dynasty, Bundelkhand (830-1289)
24.	Channamma Queen, Kittur (1778-1829)
25.	Chapotkat Dynasty, Gujrat (690-942)
26.	Chauhan Dynasty, Sakambhari (684-1194)
27.	Chaunah Dynasty, Nadol (950-1200)
28.	Chauhan Dynasty, Ranthambhot (1194-1301)
29.	Chauhan Dynasty, Jalor (1182-1311)
30.	Chauhan Dynasty, Sirohi (1311-1527)
31.	Chauhan Dynasty, Hadauti (1382-1631)
32.	Chauhan Dynasty, Bundi, (1343-1948)
33.	Chauhans Dynasty Kota, (1631-1948)
34.	Cher Purumal Dynasty, Kerala (800-1102)
35.	Chindak Nag Dynasty, Bastar (760-1324)

36. Chola Dynasty, Tanjavar (50-1279)
37. Chudasama Dynasty, Junagadh (875-1505)
38. Dogra Dynasty, Jammu- Kashmir- Laddakh- Gilgit- Baltistan (1812-1947)
39. Gaikwad Dynasty, Baroda, Gujrat (1720-1951)
40. Gajapati Dynasty, Kalinga (1434-1541)
41. Ganga Dynasty (East), Kalinga (700-1264)
42. Ganga Dynasty (west, Talkad (350-1024)
43. Gandhar Dynasty (Ancient Time)
44. Gonaditya Dynasty, Kashmir (1182 BC-631 AD)
45. Gond Dynasty (Ancient Time)
46. Gond Dynasty of Vidarbha **(1200-1550)**
47. Guhil Dynasty, Mewad (550-1303)
48. Gupta Dynasty, Patliputra (240-730)
49. Gurjar Dynasty, Rajastan (400-725)
50. Gutta Dynasty, Karnatak (1080-1262)
51. Haryak Dynasty, Patliputra (544-413 BC)
53. Hindu Shahi Dynasty, Kabul-Gandhar (867-1026)
54. Holkar Dynasty, Indore (1730-1948)
55. Hoysal Dynasty, Halebid (1026-1348)
56. Ikshavaku Dynastu (Ancient Time)
57. Shailendra Dynasty, Java (674-947)
58. Simha Shri Dynasty, Java (1222-1478)
59. SUMATRA, Shri Vijaya Dynasty, (683-1405)
60. Jadeja Dynasty, Saurashtra (1203-1948)
61. Kachhavaha Dynasty, Rajastan (1036-1948)
62. Kadamb Dynasty, Karnatak (340-610)
63. Kanva Dynasty, Patliputra (72-27 BC)
64. Kakatiya Dynasty, Warangal (1000-1323)
65. Kalchuri Dynasty, Mahismati (550-620) :
66. Kalchuri Dynasty, Tripuri (675-1210) :
67. Kalchuri Dynasty, Ratnapuri (1000-1745) :
68. Kalchuri Dynasty, Kalyani (1156-1184) :
69. Karkota Dynasty, Kashmir (631-855)
70. Kaurava Dynasty (Ancient Time)
71. Kshatrap Dynasty, Girnar, Ujjain, Nasik (78-395)
72. Kukkur Dynasty (Ancient Time)
73. Kuru Dynasty (Ancient Time)
74. Kushan Dynasty, Purushapur-Mathura (30-244)
75. Lohar Dynasty, Kashmir (1003-1172)
76. Madra Dynasty (Ancient Time)

77. Maitrak Dynasty, Saurashtra **(480-767)**
78. Majapihit Dynasty, Malaya **(1299-1391)**
79. Manikya Dynasty, AgartaLa. Tripura **(1400-1948)**
80. Maukhari Dynasty, Kannauj **(540-725)**
81. Maurya Dynasty, Patliputra **(322-184 BC)**
82. Meera Bai, Queen **(1498-1573)**
83. Nag Dynasty, Jharkhand **(83-1948)**
84. Nal Dynasty, Chhattisgadh **(290-960)**
85. Nand Dynasty, Patliputra **(344-322 BC)**
86. Narayan Dynasty, Kashi-Varanasi **(1737-1948)**
87. Nayak, Sangam Dynasty **(1336-1485)** :
88. Nayak, Saluv Dynasty **(1485-1503)** :
89. Nayak, Tuluv Dynasty **(1503-1565)** :
90. Nayak, Aravidu Dynasty **(1565-1649)** :
91. Nayak, Musunuri Dynasty **(1325-1368)** :
92. Nayak, Pemmasani Dynasty **(1423-1685)** :
93. Nayak, Jinji Dynasty **(1491-1649)** :
94. Nayak, Keladi Dynasty **(1499-1763)** :
95. Nayak, Madura Dynasty **(1509-1736)** :
96. Nayak, Vellor Dynasty **(1526-1595)** :
97. Nayak, Tanjavar Dynasty **(1532-1673)** :
98. Nayak, Penukonda Dynasty **(1565-1616)** :
99. Nayak, Chennai Dynasty **(1572-)** :
100. Nayak, Chitradurg Dynasty **(1588-1779)** :
101. Nayak, Kendy Dynasty **(1739-1815)** :
102. Nayak, Kondavidu Reddi Dynasty**(1325-1448)** :
103. Nayak, Haleri Dynasty, Coorg **(1633-1834)** :
104. NEPAL, Gopal Ahir Dynasty **(Ancient Time)**
105. NEPAL, Kirat Dynasty **(900 BC-205 AD)**
106. NEPAL, Som Dynasty **(205-305)**
107. NEPAL, Lichchhavi Dynasty **(305-605)**
108. NEPAL, Anshuvarma Dynasty **(605-879)**
109. NEPAL, Raghav Dynasty **(879-1046)**
110. NEPAL, Thakur Dynasty **(1046-1200)**
111. NEPAL, Malla Dynasty **(1200-1768)**
112. NEPAL, Shah Gurkha Dynasty **(1768-1948)**
113. Nevalkar Dynasty, Jhansi **(1838-1858)**
114. Nimi Janak Dynasty **(Ancient Time)**
115. Pal Dynasty, Mudagiri, Bengal **(750-1174)**
116. Pallava Dynasty, Kanchipuram **(315-897)**

117. Pandava Dynasty (Ancient Time)
118. Pandya Dynasty, Madura (50-1422)
119. Parivrajak Dynasty, Bagelkhand (400-528)
120. Parmar Dynasty, Dhar, Malwa (800-1305)
121. Peshva Dynasty, Maharashtra (1713-1818)
122. PHILLIPINE, Hindu Dynasties (50-1828)
123. Pradyot Dynasty, Ujjain (546-413 BC)
124. Pratapaditya Dynasty, Kashmir (167 BC-25 AD)
125. Pravargupta Dynasty, Kashmir (949-1003)
126. Pratihar-Gurjar Dynasty, Kannauj (725-1036)
127. Pudukottai Dynasty, Tamil Nadu (1673-1948)
128. Pulastya Dynasty, Shri Lanka (Ancient Time)
129. Puru Dynasty (Ancient Time)
130. Pushyabhuti-Vardhan Dynasty, Patliputra (505-647)
131. Raghu Dynasty (Ancient Time)
132. Rai Dynasty, Alor, Sindh (489-631)
133. Rashtrakut Dynasty, Malkhed (620-973)
134. Rashtrakut Dynasty, Malkhed (806-888)
135. Rathor Dynasty, Jodhpur (1250-1948)
136. Rathor Dynasty, Bikaner (1465-1948)
137. Rathor Dynasty, Kishangadh (1609-1948)
138. Ratta Dynasty, Belgaon, Karnatak (850-1240)
139. Ror Dynasty, Roruk-Sakkar (Ancient Time)
140. Saindhav Dynasty, Saurashtra (734-920)
141. Satvahan Dynasty (271 BC-195 AD)
142. Sauvir Dynasty, Sindh (Ancient Time)
143. Sen Dynasty, Nadiya, Bengal (1074-1230)
144. Shashank Dynasty, Gaur, Bengal (600-625)
145. Shakya Gautam Dynasty (Ancient Time)
146. Shalasthambha Dynasty, Kamrup, Assam (665-990)
147. Shilahar Dynasty, North Knokan (800-1265)
148. Shilahar Dynasty, South Knokan (765-1024)
149. Shilahar, Kolhapur (940-1212)
150. Shishunag Dynasty, Patliputra (413-344 BC)
151. Simha Dynasty, Imphal, Manipur (1821-1948)
152. SHRI LANKA, Pandya Rule (429-455)
153. SHRI LANKA, Chola Rule (1029-1055)
154. SHRI LANKA, Kendy Nayak Rule (1739-1815)
155. SHRI LANKA, Arya Chakravarti Dynasty (1262-1619)
156. Sikh Dynasty, Punjab (1799-1849)

157. Sindhia Dynasty, Gwalior **(1716-1948)**
158. Sindhu Dynasty **(Ancient** Time)
159. Sisodiya Dynasty, Chittor, Mewad **(1303-1948)**
160. Shunga Dynasty, Vidisha **(185-72 BC)**
161. Shurasen Dynasty, Mathura **(Ancient** Time)
162. Simha Dynasty, Bharatpur, Rajastan **(1722-1948)**
163. Solanki Dynasty, Patan, Gujrat **(942-1244)**
164. Sutiya Dynasty, Sadiya, Assam **(1187-1524)**
165. THAILAND, Funan Dynasty, Vyadhpur **(50-627)**
166. THAILAND, Indraditya Dynasty, Sukhdai **(1238-1438)**
167. THAILAND, Ram Dynasty, Ayodhya **(Ayuthia) (1351-1782)**
168. THAILAND, Ram Dynasty, Bangkok **(1782-1948)**
169. VIETNAM, Shrimar Dynasty, Champa **(192-645)**
170. VIETNAM, Bhava varma Dynasty, Chenla **(550-788)**
171. CAMBODIA, Varma Dynasty, Yashodapur **(802-1353)**
172. LAOS, Lain Zang Dynasty, Vyadhpur **(1353-1706)**
173. Tomar Dynasty, Delhi **(736-1192)**, Gwaloir **(1375-1523)**
174. Tomar Dynasty of Gwalior
175. Traikutak Dynasty, Junnar, Maharashtra **(388-492)**
176. Uchchhakalpa Dynasty, Baghelkhand **(400-533)**
177. Utpal Dynasty, Kashmir **(855-949)**
178. Wadiyar Dynasty, Mysore **(1399-1947)**
179. Waghela Dynasty, Anhilwad Gujrat **(1243-1304)**
180. Waghela Dynasty, Riwa, Bagelkhand **(1648-1948)**
181. Vakatak Dynasty, Nandivardhan, Vidarbha **(250-510)**
182. Varma Kulashekhar Dynasty, Venad Kerla **(1102-1729)**
183. Varma Dynasty, Kochin, Kerla **(1500-1947)**
184. Varma Dynasty, Travankor, kerla **(1729-1948)**
185. Varma Dynasty, Kamrup, Assam **(350-650)**
186. Velu Nachchiyar, Queen of Ramand **(1730-1790)**
187. Vivasvan Dynasty **(Ancient** Time)
188. Vrishni Dynasty **(Ancient** Time)
189. Vuppadeva Dynasty, Kashmir **(1172-1301)**
190. Yadav Dynasty, Devgiri **(850-1311)**
191. Yadu Dynasty **(Ancient** Time)
192. Yayati Dynasty **(Ancient** Time)
193. Yudhishthir Dynasty **(Ancient** Time)

Chronological Index of the Hindu Dynasties

Period of Rule	Dynasty Name	Dynasty Number
Ancient Time	Bharat Dynasty	7.
Ancient Time	Atri Dynasty	1.
Ancient Time	Ajamidh Dynasty	3.
Ancient Time	Brihadrith Dynasty, Magadh	15.
Ancient Time	Gandhar Dynasty	43.
Ancient Time	Gond Dynasty	45.
Ancient Time	Ikshavaku Dynastu	56.
Ancient Time	Kaurava Dynasty	70.
Ancient Time	Kukkur Dynasty	72.
Ancient Time	Kuru Dynasty	73.
Ancient Time	Madra Dynasty	76.
Ancient Time	NEPAL, Gopal Ahir Dynasty	104.
Ancient Time	Nimi Janak Dynasty	114.
Ancient Time	Pandava Dynasty	117.
Ancient Time	Pulastya Dynasty, Shri Lanka	128.
Ancient Time	Puru Dynasty	129.
Ancient Time	Raghu Dynasty	131.
Ancient Time	Ror Dynasty, Roruk - Sakkar	139.
Ancient Time	Sauvir Dynasty, Sindh	142.
Ancient Time	Shakya Gautam Dynasty	145.
Ancient Time	Sindhu Dynasty	158.
Ancient Time	Shurasen Dynasty, Mathura	161.
Ancient Time	Vivasvan Dynasty	187.
Ancient Time	Vrishni Dynasty	188.
Ancient Time	Yadu Dynasty	191.
Ancient Time	Yayati Dynasty	192.
Ancient Time	Yudhishthir Dynasty	193.
1182 BC - 631 AD	Gonaditya Dynasty, Kashmir	44.
900 BC - 205 AD	NEPAL, Kirat Dynasty	105.
546 BC - 413 BC	Pradyot Dynasty, Ujjain	123.
544 BC - 413 BC	Haryak Dynasty, Patliputra	51.
413 BC - 344 BC	Shishunag Dynasty, Patliputra	150.
344 BC - 322 BC	Nand Dynasty, Patliputra	85.
322 BC - 184 BC	Maurya Dynasty, Patliputra	81.
271 BC - 195 AD	Satvahan Dynasty	141.
185 BC - 72 BC	Shunga Dynasty, Vidisha	160.
72 BC - 27 BC	Kanva Dynasty, Patliputra	63.
30 BC - 244 AD	Kushan Dynasty, Purushapur - Mathura	74.

50 - 627	THAILAND, Funan Dynasty, Vyadhpur	165.
50 - 1279	Chola Dynasty, Tanjavar	36.
50 - 1422	Pandya Dynasty, Madura	118.
50 - 1828	BURMA Mynmar, Hindu Dynasties	16.
50 - 1828	PHILLIPINE, Hindu Dynasties	122.
78 - 395	Kshatrap Dynasty, Girnar, Ujjain, Nasik	71.
83 - 1948	Nag Dynasty, Jharkhand	83.
290 - 960	Nal Dynasty, Chhattisgadh	84.
305 - 605	NEPAL, Lichchhavi Dynasty	107.
315 - 897	Pallava Dynasty, Kanchipuram	116.
340 - 610	Kadamb Dynasty, Karnatak	62.
350 - 1024	Ganga Dynasty west, Talkad	42.
350 - 650	Varma Dynasty, Kamrup, Assam	185.
355 - 1826	Ahom Dynasty, Kamarup, Asaam	2.
388 - 492	Traikutak Dynasty, Junnar, Maharashtra	175.
400 - 528	Parivrajak Dynasty, Bagelkhand	119.
400 - 533	Uchchhakalpa Dynasty, Baghelkhand	176.
400 - 725	Gurjar Dynasty, Rajastan	49.
429 - 455	SHRI LANKA, Pandya Rule	152.
440 - 1070	Chalukya East Dynasty, Vengi	22.
480 - 767	Maitrak Dynasty, Saurashtra	77.
489 - 631	Rai Dynasty, Alor, Sindh	132.
505 - 647	Pushyabhuti - Vardhan Dynasty, Patliputra	130.
525 - 753	Chalukya Dynasty West, Badami	18.
540 - 725	Maukhari Dynasty, Kannauj	80.
550 - 1303	Guhil Dynasty, Mewad	47.
550 - 620	Kalchuris of Mahismati	65.
550 - 788	VIETNAM, Bhava varma Dynasty, Chenla	170.
590 - 750	Chalukya Dynasty, Lat, Gujrat	20.
600 - 625	Shashank Dynasty, Gaur, Bengal	144.
605 - 879	NEPAL, Anshuvarma Dynasty	108.
620 - 973	Rashtrakut Dynasty, Malkhed	133.
631 - 712	Chach Dynasty, Alor, Sindh	17.
631 - 855	Karkota Dynasty, Kashmir	69.
665 - 990	Shalasthambha Dynasty, Kamrup, Assam	146.
674 - 947	Shailendra Dynasty, Java	57.
675 - 1210	Kalchuris of Tripuri	66.
683 - 1405	SUMATRA, Shri Vijaya Dynasty,	59.
684 - 1194	Chauhan Dynasty, Sakambhari	26.
690 - 942	Chapotkat Dynasty, Gujrat	25.
696 - 1189	Chalukya Dynasty West, Kalyani	19.
700 - 1264	Ganga Dynasty East, Kalinga	41.
720 - 900	Bana Dynasty, Vanapuram	6.
725 - 1036	Pratihar - Gurjar Dynasty, Kannauj	126.

731 - 1948	Bhati Raval Dynasty, Jaisalmer, Rajastan	8.
734 - 920	Saindhav Dynasty, Saurashtra	140.
736 - 1192	Tomar Dynasty, Delhi	173.
750 - 1174	Pal Dynasty, Mudagiri, Bengal	115.
750 - 900	Chalukya Dynasty, Kathiawad, Saurashtra	21.
760 - 1324	Chindak Nag Dynasty, Bastar	35.
765 - 1024	Shilahar Dynasty, South Knokan	148.
800 - 1102	Cher Purumal Dynasty, Kerala	34.
800 - 1265	Shilahar Dynasty, North Knokan	147.
800 - 1305	Parmar Dynasty, Dhar, Malwa	120.
802 - 1353	CAMBODIA, Varma Dynasty, Yashodapur	171.
806 - 888	Rashtrakut Dynasty, Malkhed	134.
830 - 1289	Chandela Dynasty, Bundelkhand	23.
850 - 1240	Ratta Dynasty, Belgaon, Karnatak	138.
850 - 1311	Yadav Dynasty, Devgiri	190.
855 - 949	Utpal Dynasty, Kashmir	177.
867 - 1026	Hindu Shahi Dynasty, Kabul - Gandhar	53.
875 - 1505	Chudasama Dynasty, Junagadh	37.
879 - 1046	NEPAL, Raghav Dynasty	109.
940 - 1212	Shilahar, Kolhapur	149.
942 - 1244	Solanki Dynasty, Patan, Gujrat	163.
949 - 1003	Pravargupta Dynasty, Kashmir	125.
950 - 1200	Chaunah Dynasty, Nadol	27.
1000 - 1323	Kakatiya Dynasty, Warangal	64.
1000 - 1745	Kalchuris of Ratnapuri	67.
1003 - 1172	Lohar Dynasty, Kashmir	75.
1026 - 1348	Hoysal Dynasty, Halebid	55.
1029 - 1055	SHRI LANKA, Chola Rule	153.
1036 - 1948	Kachhavaha Dynasty, Rajastan	61.
1046 - 1200	NEPAL, Thakur Dynasty	110.
1074 - 1230	Sen Dynasty, Nadiya, Bengal	143.
1080 - 1262	Gutta Dynasty, Karnatak	50.
1102 - 1729	Varma Kulashekhar Dynasty, Venad Kerla	182.
1156 - 1184	Kalchuris of Kalyani	68.
1172 - 1301	Vuppadeva Dynasty, Kashmir	189.
1182 - 1311	Chauhan Dynasty, Jalor	29.
1187 - 1524	Sutiya Dynasty, Sadiya, Assam	164.
1194 - 1301	Chauhan Dynasty, Ranthambhot	28.
1200 - 1550	Gond Dynasty of Vidarbha	46.
1200 - 1768	NEPAL, Malla Dynasty	111.
1203 - 1948	Jadeja Dynasty, Saurashtra	60.
1222 - 1478	Simha Shri Dynasty, Java	58.
1238 - 1438	THAILAND, Indraditya Dynasty, Sukhdai	166.
1243 - 1304	Waghela Dynasty, Anhilwad Gujrat	179.

1250 - 1948	Rathor Dynasty, Jodhpur	135.
1262 - 1619	**SHRI LANKA**, Arya Chakravarti Dynasty	155.
1299 - 1391	Majapihit Dynasty, Malaya	78.
1303 - 1948	Sisodiya Dynasty, Chittor, Mewad	159.
1311 - 1527	Chauhan Dynasty, Sirohi	30.
1325 - 1368	Nayak, Musunuri Dynasty	91.
1325 - 1448	Nayak, Kondavidu Reddi Dynasty	102.
1336 - 1485	Nayak, Sangam Dynasty	87.
1343 - 1948	Chauhan Dynasty of Bundi,	32.
1351 - 1782	**THAILAND**, Ram Dynasty, Ayodhya Ayuthia	167.
1353 - 1706	**LAOS**, Lain Zang Dynasty, Vyadhpur	172.
1375 - 1523	Tomar Dynasty of Gwalior	174.
1382 - 1631	Chauhan Dynasty, Hadauti	31.
1399 - 1947	Wadiyar Dynasty, Mysore	178.
1400 - 1948	Manikya Dynasty, AgartaLa. Tripura	79.
1423 - 1685	Nayak, Pemmasani Dynasty	92.
1434 - 1541	Gajapati Dynasty, Kalinga	40.
1465 - 1948	Rathor Dynasty, Bikaner	136.
1485 - 1503	Nayak, Saluv Dynasty	88.
1491 - 1649	Nayak, Jinji Dynasty	93.
1498 - 1573	Meera Bai, Queen	82.
1499 - 1763	Nayak, Keladi Dynasty	94.
1500 - 1947	Varma Dynasty, Kochin, Kerla	183.
1503 - 1565	Nayak, Tuluv Dynasty	89.
1509 - 1736	Nayak, Madura Dynasty	95.
1526 - 1595	Nayak, Vellor Dynasty	96.
1532 - 1673	Nayak, Tanjavar Dynasty	97.
1565 - 1616	Nayak, Penukonda Dynasty	98.
1565 - 1649	Nayak, Aravidu Dynasty	90.
1572 -	Nayak, Chennai Dynasty	99.
1588 - 1779	Nayak, Chitradurg Dynasty	100.
1594 - 1848	Bhosle Dynasty, Satara	9.
1609 - 1948	Rathor Dynasty, Kishangadh	137.
1631 - 1948	Chauhan Dynasty of Kota,	33.
1633 - 1834	Nayak, Haleri Dynasty, Coorg	103.
1642 - 1948	**SIKKIM**, Namgyal Dynasty, Gangtok	14.
1648 - 1948	Waghela Dynasty, Riwa, Bagelkhand	180.
1673 - 1948	Pudukottai Dynasty, Tamil Nadu	127.
1675 - 1855	Bhosle Dynasty, Tanjavar	11.
1675 - 1855	Bhosle Dynasty, Nagpur	12.
1680 - 1844	Angre Dynasty, Kulaba, Maharashtra	4.
1689 - 1940	Bhosle Dynasty, Kolhapur	10.
1713 - 1818	Peshva Dynasty, Maharashtra	121.
1716 - 1948	Sindhia Dynasty, Gwalior	157.

1720 - 1951	Gaikwad Dynasty, Baroda, Gujrat	39.
1722 - 1948	Simha Dynasty, Bharatpur, Rajastan	162.
1729 - 1948	Varma Dynasty, Travankor, kerla	184.
1730 - 1790	Velu Nachchiyar, Queen of Ramand	186.
1730 - 1948	Holkar Dynasty, Indore	54.
1737 - 1948	Narayan Dynasty, Kashi - Varanasi	86.
1739 - 1815	Nayak, Kendy Dynasty	101.
1739 - 1815	SHRI LANKA, Kendy Nayak Rule	154.
1768 - 1948	NEPAL, Shah Gurkha Dynasty	112.
1778 - 1829	Channamma Queen, Kittur	24.
1782 - 1948	THAILAND, Ram Dynasty, Bangkok	168.
1799 - 1849	Sikh Dynasty, Punjab	156.
1812 - 1947	Dogra Dynasty, Jammu- Kashmir-Laddakh-Gilgit-Baltistan	38.
1821 - 1948	Simha Dynasty, Imphal, Manipur	151.
1831 - 1858	Avanti Bai, Queen of Ramgadh	5.
1838 - 1858	Nevaalkar Dynasty, Jhansi	113.
1907 - 1948	BHUTAN, Wangchuk Dynasty	13.

Place of Rule : Index of the Hindu Dynasties

Place of Rule	Dynasty Name	Period of Rule	Dynasty Number
Ancient Bharat	Ajamidh Dynasty	Ancient Time	3.
Ancient Bharat	Atri Dynasty	Ancient Time	1.
Ancient Bharat	Bharat Dynasty	Ancient Time	7.
Ancient Bharat	Brihadrith Dynasty, Magadh	Ancient Time	15.
Ancient Bharat	Gandhar Dynasty	Ancient Time	43.
Ancient Bharat	Gond Dynasty	Ancient Time	45.
Ancient Bharat	Ikshavaku Dynastu	Ancient Time	56.
Ancient Bharat	Kaurava Dynasty	Ancient Time	70.
Ancient Bharat	Kukkur Dynasty	Ancient Time	72.
Ancient Bharat	Kuru Dynasty	Ancient Time	73.
Ancient Bharat	Madra Dynasty	Ancient Time	76.
Ancient Bharat	Nimi Janak Dynasty	Ancient Time	114.
Ancient Bharat	Pandava Dynasty	Ancient Time	117.
Ancient Bharat	Pulastya Dynasty, Shri Lanka	Ancient Time	128.
Ancient Bharat	Puru Dynasty	Ancient Time	129.
Ancient Bharat	Raghu Dynasty	Ancient Time	131.
Ancient Bharat	Vivasvan Dynasty	Ancient Time	187.
Ancient Bharat	Vrishni Dynasty	Ancient Time	188.
Ancient Bharat	Yadu Dynasty	Ancient Time	191.
Ancient Bharat	Yayati Dynasty	Ancient Time	192.
Ancient Bharat	Yudhishthir Dynasty	Ancient Time	193.
Asaam	Ahom Dynasty, Kamarup, Asaam	355 - 1826	2.
Assam	Shalasthambha Dynasty, Kamrup, Assam	665 - 990	146.
Assam	Sutiya Dynasty, Sadiya, Assam	1187 - 1524	164.
Assam	Varma Dynasty, Kamrup, Assam	350 - 650	185.
Karnatak	Chalukya Dynasty West, Badami	525 - 753	18.
Bagelkhand	Parivrajak Dynasty, Bagelkhand	400 - 528	119.
Bagelkhand	Waghela Dynasty, Riwa, Bagelkhand	1648 - 1948	180.
Baghelkhand	Uchchhakalpa Dynasty, Baghelkhand	400 - 533	176.
Bastar	Chindak Nag Dynasty, Bastar	760 - 1324	35.
Bengal	Pal Dynasty, Mudagiri, Bengal	750 - 1174	115.
Bengal	Sen Dynasty, Nadiya, Bengal	1074 - 1230	143.
Bengal	Shashank Dynasty, Gaur, Bengal	600 - 625	144.
Bhutan	BHUTAN, Wangchuk Dynasty	1907 - 1948	13.
Bundelkhand	Chandela Dynasty, Bundelkhand	830 - 1289	23.
Burma, Mynmar	BURMA Mynmar, Hindu Dynasties	50 - 1828	16.
Cambodia	CAMBODIA, Varma Dynasty, Yashodapur	802 - 1353	171.
Chhattisgadh	Nal Dynasty, Chhattisgadh	290 - 960	84.

Delhi	Tomar Dynasty, Delhi	736 - 1192	173.
Devgiri	Yadav Dynasty, Devgiri	850 - 1311	190.
Gandhar	Hindu Shahi Dynasty, Kabul - Gandhar	867 - 1026	53.
Gujrat	Chalukya Dynasty, Lat, Gujrat	590 - 750	20.
Gujrat	Chapotkat Dynasty, Gujrat	690 - 942	25.
Gujrat	Gaikwad Dynasty, Baroda, Gujrat	1720 - 1951	39.
Gujrat	Solanki Dynasty, Patan, Gujrat	942 - 1244	163.
Gujrat	Waghela Dynasty, Anhilwad Gujrat	1243 - 1304	179.
Gwalior	Sindhia Dynasty, Gwalior	1716 - 1948	157.
Gwalior	Tomar Dynasty of Gwalior	1375 - 1523	174.
Indore	Holkar Dynasty, Indore	1730 - 1948	54.
Java	Shailendra Dynasty, Java	674 - 947	57.
Java	Simha Shri Dynasty, Java	1222 - 1478	58.
Jhansi	Nevaalkar Dynasty, Jhansi	1838 - 1858	113.
Jharkhand	Nag Dynasty, Jharkhand	83 - 1948	83.
Junagadh	Chudasama Dynasty, Junagadh	875 - 1505	37.
Kalinga	Gajapati Dynasty, Kalinga	1434 - 1541	40.
Kalinga	Ganga Dynasty East, Kalinga	700 - 1264	41.
Karnatak	Chalukya Dynasty West, Kalyani	696 - 1189	19.
Kanchipuram	Pallava Dynasty, Kanchipuram	315 - 897	116.
Kannauj	Maukhari Dynasty, Kannauj	540 - 725	80.
Kannauj	Pratihar - Gurjar Dynasty, Kannauj	725 - 1036	126.
Karnatak	Gutta Dynasty, Karnatak	1080 - 1262	50.
Karnatak	Hoysal Dynasty, Halebid	1026 - 1348	55.
Karnatak	Kadamb Dynasty, Karnatak	340 - 610	62.
Karnatak	Kalchuris of Kalyani	1156 - 1184	68.
Karnatak	Ratta Dynasty, Belgaon, Karnatak	850 - 1240	138.
Kashmir	Dogra Dynasty, Jammu-Kashmir-Laddakh-Gilgit-Baltistan	1812 - 1947	38.
Kashmir	Gonaditya Dynasty, Kashmir	1182 BC - 631 AD	44.
Kashmir	Karkota Dynasty, Kashmir	631 - 855	69.
Kashmir	Lohar Dynasty, Kashmir	1003 - 1172	75.
Kashmir	Pravargupta Dynasty, Kashmir	949 - 1003	125.
Kashmir	Utpal Dynasty, Kashmir	855 - 949	177.
Kashmir	Vuppadeva Dynasty, Kashmir	1172 - 1301	189.
Kerala	Cher Purumal Dynasty, Kerala	800 - 1102	34.
Kerla	Varma Dynasty, Kochin, Kerla	1500 - 1947	183.
Kerla	Varma Dynasty, Travankor, kerla	1729 - 1948	184.
Kerla	Varma Kulashekhar Dynasty, Venad Kerla	1102 - 1729	182.
Kittur	Channamma Queen, Kittur	1778 - 1829	24.
Knokan	Shilahar Dynasty, North Knokan	800 - 1265	147.
Knokan	Shilahar Dynasty, South Knokan	765 - 1024	148.
Kolhapur	Shilahar, Kolhapur	940 - 1212	149.
Laos	LAOS, Lain Zang Dynasty, Vyadhpur	1353 - 1706	172.

Madura	Pandya Dynasty, Madura	50 - 1422	118.
Magadh	Shakya Gautam Dynasty	Ancient Time	145.
Maharashtra	Angre Dynasty, Kulaba, Maharashtra	1680 - 1844	4.
Maharashtra	Bhosle Dynasty, Kolhapur	1689 - 1940	10.
Maharashtra	Bhosle Dynasty, Nagpur	1675 - 1855	12.
Maharashtra	Bhosle Dynasty, Satara	1594 - 1848	9.
Maharashtra	Peshva Dynasty, Maharashtra	1713 - 1818	121.
Maharashtra	Satvahan Dynasty, Maharashtra	271 BC - 195 AD	141.
Maharashtra	Traikutak Dynasty, Junnar, Maharashtra	388 - 492	175.
Mahismati	Kalchuris of Mahismati	550 - 620	65.
Malaya	Majapihit Dynasty, Malaya	1299 - 1391	78.
Malkhed	Rashtrakut Dynasty, Malkhed	620 - 973	133.
Malkhed	Rashtrakut Dynasty, Malkhed	806 - 888	134.
Malwa	Parmar Dynasty, Dhar, Malwa	800 - 1305	120.
Manipur	Simha Dynasty, Imphal, Manipur	1821 - 1948	151.
Mathura	Shurasen Dynasty, Mathura	Ancient Time	161.
Mathura-Purushapur	Kushan Dynasty, Purushapur - Mathura	30 BC - 244 AD	74.
Mewad	Guhil Dynasty, Mewad	550 - 1303	47.
Mysore	Wadiyar Dynasty, Mysore	1399 - 1947	178.
Nepal	NEPAL, Anshuvarma Dynasty	605 - 879	108.
Nepal	NEPAL, Gopal Ahir Dynasty	Ancient Time	104.
Nepal	NEPAL, Kirat Dynasty	900 BC - 205 AD	105.
Nepal	NEPAL, Lichchhavi Dynasty	305 - 605	107.
Nepal	NEPAL, Malla Dynasty	1200 - 1768	111.
Nepal	NEPAL, Raghav Dynasty	879 - 1046	109.
Nepal	NEPAL, Shah Gurkha Dynasty	1768 - 1948	112.
Nepal	NEPAL, Thakur Dynasty	1046 - 1200	110.
Patliputra	Haryak Dynasty, Patliputra	544 BC - 413 BC	51.
Patliputra	Kanva Dynasty, Patliputra	72 BC - 27 BC	63.
Patliputra	Maurya Dynasty, Patliputra	322 BC - 184 BC	81.
Patliputra	Nand Dynasty, Patliputra	344 BC - 322 BC	85.
Patliputra	Pushyabhuti - Vardhan Dynasty, Patliputra	505 - 647	130.
Patliputra	Shishunag Dynasty, Patliputra	413 BC - 344 BC	150.
Philipines	PHILLIPINE, Hindu Dynasties	50 - 1828	122.
Pudukottai	Pudukottai Dynasty, Tamil Nadu	1673 - 1948	127.
Punjab	Sikh Dynasty, Punjab	1799 - 1849	156.
Rajastan	Bhati Raval Dynasty, Jaisalmer, Rajastan	731 - 1948	8.
Rajastan	Gurjar Dynasty, Rajastan	400 - 725	49.
Rajasthan	Chauhan Dynasty of Bundi,	1343 - 1948	32.
Rajasthan	Chauhan Dynasty of Kota,	1631 - 1948	33.
Rajasthan	Chauhan Dynasty, Hadauti	1382 - 1631	31.
Rajasthan	Chauhan Dynasty, Jalor	1182 - 1311	29.
Rajasthan	Chauhan Dynasty, Sirohi	1311 - 1527	30.

Region	Dynasty	Period	#
Rajasthan	Chauhan Dynasty, Ranthambhot	1194 - 1301	28.
Rajasthan	Chauhan Dynasty, Sakambhari	684 - 1194	26.
Rajasthan	Chaunah Dynasty, Nadol	950 - 1200	27.
Rajasthan	Kachhavaha Dynasty, Rajastan	1036 - 1948	61.
Rajasthan	Meera Bai, Queen	1498 - 1573	82.
Rajasthan	Rathor Dynasty, Bikaner	1465 - 1948	136.
Rajasthan	Rathor Dynasty, Jodhpur	1250 - 1948	135.
Rajasthan	Rathor Dynasty, Kishangadh	1609 - 1948	137.
Rajasthan	Simha Dynasty, Bharatpur, Rajastan	1722 - 1948	162.
Rajasthan	Sisodiya Dynasty, Chittor, Mewad	1303 - 1948	159.
Ramgadh	Avanti Bai, Queen of Ramgadh	1831 - 1858	5.
Ratnapuri	Kalchuris of Ratnapuri	1000 - 1745	67.
Saurashtra	Chalukya Dynasty, Kathiawad, Saurashtra	750 - 900	21.
Saurashtra	Jadeja Dynasty, Saurashtra	1203 - 1948	60.
Saurashtra	Maitrak Dynasty, Saurashtra	480 - 767	77.
Saurashtra	Saindhav Dynasty, Saurashtra	734 - 920	140.
Shri Lanka	Nayak, Kendy Dynasty	1739 - 1815	101.
Shri Lanka	SHRI LANKA, Chola Rule	1029 - 1055	153.
Shri Lanka	SHRI LANKA, Pandya Rule	429 - 455	152.
Shri Lanka	SHRI LANKA, Arya Chakravarti Dynasty	1262 - 1619	155.
Shri Lanka	SHRI LANKA, Kendy Nayak Rule	1739 - 1815	154.
Sikkim	SIKKIM, Namgyal Dynasty, Gangtok	1642 - 1948	14.
Sindh	Chach Dynasty, Alor, Sindh	631 - 712	17.
Sindh	Rai Dynasty, Alor, Sindh	489 - 631	132.
Sindh	Ror Dynasty, Roruk - Sakkar	Ancient Time	139.
Sindh	Sauvir Dynasty, Sindh	Ancient Time	142.
Sindh	Sindhu Dynasty	Ancient Time	158.
Sumatra	SUMATRA, Shri Vijaya Dynasty,	683 - 1405	59.
Talkad	Ganga Dynasty west, Talkad	350 - 1024	42.
Tamil Nadu	Velu Nachchiyar, Queen of Ramand	1730 - 1790	186.
Tanjavar	Bhosle Dynasty, Tanjavar	1675 - 1855	11.
Tanjavar	Chola Dynasty, Tanjavar	50 - 1279	36.
Thailand	THAILAND, Indraditya Dynasty, Sukhdai	1238 - 1438	166.
Thailand	THAILAND, Ram Dynasty, Ayodhya Ayuthia	1351 - 1782	167.
Thailand	THAILAND, Ram Dynasty, Bangkok	1782 - 1948	168.
Thailand	THAILAND, Funan Dynasty, Vyadhpur	50 - 627	165.
Tripura	Manikya Dynasty, AgartaLa. Tripura	1400 - 1948	79.
Tripuri	Kalchuris of Tripuri	675 - 1210	66.
Ujjain	Pradyot Dynasty, Ujjain	546 BC - 413 BC	123.
Ujjain	Kshatrap Dynasty, Girnar, Ujjain, Nasik	78 - 395	71.
Vanapuram	Bana Dynasty, Vanapuram	720 - 900	6.
Varanasi	Narayan Dynasty, Kashi - Varanasi	1737 - 1948	86.
Vengi	Chalukya East Dynasty, Vengi	440 - 1070	22.
Vidarbha	Gond Dynasty of Vidarbha	1200 - 1550	46.

Vidisha	Shunga Dynasty, Vidisha	185 BC - 72 BC	160.
Vietnam	VIETNAM, Bhava varma Dynasty, Chenla	550 - 788	170.
Vijaynagar	Nayak, Aravidu Dynasty	1565 - 1649	90.
Vijaynagar	Nayak, Chennai Dynasty	1572 -	99.
Vijaynagar	Nayak, Chitradurg Dynasty	1588 - 1779	100.
Vijaynagar	Nayak, Haleri Dynasty, Coorg	1633 - 1834	103.
Vijaynagar	Nayak, Jinji Dynasty	1491 - 1649	93.
Vijaynagar	Nayak, Keladi Dynasty	1499 - 1763	94.
Vijaynagar	Nayak, Kondavidu Reddi Dynasty	1325 - 1448	102.
Vijaynagar	Nayak, Madura Dynasty	1509 - 1736	95.
Vijaynagar	Nayak, Musunuri Dynasty	1325 - 1368	91.
Vijaynagar	Nayak, Pemmasani Dynasty	1423 - 1685	92.
Vijaynagar	Nayak, Penukonda Dynasty	1565 - 1616	98.
Vijaynagar	Nayak, Saluv Dynasty	1485 - 1503	88.
Vijaynagar	Nayak, Sangam Dynasty	1336 - 1485	87.
Vijaynagar	Nayak, Tanjavar Dynasty	1532 - 1673	97.
Vijaynagar	Nayak, Tuluv Dynasty	1503 - 1565	89.
Vijaynagar	Nayak, Vellor Dynasty	1526 - 1595	96.
Warangal	Kakatiya Dynasty, Warangal	1000 - 1323	64.

Preface

Hindu Rajatarangini! In this great Sanskrit title there are two key nouns, 1. Hindu and 2. Tarangini. (1) Hindu: Hindu refers to that righteous path (Dharma) which is not a man-made religion or a dogma that is set forth by any one person, but it is a cultural system of eternal harmony of all living beings. It is the only supernatural path of life. And, in this sense only, the word Hindu has been used in this book. In this sense it is Hindu virtue, Hinduism, Hindutva, Hindu Dharma or Sanatan Dharma. 'Sanatan' means eternal, which neither has a countable beginning nor an end.

Therefore, it neither has a human founder nor it has any human destroyer. Whatever it is, we are the doers and its protectors. Our development is with our own wisdom and our destruction, if ever, will be with our own misdeeds, greed or slave mentality. Hindu culture is the divine gift of the wisdom of our eternal sages. It is the foundation of Indian decency, of which some footprints are physically visible in the Aryan civilization of the Indus Valley. This is not a "religion" like present day religious sects.

This civilization is the Indian Sanatan ideology in the sense of virtue, modesty, duty and responsibility and in that sense only Sanatan civilization is called Dharma or Arya-dharma, of which the well-defined literature is the Vedas, Puranas, Upanishads, Ramayan, Mahabharat, Gita, and other Sanskrit Shruti-Smriti scriptures. Here, the knowledge of self is the true knowledge. It enunciates the principles of truth, non-violence, mercy, forgiveness, peace, charity, chanting, penance, etc., wherein the heavens, air, water, fire, earth and the three attributes are considered to be the primary elements of the nature (*prakriti*) and the divinity (*purusha*). A person who upholds all these supreme elements in his heart and soul is called a Hindu in this book and his sound faith is Hindutva (Hinduism). Only the Royal Dynasties which followed the Hindu Culture as said above, are discussed in this book.

The Dohas[1] tell us :

Hindu Rajatarangini, in brilliant colours seven,
Stream of divine culture, came down from the heaven. 1

---

[1] Hindi Dohas, as given in the Hindi Edition of the Hindu RajTarangini.

Sacred Hindu culture, source of divine virtue.
Not a man-made cult but, a natural marvel true. 2

This Universal culture, based on humanity,
Sages gave the values, ethics and humility. 3

Scriptures told by Gods, by which people abide,
Principle of kindness, that is India's pride. 4

Peace truth honesty, non-violence simplicity,
Mercy compassion charity, forgiveness and purity; 5

Birth to Moksha Journey, provides this vehicle,
Hindu religion is the name, in the words practical. 6

On the milky ocean (क्षीर सागर) of Vaikuntha, arose from the navel of Lord Vishnu, twenty-one Prajapatis took birth who produced the beings on the earth. Thus is the evolution of Hindu civilization. It is not a foundation or creation of a man-made religion. In the flow of this Rajatarangini, Solar Dynasty of Sri Ramachandra and the Lunar Dynasty of Shri Krishna are treated as the pioneer Royal Houses. A joint table of genealogies of these two dynasties is presented below for display.

The Dohas tell us :
Seshasayi Vishnu Bhagwan, on the milky ocean,
Lotus rose from navel, on it Brahma in devotion. 7

With His four mouths He is, chanting Vaidic Mantra,
Listening to it Vishnu, silently the Trantra. 8

At this sacred time, there evolved slowly,
Twenty-one Prajapatis, from His organs holy. 9

Evolved from Prajapatis, progenies of diverse natures,
On the earth then appeared, many different creatures. 9

This was the auspicious, foundation of humanity.
Since the beginning of time, as His creativity. 10

Hindu Rajatarangini, has two main clans,
Ravi-Shashi Dynasties, as were the Brahma's plans. 11

In that early age of evolution, Lord Ramachandra's kingdom became such an auspicious model of virtue on the earth that any heavenly peaceful kingdom was called a "Rama-rajya," i.e. a kingdom ruled by humane ethics. The spread of this virtuous kingdom was not with the power of sword, but with the power of the divine values of this righteousness (*Dharma*). Its fame grew spontaneously in all directions and then as a result a wide Rama-rajya-empire was formed in the west, north, East and South of India, as depicted in the following map.

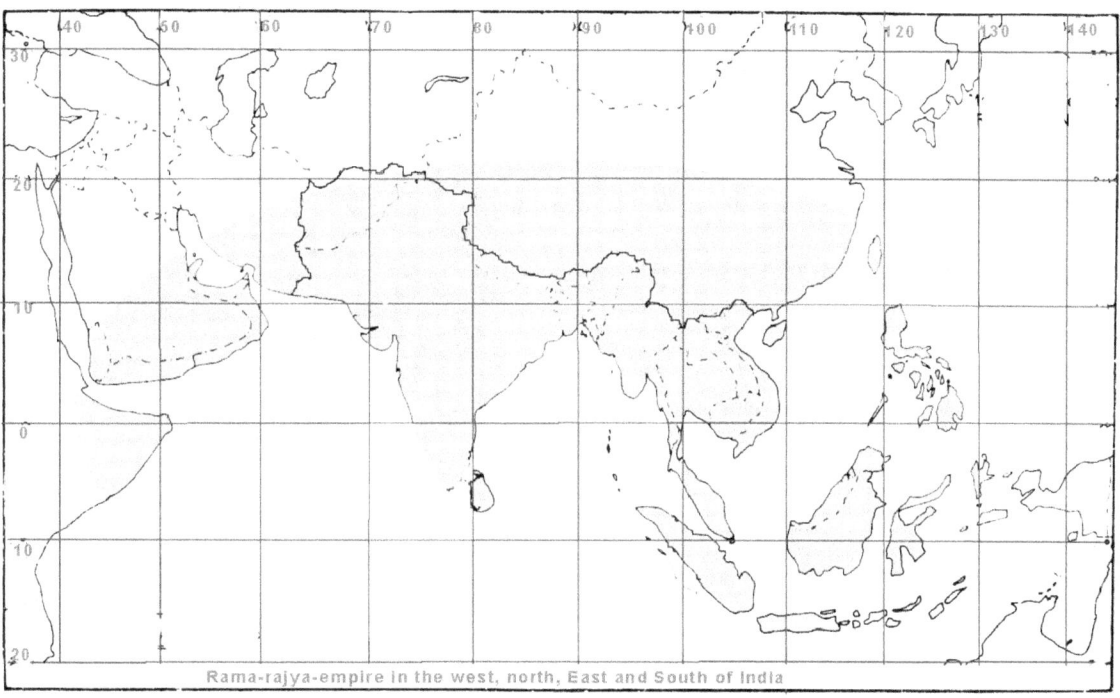
Rama-rajya-empire in the west, north, East and South of India

King is the cause of the good or bad times in the kingdom, says Mahabharat. State is just any kingdom, but Rama-Rajya is Lord Rama's righteous realm. The difference is basic. The difference is of the purity. In the history of Kali Yuga, it is frequently seen that the king of a state is often a dictator, chaotic, adulterous, rapist, inhuman, thief, marauder, fraudster, cheater, trickster, unjust, womanizer, lustful, demonic, greedy, kidnapper, saboteur, arsonist and unfit for governance. The subjects are deprived of happiness and peace during his time. There is neither such king nor such governance in Rama-rajya. Therefore, following is said about Rama-rajya :

The Dohas tell us:

Knowing the ethics and rules, of the Rama's kingdom,
subjects of its realm, earn knowledge and wisdom. 12

Keeping the given word, is the Rama's ethics,
One may lose his life, but not given promise. 13

Venerable must be the king, like the Ganga's water,
Must be straight and simple, like the ironed matter. 14

King is son of his subjects, subjects are mother-father,
Must he be obedient, peoples' servant rather. 15

He should know the weapons, and the words of Scriptures,
May he be good warrior, one in a million creatures. 16

He must be a logician, skillful and be expert,
Able to win people, intelligent stalwart. 17.

Should see truth from untruth, know the righteous deed,
discern right from the wrong, with the electric speed. 18

Ocean of wisdom he be, arts he should know all,
Polity he should know well, only then win he shall. 19

May he be efficient doer, master of polity he be,
Ever alert he should, hidden flaws all to see. 20

(and)
With money mind and soul, king should serve his people,
May stay firm in difficult times, without wave or ripple. 21

Difficult tasks of kingdom, he should make all easy,
Solving peoples' problems, he be always busy. 22

He be braver than the brave, diamond in the jewels,
Mountain of the courage, victor in the duels. 23

May his heart be humble, kind in every sector,
Words in his mouth be sweet, like Amrit nectar. 24

Shelter who seeks refuge, shower love on poor,

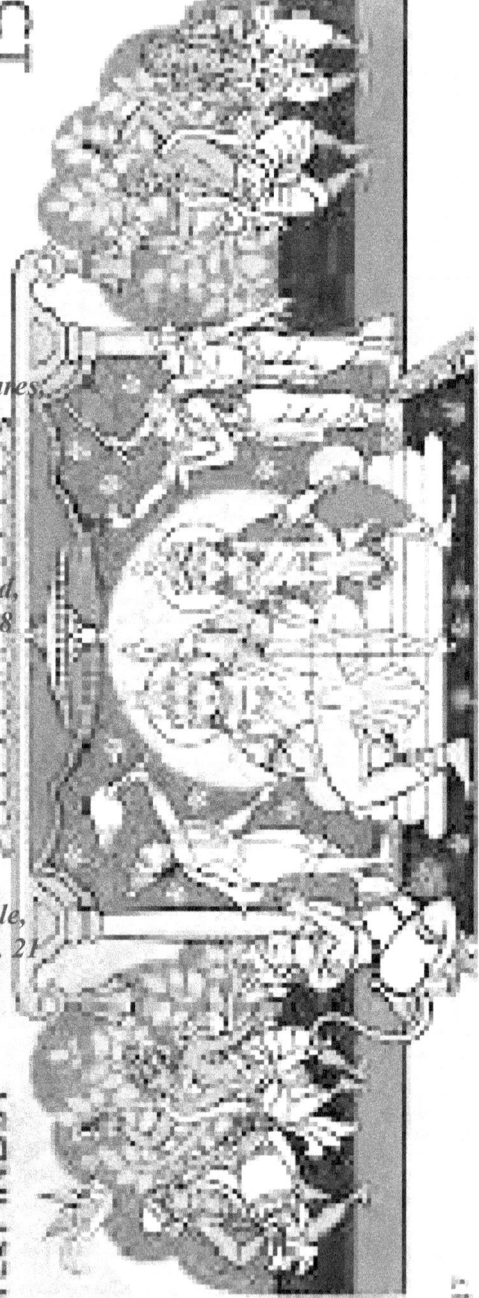

Forgive who is sorry, remorseful for sure. 25

(Also)

May he be not greedy, a jealous person King,
Neither sinful at heart, for him Rama is caring. 26

He who helps the needy, serving day and night,
Speaking kinder language, to be king he is right. 27

May he not be deceitful, dishonest and delusive,
Harsh egoist wrangler, nor should be abusive. 28

May he not be traitor, possess dirty habits,
Nor may he argue, without any merits. 29

Away from the anger, hatred and false pride,
King of righteous nature, has peace countrywide. 30

(As well)

Abducting woman is a sin, punishable by death,
No one may mistreat her, nor one may lose her faith. 31

Manu told us ethics, how to treat a sinner,
He who kidnaps a lady, death will make him dinner. 32

Never should king be cruel, nor should he be pervert,
May he not be unrighteous, nor should he act covert. 33

Idle should not be king, always devout in Karma,
In every situation king should, always follow Dharma. 34

Dharma is supreme duty, for a warrior brave,
As the scriptures tell us, selflessness he should crave. 35

Impartial should be king, balanced in his mind,
He should punish or reward, in the proper kind. 36

Justice done with ethics, gives everyone delight,
Justice that is fair, is the action right. 37

King should be loving, every subject alike,
People in the kingdom, also should him like. 38

King who is atrocious, and the king dictator,
And the king unethical, and the king, molester; 39

These four kinds of men, as well as the kings,
Are punishable alike, for the safety of the things. 40
 (and)
He who kills an innocent, is a sinful man,
He who lets go a guilty, punish him as you can. 41

Help him who seeks shelter, give him food and roof,
Treat him with the respect, do not leave him aloof. 42

A good man driven away, from his family and home,
He will join your enemy, and eat you like a gnome. 43

No one should be hungry, and no mother should cry,
Food should be plenty, wells should never dry. 44

King is servant of people, service is his job,
He who eats up taxes, that king is called a rob. 45

Everyone should be in unison, kingdom always be peaceful,
Everyone should have home, food clothing for all people. 46

No body be left hungry, may no one be left lonely,
Everyone should have peace, and the happiness only. 47

No one in the kingdom, should speak abusive words,
No one should steal or kill, people animals birds. 48

May everyone utter, sweet words with fond,
May everyone be united, in a common bond. 49

All should respect Gurus, with the open mind,
All should follow rules, regulations every kind. 50

 (Also)
In the Rama's kingdom, one should have good heart,
Loving living beings, should be well known art. 51

Truth and simplicity, and the quality,
Forgiveness and pity, and the humane quality; 52

People of four classes, should have future bright,
Women should have respect, and the equal right. 53

King should protect people, of his kingdom well,
Men women and children, like a magic spell. 54

King should serve the people, day and night diligent,
He is loved by all, the king who is efficient. 55

Famine should not occur, in the kingdom ever,
Men and women all, should be wise and clever. 56

Women men and children, should be roaming fearless,
People in the kingdom, should be all tearless. 57

There is peace and happiness, in righteousness and truth,
Walking right path wins, the earth and heaven both. 58

Atheist loses always, theist wins the world,
Everyone should have faith, and love for young and old. 59

King should adore sages, with his heart and soul,
Being pure and true, should be everyone's goal. 60

(At the same time)
Helping poor people, helpless and the hurt,
That righteous king, is the polity expert. 61

He who is not virtuous, and is wicked and evil,
Punishment should be given, to that person devil. 62

People who have love, they are wise and honest,
The are joy givers, and the friends best. 63

No one should take kickback, nor should give a bribe,
No one should be corrupt, helpless balant tribe. 64

He who is equanimous, in the pleasure and pain,
That courageous person, is equal in loss and gain. 65

Your real friend is he, in trouble who is sad,
And he is your brother, to help you who is glad. 66

Kidnapping woman is a sin, that gives death to you,
Respect women always, in whatever you do. 67

Think of other lady, your daughter sister mother,
And treat your wife, like a goddess rather. 68

Protecting a woman, who is in the need,
Gives you merit points, for your righteous deed. 69

Women should be able, to roam without fear,
Women in the kingdom, should live without tear. 70

With the Om sound, home should be Temple,
No woman should be sad, she should be happy ample. 71

If the forest catches fire, protector is the rain,
If you burn in anger, no one removes pain. 72

A wise king should always, worship holy men,
Hearing words of scriptures, there is lot to gain. 73

Understanding adherence to the righteous rule for Ram-Rajya and accepting the essence of its principle, "One may lose his life but not the given promise," we see in the Bhishma Parva of Mahabharat, the political rules of a righteous war (Dharma-yuddha), as told by Lord Shri Krishna:

The Dohas tell us :
Only aim is Victory, in a regular war,
But in righteous war, equal win and defeat are. 74

Such equanimous ethics, is called righteous war,
Same is life and death, where duty is the bar. 75

Krishna told the rules, for the righteous war,
Warriors must follow, to be a battle star. 76

Time for the battle, is morning till sunset,

In the dark periods, warfare has to wait. 77

Evening to morning, everyone is a brother,
There is no enemy, on the side either. 78

Declare your status, to choose an equal foe,
Do not strike an enemy, afflicted with woe. 79

Or who is scared, or lost his weapon,
Who is already wounded, or sword is broken. 80

 (Or)

Or has put down weapon, and has raised hands,
Ready for the surrender, agreed your demands. 81

Horseman with the horseman, may fight enemy equal,
Archer with the archer, of the same level. 82

Elephant rider may fight, with the elephant rider,
Foot soldier may fight, with the foot soldier. 83

Do not use a weapon, that is hidden under,
Laced with poison or fire, to cause a mass murder. 84

In a righteous war, remember it again!
Victory same as defeat, loss is same as gain. 85

There were sixteen Indian Mahajanapadas (Great Kingdoms) in the Ramayan-Mahabharat era. Names of the Mahajanpadas and places of their capital are known to history, but copmlete records of the dynasties of those royal houses is not properly written anywhere. It is only known that there were sixteen kingdoms from West to East namely : 1. Gandhara, capital Taxila; 2. Kamboj, Rajapur; 3. Ashmak, Pratisthan; 4. Avanti Ujjayini; 5. Matsya, Virat Nagar; 6. Kuru, Kurukshetra; 7. Shursen, Mathura; 8. Panchal, Kampila; 9. Chedi, Shuktmati; 10. Vatsa, Kaushambi; 11. Koshal, Saket (Ayodhya); 12. Kashi, Banarsi; 13. Malla, Pava; 14. Magadha, Rajgriha; 15. Videha, Mithila; and 16. Anga, Champa. This was the golden historical period of India.

(2) Tarangini : Tarangini means river. A river is not just a flow water. Also, the flow of a river does not flow always at same speed and in the same direction, otherwise it is called a canal. River flow is sometimes fast, sometimes slow, sometimes shallow, sometimes deep, sometimes narrow, sometimes wide, sometimes straight, sometimes sinuous, in the North or East or South or West direction. A river is very short or a river is very long. On the banks of the river there is sometimes a hill, sometimes a town, sometimes shrubs, sometimes a field, sometimes grass, sometimes a rock. Somewhere in the water of the river there are aquatic animals, different vegetations, soil or dirt. Somewhere the water is dirty, somewhere it is clean, There are boats on the river and fishermen somewhere. One river sometimes joins another river and the other river merges into the third river, but in the end all the rivers merge into the ocean. The river may be a flow of water or it may be the Ganges of Knowledge.

For the purpose of incorporating all these qualities of the rivers in this Hindu Rajatarangini, this book is not written in just one poem of Shlokas or Dohas, but rather it is written sometimes in Dohas, somewhere Shlokas, somewhere prose, somewhere dynastic listing, sometimes maps, coins, pictures, illustrations, etc. so that all the diverse qualities of a river appear in this Hindu Rajatarangini, as a natural river.

In this book the Hindu dynasties from the ancient times are listed alphabetically for the convenience of the readers, also they are shown in chronological order for the benefit of the scholars. Whether a royal house is very small or it is big, it is not ignored.

The dynastic and archaic practice of royalty began to be invalidated due to the corrupt, fanatic and dictatorial behavior of various kings and by the year 1920, it was rejected in many countries. In India, under the Indian Independence Act of 1948, the Family Dynasty System was abolished and considered illegal. Therefore, the flow of Hindu Rajatarangini is presented in this book only up to year 1948.

To the constitution of this river, despite of being historic, lots of Hindu cultural content and music are added to make it captivating and an educational Gyana Ganga for the purpose of increasing the knowledge of the readers.

Although thousands up on thousands of Hindu dynasties have been there in the vast history of Sanatan Hindu culture, only a tiny fraction of them are listed anywhere. 195 dynasties are included in this work.

For the convenience of the readers, 195 royal houses have been listed in the beginning of the book in alphabetical order and then chronologically according to their time period.

It is hoped that this research work will increase the knowledge of the readers and it will make an incomparable contribution of valuable material for the research scholars.

Divine Hindu culture and history have been suppressed, hidden, defied, ignored, unpublished and maligned for centuries before India's independence and for the last 70 years, even after the independence. But now our eyes have opened and the time has come for us to fulfill this important hospitality a responsibility. This is our sacred duty.

While engaged in this great auspicious task day and night, one day I suddenly felt that my hands and legs are becoming paralyzed and my neck is becoming numb. I immediately had to be rushed to the hospital at the behest of the doctor and I had to undergo a Brain Hemorrhage Surgery. At that moment my future had a chance of living, dying or disability. But due to the kind grace of God, skill of the doctors and the earnest prayers of the well wishers, my life train was brought back on track in few months. Today, it is a matter of joy that the obstacle in the accomplishment of this book is partly removed and the completion of this book became possible. Hari Om

Ratnakar Narale
Toronto, Canada

NOTES :
1. Please note that in order to save number of pages, the vast Research Reference Section is given only in the Hindi Edition of the Hindu RajTarangini. Please see the references at the end of the Hindi Edition.

2. Also, for the same reason, relationship of each king with his successor is shown only in the Hindi Edition of the Hindu RajTarangini. Please refer to the Hindi Edition.

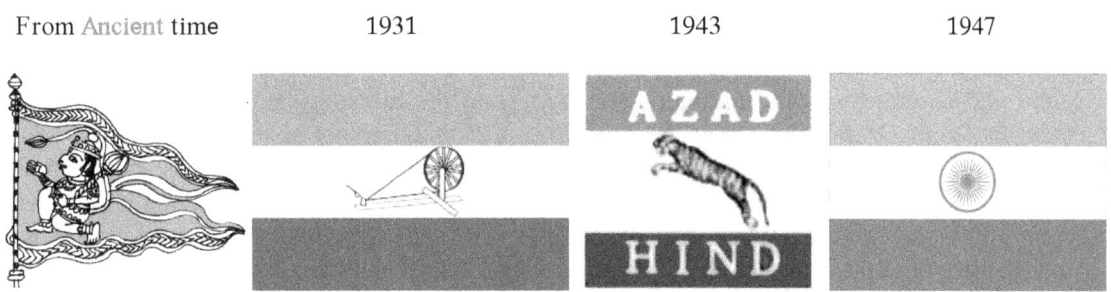

From Ancient time 1931 1943 1947

1. Atri Dynasty (Ancient Time)

1.	Brahma	ब्रह्म
2.	Brahma	ब्रह्मा
3.	Atri	अत्रि प्रजापति
4.	Chandra	चंद्र
5.	Budha	बुध
6.	Pururava	पुरुरव
7.	Ayu	आयु
7.	Nahusha	नहुष
8.	Yayati	ययाति

Hindu Philosophy

According to the Hindu philosophy, world is "evolved" from Brahma (ब्रह्म), not Brahma (ब्रह्मा) "created" the world. Brahma (ब्रह्म) is the dual principle: Prakriti and Purusha. In whichever form the living being is, moveable, non-moving, visible or invisible, the soul of all beings is one. Purusha-Prakriti and atma (आत्मा) all together are Brahma (ब्रह्म). Purusha-Prakriti are in the form of Narayana-Narayani. From the navel of Narayana a lotus emerged. Sitting on the lotus is the Four headed Brahma (ब्रह्मा). Twenty-one Prajapatis evolved from the different parts of the body of Brahma (ब्रह्मा). Prajapatis gave birth to the progenies of living beings on the earth. Such is the evolution.

For the Next Dynasty, please see : Yayati Dynasty (Ancient Time)

Atri Dynasty

Atri Maharishi was one of the nine Mnasaputra (born from mind) Prajapatis of Brahma (ब्रह्मा). The other eight Manasputra Prajapatis were Bhrigu, Pulastya, Pulah, Kratu, Angiras, Marichi, Daksha and Vasistha (Vishnu Purana 7.1). Maharaja Atri Prajapati's wife was Anasuya Devi. The names of the wives of other eight Prajapatipatis were respectively : Khyati, Bhuti, Sambhuti, Kshama, Preeti, Sannati, Urja and Prasuti. Anasuya Devi's three headed son was Dattatreya and the other son was Chandra. Pururava, the grandson of King Chandra, was a king with a very bright aura. King Ayu (आयु) was the son of King Pururava and his wife Urvashi. King Nahush and his wife Indumati's son born with the blessings of Dattatreya, was King Nahusha (Maha. Adi. 7.24). The virtuous King Ayu was famous in the three worlds. King Nahusha was a form of Lord Indra and used to fly in the plane of Indra. King Nahusha's famous son was Maharaja Yayati. Maharaja Yayati had two wives. Queen Devyani's son was king Yadu and Queen Sharmishtha's son was king Puru. There were many eminent kings in the lineage of both of these houses. King Amavasu, son of king Pururava of Atri Dynasty founded the city of Kanyakubj (Kannauj) and made it his capital.

Hindu Rajtarangini

2. Ahom Dynasty, Kamarup, Asaam (355-1826)

#	Name	(Devanagari)	Period
1.	Pushya Varma	पुष्यवर्मा	355–380
2.	Samudra Varma	समुद्रवर्मा	380–405
3.	Bala Varma-1	बालवर्मा-1	405–420
4.	Kalyan Varma	कल्याणवर्मा	420–440
5.	Ganapati Varma	गणपतिवर्मा	440–450
6.	Mahendra Varma	महेंद्रवर्मा	450–480
7.	Narayan Varma	नारायणवर्मा	480–510
7.	Bhuti Varma	भूतिवर्मा	510–555
8.	Chandra-mukh Varma	चंद्रमुखवर्मा	555–565
9.	Sthiti Varma	स्थितिवर्मा	555–585
10.	Sisthiti Varma	सुस्थितिवर्मा	585–593
11.	Supratik Varma	सुप्रतिकवर्मा	593–594
12.	Bhaskar Varma	भास्करवर्मा	594–650
13.	Chaolung Sukpha	शौलंग सुखफा	1228–1262
14.	Buddhi Svarganarayan	बुद्धि स्वर्गनारायण	1494–1539
15.	Gargeya Raj	गार्गेयान राज	1539–1525
16.	Khura Raj	खुरा राज	1552–1603
17.	Pratap Simha	प्रताप सिंह	1603–1641
18.	Bhag Raj	भाग राज	1641–1644
19.	Nar Raj	नर राज	1644–1650
20.	Jay-dhvaja Raj	जयध्वज सिंह	1650–1664
21.	Chakra-dhvaja Simha	चक्रध्वज सिंह	1664–1670
22.	Udayaditya Simha	उदयादित्य सिंह	1670–1672
23.	Rama-dhvaja Simha	रामध्वज सिंह	1672–1674
24.	Gobhar Simha	गोभर सिंह	1674–1675
25.	Arju Raj	अर्जुन राज	1675–1677
26.	Parvatiya Simha	पर्वतीय सिंह	1677–1679
27.	Ratna-dhvaja Simha	रत्नध्वज सिंह	1679–1681

Ahom Dynasty

The history of the vast region of the Brahmaputra valley, known by the names of Ahom, Aakhom, Akhom, Assam, Asam, etc., is obscure before year 450. In ancient times, there were great descendants like Bhagadatta, Madhav, Jitari, Aashmat etc.

Mahendra Varma (450-480) was the great king of Kamrup in the fourth century. In the sixth century Bhaskara Varma (594-650) was the famous king of Assam. Before Bhaskar Varma, in the thirteenth century, Govind Deva and Ishanaya Deva were well known kings and in the fourteenth century, Durlabh Narayan was also a well known ruler of Ahom kingdom.

During the reigh of King Chaolung Sukpha (1228-1262) great political reforms took place in Assam in the year 1228. The plulic of Assam supported the mass drive to bring about improvement in skills, craftsmanship and agricultural reforms. As a result, the social, economic and political changes began in Assam in a big way.

28.	Gadadhar Simha	गदाधर सिंह	1681–1696
29.	Rudra Simha Svargadev	रुद्रसिंह स्वर्गदेव	1696–1714
30.	Shiva Simha	शिवसिंह	1714–1744
31.	Pramatt Simha	प्रमत्त सिंह	1744–1751
32.	Rajeshvar Simha	राजेश्वर सिंह	1751–1769
33.	Lakshmi Simha	लक्ष्मी सिंह	1769–1780
34.	Gaurinath Simha	गौरीनाथ सिंह	1780–1795
35.	Kamleshvar Simha	कमलेश्वर सिंह	1795–1811
36.	Chandrakant Simha-1	चंद्रकांत सिंह–1	1811–1818
37.	Purandra Simha	पुरंदर सिंह	1818–1819
38.	Chandrakant Simha-2	चंद्रकांत सिंह–2	1819–1821
39.	Yogeshvar Simha	योगेश्वर सिंह	1821–1826

Ahom Dynasty

The great Dynasty of Assam, of which name was Ahom,
Ruled for six centuries, uttering Shiva Om, Shiva Om. 1

Its great king Rudrasimha, ruled the kingdom well,
Assam prospered now, history knows the tale. 2

Ahom Dynasty, continued

Peace and prosperity was established in Assam during the historic rule of King Buddha Swarganarayan (1494-1539). He had formed a bond of love through matrimonial relations with the neighboring kingdom of Manipur. Veerangana Mula Gabharu, wife of King Buddha Swarnarayan, was known as the brave queen of Assam.

King Rudrasimha (1696–1714) was the first king to hold the title of Swargadev in Assam. During his time two Enormous temples of Lord Shiva and Durga Devi, named Shiva Dhol and Goddess Dhol, were built and Shiva-Durga were worshiped as the deity of the ultimate power. Assam's prosperity reached its climax during the time of King Rudrasimha.

The ancient capital of Assam was shifted from Kamrup to Jorhat during the reign of King Gaurinath Simha (1780–1795).

Then, During the long reign of King Yogeshwar Simha (1821-1826), the capital of the kingdom of Assam was shifted from Jorhat to Guwahati. From that time the Capital of Ahom Kingdom (Assam) remained at Guwahati.

3. Ajmidh Dynasty (Ancient Time)

3a. Ajmidh Dynasty of King Kuru (Ancient Time)

For the Prevoius Dynasty, please see : Bharat Dynasty (Ancient Time)

1.	Ajmidh	अजमीढ़
2.	Raksh	रक्ष
3.	Samvarna	संवर्ण
4.	Kuru	कुरु

For the Next Dynasty, please see :
Kuru Dynasty (Ancient Time)

3b. Ajmidh Dynasty of King Drupad (Ancient Time)

1.	Ajmidh	अजमीढ़
2.	Nil	नील
3.	Shanti	शांति
4.	Sushanti	सुशांति
5.	Puruj	पुरुज
6.	Arka	अर्क
7.	Bharmyashva	भर्म्यश्व
8.	Panchal	पांचाल
9.	Mudgal	मुद्गल
10.	Divodas	दिवोदास
11.	Maitreyu	मैत्रेयु
12.	Sudas	सुदास
13.	Sahadeva	सहदेव
14.	Somak	सोमक
15.	Drupad	द्रुपद
	Dhrishtadyumna	धृष्टद्युम्न

Ajmidh Dynasty

King Kuru :

After King Hasti, King Ajmeed became the ruler of Prayagraj and Hastinapur, yet the main capital remained Hastinapur. Hastinapur was not only a political center but also a popular pilgrimage center on the banks of river Yamuna. Nil, the son of King Ajmidh, became ruler of the North-West kingdom in Ahicchapur and Kampila. Brihatsu, the other son of Ajmidh, became the ruler of South Panchal. Due to the bright historical image of king Ajmidh, in the Vana Parva of Mahabharat, Vidur and king Janhu were referred as Ajmidhites.

After King Ajmidh, the great Pandava Dynasty and Kaurava Dynasty originated from King Kuru, the great son of king Samvarna. King Kuru made Kurukshetra a Dharmasthana by performing thousands of Yajnas and cleansing the place with the holy water of the river Saraswati. King Ajmidh had also founded the pilgrimage center of Ajayameru (Ajmer).

King Drupad :

The great king Drupad was in the lineage of King Nil, the second son of king Ajmidh. Dhrishtadyumna, the intelligent son of king Drupada (Gita 1.3) was the commander-in-chief of the Pandavas in the Mahabharat war. Draupadi, the wife of Pandavas was the daughter of King Drupad.

4. Angre Dynasty, Kulaba, Maharashtra (1680-1844)

1. Kanhoji Angre-1   कान्होजी आंग्रे-1   1690–1729
2. Shekhoji   शेखोजी   1729–1733
3. Sambhaji   संभाजी   1734–1735
4. Manaji-1   मानाजी-1   1735–1758*
5. Raghuji-1   रघुजी-1   1759–1793
6. Manaji-2   मानाजी-2   1793–1799
7. Babarao   बाबाराव   1799–1813
8. Manaji-3   मानाजी-3   1813–1817
9. Raghuji-2   रघुजी-2   1817–1838
10. Kanhoji-2   कान्होजी-2   1838–1839
11. Kanhoji-3   कान्होजी-3   1839–1844

* Manaji ruled with his brother Tulaji (1735–1756)

Angre Dynasty

Angre was a famous clan from a village called Angarwadi in Maharashtra. They played an important role in the history of the Marathas.

Sekhoji Angre's son Tukoji Angre became famous in the battles along with Maratha chieftain Shri Shahaji Bhosle (1594-1664).

In 1859, Tukoji Angre became a high ranking officer (Sarkhel) of the Marine Navy in Shivaji's army. After the death of Tukoji, his son Kanhoji Angre (1690–1729) was considered as the founder of the Royal House of Angre. This Kanhoji Angra was considered as the bravest and best warrior of the Angre Maratha Dynasty, who never gave up a fight in any war.

Angre Dynasty

Kanhoji Angre of Angarvadi, was a bold Warrior,
He fought naval wars, in Western corridor. 1

The brave Angre warriors, became famous quickly,
Shivaji employed them, in his army permanently. 2

They controlled Konkan, on the Western Sea Coast,
Kanhoji held the important, Navy General's post. 3

There were no better people, to fight the naval war,
For an amphibious battle, Kanhoji was a star. 4

Angres built and guarded forts, in the Konkan region,
Kulaba was their station, for the Maratha legion. 5

Kanhoji was the best, in the Angre power,
Let us salute him, with gratitude and honor. 6

5. Queer Avanti Bai of Ramgadh (1831-1858)

1. Vikramjit Singh विक्रमजीत सिंह 1851–1857
2. Avanti Bai अवंती बाई 1857–1858

> **Rani Avanti Bai**
> *This brave woman, jumped in the freedom fight,*
> *This Queen from Mandla, never took it light.*

Rani Avanti Bai

Vikramjit Singh (1851–1857) was the king of Ramgarh region of Mandla district in central India (Madhya Pradesh). King Vikramjit Singh was married to Avant Bai, the daughter of Jagirdar Rao Jhursingh of Manekhadi area of Seoni district. King Vikramjit Singh and Avanti Bai had two sons named Sher Singh and Aman Singh.

In 1857, King Vikramjit Singh died and Queen Avantibai took the power. She stood up against the British usurpation policy.

Queen Avanti Bai mobilized her society and raised her army against the British. The ruler of Mandla, Shri Shankar Shah took the leadership of the struggle in his hands.

Queen Avanti Bai's rebellion was pioneer in the freedom struggle of 1857. She was fighting the British along with Queen Lakshmibai Newalkar (1853–1858) of Jhansi. The British captured the queen Avanti Bai's motivator, Shri Shankar Shah and killed him after giving him death penalty.

Now Queen Avanti Bai started fighting alone. In a battle, the queen was about to be caught at the hands of the British, but the heroine cut her throat with her own sword and took to heaven with pride and smile on her face. She gained heroic martyrdom.

Hindu Rajtarangini

6. Bana Dynasty, Vanapuram (720-900)

For the Earlier Dynasty, please see :
Chola Dynasty, Tanjavar (50–1279)

1.	Jaya Nandi Varma	जयनंदीवर्मा	720
2.	Vijayaditya-1	विजयादित्य-1	
3.	Malla Deva	मल्लदेव	
4.	Vidyadhara-2	विद्याधर-1	870
5.	Prabhu Meru Deva	प्रभुमेरुदेव	890
6.	Vidyadhara-2	विद्याधर-2	
		= (विक्रमादित्य-1)	
7.	Vijayaditya-2	विजयादित्य-2	
8.	Vidyadhara-3	विद्याधर-3	
9.	Vijayaditya-3	विजयादित्य-3	
		= (विक्रमादित्य-2)	900

Baana Dynasty

Perumbanappady, i.e. the great Baana country situated to the West of Andhra, extended to Kerala. The Baana Kingdom was also attached to the Tamil territory. It was a feudatory of the Tamil Chola kings. Its capital was known by the name Vanapuram or Thiruvellam.

The Baana Dynasty ruled for nearly two hundred years from the Godavari in the North to the Palar river in the south. The kings of this Dynasty stood steadfast as the shield of the kingdom from the invasions from Andhra country and Kerala.

Baana Dynasty

Almost for two centuries,
the Baana kings ruled,
Andhra and Kerala kings,
they always befooled. 1
From Godavari to Palar,
Baana kingdom spread,
Western to Eastern mountains,
was Baana dread. 2
Bananas were attached,
to the Tamils great,
They also had shelter,
from the Cholas late. 3
Their first ruler was,
Jainandi with renown,
Nine rulers of this line,
were well known. 4

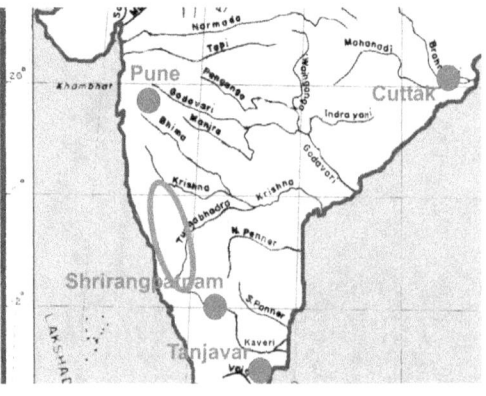

7. Bharat Dynasty (Ancient Time)

For the Earlier Dynasty, please see : पुरु राजवंश (Ancient Time)

1. Dushyant — दुष्यंत
2. Bharat — भरत
3. Suhotra — सुहोत्र
4. Bhritakshetra — भृतक्षेत्र
5. Hasti — हस्ति
6. Ajmidh — अजमीढ़

For the Next Dynasty, please see :
Ajmidh Dynasty (Ancient Time)

Bharat Dynasty

The son of Shakuntala,
was the great king Bharat,
After whose name,
this country is called Bhaarat. 1

The descendents of Bharat,
Bharatiya themselves call,
We enjoy that culture,
the rich ancient windfall. 2

Bharat Dynasty

At lEast five great men of the name "Bharat (भरत)" are found in the ancient Indian history: Bharat-1: son of Dushyant and Shakuntala; Bharat-2: King Dasaratha's son Bharata in Raghu Dynasty; Bharat-3: Son of King Rishabha (Swayambhuva Manu-Priyabrata-Agidhar-Nabhi-Rishabh-Bharat); Bharat-4: Author of Natyashastra, the Maharishi Bharata; And Bharat-5: A son of Lord Agni, the Fire God.

Bharat-1 Chakravarti, son of Dushyant and Shakuntala, was king and his country is called Bharat (भरत) or Bharatvarsha (India) after his name. The first and the only king in history, Bharat had declared that, "it is not necessary that the king should be only a son of a king." Also he said, "it should not be true that a king could be born in the king's house only."

Maharaja Hasti, son of King Bhritakshetra, built the new city of Hastinapur. He was the one who transferred his capital from Prayagraj to Hastinapur and made it the eternal capital of Bharat Varsha.

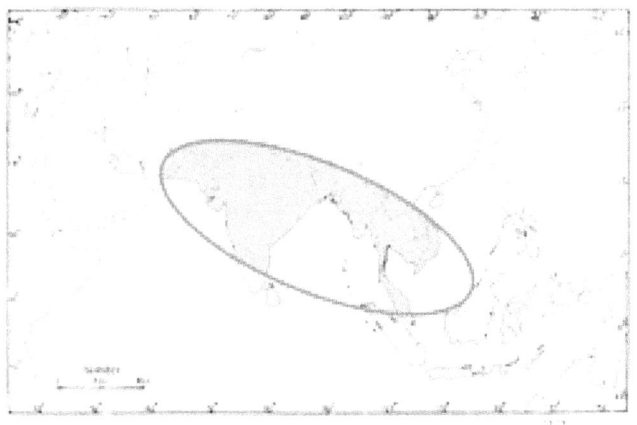

Hindu Rajtarangini

8. Bhati Raval Dynasty, Jaisalmer (731-1948)

1. Bhati — भाटी
2. Mangal — मंगल
3. Majam Rao — माजम राओ
4. Kehar Simha — केहर सिंह — 731–806
5. Tano Simha — तानो सिंह — 806–821
6. Vijay-1 — विजय-1 — 821–853
7. Devraj — देवराज — 853–908
8. Mundha — मुंध — 908–979
9. Vijay-2 — विजय-2 — 979–1044
10. Dusaj — दुसज — 1044–1123
11. Bhojdeva — भोजदेव — 1123–1155
12. Jaisal — जैसाल — 1155–1167
13. Shalivahan — शालिवाहन — 1167–1189
14. Baldev — बलदेव — 1189–1189
15. Kailan — कैलन — 1189–1218
16. Chakchakdeva-1 — चकचकदेव-1 — 1218–1242
17. Karan Simha — करन सिंह — 1242–1270
18. Lakshman Sen — लक्ष्मण सेन — 1270–1274
19. Punyapal* — पुण्यपाल — 1274–176

   Father of Maharani Padmavati of Chittor

20. Jaitsimha — जैतसिंह-1 — 1276–1293
21. Moolraj-1 — मूलराज-1 — 1293–1295
22. Dudar — दुदर — 1295–1311
23. Vishal Deva — विशालदेव — 1311–1316
24. Ghar Simha — घरसिंह — 1316–1334
25. Kehar Simha — केहर सिंह — 1334–1394
26. Lakshman — लक्ष्मण — 1394–1439

Bhati Dynasty

Brave Bhati or Bhatti were Solar Rajput kings. Bhati Rajput king Bappa Rawal was from Lahore. The Jats and Gurjars were Bhati Rajputs.

King Kehar Singh Bhati built Tantot city in Rajasthan after year 730 and made it his capital. In 853, Vijay Rawal settled the capital at Lodurwa. In 1155, the King Jaisal built the capital city named Jaisalmer and built the Jaisalmer Fort.

Later on the Bhati Rajputs were established in Ambar, Bikaner, Bundi, Jodhpur, Kannauj, Mewar, Malwa, etc. The famous Rajput queen Padmini of Chittaud was the daughter of King Punyapala (1274–1276).

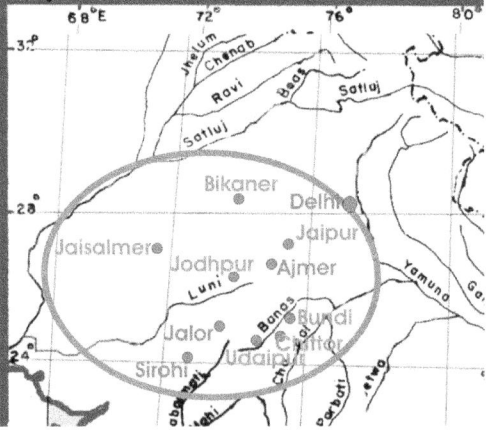

Hindu Rajtarangini

#	Name	नाम	Period
27.	Ber Simha	बेर सिंह	1439–1449
28.	Chakchakdeva-2	चकचकदेव-2	1449–1455
19.	Devidas	देवीदास	1455–1496
20.	Jait Simha-2	जैतसिंह-2	1496–1528
21.	Karan Simha	करन सिंह	1528–1528
22.	Lunkaran	लूनकरन	1528–1550
23.	Maldev	मालदेव	1550–1561
24.	Harraj	हरराज	1561–1577
25.	Bhima Simha	भीम सिंह	1577–1613
26.	Kalyan Dimha	कल्याण सिंह	1613–1627
27.	Manohar Das	मनोहर दास	1627–1648
28.	Ram Chandra	रामचंद्र	1648–1651
29.	Sabal Simha	सबल सिंह	1651–1661
30.	Amar Simha	अमर सिंह	1661–1702
31.	Yashvant Simha	यशवंत सिंह	1702–1708
32.	Budh Simha	बुध सिंह	1708–1720
33.	Tez Simha	तेज सिंह	1720–1722
34.	Sawai Simha	सवाई सिंह	1722–1722
35.	Aksha Simha	अक्ष सिंह	1722–1762
36.	Moolraj-2	मूलराज-2	1762–1819
37.	Gaja Simha	गजसिंह	1819–1846
38.	Ranjit Simha	रणजीत सिंह	1846–1864
39.	Bairisal	बैरीसाल	1864–1890
40.	Shalivahan	शालिवाहन	1890–1914
41.	Jawahar Simha	जवाहर सिंह	1914–1949
42.	Giridhar Simha	गिरिधर सिंह	1949–1950

9. Bhosle Dynasty, Satara (1594-1848)

	Bhairosimha	भैरोसिंह	
	Maloji	मालोजी	
	Shahaji-1 Raje	शहाजी राजे	1594–1664
1.	Shivaji Chhatrapati	शिवाजी छत्रपति	1674–1680
2.	Sambhaji Raje	संभाजी राजे	1680–1689
3.	Rajaram	राजाराम	1689–1700
4.	Tarabai	ताराबाई	1700–1708
5.	Sahu-1 (Shivaji)	साहू-1	1708–1749
6.	Ramraja	रामराजा	1749–1777
7.	Sahu-2	साहू-2	1777–1808
8.	Pratap Simha	प्रताप सिंह	1808–1839
9.	Shahaji-2	शहाजी	1839–1848

Bhosle Dynasty of Satara

After the death of Maratha Brave King Chhatrapati Shri Shivaji Maharaj (1680), the Dynasty of Sambhaji Raje (1656–1689), the valiant son of Queen Sayibai (1640–1659), located the capital at Satara, and Rajaram (1650–1681), son of Queen Soyarabai (1650–1681). 1670-1700) fixed his capital at Kolhapur.

King Sahu-1 of Satara was son of Sambhaji Raje (1680-1689) and Queen Yashwanta Bai (1659-1731). Ekoji or Vyankoji (1631-1685) was Shivaji's half-brother, son of Shahaji Bhosle (1594-1664) and his wife Tukabai Mohita (married 1624). Ekoji founded the Maratha kingdom (1675–1684) of Tanjavar.

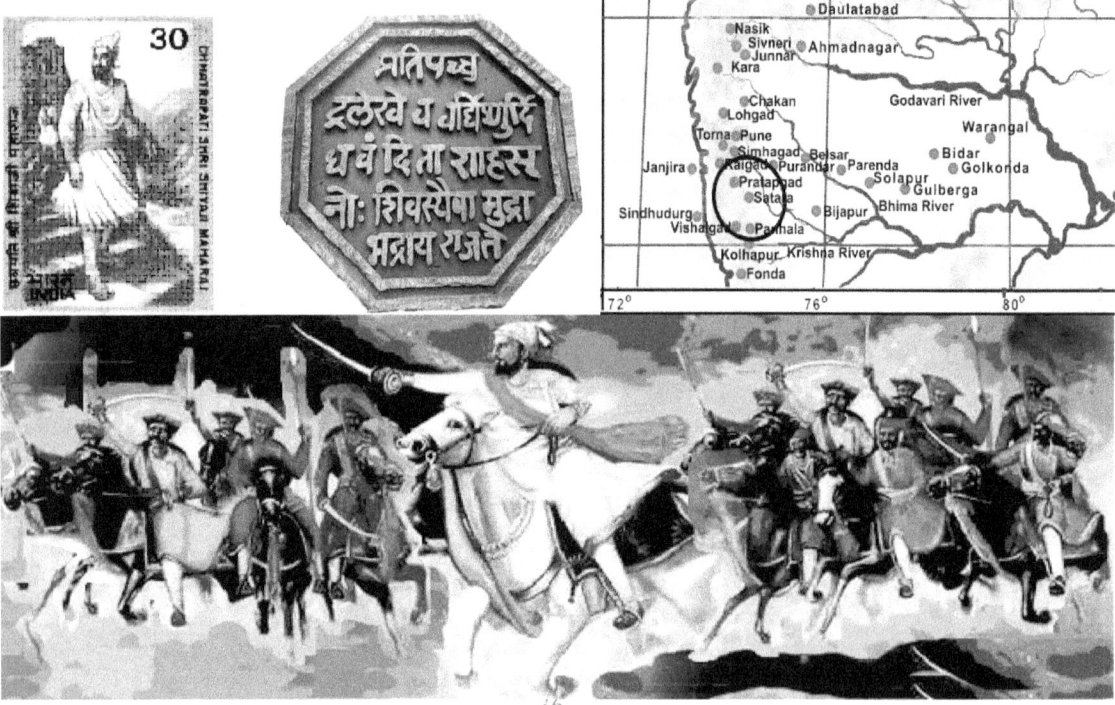

Hindu Rajtarangini

Chhatrapati Shivaji Bhosle

Whenever dharma diminishes,
and adharma takes over,
Lord appears on the earth,
to protect dharma lover. 1
For protecting truth, and removing false,
He takes birth,
when the right moment falls. 2

(Birth of Shivaji)

When the right time arrived, the holy men came,
To bless the arrival of, the Avatara of fame. 3
The attendants came,
to sweep the room with broom,
An idol of Shiv ji, installed in the room. 4
Doctors and maids came, to deliver the star,
Shivaji was born, the Shiv ji's avatar. 5
Hearing the cry, of the new born child,
People clapped with joy,
and the elation got wild. 6
The news spread around, with electric speed,
Security on the fort,
tightened with urgent need. 7
Brahma-Vishnu-Shiva,
came to bless the baby boy,
The men and women all,
sang with the joy. 8
The Maratha braves,
played the drums loud,
The boys and girls danced,
everyone was proud. 9
Reading palm of the baby, the fortune teller told,
The boy will grow, brave and very bold. 10
More and more grave, the Sultans had become,
Mother gave Shivaji, the lessons of freedom. 11
The seed he had sown, when he was ten,
Assembling his friends, young boys and men. 12
First victory was Torana, the fort that was old,
For the freedom struggle, they became bold. 13

(Jijabai's teachings)

Mother made Shivaji, a great freedom fighter,
Even the greatest danger, he made it lighter. 14
To the foreign Sultan, his father gave a bow,
But for Shivaji, it was unacceptable now. 15

Chhatrapati Shivaji Bhosle continued

In the freedom fight, help some gave,
Even though many were, happy being slave. 16
Awful events occurred, he faced them all,
His kingdom grew slowly,
up to Jinji after-all. 17
Sometimes he got trapped,
sometimes he was jailed,
But, in front of Shivaji, all efforts failed. 18
Disciple of Ramdas, Shivaji was king,
He ruled with ethics, honour to bring. 19
The lover of freedom, the fearless hero,
Even the giant Mughals,
in front of him zero. 20
He served subjects well,
with patience and calm,
Righteous king he was,
just like Shri Ram. 21

(and)

On the battlefield, he stood strong,
Acted with wisdom, and never went wrong. 22
He punished well, the idol-breaker fools,
He made public happy, with available tools. 23
He sat with saints, enjoyed their speech,
He always obeyed, the goodness they teach. 24
Never touched wine, he respected women,
He was never cruel, humanity his domain. 25
He protected cows, gave happiness to all,
He knew scriptures, he was a merciful pal. 26
Protector of Dharma, savior of Maharashtra,
Obeisance to the great, hero of his era. 27
Upholder of Dharma, destroyer of enemies,
We will never forget, his paramount aegis. 28

(Death of Shivaji)

Sixteen-hundred-eighty,
was the year very bad,
In the Maratha History,
it brought the news sad. 29
The struggle for freedom,
one chapter got closed,
On the death of Shivaji,
great dangers posed. 30

Chhatrapati Shri Shivaji the Greatest Freedom Fighter (1630-1680)

गीत : कहरवा ताल 8 मात्रा

शिवलीलामृत

स्थायी

सुना रहा हूँ गायन सुंदर, शिवलीला का कथा समुंदर ।

अंतरा-1

जन्म शिवा का शिव अवतारा, मातु-जिजा का नंदन न्यारा ।
स्वतंत्रता का अद्भुत नारा, महाराष्ट्र में पहिला नंबर ।।

अंतरा-2

श्रीगणेश है विजय-तोरणा, जीते और रचे गढ़ नाना ।
अमर-कहानी जय-कोंडाणा, हर्ष से खिले धरती-अंबर ।।

अंतरा-3

ढेर किये अरि जाने-माने, दिल्लीपति को चकमे दीन्हे ।
सुलतानों के मुश्किल जीने, कूटनीति से कीन्हे संगर ।।

अंतरा-4

पर-नारी को माँ का आदर, भूप शिवाजी सद्गुण आगर ।
सुन कर अमर कथा का सागर, आनंदित हैं भवानी-शंकर ।।

Shiva-Leelamrit

*I am singing lovely song, of Shivaji's divine deeds.
Shivaji is an avatar of Shiva, he is son of Jija,
He declared independence in the Maratha land.
He captured Torna and made holy beginning,
Then Kondhana he won, the earth is happy.
The giant enemies he killed, deluded Delhi Sultan,
He made their life difficult, won many battles.
Other women he thought, as his mothers,
Hearing his life story, Uma and Shiva are happy.*

गीत : कहरवा ताल 8 मात्रा

आदर्श शिवाजी

स्थायी

वीर शिवाजी, मंगल पावन, नीति परायण, नृपवर है - - - ।
दीनन बंधु, करुणा सिंधु, सद्गुण इंदु, सुधाकर हैं - - - ।।

अंतरा-1

संकट त्राता, हैं सुख दाता, चंचल चतुर, सुधी नर हैं - - - ।
शूर शिवाजी, तान्हा बाजी, विघ्न विनाशक, शुभंकर हैं - - - ।।

अंतरा-2

भारत गौरव, कीर्ति सौरभ, अबला रक्षक, नृपवर हैं ।
कर्म अनेक महान किए हैं, चरित्र मंगल सुंदर है ।।

अंतरा-3

मर्द मराठा जनगण प्यारा, हिंदुधर्म का रक्षक है ।
भारत माँ का सुपुत्र न्यारा, शुचि अवतारी शंकर है ।।

Noble Shivaji

Brave Shivaji is holy, and ethical king,
Brother for helpless, ocean of mercy,
infinite wisdom,
He is pleasant like the moon.
Protects from dangers, he is giver of joy,
He is quick, clever and wise.
Shivaji is great, so is Baji.
He removed dangers, his deeds are awesome.
He is the glory of India, his fame is fragrance,
He is protector of women, he is a super king,
He did many wonderful deeds,
His character is clean, noble and nice
Brave Maratha hero, loved by people,
Protector of Hindu Culture, Great son of India,
He is a holy avatar of Shiva ji.

गीत : कहरवा ताल 8 मात्रा

शिवाजी राजे

राग : भैरव, कहरवा ताल, 8 मात्रा

स्थायी

वीर शिवाजी, हैं सुख दाता, नीति परायण शासक हैं ।
दीनन बंधु, किरपा सिंधु, विपदा शत्रु विनाशक हैं ।।

अंतरा–1

कर्म अनेक महान किये हैं, संकट विघ्न निवारक हैं ।
सत्य सहायक अनुपम सज्जन, योगी तापस साधक हैं ।।

अंतरा–2

पुत्र बहादुर भारत माँ का, धर्मध्वजा का पूजक है ।
राज्य हिंदवी स्वराज्य स्थापक, शिव अवतार शुभंकर है ।।

King Shivaji

Brave Maratha hero, loved by people,
Protector of Dharma, dear son of India.
Holy avatar of Shiva Shankar.
Brave Shivaji, giver of happiness,
he is ethical ruler.
Friend of the needy, merciful protector.

Many amazing deeds, he has performed,
Many giant enemies, he has destroyed.
Protector of truth and good people,
He is a Yogi and divine soul.

He is a brave son, Carrier of Bhagva Flag,
Founder of Hindu Rashtra.

Homage to Chhatrapati Shri Shivaji maharaj

(सन 1680)

प्रार्थना

स्थायी
देना प्रभो! शांति इस आत्मा को ।
तुमको हमारी, यह वंदना है ।।

अंतरा–1
आत्मा मिले ये परमात्मा से ।
लेना चरण में, यह प्रार्थना है ।।

अंतरा–2
सारे जगत के, आनंद दाता ।
गोविंद! देना, सुख आत्मा को ।।

अंतरा–3
हे कृष्ण! दामोदर! चक्रपाणि! ।
इसे मोक्ष देना, यह अर्चना है ।।

अंतरा–5
इसे पुण्य की तू, घनी छाँव देना ।
तुझसे भवानी! यही माँगना है ।।

अंतरा–6
नीति सदाचार का ये पुजारी ।
आजन्म इसकी, हृद् स्पंदना है ।।

(Year 1680)

Homage to Chhatrapati Shivaji

A Prayer

Sthayi
O Lord! please give eternal peace to this departed soul, this is our humble prayer to you.

Antara
O Lord!, may you keep this person in your shelter,
it is our request to you. 1

O Govind! the Joy giver, please bestow peace on
this departed soul. 2

O Lord Krishna!
O Damodar! O Chakrapani!
please liberate this soul. 3

O Amba Bhavani! O Lord Shiva!
please place this soul
in the heaven. 4

O Lord! this soul worshipped ethics and humanity,
It has been his
life long heart beat. 5

10. Bhosle Dynasty, Kolhapur (1689-1940)

	Name	Devanagari	Years
	Bhairo Simha	भैरोसिंह	
	Maloji	मालोजी	
	Shahaji Raje	शहाजी राजे	(1594–1664)
	Shivaji Chhatrapati	शिवाजी छत्रपति	1674–1680
	Rajaram	राजाराम	1689–1700
1.	Shivaji-1	शिवाजी-1	1700–1712
2.	Shambhuji-1	शंभुजी-1	1712–1760
3.	Shivaji-2	शिवाजी-2	1760–1813
4.	Shambhuji-2	शंभुजी-2	1813–1821
5.	Shivaji-3	शिवाजी-3	1821–1822
6.	Shahaji-1	शहाजी-1	1821–1837
7.	Shivaji-4	शिवाजी-4	1837–1866
8.	Rajaram-1	राजाराम-1	1866–1870
9.	Shivaji-5	शिवाजी-5	1870–1883
10.	Shahu	शाहू	1883–1922
11.	Rajaram-2	राजाराम-2	1922–1940
12.	Rajasbai	राजसबाई	1940–1942
13.	Shivaji-6	शिवाजी-6	1942–1947
14.	Shahaji-2	शहाजी-2	1947–1949

Bhosle Dynasty of Kolhapur

After the death (1680) of Maratha Brave Chhatrapati Shri Shivaji Maharaj, the Dynasty of Rajaram (1670–1700), son of Queen Soyarabai (1650–1681), fixed their capital at Kolhapur. After Rajaram, Shivaji (1696–1726), son of Rajaram-Tarabai, was declared king.

After the death of this Shivaji of Kolhapur, Rajaram's second wife Queen Rajasabai appointed her son Shambhu-1 (1696-1760) to rule Kolhapur (1712-1760). On 1 March 1949, Kolhapur merged with the Mumbai province.

Bhosle Dynasty of Kolhapur

The descendents of Sambhaji,
founded Satara Kingdom,
Descendents of Rajaram,
founded Kolhapur Kingdom. 1

Kolhapur House had,
internal struggles,
Still they survived,
in spite of the troubles. 2

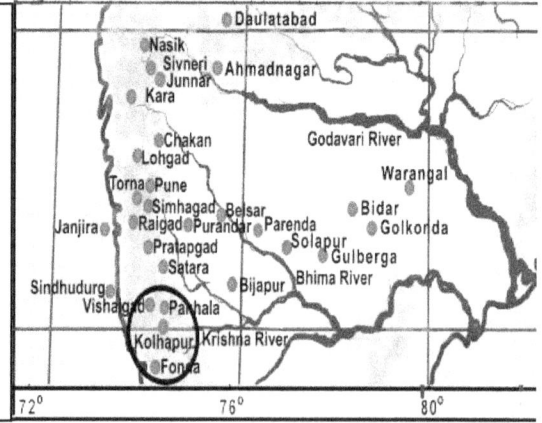

Hindu Rajtarangini

11. Bhosle Dynasty, Tanjavar (1675-1855)

	Bhairo Simha	भैरोसिंह	
	Maloji	मालोजी	
	Shahaji Raje	शहाजी राजे	(1594–1664)
1.	Ekoji	एकोजी राजे	1675–1684
2.	Shahaji	शहाजी	1684–1712
3.	Sarfoji-1	सरफोजी-1	1712–1728
4.	Tukoji	तुकोजी	1728–1735
5.	Baba Saheb	बाबा साहेब	1735–1736
6.	Sujana Bai	सुजनाबाई	1736–1738
7.	Savai Shahaji	सवाई शहाजी	1738–1738
8.	Sayaji	सयाजी	1738–1739
9.	Pratap Simha	प्रताप सिंह	1739–1763
10.	Tuljaji	तुलजाजी	1763–1787
11.	Amar Simha	अमर सिंह	1787–1798
12.	Sarfoji-2	सरफोजी-2	1798–1824
13.	Shivaji	शिवाजी	1824–1855

Bhosle Dynasty of Kolhapur

Jijabai (1595-1674), the first wife of Shahaji Bhosle (1594–1664) was the mother of Chhatrapati Shivaji Maharaj (1630–1680), the son of Jijabai (1595–1674), and the second wife was Tukabai Mohite (married. 1624). Her son was Ekoji or Vyankoji Bhosle (1631–1685). He established the Maratha kingdom of Thanjavar.

The work of this family was carried out only with the help of non-resident foreigners, and Bhosle power was established here with the help of them. The last king Sarfoji Bhosle (1824–1855) was a lover of art and a patron of dance and music.

Bhosle Dynasty of Tanjavar

Ekoji Bhosle Maratha, ruled from Tanjavar,
Many enemies of Shivaji,
friends of Ekoji they were. 1
This kingdom he ruled,
with the help of foreign hands,
Foreigners were his supporters,
who managed his lands. 2
At the court of Ekoji, many arts flourished,
Dance and music,
artists were nourished. 3

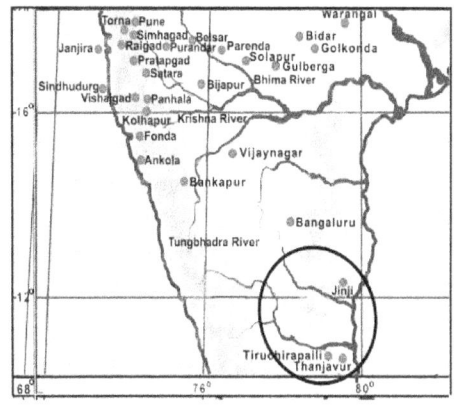

12. Bhosle Dynasty, Nagpur (1675-1855)

	Bimbaji	बिंबाजी	
	Mudhohi-1	मुधोजी–1, अमरावतीकर	
	Bapuji	बापूजी	
1.	Parsoji-1	परसोजी–1 नागपुरकर	1699–1707
2.	Kanhoji	कान्होजी	1709–1731
3.	Raghuji-1	रघुजी–1	1731–1755
4.	Janoji-1	जानोजी–1	1755–1772
5.	Raghuji-2	रघुजी–2	1772–1775
6.	Mudhoji-2	मुधोजी–2	1775–1778
7.	Raghuji-3	रघुजी–3	1788–1816
8.	Parsoji-2	परसोजी–2	1816–1817
9.	Appa Saheb	आप्पा साहेब, मुधोजी–3	1817–1818
10.	Raghuji-4	रघुजी–4, बाजीबा	1818–1853
11.	Janoji-2	जानोजी–2, यशवंतराव	1853–1854

Bhosle Dynasty of Nagpur

The ancestors of the Bhosle Dynasty of Nagpur, served in Chhatrapati Shri Shivaji Maharaja's army and earned a place in the Maratha kingdom by their valor. Thus they secured a place of rule in Vidarbha. Mudhoji-1 Bhosle was located in Amravati.

Parsoji-1 was in the army of King Chhatrapati Shivaji (1674–1680). Hence, after the death of Chhatrapati Shivaji, Parsoji Bhosle was given the authority of Nagpur (1699–1707) by Rajaram Bhosle (1689–1700), the king of Satara. In 1867, Janoji-2 got the title of Raja. In their internal battles, the Bhosle of Nagpur got their Dynasty destroyed and their important rule was ruined.

Bhosle Dynasty of Nagpur

The Bhosle of Nagpur,
believed they are Rajputs,
But they were Gonds,
ancient were their roots. 1
Employed by Shivaji, at a level lower,
But with their bravery, they rose to power. 2
At the service of the Marathas,
they earned respect,
They proved themselves fit,
in every war aspect. 3
From Chanda Deogadh, and Gondwan forest,
They settled in Nagpur,
and became rulers best. 4
But they ruined themselves,
with the internal struggle,
They lost their power,
diplomacy they couldn't juggle. 5

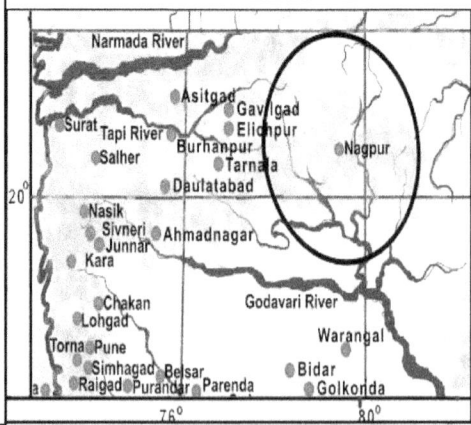

Bhutan and Sikkim, Hindu Dynasties (1591-1948)

1. Bhutan, Devraj and Wangchul Dynasty (1591-1948)
2. Sikkim, Namgyal Dynasty (1642-1948)

13. Wangchuk Dynasty, Thimphu, Bhutan (1907-1948)

1. Yugen Wangchuk — युगेन वांगचुक — 1907–1926
2. Jigme Dorgi Wangchuk — जिग्मे दोरजी वांगचुक — 1926–1948

14. Namgyal Dynasty, Gangtok, Sikkim (1642-1948)

1. Futsog Namgyal-1 — फुंटसोग नामग्याल-1 — 1642–1670
2. Tensung Namgyal — तेनसुंग नामग्याल — 1670–1700
3. Chador Namgyal — चदोर नामग्याल — 1700–1717
4. Gurmed Namgyal — गुरमेद नामग्याल — 1717–1733
5. Futsog Namgyal-2 — फुंटसोग नामग्याल-2 — 1733–1780
6. Tensing Namgyal — तेनसिंह नामग्याल — 1780–1793
7. Sugfud Namgyal — सुगफुद नामग्याल — 1793–1863
8. Sidkang Namgyal-1 — सिदकंग नामग्याल-1 — 1863–1874
9. Thutob Namgyal — थुतोब नामग्याल — 1874–1914
10. Sidkang Namgyal-2 — सिदकंग नामग्याल-2 — 1914–1914
11. Tashi Namgyal — ताशी नामग्याल — 1914–1948

Bhutan, Sikkim

The Devaraja Dynasty (1591– 1907) of Bhutan was founded in the sixteenth century by a branch of the Dynasty of the Hindu king Rajamuda Lumay (1621–1622) of the Khmer kingdom from the island of Chebu, Philippine.

After defeating the last king of this Devaraja Dynasty, Yugen Wangchuk (1907–1926) king of Bhutan established the Wangchuk Dynasty (1907–1948) of Bhutan in the capital Thinphu.

In the seventeenth century, King Gawang Namgyal of this Wangchuk family established the Namgyal or Chogayal Dynasty of Sikkim, the Royal House of the monarchy in the capital Gangtok (1642–1948).

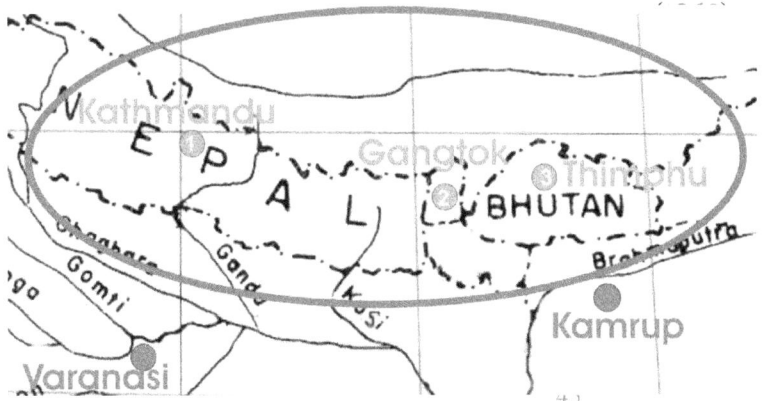

Hindu Rajtarangini

15. Brihadrith Dynasty, Magadh (Ancient Time)

1. Vasu — वसु ...
2. Brihadrath — बृहद्रथ
3. Amana Devi — अमना देवी
4. Kushagra — कुशाग्र
5. Vriksha — वृश्व
6. Pushyant — पुष्यवंत
7. Satyadhrita — सत्यधृत
8. Sudharma — सुधर्म
9. Dhanush — धनुष
10. Urja — उर्ज
11. Sambhava — संभव
12. Jarasandha — जरासंध
13. Sahadeva — सहदेव
14. Ripunjaya — रिपुंजय
15. Bimbisar — बिंबिसार   554–492 BC.

For the Next Dynasty, please see :
Haryak Dynasty, Magadh (544–413 ई.पू.)

Brihadrath Dynasty

The oldest Dynasty of Magadha kingdom was the Royal House of Brihadrath (Maha. Adi. 30.63). Brihadrath was the son of King Jarasandha. He was the most majestic and illustrious king of this Dynasty. Jara Devi had given birth to Jarasandha by joining two eggs together, so his name became Jarasandha.

The mighty Pandava Bhima killed Jarasandha in a wrestling war that occurred due to the sin of Jarasandha of committing heinous insults of Shri Krishna in a court meeting. The last king of the Brihadrath Dynasty was Ripunjaya, who was murdered by his minister Pulik. Pulik then put his son on the throne, but he was also killed by his subordinate named Bhattiya who made his son Bimbisara king over the empire of Magadha. Emperor Bimbisara founded his new Harayak Dynasty (544–413 BC).

Brihadrath Dynasty

Yayati's son Puru,
Puru's son was Dushyant,
And their Lunar Dynasty,
was significant. 1
Brihadrath ruled Magadha,
and he was efficient,
This Dushyanta's Dynasty,
was a family ancient. 2
Jarasandha of this lineage,
was valiant sinful king,
like the Kamsa menacing. 3
Jarasandha insulted Krishna,
in the kings court,
Bhima the Pandava, killed him in a spurt. 4

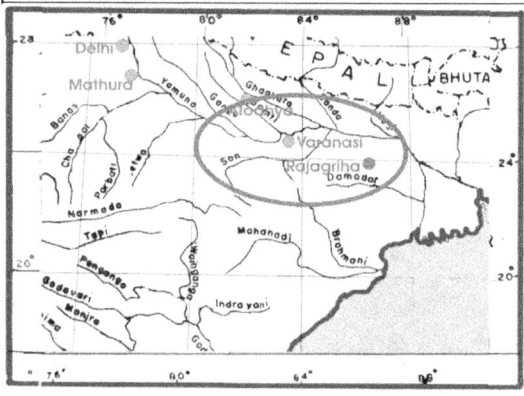

16. Burma (Mynmar), Hindu Dynasties (50-1828)

1. Funan Dynasty (50-627)
2. Kamrup Varma Dynasty (350-350)
3. Khmer Dynasty (802-1431)
4. Sen Dynasty (1185-1498)
5. Ahom Dynasty (1228-1828)
6. Manikya Dynasty (1400-1948)
7. Khen Dynasty (1440-1498)

Hindu Dynasties of Burma

It is known from the documents of history that the first of the kingdoms of Hindu culture over Burma was the power of the Funan (50-627) kings of Vyadhpur over Yangon (Rangoon) and Mandalay. after the Funan kings, the authority of Varma Royal House of Kamrup-Pragjyotishpur remained steady for one year (350-350).

After the Kamrup kings of Pragjyotishpur, the rulers of Burma were the great Khmer kingdom of Yashodapur (802-1431). From 802 to 1140, the power of Burma was divided among the Kamrup feudatory kings and the Khmer kings. Along with that, the Sena rulers of Bengal also asserted their authority (1185-1498) over the territory of Burma. In addition to Sena rule, Ahom kings of Rangpur Assam started establishing power (1228-1828). From time to time, the Manikya Dynasty of Tripura (1400–1948) also established authority in Burma. Finally, the Khen kings of Kamata (Kamrup) (1440–1498) had taken possession of some areas of Burma for a short time. There were only three kings of this Khen Dynasty: 1. Niladhvaja (1440–1460), Chakradhwaja (1460–1480) and Nilambar (1480–1498).

Among the ancient Hindu temples of Burma is the 11th century Nath Linga Vishnu temple of Bagan. In other temples, temples of Indra Bhagwan, Ramsatattva (Adhana), Saraswati Devi, Shiva Parmeshwar, etc. Gods and Goddesses are extant.

17. Chach Dynasty, Alor, Sindh (631-712)

For the Pervious Dynasty, please see :
Rai Dynasty of Sindh (489–631)

1. Maharaja Chach   महाराजा चाच   643–671
2. Chandra   चंद्र   671–679
3. Maharaja Dahir   महाराजा दाहीर   679–712
4. Hillu   हिल्लु   712–712
5. Shisha   शीश   712–724

Chach Dynasty, Sindh

Maharaja Chach: Maharaja Chach of Sindh region was a great and ideal suzerain in Hindu history. Maharaja Chach's younger brother Chandra was the Prime Minister of Alor. The glory of Maharaja Chach was omnipresent in all four directions.

Maharaja Dahir: The great King Dahir, the son of Maharaja Chach was the best king of Sindh. A famous lion like Maharaja Dahir was brave and his brave lioness was his Empress Ladi. The ideals of Dahir's valor were a source of inspiration and enthusiasm for the Rajput Maharanas of Rajastan.

Maharaja Chach

In year six-hundred-thirty-six,
came Arab warlords,
To capture Hindu lands,
with the force of their swords. *1*
Khalifa's horsemen, won many wars,
Now they came to Sindh, without any bars. *2*
Came Arab invader, marching like a despot,
Winning Iran and Syria, Sindh next spot. *3*
This was the Arabic first,
invasion worth known,
Defenders were strong,
the war Hindus won. *4*
Ruler of the Sindh was, famous king Chach,
Country was so peaceful,
there was no match. *5*
He was a glorious king, well known his name,
Ethical and righteous, everywhere his fame. *6*
Chach was sovereign king, illustrious ever,
Opulent his kingdom was,
on the Sindu river. *7*
When those Arabs came,
with the military pack,
King Chach defeated them,
and turned them back. *8*
Chach was a mighty king, jewel in the crown,
King of Sindh Alore, loved in every town. *9*
Multan was other place, not far from Alor,
It was a battlefield, with the fame galore. *10*

Maharaja Dahir

When the king of Sindh, was Dahir the Great,
On the battlefield, Queen Ladi was his mate. *1*
When the Arabs came, to fight again,
Spreading their own faith,
their aim was main. *2*
Blinded with the faith,
and bearing the swords,
They wanted everyone,
to obey their words. *3*
They demolished temples,
vandalized the towns,
converted the people,
and burnt the godowns. *4*
Dahir came to fight, and the queen also came,
King Dahir was a lion, lioness was her fame. *5*
With one stray arrow, Dahir got shot,
He fell on the ground, and was bleeding a lot. *6*
Queen was still fighting, but unable to win,
Ladi got caught and fell, in the hands of sin. *7*
Dahir was beheaded, with the utter hate,
Khalifa received the Queen, to spoil her fate. *8*
Multan town was slaughtered,
the ground ran red,
Who refused to convert, they became dead. *9*
The temples were sacked, Hindus were killed,
On the land of the Sindh, terror was filled. *10*

18. Chalukya Dynasty (West), Badami (525-753)

There were 16 earlier Kadamba kings following the 59 Kings of Raghu Dynasty of Ayodhya.

For the Previous Dynasty, please see :
Kadamb Dynasty of Vaijayanti (340–610)

1. Jaya Simha — जयसिंह — 500–525
2. Ranaraga — रणरंगा — 525–543
3. Pulakeshi-1 — पुलकेशी–1 — 543–566
4. Kirtivarma-1 — कीर्तिवर्मा–1 — 566–597
5. Manglesha — मंगलेश — 597–608
6. Pulakeshi-2 — पुलकेशी–2 — 608–642
7. Vikramaditya-1 — विक्रमादित्य–1 — 642–680
8. Vinayaditya — विनयादित्य — 680–696
9. Vijayaditya — विजयादित्य — 696–733
10. Vikramaditya-2 — विक्रमादित्य–2 — 733–746
11. Kirtivarma-2 — कीर्तिवर्मा–2 — 746–753

For the Next Dynasty, please see :
Chalukya Dynasty, Kalyani (696–1189)

Chalukya Dynasty of Badami

The great historical Chalukya Dynasty of Badami (Bijapur) was established in the whole of Karnataka, a large part of Andhra Pradesh, Western Maharashtra, South Madhya Pradesh and South Gujarat. It is believed that it was founded by Maharaja Jayasimha (500-525), even though 75 kings had descended before him.

Among the seven main branches of the Chalukya Dynasty, the Badami branch is known to be the most ancient. The reign of this Dynasty is considered to be a golden period of South India due to the flourishing of art and prosperity. The greatest king of this family was Satyashraya Pulakeshi (608-642).

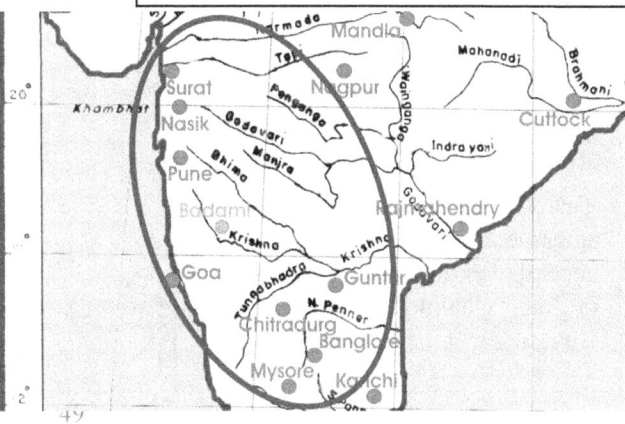

Hindu Rajtarangini

Badami Chalukya King Satyashraya Pulakeshi (608-642)

Satyashraya Pulakeshi

The great king of the Chalukya Dynasty of Badami (Vatapi) was Satyashraya Pulakeshi-2 (608-642), a very powerful ruler. He had won many battles. His victory over Pushyabhuti King Harshavardhana (606-664) of Kannauj was the most important achievement of his life. Emperor Pulakeshi defeated King Bhogivarma (566-610) of the Kadamb Dynasty and established his power over Vaijayanti (Karnataka).

Vengi king Vardhan-1 (615-632), the brother of King Pulakeshi and the Governor of Vengi (Rajahmundry), revolted and established Vengi as an independent kingdom of the former Chalukyas (615-945). Pulakeshi established trade relations with the Sasanian king of Persia, Khusru (590–628), which is mentioned in the inscription of the cave of Ajanta.

The Chalukya king Pulakeshi of Vatapi (Badami) was killed by the Pallava king Narasimhavarma-1 (630-668) of Kanchipuram in a battle in 642 AD and he assumed the title Vatapikonda (Conqueror of Vatapi). Nevertheless, as per the agreement Narasimha Varma handed over the kingdom of Badami to the Chalukya crown prince Vikramaditya-1 (642–680).

Satyashraya Pulakeshi

On the decline of Kadambas, revolt became possible,
Chalukyas became free, without much tussle. **1**

Chalukyas of Badami, was the oldest branch,
From the sixth century, with a divine touch. **2**

Chalukyas loved arts, sculpture of styles eight,
They built many temples, beautiful and great. **3**

No one in the world, was so able,
Glory of Karnataka, grew like fable. **4**

Precious than the gold, was their sculpture,
It was a golden age, for India's future. **5**

Gods Goddesses depicted, in multiple kinds,
They sculpted the idols, with intelligent minds. **6**

Elephants horses flowers, numerous divine figures,
Artists designed forms, gave the eyes pleasures. **7**

Chalukyas were praised, in the world of arts,
From earth to heaven, in several sorts. **8**

Pulakeshi was the king, greatest of his time,
People were busy, there was no crime. **9**

Sculptors and artists, received royal support,
They built the temples, with monumental effort. **10**

Their pillars were smooth, the peaks were high,
The domes were majestic, sculptors took sigh. **11**

They chiseled mountains, they carved the caves,
They cut the rocks, they were braves. **12**

Pulakeshi won enemies, in directions four,
He collected wealth, millions and more. **13**

He expanded the kingdom, from Vindhya in the North,
To the East-West oceans, to Kaveri in the South. **14**

19. Chalukya Dynasty (West), Kalyani (696-1189)

For the Previous Dynasty, please see :
Chalukya Dynasty of Badami (525–753)

Feudatories of Rashtrakut Dynasty of Malkhed (696–973)

1. Vijayaditya — विजयादित्य — 696–733
2. Bhima-1 — भीम–1
3. Kirtivarma-3 — कीर्तिवर्मा–3
4. Tailap-1 — तैलप–1
5. Vikramaditya-3 — विक्रमादित्य–3
6. Bhima-2 — भीम–2
7. Ayyanna-1 — अय्यन्ना–1
8. Vikramaditya-4 — विक्रमादित्य–4

Independent from Rashtrakut Dynasty of Malkhed (620–973)

9. Tailap-2 — तैलप–2 आहवमल्ल नुरमाडी — 973-997
10. Satyashraya Irivabedanga — सत्याश्रय इरिवबेदंगा — 997–1009
11. Vikramaditya-5 — विक्रमादित्य–5 जगदेकमल्ल — 1009–1014
12. Ayyanna-2 — अय्यन्ना–2 — 1014–1018
13. Jayasimha — जयसिंह — 1018–1040
14. Someshvara-1 — सोमेश्वर–1 त्रैलोक्यमल्ल — 1040–1069
15. Someshvara-2 — सोमेश्वर–2 भुवनैकमल्ल — 1069–1076
16. Vikramaditya-6 — विक्रमादित्य–6 त्रिभुवनमल्ल — 1076–1127
17. Someshvara-3 — सोमेश्वर–3 भुलोकमल्ल — 1127–1138
18. Jagadekmalla-2 — जगदेकमल्ल–2 — 1138–1150
19. Tailap-3 — तैलप–3 त्रैलोक्यमल्ल — 1150–1156

Rule of Kalchuri Dynasty of Kalyani (1156–1184, See)

20. Someshvara-4 — सोमेश्वर–4 त्रिभुवनमल्ल — 1184–1189

For the Next Dynasty, please see :
Yadav Dynasty of Devgiri (850–1311)

Chalukyas of Kalyani

The Chalukya Dynasty of Kalyani emerged from the decline of the Rashtrakuta empire (620-973). The original capital of the Western Chalukya Dynasty of Kalyani was Manyakhet or Malkhed. The first ruler of this clan, Vijayaditya (696–733), was the son of Badami Chalukya Vinayaditya (680–696). The great king of this Dynasty, Someshwar-1 (1040 - 1069), established his rule by founding the city of Kalyani. The range of the kingdom extended from the West Sea to Kaushal and Kalinga in the Northeast. The Chalukya king Vikramaditya-6 (1076-1127) started the Chalukya Samvat era by invalidating the Saka Samvat. Mahakavi Bilhan was seated in his court. Mayuradhwaj was ornamented in the Chalukya-emblems. The family insignia of the Chalukya Dynasty was Varaha (Boar).

Chalukya Dynasty, Kalyani

The Kalyani Chalukyas ruled,
years five hundred,
But, under the Rashtrakutas,
for years three hundred. 1
Decline of Rashtrakutas,
gave Chalukyas rise,
They became strong,
and grew in big size. 2
From Kalyani they ruled,
for first two hundred years,
Their glory made happy,
people's eyes and the ears. 3
Kalyani Vikramaditya,
was a brave man,
Kalyani to Kalinga,
was his kingdom's span. 4
Chalukya arts literature and sculptures,
They built supreme, temple structures. 5
Their temple pillars, are glazing smooth,
Chalukya polished stones,
makes your mind soothe. 6
Poet laureate Bilhan, honored at the court,
Poet Jagannath had, honor special sort. 7
Vikramankdev Charitra,
was creation of this age,
Mitakshara was written,
under Chalukya patronage. 8
In such prosperous kingdom,
General Bijjal was traitor,

He caused rebellion,
and destroyed Chalukya power. 9
Chalukyas kingdom broke,
in to three parts,
Then the revolution stopped,
when it quitened their hearts.

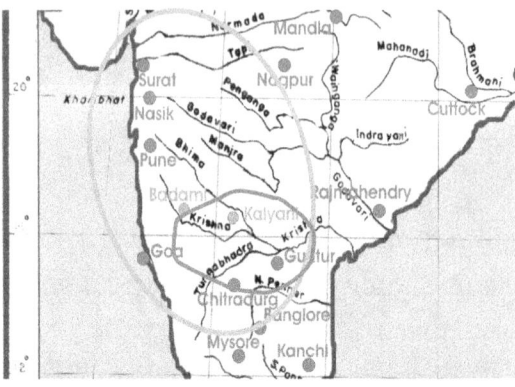

Hindu Rajtarangini

20. Chalukya Dynasty, Lat, Gujrat (590-750)

For the Prior Dynasty, please see :
Chalukya Dynasty of Badami (525–753)

Feudatories of Rashtrakut Dynasty of Malkhed (620–750)

1.	Jayasimha Raja	जयसिंह राजा	590–610
2.	Buddhavarma Raja	बुद्धवर्मा राजा	610–643
3.	Vijaya Raja	विजय राजा	643–655
4.	Jayasimhavarma	धाराश्रय जयसिंहवर्मा	655–669
5.	Satyashraya	सत्याश्रय शीलादित्य	669–738
6.	Pukakeshi	पुलकेशी	738–750

For the Next Dynasty, please see :
Rashrtakut Dynasty, Malkhed (620–973)

Lat Chalukya Dynasty

The Chalukya Rajput kings of Lat were initially ruling under the Western Badami Chalukyas. Lat King Dharashraya Jaisimha Varma (655-669) was the brother of Vikramaditya-I of West Chalukya of Badami.

The Lat king Satyashraya (669–738) attained independence from the Badami Chalukyas but later on he was defeated by the Chalukya kings of Saurashtra Naksisapur (750–900) and again made them his feudatories.

Taking advantage of this opportunity, Rashtrakuta King Dantidurga-2 (710-757) of Malkhed defeated the last king of Gujarat's Lat Dynasty, Pulakeshi (738-750) and annexed the Lat kingdom.

Lat Chalukyas

The Chalukyas of Lat,
were brave and virtuous,
Their king Jaisimha,
made the kingdom pious. 1

Six kings of Lat Chalukyas,
were autonomous semi,
They were related to,
Chalukyas of Badami. 2

Pulakeshi was the king,
of the Chalukyas Lat,
Rashtrakutas defeated him,
he was the king last. 3

21. Chalukya Dynasty, Kathiawad, Saurashtra (750-900)

For the Prior Dynasty, please see :
   Chalukya Dynasty, Badami (525–753)

1. Mahalla   महल्ल   …
2. Kalla   कल्ल राजा   750–
3. Mahalla Raja   महल्ल राजा
4. Vahuk Dhaval   वाहुकधवल
5. Avani Varma-1   अवनिवर्मा-1
6. Balavarma   बालवर्मा
7. Avani Varma-2   अवनिवर्मा-2, योग   –900

Chalukya Dynasty of Saurashtra

Who was the king for a short time after King Mahall the second king of the Chalukya Dynasty of Saurashtra is not known to the history.

Nevertheless, it is certain that the grandson of King Kalla was King Vahukadhaval. The currrency of this kingdom was called Gadharia Paisa.

22. Chalukya (East) Dynasty, Vengi (440-1070)

1.	Madhava Varma-1	माधववर्मा-1	440-460
2.	Vikramendra Varma-1	विक्रमेंद्रवर्मा-1	460-480
3.	Indra Varma	इन्द्रवर्मा	480-515
4.	Vikramendra Varma-2	विक्रमेंद्रवर्मा-2	515-535
5.	Govind Varma	गोविंदवर्मा	535-555
6.	Madhava Varma-2	माधववर्मा-2	555-615
7.	Vishnu Vardhan-1	विष्णुवर्धन-1, कुब्ज	615-632
8.	Jaya Simha-1	जयसिंह-1	632-663
9.	Indra Bhattarak	इन्द्र भट्टारक	663-663
10.	Vishnu Vardhan-2	विष्णुवर्धन-2	663-672
11.	Mangi Yuvaraja	मंगी युवराजा	672-696
12.	Jaya Simha-2	जयसिंह-2	696-709
13.	Kokkili	कोक्किली	709-709
14.	Vishnu Vardhan-3	विष्णुवर्धन-3	709-746
15.	Vajayaditya-1	विजयदित्य-1	746-764
16.	Vishnu Vardhan-4	विष्णुवर्धन-4	764-799
17.	Vijayaditya-2	विजयादित्य-2	799-843
18.	Vishnu Vardhan-5	विष्णुवर्धन-5, काली	843-844
19.	Vijayaditya-3	विजयादित्य-3, गुणक	844-892
20.	Chalukya Bhima-1	चालुक्य भीम-1	892-918
21.	Vijayaditya-4	विजयादित्य-4	918-918
22.	Ammaraja-1	अम्मराजा-1	918-925
23.	Vijayaditya-5	विजयादित्य-5, कण्ठिका	925-926
24.	Vikramaditya	विक्रमादित्य	926-934
25.	Chalukya Bhima-1	चालुक्य भीम-1	926-934
26.	Chalukya Bhima-2	चालुक्य भीम-2	934-945
27.	Ammaraja-2	अम्मराजा-2	945-973

Chalukya Dynasty, Vengi

When the West Chalukya Badami King Pulakeshi-2 (608-642) won Vengi in year 615 and retained the power of his brother Vishnuvardhan-1 Kubja (615-632), the former Chalukya household of the Vengi became stable.

The ninth king of Vengi Chalukya, Indra Bhattarak (663) was in power for only seven days. Satyashraya Uttam, son of Vijayaditya-5 (925-926), established the Eastern Chalukya Dynasty (925-1225) of Pithapuram.

In 973, King Danarnava of Vengi was assassinated by Telugu Chola Bhima and then after some chaos, Vengi was empowered by the Chola Rajaraja-1 the Great, of Tanjavar (985-1014) for 27 years, after which Shaktivarma (1000–1010) made Vengi independent kingdom again in year 1000.

| 28. | Danarnava | दानार्णव | 973– |

Tanjavar Chola Rajaraja-1 (985-1014) ruled over Vengi for 27 years (975-1000)

29.	Shalti Varma-1	शक्तिवर्मा-1	1000–1010
30.	Vimaladitya	विमलादित्य	1010–1022
31.	Narendra Rajaraj	नरेंद्र राजाराज	1022–1062
32.	Rajendra	राजेन्द्र	1062–1062
33.	Vijayaditya-4	विजयादित्य-4	1062–1070

For the Next Dynasty, please see :
Chola Dynasty, Tanjavar (50–1299)

Chalukyas of Vengi

Pulakeshi was the greatest, king of Badami line,
He gave the rule of Vengi, to his brother pristine. 1

Obtaining the Vengi kingdom,
the brother ruled best,
New Chalukya community,
he founded in the East. 2

The kingdom of Vengi, was a great success,
People were gallant, desirous of progress. 3

For five hundred years, Vengi kingdom lasted,
Cholas took Vengi, Chalukyas were blasted. 4

Chalukya Dynasty, Vengi

The Chalukyas of Vengi were devotees of Shiva, even then Shiva, Vishnu, Agni, Surya, etc. were present in their temple crafts.

King Vijayaditya-2 (799-843) built 108 grand temples. King Vijayaditya-5 (925-926) built the Kartikeya temple. King Chalukya Bhima-1 (892-918, 926-934) built the Draksharaj temple. Narendra. Rajaraja (1022-1062) built the Kalindi temple and carried forward the tradition of great temple work of Badami Chalukya and Kalyani Chalukya Dynasties.

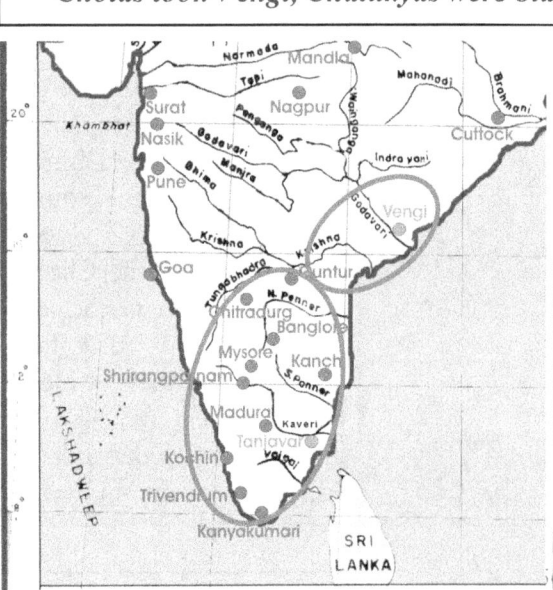

23. Chandela Dynasty, Bundelkhand (830-1289)

For the Pervious Dynasty, please see :
Pratihar Dynasty (725-1036)

1. Nannuka Chandravarma — नन्नुक चंद्रवर्मा — 831–845
2. Vakpati — वाक्पति — 845–865
3. Jayashakti — जयशक्ति — 865–885
4. Vijayashakti — विजयशक्ति — 865–885
5. Rahila — राहिला — 885–914
6. Harshadeva — हर्षदेव — 914–948
7. Yasha Varma — यशवर्मा — 948–954
8. Dhanga — धंग — 954–1000
9. Ganda — गंड — 1000–1019
10. Vidyadhara — विद्याधर — 1019–1037
11. Vijayapaldeva — विजयपालदेव — 1037–1051
12. Devendra Varma — देवेंद्रवर्मा — 1051–1098
13. Kirti Varma — कीर्तिवर्मा — 1098–1100
14. Sulakshan Varma — सुलक्षणवर्मा — 1100–1117
15. Jaya Varma — जयवर्मा — 1117–1125
16. Prithvi Varma — पृथ्वीवर्मा — 1125–1129
17. Madan Varma — मदनवर्मा — 1129–1165
18. Parmardi Deva — परमारदीदेव — 1165–1203
19. Trailokya Varma — त्रैलोक्यवर्मा — 1203–1245
20. Vira Varma-1 — वीरवर्मा–1 — 1245–1286
21. Bhoja Varma — भोजवर्मा — 1286–1288
22. Hammira Varma — हम्मीरवर्मा — 1288–1311
23. Vira Varma-2 — वीरवर्मा–2 — 1315– ...
24. Mohansimha — मोहनसिंह — 1470– ...
25. Kiratrao — कीरतराव — 1520–1524
26. Queen Durgavati — रानी दुर्गावती — 1524–1565

She was the brave wife of King Dalpat of Mandla

Chandela Dynasty

The Chandela Dynasty is an unforgettable and important Rajput Dynasty of central India, Bundelkhand. They received the titles of Deva and Rao. The Lunar Chandela kings belonged to Atri gotra and are considered to be the descendants of Chandradev Rishi.

Their main areas were Khajuraho, Kalanjar and Mahoba. These kings were as much lovers of art, music and craftsmanship as they were brave warriors.

Their 85 great temples including the grand and beautiful Kandariya Mahadev Temple, Laxman Temple, Vishwanath Temple, Vaman Temple, Chitragupta Temple, etc. are all world famous.

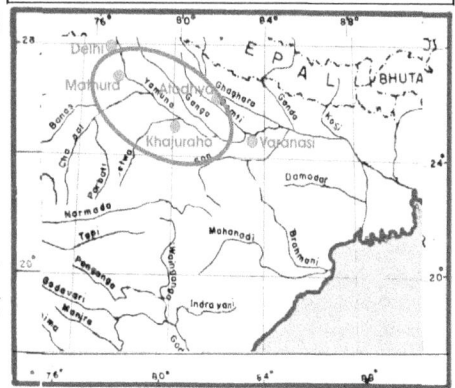

Hindu Rajtarangini

Chandela Dynasty

Descendents of Chandratreya,
Chandelas were well known,
They were Rajput braves,
famous on their own. 1
Pratiharas were their lords,
for some time it was fine,
Nannuka rebelled and said,
this kingdom is mine. 2
Khajuraho was their place,
in the Bundelkhand,
Against all the enemies,
they protected their land. 3
Harshadeva was the king,
of the Chendelas strong,
He left the Pratiharas,
but didn't go wrong. 4
At the time of Vidyadhara,
arts esteemed high,
Many temples were built,
touching the sky. 5
King Yashovarma built,
Lakshmana Temple large,
King Dhanga then built,
Vishvanath Temple huge. 6
Vidyadhara was a man,
learned and wise,
Great builders always were,
searching his eyes. 7
Vidyadhara was a king,
devoted to Shiva,
He built colossal Temple,
Kandaria Mahadeva. 8
These temples are praised by,
Chand Bardai poet,
He said, these temples supreme,
are the world asset. 9

24. Channamma Queen, Kittur (1778-1829)

1. Raja Mallasaraja   राजा मल्लसराजा   ...
2. Qieen Channamma   रानी चन्नम्मा   778-1829

Queen Channamma of Kittur

Queen Channamma was born in Belgaum in Karnataka in the year 1778. She married King Mallasaraja of Kittur. King Mallasaraja was the feudatory of Wadiyar Maharaja Chamaraja-7 (1770–1776) and Maharaja Chamaraja-8 (1776–1796) of Mysore. King Mallasaraja and Queen Channamma had a son who died along with the death of his father.

The queen adopted a second son named Shivlingappa in 1824 and launched an armed movement against the British policy of appropriation. Queen was expert in horse riding, fencing and archery since her childhood.

The queen started winning battles constantly against the British. The queen started giving evidence of extreme valor, but in a battle she was caught at the hands of the British and was lodged in the fort of Belhongal.

In year 1829, facing torture and tyranny in the prison, the queen gave up her life and died with a smiling face. In India, that adventuress became an example of female power and remained in the minds of millions of Hindus.

रानी चेनम्मा

जै जै बोल जै जै बोल, जै जै बोल जै जै बोल ।
जै जै बोल जै जै बोल, जै जै बो- - - - ल ॥

मर्दानी वह चन्नम्मा थी, कर्नाटक की रानी ।
कूद पड़ी वो अंग्रेजों पर, पराक्रमी तूफानी ।
शत्रु देखता सुन्न रह गया, दीन्हा पीछा छो- -ड़ ॥ 1

बोली किटूर मैं ना दूँगी, प्राण भले ही जाए ।
अंगैरज़ों की एक ना चली, कुछ भी कर ना पाए ।
रणचंडी बन टूट पड़ी वो, विद्युत गति को जो- -ड़ ॥ 2

दुश्मन उसको पकड़ न पाते, भौचक सब रह जाते ।
कभी यहाँ पर, कभी वहाँ वो, लीला समझ न पाते ।
पवन वेग से घोड़ा उसका, दौड़े मन की तौ- - र ॥ 3

जो भी उससे लड़ने आता, उसे चटाती धूल ।
अँग्रेज़ों से गोली बरसी, भारतियों से फूल ।
वंदन वंदन देवी! तुझको, तन मन कर को जो- -ड़ ॥ 4

Queen Channamma

Say Victory to Queen Channama!
She was a brave heroin,
She fought the British Raj,
The British gave up, and left her alone. 1

She said, I will give my life,
But I will not give my Kittur,
She became Goddedd Bhavani,
And attacked the British force. 2

Enemy could not catch her,
They were greatly surprised,
Her horse ran with electric speed,
Leaving the enemy behind. 3

Whoever came to catch her,
She made him sad and sorry,
The British showered bullets,
And the Indians showered flowers.
They hailed her and saluted her,
With their folded hands. 4

25. Chapotkat Dynasty, Gujrat (690-942)

1. Jai Shekhar — जयशेखर — 690
2. Vamraj — वनराज — 746–806
3. Yogaraj — योगराज — 806–841
4. Kshemaraj — क्षेमराज — 841–866
5. Bhuyad — भूयाद — 866–895
6. Vairi Simha — वैरिसिंह — 895–920
6. Ratnaditya — रत्नादित्य — 920–935
7. Samant Simha — सामंतसिंह — 935–942

For the Next Dynasty, please see :
Solanki Dynasty, Anhilwad (942–1244)

Chapotkat Dynasty

Chap Chalukya Chawda,
Chapran are all same, Chapotkat king,
Jayshakher was his name. 1
One day came an invasion,
fierce was the battle,
Jayshakher got killed,
before the war could settle. 2
The Queen was pregnant,
she ran away to forest,
She had no choice,
at that time it was the best. 3
Her child was born,
Vanaraj she named,
She trained him to fight,
as she had arranged. 4
Child became adult, expert in war,
He won back the kingdom,
and became a star. 5
More than two centuries,
they ruled with grace,
Solanki became kings, then in their place. 6

Chapotkat Dynasty of Patan

The Royal House of Patan was established by King Jaishekhar. One day during Jaishekhar's period of peace, a sudden attack was launched by his neighbor and the king was killed in battle. His wife, who was pregnent at that time, shrewdly ran away and hid herself somewhere in the forest.

Later, he had a son named Vanaraja. The queen was a visionary. In year 746 she reclaimed the kingdom of Patan by making her son a war hero. This Dynasty ruled for almost two-and-a-half centuries, but the last king, Samantasimha died childless. Taking advantage of this opportunity, his nephew named Moolraj (942-995) seized the power of Patan and established an independent Solanki Dynasty in Anhilwad (942-1244).

In the Chapotkat Dynasty of Vardhman (820-914) - Vikramaraka, Addak, Pulakeshi, Dhruvabhatta, Dharanivaraha - were the known kings.

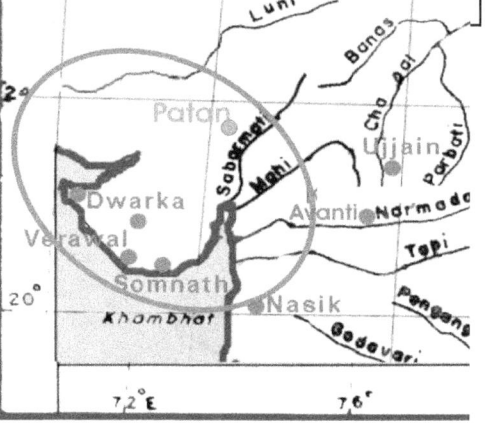

26. Chauhan Dynasty, Sakambhari (684-1194)

1.	Vasudev	वासुदेव	In the 6th century
2.	Guvak-1	गुवक–1	… …
3.	Samantraj	सामंतराज	684–709
4.	Purnatalla	पूर्णतल्ल	709–721
5.	Jairaj	जयराज	721–734
6.	Vigraharaj-1	विग्रहराज–1	734–759
7.	Chandraraj-1	चंद्रराज–1	759–771
8.	Gopendraraji1	गोपेंद्रराज	771–784
9.	Durlabhraj-1	दुर्लभराज–1	784–809
10.	Guvak-2	गुवक–2	809–836
11.	Chandraraj-2	चंद्रराज–2	636–863
12.	Guvak-3	गुवक–3	863–890
13.	Chandraraj-3	चंद्रराज–3	890–917
14.	Vakpatiraj-1	वाक्पतिराज–1	917–944
15.	Simharaj	सिंहराज	944–971
16.	Vigraharaj-2	विग्रहराज–2	971–998
17.	Durlabhraj-2	दुर्लभराज–2	998–1012
18.	Govindraj	गोविंदराज	1012–1026
19.	Vakpatiraj-2	वाक्पतिराज–2	1026–1040
20.	Viryaram	वीर्यराम	1040–1040
21.	Chamundraj	चामुंडराज	1040–1065
22.	Durlabhraj-3	दुर्लभराज–3	1065–1070
23.	Virsimha	वीरसिंह	1070–1070
24.	Vigraharaj-3	विग्रहराज–3	1070–1090
25.	Prithviraj-3	पृथ्वीराज–1	1090–1110
26.	Ajaydev	अजयदेव	1110–1130
27.	Arnoraj	अर्णोराज	1130–1153
28.	Vigraharaj-4	विग्रहराज–4	1153–1166

Chauhan Dynasty Sakambhari

According to the old stories the great Chauhan Dynasty originated from the Yajnas performed by the sages on Abu Mountain. Later on, 24 Rajput branches of this Dynasty were produced.

Politically and historically, the three main branches of the Chauhan Dynasty are known :

(1) the first, the branch of Sakambhari-Ajmer (684-1194),

(2) the second, the branch of Ranthambor (1194-1301), and

(3) the third, the branch of Nadol (950–1200).

King Vasudeva founded the Chauhan Dynasty of Sakambhari in Rajasthan in 551 AD in Nagaur near Sambar lake. After that Ajayadev Chauhan (1110-1130) founded the city of Ajmer in the Aravali hills and made it his capital (1130). The greatest Maharana of this Dynasty was Rai Pithaura Prithviraj Chauhan-3 (b. 1163-d. 1192) whose immortal and thrilling saga is written by Prithviraj's best friend Chand Bardai (1149-1200) in his epic called Prithviraj Raso.

29. Prithviraj-2	पृथ्वीराज-2	1166–1169
30. Someshvar	सोमेश्वर	1169–1177
31. Prithviraj-3	पृथ्वीराज-3	1177–1192
32. Govindraj-2	गोविंदराज-2	1192–1193
33. Hariraj	हरिराज	1193–1194

Chauhan Dynasty, Ajmer
Chauhans of Ajmer conquered Delhi from the Gahadwal Tomars. Govindaraj-2, son of Prithviraj-3 Chauhan, left Ajmer and established the Chauhan Dynasty of Ranthambor.

27. Chaunah Dynasty, Nadol (950-1200)

1. Lakshmanraj	लक्ष्मणराज	950–962
2. Shobhitraj	शोभित	962–986
3. Balirajraj	बलिराज	986–990
4. Vigrahapal	विग्रहपाल	990–994
5. Mahendrapal	महेंद्रपाल	994–1015
6. Ashvapal	अश्वपाल	1015–1019
7. Ahil	अहिल	1019–1024
8. Ajnipal	अहनिपाल	1024–1055
9. Balprasad	बालप्रसाद	1055–1070
10. Jayendraraj	जयेंद्रराज	1070–1080
11. Prithvipal	पृथ्वीपाल	1080–1091
12. Yojaldev	योजलदेव	1091–1110
13. Ashvaraj	अश्वराज	110–1119
14. Ratnapal	रत्नपाल	1119–1132
15. Rajyapal	राज्यपाल	1132–1145
16. Katukraj	कटुकराज	1145–1153
17. Alhandev	आल्हणदेव	1153–1161
18. Kelhandev	केल्हणदेव	1161–1165
19. Kirtipal	कीर्तिपाल	1165–1193
20. Jaitsimha	जैतसिंह	1193–1197
21. Samantsimha	सामंतसिंह	1197–1200

Chauhan Dynasty, Nadol
Nadol was the capital site of the Chauhan Rulers of Sonagara village situated on the Swarnagiri hills in the Rajasthan. Kirtipal Singh Chauhan (1165-1193), son of Rana Alhandev Chauhan (1153-1161), founded the city of Jalor in 1182 and made the city his capital.

The ancient name of Jalor was Jabalipur. The dominance of this Dynasty continued for more than a hundred years.

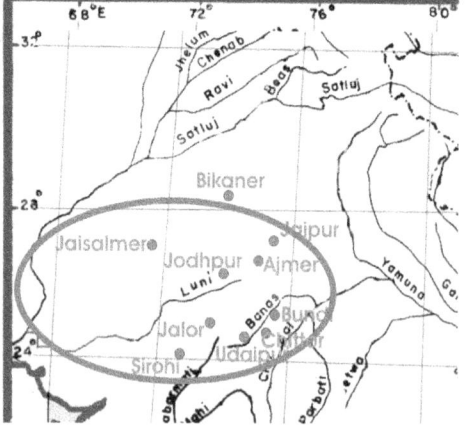

28. Chauhan Dynasty, Ranthambhor (1194-1301)

1. Govindraj   गोविंदराज   1194 ...
2. Balhandev   बल्हणदेव
3. Pralhad   प्रल्हाद
4. Vira Narayan   वीर नारायण
5. Vagbhat   वागभट
6. Jaitrasimha   जैत्रसिंह   1248–1283
7. Hammir Dev   हम्मीरदेव   1283–1301

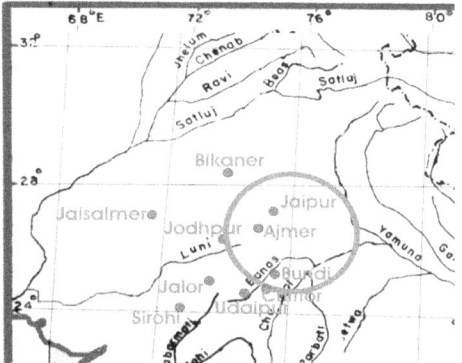

29. Chauhan Dynasty, Jalor (1182-1311)

1. Kirtipal Simha   कीर्तिपाल सिंह   1182 (Son of Alhandev 1153-1161 of Nadol)
2. Samar Simha   समर सिंह   1182–1205
3. Uday Simha   उदय सिंह   1205–1257
4. Chachan Simha   चाचन सिंह   1257–1282
5. Samant Simha   सामंत सिंह   1282–1305
6. Kanhaddev Simha   कान्हड़देव सिंह   1305–1311

> **Chauhan Dynasty, Jalor**
> Kirtipal Singh Chauhan (1165-1193), son of Rana Alhandev Chauhan (1153-1161), the ruler of Nadol kingdom founded Jalor in 1182 and made the city his capital.
> The ancient name of Jalor was Jabalipur. The dominance of this Dynasty continued for more than a ceentury (1182-1311). The reign of king Uday Simha was the longest (1205-1257) in this dynasty.

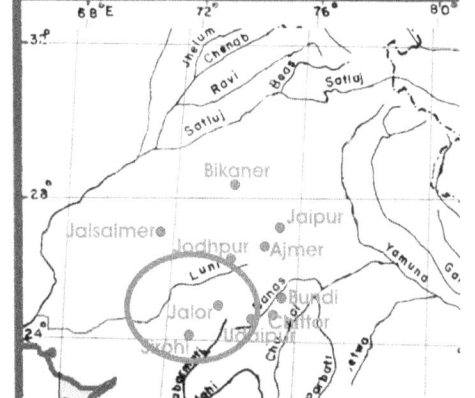

30. Chauhan Dynasty, Sirohi (1311-1527)

1. Lumba   लुम्बा   1311 ...
2. Sahasmal   साहसमल   1425 ...
3. Akhairaj   अखैराज   1527 ...

> **Chauhan Dynasty, Sirohi**
> In ancient times, Sirohi area was called Arbud Desh. At that time Sirohi town was called Shivpuri.

31. Chauhan Dynasty, Hadauti (1382-1631)

1. Hada Chauhan — हाड़ा चौहान — 1342 ...
2. Sujan Simha — सुरजन सिंह — 1569 ...
3. Madho Simha — माधो सिंह — 1631 ...

Chauhan Dynasty, Hadauti
Bundi, Kota, Jhalawar etc. areas of Rajasthan came in Hadoti. Hada Chauhans defeated Mina chieftains in 1342 and made Hadoti the center of their rule.

Chauhan of Bundi and Kota

32. Chauhan of Bundi : 1. Dewas Singh, 2. Samarsingh (1343–1346), 3. Narpal Singh (1346–1370), 4. Rao Hama (1370–1403), 5. Veerasingh (1403–1413), 6. Rao Beshilal (1413–1459), 7. Rao Bhanda (1459–1503), 8. Rao Narayan (1503–1527), 9. Surajmal (1527–1531), 10. Rao Surtana (1531–1554), 11. Surjan Singh (1554–1585), 12. Rao Bhoja (1585–1607), 13. Ratan Singh (1607–1631), 14. Rao Shatarshal (1631–1658), 15. Bhavsingh (1658–1681), 16. Rao Anirudh (1658–1695), 17. Buddha Singh (1695–1739), 18. Umed Singh (1739–1771), 19. Vishnusingh (1771–1821), 20. Ramsingh (1821–1889), 21. Raghuvir Singh (1889–1927), 22. Ishwar Singh (1927–1945), 23. Bahadur Singh (1945–1948).

33. Chauhans of Kota : 1. Madhosingh (1631–1649), 2. Mukund Singh (1649–1658), 3. Jagatsingh (1658–1683), 4. Prem Singh (1683–1684), 5. Kishor Singh – 1 (1684–1696), 6. Ramsingh – 1. (1696–1707), 7. Bhimsingh-1 (1707–1727), 8. Arjun Singh (1727–1756), 9. Ajitsingh (1756–1758), 10. Shatarshal-1 (1758–1764), 11. Guman Singh (1764-1771), 12. Umed Singh-1 (1771–1819), 13. Kishor Singh-2 (1819-1827), 14. Ramsingh-2 (1827-1865), 15. Shatarshal-2 (1865-1888), 16 Umed Singh-2 (1888–1940), 17. Bhim Singh-2 (1940–1948).

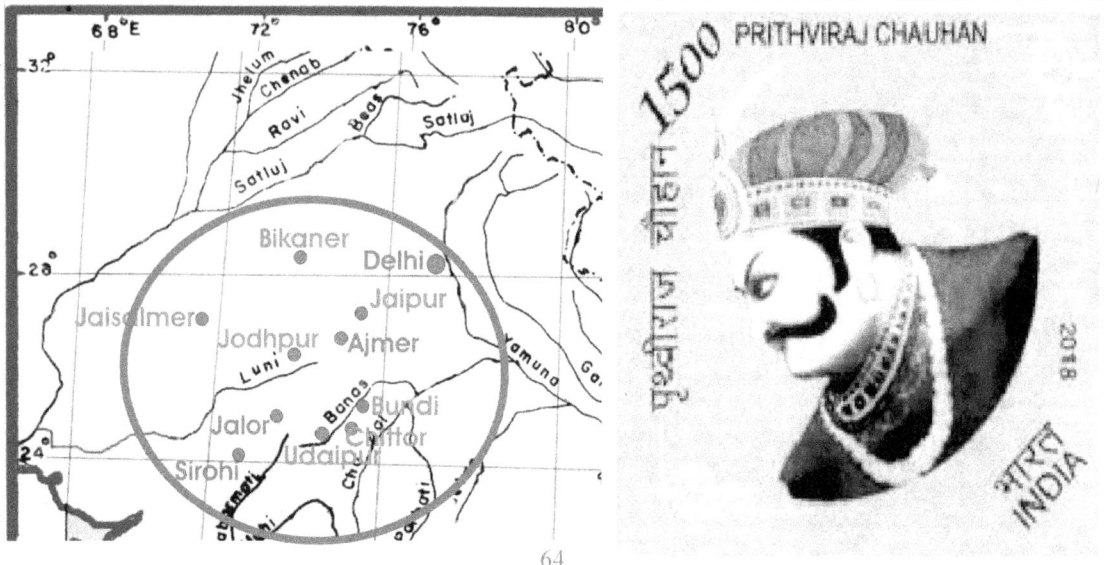

Hindu Rajtarangini

Prithviraj Chauhan

A brave warrior great,
was Prithviraj Chauhan,
Neither was nor will be,
like him ever a brave man. 1
Against the norms he acted,
one day ever he had,
He forgave the unforgivable,
result was very bad. 2
Permanent that result,
infinite damage was done,
Enemy became king,
millions of lives were gone. 3
The arrow that is shot, never returns back,
Cancer if infects, incurable is the attack.

(Therefore)
King of Delhi and Ajmer,
was Prithviraj Chauhan,
Very brave hero he was,
everyone his fan. 5
Prithviraj, the king of Ajmer,
was a Rajput brave,
Also he was Delhi king,
the authority Tomars gave. 6
Super hero of the heroes,
multiple talents he had,
Best archer Prithviraj was,
to see it world was glad. 7
Best horseman Prithviraj,
he was a potent man,
Fight with both hands,
holding two swords he can. 8
Handsome he was, like Indra Lord,
He was a daring king,
victorious was his sword, 9
Lover of all arts, he cherished his wife,
Eyes closed he could shoot,
and take enemy's life. 10
Prithviraj was big hearted,
and a forgiving man,
Devoted to Lord Shiva,
as much as he can. 11

(Sultan)
Eleven Hundred Ninety two, was a terrible year,
Sultan broke his promise,
struck India with fear. 12
Prithviraj was kind to him, and let him go free,
But that traitor made, again savage entree. 13
Prithviraj didn't foresee it,
and got destroyed himself,
He fell flat on face, and caused lot of grief. 14
Made a show of big heart, and was kind to wicked,
He didn't see the fault, horrible mistake made. 15
These are the principles, one has to remember,
Remembering it all the time,
won't fall in slumber. 16

(Thus)
Who is good, and who is bad,
Who makes you happy, and who makes you sad. 17
What is his standard, and his heritage,
What are his vices, how much he has rage. 18
What revenge does he want,
what evil on his mind,
How much can you trust, you have to first find. 19
Who can be a good friend, and who is not,
Who is poisonous, dangerous boiling pot. 20
Whose pedigree is bad, whose history is adverse,
Who is an imposter, and who is averse. 21

(Principles)
Who is a sage, and who is a snake,
Who is a fraud, and who is a fake; 22
Who has held poison, deep in his heart,
Who is shameless, and who is an upstart; 23
Who is a villain, and who is mean,
Who is a crook, and who is not clean; 24
Who should be punished, and up to what length,
Who is wicked, and deserves the death. 25
With a man unscrupulous, why make a deal,
Deny his request, his fate you should seal. 26
Left in the body, even a small sliver,
Will become septic, and will give you fever. 27
Even a small spark, is cause of fire,
Could burn your house, or the forest entire. 28
Even one rotten apple, spoils the complete stock,
One drop of a poison, kills the whole flock. 29

Even slight negligence can, put you in noose,
Error at wrong time, your life you may lose. 30

(and)
Even if you are brave, and powerful,
Not knowing enemy, you will be a fool. 31
Leaving the principles, if you act with vice,
Your coming generations, will pay the price. 32
Trusting him who is a crook, and has bad blood,
Such suicidal action will, sink you in the mud. 33

(History)
Trusting the enemy, of innocent face,
Fortune runs away, that you can't chase. 36
Miyas-ud-din was evil, Sultan of Ghor,
Invaded India, ten times and more. 37
He marched on Delhi, when tenth time,
He got caught again, doing the same crime. 38
He begged pardon and,
promised he will not come,
Prithviraj trusted him, without thinking some. 39
Prithviraj let him go, though aware of his past,
Released him with honour, as if it was last. 40
At the time of downfall, wicked appears good,
False looks like truth, filth feels like food. 41
Forgetting your principles, acting like a noble,
The very bitter outcome, to you it will gobble. 42
He who attacks you, equipped with a weapon,
How can you pardon him, and act like a moron. 43
He who is on battlefield, to take your life,
How can you ignore him, who is holding knife. 44

(Also)
Sin that one earns, for punishing innocent,
Same sin is told for, not punishing indecent. 45
For spreading his faith, to India Sultan came,
What he did at home, he did here same. 46
Defeated and turned back, every time he came,
Keep doing again, the Sultan had no shame. 47
He came eleventh time, with a big force,
He was determined, his ambition to enforce. 48
With him he brought a slave, Kutb-ud-din Aybak,
As evil as Ghori he was,
watching Sultan's back. 49
When Sultan reached India, Jaichand joined him,
Traitor in the family,
Jaichand's insight was dim. 50

He messaged Ghori, Prithviraj is in the grove,
He is having good time, in his wife's love. 51

(then)
Seeing Ghori's army, Prithviraj was awed,
Prithviraj was not ready,
thus his cool was thawed. 52
Quickly he got ready,
and fought back like a hound,
By chance he got shot,
and he fell on the ground. 53
Ghori imprisoned Prithviraj,
and broke his eyes both,
That ungrateful Sultan, was blinded with loath. 54
When he was going home,
he took Prithviraj with him,
Aybak now Delhi Sultan, acted with his whim. 55
Aybak slaughtered Hindus,
demolished temples holy,
Built a tower in own name,
midst of the melancholy. 56

(In Afghanistan)
When they came to Ghor, excited was that Sultan,
People came to see,
the brave Prithviraj Chauhan. 57
Sultan was very proud, he arranged a big show,
Blind Prithviraj king,
was standing with his bow. 58
Sultan stood on a dais,
people standing on the lawn,
Prithviraj and Bardai, were facing the Sultan. 59
People wanted to witness, skill of the blind archer,
All people shouting,
noise was getting louder. 60
(that time)
Bardai said a couplet, to tell Prithviraj blind,
Where Sultan is, the target how he can find. 61
"Four poles twenty-four yards,
eight bits is the range,
Sultan is standing ahead,
miss not to take revenge. 62

(Final)
Doing the estimate precise, he shot arrow at aim,
Arrow hit the target, it was the end of the game. 63
Arrow shot the Sultan, and made him fatal wound,
Sultan got shot,
and fell on the ground. 64

34. Cher Purumal Dynasty, Kerala (800-1102)

1. Udayanjeral उदियंजेराळ 130–
2. Nedunjeral नेडुंजेराळ आदान
3. Kattuvan कट्टुवन
4. Shettuven शेंगुट्टुवन
5. Kuduki Iranjeral कुडुकी इरंजेराळ इरुंपोडई 190–210
6. **Mandarjeral** मांदरजेराळ इरुंपोडई 210–
7. Cheraman चेरमान् पेरुमल् 742–800
2. Kulashekhar कुलशेखर अलवार 800–820
2. Rajshekhar Varma राजशेखरवर्मा 820–844
3. Sthanuravi Varma स्थाणुरविवर्मा 844–885
4. Rama Varma-1 रामवर्मा–1 885–917
5. Ravi Varma-2 रविवर्मा 917–944
6. Kotha Varma कोठवर्मा 944–962
7. Bhaskararavi Varma-1 भास्कररविवर्मा–1 962–979
8. Bhaskararavi Varma-2 भास्कररविवर्मा–2 979–1021
9. Vira Keralvarma वीर केरलवर्मा 1021–1028
10. Rajsimha राजसिंह 1028–1043
11. Bhaskararavi Varma-3 भास्कररविवर्मा–3 1043–1082
12. Rama Varma-2 रामवर्मा–2 1082–1090
13. Ravivarma Kulashekhar रविवर्मा कुलशेखर 1090–1102

Chera Dynasty

In ancient times, the name of Kerala was Chera. In the inscriptions of Ashok Maurya (269–232 BC), the Chera kings were called Keralaputra. Travankor, Cochin and Malabar areas of the western sea shore were under the power of the Chera Dynasty. Their capital was at Vanji. Later on it was located at Thiruvarikamalai and then at **Kollam**. The first known Chera ruler in the Sangam era (100–200 AD) was Udiyanjera (130 AD). From the fourth century to the ninth century the Chera kings started prospering along the Malabar shore and started trading with foreign countries.

The Chera King Kulasekhar Alwar (800-820) was a contemporary of Jagadguru Shri Shankaracharya (788-820). The emblem of the rule of the Chera Dynasty was bow and arrow and the same symbol was enshrined on their flag.

Chera Dynasty

The Chera Dynasty of Kerala,
was very ancient,
From Travankor to Malbar,
to Cochin they were prevalent. 1

Since the Sangama Age,
three dynasties had smarts,
Chera Chola Pandya,
all were dedicated to arts. 2

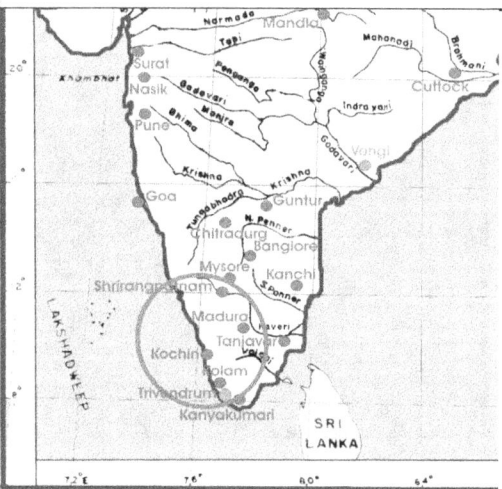

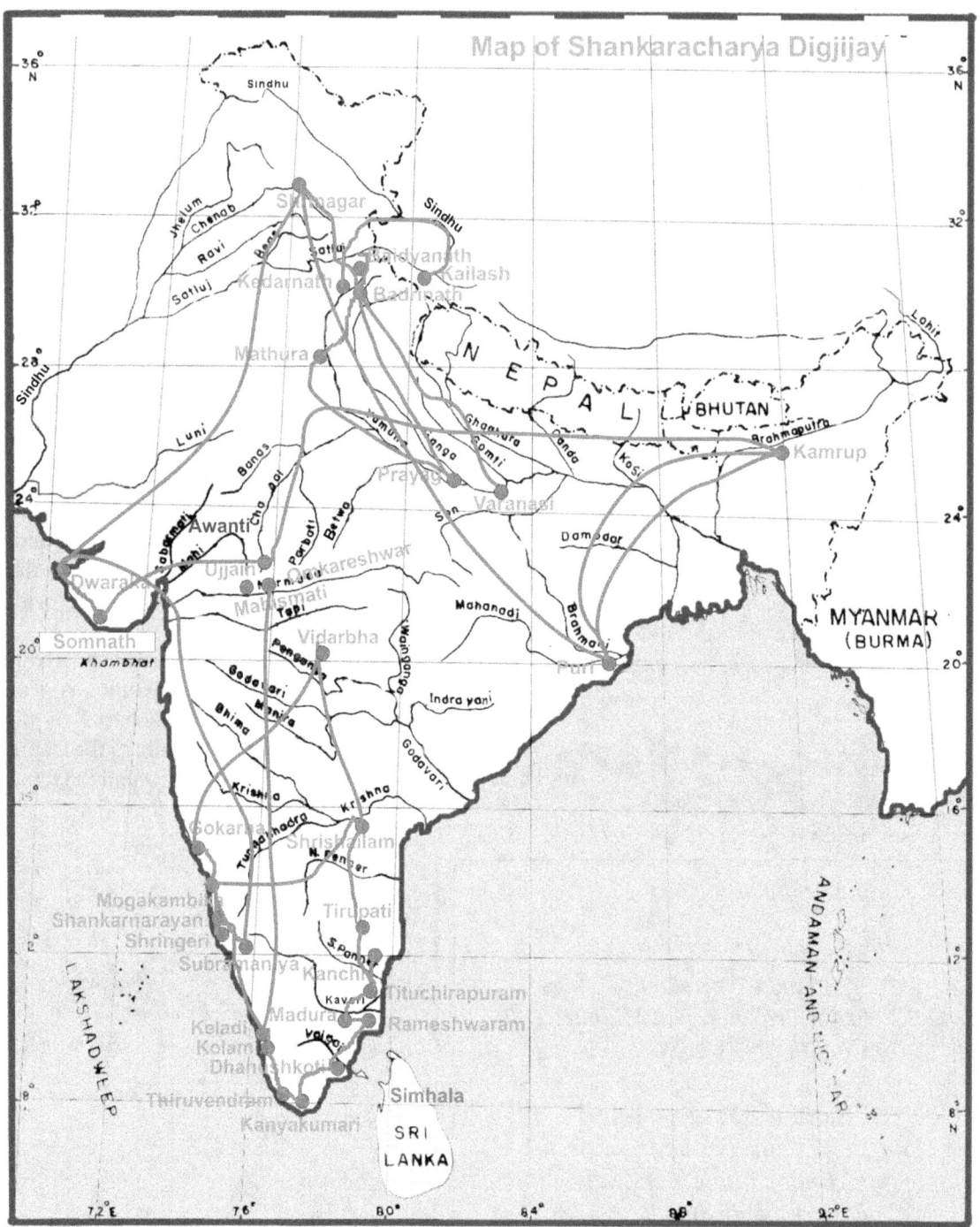

35. Chindak Nag Dynasty, Bastar (760-1324)

For the Prior Dynasty, please see : Gond Dynasty (800–1781)

1. Nripatibhushan — नृपति भूषण — 945–1023
2. Dharavarsha — धारावर्ष
3. Madhurantak — मधुरांतक देव
4. Someshvar Deva — सोमेश्वर देव — 1069–1111
5. Kalhar Deva — कन्हार देव-1 — 1111–1122
6. Jaisimha Deva — जयसिंह देव
7. Narsimha Deva — नरसिंह देव
8. Kanhar deva — कन्हार देव-2
9. Harishchandra Deva — हरिश्चंद्र देव — –1324

For the Next Dynasty, please see :
Kakatiya Dynasty (1000–1323)

Chhindak Nag Dynasty

Chakrakot was their Capital,
from where their kings ruled,
It was in Bastar State,
like Nagas it was moduled. 1
The Chhindak Nagas had,
Sindaka Nagas name,
Ruled from the eighth century,
Unique was their fame. 2
In the Kosal State, Foes were the King,
In Chhattisgarh, Chhindakas were ruling. 3
Chhindakas were devout, and lovers of arts,
They built nice temples,
in the kingdom's every part. 4

Chhindak Nag Dynasty

Chhindak Nag people of Chhattisgarh are considered descendants of Sanatan Gond (see No. 35-36) Dynasty.

The rule of Chhindak Nags in Bastar lasted for about 400 years in Chakrakote. When the Kalchuri Dynasty was ruling in Tripuri (825-1180), Chhindak Nag Dynasty was ruling in Bastar (760-1324).

Although the Chhindak Nag Dynasty was in power since year 760 CE, the founder of this Dynasty is known to be King Nripatibhushan (945-1023).

King Someshwar Deva (1069–1111) was a religious and art-loving ruler. Many beautiful temples and ponds built by him still exist.

Chhindak Nag were a compotators of the Dynasty of Kalchuris (1000-1745) of Ratanpur, South Kosala, for three centuries.

In 1324, Harishchandra Dev, the last ruler of the Chhindak Nag Dynasty was defeated by the last Kakatiya king Prataparudradeva-2 (1295-1325) of Anumkonda (Warangal). As a result, the territory of the Chhindak Nag Dynasty merged into the Kakatiya kingdom and the Chhindak Nag Dynasty came to end.

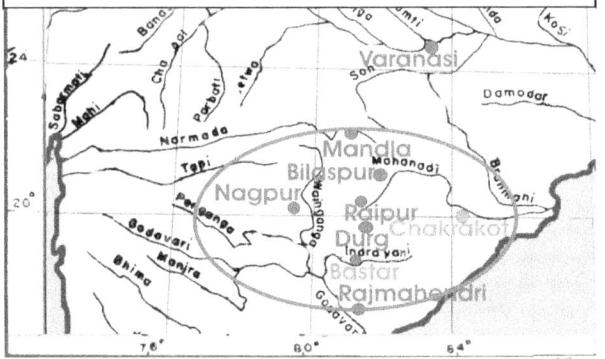

Hindu Rajtarangini

36. Chola Dynasty, Tanjavar (50-1279)

#	Name	Devanagari	Period
1.	Ilanjetsernni	इलंजेटसेर्न्नी	before 50
2.	Karikal	करिकाल	after 50–
3.	Shetshreni Nalangili	शेत्श्रेण्णी नाळंगिळी	about 100
4.	Kilivalan	किळिवळन	about 105
5.	Perunarkili	पेरुनारकिळी	...

.....

#	Name	Devanagari	Period
1.	**Vijayaditya Parakesari**	विजयादित्य पराकेसरी वर्मा	846–881
2.	Aditya Rajkesari	आदित्य राजकेसरी वर्मा	881–907
3.	Parantaka-1	परांतक-1	907–948
4.	Rajaditya	राजादित्य	948–949
5.	Gandaraditya	गण्डरादित्य	949–956
6.	Arinjay	अरिंजय	956–956
7.	Parankaka-1	परांतक-2	956–970
8.	Uttam	उत्तम	970–969
9.	Madhurantak	मधुरांतक	969–985
10.	Rajara-1, the Great	**राजाराज-1 (महान)**	985–1014
11.	Rajendra-1	राजेंद्र-1 पराकेसरी वर्मा	1014–1044
12.	Rajadhiraj-1	राजाधिराज-1	1044–1052
13.	Mahendra	महेंद्र	1052–1062
14.	Virarajendra	वीरराजेंद्र राजकेसरी वर्मा	1062–1067
15.	Adhirajendra	अधिराजेंद्र पराकेसरी वर्मा	1067–1070
16.	Rajendra-2	राजेंद्र-2 कुलोतुंग	1070–1118
17.	Vikrama Parakesari	विक्रम पराकेसरी वर्मा	1118–1133
18.	Kulottunga	कुलोतुंग-2	1133–1146
19.	Rajaraj-2	राजाराज-2	1146–1163
20.	Rajadhiraj-2	राजाधिराज-2	1163–1178
21.	Kulottunga-3	कुलोतुंग-3	1178–1216

Chola Dynasty

The ancient reference to the Chola Dynasty is found in the sources of sage Katyayana, the son of Yajnyavalkya, of the Vishvamitra Dynasty. The history of the Chola Dynasty from there to the late Sangam era (சங்ககாலம்) (600 B.C. to 300 A.D.) is unknown. However, some excerpts are available in the edicts of Ashok Maurya (269–232 B.C.) and the name of the Chola kingdom (50 A.D.) of the Sangam period is well known.

The renaissance of the Chola Dynasty began from the middle of the ninth century and the founder of the new generation Vijayaditya Parakesari Varma (846-881) settled in Tiruchirapalli (Uraiyur) and later the Cholas ruled at Tanjavar for 400 years. At this time, the kingdom of the Pallavas (315-897) and Pandyas (50-1463) were established in Tamil

22. Rajaraj-3   राजाराज–3   1216–1246
23. Rajendra-3   राजेंद्र–3   1246–1279

Chola Dynasty

Royal House of Cholas,
was greatest in the South,
Tamil Kerala and Andhra kings,
shut up their mouth. 1

Rajaraja was the noblest,
king in the world,
He was a sovereign monarch,
no one was so bold. 2

Cholas revered Shiva,
Vishnu was also worshipped,
The built great temples,
unique arts were equipped. 3

Cholas gave shelter,
to poets and sages,
Rich literature was written,
millions of pages. 4

Chola Dynasty

Although the Chola emperors were devotees of Shiva, at the time of the first great Chola Rajaraja-1 (985-1014), Nambi Andar Nambi established Vaishnava devotion as well in Tamil Nadu. In Chola empire, the principal Acharya were Shrimat Nathamuni (823-951), Yamunacharya (918-1038) and Ramanuja (1017-1137). Unique Tamil literature was composed in this period. The exquisite temple crafts of Shiva, Nataraja, Vishnu, Shri Krishna etc. of the Chola period were created.

The Chola emperor Rajaraja-1 defeated the West Chalukya king Satyashraya Irivabedanga (997- 1009) of Kalyani and the former Chalukya king Vimaladitya (1010-1022) of Vengi and established his sovereignty beyond Kalinga to Sayam, Malaya, Java, Sumatra, Bali. He defeated Vengi's enemy Telugu King Chola Bhima (973–1000) and then Bhima gave his daughter to Vengi's Maharaja Vimaladitya Chalukya to establish good relations.

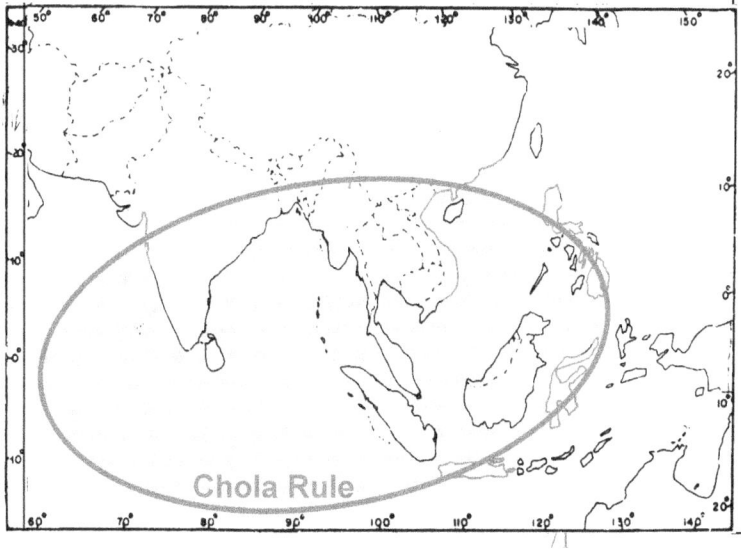

Hindu Rajtarangini

Chola Rajaraja, the Great of Tanjavar (985-1014)

Rajaraja Chola (985-1014) was the greatest emperor of South India. Rajaraja's birth name was Arulaamojahivarma and his other names were Shivpada Shekhar, Telungana Kulakavi, Pennian Selvan, etc. He has received the title of "Great" in history, seeing the expansion of his kingdom, the shelter of arts and crafts, the personality and skillful governance. At lEast 74 huge temples built by Rajaraja mentioned in the records. The grand Rajarajeshwar temple of Tanjavar also known as Brihadeeswarar Temple is a perfect example of Chola craftsmanship.

Emperor Rajraja Chola had kept a very large navy in which women and nine soldiers were also used. Through this navy, Rajaraja and his descendants of Shri Lanka continued to spread Hindu culture in the East-South Islands of Cambodia, Malaya, Sayam, Sumatra, Java, Bali, Philippine, etc.

Rajaraja was an ardent warrior. He had won many kings in the war and brought them under his power, among which special names were :

Vengi's former Chalukya king Vimaladitya (1010-1022),
Kalyani's West Chalukya king Satyasraya Irivabedanga (997-1009),
Pandya king Marvarma Raja Simha-2 (900-920) of Madura,
Chera Presidency of Kerala Bhaskar Ravivarma-2 (979-1021),
Former Gang king Vajrahasta-3 of Kalinga country (980-1015),
Pachim Ganga king Rakkas of Karnataka, Talkad (985-1024).

Chola Dynasty of Tanjavar

In the history of the South, no king was so Great,
Neither a warrior nor, a builder of supreme fate. 1

Brihadeshvara of Tanjavar, temple so marvelous,
Emperor Rajaraja built, sculptures sagacious. 2

He spread Hindu Culture, in the Far East,
Result was far reaching,
profound to say the least. 3

https://www.facebook.com/wakeupsleepinghindus/photos/a.104727547727602/189102762623413/

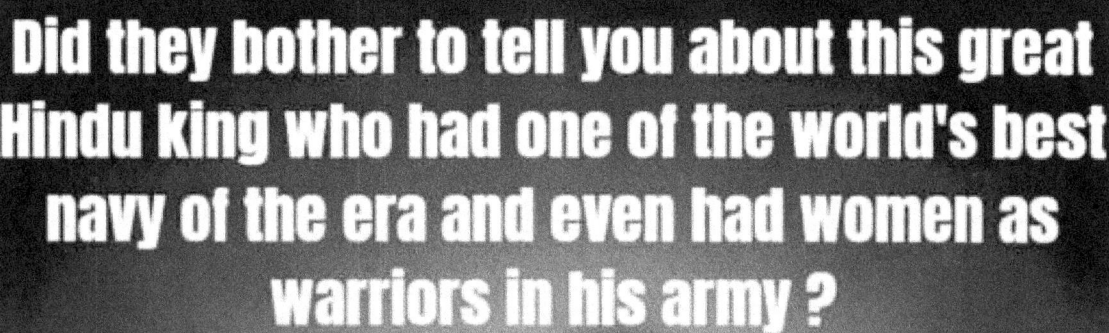

37. Chudasama Dynasty, Junagadh (875-1505)

For the Previous Dynasty, please see :
Maitrak Dynasty, Saurashtra (480–767)

	Chudachandra	चुडाचंद्र	875–907
1.	Ra Khengar-1	रा खेंगार–1	1098–1114
2.	–	–	1114–1125
3.	Ra Navaghan-1	रा नवघण–1	1125–1140
4.	Ra Kavant	रा कवांट	1140–1152
5.	Ra Jayasimha-1	रा जयसिंह–1	1152–1180
6.	Ra Rayasimha	रा रायसिंह	1180–1184
7.	Ra Mahipal-1	रा महीपाल–1	1184–1201
8.	Ra Jayamalla	रा जयमल्ल	1201–1230
9.	Ra Mahipal-2	रा महीपाल–2	1230–1253
10.	Ra Khengar-2	रा खेंगार–2	1253–1260
11.	Ra Mandlik-1	रा मांडलिक–1	1260–1306
12.	Ra Navghan-2	रा नवघण–2	1306–1308
13.	Ra Mahipal-2	रा महीपाल–3	1308–1325
14.	Ra Khengar-3	रा खेंगार–3	1325–1351
15.	Ra Jayasimha-2	रा जयसिंह–2	1351–1373
16.	Ra Mahipal-4	रा महीपाल–4	1373–1373
17.	Ra Muktasimha	रा मुक्तसिंह	1373–1397
18.	Ra Mandlik-2	रा मांडलिक–2	1397–1400
19.	Ra Mangaldeva	रा मंगलदेव	1400–1415
20.	Ra Jatsimha-3	रा जतसिंह–3	1415–1440
21.	Ra Mahipal-5	रा महीपाल–5	1440–1451
22.	Ra Mandlik-3	रा मांडलिक–3	1451–1472
23.	Ra Bhupatsimha	रा भुपतसिंह	1472–1505

Raizada Dynasty

Chudasama Dynasty

Girinagar (future Junagadh), the capital of the Chudasama Dynasty of Saurashtra (875-1505), has been a geographical and historical center in the history of Gujarat. This Golden city of Saurashtra received the name Junagadh during the period of Chudasama Dynasty.

After the fall of the Maurya Dynasty (322–184 BC), the Maitraka (480–767) kings in Saurashtra made Vallabhi the capital. After the Maitrakas, the Chudasama Dynasty of Saurashtra ruled from Junagadh from the ninth century to the sixteenth century.

In the Yadu lineage of the Chandra Dynasty, 140th King Devendra was ruling in Sonitpur in Saurashtra. In his father-son tradition, **Gajpat, Shalivahana, Yadabhana, Jaskarna, Sama and then** Chudachandra became kings. Chudachandra (875-907) became the king of Vanthali and was considered as the Chandrachud or the Adi Purusha of the Dynasty.

After King Chudachandra, King Graharipu (940-982) conquered all the territory of Saurashtra and the Chudasama started prefixing Ra or Maharana before their name. King Ra Khengar-1 (1098–1114) shifted the capital from Vanthali to Junagad and the same capital remained for the Chudasama Dynasty up to Ra Bhupatsingh (1472–1505). After King Bhupat Singh, his descendants became the separate Raizada Dynasty.

Chudasama Dynasty

In the Solar Dynasty,
of the Atri Gotra,
Shri Krishna was born,
as Vishnu's Avatara. 1
In this Yayati's family,
great Yadavas belong,
On the land of Saurashtra,
says their history long. 2
The Chudasama kings,
worshipped Shiva's form,
They had Chandrachud title,
it was their norm. 3
Vanasthali was the place,
where they ruled first,
Chandrachuda was the king,
who quenched their thirst. 4
Chandrachud won,
the entire Saurashtra land,
He became powerful,
Sovereign King Grand. 5
It was the Golden Age,
of the Gujrat State,
Chudasama was the name,
foremost on that date. 6
Saurashtra made progress,
and received many cheers,
From the ninth century,
six hundred years. 7
Of the Chudasama Dynasty,
Girigram was place,
Girigram became Junagadh,
of this Gujrati race. 8

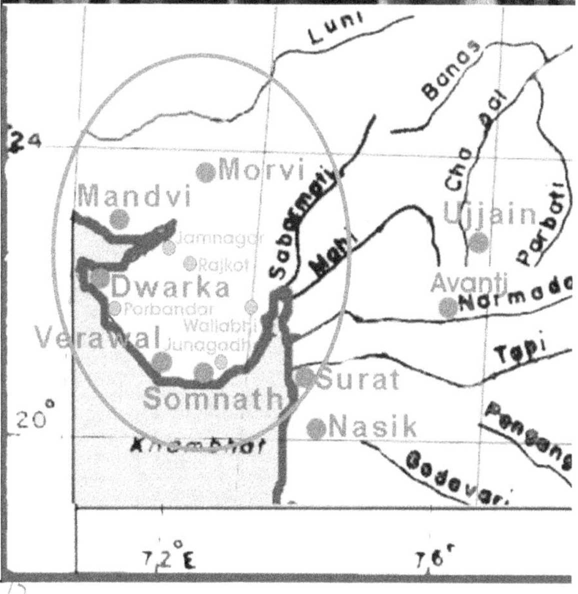

Hindu Rajtarangini

38. Dogra Dynasty, Jammu-Kashmir-Laddakh-Gilgit-Baltistan (1812-1947)

For the Prior Dynasty, please see :
Sikh Dynasty (1799–1849)

1. Gulab Singh   गुलाब सिंह   1822–1856
2. Ranbir Singh   रणबीर सिंह   1856–1885
4. Pratap Singh   प्रताप सिंह   1885–1925
5. Hari Singh   हरि सिंह   1925–1947
   Karan Singh

Dogra Dynasty

Born in Ikshavaku Dynasty, they were warrior guild,
They were Dogra heroes, lions on battlefield. 1
They wore long silk shirt, and turban on the head,
A shawl on the shoulder, and shoes with lining red. 2
Vegetarian their diet,
they ate "Kachur" what they call,
"Halva Pudi Thekur," Rice "Roti Daal." 3
They like Lassi of Curd, which gave them tickle,
They loved eating in groups,
they liked Mango Pickle. 4
They liked music and singing, in their Desi tune,
They liked folk singing,
in the sky when there is moon. 5

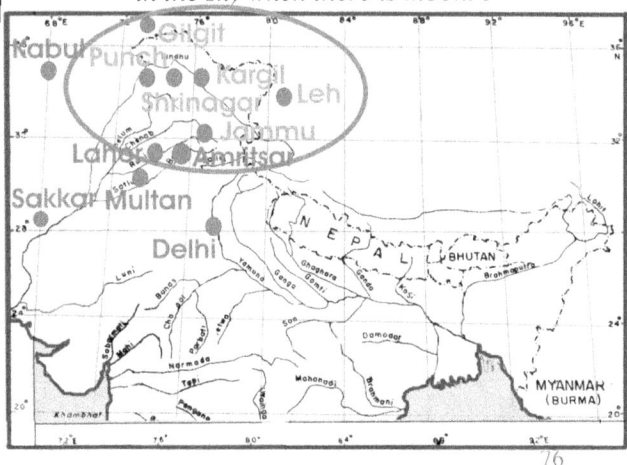

Dogra Dynasty

The Rajput kings of Jammu, Kashmir, Laddakh and Gilgit-Baltistan was Maharaja Gulab Singh (1792–1857), the founder of the Dogra Dynasty. Maharaja Gulab Singh was a Kshatriya of the Jamwal clan. He was initially employed in the army of Sikh Maharaja Ranjit Singh (1780–1839) and later became the king of Jammu.

In 1822, Gulab Singh Dogra bought Jammu, Kashmir, Laddakh and Gilgit-Baltistan regions from the East-India Company after the Sikh Empire fell in the British hands. He then became the authorized Maharaja of the Dogra Empire.

In 1843, Gulab Singh conquered Laddakh from the Namgyal Dynasty of Laddakh (1460–1842) along with Baltisthan and established Dogra power (1843–1947) there.

On October 26, 1947, the last Maharaja of Dogra Dynasty Hari Singh (1895–1961, power 1925–1947) transferred his entire empire to the Republic of India and his son Karan Singh Dogra (b. 1931) became a minister of the Independent Indian Government.

39. Gaikwad Dynasty, Baroda, Gujrat (1720-1951)

For the Prior Dynasty, please see :
Bhosle Dynasty, Satara (1594–1848)

1. Damaji Rao-1 — दामाजीराव-1 — 1720–1721
2. Pilaji Rao — पिलाजीराव — 1721–1732
3. Damaji Rao-2 — दामाजीराव-2 — 1732–1767
4. Govind Rao-1 — गोविंदराव-1 — 1768–1771
5. Sayaji Rao-1 — सयाजीराव-1 — 1771–1789
6. Manaji Rao — मानाजीराव — 1789–1793
7. Govind Rao-2 — गोविंदराव-1 — 1793–1800
8. Anand Rao — आनंदराव — 1800–1818
9. Sayaji Rao-2 — सयाजीराव-2 — 1818–1847
10. Ganpat Rao — गणपतराव — 1847–1856
11. Khande Rao — खंडेराव — 1856–1870
12. Malhar Rao — मल्हारराव — 1870–1875
13. Sayaj Rao-3 — सयाजीराव-3 — 1875–1939
14. Pratap Simha — प्रतापसिंह — 1939–1951

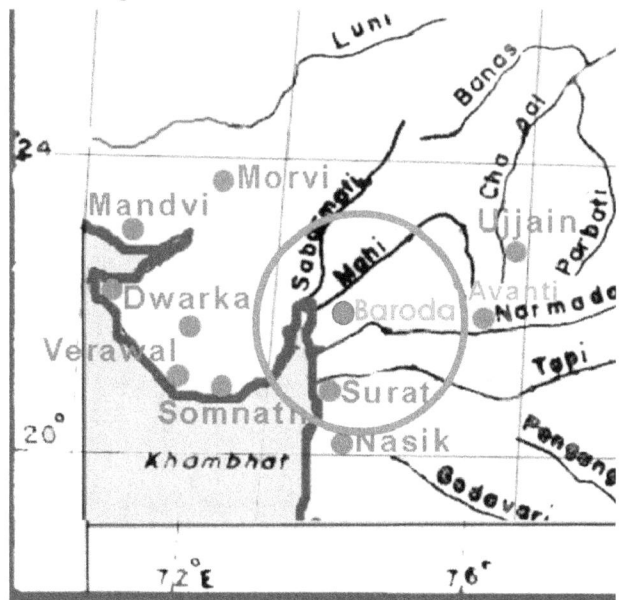

Gaikwad Dynasty

Damaji Gaikwad-1 (1720-1721) was a fighter in the army of Maratha Sardar Dabhade in the service of Chhatrapati Sahu-1 (1708-1749) of Satara. Later, he started an independent campaign in Gujarat and for his valor, Chhatrapati Sahu gave him the title of Samsher Bahadur. After his death, his nephew Pilaji Gaikwad built a fort in Sonegarh and settled his capital there.

Gaikwad rule started when Pilaji won Baroda from the power of Delhi Sultanate in 1721. In 1732, Pilaji was killed and Damajirao-2 (1732-1767) became king. In 1761, Damaji returned alive from the battle of Panipat-3.

The most famous and great majestic ruler of the Gaikwad family was Maharaja Sayajirao-3 Gopalrao Gaikwad (1875–1939).

Inspired by the ideals of social worker Mahatma Jyotiba Govindrao Phule (1827-1890), Maharaja Sayajirao-3 agitated against the unsociability in Pune in 1918. in 1913 Gopalro had given scholarship to Baba Saheb Bhimrao Ambedkar (1891–1956) for further education.

40. Gajapati Dynasty, Kalinga (1434-1541)

For the Prior Dynasty, please see :
Ganga Dynasty, East, Toshali (700–1264)

1. Kapilendra Deva — कपिलेन्द्र देव — 1434–1466
2. Purushottam Deva — पुरुषोत्तम देव — 1466–1497
3. Prataprudra Deva — प्रतापरुद्र देव — 1497–1540
4. Kalua Deva — कालुआ देव — 1540–1541
5. Kakharua Deva — कखरुआ देव — 1541–1541

Gajapati Dynasty

The Gajapati Dynasty,
lasted hundred years,
It was a golden era, without any fears. 1
Devoted to Krishna, were all people,
Chaitanya Mahaprabhu,
spread the love ample. 2
Good people in the world, do not last long,
Bad people make, the things go wrong. 3
Govind was a minister,
at the Gajpati court,
He was an evil man,
who sabotaged the fort. 4

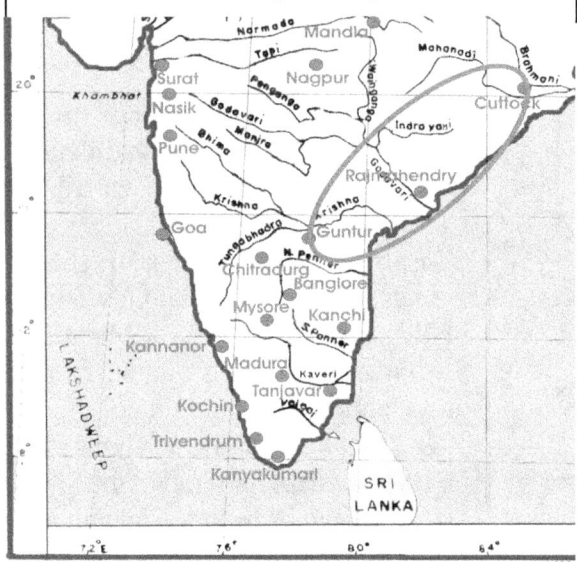

Gajapati Dynasty

The Suryavamshi Kalinga Gajapati Dynasty (1434–1541) was founded by king Kapilendra Deva (1434–1466). In the absence of the Ganga king Rakkas (985-1024) in the kingdom, Gajapati King Kapilendra Deva seized the chace to establish his power over Kalinganagar. The kingdom of the Gajapati Dynasty became immense from the Ganges River to the Kaveri River.

After Kapilendra Deva, king Purushottam Deva (1466–1497) and King Prataparudra Deva (1497–1540) became rulers. Purushottam Deva was a close relative of Chaitanya Mahaprabhu (1486-1534). When he became king, with the influence of Chaitanya, Purushottam Deva had spread Jagannath consciousness in the kingdom.

It is seen again and again in the history that many times more destruction is caused by our own Jaichandi people than the outsiders. The same happened to this Dynasty. When Kalua Deva (1540–1541) came to power, his minister Vidyadhar killed king Kalua Deva and installed Kakharua Deva on the throne (1541–1541). But the insidious Govind Vidyadhar killed Kakharua Deva and put an end to the Gajapati Dynasty.

Hindu Rajtarangini

41. Ganga Dynasty (East), Kalinga (700-1264)

1.	Virasimha	वीरसिंह	700–
2.	Kamarnava-1	कामार्णव–1	–
3.	Danarnava	दानार्णव	–
4.	Kamarnava-2	कामार्णव–2	–
5.	Ranarnava	राणार्णव	–
6.	Vajrahasta-1	वज्रहस्त–1	–
7.	Kamarnava-3	कामार्णव–3	–
8.	Gunamaharnava	गुणमहार्णव	871–898
9.	Vajrahast-2	वज्रहस्त–2	898–942
10.	Gundamma-1	गुण्डम्मा –1	942–945
11.	Kamarnava-4	कामार्णव–4	945–977
12.	Vinayaditya	विनयादित्य	977–980
13.	Vajrahasta-3	वज्रहस्त–3	980–1015
14.	Kamarnava-5	कामार्णव–5	1015–1016
15.	Gundamma-2	गुण्डम्मा–2	1016–1019
16.	Madhukamarnava	मधुकामार्णव	1019–1038
17.	Vajrahasta-4	वज्रहस्त–4	1038–1050
18.	Rajaraj-1	राजाराज–1	1050–1078
19.	Anant Varma	अनंतवर्मा	1078–1100
20.	Kamarnava-6	कामार्णव–6	1100–1151
21.	Raghav	राघव	1151–1165
22.	Rajaraj-2	राजाराज–2	1165–1189
23.	Ainyankbhima-1	ऐन्यंकभीम–1	1189–1197
24.	Rajaraj-3	राजाराज–3	1197–1200
25.	Ainyankbhima-2	ऐन्यंकभीम–2	1200–1238
26.	Narasimha-1	नरसिंह–1	1238–1264
27.	Bhanudeva-1	भानुदेव–1	1264–1279
28.	Narasimha-2	नरसिंह–2	1279–1306

Ganga Dynasty (East)

The Ganga Dynasty of East India ruled in the Kalinga country, with capital at Toshali. Along with the Kalinga country, the power of this kingdom was spread wide up to Bengal, Chhattisgarh and East Andhra.

Later on, Gang kings located their capital at Kalinganagar. What relationship the East Ganga Dynasty (700–1434) had with the Western Ganga Dynasty of Karnataka (350–1004), whose capital was in Talkad, is not fully known in the history.

The kings of Kalinga Nagar were known as Trikalingadhipati. The Kalinga kings had their own separate Rajshwari era, which was about 500 years ahead of the AD count.

The divine temple of the great Jagannathpuri was built at the time of Ganga King Anantavarma Chodagangadeva (1078–1100), and then the Sun Temple of Odisha was built during the time of Ganga King Narasimha-1 (1238-1264).

29. Bhanudeva-2   भानुदेव-2   1306–1328
30. Narasimha-3   नरसिंह-3   1328–1352
31. Bhanudeva-3   भानुदेव-3   1352–1378
32. Narasimha-4   नरसिंह-3   1378–1414
33. Bhanudeva-4   भानुदेव-4   1414–1434

Ganga Dynasty, Kalinga

Gangas ruled Kalinga,
without any feud,
Their place was Toshali,
near Chhattisgarh. 1

Gangas had their era,
and own Date Count,
They were self sufficient,
keeping their account. 2

In addition to East,
Gangas were in the West,
Not much we have known,
about the lineage and the rest. 3

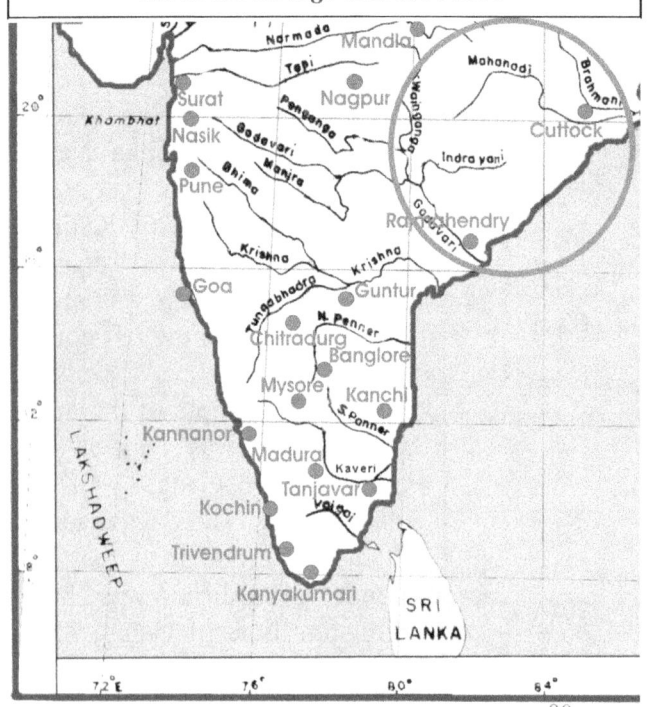

Hindu Rajtarangini

42. Ganga Dynasty (west, Talkad (350-1024)

1.	Konguni Varma	कोंगुनिवर्मा	350–400
2.	Madhava-1	माधव-1	400–450
3.	Hari Varma	हरिवर्मा	450–460
4.	Madhava-2	माधव-2	460–500
5.	Avinit	अविनीत	500–540
6.	Mushkar	मुष्कर	
7.	Shri Vikram	श्रीविक्रम	
8.	Bhu Vikram	भूविक्रम	
9.	Shivamara-1	शिवमार-1	750–760
10.	Shri Purusha	श्रीपुरुष	760–788
11.	Shivamara-2	शिवमार-2	788–817
12.	Rajmalla-1	राजमल्ल-1	817–853
13.	Nitimarga-1	नीतिमार्ग-1	853–870
14.	Rajmalla-2	राजमल्ल-2	870—907
15.	Nitimarga-2	नीतिमार्ग-2	907–935
16.	Narasimha	नरसिंह	935–936
17.	Rajmalla-3	राजमल्ल-3	936–937
18.	Butuga	बूतुग	937–955
19.	Malladeva	मरुलदेव	955–960
20.	Marasimha	मारसिंह	960–974
21.	Rajmalla-4	राजमल्ल-4	974–985
22.	Rakkas	रक्कस	985–1024

For the Next Dynasty, please see :
Chola Dynasty, Tanjavar (50–1279)

Ganga (West) Royal House

The capital of the Western Ganga Dynasty of Karnataka was Kolar. It was then located at Talkad or Talvanpur on the bank of the river Kaveri. The first king of Western Ganga Dynasty, Kongunivarma (350-400) and his son Madhava-1 (400-450) were experts in ethics and Upanishads. Madhav-1 has written a commentary on Vatsayan's Kamasutra. His son Harivarma transferred the Ganga capital from Kolar to Talakad. At the time of King Avinit (500-540), Sanskrit was predominant language. Mahakavi Bharavi was a royal poet at the Ganga Court. King Shripurusha's period (760-788) was considered to be the golden age of the Western Ganga Dynasty. King Shripurusha had the title of "Shri Rajya." Due to this great fame, the invasions of Rashtrakuta and Chola kings on the Ganga kingdom the Cholas annexed Ganga kingdom in the year 1004. This ended the Ganga Dynasty of the Talakad.

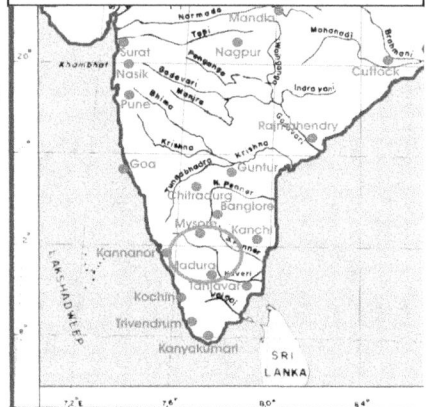

Ganga Dynasty (West)
Kolar was the capital, of the Gangas West,
It was moved the Talkad, at strategic place best. 1
On the banks of Kaveri, it was a nice place,
learned received honour, and poets had a base. 2

43. Gandhar Dynasty (Ancient Time)

1. Dushyant   दुष्यंत   ...
2. Varudha   वरूढ
3. Gandir   गाण्डीर
4. Gandhar   गांधार
5. Subal   सुबल
6. Shakuni   शकुनि

For the Next Dynasty, please see :
Hindu Shahi Dynasty (867–1026)

Gandhar Dynasty
Taxila was a super,
University in the world,
It made name of Gandhar,
shine like the gold. 1

But evil Shakuni ruined,
Gandhar's good name,
With his wicked actions,
he spoiled the fame. 2

Of the King Subal,
Gandhari was the daughter,
Dhritarashtra's wife,
Duryodhan's mother. 3

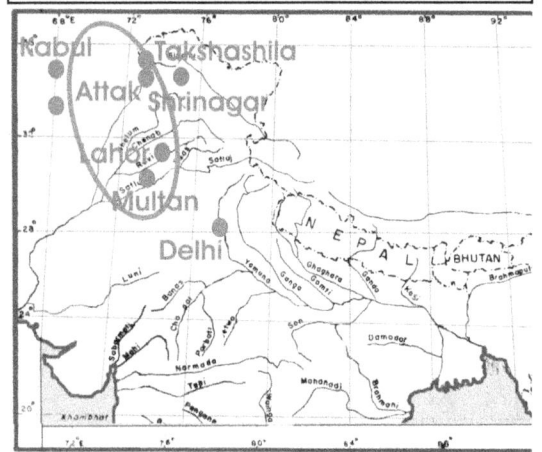

Gandhar Dynasty

The principal center of Sanatan Gandhar Mahajanapada was Purushapur and the capital was Takshashila. In the Mahabharata period, the ruler of Gandhar was the Mahabharata's infamous villain Shakuni. Gandhari, the wife of blind king Dhritarashtra of Hastinapur was the princess of this country. Shakuni and her sister Gandhari were considered to be masters of economics (Maha. Adi. 63).

Sindhu King Shakuni was the son of King Subal and Queen Sudarma. As Gandhari's husband Dhritarashtra was blind, Gandhari also put blindfold on her eyes as a sacrifice.

Shakuni, the evil king of Gandhar, was the ill-fated uncle of the wicked Duryodhan, who pulled the strings of Duryodhana's misdeeds. In the Mahabharata War, the gambler Shakuni was killed at the hands of Sahadeva (Maha. Surg. 28.61) and Shakuni's five brothers were killed at the hands of Bhima.

After the Mahabharata War, Gandhari, Dhritarashtra, Kunti, Vidur and Sanjay retired to the forest where Gandhari and Dhritarashtra were consumed by a forest conflagration (Maha. Ashram. : 32).

44. Gonaditya Dynasty, Kashmir (1182 BC-631 AD)

#	Name	(Devanagari)	Dates
1.	Gonand	गोनन्द –2	1182–1147 BC
2.	Vibhishan-1	विभीषण–1	1147–1094
3.	Indrajit	इंद्रजीत	1094–1059
4.	Ravan	रावण	1059–1058
5.	Vibhishan-2	विभीषण–2	1058–1023
6.	Nar-1	नर–1	1023–983
7.	Siddha	सिद्ध	983–923
8.	Utpalaksha	उत्पलक्ष	923–893
9.	Hiranyaksha	हिरण्याक्ष	983–855
10.	Hiranyakula	हिरण्यकुल	855–795
11.	Mukul	मुकुल	795–735
12.	Mihirakul	मिहिरकुल	735–665
13.	Bak	बक	665–602
14.	Kshitinand	क्षितिनंद	602–572
15.	Vasunand	वसुनंद	572–520
16.	Nara-2	नर–2	520–460
17.	Aksha	अक्ष	460–400
18.	Gopaditya	गोपादित्य	400–340
19.	Gokarna	गोकर्ण	340–282
20.	Narendraditya-1	नरेंद्रादित्य–1	282–246
21.	Yidhishthira-1	युधिष्ठिर–1	246–212 BC
22.	Meghavarna	मेघवर्ण	25–59 AD
23.	Shreshthasen	श्रेष्ठसेन	59–89
24.	Hiranya	हिरण्य	89–120
25.	Mitragupta	मित्रगुप्त	120–125
26.	Pravarasen	प्रवरसेन	125–185
27.	Yudhishthir-2	युधिष्ठिर–2	185–206
28.	Narendraditya-2	नरेंद्रादित्य–2	206–219
29.	Ranaditya	रणादित्य	219–261
30.	Vikramaditya	विक्रमादित्य	261–297
...	Baladitya	बालादित्य	–631 AD

For the Next Dynasty, please see :
Karkota Dynasty, Kashmir (631–855)

Gonaditya Dynasty

From the Rajatarangini of Mahakavi Kalhan, we know the dynastic records from the early period of Kashmir to AD 1151. According to him, Kushan king Kanishka had settled Kanishka city in Kashmir and then Ashok Maurya (269-232 BC) settled the city of Shrinagar. According to Kalhan, at the time of Mahabharata, King Yudhishthir's contemporary was King Gonanda-1. After him, the names of 53 kings have been mentioned, but their dates are not given. This Dynasty is known as Gonaditya Dynasty for its first known King was Gonanda.

During the reign of King Yudhishthir-I (246–212 BC) of Kashmir, the kingdom of Maurya emperor Chakravarti Ashok Maurya (269–232 BC) came to power in Kashmir and Chakravarti Ashok established the city of Shrinagar. From 212–167 BC, Kashmir was ruled by the Maurya Dynasty and then the Sunga (185–72 BC) kings. After them, the power of the kings of Pratapaditya Dynasty (167 BC-25 AD) was established over Kashmir.

The Gond Dynasty (Ancient Time)

45. The Gond Dynasty of Mandla (900–1781)

1.	Narasimha	नरसिंह	900–
2.	Ramachandra	रामचंद्र	
3.	Krishna	कृष्ण	
4.	Rudra	रुद्र	
5.	Jagannath	जगन्नाथ	
6.	Vasudeva	वसुदेव	
7.	Madansimha	मदन सिंह	1116
8.	Arjun	अर्जुन	
9.	Sangram	संग्राम	
10.	Dalpat	दलपत	1550
11.	Queen Durgavati	रानी दुर्गावती	1550–1564
12.	Vira Narayan	वीर नारायण	
13.	Chandra	चंद्र	
14.	Madhukar	मधुकर	
15.	Prem Narayan	प्रेम नारायण	
16.	Narahar	नरहर	1742–1781

Gond Dynasty

The Gond-Bhil Dynasty of central India was very large. It extended from Orissa, Chhattisgarh, Vidarbha to Telangana. Its main centers are historical in places like Chandrapur, Ballarsha, Kalamb, Devgad, Baitul, Shivni, Ramnagar, Mandla, etc. Gond and Bhil tribal people are considered to be of the same origin.

Guh Nishad Bhil of Shringevarpur of ancient times is seen in Valmiki Ramayana at the time of King Shri Ram Chandra's exile.

The Gondi language has its own script which looks like the Modi language, and which bears some resemblance to the Devanagari and Telugu characters.

Gond people are brave, self-respecting, strong and extremely patient.

46. The Gond Dynasty of Vidarbha (1200–1550)

1.	Bhilraja	भिल राजा	
2.	Bhima	भीम	
3.	Kharja	खरजा	
4.	Hir-1	हीर–1	
5.	Andiya	अंदिया	
6.	Talvar	तलवार	
7.	Kesar	केसर	
8.	Dinkar	दिनकर	
9.	Ramsimha	राम सिंह	
10.	Suraj	सूरज	1445–1470
11.	Khando	खंडो	1470–1495
12.	Hir-2	हीर–2	1495–1521
13.	Queen Hira Bai	हीराबाई	1521–1550

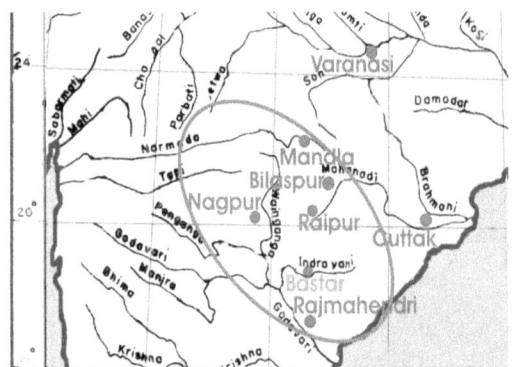

47. Guhil Dynasty, Mewad (550-1303)

For the Previous Dynasty, please see : Raghu Dynasty (Ancient Time)

1. Guhadatta (Guhila) गुहदत्त (गुहिल) 550 ... ...
2. Bappa Raval बप्पा रावल 730-753
3. Sumitsimha सुमितसिंह 753-773
4. Rajatsimha रजतसिंह 773-793
5. Chetansimha चेतनसिंह 793-813
6. Ravalsimha रावलसिंह 813-828
7. Khummanasimha-1 खुम्मणसिंह-1 828-853
8. Mahayaksimha महायक 853-878
9. Khummanasimha-2 खुम्मणसिंह-2 878-903
10. Bhirtribhatta भर्तृभट्ट 903-951
11. Allat अल्लट 951-972
12. Naravahan नरवाहन 972-973
13. Shalivahan शालिवाहन 973-977
14. Shaktikumar शक्तिकुमार 977-993
15. Ambaprasad अम्बाप्रसाद 993-1007
16. Suchivarma शुचिवर्मा 1007-1021
17. Naravarma नरवर्मा 1021-1035
18. Kirtivarma कीर्तिवर्मा 1035-1051
19. Yogivarma योगिवर्मा 1051-1068
20. Vairat वैरट 1068-1088
21. Vamshapal वंशपाल 1088-1103
22. Vairisimha वैरीसिंह 1103-1108
23. Vijaysimha विजयसिंह 1108-1127
24. Arisimha अरिसिंह 1127-1138
25. Chaudsimha चौडसिंह 1138-1148
26. Vikramsimha विक्रमसिंह 1148-1158
27. Ranasimha रणसिंह 1158-1168

Guhil Dynasty of Mewad

The most powerful Dynasty of Mewar was the Guhil Dynasty. This Dynasty is considered to be a descendant of the Raghu Dynasty of Shri Rama. In 550 AD, Guhiladitya established Guhil Rajput kingdom with Nagda as their capital. His great descendant Bappa Rawal (730-753) is considered to be the first Maharaja of the Guhil Dynasty. Bappa Rawal Ekling was a devotee of Shiva. He minted his gold coins to prove his sovereignty over Mewar.

Bappa Rawal died in Nagda when the Amra poet wrote a singular commendation in his praise. Mahalakshmi, the wife of King Bhartribhatta (903-951) of Mewar, was a Princess of the Rathor Dynasty. His son King Alhat (951-972) shifted the capital of Guhil kingdom from Nagda to Ahad. Her son Raja Narvahana (972-973) had established political relations with Sakambhari Chauhans by marrying the daughter of Jejay Chauhan of Sakambhari Dynasty.

Rana Samant Singh of Mewar (1171–1179) married Prithvi Bai, the sister of Rana Prithviraj Chauhan-2 (1166–1169) of Sakambhari-Ajmer. Moreover, King Tej Singh (1256-1273), son of Rana Jaitrasingh of Mewar, married Rupadevi, daughter of Udai Singh Chauhan, a descendant of the Chauhan Dynasty of Nadol, to establish Guhil-Chauhan relationship. In year AD 1303, Maharani Padmini of Chittor performed Jauhar along with 16000 Rajput women. It is a glittering event in the history of Rajastan and India.

28. Kshemsimha	क्षेमसिंह	1168–1171
29. Samantsimha	सामंतसिंह	1171–1179
30. Kumarsimha	कुमारसिंह	1179–1191
31. Manthanasimha	मंथनसिंह	1191–1211
32. Padmasimha	पद्मसिंह	1211–1213
33. Jaitrasimha	जैत्रसिंह	1213–1256
34. Tejsimha	तेजसिंह	1256–1273
35. Samarsimha	समरसिंह	1273–1301
36. Ratnasimha	रत्नसिंह	1301–1303

For the Next Dynasty, please see :
Sisodiya Dynasty, Mewad (1303–1948)

Bappa Rawal

When the Sindh province, fell in Arab hands,
New aggressions began, in the Sindh lands. 1
Attacks also occurred, in Rajasthan,
But they were defended, by this brave man. 2
He was Bappa Raval, the king of Mewad,
Arabs stopped missions, defeat they had. 3
Bappa was a Guhil, Rajput hero,
Warrior he was great, battlefield pro. 4
He protected land, with mighty courage,
King of the Mewad, with a divine image. 5
Chittor was rich, people were happy,
Peace in the country, heaven was a copy. 6

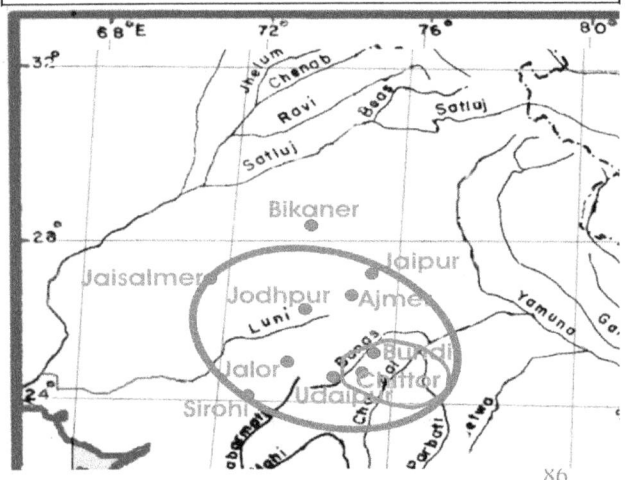

चितौड़ की महारानी पद्मावती

स्थायी
राजस्थान की पावन देवी, रानी पद्मावती ।
वो तो, नारी जगत महान थी ।
जिसे, सानी कोई न थी ।।

अंतरा–1
जग में सुंदर, नारी अनुपम,
नैतिक उसकी बुद्धि ।
धर्मचारिणी वह तो नारी,
सीता जैसी सती ।। जिसे …

अंतरा–2
पतिव्रता वह, नीति निपुण थी,
राजस्थान की शान थी ।
लक्ष्मी का अवतार धरा पर,
मेवाड़ की जान थी ।। जिसे …

Maharani Padmini

The Goddess of Rajasthan,
Queen Padmavati,
She is noblest woman in the world,
Whom there is no match.

She is most beautiful in the world,
She is ethical woman,
She is moral woman,
Like the Goddess Sita,
whom ... 1.

The devoted woman, she is skillful,
She is the honour of Rajasthan,
She is the Lakshmi on the earth,
She the life of Mewad,
whom ... 2.

48. Gupta Dynasty, Patliputra (240-730)

For the Prior Dynasty, please see :
   Kanva Dynasty (72 BC-27 BC)
   Shunga Dynasty (185 BC-72 BC)
   Maurya Dynasty (322 BC-184 BC)

Earlier Gupta Dynasty (240–530)

#	Name		Years
1.	Shrigupta	श्रीगुप्त	240–280
2.	Ghatotkacha	घटोत्कच	280–319
3.	Chandragupta-1	चंद्रगुप्त-1	319–350
4.	Samudragupta	समुद्रगुप्त (पराक्रमांक)	350–375
5.	Ramagupta	रामगुप्त	375–375
6.	Chandragupta-2	चंद्रगुप्त-2 (विक्रमादित्य-1)	375–415
7.	Kumaragupta-1	कुमारगुप्त-1	415–455
8.	Skandagupta	स्कन्दगुप्त	455–467
9.	Narasimhagupta	नरसिंहगुप्त (बालादित्य)	467–473
10.	Kumaragupta-2	कुमारगुप्त-2	473–477
11.	Narasimhagupta	नरसिंहगुप्त (बालादित्य)	495–530

Later Gupta Dynasty (530–730)

#	Name		Years
12.	Krishnagupta	कृष्णगुप्त	530–540
13.	Harshagupta	हर्षगुप्त	540–
14.	Jivitagupta	जीवितगुप्त	–550
15.	Kumaragupta-3	कुमारगुप्त-3	550–560
16.	Damodargupta	दामोदरगुप्त	560–562
17.	Maheshagupta	महेशगुप्त	562–601
18.	Madhavagupta	माधवगुप्त	601–655
19.	Adityasen	आदित्यसेन	655–680
20..	Devagupta	देवगुप्त	680–700
21.	Vishnugupta	विष्णुगुप्त	700–
22.	Jivitagupta	जीवितगुप्त	–730

For the Next Dynasty, please see :
   Pushyabhuti Dynasty (505–647)

Gupta Dynasty

After the dominant Maurya period (322BC-184BC), two great Royal Houses came to power, Vakataka Dynasty (255–510) in the South and Gupta Dynasty (240–730) in the east. In Kaushambi near Prayagraj, King Shrigupta (240–280) founded the Gupta Dynasty (240–730). He ruled over Saket (Ayodhya) and Magadha region. Samudragupta (350-375), the son of the Gupta emperor Chandragupta-1 (319-350) and Queen Maharani Kumaradevi was a great mighty king. Therefore, he got the honour of Maharajadhiraja. Samudragupta himself was a high-quality poet and musician. The scholar Vasubandhu was appointed in his cabinet. Poet Harishen was his court poet. Samudragupta's empire had grown from the Himalayas in the North to the Vindhya Mountains in the South and from Bengal in the East to Malwa in the west. The son of Maharaja Samudragupta and his Queen Maharani Dattadevi was called Chandragupta-2 Vikramaditya (375-415). After King Samudragupta's death, his grandson Chandragupta II became a great king in the Indian history.

Emperor Chandragupta Vikramaditya (375-415)

Emperor Chandragupta Vikramaditya (375-415)

Emperor Chandragupta-2 Vikramaditya (375-415), the grandson of Emperor Parakramanka Samudragupta (350-375) in the Gupta Dynasty of Patliputra and Ujjain (240-730), was a great scholar and patron of art, like his father Emperor Samudragupta. During the time of Chandragupta Vikramaditya, the area of Gupta Empire was at its maximum and very large. Chandragupta-2 made his mark by adding family ties to Jharkhand's Nag Dynasty (83-1948), Nandivardhan's Vakataka Dynasty (250-510) and Karnataka's Kadamba Dynasty (340-610), etc. He subdued the kingdoms of Malwa and Kathiawar from Shaka Kshatrap Rudrasimha-2 (388-395) and established his second capital in Ujjain.

Chandragupta married the Nag princess Kubernaga and gave his daughter Prabhavati Devi to the Vakataka king Rudrasen-2 (400-405) in marriage. Chandragupta-II got his son Kumaragupta-1 (415-455) married to Princess of the Kadamba Dynasty (340-610) of the Vanvasi and established the influence of his power up to the West coast. He made Ujjain his second capital.

The reign of Chandragupta II was considered as the golden period of literature, art and music. Kalidas, Dhanvantari, Kshanpaka, Amarasimha, Shanku, Varahamihir, Varruchi, Aryabhatta, Visakhadatta, Shudraka, Brahmagupta, Bhaskaracharya, Vishnusharma, etc. were honoured in his court.

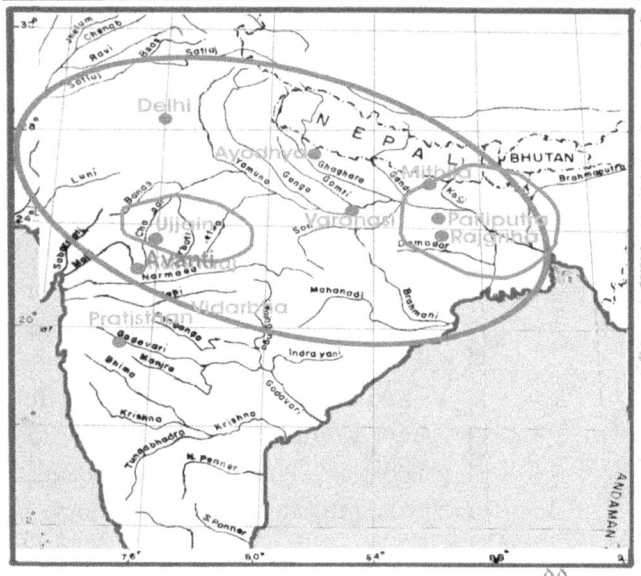

Hindu Rajtarangini

https://www.facebook.com/TheHinduWarriors/photos/a.103761384693990/211735557229905/

49. Gurjar Dynasty, Rajastan (400-725)

For the Prior Dynasty, please see :
Gupta Dynasty (240–730)

1. Dadda-1 — दद्दा–1 — 400 ...
2. Jayabhatta-1 — जयभट्ट –1
3. Dadda-2 — दद्दा–2 (प्रशान्तराग) — 478–
4. Dadda-3 — दद्दा–3
5. Dadda-4 — दद्दा–4 (प्रशान्तराग) — 580–
6. Jayabhatta-2 — जयभट्ट–2 (वीतराग)
7. Dadda-5 — दद्दा–5 (सुसहाय) — 628–640
8. Jayabhatta-3 — जयभट्ट–3 — 640–
9. Dadda-6 — दद्दा–6
10. Jayabhatta-4 — जयभट्ट–4 — 706–725

For the Next Dynasty, please see :
Pratihar-Gurjar (725–1036)

Gurjar Dynasty of Bhinmal

According to the history, along with the shrinking territory of the Gupta kingdom of Rajasthan in the fifth century, his feudal Gurjar Kshatriyas established their reign at Bhinmal on the land between Loni River and Abu Mountains. They fixed their capital at Jodhpur and made the port of Bharuch as their trade hub. In the early eighth century, the land of Gujarat and Rajasthan was called Gurjar Rakshit Desh i.e. Gurjararatra (Gujarat) due to their valor of repulsing the foreign Arab aggressors. The Gurjars were considered to be a faction of the Chapotkat Rajputs.

The territory of the Gurjars was growing, but the expansion of the Gurjars was stalled for some time due to the victories of Pushyabhuti Prabhakar Vardhan (580-605). Then, the Gurjars attained oneness with the Pratiharas in the eighth century (725 AD) during the reign of Pratihara king Harishchandra. After that, the Gurjars conquered the Lat Chalukyas of Gujarat (590–750) and established authority across the Vindhya Mountains up to river Tapi.

Hindu Rajtarangini

50. Gutta Dynasty, Karnatak (1080-1262)

For the Prior Dynasty, please see :
Chalukya Dynasty, Kalyani (696–1189)

1. Mahaguttal — महागुत्तल — 1080–
2. Gutta-1 — गुत्त–1
3. Mallideva — मल्लीदेव — 1115–
4. Vira Vikramaditya-1 — वीर विक्रमादित्य–1
5. Jaya Deva-1 — जयदेव–1
6. Gutta-2 — गुत्त–2 — 1181–1187
7. Vira Vikramaditya-2 — वीर विक्रमादित्य–2 — 1187–1238
8. Jaya Deva-2 — जयदेव–2 — 1238
9. Vira Vikramaditya-3 — वीर विक्रमादित्य–3
10. Gutta-3 — गुत्त–3 — 1262
11. Hariya Deva — हरीयदेव
12. Jaya Deva-4 — जयदेव–4

For the Next Dynasty, please see :
Yadav Dynasty, Devgiri (850–1317)

Gutta Dynasty

In the Guttal region of Karnataka, King Mahaguttal founded his Dynasty as a feudatory in territory of the powerful Chalukya king Vikramaditya-6 (1076-1127) of Kalyani, in the year 1080.

After the Chalukyas, Guttal kings rose to power in the kingdom of Yadava Dynasty of Devgiri (1069-1317) and in the shadow of the Yadavas, 1. the Sindas of Yelaburg, 2. the Rattas of Belgaum, 3. the Pandyas of the highlands, 4. the Kadambas of Hangal, 5. the Silchars of Konkan and 6. the Guttas of Guttals started ruling the Guttal area of Kaveri district of Karnataka. At that time Guttal area was called Gottamgadi.

The most powerful ruler of the Gutta Dynasty was King Gutt-2 (1181–1187), the grandson of Gutta King Vikramaditya-1, who was a feudatory under the Kalyani Chalukya king Somesvara-4 (1183–1189). After this, the Gutta Dynasty became feudatories of the Yadava king Bhillama of Devgiri (1187–1191).

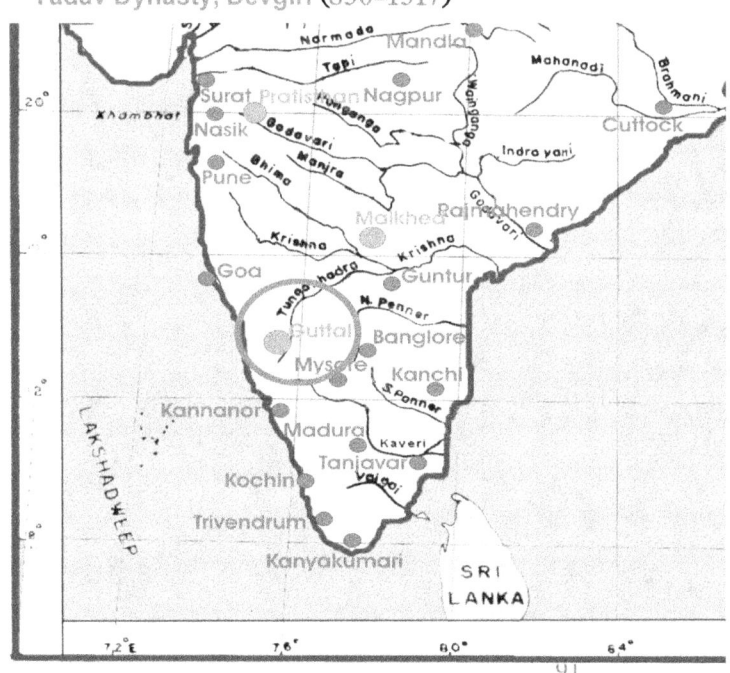

Hindu Rajtarangini

51. Haryak Dynasty, Patliputra (544-413 BC)

For the Earlier Dynasty, please see :
Brihadrath Dynasty, Magahd (Ancient Time)

1. Bimbisar   बिंबिसार (श्रेणिक)   546–494 BC.
2. Ajatshatru   अजातशत्रु   494–462 BC.
3. Udayibhadra   उदायीभद्र   462–442 BC.
3. Aniruddha   अनिरुद्ध
4. Mund   मुंड
5. Nagdarshak   नागदर्शक   437–413 BC.

For the Earlier Dynasty, please see :
Shishunag Dynasty, Patliputra (413–344 BC)

Haryaka Dynasty

Bimbisara, the son of Bhattiya, the minister of Rajagriha Magadha, ended the Brihadratha Dynasty and established the Harayak or Haryanka Dynasty. King Bimbisara had met Gautama Buddha (563-483) and the 24th Tirthankar Vardhaman Mahavir Swami (540-468), in person.

Ajatashatru, son of the Haryak emperor Bimbisara, built the city of Pataliputra and his son Udayi (462–442 BC) moved the capital from Rajgriha to Patliputra. During the reign of this king, the power of Haryak Dynasty was extended to Champa, Kaushambi, Vidisha, Varanasi, Ujjain. The Harayak Dynasty ended at the hands of Shishunag Dynasty in 413 BC.

Haryaka Dynasty

Magadha king Bimbisar,
was also called Shrenik,
He began Haryak Dynasty,
at Rajgriha in panik. 1

He built nuw city, Patliputra name,
His son moved there,
and brought it to fame. 2

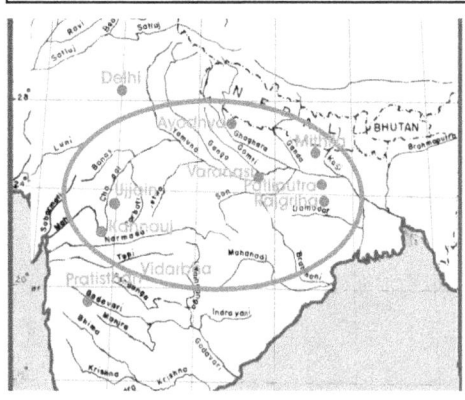

Hindu Rajtarangini

Emperor Ajatashatru, of Magadh (494-462 BC)

Emperor Ajatshatru

Son of King Bimbisara,
the Magadha ruler mighty,
Ajatshatru built,
the great Pataliputra city. 1

King Ajatshatru met,
Gautama Buddha in person,
He also met Mahavira,
whose blessings he had won. 2

Ajatshatru created, Rathamusala weapon,
It was a war machine, to depend up on. 3

Ajatshatru of Magadha, was a great warrior,
He won many kings, there was no barrier. 4

Ajatshatru's influence, spread far and wide,
From Nepal to Bengal kings,
became on his side. 5

Emperor Ajatshatru

King Ajatashatru (494–642 BC) of the Harayak Dynasty was the noted king of the Magadha Empire. His capital was at Patliputra. Ajatashatru was also called Kuniya. Emperor Bimbisara (546–494 BC) and his son Ajatashatru were contemporaries of the 24th Tirthankara Mahavir Swami (540–468 BC) and Mahatma Gautama Buddha (563–483 BC). King Ajatshatru was directly associated with Lord Buddha. Ajatashatru's mother was related to Chellana Vardhaman Mahavir, the princess of the Vaishali kingdom. Mahatma Gautama Buddha and Vitarag Mahavir died during Ajatshatru's tenure.

King Ajatshatru was the Governor of the country of Emperor Bimbisara. After the death of his father, Emperor Ajatshatru won the Lichchhavi kingdom of Tirhat and enlarged his kingdom from Anga country to the Himalayas. To prevent the possibility of Lichchhavi invasion from Nepal, Ajatshatru built a fort called Patal at the confluence of the Ganges River on the banks of the Shone River and built a fort there. This Patal city was the fortified city of Pataliputra.

Hindu Rajtarangini

52. Hemachandra Vikramaditya, Delhi (1555-1556)

For Earlier Dynasty, see : Chauhan Dynasty, Sakambhari (648–1192)

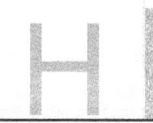

Hem Chandra Vikramaditya, Panipat Wars-1, 2

(The first war of Panipat, 1526)

Year Fifteen hundred-twenty-six,
was the war of Panipat first,
Fought between two Afghans,
both had power thirst. 1
Ibrahim Lodi was, the Delhi Sultan,
Babar the Mughal, came from Afghanistan. 2
Babar reached Panipat, with a huge force,
Lodi went from Delhi, try to change the course. 3
War was terrible, red blood river ran,
Lodi got killed and, Babar became Sultan. 4

(The second war, 1556)

When Sikandar Sur was Sultan,
Hemu was his minister,
With his prowess then, Hemu became ruler. 5
Hemu was a Brahmin,
a brave man with no fame,
He became Delhi King, Vikramaditya name. 6
Year Fifteen-hundred-fifty-six,
brought second Panipat war,
Mughal from Kabul came,
to fight so much far. 7
Battlefield Panipat, fierce was the battle,
An arrow struck Hemu,
and gave a wound fetal. 8
Hemu fell on the ground, unconscious he was,
Akbar didn't have to fight,
finished was his cause. 9
Akbar caught Hemu, and beheaded the dead,
In order to scare people,
exhibited the severed head. 10
Akbar became Sultan, in the Mughal style,
He was now free to spread,
terror quite a while. 11

Emperor Hem Chandra Vikramaditya

Hem Chandra or Hemu (1501-1156), the gallant man of Alwar, was the commander in Mughal army at Mirzapur. On hearing the news of Humayun's death (1555–1555), he immediately marched on Delhi with his army. Emperor Hem Chandra Vikramaditya himself became King of Delhi by establishing his authority over Agra and Delhi, and for the first time after Maharana Puthviraj Chauhan (1166-1169) put the saffron flag of Indian independence in the Capital Delhi. Maharaja Hemu had a huge army adorned with 1500 elephants.

On hearing the news of Hemu becoming Sovereign Ruler of Delhi, Akbar (1542–1605) left Kabul and the second battle of Panipat with Hemu (1556) broke out. While fighting, unfortunately, an arrow hit Maharaja Hemu seated on elephant. Hemu fell on the ground and the war and Indian independence was overturned.

Vikramaditya Hem Chandra was an influential ruler, shrewd politician, successful fighter and visionary of diplomacy. Born at the home of Purohit Rai Purnadas of Alwar, Hemu started his bright life journey. Hem Chandra became a scholar of Sanskrit and Mathematics and a bulwark of fencing and horse riding. As soon as he became Delhi King, he attained the title of Chakravarti by Vedic coronation in the old fort of the Pandavas. He imposed ban on cow slaughter in the state. After the death of Maharaja Hemu, there was concern and question in the minds of the Hindu nationalists as to when and if such a great Hindu Chakravarti king would rule from Delhi ever again.

53. Hindu Shahi Dynasty, Kabul-Gandhar (867-1026)

For the Earlier Dynasty, please see : गांधार राजवंश (Ancient Time)

1. Kalhar — कहार — 867–870
2. Samant — सामंत — 870–895
3. Kamal Varma — कमलवर्मा — 895–921
4. Bhima Jetripal — भीम जेतृपाल — 921–960
5. Jaipal — जयपाल — 960–1002
6. Anandpal — आनंदपाल — 1002–1021
7. Trilochalpal — त्रिलोचनपाल — 1021–1026

Hindu Shahi Dynasty
Hindu Shahi Dynasty kings,
were Kabul rulers,
Seven kings of this House,
ruled for Hundred-sixty years.

Hindu Shahi Dynasty

After seizing power from the Buddha king Laghturma of Kabul-Gandhara, his minister Spalapati Kahlar established the Hindu Royal Dynasty on Kabul-Gandhar with the help of the Pratihara king Mihir Bhoj (843-893) of Kannauj. Kahlar's kingdom centers were Kabul, Udbhandapur and Nagarkot. The political relations of the Kahlar king were closely related to the Karkota Dynasty (631–855) and then the Utpal (855–949) Dynasty of Kashmir.

After the death of king Kahlar, Samanta (870–895) and then Kamalar's son Kamalavarma (895–921) became kings. After Kamalavarma's death, his son Jetripal Bhima (921-960) came to power. Nagarkot was named Bhimnagar by King Bhima. He had solidified Kabul's political relations with Kashmir by marrying his daughter to Utpal Prince Simha of Kashmir. After the death of King Anandpal, his son Trilochanpal also gave his daughter Bimba to Kandar Simha, the son of the Prime Minister of Sangramaraja (1003-1028) of Lohar Dynasty (1003-1172) of Kashmir.

Hindu Rajtarangini

54. Holkar Dynasty, Indore (1730-1948)

For the Earlier Dynasty, please see : Peshwa Dynasty, Pune (1713–1818)

1. Hingoji Holkar — हिंगोजी होळकर ...
2. Khandoji — खंडोजी
3. Malharrao-1 — मल्हारराव-1 — 1731–1766
4. Tukojirao-1 — तुकोजीराव-1 — 1766–1767
5. Malerao — मालेराव — 1767–1767
6. Ahalya Bai — रानी अहल्याबाई — 1767–1795
7. Tukojirao-2 — तुकोजीराव-2 — 1795–1797
8. Malharrao-2 — मल्हारराव-2 — 1797–1797
9. Kashirao — काशीराव — 1797–1798
10. Yashvantrao-1 — यशवंतराव-1 — 1798–1807
11. ... Chaos — अराजकता — 1807–1811
12. Malharrao-3 — मल्हारराव-3 — 1807–1833
13. Martandrao — मार्तण्डराव — 1834–1834
14. Harirao — हरिराव — 1834–1843
15. Khanderao — खंडेराव — 1843–1844
16. Tukojirao-3 — तुकोजीराव-3 — 1844–1886
13. Shivajirao — शिवाजीराव — 1886–1903
14. Tukojirao-4 — तुकोजीराव-4, — 1903–1926
15. Yashvantrao-2 — यशवंतराव-2 — 1926–1948

Holkar Dynasty

The pioneer men of the Holkar Dynasty were Hingoji and Khandoji Holkar of Wafgaon in Maharashtra, but Malharrao Holkar (1693–1766) is considered as the founder of the Holkar Dynasty. In 1730, Peshwa Bajirao-1 (1720–1740) appointed Malharrao as the governor of Malwa province and Malharrao made Indore (Indur) his capital. In 1733, Malharrao married his son Khanderao (1723–1754) to Mankoji Shinde's daughter Ahalyabai (1725–1795) of Jamkhed, Maharashtra. From year 1740, Ahalyabai started taking armed part in many battles. In 1754, Khanderao was killed in the battle of Kumbher and Malharrao's adopted son Tukojirao-1 (1766-1767) came to throne in Indor. Tukojirao-1 died in 1767 and Ahalyabai rose to power (1767–1795). In 1795, Ahalyabai retired and soon died. In 1795, Tukoji-2 came to power. Tukoji-2 served Peshwas from Bajirao-1 (1720-1740) to Madhavrao-2 (1774-1795) in many events : 1. Rohila war (1769), 2. Barabhai Affair (1174), 3. Tipu War (1786), 4. British War (1778-1779), 5. Nizam war (1795), etc.

Hindu Rajtarangini

Queen Ahilyabai Holkar of Indore (1725-1795)

Punyashlok Ahalyabai Holkar (1767–1795)

Ahalyabai Holkar was a skilled, dutiful and religious Hindu queen. This warrior and religious woman built temples of Ayodhya, Nashik, Dwarka, Pushkar, Hrishikesh, Jejuri, Pandharpur, Gaya, Udaipur, etc.; and she renovated the fractal temples of Sorti Somnath, Omkareshwar, Mallikarjuna, Vishveshwar, Kashi, Vishnupada, Mahakaleshwar, etc. She built huge pilgrimage ghats for travelers at the banks of the rivers at holy places such as Varanasi, Prayagraj, Pantambe, Chaundhi, Nashik, Indore, Trimbakeshwar, etc.

Maharaja Malhar Rao Holkar, Indore (1693-1766)

मल्हारराव होलकर
जय बोल, जय बोल, जय बोल,
जय जय बो - - - ल ।।
देशभक्ति का जुनून जिस पर,
सवार हो बचपन से ।
सैनिक बन कर सब अर्पण कर,
लड़ता जो तन मन से ।
ऐसा सेनानी हो या राजा,
जीवन वो अनमोल ।। जय बोल
खेला बावन युद्ध समर वो,
श्री होलकर मल्हार ।
मातृभूमि की सेवा करता,
जीत मिले या हार ।
आओ गीत स्तुति के उसकी,
गाएँ हिरदय खोल ।। जय बोल

Malharrao Holkar
Say jai Jai Jai!
He who had the craze
of patriotism from childhood,
He became a soldier
and served the country,
With is body mind and soul.
He fought fifty-two wars,
and served his Motherland,
He may win or he may lose,
Let's sing song for that Malharrao Holkar.

Maharaja Malharrao Holkar (1731–1766)

For the first time in history, Shakuntala's son King Bharata said that "King should not only be the son of the king, it should not be true that the king takes birth in the king's house". This is a perfect example in the case of Malharrao Holkar of Indor (Holkar)) (1731–1767).

Malhari (1693–1766), son of Khandoji Holkar, a poor Maratha Sheppard from a village called Hol in Maharashtra, became a spontaneous fighter with patriotism and thirst for service to his birthplace. Following the childhood footprints of Chhatrapati Shivaji (1630–1680), Malhari also started fighting with his friends against the Nizam foreigners by forming a small military force.

Seeing the courage and valor of Malhari, the great Peshwa Bajirao-1 (1720–1740) gave him a place in his cavalry in 1721. Then, seeing the war skills and fame of Malhari, Bajirao Peshwa made Malharrao a commander of five-hundred cavalry and head of Uttar Khandesh in 1725. Malharrao fought a total of 52 miscellaneous wars and rendered valuable service to Peshwa Bajirao-1 and Peshwa Nana Saheb (1740–1761).

In 1761, Malharrao participated in the battle of Panipat-3 with Sadashivrao Peshwa (1730–1761) along with Mahadaji Scindia (1727–1794) of Gwalior. Khanderao (1723–1764), the only son of Maharaja Malharrao and Queen Gautamibai Holkar, was the husband of Queen Ahilyabai Holkar (1725–1795).

55. Hoysal Dynasty, Halebid (1026-1348)

For the Earlier Dynasty, please see : Yadav Dynasty, Devgiri (850–1311)

1. Sal — सळ — 1006–1022
2. Nripakam — नृपकाम — 1022–1047
3. Vinayaditya — विनयादित्य — 1047–1063
4. Ereyang — एरेयंग — 1063–1100
5. Vira Ballal-1 — वीर बल्लाळ-1 — 1100–1110
6. Vishnuvardhan — विष्णुवर्धन त्रिभुवनमल्ल — 1110–1152
7. Narasimha-1 — नरसिंह-1 — 1152–1173
8. Vir Ballal-2 — वीर बल्लाळ-2 — 1173–1220
9. Narasimha-2 — नरसिंह-2 — 1220–1233
10. Someshvar — सोमेश्वर — 1233–1254
11. Narasimha-3 — नरसिंह-3 — 1254–1291
11. Vir Ballal-3 — वीर बल्लाळ-3 — 1291–1342
12. Vir Ballal-4 — वीर बल्लाळ-4 (वीरुपक्ष) — 1342–1348

For the Next Dynasty, please see :
Nayak Dynasty, Vijaynagar (1336–1565)

Hoysala Dynasty

Hoysala were kings in, Karnataka stronghold,
The rulers were great, in the history old. 1

Sculptures of this period, had world fame,
Idols Pillars Arches, Peaks Designs Dome; 2

The temples they built big, beautiful and perfect,
In the architectural annals, they have high respect. 3

Hoysala Dynasty

The Hoysala Dynasty (1024–1348) is a Lunar branch of the Yadava Dynasty (850–1311) of Devgiri. The Hoysala chief ruled as a feudatory ruler under Western Chalukyas (696–1189) of the Kalyani.

During the time of Kalyani Chalukya King Someshwar-3 (1127-1138), Hoysala King Vishnuvardhana Tribhuvanamall (1110-1152) conquered the Chalukya kingdom and gave independence. He established his capital at Dvarasamudra (Halebid). King Vishnuvardhana was a follower of the Vaishnava Ramanujacharya (1017– 1137). He built the Chennakeshava temple at Belur and the great temple of Hoysaleshwara at Halebid to commemorate his great victory.

King Vir Balla-2 (1173-1220) became the most famous king of the Hoysala Dynasty. He made the kingdom huge and prosperous. His effective attacks weakened the ability of the Chalukyas and taking advantage of it, the Yadava king Bhilam-5 (1173–1192) conquered the Chalukya king Someshwar-4 (1183–1189) and gained authority over Kalyani.

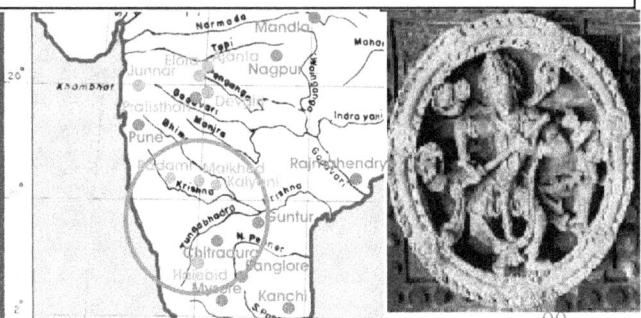

Hindu Rajtarangini

Hoysala king Vishnuvardhana Tribhuvanamall (1110-1152)

The Hoysala king Tribhuvanamalla Vishnuvardhana (1110–1152) of Dvarasamudra (Halebid) was once a feudatory of the Chalukya king Vikramaditya Tribhuvanamalla Bittideva (1076–1127) of Kalyani. King Vishnuvardhana came under the influence of Vaishnava Acharya Ramanujacharya (1017–1137) and became a Vaishnava devotee. As a result, the Vishnu devotee king Tribhuvanamall was known by the name Vishnuvardhana since then. Vishnuvardhan started building the ravishing Vishnu temple.

The capital of the Hoysala king Vishnuvardhana was in Belur. Vishnuvardhan's Chennakeshava Tri-mandir made in Belur is a testimony to the culmination of this art. Adorned with the beautiful Apsaras and Yaksha statues of the Chennakeshava temple, the Arches and beautiful pillars are known for their high quality of craftsmanship.

King Vishnuvardhana then built the city of Dvarasamudra (Halebid) and built the great Kedareshwar temple with sixteen corners in the form of a star. After this, by creating the second grand Keshava temple at Somanathapuram near Shrirangapatnam, the greatness of the Hoysala Dynasty became eternal in the history.

56. Ikshavaku Dynasty (Ancient Time)

For the previous dynasty, please see the Vivasvan Dynasty.

1. Vaisvat Manu — वैवस्वत मनु
2. Ikshvaku — इक्ष्वाकु
3. Shashad — शशाद
4. Kakutsa — ककुत्स्थ
5. Anena — अनेन
6. Prithulashva — पृथुलाश्व
7. Prashnajit — प्रश्नजीत
8. Yuvanashva — युवनाश्व
9. Mandhata — मांधाता
10. Purukutsa — पुरुकुत्स
11. Trasadasyu — त्रसदस्यु
12. Anaranya — अनारण्य
13. Haryashva — हर्यश्व
14. Vasuman — वसुमन
15. Sutanva — सुतन्व
16. Trayyarunya — त्रय्यरुण्य
17. Satyavrat — सत्यव्रत
18. Harishchandra — हरिश्चन्द्र
19. Rohit — रोहित
20. Chanchu — चंचु
21. Sudeva — सुदेव
22. Bharuk — भरुक
23. Bahuk — बाहुक
24. Sagar — सगर
25. Asamanjas — असमंजस
26. Anshuman — अंशुमान
27. Bhagirath — भगीरथ

Ikshavaku Dynasty

Shri Ram's Raghuvamsha originated from King Vikukshi, the son of King Ikshvaku, the son of Manu Vivaswan. The Videha Dynasty of King Janaka originated from Ikshvaku's second son King Nimi. King Kakutsa was the pioneer for heroism and polity, and therefore, Shri Ram was known as Kakutastha (Ram Raksha 22). King Mandhata was well known for the rule of virtues and his kingdom was very well known all around for prosperity. He was charitable and eloquent. He used to converse with Brihaspati (Maha. Adi. 4.76).

King Satyavrat was same as king Trishanku, whose great son was truth speaking King Harishchandra. Lord Indra used to travel in the airplane to King Trishanku. King Harishchandra was considered to be the true genius of truth and honesty, for which he was blessed by Brahma-Vishnu-Mahesh. Whenever there is a discussion of truth, the name of King Harishchandra definitely comes and will continue to come for ever. The son of King Harishchandra and his Queen Taramati received by the grace of Lord Varun, was Rohitashv or Rohit. The head priest of King Rohit was Vasistha Muni.

Maharaja Sagar, the son of the great King Bahuk of Ayodhya and his wife Yadavi, was a divine person. King Bahuka used to worship Yamraj in his court (Maha Sabha. 8.19). King Bahuka had expelled his son Asmanjas from the kingdom for the sin of being vicious (Maha. Adi. 107.89). Sagar Maharaja was righteous and he was vegetarian (Maha. Anu. 115.89). Virtue is attained even by just uttering the name of King Sagara (Maha. An. 165.49).

Great sage Maharishi Bhagiratha was a great king of the Ikshavaku Dynasty who had place in the court of Yama (Maha Sabha 8.11). Maharaja Bhagiratha gave Ganga Devi a place on earth from the head of Lord Shiva. Therefore, river Ganga is called Bhagirathi. King Janhu drank Ganga and released her from his ear, therefore, Ganga is known as Janhavi.

For the Next Dynasty, please see : 1. Raghu Dynasty; 2. Nimi Dynasty

गंगा देवी

गंगा देवी! तू मंगल है माता,
तेरा अँचल है कितना सुहाना ।
तेरी लहरों में है गुनगुनाता,
मैया! संगीत सरगम सुहाना ।। धृ.
निकली शंकर की काली जटा से,
तुझको भगिरथ ने लाया धरा पे ।
तुझको जन्हू की कन्या है माना,
तेरा इतिहास पावन पुराना ।। 1
तेरे जल में हिमालय की माया,
तुझमें जमुना का पानी समाया ।
सरयु को भी गले से लगाया,
तूने उनको भी दीन्ही गरिमा ।। 2
तेरा तीरथ है लीला जगाता,
सारे पापों से मुक्ति दिलाता ।
है सनातन तेरा मेरा नाता,
बड़ी पावन नदी तू मेरी माँ ।। 3

Goddess Ganga

Sthayi
O Ganga Devi! you are our holy mother.
Your blessings are so loving.
There is beautiful music in your waves.

Antara
You arose from the hair of Shiva.
Sage Bhagirath brought you to the earth.
You are the daughter of King Janhu.
Your history is auspicious and ancient. 1

There is divinity of Himalaya in you.
Water of river Yamuna merges in you.
You have hugged the river Sharayu.
You have given fame to them all. 2

Your holy water is magical,
it cleanses all our sins.
I have an ancient relationship with you,
you are our holy mother. 3

O Ganga! you are our holy mother.

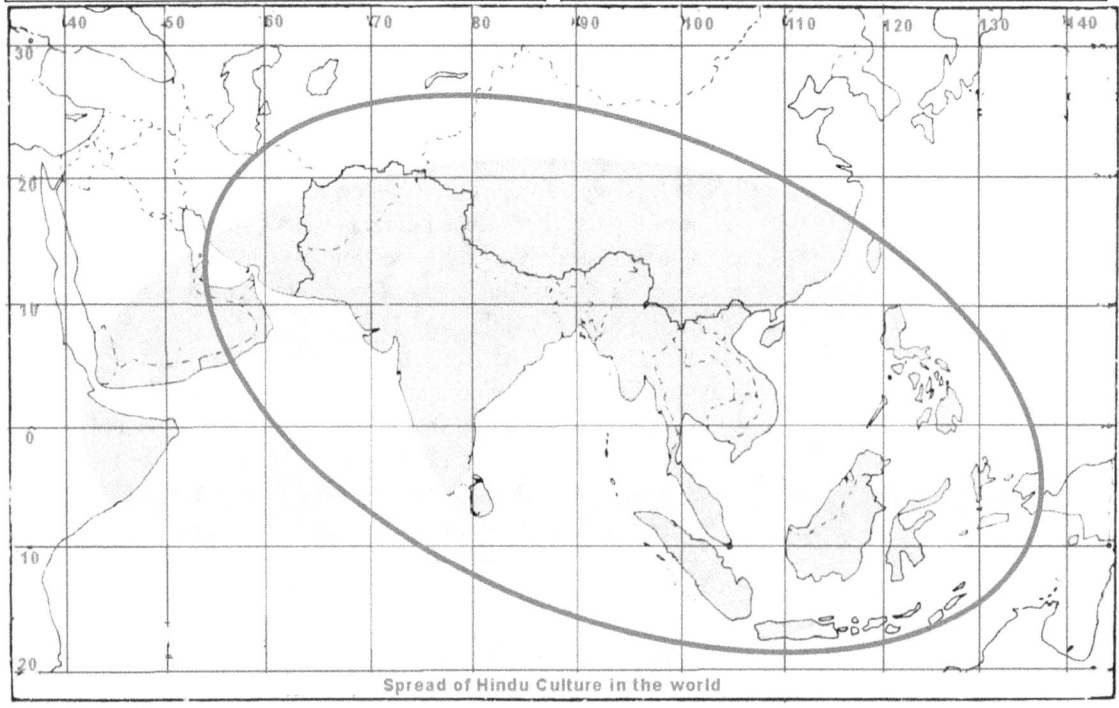

Spread of Hindu Culture in the world

King of the Gods, Lord Indra (Ancient Time)

Lord Indra

Lord Indra, the son of Prajapati Marichi's son Kashyapa and his wife Aditi, was the king of the Gods. Indra was the eldest of Aditi's 32 sons (Maha. Adi. 65-15). Among the other 31 sons of Aditi were twelve Adityas, eight Vasus and eleven Rudras. Indra's chariot was an aerial aircraft. The garden of Indra was called Nandanvan in which Kalpavriksha (Wish granting tree) used to be. Indra was also known as Shakra and Purandar.

The elephant of Lord Indra was Airavat (Gita 10.27), the name of his horse was Uchhaishrava (Gita 10.27), the name of his weapon was Vajra, the name of his bow was Indradhanush and the name of his sword was Paranjaya (Maha. Adi. 18, Agnipuran 51). Lord Indra's court was resplendent and graceful. At this court, great sages like Udalaka, Galav, Gaurashiras, Dirghatamas, Durvasa, Parashar, Pritpani, Yagyavalkya, Shankha, Shyen, Shvetketu, Savarni, etc. had great honour.

Lord Indra was very proud of the fact that he is the king of the Gods, but when child Shri Krishna became more popular in Vrindavan, one day Indra poured torrential rain on the village to teach a lesson to Shri Krishna and the people of the village. The village became inundated and the people got scared. Shri Krishna then lifted the Govardhan mountain and saved people of the village under the shelter of the mountain. In a while, Indra's pride was crushed and Indra begged for pardon to Shri Krishna. The event of this defeat was a great insult in Indra's life.

गीत राग : भैरवी, कहरवा ताल

गोवर्धनधारी

गोवर्धन उठाए हरि, देखो देखो जी लीला खरी ।
उँगली पर धरे, वो समूचा गिरी, और बजाए मीठी बाँसुरी ।।

मथुरा के परे पास में, मधुबन की हरी घास में ।
गोप गोपी सगे, खेल में जब लगे, साथ में थे सखा श्री हरि ।
मूसला वर्षा अचानक गिरी, व्रज में चिंता भयानक पड़ी ।। 1

व्रज वासी खड़े आस में, थे बड़े आज विश्वास में ।
सब गिरि के तले, लगे सुख से गले, सबने मन में थी आशा धरी ।
चाहे जितनी भी बारिश गिरी, दुख में सब को बचाए हरि ।। 2

इन्द्र भगवान जब थक गए, बरसा कर बादल अक गए ।
शक्र हार गए, शर्मिंदा भये, झट से वर्षा फिर बंद करी ।
बोले तेरी हो जै जै हरि, तेरी लीला है जादू भरी ।
उँगली पर धरे, तू समूचा गिरी, और बजाए मीठी बाँसुरी ।। 3

गोवर्धन उठाए हरि, ...

Govardhan

Krishna has picked up the Govardhan Mountain.
Behold the true Divine Power.
He picked up the mountain on his little finger,
And played the sweet flute with the other hand.

Beyond Mathura, in the green pasture of Madhuban,
While the Gops and the Gopis were playing,
And when Shri Hari Krishna was with them,
Torrential rain suddenly poured on the village.
The village dwellers became worried.
Krishna picked up the mountain on his little finger,
and played the sweet flute with the other hand. 1

The people are waiting eagerly for Krishna's help.
Today they have great confidence in him.
All are standing under the mountain.
They are sure that, doesn't matter how hard it rained,
Krishna will save them from the trouble.
Krishna picked up the mountain on his little finger,
and played the sweet flute with the other hand. 2

When Lord Indra got tired,
Aand the clouds got fed up of pouring the rains,
Indra lost the contest, he quickly stopped the rain,
And said, O Krishna, yours is true victory.
Your divine power is great. 3

Hindu Dynasties of Indonesia (Hindesia) (674-1478)

1. Shailendra Dynasty, Java (674-947)
2. Simhashri Dynasty, Java (1222-1478)
3. Shri Vijaya Dynasty Sumatra (683-1405)
4. Shri Kesari Dynasty, Bali (914-1119)
5. Jay Dynasty, Bali (1133-1284)

57. Shailendra Dynasty, Java (674-947)

For the previous dynasty, please see the Chola Dynasty (50-1279)

#	Name	Devanagari	Years
1.	Shantanu	शान्तनु	...
2.	Shailendra	शैलेन्द्र	674–717
3.	Pangkaran	पंगकरन	760–780
4.	Panungalan	पनुंगलन	780–800
5.	Samar Gravir	समर ग्रवीर	800–819
6.	Garung	गरुंग	819–838
7.	Piktan	पिकतन	838–850
8.	Lokpal	लोकपाल	850–898
9.	Balitung	बालितुंग	898–910
10.	Daksha	दक्ष	910–919
11.	Tulodang	तुलोदंग	919–924
12.	Vava	वावा	924–929
13.	Sindok	सिंडोक	929–947

58. Simha Shri Dynasty, Java (1222-1478)

#	Name	Devanagari	Years
1.	Rajas	राजस	1222–1227
2.	Anushyati	अनुष्यति	1227–1248
3.	Vishnuvardhan	विष्णुवर्धन	1248–1268
4.	Kirtnagar	कीर्तनगर	1268–1292
5.	Jayakatvang	जयकत्वंग	1292–1293
6.	Jayavardhan	जयवर्धन	1293–1309

> **Royal Hindu Houses of Java, Sumatra, Bali**
>
> The influence of Hindu culture has been known on the archipelago of Java, Sumatra and Bali since the time of Gupta Emperor Chandragupta (319–350). This influence continued with the stories of the Ramayana and with the Tamil maritime traders, travellers and the trade workers.
>
> In the ninth century, the largest Shiva temple of Hindeshia (Indonesia) was built. By the fifteenth century, there were many Hindu dynasties in Java-Sumatra, such as Shailendra, Shrivijaya, Holing, Medang, Koderi, Sunda, Simhashri, Majpahit, etc., but the clear dynastic accounts of all these are not known or written.
>
> In Harshavijaya chronicle it has been said that the influence of Shiva-Vaishnav Hindu culture has been on the islands of Java, Sumatra, Bali etc. since Mahabharata time. And, it is also said that the influence of Vedas, Upanishads, Shiva Samhita and Bhakti Marg have been indelible on the island of Bali by the descendants of Lord Shri Krishna Himself.

7. Jayanagar	जयनगर	1309–1329
8. Tribhuvan	त्रिभुवन	1329–1350
9. Rajsangar	राजसंगर	1350–1389
10. Vikramavardhan	विक्रमवर्धन	1389–1429
11. Suhit	सुहित	1429–1447
12. Kartavijay	कार्तविजय	1447–1451
13. Rajasvardhan	राजसवर्धन	1451–1456
14. Purvavishesh	पूर्वविशेष	1456–1466
15. pandan	पंदन	1466–1478

59. Shri Vijaya Dynasty, Sumatra (683-1405)

1. Shrivajay	श्रीविजय	683–
2. Dharmasetu	धर्मसेतु	725–
3. Samartung	समरतुंग	792–
4. Jayavarma	जयवर्मा	825
4. Balaputra	बालपुत्र	835–
5. Chudamani	चुडामणि	988–

the Shri Vijaya Dynasty ruled Java-Sumatra-Bali as the feudatories of the Cholas of Tanjavar, up to year 1279 and then under the Pandyas of Madura up to year 1405..

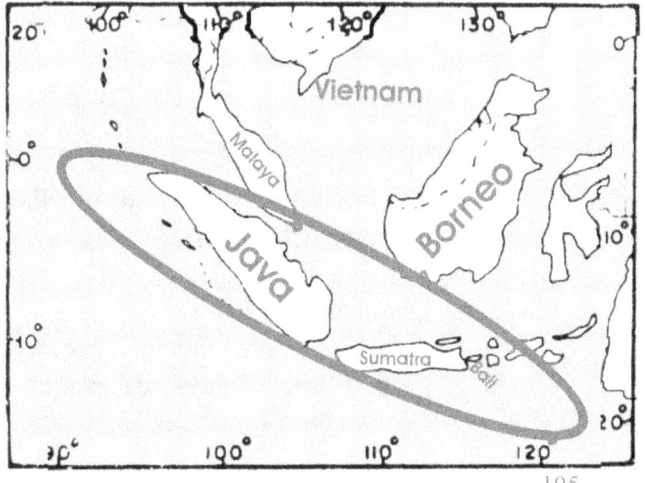

The Hindu Dynasty of Sumatra

The Hindu Dynasty of Sumatra raised their flag in Hindeshia by establishing a capital named Shrivijaya. Through the stories of Ramayana-Mahabharata, the drama-music-musical-arts of all the society of Indonesia (Hindeshia) had been emanated.

The Parabrahma Trimurti temple group, built around year 830 AD at the time of King Jayavarma of Sumatra (825-835), is a living example of this. Gods of Shiva, Vishnu, Ganesh, Saraswati, Durga, Arjuna, etc. are seen adorned in the temples of Bali. Shri Kesari Vamdev Dynasty (914-1119) and Jai Dynasty (1133-1284) of Bali are known to history prominently.

The Dohas tell us :
Java-Sumatra

*The islands of Java-Sumatra,
became holy lands,
Influence of Hindu Culture,
eradicated evil hands. 1*

*The joy Harshavijaya gave,
beyond the oceans seven,
With the touch of Hinduism,
Java became heaven. 2*

*People built the temples, studying
scriptures first,
Reading Ramayana stories,
quenched knowledge thirst. 3*

60. Jadeja Dynasty, Saurashtra (1203-1948)

#	Name	Hindi	Years
1.	Lakhaji-1	लाखोजी-1	1203–1231
2.	Lakha Ghurara-1	लाखा घुरारा-1	1231–1270
3.	Jam Moodha	जाम मूड़ा	1270–1295
4.	Jam Sara	जाम सारा	1295–1300
5.	Jam Fula	जाम फूला	1300–1320
6.	Jam Lakha-1	जाम लाखा-2	1320–1350
7.	Jam Pura	जाम पूरा	1350–1365
8.	Jam Raydhan-1	जाम रायधन-1	1365–1385
9.	Jam Athoji	जाम आठोजी	1385–1405
10.	Jam Godaji	जाम गोदाजी-1	1405–1430
11.	Jam Vehanji	जाम वेहांजी	1430–1450
12.	Jam Madraji	जाम मदराजी	1450–1470
13.	Jam Kanhoji	जाम कान्होजी	1470–1490
14.	Jam Amarji	जाम अमरजी	1490–1510
15.	Jam Bhimaji	जाम भीमजी	1510–1525
16.	Jam Hamirji	जाम हमीरजी	1525–1537
17.	Jam Ravalji	जाम रावलजी	1537–1548
18.	Jam Khengar-1	राव खेंगार-1	1548–1585
19.	Rao Bharmal-1	राव भरमल-1	1585–1631
20.	Rao Bhojraj	राव भोजराज	1631–1645
21.	Rao Khengar-2	राव खेंगार-2	1645–1654
22.	Rao Tamachi	राव तमाची	1654–1662
23.	Rao Raydhan-2	राव रायधन-2	1662–1697
24.	Rao Pragmal-1	राव प्रागमल-1	1697–1715
25.	Rao Godaji-2	राव गोदाजी-2	1715–1718
26.	Rao Desal-1	राव देसल-1	1718–1741
27.	Rao Lakha-3	राव लाखा-3	1741–1760
28.	Rao Godaji-3	राव गोदाजी-3	1760–1778

Jadeja Dynasty

The Royal House of the Jadeja Dynasty came from the Lunar Line of Pururava, Nahush and Yayati. lineage of Yadu, Kuru, Vidurth, Shursen, Vasudeva, Shri Krishna, Pradyumna, Anirudh, Gajpat, Bhupat, etc. After them came Jadeja Dynasty kings Jam Narapat Sawant (683-701), Jam Sama Sawant (701-757), Jam Jeho Sawant (757-831), Jam Neto Sawant (831-855), Jam Notiyar (865-870), Jam Oghar (870-881), Jam Otho (881-898), Jam Rahu (898- 918), Jam Odhar (931-942), Jam Lakhiar (942-956), Jam Dhurari (956-986), Jam Unnad (986-991), Jam Samo (991-1041), Jam Kaku (1041-1062), Jam Raidhan-1 (1062- 1092), Jam Pratap (1092-1112), Jam Samadhad (1112-1182), Jam Jado (1182–1203), etc. were the kings. After them, Jam Lakhoji Jadeja (1203–1231). All were well known Kings.

This great Jadeja Dynasty ruled the region of Kutch-Saurashtra for about 750 years.

29. Rao Raydhan-3	राव रायधन-3	1778-1814
30. Rao Bharmal-2	राव भरमल-2	1814-1819
31. Rao Desal-2	राव देसल-2	1819-1860
32. Rao Pragmal-2	राव प्रागमल-2	1860-1876
33. Rao Khengar-3	राव खेंगार-3	1876-1942
34. Rao Vijayraj	राव विजयराज	1942-1947
35. Rao Pradyumna	राव प्रद्युम्न	1947-1948

Jadeja Dynasty

Jadeja Dynasty of Gujrat,
was a Rajput clan,
Kachcch Bhuj and Saurashtra,
was their territory span. 1
They belonged to Yadu lineage,
brave warrior heroes,
They fought with the swords,
and with bows and arrows. 2

Jadeja Dynasty continued

Sawant's son was Jado Sawant, whose descendants were called Jadeja. In Jadeja branch of Rajkot, Jam Rawal Sawant (1561-1618), Jam Vibhaji Sawant (1618-1625), Jam Chhatrasal Sawant (1625-1664), etc. were the great ancestors.

Jam Lakhadhiraj (1907-1930) of this royal family gave importance to modern education in Rajkot and brought social reforms like adult marriage etc. in the kingdom. Lakhadhiraj brought farming to a very high level in the agricultural sector and gained popularity in the kingdom. Lakhadhiraj had affection for Mahatma Gandhi (1869–1948).

The movement started in Rajkot during the time of Thakur Dharmendrasingh (1930–1940) after Lakhadhiraj In 1938 Gandhi sat down on Satyagraha against the power. As a result, the kingdom administration delegation came into the able hands. Rail, roads, clothes factory, hospital, print shop, etc. opened up in a big way in Kathewad and progress increased in Rajkot.

61. Kachhavaha Dynasty, Rajastan (1036-1948)

For the Previous Dynasty, please see :
Sangram Simha-1, Sisodiya Dynasty, Chittor, (1473–1527)

#	Name	(Hindi)	Reign
1.	Sodha Singh	सोढ़ासिंह	–
2.	Dulhe Rai	दूल्हेराय	1036–1037
3.	Kankil Deva	कांकिल देव	1037–1038
4.	Huna Deva	हूण देव	1038–1053
5.	Janha Deva	जान्ह देव	1053–1070
6.	Poojan Deva	पूजन देव	1070–1084
7.	Malsi Deva	मलसी देव	1084–1146
8.	Jaital Deva	जैतल देव	1146–1179
9.	Raj Deva	राज देव	1179–1216
10.	Kilhan Deva	किल्हण देव	1216–1276
11.	Kuntal Deva	कुन्तल देव	1276–1317
12.	Junsi Deva	जुणसी देव	1317–1366
13.	Ubhaya Karan	उदयकरण	1366–1388
14.	Naro Singh	नारोसिंह	1388–1413
15.	Banbir Singh	बनबीरसिंह	1413–1424
16.	Udha Rao	उधाराव	1424–1453
17.	Chandra Sen	चंद्रसेन	1453–1502
18.	Prithvi Raj Singh-1	**पृथीराजसिंह-1**	1502–1527
19.	Bhim Singh	भीमसिंह	1527–1534
20.	Ratna Singh	रतनसिंह	1534–1537
21.	Bharmal	भारमल	1537–1573
22.	Bhagavan Das	भगवानदास	1573–1589
23.	Man Singh-1	मानसिंह-1	1589–1614
24.	Jagat Singh-1	जगतसिंह-1	1614–1614
25.	Bhao Singh	भाओसिंह	1614–1621

Kachhawaha Dynasty

The Kachhwaha Dynasty was founded by King Dulhe Rai (1036-1037) of the Rajput Narwar branch in 1036 AD. His son King Kankil Deva (1037-1038) established his capital at Amer (Ambar), which remained there for the next five centuries.

Kachwaha king Prithviraj Singh-1 (1502-1527) was feudatory of Sisodiya Maharana Sanga (1473-1527) of Chittor, therefore, after the retreat of Rana Sanga form the battle of Khanwa in 1527, Prithviraj Singh returned from that war and established his independent rule in a place called Manchi. .

After King Bhagwandas Kachhwaha (1573–1589), his son King Mansingh-1 (1589–1614) became a respectable feudatory of the Mughals. After Mansingh, the next ruler Mirza Jaisingh-1 (1621–1666) as a chieftain of the Mughals signed the famous Treaty of Purandar with the Maratha King Shivaji (1630–1680).

26. Jai Singh-1	जयसिंह–1	1621–1666
27. Ram Singh-1	रामसिंह–1	1666–1688
28. Bishna Singh	बिशनसिंह	1688–1700
29. Savai Jai Singh-2	सवाई जयसिंह–2	1700–1743
30. Ishvar Singh	ईश्वरीसिंह	1743–1750
31. Madho Singh-1	मधोसिंह–1	1750–1768
32. Prithvi Singh-2	पृथ्वीसिंह–2	1768–1778
33. Pratap Singh	प्रताप सिंह	1778–1803
34. Jagat Singh-2	जगतसिंह–2	1803–1818
35. Jai Singh-3	जयसिंह–3	1818–1835
36. Ram Singh-2	रामसिंह–2	1835–1881
37. Savai Madho Singh-2	सवाई मधोसिंह–2	1881–1922
38. Savai Man Singh-2	सवाई मानसिंह–2	1922–1948

Kachhawaha Dynasty continued

After the treaty of Purandar, Jai Singh persuaded Shivaji to go to Agra court, with good intensions. But there, the Mughals imprisoned Shivaji. However, with the help of Jai Singh's son King Ramsingh Kachhwaha (1666-1688), Shivaji escaped from the prison and returned to Rayagad.

Knowing that Shivaji is imprisoned in Agra by the Mughal Sultan and Sultan is about to kill the Maratha king, Rajput Mirza Jai Singh regretted his inferior position of slavery with the Mughals.

Mirza Raja Jai Singh became the ultimate victim of sorrow. As a result, he had a heart disorder and after getting sick, that great leader died with sorrow.

Kacchavaha Dynasty

Descendents of Rana Sanga, the Solar Dynasty braves,
Belonged to Rama's lineage, famous for battle waves. 1

When the Mughals spread, destruction everywhere,
The Rajputs became slaves, keeping their pride spare. 2

Jaisingh convinced Shivaji, promising as much he can,
Shivaji went to Agra, to meet the Mughal Sultan. 3

The Mughal insulted Shivaji, and put him in the jail,
Installed mighty guards, to kill him without fail. 4

Promises made by Jai Singh, turned out to be false,
Jai Singh became sorry, and very sick then he falls. 5

He repented his mistake, he was in disbelief,
He realized he is a slave, with a serious grief. 6

Mughals call me Mirza, only for name sake,
They treat me like king, but the show is fake. 7

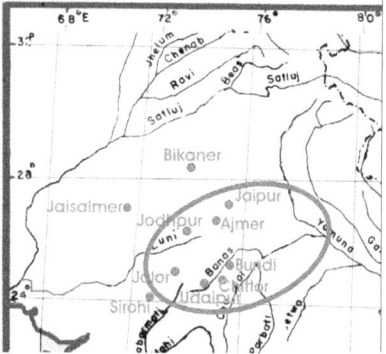

62. Kadamb Dynasty, Karnatak (340-610)

For the Previous Dynasty, please see : Pallava Dynasty (315–897)

1. Mayur Sharma — मयूरशर्मा — 340–360
2. Kang Varma — कंगवर्मा — 360–385
3. Bhag Varma — भागवर्मा — 385–410
4. Raghu Nath Varma — रघुनाथवर्मा — 410–425
5. Kakustha Varma — काकुस्थवर्मा — 425–450
6. Shanit Varma — शांतिवर्मा — 450–475
7. Mrigendra Varma — मृगेंद्रवर्मा — 475–490
8. Mandhatri Varma — मंधातृवर्मा — 490–497
9. Ravi Varma — रविवर्मा — 497–537
10. Hari Varma — हरिवर्मा — 537–547
11. Krishna Varma — कृष्णवर्मा — 547–565
12. Aja Varma — अजवर्मा — 565–566
13. Bhogi Varma — भोगीवर्मा — 566–610

For the Next Dynasty, please see :
Chalukya Dynasty, Badami (525–753)

Kadamb Dynasty

Kadambas were Brahmins, but were warriors best,
They defeated Pallavas, and captured South-West. 1
They were Vaidic Scholars, they took Sharma title,
They were excellent fighters, a quality that is vital. 2
Three centuries they ruled, with a great honour,
Protected their kingdom, in the best manner. 3

Kadamb of Gova, Hangal	
Guhalla	980–1007
Shatdev-1	1007–1052
Jaykeshi-1	1052–1080
Vijaydityа-1	1080–1110
Jaykeshi-2	1110–1147
Shivachitta	1147–1174
Vijaydityа-2	1174–1187
Jaykeshi-3	1187–1220
Tribhuvan	1220–1146
Shatdev-2	1246–1250

Kadamba Dynasty

The power of the Pallavas of Kanchi (315–897) was weakened after the South expedition of Emperor Chandragupta-1 (319–350) of the Gupta Dynasty (240–730). Then, on the southwestern part of the Dakshinapath, Kadamb Mayur Sharma (340–360) declared independence from the Pallavas and established the Kadamb Dynasty (340–610) at Vyjayanti (Vanvasi). Mayurasharma strengthened the Vedic culture and tradition by performing eighteen Ashwamedha Yagyas. His descendants gained power over the Chalukya and Rashtrakuta kingdoms. The Kadamba people then spread to Goa and Hangal.

The Brahmana Kadamb kings were devotees of Lord Shiva and Vishnu, however, they considered themselves to be Kshatriyas with the desire of political power. For the same purpose, they also bore the title of Varma. Like the ancient Satavahana rulers (271 BC-195 AD), the administrative system of Kadamb rulers was also based on religion and the scripture

63. Kanva Dynasty, Patliputra (72-27 BC)

For the Previous Dynasty, please see :
Shunga Dynasty **(185 BC - 72 BC)**

1. Vasudev   वसुदेव   72-63 **BC**
2. Bhumi Mitra   भूमिमित्र   63-51 **BC**
3. Narayan   नारायण   51-37 **BC**
4. Susharma   सुशर्मा   37-27 **BC**

For the Next Dynasty, please see :
Satvahan Dynasty **(271 BC - 195 AD)**

Kanva Dynasty

Kanva Dynasty grew, wiping Shunga glamour,
Hundred years ruled, Kanva kings four.

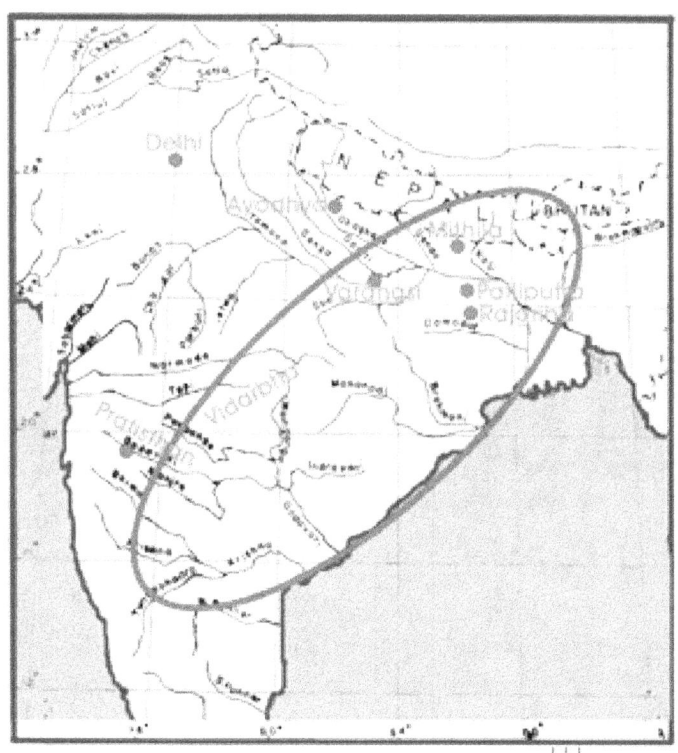

Hindu Rajtarangini

Kanva Dynasty

Devabhuti (82-72 BC), the unworthy ruler of the Pushyamitra Dynasty of Magadha, was killed by his minister Vasudeva (72-63 BC) and he became the king himself. He founded the new Kanva Dynasty in Patliputra (72-27 BC).

The drive which was initiated by the Pushyamitra Dynasty to revive Vedic culture from Buddhist influence, was carried forward by Kanva kings, the descendants of sage Kanva.

The last ruler of Kanva Dynasty was also extremely useless and inept. Therefore, this bright Dynasty also ended in a rule of meager 55 years, one of the short lived dynasties.

The Magadha Empire rapidly eroded and narrowed, and at the end, King Pulumavi-1 (43-07 BC) of the mighty Satavahana Dynasty (271 BC-195 AD) of Maharashtra. Susarma (37-27 B.C.) of the Kanva Dynasty, the last king.

64. Kakatiya Dynasty, Warangal (1000-1323)

For Previous Dynasty, please see :

Rashtrakuta Dynasty (600–973)

Chalukya Dynasty, Kalyani (696–1189)

1. Yarraya Vetaraj — यर्रया वेतराज — 1000-1030
2. Prodaraj-1 — प्रोदराज-1 — 1030-1075
3. Vetraj Tribhuvanmalla — वेतराज त्रिभुवन — 1075-1110
4. Prodraj-2 — प्रोदराज-2 — 1110-1163
5. Prataprudra Deva-1 — प्रतापरुद्रदेव-1 — 1163-1196
6. Mahadeva-1 — महादेव-1 — 1196-1199
7. Ganapati — गणपति — 1199-1262
8. Queen Rudramma Devi — रानी रुद्रम्मा देवी — 1262-1295
9. Prataprurda Deva-2 — प्रतापरुद्रदेव-2 — 1295-1323

Kakatiya Dynasty

Prolaraja was Chalukya, who left the clan,
Became king of Warangal, as a Kakatiya man. 1

A Kakatiya princess, married Chalukya prince,
Brought two houses together, to strengthen the province. 2

Kakatiyas of Andhra, worshipped Vishnu and Shiva,
They were called Lingayats, they were like molten lava. 3

Kakatiya Dynasty

When Chalukyas of Kalyani began to crumble and split after year 1190, the first lord of that crumbling kingdom was the (1) Kakatiya king (1000-1323) of Warangal (Orugallu), the second was (2) the Yadavas of the Dvarasamudra (Halebid) (1026-1348) and the third was Yadavas of Devgiri (850-1131).

The Kakatiya Telugu empire was active in the regions of Andhra Pradesh and Vidarbha. The Kakatiya king Pratapa Rudradeva-1 (1163–1196) was the famous ruler who extended his kingdom beyond the North bank of river of Godavari. King Ganapati (1199–1262) was the best Kakatiya ruler. He bore the title of Rajagajakesari. He made his daughter Rudramma Devi (1262–1295) queen. Rudramma had no son. He gave his other daughter Mammadamba to Chalukya prince Mahadev of Anhilwad Gujarat in marriage and strengthened the Chalukya-Kakatiya unity. Queen Mammadamba's son Annadev was the ancestor of Praveerchandra Bhanjadeva (1929–1966), the famous Maharaja of Bastar.

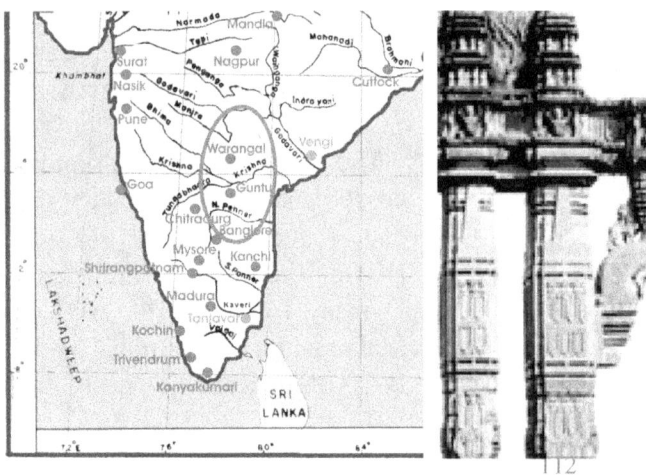

Hindu Rajtarangini

65-66-67 Kalchuri Dynasty (550-1745)

For Previous Dynasty, please see :
Vakatak Dynasty of Nandivardhan (250–510)

65. Kalchuris of Mahismati (550–620) :

#	Name	Devanagari	Years
1.	Krishna Raj	कृष्णराज	550–575
2.	Shankargan	शंकरगण	575–600
3.	Buddha Raj	बुद्धराज	600–620

66. Kalchuris of Tripuri (675–1210) :

#	Name	Devanagari	Years
1.	Vamdev Rai	वामदेवराय	675–700
2.	Shankargan Deva-1	शंकरगणदेव-1	750–775
3.	Lakshman Rai-1	लक्ष्मणराय-1	825–850
4.	Kokkal Deva-1	कोक्कलदेव-1	850–890
5.	Shankargan Deva-2	शंकरगणदेव-2	890–910
6.	Balaharsha Deva	बालहर्षदेव	910–925
7.	Yuvaraj Deva-1	युवराजदेव-1	925–950
8.	Lakshman Rai-2	लक्ष्मणराय-2	950–970
9.	Shankargan Deva-3	शंकरगणदेव-3	970–974
10.	Yuvaraj Deva-2	युवराजदेव-2	974–1000
11.	Kokkal Deva-2	कोक्कलदेव-2	1000–1037
12.	Gangeyadeva	गंगयदेव विक्रमादित्य	1037–1042
13.	Karna Deva	कर्णदेव	1042–1120
14.	Yashakarna Deva	यशकर्णदेव	1120–1151
15.	Gayakarna Deva	गयकर्णदेव	1151–1155
16.	Narsimha Deva	नरसिंहदेव	1155–1175
17.	Jayasimha Deva	जयसिंहदेव	1175–1180
18.	Vijayasimah Deva	विजयसिंहदेव	1180–1210
19.	Trailokyamal Deva	त्रैलोक्यमलदेव	1210–1212

Kalchuri Dynasty

The Kalchuri Dynasty : Four families of Kalchuri Dynasty were ruling from year 550 to 1745. The first branch was (1) the Kalchuris (550-620) at Mahishmati, the second branch was (2) Kalchuris (675-1210) at Tripuri, the third branch was (3) Kalchuris (1000-1745) at Ratnapur and the fourth branch was (4) Kalchuris (1156-1184) at Kalyani.

1. The Kalchuris of Mahishmati (550-620) :

King Krishnaraja (550-575), the ruler of the branch that ruled from Mahishmati (Maheshwar) in the valley of the Narmada River ruled after the Vakataka (250–500) Dynasty. He took power and extended his authority as far as Konkan, Western Maharashtra, Gujarat and Malwa. During the advancement of the Badami Chalukya (525-753) Dynasty, the Mahishmati Kalchuri Dynasty started coming to end.

67. Kalchuris of Ratnapuri (1000–1745) :

1.	Kalinga Raj	कलिंगराज	1000–1020
2.	Kamal Raj	कमलराज	1020–1045
3.	Ratna Deva-1	रत्नदेव-1	1045–1065
4.	Prithvi Deva-1	पृथ्वीदेव-1	1065–1114
5.	Jajjala Deva-1	जाजल्लदेव-1	1114–1141
6.	Ratna Deva-2	रत्नदेव-2	1141–1145
7.	Prithvi Deva-2	पृथ्वीदेव-2	1145–1167
8.	Jajjala Deva-2	जाजल्लदेव-2	1167–1181
9.	Ratna Deva-3	रत्नदेव-3	1181–1190
10.	Prithvi Deva-3	पृथ्वीदेव-3	1190–1220
11.	Pratapmalla	प्रतापमल्ल	1220–1222
12.	Baharendra Say	बाहरेंद्र साय	1480–1535
13.	Kalyana Say	कल्याणसाय	–
14.	Takhta Simha	तख्तसिंह	–
15.	Raj Simha	राजसिंह	–
16.	Sardar Simha	सरदारसिंह	1712–1732
17.	Raghu Nath Simha	रघुनाथसिंह	1732–1741
18.	Mohan Simha	मोहनसिंह	1741–1745

68. Kalchuris of Kalyani (1156–1184) :

1.	Bijjal	बिज्जल	1156–1167
2.	Someshvar	सोमेश्वर	1167–1177
3.	Shankam	शंकम	1177–1180
4.	Ahavamalla	आहवमल्ल	1180–1183
5.	Singhan	सिंघण	1183–1184

Kalchuri Dynasty

2. The Kalchuris of Tripuri (675-1210) :

The Kalchuri Dynasty of Tripuri is also called the Haihaya Dynasty. In the seventh century, the Chalukyas of Badami (525-753) prevailed in the kingdom of Maharashtra, Vidarbha, Gujarat and the Kalchuri Dynasty won the fort of Kalanjar near Jabalpur in Tripuri.

Their capital was settled at Kalanjar. For this noble work of the founder of the Tripuri branch Vamdevaraya (675-700), his descendants salute Vamdevaraya by calling themselves Vamadeva-padanudhyat. Laxmanaraya (825–850), the younger brother of Vamdevaraya, expanded the kingdom by winning the territories up to the river Sarayu.

3. The Kalchuris of Ratnapuri (1000-1745) :

In the early eleventh century, Kalingaraja (1000-1020), son of King Kokkaldev-2 (1000-1037) of Kalchuris of Tripuri, conquered Chhattisgarh and started a new branch of Kalchuris at Ratnapur (1000-1745). This branch was in power of the Kalchuri family of Ratnapur until Bhosale King Raghuji-1 of Nagpur (1731-1755) won Chhattisgarh.

Kalchuri Dynasty
Mahismati, Tripuri
Ratnapuri, Kalyani

Dynasty of Kalchuris, had branches many,
It was a big family, like no monarch any. 1

Lasted twelve centuries, their reign was long,
They served people well, people loved them all along.

One branch at Mahismati, other was at Tripuri,
Third branch at Kalyani, fourth one at Ratnapuri. 3

Kalchuris were famous for, Architecture and art,
Devoted to Shiva and Vishnu, religious on their part.

Kalchuri kings were adored, like a precious jewel,
Women were respected, in their kingdom well. 5

Kalchuri Dynasty

4. The Kalchuris of Kalyani (1156-1184) :

Bijjal (1156-1167), the founder of Kalchuri family of Kalyani, was a descendant of Krishnaraja (550-575), Kalchuri of Mahishmati. Bijjal was originally a feudatory of the Kalyani Chalukya Tailap-3 (1150–1183), who seized power from his master and gained authority over Kalyani. However, after Bijjal (1156–1167), King Singhan (1183–1184) had to return the power to Chalukyas of Kalyani.

Hindu Rajtarangini

69. Karkota Dynasty, Kashmir (631-855)

For the Previous Dynasty, please see :
Gonaditya Dynasty, Kashmir (1182 BD-631 AD)

1. Durlabh Vardhan — दुर्लभवर्धन — 631–680
2. Pratapaditya — प्रतापादित्य — 680–712
3. Vajraditya Chandrapid — वज्रादित्य चंद्रपीड़ — 712–720
4. Udayaditya Tarapid — उदयादित्य तारपीड़ — 720–725
5. Lalitaditya Muktipid — ललितादित्य मुक्तिपीड़ — 725–767
6. Kuvalayapid — कुवलयापीड़ — 767–768
7. Varjaditya Bappiyak — वज्रादित्य बप्पीयक — 768–775
8. Prithvipid — पृथ्वीपीड़ — 775–780
9. Sangramapid-1 — संग्रामपीड़-1 — 780–780
10. Jayapid, Jajja — जयपीड़, जज्जा — 780–810
11. Lalitpid — ललितपीड़ — 810–820
12. Sangrampid-2 — संग्रामपीड़-2 — 820–825
13. Brihaspati — बृहस्पति — 825–840
14. Ajitpid — अजीतपीड़ — 840–850
15. Anangpid — अनंगपीड़ — 850–851
16. Utpalpid — उत्पलपीड़ — 851–855

For the Next Dynasty, please see :
Utpal Dynasty, Kashmir (855-949)

Karkota Dynasty

Baladitya, the last king of the Gonaditya Dynasty of Kashmir (1182 BC-631 AD), died childless. After him, his son-in-law Durlabhvardhan Karkota came to power in Shrinagar in 631 AD.

King Durlabhvardhan was a contemporary of Maharaja Harshavardhan (606–647), the great Pushyabhuti king of Kannauj. Lalitaditya Muktiped (725-767) was the most powerful king of this Karkota Dynasty.

Anantivarma (851-855) seized power from Utpalpeed (851-855), the last king of Karkota Dynasty of Kashmir. King Avantivarma established his separate Utpal Dynasty of Kashmir (855-949).

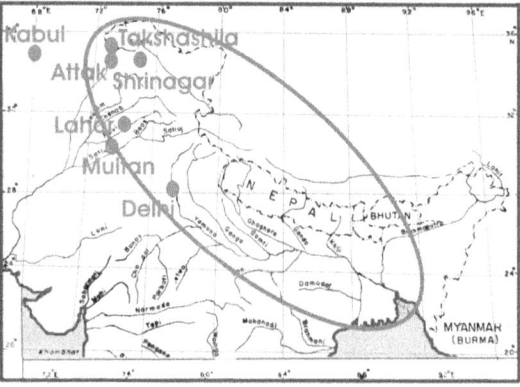

Ref. : facebook_1613914202632_6769246795756245173

Hindu Rajtarangini

70. Kaurava Dynasty (Ancient Time)

For the Previous Dynasty, please see :
Kuru Dynasty (Ancient Time)

1. Vichitravirya   विचित्रवीर्य ...
2. Dhritarashtra   धृतराष्ट्र
3. Duryodhan   दुर्योधन

Kaurava Royal House

Maharaja Shantanu had two wives, Ganga and Satyavati. The son of Ganga was Bhishma, so he was called Gangeya. Satyavati had three sons: Vyas, Chitrangad and Vichitravirya. Dhritarashtra was the son of Vichitravirya and his wife Ambika. Dhritarashtra was blind from birth.

Queen Gandhari, the wife of King Dhritarashtra, was the daughter of Subal, the king of Gandhar. Dhritarashtra had a daughter named Dushshila who was the wife of King Jayadratha of the Sindhu country. Gandhari was sister of Shakuni, the king of Gandhara kingdom.

The names of Dhritarashtra's one hundred Kaurava sons were :
1. Duryodhan, 2. Dushashan, 3. Duhasah, 4. Dushal, 5. Jalsangha, 6. Sama, 7. Sah, 8. Vind, 9. Anuvind, 10. Durdarsha, 11. Subahu, 12. Dushpradhrshana, 13. Dharmarshana, 14. Durmukh, 15. Dushkarna, 16. Vikarna, 17. Shal, 18. Satvana, 19. Sulochan, 20. Chitra, 21. Upachitra, 22. Chitraksha, 23. Charuchitra, 24. Sharasana, 25. Dermad, 26. Durvigaha, 27. Vivitsu, 28. Viktananda, 29. Urnanabh, 30. Sunabha, 31. Nand, 32. Upananda, 33. Chitrabana, 34. Chitravarma, 35. Suvarma, 36. Durvimochan, 37. Ajobahu, 38. Mahabahu, 39. Chitrang, 40. Chitrakundal, 41. Bhimaveg, 42. Bhimabala, 43. Balaki, 44. Balwardhana, 45. Ugrayudha, 46. Sushena, 47. Kundadhara, 48. Mahodara, 49. Chitrayudha, 50. Nishangi, 51. Pashi, 52. Vrindaraka, 53. Dridhavarma, 54. Dridhakshatra, 55. Somakirti, 56. Anudar, 57. Dridhasandha, 58. Jarasandha, 59. Satyasandha, 60. Sadsuvaka, 61. Ugrashrava, 62. Ugrasena, 63. Senani, 64. Dushparajaya, 65. Aparajitha, 66. Kundashayi, 67. Vishalaksha, 68. Duradhara, 69. Dridhahasta, 70. Suhast, 71. Vatavega, 72. Suvarcha, 73. Adityaketu, 74. Bahwashi, 75. Nagadatta, 76. Ugrashayi, 77. Kavachi, 78. Krathana, 79. Kundi, 80. Bhimavikra, 81. Dhanurdhara, 82. Veerabahu, 83. Alolupa, 84. Abhaya, 85. Dridhakarma, 86. Dridharathashraya, 87. Anadrishya, 88. Kundabhedi, 89. Viravi, 90. Chitrakundala, 91. Pradhama, 92. Amapramathi, 93. dirgharome, 94. Suviaryavana, 95. Dirghabahu, 96. Sujata, 97. Kanakadhvaja, 98. Kundashi, 99. Veeraja, 100. Yuyutsu.

Evil King Duryodhana (Ancient Time)

In the Shrimad Bhagavad Gita (1.23) Duryodhan is called Durbudhi. He was the son of the blind Kaurava king Dhritarashtra and Maharani Gandhari. He was the eldest of the hundred Kaurava brothers but he was younger than Pandava prince Dharmaraja Yudhishthir. Despite of not being the eldest son, he was trying to become a prince of Hastinapur by deceit and violence. Kuntiputra Karna had full support for him in this misdeed, due to which Duryodhan was steadfast in his final victory and as a result Mahabharatiya Mahabharat war could not be averted. Duryodhan was supreme ignorant. The world thought of him as a fool.

गीत

अज्ञानी दुर्योधन

मैं ही एक सयाना, बाकी,
दुनिया उल्लू की पट्ठी ।

मैं बलशाली, सबसे जाली ।
मैं हूँ ज्ञानी, बड़ा तूफानी ।
दुनिया वालों की सत्ती पर,
होगी मेरी अड़ी ।। 1
मुझमें बुद्धि, मुझमें सिद्धि ।
होगी मेरी, निश-दिन वृद्धि ।
चोर फरेबों की है टोली,
करली मैंने कट्ठी ।। 2
मैं हूँ नास्तिक, मन का मालिक ।
मुझको कुछ भी नहीं अनैतिक ।
कोई मेरा भेद न जाने,
बंधी मेरी मुट्ठी ।। 3
(हे प्रभो!)
दुष्ट बुद्धि ये क्यों हैं आते ।
भद्र जनों को जो तरसाते ।
या प्रभु! इसको दो सद्बुद्धि,
या हो इनकी छुट्टी ।। 4

Ignorant Duryodhan

Sthayi
I am the one who is wise,
The rest of the world is foolish.

Antara
I am powerful. I am a cheat.
I am wise. I am stormy,
I will always have
One better over theirs. 1

I am smart. I am successful.
I progress day and night.
Thieves, bobbers, guileful,
And rogues are in my gang.
No one knows my secret. 2

I am atheist, stubborn, immoral.
No one knows my secret. 3

Ratnakar says,
O Lord! where these evils
come from
To oppress virtuous people?
O Lord! Either give them good sense,
Or remove them from the earth. 4

71. Kshatrap Dynasty, Girnar, Ujjain, Nasik (78-395)

For the Previous Dynasty, please see :
Satvahan Dynasty (271 BC-195 AD)

1. Nahapana — नहपान — 78-126
2. Jayadaman — जयदामन — 126-145
3. Rudradaman-1 — रुद्रदामन-1 — 145-150
4. Damadaksha-1 — दामक्षद-1 — 150-178
5. Satyadaman — सत्यदामन — 178-188
6. Rudrasimha-1 — रुद्रसिंह-1 — 188-199
7. Rudrasen-1 — रुद्रसेन-1 — 199-222
8. Sanghadaman — संघदामन — 222-223
9. Damasen-1 — दामसेन-1 — 223-236
10. Ishvardatta — ईश्वरदत्त — 236-239
11. Yashodaman — यशोदामन — 239-240
12. Vijaysen — विजयसेन — 240-250
13. Damasen-2 — दामसेन-2 — 250-265
14. Rudrasen-2 — रुद्रसेन-2 — 256-279
15. Vishvasen — विश्वसिंह — 279-282
16. Bhartridaman — भर्तृदामन — 282-332
17. Rudradaman-2 — रुद्रदामन-2 — 332-348
18. Rudrasen-3 — रुद्रसेन-3 — 348-378
19. - — – — 378-382
20. Simhasen — सिंहसेन — 382-388
21. Rudrasimha-2 — रुद्रसिंह-2 — 388-395

Kshatrapa Royal House

The ancient people who settled on the Shakal island belonging to the Vaidic period of the Aryans were called Kshatrapas, Shakas or Shakas. King Kujulak, who was of the Kshaharapa Dynasty, was the ruler of the Mathura-Nasik region and Ujjain. The record of this rule is present in Taxila.

The Kshaharapa Dynasty was established by the Kshatrapa king Rudradaman-1 (145–150). King Rudrasingh-2 (388-395), the last Kshatrapa king of Ujjain, was conquered by Gupta Emperor Chandragupta-2-Vikramaditya-1 (375-415) of Ujjain and ended his 400-year rule of the Kshatrapas and annexed it to his kingdom.

Kshatrapa Dynasty

Flourished in the Aryan, ancient Vaidic visions,
Kshatrapas were rulers, in three regions. 1
Kshatrapa kings ruled, at Nasik in the West,
Ujjain in the North, and Mathura in the East. 2
Vaidic their culture, they were Aryan Kings,
They followed scriptures, to do their things. 3

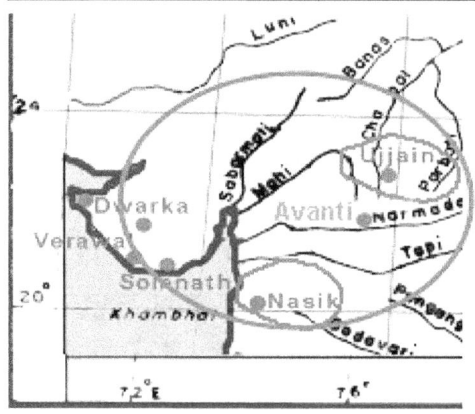

72. Kukkur Dynasty (Ancient Time)

For the Previous Dynasty, please see :
Vrishni Dynasty (Ancient Time)

1. Chitrarath — चित्ररथ ...
2. Kukkura — कुक्कुर
3. Vanhi — वन्हि
4. Vilom — विलोम
5. Kapotrom — कपोतरोम
6. Tumbru — तुंबरु
7. Dundhubhi — दुंदुभी
8. Daridra — दरिद्र
9. Vasu — वसु
10. Nahuk — नाहुक
11. Ahuk — आहुक
12. Ugrasen, Mathura King — उग्रसेन
13. Kamsa, Mathura King — कंस, मथुराधिपति
14. Ugrasen (2nd time) — उग्रसेन

For the Next Dynasty, please see :
Vrishni Dynasty (Ancient Time)

Kukkur Dynasty

Shri Krishna was born, in the House of Yadu,
Pandavas were born, in the family of Kuru. 1

Shursen was the king, of the Mathura kingdom,
This great monarch, well known for wisdom. 2

Kamsa was the wicked, son of Ugrasen,
He was evil king, who killed many men. 3

Kamsa was incarnation, of Kalanemi demon,
Of a righteous father, he was a wicked son. 4

Kukkur Dynasty

King Vidura and King Kukkura, the two sons of King Chitraratha (see: Vrishni Dynasty, No. 10 Chitraratha) of the Vrishni clan of the Yadava Dynasty, were the founders of two different Royal Houses. Yadava clan of Lord Krishna was originated form King Vidurtha. The Yadava Dynasty of the evil Kamsa originated from King Kukkura. In the Yadava family of Kamsa was the virtuous Maharaja Ugrasen, whose brother Devak's daughter Devaki was the sister of Kamsa.

Just as Ravan had a villain's role in Shri Ramayana, Kamsa had a villain's role in Shri Krishnanayan (see: Ratnakar's Shri Krishnanayan (ISBN 987 4897 416 82 2). A part of Ravan was known as a learned Pundit, but Kamsa had no connection with knowledge and ethics.

Kamsa, the king of Mathura, was the incarnation of demon Kalanemi of ancient times (Devi Bhagwat, Skanda 4). On the banks of the river Yamuna, there was a forest called Madhuban, where a demon named Madhu ruled. His capital was named Mathura. After slaughter of Demon Madhu, Mathura came into the hands of King Shursen. When Kamsa was the king of Mathura at the time of Devaki's marriage, a celestial voice said, O Kamsa! You will die at the hands of Devaki's eighth son.

73. Kuru Dynasty (Ancient Time)

For the Previous Dynasty, please see :
Ajmid Dynasty (Ancient Time)

1. Ajmidh — अजमीढ़
2. Kuru — कुरु
3. Janhu — जन्हू
4. Surath — सुरथ
5. Vidurth — विदूरथ
6. Sarvabhaum — सार्वभौम
7. Jayatsen — जयत्सेन
8. Ranya — रण्य
9. Bhavuk — भावुक
10. Shakriddhava — शक्रोद्धत
11. Devatithi — देवातिथि
12. Riksha — ऋक्ष
13. Bhimsen — भीमसेन
14. Pratip — प्रतीप
15. Shantanu — शान्तनु
16. Vichitravirya — विचित्रवीर्य
17. Pandu & Dhritarashtra — पांडु और धृतराष्ट्र

For the Next Dynasty, please see :
Kaurav Dynasty and Pandav Dynasty
(Ancient Time)

Kuru Dynasty

The Kauravas and Pandavas were born in the Dynasty of the great majestic king Kuru. When King Bhagiratha brought Ganga Devi from heaven to earth. Then Janhu, the son of Maharaja Kuru and his wife Maharani Keshini, drank Ganga and released her from his ear. Therefore, Ganga received the names Bhagirathi and Janhavi.

King Shantanu (Maha. Adi. 94.61) was the great son of King Pratip and his wife Sunanda. King Shantanu gave Kripacharya a place in his kingdom (Maha. Adi. 95.46). Like King Harishchandra, King Shantanu was also considered an image of truth (Maha. Adi. 96.1). Being the son of King Pratip, King Shantanu is called King Pratip in Mahabharata. King Vichitravirya, son of King Shantanu and Queen Satyavati, was considered as originator of Kuru Dynasty. But his son Dhritarashtra was blind from the birth, therefore Pandu, the son of Ambalika, got the kingship.

Kurukshetra was considered holy by virtue of the King Kuru's severe penance (Maha. Adi. 94.80). Kurukshetra was also considered as a Dharmakshetra because sacred water of river Sarasvati was used for the purpose of the Yajnas performed at Kurukshetra (Maha Surg. 39.26-27).

74. Kushan Dynasty, Purushapur-Mathura (30-244)

1. Kujula Kadphises — कुजूला कडफिसेस — 30–80
2. Vema Kadphises — वेमा कडफिसेस — 80–103
3. Kanishka-1 — कनिष्क–1 — 103–126
4. Vashishka — वशिष्क — 126–130
5. Huvishka-1 — हुविष्क–1 — 130–143
6. Kanishka-2 — कनिष्क–2 — 143–150
7. Huvishka-2 — हुविष्क–2 — 150–166
8. Vasudeva-1 — वसुदेव–1 — 166–200
9. Kanishka-3 — कनिष्क–3 — 200–222
10. Vasudeva-2 — वसुदेव–2 — 222–244

Kushan Dynasty

Kushan king Kanishka, in Arya Dharma he enters,
Purushapur and Mathura,
became his capital centers. 1

Nagarjuna and Ashvaghosha, had a place of honour,
In the kingdom of Kanishka, in the every corner. 2

Kanishka won Kashmir, and built a city there,
Kanishkapur its name, Huvishkapur was its pair. 3

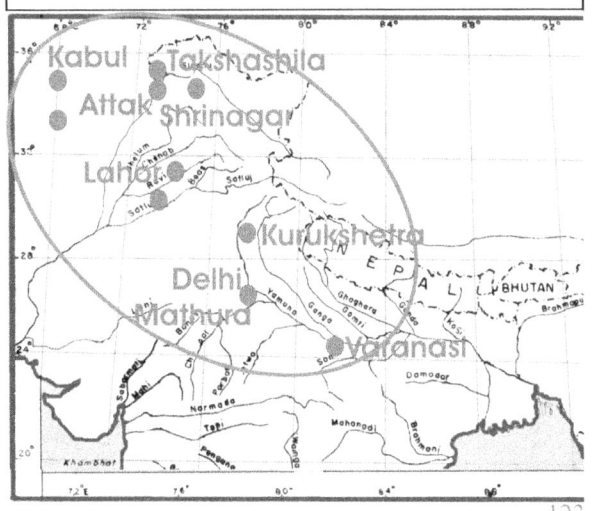

Kushan Dynasty

The name of Emperor Kanishka-1 (103-126) of the Kushan Dynasty is at a high level among the great kings of ancient India. The descendants of Kanishka ruled the kingdom with Aryan culture.

The main capital of Emperor Kanishka was in Purushapur (Peshawar) and the second eastern capital was Mathura. Kanishka had conquered Kashmir. Sculpture and arts has shelter and growth in the kingdom of King Kanishka.

After the death of King Kanishka, King Vasishaka (126–130) was ruling in the adjacent areas of Mathura. The authority of King Vasishka was asserted over Saket (Ayodhya), Prayag and Magadha regions. Religion, art, literature. of Indian culture progressed in the vast Kushan Empire.

Philosophical and scientific great scholars such as Ashwaghosh (80–150) and Nagarjuna (150–250) were honoured during the Kushan period.

King Huvishka (130-143) established a city called Huvishkapur in Kashmir, which is mentioned in Kalhan's Rajatarangini. Figures of Shiva, Skanda, Vishnu etc. are found on Kushan coins.

75. Lohar Dynasty, Kashmir (1003-1172)

For the Earlier Dynasty, please see :
Pravargupta Dynasty of Kashmir (949–1003)

1.	Sangramaraja	संग्रामराजा	1003–1028
2.	Hariraja	हरिराजा	1028–1028
3.	Anantraja	अनंतराजा	1028–1063
4.	Kalasharaja	कलशराजा	1063–1089
5.	Utkarsharaja	उत्कर्षराजा	1089–1089
6.	Harsharaja	हर्षराजा	1089–1101
7.	Ucchharaja	उच्छराजा	1011–1111
8.	Radhashankar	राधाशांकर	1111–1112
9.	Salhan	सलहण	1112–1112
10.	Sussaharaja	सुश्शलराजा	1112–1123
11.	Jayasimha	जयसिंह	1128–1155
12.	Parmanuk	परमाणुक	1155–1165
13.	Vantideva	वंतीदेव	1165–1172
14.	Vuppadeva	वुप्पदेव	1172–

For the Next Dynasty, please see :
Vuppadeva Dynasty of Kashmir (1172–1286)

Lohar Dynasty

Kalhan wrote history, of the Kashmir long,
From ancient time, to twelfth century along. 1
Kalhan's precious work, begins with king Gonand,
Written in Sanskrit Shlokas, like a flower garland. 2
History of the Pandavas, in his chronicle,
Names of the rulers, as much possible. 3
Rule of Pratapaditya, written clearly well,
The first dynasty local, he was the first to tell. 4
Then the Karkota Dynasty, for centuries six,
Sixteen kings of this line, of the attitudes mixed. 5
Then ruled the Utpals, rulers seventeen,
Then the Pravarguptas, and then Didda queen. 6
Didda gave her kingdom, to her nephew Sangram,
Lohar dynasty started, in a total jam. 7
Kalhan Royal Poet, was great history writer,
He was Sanskrit pundit, no one became greater. 8

Lohar Dynasty

Didda, the last queen of the Pravargupta Dynasty of Shrinagar, retired herself and gave power to her nephew Sangram Raja in 1003. From there the Lohar Dynasty of Shrinagar Kashmir started. Udayaraja, the father of Sangramraja (1003-1028) was the brother of Queen Didda.

The Lohar Chiefs were from Khasa tribe. Their original place of rule was a hill-fort called Loharakotta.

Queen Didda was a daughter of Lohar king Simharaja. She married the king Ksemgupta and she united the two Kashmir Houses. Queen Didda adopted nephew Vigraharaja who was then installed on the throne of Kashmir.

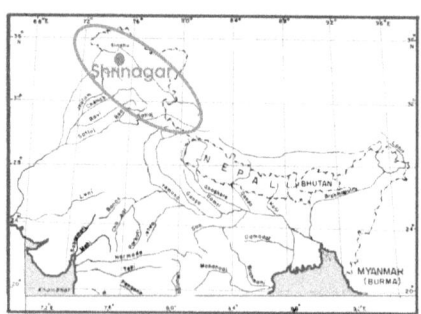

76. Madra Dynasty (Ancient Time)

1. Shalya शल्य ...

Madra Dynasty

On the bank of Jhelum,
stood Madra at that date,
Madri was sister of Shalya,
the king of that state. 1
Madri was wife of Pandu,
she was a dedicated lady,
On Pandu's death,
for self-immolation she was ready. 2
At the Great War, Shalya
fought on Kaurava side,
Though Madri was Pandu's wife,
jealousy he couldn't hide. 3
Shalya was Karna's charioteer,
and Kaurava Commander,
He fought with Yudhishthir,
and got killed asunder. 4

Madra Dynasty

Madra kingdom was one of the sixteen ancient Mahajanapadas in Madra kingdom. Madra Mahajanapada was situated on the banks of the river Vistasta (Jhelum).

Madra King was the brother of Maharani Madri, King Pandu's second wife (Maha. Adi. 112). However, impressed with the deceits of Duryodhan, Madra King Shalya fought in Mahabharatiya war on behalf of Kauravas.

He became the charioteer of Karna in the great war and after the death of Kaurava Commander Karna, he became the commander-in-Chief of the Kauravas (Maha. Karna 32). Shalya was killed by Dharmaraja Yudhishthir the same day as he became the Kaurava Commander (Maha Surg. 17.52).

Nakula and Sahadeva were the twin sons of Queen Madri. On the death of the retired King Pandu in exile, Maharani Madri became immolated herself on the funeral pyre with her husband (Maha. Adi. 115-126).

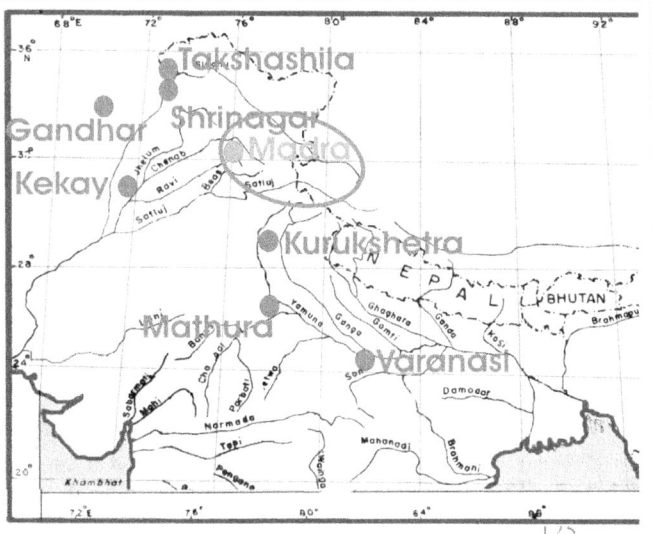

77. Maitrak Dynasty, Saurashtra (480-767)

For the Earlier Dynasty, please see:
Pallava Dynasty (315–897)

1. Bhattarak — भट्टारक — 480–492
2. Dharmasen-1 — धर्मसेन–1 — 492–500
3. Drona Simha — द्रोणसिंह — 500–526
4. Dhruvasen-1 — ध्रुवसेन–1 — 526–540
5. Dharapatta — धारपट्ट — 540–559
6. Guhasen — गुहसेन — 559–571
7. Dharmasen-2 — धर्मसेन–2 — 571–605
8. Shiladitya-1 — शीलादित्य–1 — 605–609
9. Khdagagraha-1 — खड्गग्रह–1 — 609–623
10. Dharmasen-3 — धर्मसेन–3 — 623–629
11. Dhruvasen-2 — ध्रुवसेन–2 — 629–645
12. Dharmasen-4 — धर्मसेन–4 — 645–653
13. Dhruvasen-3 — ध्रुवसेन–3 — 653–656
14. Khadgagraha-2 — खड्गग्रह–2 — 656–669
15. Shiladitya-2 — शीलादित्य–2 — 669–691
16. Shiladitya-3 — शीलादित्य–3 — 691–722
17. Shiladitya-4 — शीलादित्य–4 — 722–760
18. Shiladitya-5 — शीलादित्य–5 — 760–766
19. Shiladitya-6 — शीलादित्य–6 — 766–767

Maitraka Dynasty, Vallabhi

The Gurjar governor of Saurashtra province of Ujjain's Gupta Empire (240-730), Bhattarak (470-492), declared independence in 480 and established his Maitraka Dynasty (480-767).

The immortal hospitality of this great army General was that on an old site he **built the divine Shiva temple of Somnath**, the most holy historical temple in Saurashtra, on the land of Veraval port. In addition, the Maitraka kings built more than hundred beautiful temple craft art after the establishment of Somnath Temple in Saurashtra. Encouraged by the same spirit, Maitrakas did the pious work of propagating Vedic culture by building Vallabhi University like the Nalanda University.

सोमनाथ जी

सोमनाथ का पावन धाम, ज्योतिर्लिंग श्री शिव भगवान ।
एकलिंग जी! शुभ दो वरदान, शंकर भोले किरपावान ।।
तुमरा मंदिर स्वर्ग समाना, तुमरी मूरत स्वर्ण ललामा ।
पूजन कीर्तन तुमरे, भोले! भगतन को देता सुखदान ।। 1
शिव का मंदिर सर्वसनातन, ऋषि मुनियों ने कीन्हा स्थापन ।
नंदीश्वर! तुम भाते मोहे, सबसे मंगल तुमरा नाम ।। 2
त्रिशूलधारी तुम त्रिपुरारी! डमरूधर तुम जय गंगाधर! ।
विघ्नविनाशक तुमको माना, भव में ऊँचे तुमरे काम ।। 3

Somnath Ji

The divine Shiva Temple of Somnath,
is a Jyotirlinga,
O Ekling ji! please give us auspicious boons.
This Somnath abode is like heaven,
your image is of gold,
Your worship and songs give us happiness.
This Shiva temple is heavenly, built by sages,
O Nandishvara! your name give us joy.
O Trishuldhari! O Tripurari! O Damrudhar!
You remove our misery, your deeds are divine.

Malesia (Malaya + Singapore), Hindu Dynasties

78. Majapihit Dynasty, Malaya (1299-1391)

1. Shri Tribhuvan	श्री त्रिभुवन	1299–1347
2. Shri Vikram Besar	श्री विक्रम बेसर	1347–1362
3. Shri Rana Vir Vikram	श्री राणा वीर विक्रम	1362–1375
4. Shri Paduka	श्री पादुका	1375–1388
5. Shri Parameshwar	श्री परमेश्वर	1388–1391

NOTE : The Majpihit Dynasty was also wide spread on the island group of Java, Sumatra, Bali, etc.

Royal House of Malaya and Singapore

The Tamil culture of the Chola-Pallava Empire brought Hindu culture to the Malaya Peninsula (Malaysia + Singapore) Islands. Wherever the Hindus go, they put their divine imprint through their temples, sculptures and cave carvings.

These are the best example of cave craft in Malaya, making them eternal in the Batu cave temple community. In Malaya, by connecting the festivals of Deepawali, Murugan and Navaratri, the society has been endured.

The snake shaped Malaya Peninsula, covered with ancient ruins, is called Bhujangadhari and is associated with Shiva Bhakti. The Ganga Nagar Dynasty of Malaya existed in the written pages of history till **1025**, but its clear record is not available. The Majapahit Dynasty of Malaya was also prevalent on the islands of Java, Sumatra and Bali. Singapore is a new country.

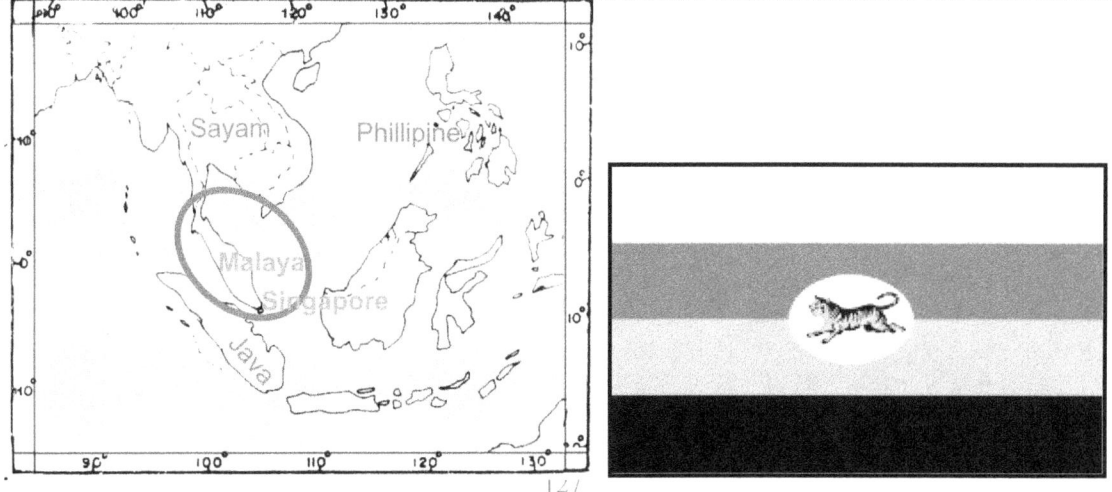

Hindu Rajtarangini

79. Manikya Dynasty, Agartala, Tripura (1400-1948)

For the Prior Dynasty, please see :
Yayati Dynasty (Ancient Time)

#	Name	Hindi	Period
1.	Mahamanikya	महामाणिक्य	1400-1431
2.	Dharma Manikya-1	धर्म माणिक्य-1	1431-1462
3.	Ratna Manikya-1	रत्न माणिक्य-1	1462-1487
4.	Pratap Manikya	प्रताप माणिक्य	1487-1487
5.	Vijay Manikya-1	विजय माणिक्य-1	1487-1488
6.	Mukut Manikya	मुकुट माणिक्य	1488-1489
7.	Dhanya Manikya	धन्य माणिक्य	1489-1515
8.	Dhvaj Manikya	ध्वज माणिक्य	1515-1520
9.	Dev Manikya	देव माणिक्य	1520-1530
10.	Indra Manikya	इन्द्र माणिक्य	1530-1532
11.	Vijay Manikya-2	विजय माणिक्य-2	1532-1563
12.	Anant Manikya	अनंत माणिक्य	1563-1567
13.	Uday Manikya	उदय माणिक्य	1567-1573
14.	Jay Manikya	जय माणिक्य	1573-1577
15.	Amar Manikya	अमर माणिक्य	1577-1585
16.	Rajdhar Manikya	राजधर माणिक्य-1	1585-1600
17.	Ishvar Manikya	ईश्वर माणिक्य	1600-1600
18.	Yashodhar Manikya	यशोधर माणिक्य	1600-1618
19.	Kalyan Manikya	कल्याण माणिक्य	1618-1660
20.	Govind Manikya-1	गोविंद माणिक्य-1	1660-1661
21.	Chhatra Manikya	छत्र माणिक्य	1661-1667
22.	Govind Manikya-2	गोविंद माणिक्य-2	1667-1673
23.	Ram Manikya	राम माणिक्य	1673-1684
24.	Ratna Manikya-2	रत्न माणिक्य-2	1684-1693
25.	Narendra Manikya	नरेंद्र माणिक्य	1693-1695
26.	Ratna Manikya-2	रत्न माणिक्य-3	1695-1712

Manikya Dynasty

Babhru, son of the lunar king Druhu, was anointed with the land of Kirat by sage Kapila. King Prasen, the fifteenth king of this Dynasty was present at the Ashwamedha yajna of King Dashrath. In the Mahabharata period, a divine descendant named Tripura of king Prasen was a student of Ashwatthama. The 39th descendant of this Tripura lineage had received the title Manikya (Jewel).

This kingdom of Yayati received the name Tripura with the grace of Tripura Devi. This place was one of the 51 Shakti Peethas of Hinduism.

The original capital of the kingdom of Tripura was Udaipur on the banks of the Gomati River, which was shifted to Agartala in the 18th century.

The 144 kings of this kingdom extended the kingdom to Assam and Burma. It is mentioned in the Rajmala chronicle. According to the Rajmala, there were Khasi Hills in the North of the Tripura State, Manipur State in the North East, Arakan Hills

27.	Mahendra Manikya	महेन्द्र माणिक्य	1712-1714
28.	Dharma Manikya-2	धर्म माणिक्य-2	1714-1725
29.	Jagat Manikya	जगत माणिक्य	1725-1729
30.	Dharma Manikya	धर्म माणिक्य-2	1729-1733
31.	Mukund Manikya	मुकुन्द माणिक्य	1733-1739
32.	Jaya Manikya-2	जय माणिक्य-2	1739-1744
33.	Indra Manikya-2	इन्द्र माणिक्य-2	1744-1746
34.	Vijay Manikya-3	विजय माणिक्य-3	1746-1748
35.	Lakshman Manikya	लक्ष्मण माणिक्य	1748-1760
36.	Krishna Manikya	कृष्ण माणिक्य-1	1760-1783
37.	Rajdhar Manikya	राजधर माणिक्य-2	1783-1804
38.	Ram Ganga Manikya-1	राम गंगा माणिक्य-1	1804-1809
39.	Durga Prasad Manikya	दुर्गाप्रसाद माणिक्य	1809-1813
40.	Ram Ganga Manikya-2	राम गंगा माणिक्य-2	1813-1826
41.	Kashi Chandra Manikya	काशी चंद्र माणिक्य	1826-1829
42.	Krishna Manikya-2	कृष्ण माणिक्य-2	1829-1849
43.	Ishan Chandra Manikya	ईशानचंद्र माणिक्य	1849-1862
44.	Vir Chandra Manikya	वीरचंद्र माणिक्य	1862-1896
45.	Radha Kishor Manikya	राधाकिशोर माणिक्य	1896-1909
46.	Virendra Manikya	वीरेन्द्र माणिक्य	1909-1923
47.	Vikram Manikya	विक्रम माणिक्य	1923-1947
48.	Kirit Manikya	किरीट माणिक्य	1947-1948

> **Manikya Dynasty continued**
>
> Among the 48 kings of this state, the best known kings were Vijay Manikya-2 (1532-1563) and Dharma Manikya-2 (1714-1725).
>
> King Veerachandra Manikya Devavarma (1862–1896) modernized his kingdom in the 19th century.
>
> In the twentieth century, Manikya kings had assumed the title of Maharaja since the time of king Virendra Manikya (1909–1923).

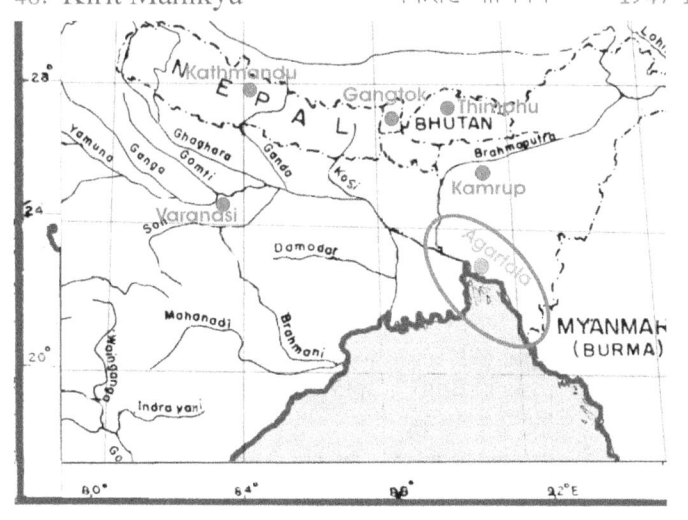

80. Maukhari Dynasty, Kannauj (540-725)

For the Earlier Dynasty, please see :
Gupta Dynasty, (240–730)

1. Hari Varma — हरिवर्मा — 500–
2. Aditya Varma — आदित्यवर्मा
3. Ishvar Varma — ईश्वरवर्मा — 540–550
4. Ishanya Varma — ईशान्यवर्मा
5. Susthita Varma — सुस्थितवर्मा
6. Avanti Varma — अवंतिवर्मा — 580–600
7. Graha Varma — ग्रहवर्मा — 600–612
8. Bhog Varma — भोगवर्मा
9. Yasho Varma — यशोवर्मा — –725

For the Next Dynasty, please see :
Pratihar Dynasty (725–1036)

Maukhari Dynasty
Maukhari of Kannauj,
were in Gupta subordination,
Maukhari king Ishanyavarma,
ended this domination. 1
Now Maukhari kings, became independent,
They ruled up to Magadha,
with great ambition. 2

Maukhari Dynasty

At the time of the decline of the Gupta Empire (240-730), the Maukhari Dynasty started independent rule from the feudal rank. Originally residents of Gaya region were feudatories of Gupta Dynasty. In the service of the Gupta kings, the Maukhari people settled in Kannauj and Barawa region of Rajasthan. The first leader of the Maukhari people, Harivarma, was a feudal partner of the Gupta kings of around the year 500 in the Kannauj region and his marital relationship was connected with the Gupta royal family.

Adityavarma, son of Maukhari king Harivarma, married the daughter princess Harshagupta of Gupta Emperor Krishnagupta (530-540). Ishwarvarma (540-550), a descendant of Harivarma, married Gupta Princess. Till now the border of Maukhari kingdom was limited to Kannauj region.

Ishvarvarma's younger brother Ishaanyavarma was an ambitious and majestic king. He minted his gold coins and bore the title of Maharajadhiraja. King Grahagavarma (600-612) married the daughter of Prabhakargupta of the Gupta Dynasty. During Ishanyavarma's reign, the Maukhari Dynasty was completely independent of the Gupta kingdom and became the universal ruler of Kannauj. Ishanyavarma also conquered Magadha by defeating Gupta monarch Damodagupta (560-562).

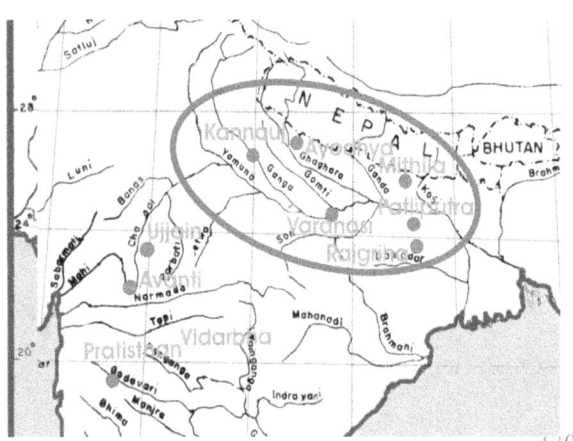

81. Maurya Dynasty, Patliputra (322-184 BC)

For the Earlier Dynasty, please see :
Nand Dynasty (344 BC –322 BC)

1.	Chandragupta	चंद्रगुप्त	322–298 BC
2.	Bindusar	बिंदुसार	298–271 BC
3.	Ashok	अशोक	269–232 BC
4.	Kunal	कुणाल	232–228 BC
5.	Dashrath	दशरथ	228–224 BC
6.	Samprati	संप्रति	224–215 BC
7.	Shalishuk	शालिशुक	215–202 BC
8.	Deva Varma	देववर्मा	202–195 BC
9.	Shata Dhanva	शतधन्वा	195–187 BC
10.	Brihadrath	बृहद्रथ	187–184 BC.

For the Next Dynasty, please see :
Shung Dynasty (185 BC–72 BC)

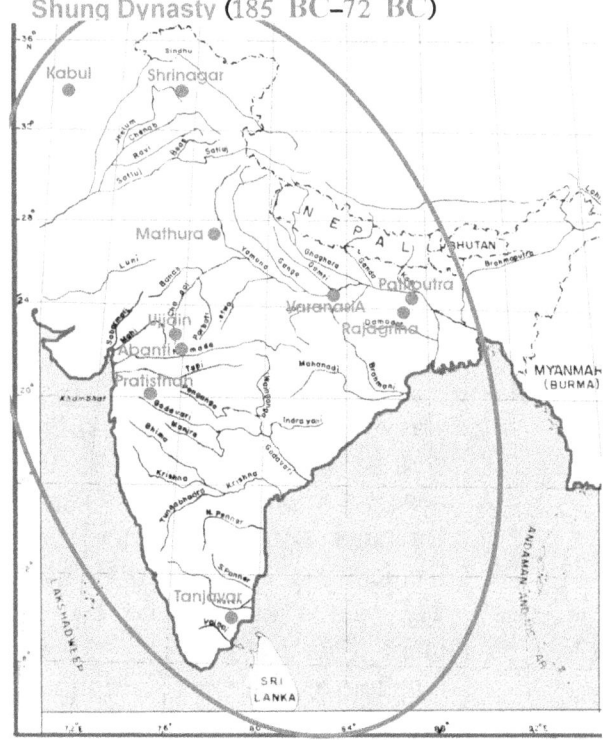

Maurya Dynasty

Emperor Chandragupta Maurya (340–298 BC) Pataliputra ended the ancient Nanda Dynasty of Magadha (344–322 BC) and established the mighty and world-famous Royal House of the Maurya (322–184 AD). The credit for this splendid victory goes to his intelligent minister Chanakya or Kautilya i.e. Vishnugupta (375–283 BC).

Soon after coming to power, Chandragupta's empire spread rapidly in the West direction, Chandragupta's army campaigned against Alexander (365-323 BC) and took possession of the Sindh and Punjab regions. After this great victory, Chandragupta and Chanakya attacked the Nanda king Dhanananda (329–322 BC) and killed him.

Soon after becoming monarch of the Magadha Empire, Chandragupta recaptured Alexander's army (305–303 BC). Chandragupta defeated Alexander and expanded Maurya power until Kabul. Then Alexander's minister Seleucos Nicatoro (305–281 BC) married his daughter Helena (358–281 BC) to Chandragupta. Now in the Maurya Empire, all the land from Kabul to Bengal and from Kashmir to Narmada was ruled by the Mauryas.

Maurya Dynasty continued

Chandragupta Maurya was succeeded by his son Bindusar (298–271 BC). The ambassadors of Asiriya (Syria) and Misr (Egypt) were present at his court. After 25 years of Bindusar rule, The mighty son of King Chandragupta and Queen Subhadrangi (304-232 BC, power 269-232 BC) emerged as the second great Maurya Emperor. The son of Emperor Bindusar was Devanapriya Ashok Maurya, the influential, talented and super-powerful emperor-of-emperors i.e. a Chakravarti King in the Indian history . His empire was widely spread from Hindukush in the north, Iran in the west, Assam in the East and Kanyakumari in the south.

The most important event of Emperor Ashok's reign was the invasion of Kalinga (261 BC) in which one hundred thousand persons got killed. Ashok's heart was moved by this horrific killing and he was impressed with the peaceful message of Lord Gautama Buddha. After this incident, he accepted Buddhism and started a new and eternal phase of history by writing kingdom orders in his inscriptions.

Emperor Chandragupta Maurya, Magadh (322-298)

Chandragupta Maurya : He was the great Army Commander of Nanda king Dhanananda (329–322 BC) of Pataliputra. The commander attempted to depose King Dhanananda but due to failure he had to leave Magadha with his secretary Vishnugupta (Kautilya, Chanakya 375–283 BC) and flee across the Vipasa (Bias) river. Following the policies of his minister Kautilya, Chandragupta mobilized a large army and invaded Magadha. He won the war. After killing King Dhanananda, Chandragupta established his Maurya Dynasty in Pataliputra (322–184 BC).

Chandragupta (322–298 BC) extended his empire across the rivers Magadha, Anga, Kosala, Kashi and the Indus. Kautilya made the four fold (Chaturangini) powerful army of Magadha and by formulating the political science and politics he built the nation.

Kautilya's Arthashastra is a great text of 115 chapters written in the cent percent interest

of the king. In this, Kautilya excelled in the quality and capacity of the king and his ministers, the rules and duties of government offices, the laws of civilization, the right diplomacy, the security of the kingdom and the treasury, the rules of the army, the dealings with neighboring states, the system of aggression and retaliation with precision. Kautilya says: Self-control is mandatory before a king can control the subjects. He is required to have Vaidic knowledge, economics, politics and mathematics. After Chandragupta, his grandson Ashok Maurya (269-232 BC) is considered the great emperor of history.

Ashoka Maurya (373–232 BCE) : The biography of Emperor Ashok Maurya (269–232 BCE), the son of the Maurya emperor Bindusar (298–271 BCE), is derived from the inscribed orders of King Ashok himself. The autobiography of a king inscribed on rocks by the king himself is seen for the first time in the global history. In year 269 BC coronation of Ashok Maurya took place. The year 261 BC Ashok won the Kalinga country. The terrible violence that had taken place in the Kalinga war caused King Ashok's heart to be shaken and moved towards non-violence. In 259 BC he accepted the peaceful message of Shakyamuni Lord Buddha (653-483 BC).

82. Meera Bai, Queen (1498-1573)

For the Earlier Dynasty, please see :
Sisodiya Dynasty, Chittor (1303–1948)

1. Maharana Sanga — महाराणा संग — 1473–1527
2. Rana Bhoj Raj — राणा भोजराज — 1495–1530
2. Meera Bai — मीरा बाई — 1498–1573

भक्त मीरा : खयाल

स्थायी
मीरा पी गई बिस का प्याला, ना हुई उईमा ना भई पीरा,
केसब की सब लीला ।

अंतरा–1
राणा जी से नाता तोरा, जग जन से मीरा मुख मोरा,
मोहन संग मन जोड़ा ।

Meera

Meera drank the glass of poison.
She neither felt burning,
nor any pain,
It is the magic of Shri Krishna, Keshava.

She broke off with Rana ji,
And turned away her face
from the world,
And made company with
Shri Krishna Mohan 1.
Meera sang the loving names of Hari.
And she ended her life with a smile. 2

Meera Bai

Meera Bai (1498-1573) was the daughter of Ratan Simha, younger brother of Maharaj of Merta, Jodhpur. After the death of her mother, Meera was brought up by Rao Duda of Kurdi village, when she was only two years old. Meera was married to Rana Bhojraj (1495–1530), son of Sisodiya Maharana Sanga (1509–1527) of Mewar, around 1530. The famous war of Khanwa took place at this time (1527). Soon after marriage Rana Bhojraj died. On his death Meera refused to go Sati. She considered Giridhar Shri Krishna as her spiritual husband. She engaged herself in Krishna devotion.

Saint Tulsi Das ji (1497-1624) had preached Shri Ram bhakti to Meerabai and she also started writing songs of Ram bhakti, such as "*Ram Ratan Dhan Payo.*"

Fed up with Meera's spiritual devotion, her family members tried poison her. Meera left home and went to Dwarka-Vrindavan to spend her time in Krishna devotion. Meera Bai's songs *Govind Teek, Sorath's ke pad, Raga Govind, Narsi ii ro mayaro,* etc. are immortal compositions.

83. Nag Dynasty, Jharkhand (83-1948)

1. Fani Mukut Rai   फणी मुकुटराय   83–177
2. Mukut Rai   मुकुटराय   177–232
3. Dhat Rai   धटराय   232–273
4. Madan Rai   मदनराय   273–326
5. Pratap Rai   प्रताप राय   326–353
...
6. Gondu Rai   गोंडुराय   548–563
7. Hari Rai   हरिराय   563–601
8. Gajraj Rai   गजराजराय   601–627
9. Sundar Rai   सुंदरराय   627–635
10. Mukund Rai   मुकुन्दराय   635–653
11. Udaya Rai   उदायराय   653–710
12. Kundan Rai   कुन्दनराय   710–756
13. Jagan Rai   जगनराय   756–772
14. Bhagan Rai   भगनराय   772–811
15. Mohan Rai   मोहनराय   811–869
16. Jagdhat Rai   जगधटराय   869–905
17. Chandra Rai   चंद्रराय   905–932
18. Andund Rai   अंदुंदराय   932–969
19. Shripati Rai   श्रीपतिराय   969–997
20. Yogendra Rai   योगेंद्रराय   997–1004
21. Nripendra Rai   नृपेंद्रराय   1004–1047
22. Gandharva Rai   गंधर्वराय   1047–1098
23. Bhimakarna   भीमकर्ण   1098–1132
24. Jashkarna   जाशकर्ण   1132–1180
25. Jalakarna   जलकर्ण   1180–1218
26. Gokarna   गोकर्ण   1218–1236
...

Nag Dynasty

The first ruler of the Nag Dynasty Phani Makutarai (83-177) was born in Sutiyambe in AD 64. From Chota Nagpur of Chhattisgarh to Nagpur of Vidarbha, the Panchayat of the society of Nag tribes had considered Phani Mukutarai as the blessed God of the Nag Devta, and regarded him as their king for life. Phani Mukutarai was the son of a Pandit named Pundarik. King Phani Mukutarai wore the crown of King in year 83. In the fourth century AD, King Vishwanath Shah (1724-1733), founded capital city for the tribal Nag Dynasty. They attached the title Rai before their names. They founded the town of Chutia on the banks of the river Swarnarekha and built a famous temple there. With the passage of time, the capital of the Nag Dynasty was shifted from Sutiyambay to Chutia, Khokhra, Palkot and then to Ratugad.

The name of the kings of the Nag Dynasty was suffixed with the title of Rai from the eleventh century, then from the twelfth century to the sixteenth century they held the title Karna for about five hundred years, and after them the king was adorned with the titles of Shah, Sal and Dev. The father-son lineage tradition has continued in the Nag Royal family. This Dynasty can be considered the world's longest genealogy.

27.	Shivadaskarna	शिवदासकर्ण	1367–1389
28.	Udaykarna	उदयकर्ण	1389–1451
29.	Pratapkarna	प्रतापकर्ण	1451–1469
30.	Chhatrakarna	छत्रकर्ण	1469–1496
31.	Bhiratkarna	भिरातकर्ण	1496–1501
32.	Panetu Rai	पानेतुराय	1501–1512
33.	Baudshal	बौदाशाल	1512–1530
34.	Madhusimha	मधुसिंह	1530–1599
35.	Bairisal	बैरीसाल	1599–1614
36.	Durjansal	दुर्जनसाल	1614–1640
37.	Ramshah	रामशाह	1640–1665
38.	Raghunathshah	रघुनाथशाह	1665–1706
39.	Yadunathshah	यदुनाथशाह	1706–1724
40.	Shivanathshah	शिवनाथशाह	1724–1733
41.	Udaynathshah	उदयनाथशाह	1733–1740
42.	Shyamsundarnathshah	श्यामसुंदरनाथशाह	
43.	Balramnathshah	बलरामनाथशाह	
44.	Mahinathshah	महीनाथशाह	
45.	Dhripanathshah	धृपनाथशाह	
46.	Devnathshah	देवनाथशाह	
47.	Govindnath	गोविंदनाथशाहदेव	1806–1822
48.	Mahajagannath	महाजगन्नाथशाह	1822–1872
49.	Mahaudaynath	महाउदयनाथशाह	1872–1950

Nag Dynasty

Five families of snakes,
the scriptures often quote,
Shesha Vasuki Pingala,
Takshak and Karkot. 1
Devotion to snakes, is our culture rich,
Naga is the deity,
a festival is there for which. 2
The Shiva devotees think,
Shesha is foremost snake,
Nagpur, the town of snakes,
was founded on a lake. 3
Mathura and Vidisha, were Nag lands,
say many Puranas, as the History stands. 4
In the area of Bastar,
in Chhatisgadh State,
Naga kingdom founded at,
Sutiyambe perfect. 5
Son of Shri Pundarika,
Parvati was his mother,
Their son was Mukut Rai,
at place called Ratugar. 6
This new born child Mukut,
was blessed by a Snake,
"You will be a king for life,"
message world will take. 7
One day the leaders said,
to Mukut Rai child,
You are the chosen king,
of the Nag people mild. 8
Then after Mukut Rai,
there were fifty kings,
This was the longest Dynasty,
thus the history sings. 9
Their seat was in Chutiya,
and here was their palace,
A temple built of stones,
it was a holy place. 10
From Bastar to Nepal,
Vidarbha and place any,
Naga tribe grew, in the countries many. 11

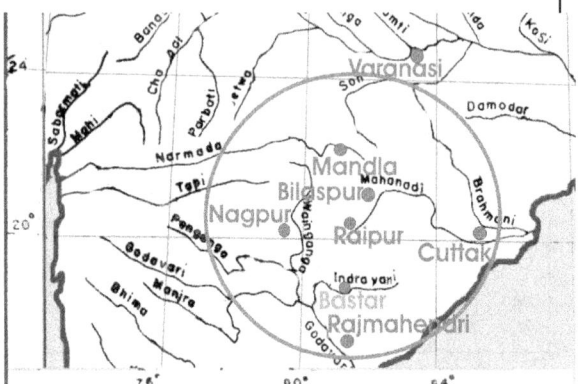

84. Nal Dynasty, Chhattisgadh (290-960)

1.	Shishuk	शिशुक	290–330
2.	Varaharaj	वराहराज	330–370
...			
3.	Bhavadatta	भवदत्त वर्मा	
4.	Adhipati	अधिपति	
5.	Skand Varma	स्कन्दवर्मा	
6.	Nandan Varma	नंदन वर्मा	
7.	Prithviraj	पृथ्वीराज	600–630
8.	Virupaksha	विरूपाक्ष	630–630
9.	Vilastung	विलासतुंग	630–642
...			
10.	Prithvivyaghra	पृथ्वीव्याघ्र	
11.	Narendra Dhaval	नरेंद्र धवल	935–960

For the Next Dynasty, please see :
Chalukya Dynasty, Badami (525–753)

Nal Dynasty

The kings of Nal Dynasty, were rulers of Bastar,
They were opulent, and honoured near and far. 1
Jealous for their richness, the Vakataka rulers,
Often invaded their kingdom,
and became well known looters. 2
The Nal kings one time, won Vakataka lands,
Expanded their kingdom, and chopped their hands. 3

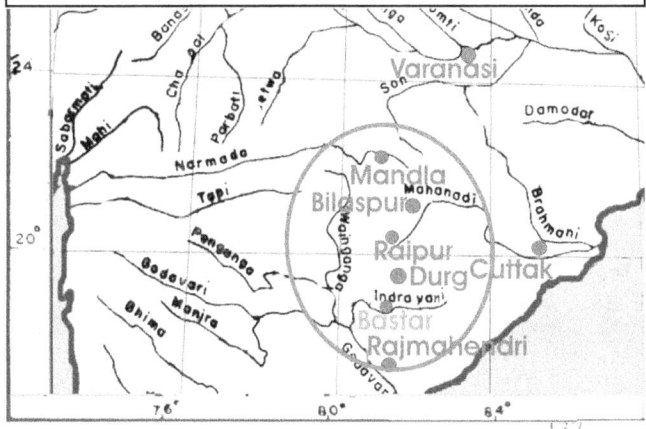

Nal Dynasty

The kings of the Nal Dynasty were in power from the 3rd century to the tenth century in Pushkari of Bastar region of Chhattisgarh. The Royal House of Vakatakas (250-510) was contemporary as well as competitors.

The reign of King Varaharaj (330–370) was a prosperous period of the Nal Empire. King Bhavadatta Varma defeated the Vakataka king Narendra Sen (450–470) and captured Nandivardhan (Nanded), the capital of Vakatakas.

The power of the Nal Dynasty was vast from Morshi village in Amravati district of Vidarbha to Odisha across Chhattisgarh. King Vilasatunga (630-642) accepted suzerainty of Chalukya dominance. It is mentioned that King Nandan Varma had received education and initiation at Nalanda University.

Hindu Rajtarangini

85. Nand Dynasty, Patliputra (344-322 BC)

For the Next Dynasty, please see :
Shishunag Dynasty (413–344 ई.पू.)

1. Mahapadma — महापद्म — –362 BC.
2. Panduka — पांडुक
3. Pandugati — पांडुगति
4. Bhutapal — भूतपाल
5. Rashtrapal — राष्ट्रपाल
6. Devanand — दैवानंद
7. Yajnabhag — यज्ञभंग
8. Mauryanand — मौर्यानंद
9. Dhananand — धनानंद — 329 –322 BC

For the Next Dynasty, please see :
Maurya Dynasty (322–184 BC)

Nanda Dynasty

The contribution of Nandas, is well known all over,
Mahapadma was a warrior, not to forget ever. **1**

He was a holy person, say the Puranic words,
Nanda kingdom was rich, tell the written records. **2**

Nanda Dynasty

Till the year 362 BC, Mahapadma, the first king of the Nanda Dynasty, conquered the kings of Panchal, Kashi, Kalinga, Ashmak, Mithil, Kuru etc. by love or war and extended his power in North India as well as South of the Vindhya mountain.

The Nanda kings introduced new measurement methods for trade in their states, it is known from the Kartikas of Panini's (2, 2, 21) sutras.

Their Chaturangini army of elephants, horses, soldiers and chariots of Nanda kingdom was very large. Its evidence is found in the history. The description of Nanda kingdom being prosperous and wealthy is also present in the Puranas.

In the early fourth century, the Nanda rule collapsed in 322 BC. In the guidance of the great strategist Kautilya, Priyadarshan Chandragupta Maurya (322–298 BC) defeated the Nanda king Dhanananda (329–322 BC) and established the Maurya Empire (322–184 BC) at Patliputra.

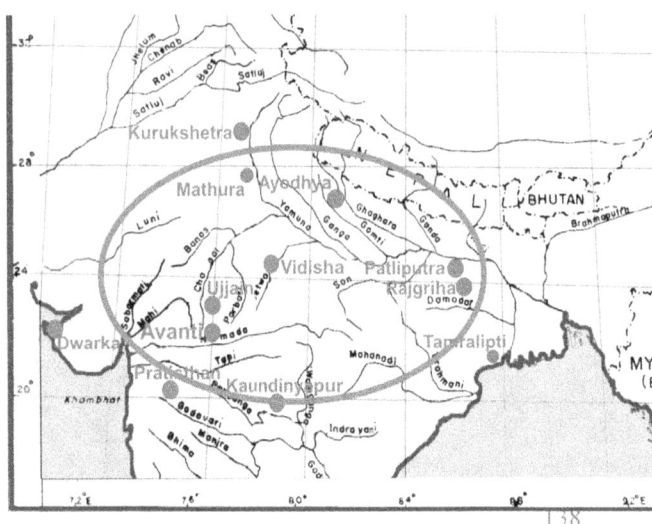

Hindu Rajtarangini

86. Narayan Dynasty, Kashi-Varanasi (1737-1948)

For the Earlier Dynasty, please see : Shakya Dynasty (Ancient Time)

1. Mansaram — 1737–1739
2. Balvant Narayan Simha — 1739–1770
3. Chait Narayan Simha — 1770–1780
4. Mahip Narayan Simha — 1780–1794
5. Udit Narayan Simha — 1794–1835
6. Ishvari Narayan Simha — 1835–1889
7. Prabhu Narayan Simha — 1889–1931
8. Aditya Narayan Simha — 1931–1939
9. Vibhuti Narayan Simha — 1939–1948

Narayan Dynasty

Kashi is the most ancient,
holy place in the world,
Lord Shiva founded Himself,
this pilgrimage old. 1
The holy city Varanasi,
is the Vishvanath abode,
Standing on the bank of Ganges,
to heaven it is a road. 2
It is a Shaktipeeth,
it is seat of learning,
It is a jyotirlinga,
it is the pilgrimage-king. 3

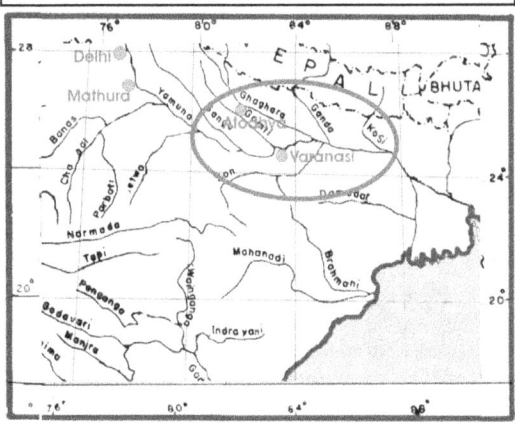

Narayan Dynasty

The city of Kashi, situated on the banks of river Ganges, is oldest in the ancient cities of the world, which was founded by Lord Shiva himself. Since then it has become a holy shrine. The same Sanatan Kashi is today called Varanasi or Banaras.

One of the seven holy cities, one of the twelve Jyotirlingas, the oldest in the Sixteen Mahajanapadas and the abode of the Vishwanath Temple is the Kashi or Varanasi. Its location being between the river Varuna and the river Ashi, it is called Varanasi. Skanda Purana 26.67, Panini Ashta. 4.2.116, Patanjali Mahabhashya 2.1.1, Atharva-veda 5.22.4, Shatapatha Brahmin 13.5.4.19, Jaiminiya Brahmin 2.3.19, Brihadaranya Upanishad. 2.1.1, Ramayana 4.40.22, Mahabharata. etc. 102, Gita 1.51 1.17 have mentioned the kings and people of Kashi. The royal Dynasty of Kashi begins with Divodasa, the King of the Rigveda, Kashi was the capital of the Shakya king Shuddhodhana.

The power of the Narayana Dynasty was founded about AD 1000 in Banaras. In 1737, Mansaram of Varanasi became a powerful king (1737–1739). His son Balwant Singh (1739–1770) became king and Jaunpur, Ghazipur and Chunar came in his kingdom. King Balwant Singh settled the capital at Gangapur on the banks of the Ganges and later at Ramnagar.

Udit Narayan Singh built Ghats and palaces on the banks of the Ganges in Varanasi, which got the name Ganga Mahal. King Prabhu Narayan Singh (1889–1931) was a great propagator of Hinduism and culture. He had provided 1300 acres of land for the Banaras Hindu University Scheme (1916) of Mahamana Pundit Madan Mohan Malaviya (1861–1946). King Vibhuti Narayan Singh (1939–1948) was also a scholar of the Vedas and Puranas. He remained the Vice Chancellor of the Banaras Hindu University until his death (1992).

Nayak Dynasty, Vijayanagar (1336-1565)
Vijayanagar, Musunuri, Pammasani, Jingi, Keladi Vellor, Tanjavar, Madura, Penukonda, Chennai, Chitradurg, Kondavidu, Haleri.

87. Sangam Nayak Dynasty (1336–1485) :

For the Previous Dynasty, please see :
Hoysal Dynasty, Halebid (1026–1343)

1. Sangam-1 — संगम–1
2. Harihar-1 — हरिहर–1 — 1336–1356
3. Bukka-1 — बुक्क–1 — 1356–1377
4. Harihar-2 — हरिहर–2 — 1377–1404
5. Vrupaksh-1 — विरूपक्ष–1 — 1404–1405
6. Bukka-2 — बुक्क–2 — 1405–1406
7. Devaraya-1 — देवराया–1 — 1406–1413
8. Virvijay-1 — वीरविजय–1 — 1413–1422
9. Ramchandrray — रामचंद्रराय — 1422–1425
10. Devaraya — देवराया–2 — 1425–1446
11. Mallikarjun — मल्लिकार्जुन — 1446–1465
12. Virupaksha — विरूपक्ष–2 — 1465–1485

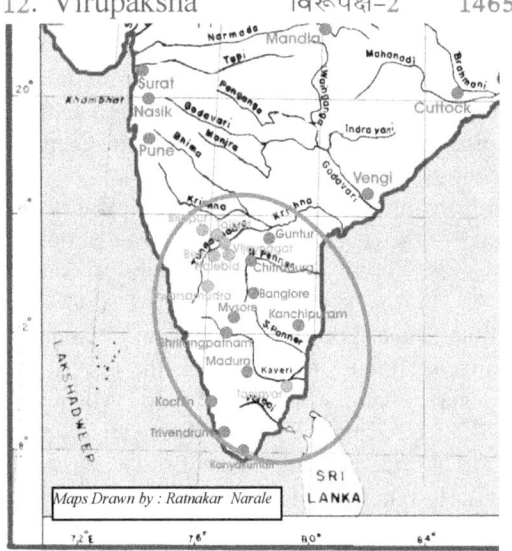

Maps Drawn by : Ratnakar Narale

Nayak Dynasty
1. Sangam Nayak Dynasty :

In 1335 Mussunuri Kapay Nayak, the hero of Telangana and the heroic leader of the Reddy clans, defeated the foreign (Arab) subedar of Warangal and assumed the title of Andhra Pradeshadhish. The flame of this revolt flared all around. In the year 1336, with the blessing of the 12th Jagadguru Swami Vidyaranya Saraswati (1268-1391) of Sharda Peeth of Shringeri (1380-1386), Harihara and Bukka, the son of Sangam Nayak established a new kingdom on the South bank of the Tungabhadra River. They named it Vijayanagara and started a new Royal House.

Along with the origin of Vijayanagar, many feudatory institutions of Vijayanagar and many independent Nayak institutions emerged in Andhra and Tamil countries. The ten main names of those Nayak Dynasties were : Mussunuri, Pemmasani, Jinji, Keladi, Vellore, Tanjavar, Madura, Penugonda, Chennai and Chitradurga. Their brief discussion and genealogy are presented ahead.

Nayak Dynasty

Vijayanagar was, a magnificent empire,
It has many provinces, Nayaks their sire. 1

Harihar founded this, house of Vijayanagar,
Reddi braves joined them, in a large number. 2

Four provinces were main, in this vast empire,
Ikkeri Madura Jinji, and the Tanjavar. 3

After seventeenth century, Jinji and Tanjavar,
Became Maratha kingdoms,
in the South very far. 4

Fifteen Hundred Sixty Five,
was the fateful year,
It will annihilate, the glory of Vijayanagar. 5

Five Sultans joined, each one was a zealot,
To demolish Hindu Kingdom,
was the heinous plot. 6

Vijayanagar was a kingdom,
heaven on the earth,
It was splendid realm, right from its birth. 7

When Ramdev was away, behind then his back,
The Sultans got a chance,
to launch sudden attack. 8

The five Sultans together,
made a thunderous attack,
The thirst for the blood, they did not lack. 9

Mass murder they caused, of the Hindus all,
Looted whole kingdom,
destruction wasn't small. 10

This Talikot war, the Hindu people lost,
The Sultans ruled South,
Hindus paid the cost. 11

Nayak Dynasty
continued

King Harihar (1336–1356), the first hero of Vijayanagar, defeated Hoysala King Brave Balla-4 (1342–1348) and took control of Halebid.

Harihara's younger brother Bukka (1356-1377) conquered Penukonda, Goa, Madura areas and dominated the region South of Tungabhadra. He started the renaissance of Vaidic religion. Thereafter, Harihar Rai (1377–1404), son of Bukka, took possession of Konkan, Tamil, Mysore, Bangalore, Tiruchirapalli, Kanchi areas. He bore titles like Vedic Margahasthaan Acharya, Maharajadhiraj, Rajparameshwar, etc. After that, during the time of King Devarai-2 (1425-1446), the Vijayanagar kingdom was at the height of prosperity.

Foreign travelers used to say that, like Vijayanagar, a prosperous and magnificent kingdom has not been seen anywhere else or heard before. The Nayak kingdom expanded from the Krishna River to Shri Lanka and from the East Valley to the Bay of Bengal. The last king of the Sangam Dynasty, Virupaksha (1465–1485), being weak and corrupt, his minister Narasimha Saluva got Virupaksha killed at the hands of the son of Virupaksha himself and Narasimha Saluva established the Saluva Nayak Dynasty (1485-1503) of Vijayanagar.

88. Saluv Nayak Dynasty (1485–1503):

1. Narasimharay   नरसिंहराय   1485–1490
2. Timma Bhupal   तिम्म भूपाल   1490–1492
3. Immadi   इम्मादी नरसिंहराय 1492–1505

89. Tuluv Nayak Dynasty (1503–1565):

1. Narsa Nayak   नरसा नायक   1491–1505
2. Vir Narasimha   वीर नरसिंह   1505–1509
3. Krishnadeva Raya   कृष्णदेवराया   1509–1530
4. Acyutadevaraya   अच्युतदेवराया   1530–1542
5. Venkataraya   वेंकटराया   1542–1543
6. Sadashivaraya   सदाशिवराया   1543–1565
   and Ramaraya   और रामराया   1543–1565

90. Aravidu Nayak Dynasty (1565–1649):

1. Tirumal Nayak   तिरुमल नायक   1565–1572
2. Shrirang-1   श्रीरंग-1   1572–1585
3. Venkat-1   वेंकट-1   1585–1614
4. Shrirang-2   श्रीरंग-2   1614–1618
5. Ramdevaraya   रामदेवराय   1618–1630
6. Venkat-2   वेंकट-2   1630–1642
7. Shrirang-3   श्रीरंग-3   1642–1649

Nayak Dynasty continued

2. Saluva Nayak Dynasty (1485): The last king of this family, Narasimharaya Nayak (1492-1505) was very weak. He made his minister Narasa Nayak of the Tuluva lineage a patron of Vijayanagar to look after his kingdom. Narasa Nayak took the power of Vijayanagar in his own hands and started his Tuluva Dynasty (1503-1565).

3. Tuluva Nayak Dynasty (1503): King Krishnadevaraya (1509-1530) of the Tuluva Dynasty made the empire of Vijayanagar most prosperous and world class. Sadashiv Rai (1543–1565), the last king of the Tuluva household, was not able to rule the great kingdom, so he placed the kingdom on the shoulders of his minister Salakam Timmaray. Timmaray turned out to be "Jaichand" of the south. He conspired with the five foreign Sultans. As a result, the five aggressors massacred and looted Vijayanagar Empire (Battle of Talikot, 1565). They burnt, mutilated, raped, corrupted, destroyed it for many months. Vijayanagar minister Tirumal Nayak (1584–1658) kept Sadashiv Rai safe in Penukonda. The Timm Nayak (1540–1565) killed Jaichandi Timmaray and he placed King Ramaraya (1565–1585) on the throne.

91. Musunuri Nayak Dynasty (1325–1368):

1. Prolay Nayak   प्रोलय नायक   1325-1333
2. Kapay Nayak   कापय नायक   1333-1368

92. Pemmasani Nayak Dynasty (1423–1685):

1. Kumar Timma Nayak-1   तम्म-1   1423-1462
2. Chenna Vibhudu   चेन्न विभुदु   1505-1540
3. Bangaru Timma Nayak   बंगरु   1540-1565
4. Narsima Nayak   नरसिंह नायक   1565-1598
5. Timma Nayak   तिम्म नायक   1598-1623
6. Chinna Timma Nayak   चिन्न तिम्म   1623-1652
7. Kumar Timma Nayak-2   तिम्म-2   1652-1685

93. Jinji Nayak Dynasty (1491–1649):

1. Vaiappa Nayak   वैयप्पा नायक   1491-1509
2. Bala Krishnappa   बाल कृष्णप्पा   1509-1521
3. Vijaya Ramchandra   विजय रामचंद्र   1521-1540
4. Mutailu   मुतैलु   1540-1550
5. Venkatappa   वेंकटप्पा   1550-1570
6. Tryambak Krishnappa   त्र्यंबक   1570-1600
7. Varadappa   वरदप्पा   1600-1620
8. Ramakrishnappa   रामकृष्णप्पा   1620-1649

94. Keladi Nayak Dynasty (1499–1763):

1. Chaudappa Nayak   चौदप्पा नायक   1499-1530
2. Sadashiv Nayak   सदाशिव   1530-1566
3. Shakanna   शंकन्ना   1566-1570
4. Chikka   चिक्का   1570-1580
5. Ramaraja   रामराजा   1580-1586

Nayak Dynasty continued

4. Aravidu Nayak Dynasty (1565):

Shrirang-1 (1572–1585), the eldest son of Tirumal Nayak (1565–1572), began to restore the kingdom of Vijayanagar at Penukonda. The last king of this Dynasty was Shrirang-3 (1642–1649).

5. Musunuri Nayak Dynasty (1325):

Mussunuri Nayak (1325-1368) of Telangan, a descendant of the Kakatiya (1000-1323) Dynasty, ruled around Bhadrachalam. Their first known leader was Praloy Nayak (1325–1333). His son Kapayya Nayak became king by conquering Warangal in 1333. Kapay Nayak (1333-1368) had given a decree of rebellion against the foreign Sultans in Andhra.

6. Pemmasni Nayak Dynasty (1423):

The Nayaks of Gandikota were feudatories of Vijayanagar and used to help them in the battles. After the fall of Vijayanagar (1565), They ruled from Pemmasani for about 150 years. The king of this Dynasty, Ramalinga Nayak (1505–1540), was a great warrior. He helped the Tuluva king Krishnadevaraya (1509-1530) to win the Golconda and Ahmadnagar wars. Foreign Nizam enemies of Golconda, Ahmadnagar, Bijapur used to tremble with his name.

6.	Venkatappa-1	वेंकटप्पा-1	1586–1629
7.	Virabharda-1	वीरभद्र-1	1629–1645
8.	Shivappa	शिवप्पा	1645–1660
9.	Venkatappa-2	वेंकटप्पा-2	1660–1662
10.	Someshvara-1	सोमेश्वर-1	1662–1697
11.	Queen Channamma	रानी चन्नम्मा	1672–1697
12.	Basavappa-1	बासवप्पा-1	1697–1714
13.	Someshvar-2	सोमेश्वर-2	1714–1739
14.	Basavappa-2	बासवप्पा-2	1739–1754
15.	Chenna Basavappa	चेन्नबासवप्पा	1754–1757
16.	Queen Viramma	रानी वीरम्मा	1757–1763

95. Madura Nayak Dynasty (1509–1736):

1.	Narasa Pillai	नरसा पिल्लई	1509–1519
2.	Kuru Timmappa	कुरु तिम्मप्पा	1519–1524
3.	Kamaiya	कामय्या	1524–1526
4.	Chinnappa	चिन्नप्पा	1526–1531
5.	Ayyakarai Vayyappa	अय्याकरै	1531–1535
6.	Vishvanath Ayyar	विश्वनाथ अय्यर	1535–1544
7.	Nagam Nayak	नागम नायक	1544–1558
8.	Vishvanath Nayak	विश्वनाथ नायक	1558–1563
9.	Periya Krishnappa	कृष्णप्पा	1563–1573
10.	Periya Virappa	वीरप्पा	1573–1602
11.	Muttu Krishnappa	मुत्तु कृष्णप्पा	1602–1609
12.	Muttu Virappa	मुत्तु वीरप्पा	1609–1623
13.	Tirumal Nayak	तिरुमल नायक	1623–1659
14.	Virappa Nayak	वीरप्पा नायक	1659–1670
15.	Chokannath	चोकन्नाथ	1670–1685
16.	Rang Krishna	रंग कृष्ण	1685–1689
17.	Queen Mangammal	रानी मंगम्मल	1689–1704

Nayak Dynasty continued

7. Ginji Nayak Royal House (1491):

During the time of the Tuluva king Narasa Nayak (1491–1505) of Vijayanagar, the Tuluva fighter Vaiyappa Nayak (1491–1509) established the feudatory Nayak Dynasty of Jinji in Tamil Nadu. After the fall of Vijayanagar in 1565, the heroes at Jinji became independent.

8. Keladi Nayak Dynasty (1499): The heroes of Keladi-Ikkeri were the feudatories of Vijayanagar from 1499. After the battle of Talikot (1565), they gained independence in the West Valley. In their kingdom came the areas of Kerala along the banks of river Tungabhadra and the kingdom of Malabar. In 1763, they merged with the Wadiyar Sarkar (1399–1947) of Mysore, but a Keladi branch (1600–1834) in the Kurg province remained independent.

Chaudappa Nayak of Keladi (1499–1530) was the first king of this Dynasty. His son Sadashiv Nayak (1530–1566) shifted the capital from Keladi to Ikkeri. Queen Channamma (1672–1697) supported the Maratha King Chhatrapati Shri Shivaji Bhosle (1674–1680) in the wars of the South against the Nizams. Later also (1680) she gave shelter to Rajaram Raje Bhosle (1689–1700).

18. Vijay Rang विजय रंग चोकन्नाथ 1704-1731
19. Rang Krishna रंग कृष्ण 1731-1734
20. Quuen Minakshi मीनाक्षी अम्मल 1734-1736

96. Vellor Nayak Dynasty (1526-1595):
1. Chinnabhumi Nayak चिन्नभूमि नायक 1526-

97. Tanjavar Nayak Dynasty (1532-1673):
1. Timmappa Nayak तिम्मप्पा नायक ...
2. Shivappa Nayak शिवप्पा 1532-1580
3. Achyutappa अच्युतप्पा 1580-1600
4. Raghunathy Nayak रघुनाथ 1600-1634
5. Vijay Raghav विजय राघव 1634-1673

98. Penukonda Nayak Dynasty (1565-1616):
1. Sadashivray सदाशिवराय 1565-1585
2. Venkatapati वेंकटपति 1585-1614

99. Chennai Nayak Dynasty (1572-):
1. Chennappa Nayak चेन्नप्पा नायक
2. Venkatappa वेंकटप्पा
3. Ayyappa अय्यप्पा
4. Ankbhupal अंकभूपाल
5. Timmappa तिम्मप्पा
6. Chenna Venkat चेन्न वेंकट

Nayak Dynasty continued

9. Madura Nayak Dynasty : (1509): Queen Mangammal (1689-1704) and Queen Minakshi Ammal (1734-1736) were the two brave women among the Nayak rulers of Madura. Queen Mangammal established trade relations with Dutch Governor Willian-van-Othurn (1731-1736) and Portuguese viceroy Sitona Demelo-e-Castro (1702-1707 See). Any British governor was not yet established in this area until 1732.

10. Vellore Nayak Dynasty : (1526):
Feudatory Vellor Nayak (1526-1595) of the Vijayanagar kingdom, King Chinnabhumi Nayak of the royal family was the most eminent king who established his capital in 1526 at the Fort of Vellor. Vellor Fort was famous in history from the time of Chinnabhoomi to the period of Chhatrapati Shivaji (1674-1680).

11. Tanjavar Nayak Dynasty (1532): Shivappa Nayak (1532-1580), son of Timmappa Nayak, the Governor of Arcot for King Achyutdevaraya (1530-1542) of the Tuluva house of Vijayanagar, established the Dynasty of Tanjavar. Wife of Shivappa Nayak was sister of the queen of King Achyutdevaraya of Vijayanagar. Shivappa's son Achyutappa (1580-1600) was managing the kingdom with his father for twenty years (1560-1580).

100. Chitradurg Nayak Dynasty (1588–1779)

1. Timmanna — तिम्मन्ना — –1588
2. Obanna-1 — ओबन्ना-1 — 1588–1602
3. Rangappa-1 — रंगप्पा-1 — 1602–1652
4. Madakari-1 — मदकरी-1 — 1652–1674
5. Obanna-2 — ओबन्ना-2 — 1674–1675
6. Kanta — कांता — 1675–1676
7. Chikanna — चिकन्ना — 1676–1686
8. Madakari-2 — मदकरी-2 — 1686–1688
9. Rangappa-2 — रंगप्पा-2 — 1688–1689
10. Bharamanna — भरमन्ना — 1689–1721
11. Madakari-3 — मदकरी-3 — 1721–1748
12. Rangappa-2 — रंगप्पा-3 — 1748–1754
13. Madakari-4 — मदकरी-4 — 1754–1779

101. Kendy Nayak Dynasty (1739–1815):

1. Vijaya Rajsimha — विजय राजसिंह — 1739–1747
2. Kirti Shri Rajsimha — कीर्ति — 1747–1782
3. Shri Rajsimha — राजसिंह — 1782–1798
4. Vikram Rajsimha — विक्रम — 1798–1815

102. Kondavidu Reddi Dynasty (1325–1448)

1. Prolaya Vema Reddi — वेमा — 1325–1353
2. Anna Vota Reddi — अन्ना — 1353–1364
3. Anna Vema Reddi — अन्ना — 1364–1386
4. Komaragiri Reddi — रेड्डी — 1385–1402
5. Peda Komargiri Reddi — पेडा — 1402–1420
6. Raja Vema Reddi — राजा — 1420–1423
7. Virabhadra Reddi — वीर — 1423–1448

Nayak Dynasty continued

12. Penukonda Nayak Dynasty (1565): At the time of the fall of Vijayanagar (1565), Tirumal Devaraya (1584–1659), son of Muttu Krishnappa Nayak of the Aravidu house, left Vijayanagar with King Sadashivaray (1543–1565) and came to Penukonda to reestablish the Vijayanagar Empire. King Sadashivaray of Penukonda (1565–1585) was succeeded by Venkatapathi (1585–1614), the junior son of Tirumal, who consolidated and strengthened the kingdom of Penukonda Nayaks.

13. Chennai Nayak Dynasty (1572): After the fall of Vijayanagar (1565), Chennappa Nayak, the commander of King Shrirang-Devaraya (1572–1585) of the Aravidu house established his Chennai Nayak Dynasty in Kalahati in 1572.

14. Chitradurga Nayak Dynasty (1588): After the fall of Vijayanagar (1565), the first king of Chitradurga Nayak, Timmanna Nayak, was the nephew of Vishwanath Nayak (1558–1563), the founder of the Nayak Dynasty of Madura. Bharmanna Nayak (1689–1721) was a feudatory of Vyankoji Bhosle (1675–1684) of Tanjavar. After that Kasturi Rangappa Nayak of Chitradurga (1748–1754) was also an assistant of the Marathas.

15. Kandy Nayak Dynasty (1588): The Tamil-speaking Shiva devotees of the Telugu Nayak Dynasty of the Madura They established the Nayak Dynasty in Kandy Shri Lanka (1739–1815). They had the military base of the Nayak kings of Madura and Tanjavar.

103. Haleri Nayak Dynasty, Coorg (1633–1834) :

1. Viraraja — वीरराजा
2. Apparaja — अप्पाराजा
3. Mudduraja — मुदूराजा–1 — 1633–1687
4. Doddaraja — दोद्दा वीरप्पा — 1687–1736
5. Chikka Virappa — चिक्क वीरप्पा — 1736–1766
6. Mudduraja-2 — मुदूराजा–2 — 1766–1770
7. Devapparaja — देवप्पाराजा — 1770–1774
8. Lingaraja-1 — लिंगराजा–1 — 1774–1780
9. Vira Rajendra-1 — वीरराजेन्द्र–1 — 1780–1809
10. Lingraja-2 — लिंगराजा–2 — 1809–1820
11. Vira Rajendra-2 — वीरराजेंद्र–2 — 1820–1834

Nayak Dynasty continued

16. Kondavidu Reddy Nayak Dynasty (1325):

Kondavidu Reddy State (1325-1448) was established along the Nayaks on the East coast of Andhra Pradesh after the fall of the Kakatiya Empire. The Reddy society of this Warangal is also called Komati Samaj.

17. Haleri Nayak Dynasty of Coorg (1633):

King Veeraraja, of a branch of the Arasu Nayak Dynasty of Ikkeri, ruled as the feudatory of the Wadiyar (1399–1947) kings of Mysore in the Haleri region of Coorg.

In 1633, Muduraja-1 (1633-1687) of Haleri established his kingdom in the Coorg State, independent of Mysore. Later, in 1681, he shifted his capital to Madikeri and fortified it.

During the reign of Dodda Veerappa (1687–1736), the Wadiyar King Chikka Devaraja Wadiyar (1673–1704) made a sudden attack and occupied some part of the eastern border of Coorg, but had to retreat when thousands of Wadiyar soldiers were killed.

In 1734, Dodda Veerappa (1687-1736) attacked the Kingdom of Mysore and won seven forts of the Wadiyar kingdom. At this time the capital of the Wadiyar kings was at Shrirangapatnam (1610–1799). Wadiyar King Krishnaraja-3 (1799-1868) shifted the capital back to Mysore.

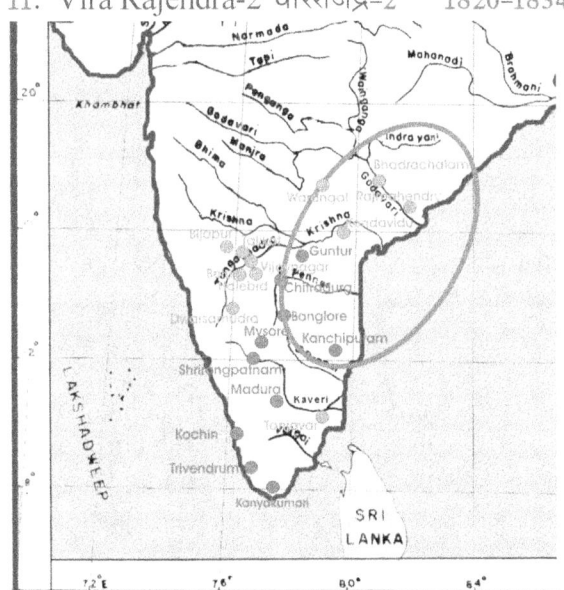

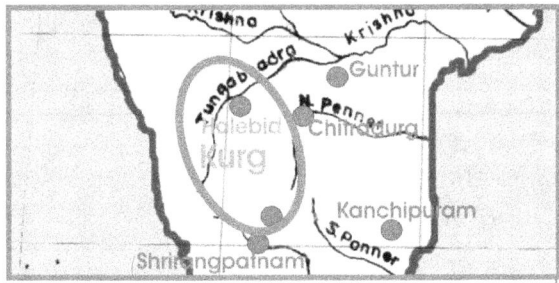

Hindu Rajtarangini

Nepali Hindu Dynasties (900BC-1948AD)

1. Gopal Ahir Dynasty (**Ancient** Time)
2. Kirat Dynasty (900 BC-205 AD)
3. Som Dynasty (205-305)
4. Lichchhavi Dynasty (305-605)
5. Anshuvarma Dynasty (605-879)
6. Raghav Dynasty (879-1046)
7. Thakur Dynasty (1046-1200)
8. Malla Dynasty (1200-1768)
9. Gurkha Dynasty (1768-1948)

The Nine Hindu Royal Houses of Nepal

The Hindu country of Nepal is a ten-thousand-foot-high kingdom stretched between the Terai plain and the Himalayan peaks. It includes rivers, mountainous terrain, dense forests, flat and fertile land.

Some of the inaccessible peaks of this region are Everest (29,200 ft.); Kanchanganga (28,100); Makalu (27,700); Mansalu (27,000); Dhavalagiri (26,800); Gusainath (26,300); Himachuli (25,800); Gaurishankar (23,400); etc. The rivers Sarada, Sharyu, Gandaki and Kori, originating from these high peaks meet the river Ganges.

Nepal, the only Hindu country in the world, is mentioned with respect in the Mahabharata (Van. 254.7) and Puranas. The history of the Nepali tribes are divided into at lEast nine major dynasties from the ninth century BC.

The Hindu kingdom of Nepal
Nepal is the world's, only Hindu Nation,
Its neighbor is Bharat, with Hindu population.

104. Gopal Ahir Dynasty of Nepal (Ancient Time)

Gopal Dynasty

The Yaduvamshi Gopal Dynasty which came to Nepal from Mathura-Magadha region, settled in Nepal. This ancient Gopal Ahir Royal House started ruling in Nepal from place to place.

105. Kirat Dynasty of Nepal (900 BC-205 AD)

Kirat Dynasty

The Kirat people were native tribe of Nepal. King Nimikh was the first ruler of the Kirat Dynasty after the ancient Gopal Ahir Dynasty. After King Nimikh, in the next two hundred years, there were 29 rulers of Kirat Dynasty. King Yalambar defeated King Bhuvan Singh of the Gopal Dynasty. In 900 AD, and the Kirat Dynasty was founded.

The next 28 kings of this Kirat Dynasty (900 BC-205 AD) were: King Pavi, Skandha, Balamb, Hriti, Humati, Jitedasti (540 BC), Galinj, Pushk, Suyarm, Pap, Bunk, Swanand, Sthunko (250 BC), Ginghari, Nen, Luk, Thor, Yoko, Varma, Guj, Pushkar, Keshu, Shuj, Sans, Gunam, Khimbu, Patuk and King Gasti.

106. Som Dynasty of Nepal (205-305)

Som Dynasty

When the king Patuk of Kirat Dynasty of Nepal ruled, the kings of Som Dynasty tried to seize the Kirat throne.

Later Soma king Nimish defeated the last Kirat king Gasti in year 205 and established the Soma Dynasty in Nepal (205-305).

The next four kings after Soma King Nimish were: King Mitaksha, King Kakavarma, King Pashupraksha and King Bhaskaravarma.

107. Lichchhavi Dynasty of Nepal (305-605)

Lichchhavi Dynasty

When the Kushan Empire (30–244) prevailed in the adjacent areas of Mathura, in the third century the Lichchhavi people in the Kushan Empire, fled to Nepal to be safe and secure. Among these Lichchhavi people, Bhumivarma became the ruler of Nepal in 305 AD.

The descendants of King Bhumivarma who ruled Nepal for three hundred years from year from year 305 to 605 were the kings: Bhumivarma, Dharmadeva, Matdev, Brishadeva, Mahidev, Basantdev, Shivdev, Jayadeva, etc. The Lichchhavi king Brishadeva was a very powerful ruler. He was a contemporary king of the Gupta emperor Chandragupta-2 Vikramaditya (375–415). Chandragupta married King Brishadeva's daughter Kumara Devi and established peace with Nepal.

108. Anshuvarma Dynasty of Nepal (605-879)

Anshuvarma Dynasty

In 605, Anshuvarma of Shivadev, the son-in-law of the last king of Lichchhavi Dynasty, defeated his father-in-law Shivadev and established his Anshuvarma Royal House (605-879) in Nepal.

Uday Dev, Dhruv Dev, Narendra Dev, Shivadev, Jayadev, Baradev, etc. were the main kings in this Anshuvarma Dynasty of Nepal.

109. Raghav Dynasty of Nepal (879-1046)

Raghav Dynasty

In the year 879, the last king of the Anshuvarma Dynasty of Nepal was defeated by Raghavavarma and established his Raghava Dynasty (879-1046). King Gunakamadev (949-994) of this Dynasty established his capital at Katmandu. The ten well known kings of this Raghava royal family were as follows:

1. King Raghavdev, the founder, 2. King Jayadeva, 3. King Vikramdev, 4. King Narendradev, 5. King Gunakamdev, 6. King Udayadeva, 7. King Rudradeva (1008-1015), 8. King Bhojdev (1015-1015) 9. King Lakshmikarmadeva (1015–1039), and 10. King Vijayakamdev (1039–1046).

110. Thakur Dynasty of Nepal (1046-1200)

Thakur Dynasty

In 1046, King Bhaskaradeva (1046-1059) defeated the last king of Nepal's Raghava Dynasty, Vijayakamadeva (1039-1046), and established the Thakur Dynasty in Katmandu (1046-1200). King Shankar Deva (1067–1080) was the most powerful king of the Thakur Dynasty. He started the festival of Nagpanchami in Nepal by worshipping Vasuki Naga. He had a cultural connection with the Nag Dynasty of Jharkhand (83-1948).

King Shiva Deva (1099–1126) was the heroic king after King Shankar Deva. He had installed gold umbrella at the ancient Pashupatinath temple. He built many temples and ponds.

Apart from the above three kings, the main kings of the Thakur Dynasty were: King Baldeva (1059-1064), King Vamadeva (1080-1090), King Harishchandra (1090-1099), King Gunakamadev (1187-1193), King Lakshmikamadev (1193-1196) and King Vijayakamadev (1196–1200).

King Vijayakamdev was the last king of the Thakur Dynasty of Nepal. After him, King Aridev (1220-1216) established the Malla Royal House of Nepal (1200-1768).

111. Malla Dynasty of Nepal (1200-1768)

For the Earlier Dynasty, please see :
Thakur Dynasty of Nepal (1046–1200)

1. Ari Malla Deva   अरि मल्ल   1200-1216
2. Abhay Malla Deva   अभय मल्ल   1216-1235
3. Jai Malla Deva   जय मल्ल देव   1235-1258
4. Jai Bhima Malla Deva जय भीम   1258-1271
5. Jai Simha Malla Deva   जय सिंह   1271-1274
6. Anant Malla Deva अनंत मल्ल देव   1274-1310
7. Jai Nand Malla Deva जय नंद देव   1310-1320
8. Jai Rudra Malla Deva जय रुद्र देव 1320-1326
9. Jai Ari Malla Deva   जय अरि देव   1326-1347
10. Jai Raj Malla Deva   जय राज देव   1347-1361

Thakur Dynasty of Nepal

King Ari Malla Deva (1200–1216) defeated the Thakur King Vijayakamadeva (1196–1200) and established the Malla Dynasty (1200–1768) in Katmandu and Patan, Nepal. King Ari Malla Deva extended the boundaries of his kingdom and gave dominance to Sanskrit language in the kingdom.

The last king of the Malla Dynasty, Jai Prakash Malla Deva (1736–1768), was defeated by Gurkha King Prithvi Narayan Shah (1768–1775) and established the Shah Dynasty (1768–1948).

#	Name	Reign
11.	Jai Arjun Malla Deva जय अर्जुन	1361–1382
12.	Jai Sthiti Malla Deva जय स्थिति	1382–1395
13.	Jai Dharma Malla Deva जय धर्म	1395–1408
14.	Jai Jyoti Malla Deva जय ज्योति	1408–1428
15.	Jai Yaksha Malla Deva जय यक्ष	1428–1482
16.	Ratna Malla Deva रत्न मल्ल देव	1482–1520
17.	Surya Malla Deva सूर्य मल्ल देव	1520–1530
18.	Amar Malla Deva अमर मल्ल देव	1530–1538
19.	Narendra Malla Deva नरेंद्र मल्ल	1538–1560
19.	Mahendra Malla Deva-1 महेंद्र-1	1560–1574
20.	Sadashiva Malla Deva सदाशिव	1574–1578
21.	Shiva Simha Malla Deva शिव	1578–1620
22.	Lakshmi Narayan Malla Deva	1620–1641
23.	Pratap Malla Deva प्रताप मल्ल	1641–1674
24.	Jai Nripendra Malla Deva जय	1674–1680
25.	Parthivendra Malla Deva पार्थिवेंद्र	1680–1687
26.	Bhupendra Malla Deva भूपेंद्र	1687–1700
27.	Bhhaskar Malla Deva भास्कर	1700–1714
28.	Mahendra Malla Deva-2 महेंद्र-2	1714–1722
29.	Jagat Jai Malla Deva जगत जय	1722–1736
30.	Jai Prakash Malla Dev जय प्रकाश	1736–1768

Thakur Dynasty of Nepal

During the reign of Malla King Jai Malla Deva (**1235-1258**), there was a great earthquake in Nepal and NorthEast India in **1255** AD. Approximately one-third of Nepal's population perished in it. In year **1258** King Jai Malla died. Destruction was even greater in India and thousands of people fled to the hills of Nepal for protection. After this great crisis, King Jai Sthiti Mall Deva (**1382–1395**) re-established the kingdom.

Before the death of King Jayasthiti Malla, he established three dynasties by dividing the kingdom of Nepal between his two sons and one grandson. **1.** Son Ratnamalla got the kingdom of Katmandu (**1482–1768**), **2.** King Rai Malla, received Bhatgaon (**1482–1768**), **3.** And later, grandson Siddhi Narayan Malla got the kingdom of Patan (**1620–1768**).

112. Shah Gurkha Dynasty of Nepal (1768-1948)

For the Earlier Dynasty, please see:
Malla Dynasty of Nepal (1200–1768)

1. Prithvi Narayan Shah पृथ्वी नरायण 1768–1775
2. Pratap Simha Shah प्रताप सिंह शाह 1775–1778
3. Rana Bahadur Shah राणा बहादुर 1778–1799
4. Girvan Shuddha Vikram Shah 1799–1816
5. Rajendra Vir Vikram Shah राजेंद्र 1816–1847
6. Surendra Vir Vikram Shah सुरेन्द्र 1847–1881
7. Prithvi Vir Vikram Shah पृथ्वी 1881–1911
8. Tribhuvan Vir Vikram Shah 1911–1948

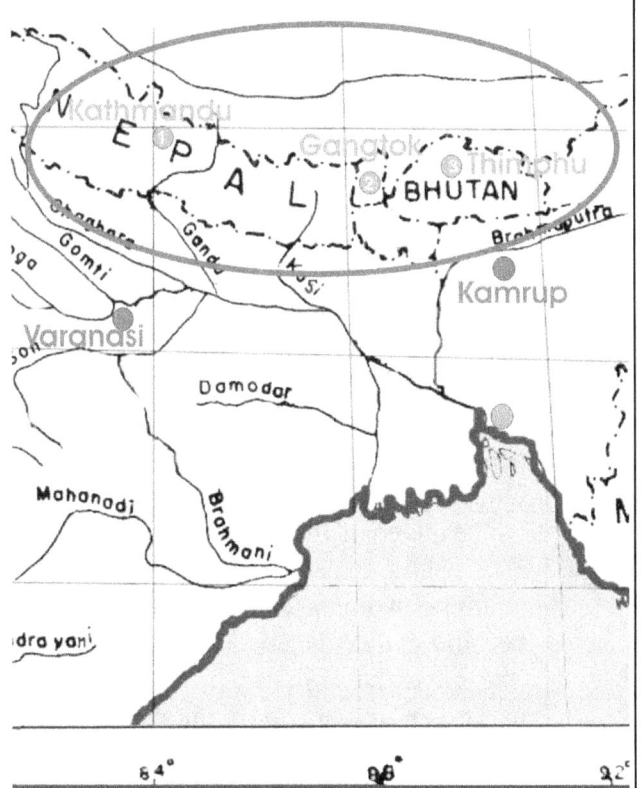

Shah Gurkha Dynasty of Nepal

The region where the followers of Guru Gorkha Nath settled in Nepal is called Gorkha and those families of the settlers are called Gurkhas. In the eighteenth century in Nepal, Brave Prithvi Narayan Shah (1723–1775) did the work of connecting all Gurkha people. By conquering Katmandu he became the first king (1768–1775) of the Royal House of Nepal (1768–1948).

Maharaja Prithvi Narayan Singh gathered various federations of Nepal and started to form a united nation. After him, the post of Prime Minister commenced during the time of Maharaja Rajendra Vikram Shah (1816–1847). The post of the first Prime Minister was handled by Rana Jung Bahadur (1846–1877). The Dynasty of Rana Jung Bahadur was a descendant of Sisodiya Rana Kumbh (1433–1468) of Chittor.

Rana Jung Bahadur was followed by Rana Randeep Singh (1877–1885), Rana Shamsher Jung Bahadur (1885–1901), Rana Chandra Shamsher Jung Bahadur (1901–1929), Rana Bhim Shankar Jung Bahadur (1929–1932), Rana Yudh Shamsher Jung Bahadur (1932–1945), and Rana Padma Shamsher Jung Bahadur (1945–1948) became Prime Ministers.

Hindu Rajtarangini

113. Nevalkar Dynasty, Jhansi (1838-1858)

For Earlier Dynasty, see : Peshwe (1713–1818)

1. Raghunath Hari   रघुनाथ हरि   ...
2. Shivaram Bhau   शिवराम भाऊ   –1838
3. Raja Gangadhar Rao   गंगाधरराव   1838-1853
4. Queen Lakshmi Bai   लक्ष्मी बाई   1853-1858

स्वातंत्र्य वीरांगना लक्ष्मीबाई

जाओ माता पुकारे, जाओ तुमको वतन बुलाए ।
योद्धा वीर हमारे ।।

बैरी देश का गौरव लीन्हो, स्वाभिमान को जागृत कीन्हो ।
प्राणों को कर अर्पण प्यारे, जीतो या फिर स्वर्ग के द्वारे ।। 1

शोले बारूद गोले खेलो, शस्त्र-अस्त्र सब हँस कर झेलो ।
विजय पताका हाथ में लेलो, जय जय माता भवानी, बोलो ।। 2

याद करो शहीदों की होली, खेली थी जिन्ह माता काली ।
रणचंडी से आँख मिचौली, राणा, शिवाजी, झाँसी वाली ।। 3

कार्य परायण आर्यों जागो, धर्म नीति से कर्म निभाओ ।
त्याग इसी में याग मनाओ, भवानी का भगवा फहराओ ।। 4

The Brave Freedom Fighter, Queen of Jhansi

Go! Mother India is calling you.
Go! Go! Mother is calling, O Brave Queen!
The enemy has insulted the nation's dignity,
and has awakened our pride,
Sacrificing your dear life,
either win or reach the door of the heaven. 1
Bare the bombs, bullets and shots of the weapons
with smiling face.
Holding the flag of victory, say Jai Jai Mother Bhavani. 2
Remember the sacrifices made by the martyrs,
blessed on the battlefield by Kali Mata,
Remember those brave Rana Pratap, Shivaji and the
Queen Avanti Bai. 3
O Great Queen! please keep up.
Do your duties, Call it a sacrifice,
and unfurl the Orange flag of Mata Bhavani.

Queen Lakshmi Bai of Jhansi

Lakshmi Bai Gangadharrao Newalkar, the queen of Jhansi, was the wife of King Gangadharrao of Jhansi (1838–1853). Gangadharrao's father Shivram Bhau was a descendant of Raghunath Hari, the first Maratha ruler of Jhansi. Lakshmi Bai was the daughter of the Maratha Moropant Tambe of Kashi and Bhagirathi Bai (Sapre). Her ancestral name was Manikarnika Bai (1828–1858). Manikarnika was married in 1842 and after marriage she received the name Lakshmi Bai. Lakshmi Bai had a son named Damodar who died close to the death of his father. Lakshmi Bai adopted a second child named Anandrao and then she renamed him Damodar.

The ancestors of Gangadharrao were in Ratnagiri, Maharashtra, where they had important positions in the Peshwa and Holkar armies. Raghunathrao established the Maratha kingdom at Jhansi in Bundelkhand, which he handed over to his brother Shivram Bhau. After the death of Shivram Bhau in 1838, Gangadharrao became king and after his death in 1853 Lakshmi Bai became the Queen of Jhansi.

The queen of Jhansi was brave, ethical, clever and expert in war. She was a stunning woman. She was the leading heroine in the freedom struggle of 1857. She gave the British a final fight, and had given up her life on the battle while carrying her baby on her back

114. Nimi Janak Dynasty (Ancient Time)

For the Earlier Dynasty, please see :
Ikshavaku Dynasty (Ancient Time)

1. Ikshavaku — इक्ष्वाकु …
2. Nimi — निमि
3. Mithi — मिथि
4. Udavasu — उदावसु
5. Nandivardhan — नंदिवर्धन
6. Suketu — सुकेतु
7. Devrat — देवरात
8. Brihadrath — बृहद्रथ
9. Mahavir — महावीर
10. Sudhriti — सुधृति
11. Dhrishtaketu — धृष्टकेतु
12. Haryashva — हर्यश्व
13. Maru — मरु
14. Pravartak — प्रवंतक
15. Kirtirath — कीर्तिरथ
16. Devamidh — देवमीढ़
17. Vibudh — विबुध
18. Mahidhrak — महीध्रक
19. Kirtirat — कीर्तिरात
20. Maharoma — महारोम
21. Swarnaroma — स्वर्णरोम
22. Hrasvaroma — ह्रस्वरोम
23. Janak (Shiradhvaja) — जनक (शीरध्वज)
    Janaki (Sita) जानकी (सीता)

For the Next Dynasty, please see :
Raghu Dynasty (Ancient Time)

Janak Videha Dynasty

Ikshavaku's son Nimi was a benevolent king. Maharishi Bhrigu, Angiras, Vamdev, Pulastya, Pulah, Hrishik Maharishis were present at the Yajna rituals of King Nimi. Mithila received its name from King Mithi, the great son of Ikshavaku. It became the Queen City of Videha Kingdom. Mithila was rich in wealth as well as spiritual knowledge wealth. Farming was successful.

In the court of Mithila King Janak, the great philosophers Yajnavalkya, Mandavya, Parashar, Ashtavakra, etc. conducted philosophical and spiritual discussions. Maharaja Janak Shirdhwaj was the father of Sita Devi. King Shirdhwaja's brother was Kushadhwaja, whose three daughters were Mandvi, Urmila and Shrutkiti. They were the wives of Bharata, Lakshmana and Shatrughna respectively (Valmiki Ramayana. Bal. **71**). King Janak was also considered an ideal king in the Gita (Gita **3.20**). Mithila king Janak is honorably known as Dharmadhvaj, Mithilesh, Videha etc. in the scriptures.

Raja Janak of Mithila

King Janak of Mithila

King Janak of Mithila, was a virtuous person,
The great Yajnyavalkya, called him the Sun. 1
Janak was Ganesha, of knowledge-of-self,
He was a great scholar, in the world, himself. 2
Mithila King Janak was,
the philosopher multifold.
A Jewel of the Videha, Janak was real gold. 3
At the court of Janak,
sat philosophers and scholars.
Yajnayavalkya, Jamasagni,
Yami Parashar seers. 4
(Janak's Kingdom)
The kingdom of Janak, was full of splendor,
The learned and wise,
understood its grandeur. 5
The court of King Janak, pundits decorated.
Like thinker Ashtavakra, wise men celebrated. 6
In the Janak's kingdom, people were prudent,
Each man and women, was a decent student. 7
People were happy, pleased and gay,
Janak was righteous,
and satisfied in every way. 8
People were contented, and joyful in every way,
Janak was ethical king, pure like sun ray. 9
There was no superior, or person inferior,
There no arbitrary, or injustice factor. 10

King Janak of Mithila

Vedas were recited, yoga Yajnas performed,
Company of saints, spiritually charmed. 11
As the king was faithful, so was his every subject,
Each will lay down life,
to keep the every aspect. 12
People were learned, blessed by Goddess,
Everyone was busy, achieving progress. 13
Peace and joy everywhere, all had good health,
Everyone had honour,
food and enough wealth. 14
(Janak's Mithila)
In Janak's kingdom, cities and towns were clean,
Gardens full of flowers,
it was beautiful scene. 15
Boys and girls were healthy, played many sports,
Students knew subjects, arts of various sorts. 16
Everyone in the kingdom, spoke soft and sweet,
Like the King they were, always at God's feet. 17
People hailed the king, who fulfilled their needs,
Janak has honour in Gita,
for his selfless deeds. 18
(Sita Devi)
Janak's daughter Sita, is Lakshmi Goddess,
Daughter of Mother Earth, Sita blesses grace. 19
Janak was the greatest, in the worlds seven,
With the wealth of wisdom,
Mithila was heaven. 20

115. Pal Dynasty, Mudagiri, Bengal (750-1174)

1. Dayit Vushnu — दयितविष्णु
2. Bappat — बप्पत
3. Gopal-1 — गोपाल–1 — 750–769
4. Dharmapal — धर्मपाल — 769–815
5. Devpal — देवपाल — 815–850
6. Vigrahapal-1 — विग्रहपाल–1 — 850–875
7. Narayanpal — नारायणपाल — 875–908
8. Rajyapal — राज्यपाल — 908–935
9. Gopal-2 — गोपाल–2 — 935–952
10. Vigrahapal-2 — विग्रहपाल–2 — 952–995
11. Mahipal-1 — महीपाल–1 — 995–1048
12. Nayapal — नयपाल — 1048–1055
13. Vigrahapal-3 — विग्रहपाल–3 — 1055–1070
13. Mahipal-2 — महीपाल–2 — 1071–1075
14. Shurpal — शूरपाल — 1075–1080
15. Rampal — रामपाल — 1080–1120
16. Kumarpal — कुमारपाल — 1120–1125
17. Mahendrapal — महेंद्रपाल — 1125–1144
18. Madanpal — मदनपाल — 1144–1161
19. Givindpal — गोविंदपाल — 1161–1174

For Next Dynasty, see : Sen Dynasty (1074–1230)

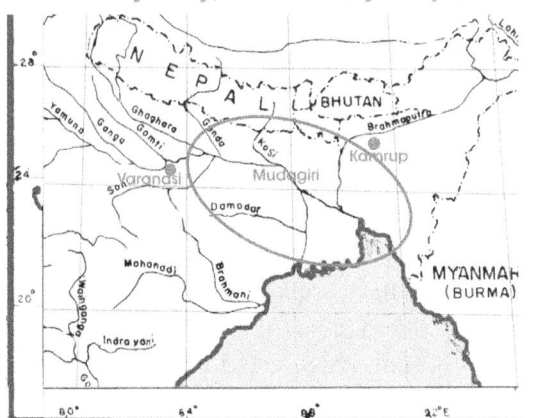

Pal Dynasty

The most influential kingdom of NorthEast India was the Pala Empire (750–1174) of Bengal. The people of Bengal placed Gopal, the son of the great majestic and skilled social worker Bappat, on the throne of Munger (Mudagiri) (750–769) and founded the Pala Dynasty (750–1174).

King Gopal built a university called Vikramashil University in Aundatipur, like the Nalanda University. It attracted students from all around, especially from Tibet.

The Pal rulers were successful war winners. They used to have a huge elephant army. King Gopal was a lover of craft and a great founder of temples. Their power was vast from West and East Bengal to Nepal. In the twelfth century Sen (1074–1230) rulers took it away.

The second branch of the Pala Empire was located at Kamrup in Assam (900–1100). These kings had the title Narakasura. They were also called Bhaum Dynasty. Their influence was all the way to Shiva worshipers of Java and Sumatra.

Pala Dynasty

Pala kings of Bengal,
to Mudagiri they came,
Other branch in Assam,
Bhaum was its name. 1
Palas were supporters,
of learning arts and sculpture,
They built University,
like Nalanda culture. 2
The sway of Palas,
was Bengal and beyond,
Pala Elephant Troops were big,
their repute was grand. 3

116. Pallava Dynasty, Kanchipuram (315-897)

For the Earlier Dynasty, please see :
Pandya Dynasty, Madura (50–1310)

1.	Shiva Varma-1	शिववर्मा-1	315–345
2.	Skand Varma-1	स्कन्दवर्मा-1	345–350
3.	Visnho Gopa	विष्णुगोप	350–355
4.	Kumar Vishnu	कुमारविष्णु-1	355–370
5.	Skand Varma-2	स्कन्दवर्मा-2	370–385
6.	Vira Varma	वीरवर्मा	385–400
7.	Skand Varma-3	स्कन्दवर्मा-3	400–435
8.	Simha Varma-1	सिंहवर्मा-1	435–460
9.	Skand Varma-4	स्कन्दवर्मा-4	460–480
10.	Nandi Varma-1	नन्दीवर्मा-1	480–510
11.	Kumar Vishnu-2	कुमारविष्णु-2	510–530
12.	Buddha Varma	बुद्धवर्मा	530–540
13.	Kumar Vishnu-3	कुमारविष्णु—3	540–560
14.	Simha Vishnu	सिंहविष्णु	560–580
15.	Mahendra Varma-1	महेंद्रवर्मा-1	580–630
16.	Narsimha Varma-1	नरसिंहवर्मा-1	630–668
17.	Mahendra Varma-2	महेंद्रवर्मा-2	668–674
18.	Parameshvara Varma-1	परमेश्वरवर्मा-1	674–700
19.	Narasimha Varma-2	नरसिंहवर्मा-2	700–728
20.	Mahendra Varma-3	महेंद्रवर्मा-3	728–731
21.	Parameshvara Varma-2	परमेश्वरवर्मा-2	731–731
22.	Nandi Varma-2	नन्दीवर्मा-2	731–796
23.	Danti Varma	दंतीवर्मा	796–847
24.	Nripottunga Varma	नृपोतुंगवर्मा	847–872
25.	Aparajita	अपराजित	893–897

For the Next Dynasty, please see :
Chola Dynasty, Tanjavar (50–1279)

Pallava Dynasty

The Pallava Dynasty became famous in the Tamil country after the fall of Pandyas at the end of Sangama Period. The Sanskrit word "Pallava" came into existence from the Tamil word "Tondaiyar." The Royal House that became independent after the Satavahana (271 BC-195 AD) kings won the Tondaimandalam from the Pandyas is the Tondaiyar or Pallava Dynasty. The Pallava king Skandavarma-1 (345–350) conquered the area from river Krishna to river Pennar and annexed the kingdom of Kanchi by performing the Ashwamedha Yajna. Mahendravarma-1 (580-630) extended the power to Tiruchirapalli. He was the patron of arts and sculpture. He had titles such as Chaityakari, Chitrakalaripi, Mattavilas, Vichitrit, etc. During the period of Pallava king Narasimhavarma-2 (700-728), great temples like Mahabalipuram emerged. In his court was Sanskrit Mahakavi Dandi honoured.

When the Badami Chalukya king Vikramaditya-2 (733-746) won Kanchi, the capital of the Pallavas was Nandipuram. Then the Chola (50-1279) kings of Tanjavar wrested the power of the remaining Pallavas.

Pallava King Narsimhavarma, Kanchipuram (700-728)

गीत : दादरा ताल
*गंगा अवतरण

गंगा देवी! तू मंगल है माता, तेरा अँचल है कितना सुहाना ।
तेरी लहरों में है गुनगुनाता, मैया! संगीत सरगम सुहाना ।।
निकली शंकर की काली जटा से, तुझको भगिरथ ने लाया धरा पे
तुझको जन्हू की कन्या है माना, तेरा इतिहास पावन पुराना ।।
तेरे जल में हिमालय की माया, तुझमें जमुना का पानी समाया ।
सरयू को भी गले से लगाया, तूने उनको भी दीन्ही गरिमा ।।
तेरा तीरथ है लीला जगाता, सारे पापों से मुक्ति दिलाता ।
है सनातन तेरा मेरा नाता, बड़ी पावन नदी तू मेरी माँ ।।

Ganga Avataran

O Ganga Devi! you are our holy mother.
Your blessings are so loving.
There is beautiful music in your waves.
You arose from the hair of Shiva.
Sage Bhagirath brought you to the earth.
You are known as the daughter of King Janhu.
Your history is auspicious and ancient. 1
There is magic of the waters of Himalaya in you.
Water of river Yamuna merges in you.
You have hugged the river Sharayu.
You have given fame to them all. 2
Your holy water is magical,
it cleanses all our sins.
I have an ancient relationship with you,
you are our holy mother. 4

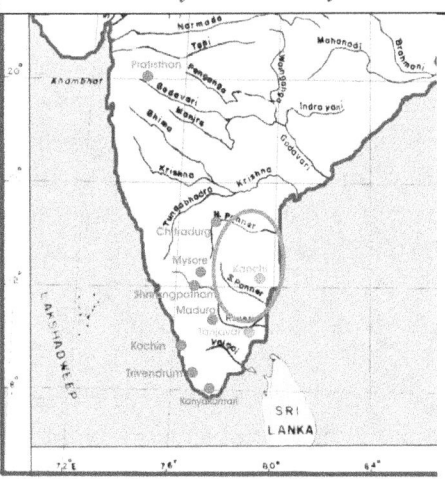

Pallava king Narasimhavarma-2

The Pallavas of Kanchipuram originated from the great sage Bharadwaja. The Pallavas were devotees of Ganga Devi.

The kingdom of the Pallava king Mahendravarma-2 (668-674) was vast spread from river Krishna to Kaveri. He made Mahabalipuram (Mamallapuram) port his trade center.

Mahendravarma's son Rajsimha Narasimhavarma-2 (700-728) had built a grand and divine temple made of stone sculptures famously known as the stone cut art of in Mahabalipuram. The scenes at this temple group include the history of the Pandavas, the ascetic Arjun and his family, and particularly the context of Ganga Devi Avataran (Ganga's coming to Earth).

In the Ganga Avataran rock cut art, the penance of King Bhagiratha and the arrival of Ganga Devi on earth are depicted alive. Ganesha, Vishnu, Narasimha, Mahishasura-mardini, Uma-Mahesh, Lakshmi, etc. are the deities carved in this temple group.

117. Pandava Dynasty (Ancient Time)

For the Earlier Dynasty, please see :
Ajmidh Dynasty (Ancient Time)
1. Vichitravirya विचित्रवीर्य
2. Pandu पांडु
3. Yudhishthir युधिष्ठिर

For Next Dynasty, please see :
Yudhishthir Dynasty (Ancient Time)

Pandava Dynasty

In the Pandava Dynasty,
was born Kuru, the virtuous,
Kuru's grandson Shantanu,
all were kings righteous. 1
Shantanu had three sons,
all three were dignified,
Vichitravirya was king,
Bhishma and Vyasa glorified. 2
Vichitravirya had three sons,
Pandu was polite,
Dhritarashtra devious,
and Vidura erudite. 3
Dhritarashtra was blind,
Vidura was illegitimate,
Thus, Pandu became
king, as was their fate. 4
Shursen's daughter Kunti,
from Mathura Royal House,
Sister of Vasudeva,
she was Pandu's spouse. 5
Madri was the second wife,
and Pandu's mate,
Pandu had five sons,
all were brave and great. 6
Kunti had three sons,
Yudhishthir Bhim Arjun brave,
Madri had two sons,
twins Nakul and Sahadev. 7

Pandava Dynasty

Kunti, the sister of Vasudeva of the Vrishni clan, was the wife of Pandu, the son of king Vichitravirya and his wife Ambalika. Kunti had three sons, Yudhishthir, Bhima and Arjun. Madri, the second wife of King Pandu, the daughter of the King of Madra (Maha. etc. 67.111), was mother of twin sons Nakul and Sahadeva. In childhood, Nakul and Sahadev learned archery from Shuk Muni. Pandu's son Yudhishthir was the eldest of the 105 Kaurava-Pandava brothers. Thus, Dhritarashtra made Yudhishthir the crown prince. In Mahabharata, Yudhishthir is glorified with names such as Ajmiadh, Ajatashatru, Bharat, Bharat Shardul, Bharatarshabh, Bharatsattam, Dharma, Dharmaraja, Dharmaputra, Pandava, Parth, etc. Yudhishthir's conch was named Panchajanya (Gita 1.5).

Bhima was a mightiest person (Maha. Udyog. 50). In the Mahabharat, Bhim is known as Kanteya, Kaurava, Kushsardul, Maruti, Pandava, Partha, Pavanatmaj, Vayuputra, Vayusut, etc. The name of Bhima's great shankha was Poundra (Gita 1.5).

Arjun was the best archer among the men. Arjuna's divine conch was named Devadatta (Gita 1.5). In Mahabharata, Sanjay had warned Dhritarashtra to refrain from war, as the victory is certain where Shri Krishna and Ajun are (Gita 18.72), yet Dhritarashtra stayed in favor of war. In Mahabharata, Arjuna is called Andri, Bharat, Dhananjaya, Gandivadhanva, Gudakesh, Jishnu, Kapidhwaja, Kaunteya, Kaurava, Kaurvasrestha, Kiriti, Kuntiputra, Pandava, Parth, Paurava, Falgun, Savyasachi, Vijay, etc.

At the time of the Great War of Mahabharata

1. There were 34 allied Kingdoms on the side of the Pandavas: -

Panchal, Chedi, Kashi, Karusha, Matsya, Kekaya, Kosal, Srnjaya, Daksharna, Somak, Kunti, Anapt, Shibi, Dasherak, Prabhadraka, Anupak, Kirat, Patcchar, Tittira, Chola, Pandya, Agniveshya, Hunda, Danabhari, Shabar, Udbhasa, Vatsa, Paundra, Paundra, Kundavish, Marut, Dhenuka, Teganna and Parathaganna.

The allied Warriors on the side of the Pandavas :

Bhima, Nakula, Sahadeva, Arjuna, Yudhishtar, the five sons of Draupadi, Satyaki, Uttamauja, Virat, Drupada, Dhrishtadyumna, Abhimanyu, Kashi-raj, Shikhandi, Yuyudhan, Dhritketu, Chekitan, Purujita, Yudhamanyu, Pandya-Raj, Ghatotkach, Shikhandi, Yuyutsu, Uttamauja, Shaibya and Anup-raj Neel.1.

2. There were 38 allied Kingdoms on the side of the Kauravas: -

Gandhar, Madra, Sindh, Kamboj, Kalinga, Sinhal, Darad, Abhishah, Magadha, Pishash, Pratichya, Bahlik, Udichya, Ansh, Pallava, Saurashtra, Avanti, Nishad, Shursen, Vasati, Paurava, Tushar, Chuchupadesh, Ashwak, Pulind, Parad, Kshudrak, Pragjyotisha, Mekal, Kuruvind, Tripur, Shal, Ambastha, Kaitava, Yavana, Trigarta, Sauvira and Prachya.

The allied Warriors on the side of the Kauravas :

Bhishma, Dronacharya, Kripacharya, Karna, Ashwatthama, Vikarna, Saumadatta, Madra-naresh Shalya, Bhurishrava, Alambush, Krittavarma, Kalinga-raja, Shrutayudha, Shakuni, Bhagadatta, Jayadratha, Vind-Anuvind, Kamboja-raja, Sudakshin, Brihadvala, Duryodhana, Brihadala and Duryodhana's 99 brothers.

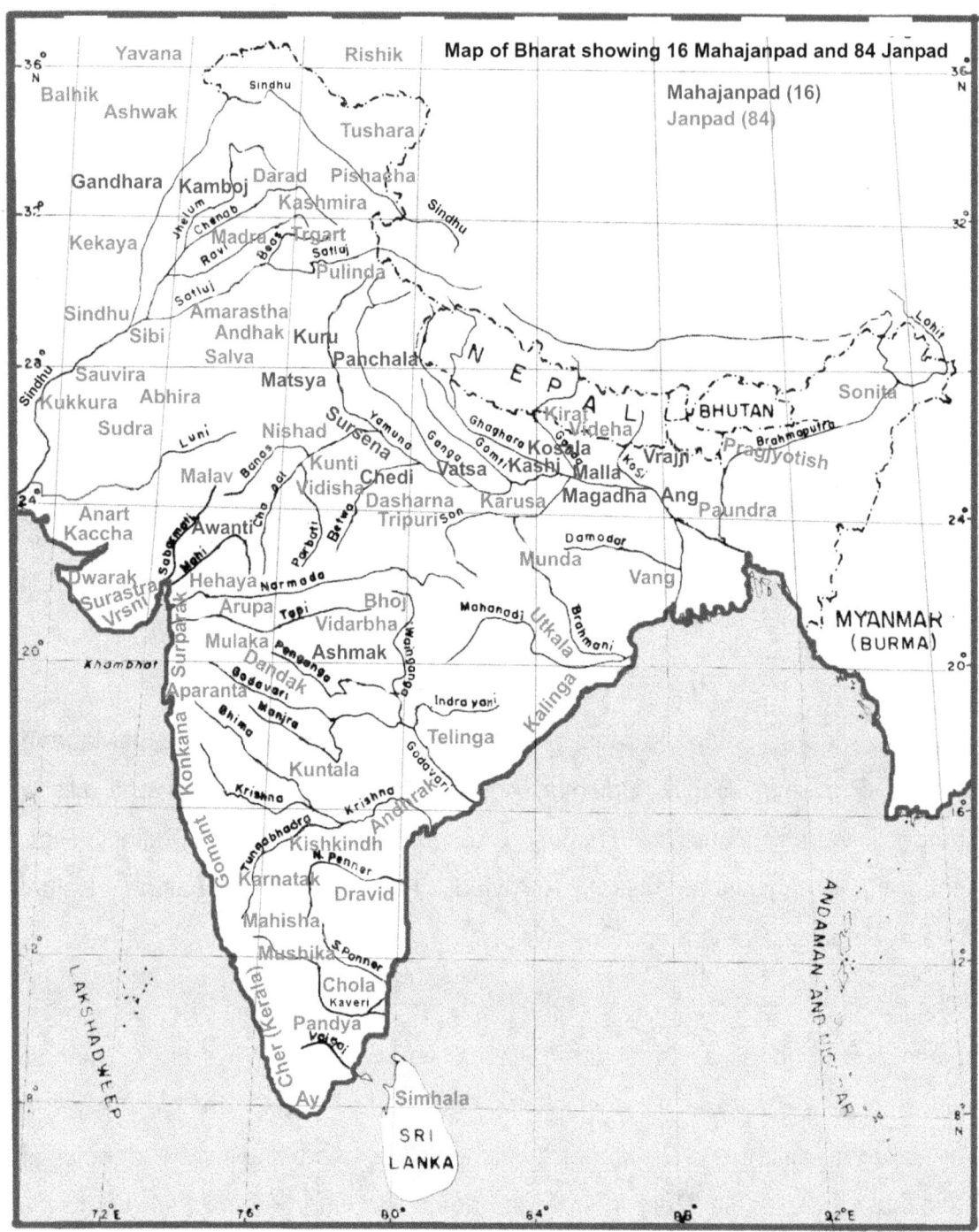

118. Pandya Dynasty, Madura (50-1422)

For the Earlier Dynasty, please see :
Satvahan Dynasty, Pratisthan (271–195 BC)

#	Name	Devanagari	Period
1.	Nedunjalaiyan-1	नेडुंजलैयन-1	...
2.	Verivarshelaiyan	वेरीवरशेलैयन	75-
3.	Nedunjalaiyan-2	नेडुंजलैयन-2	
4.	Ugraperu Veladi	उग्रपेरु वेलाडी	150-
5.	Varaguna-1	वरगुण-1	...
6.	Kadungona	कदुंगोन	590-620
7.	Mara Varma-1	मारवर्माअवनिशूलमणि	620-645
8.	Jayanti Varma	जयंतीवर्मा	645-670
9.	Maravarma-2	मारवर्मा अरिकेसरी	670-700
10.	Kochchhalaiyan	कोच्छलैयन रणधीर	700-730
11.	Maravarma-3	मारवर्मा राजसिंह-1	730-775
12.	Nedunjalaiyan-2	नेडुंजलैयन-2	775-815
13.	Shrimar Shrivallabh	श्रीमार श्रीवल्लभ	815-862
14.	Varaguna-2	वरगुण-2	862-880
15.	Parantak Viranarayan	वीरनारायण	880-900
16.	Maravarma-4	मारवर्मा राजसिंह-2	900-920
...	Under Chola Rule		920-1190
17.	Jatavarma-1	जटावर्मा कुलशेखर	1190-1216
18.	Maravarma-5	मारवर्मा सुंदर-1	1216-1238
19.	Maravarma-6	मारवर्मा सुंदर-2	1238-1251
20.	Jatavarma-2	जटावर्मा सुंदर	1251-1253
21.	Jatavarma-3	जटावर्मा वीर पांड्या	1253-1275
22.	Maravarma-7	मारवर्मा कुलशेखर	1275-1310
...			
23.	Jatavarma-4	जटावर्मा पराक्रम	1422-1429
24.	Jatavarma-5	जटावर्मा कुलशेखर	1429-1473

Pandya Dynasty

Dravid-vansi Pandya Royal House is famous since the time of Panini. The kingdom of this Dynasty has been in Madura, Tirunelveli and Tiruchirapalli from time to time. The mention of this Dynasty is found in the inscriptions of Ashok Maurya (269–232 BC) and in the Katyayana writings.

The history of the Pandya Royal Family is well known from the time of Marvarma Arikesari Varma (670–700). During the period of Nedunjalayan-2 (775–815), the kingdom of Pandya expanded from Malabar in the South of the Kaveri River to Tanjavar, Tiruchirapalli, Salem, Koimbtur and South Travankor. There was richness of poetry and craftsmanship in the Pandya kingdom. This kingdom was famous for pearls. King Shrimar Shrivallabh (815-862) had authority from the South of the Krishna river to North Shri Lanka.

The great Pandya king Marvarma Kulasekhar (1275–1310) made the Chola king Udaya Martand Rajendra (1246–1279) of Tanjavar his feudatory.

25. Perumal Parakram	पेरुमाल पराक्रम	1473–1479
26. Kulashekhardeva	कुलशेखरदेव	1479–1534
27. Jatavarma-6	जटावर्मा श्रीवल्लभ	1534–1543
28. Parakram Kulashekhar	पराक्रम	1543–1552
29. Nelvelli Maran	नेल्वेली मारन्	1552–1564
30. Jatavarma-7	जटावर्मा अतिवीरराम	1564–1604
31. Varattunga	वरतुंग	1604–1612
32. Varagunaram	वरगुणराम	1612–1618

Pandya Dynasty

This famous kingdom of South India was beyond the vast empire of Ashok Maurya (269-232 BC), and the mention of Pandya kingdom is found in the inscriptions of Ashok. Also, there is mention of Pandya power in the Raghuvamsha, the epic of Mahakavi Kalidasa.

King Marvarma Sundar Pandya-2 (1238–1251) defeated Chola Rajaraja-3 (1216–1246) and annexed the territories near Tiruchirapalli and Pudukottai.

The Pandya kingdom had conquered many territories of the Kakatiya kingdom (1000–1323) and the Hoysala kingdom (1026–1348).

Like many other Indian kings, the Pandya king of Madurai was also a lover and patron of art and Vaidic scripture. The great and unique Meenakshi Temple and the Divine Shrirangam Temple of Madurai are the contributions of the Pandya kings.

The Pandya kings have a special place in Indian craftsmanship in their divine temples and cave crafts and mural paintings.

Pandya Dynasty

Great Pandya kings,
of the Dynasty of the South.
Were surrounded by enemies,
to choke their mouth. 1
Cholas were their rivals,
supremacy was their goal,
There were always clashes,
between Pandya and the Chol. 2
Pandyas built Meenakshi,
the greatest temple of all,
They also built Shrirangam,
the golden temple tall.

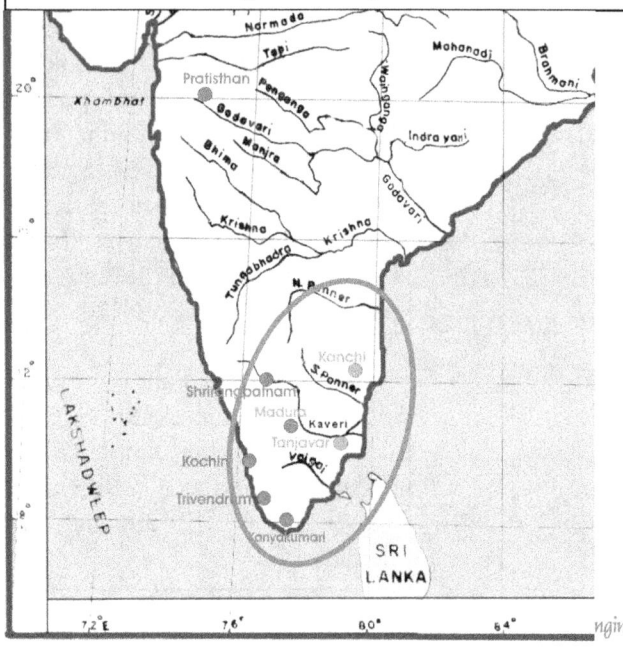

119. Parivrajak Dynasty, Bagelkhand (400-528)

For the Earlier Dynasty, please see :
Gupta Dynasty (240-730)

1. Susharma — सुशर्मा — 400–
2. Devadhya — देवाढ्य
3. Prabhanjan — प्रभंजन
4. Damodar — दामोदर
5. Hasti — हस्ती — 475–518
6. Sankshobha — संक्षोभ — 518–528

For the Next Dynasty, please see :
Pushyabhuti Dynasty (500-647)

Parivrajak Dynasty

Parivrajak kings ruled, during the Gupta time,
Six kings of this family, are know to be prime. 1

Out of these six kings, all were great,
They were charitable,
the history records indicate. 2

They were Shiva devotees,
Bharadvaj was the lineage,
Devotion to Lord Shiva, was their heritage. 3

Maharaja Hasti ruled, for forty years,
Many invasions came,
he faced all without fears. 4

The downfall of the Guptas, gave end to them,
Pushyabhutis became kings,
Parivrajaks lost the fame. 5

Parivrajak Dynasty

The Parivrajak Dynasty of central India was a neighbor of Baghelkhand's Ucchakalp Royal House on its West side. Like the Ucchakalp rulers, the kings of the Parivrajak Dynasty were feudal kings under the Gupta Emperors.

The greatest two kings of this Dynasty were Maharaja Hasti (475–518) and Maharaja Shankshobh (518–528). During the 42-year-long reign of King Hasti, there was a family change in the Gupta Empire (original 240–530) (Later 530–730).

Parivrajak Kings were Shiva devotees. All the kings of this clan were charitable. Along with the original Gupta Empire (290–530), the Parivrajak Dynasty was also extinguished and in their place Pushyabhutis became the kings.

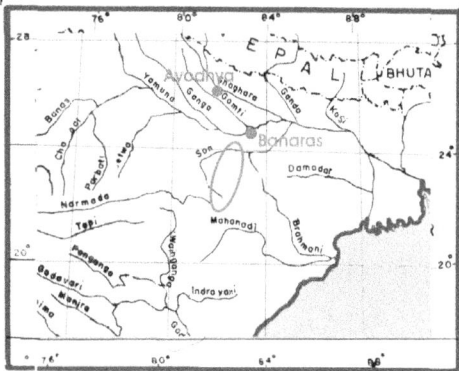

120. Parmar Dynasty, Dhar, Malwa (800-1305)

For the Earlier Dynasty, please see :
Rashtrakut Dynasty, Malkhed (620–973)

1. Upendraraj — उपेंद्रराज (कृष्णराज) — 800–818
2. Vairi Simha-1 — वैरीसिंह-1 — 818–843
3. Siyak-1 — सीयक -1 — 843–893
4. Vakpatiraj — वाक्पतिराज — 893–918
5. Vairi Simha-2 — वैरीसिंह-2 — 918–948
6. Siyak-2, Harsha — सीयक-2 हर्ष — 948–972
7. Vakpatiraj-2, Munja — वाक्पतिराज-2 मुंज — 972–995
8. Sindhuraj — सिंधुराज — 995–1010
9. **Bhoja Deva-1** — भोजदेव-1, राजा भोज — 1010–1055
10. Jai Simha-1 — जयसिंह-1 — 1055–1059
11. Udayaditya — उदयादित्य — 1059–1087
12. Lakshman Deva — लक्ष्मणदेव — 1087–1097
13. Nara Varma — नरवर्मा — 1097–1134
14. Yashovarma — यशोवर्मा — 1134–1135
15. Jai Varma-1 — जयवर्मा-1 — 1135–1138
16. Ajay Varma — अजयवर्मा — 1138–1143
17. Vindhya Varma — विंध्यवर्मा — 1143–1178
18. Subhatavarma — सुभटवर्मा — 1178–1200
19. Arjun Varma — अर्जुनवर्मा-1 — 1200–1218
20. Devapal — देवपाल — 1218–1236
21. Jaitug Deva — जैतुगदेव — 1236–1255
22. Jai Varma-2 — जयवर्मा-2 — 1255–1265
23. Jai Simha-2 — जयसिंह-2 — 1265–1270
24. Arjun Varma-2 — अर्जुनवर्मा-2 — 1270–1285
25. Bhoja Deva-2 — भोज देव-2 — 1285–1300
26. Mahalak Deva — महलकदेव — 1300–1305

Parmar Dynasty

This is one of the best Agnivamshi Dynasty of Indian history which ruled Ujjain city of Malwa by making it the capital. The first king of this Dynasty was Upendraraj or Utpalraj Krishnaraja (800-818). Earlier, the kings of this Dynasty were feudatories of the Rashtrakutas of Malkhed (620–973).

At the time of the decline of the Rashtrakutas, King Vakpati Munja (972-995) declared independence. King Munja was a very knowledgeable and brave man. He had managed the kingdom very well.

King Bhoj (1010-1055), the nephew of King Vakpatiraja Munja, was the most powerful and effective ruler of the Parmar Dynasty. He was considered to be the best pundit and the patron of art literature among the medieval rulers.

The Parmar Rajputs of Malwa were relatives of the Parmar royal family of Abu, whose capital was Chandravati. Some other families of Parmars were Parmar of Jalore, Parmar of Kiradu, Parmar of Danta, Parmar of Sirohi, etc.

The Great Raja Bhoj of Malwa (1010-1055)

The most learned, philanthropic, holy, heroic and great king of the Paramara royalty of Malwa was Tribhuvana Narayana Bhoja or Raja Bhoja (1010-1055). He was the son of Raja Sindhu Raj (995-1010), the younger brother of Vakpati Raja Munja (972-995). After the coronation, Raja Bhoj shifted his capital South from Ujjain to the city of Dhar. Raj Bhoj had expanded his power by subduing the kings of Chittor, Bundelkhand, Baghelkhand and Khandesh, Konkan etc. of the south.

Raja Bhoj was constantly busy in wars, yet he was a lover of learning and poetry. He himself was a high-quality poet lauret and the supporter of arts. There was no other Sanskrit poet and virtuous king in the Indian history. He was also a great builder of temples and sculptures.

Maharani Lilavati, wife of Raja Bhoj, was also an eminent scholar like her husband. In the court of Raja Bhoj, the great poet-scholars such as Sri Vallabh, Merutung, Varruchi, Subandhu, Rajashekhar, Magha, Dhanapala, Manatung, Padmagupta, Bhattagovind, Vidyapati Bhaskar, etc. had place of honor. The great texts written by Raja Bhoja himself include Saraswati Kanthabharana, Rajamriganka, Vidvajjanamandal, Samaranga Sutradhara, Shringar Manjusha, Kurmashtak, Prashnajnana, Rajamandand, Adityapratapasiddhanta, Vyavaharasamapuchya, Charuacharya, Muktikalapataru, Vishranta-vidya-vinod, Champu Ramayana, Shalihotra, Shabdanushasan, Siddhanta Samgraha, Subhashita Prabandha, etc. 84 books were composed by Raja Bhoj.

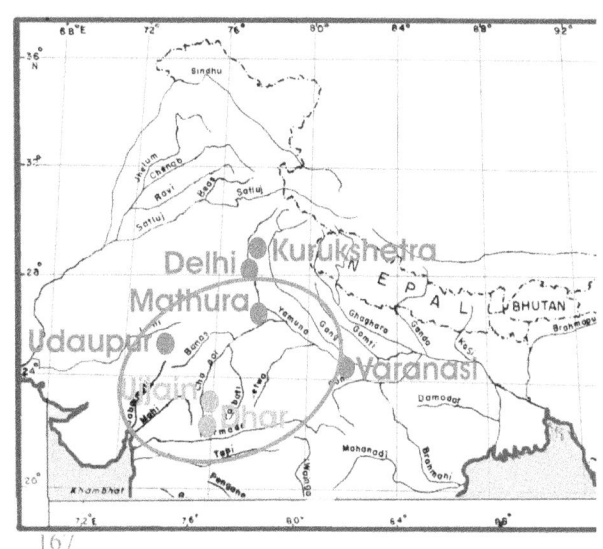

Tribute to Raja Bhoj

*With the death of King Bhoj,
today the earth is aloof,
The Goddess Sarasvati has lost, her
super intelligent child!*

In other words)
*With the departure of King Bhoj,
today the earth is helpless,
The Pundits are orphaned,
the Goddess of Learning is sorry!*

Hindu Rajtarangini

121. Peshva Dynasty, Maharashtra (1713-1818)

For the Earlier Dynasty, please see :
Bhosle Dynasty, Satara (1689–1848)

#	Name	Marathi	Years
1.	Sonopant	सोनोपंत विश्वनाथ बहुलकर	1638–1640
2.	Shyamrao	शामराव निळकंठ रांझेकर	1640–1661
3.	Narhari	नरहरी आनंदराव	1661–1662
4.	Moropant	मोरोपंत त्र्यंबक पिंगळे	1662–1681
5.	Nilopant	निळोपंत मोरेश्वर पिंगळे	1681–1707
6.	Bahirji	बहिरजीपंत मोरेश्वर पिंगळे	1707–1713
7.	Balaji Vishvanath	बाळाजी विश्वनाथ	1713–1720
8.	Bajirao-1	बाजीराव-1, विश्वास बल्लाळ	1720–1740
9.	Babuji Naik	बाबूजी नाईक जोशी	1740–1740
10.	Nanasaheb	बाळाजी बाजीराव, नानासाहेब	1740–1761
11.	Madhavarao	माधवराव बल्लाळ	1761–1772
12.	Narayanrao	नारायणराव बल्लाळ	1772–1773
13.	Raghoba	राघोबादादा बाजीराव बल्लाळ	1773–1774
14.	Savai Madhavrao	सवाई माधवराव	1774–1795
15.	Bajirao-2	बाजीराव रघुनाथ बल्लाळ	1795–1818
16.	Govind Bajirao	गोविंद बाजीराव	1851–1857

Peshwa Dynasty

The Prime Minister was called "Peshwe" in the Cabinet of the Maratha Empire. He was the representative of the king in kingdom affairs. This practice started in the era of Shahaji Raje (1594-1664) when Shivaji (1630-1680) got the jagir of Pune in 1640. During the reign of King Shahu-1 Shivaji (1708–1749) of Satara, Balaji Vishwanath Ballal Bhat (1662–1720) became Peshwa (1713–1720) and from 1714 he based his government in Pune and took over the reins of the Maratha Empire. By 1759, the heroic Peshwas had extended the Maratha empire from Tanjavar-Cuttack to Attock.

The House of Peshwa

Peshwa is the Prime Minister,
in the cabinet of eight,
He represents the King,
he is the warrior great. 1
From Tanjavar to Attock,
the saffron flag was raised,
The soldiers fought well,
everywhere they were praised. 2
He who never lost a battle,
Bajirao is his name,
He is the greatest Peshwa,
he gave the Marathas fame. 3

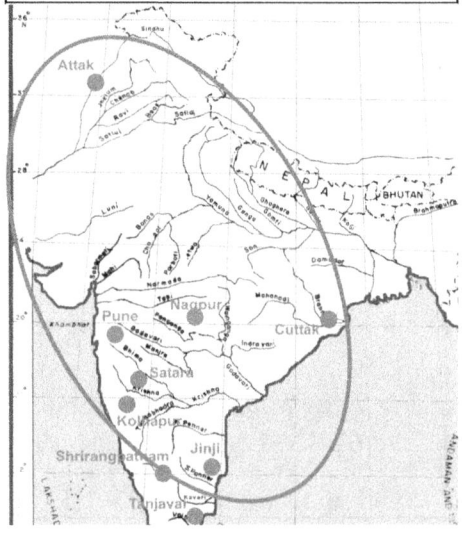

Brave Bajirao Peshwa (1720-1740)

Bajirao Peshwa (1720-1740), the mighty son of Peshwa Balaji Vishwanath Ballal (1713-1720), was a great war-skilled hero. From childhood, he learned polity, diplomacy, skillful swordsmanship and horse riding by going on campaigns along with his father. Like Chhatrapati Shivaji Maharaj (1630–1680), Bajirao was so busy whole life in battles that he had no luxury of rest.

Seeing this allegiance, determination and fighting prowess of Bajirao, Maharaja Sahu Bhosle of Satara (Shivaji Bhosle 1708-1749) selected Bajirao for the post of Peshwa in 1720 and provided him with the Royal Garments. The fate of Maharashtra immediately shone with this selection. The goal of Hindu-padapada-shahi, established by Chhatrapati Shivaji Maharaj, began to move forward at a fast pace. However, this selection was retaliated by Kanhoji Bhosle (1709-1731) of Nagpur and after that Raghuji Bhosle (1731-1755) was expressing unhappiness. In 1730–31, Bajirao built the magnificent Shaniwar Wada Rajmahal in Pune and made it the residence and center of the capital. Seeing the war fame and national love of Bajirao, King Ranoji Scindia (1716-1745) of Gwalior, Malharrao Holkar (1693-1766) of Indore and King Damajirao Gayakwad of Baroda (1720-1721), Pilajirao Gayakwad (1721-1732) and Damajirao -2 (1732-1767), etc., all found the excitement of making Hindu Nation, a reality again. As a result, the influence of the Marathas spread to Malwa, Bundelkhand, Rajputana, and other regions.

Bajirao was married in 1713 to Kashibai, the daughter of Mahadji Joshi of Chas village. Kashibai died in 1758 after Bajirao's death (1740).

बाजीराव पेशवा

शिवाजी रूप ये बाजी, मराठों की गरिमा है ।
मराठा पेशवा बाजी, शिवाजी की प्रतिमा है ॥

जहाँ में वीर ये ऐसा, युगों में एक आता है ।
कभी ना युद्ध जो हारा, विजय ही जिसकी सीमा है ॥
बचाने हिंदूभूमि को, लगाई जान की बाज़ी ।
जिसे ना डर है मरने का, उसे लोहे का सीना है ॥
हमारी हिंदूभूमि का, पियारा पुत्र है बाजी ।
भवानी! स्वर्ग दो उसको, हमारी ये तमन्ना है ॥
कहो जय! शूर बाजी की, कहो जय! उस भवानी की ।
दिया आशीष है जिसने, उसी की ये महिमा है ॥

Bajirao Peshwa
*Bajirao is an image of Shivaji,
he is the honor of Marathas.
In the world such hero comes only once,
He who never lost battle,
victory is his only chance.
To save the Hindu land,
he put his life on the line,
He is not afraid of death,
for him everything is fine,
He is the dear child of Hindu Land,
O Lord! Please give him heaven,
We pray with our folded hands.
Say, Victory to Baji! Say,
hail Bhavani Goddess!
She is blessing us, it is her greatness.*

https://www.facebook.com/photo?fbid=10222742906628780&set=gm.1501189950076038

122. Phillipine, Hindu Dynasties (50-1828)

Hindu Dynasties of the Philippine

Hinduism in Philippine came from the Ramayana stories of Java when Nepal, Bhutan and Burma were the kingdoms of India. People used to travel to Thailand, Bali regions for seven hundred centuries and used to travel to . It is also said that the movement of Shaivite-Vaishnav people from Odisha was also considerable.

Along with this, it is also known that Tamil Chakravarti Emperor Rajendra Chola (1014-1044) had an equally important contribution in bringing Hindu culture to this region. Due to these travel activities, the royal family of Bhutan originated from the descendants of the Khmer Empire of the island of Chebu, Philippine.

The names of some descendants of Bhutan were King **Shri Lume, King Shri Alho, King Shri Bantung, King Shri Lamrao, King Shri Ukbo**, etc.

Philippine is not just a single island but a country of about seven-thousand islands of which economic and intellectual trade was unbreakable with Vietnam.

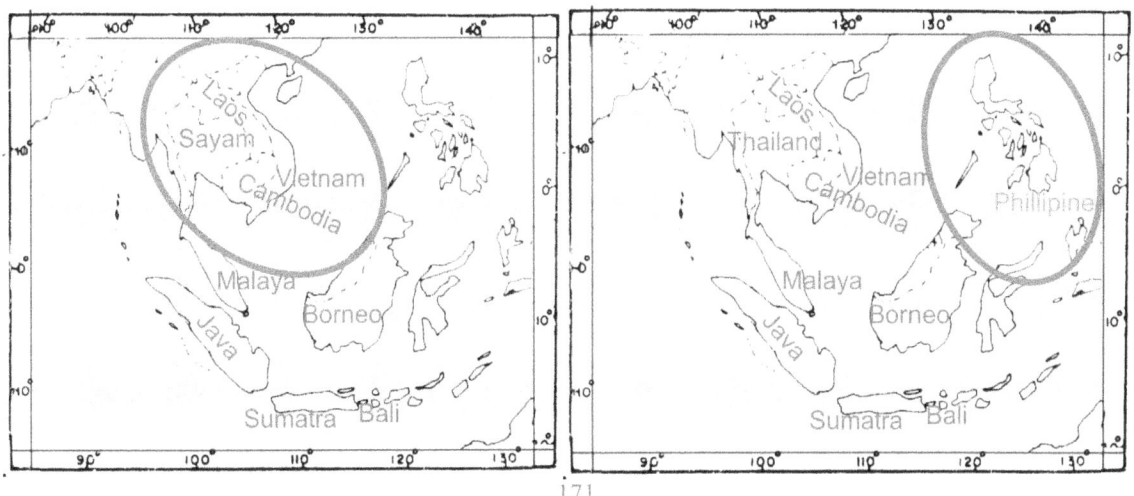

123. Pradyot Dynasty, Ujjain (546-413 BC)

1. Pradyot   प्रद्योत   546 BC. ...
2. Gpoal   गोपाल
3. Palak   पालक
4. Aryak   आर्यक
5. Nandi vardhan   नंदिवर्धन   413 BC.

For the Next Dynasty, please see :
Shishunag Dynasty (413–344 BC)

> **Pradyot Dynasty**
> *A great warrior was Pradyot,*
> *the Avanti monarch,*
> *His kingdom had glory,*
> *other kingdoms could not match. 1*
> *King Pradyot belonged to,*
> *the Hehaya Dynasty,*
> *Of Western India, the Yadava variety. 2*

Pradyot Dynasty

King Pradyot was the victor of the Avanti (Ujjain) and Mahismati. The capital of North Avanti was Ujjayini and the capital of South Avanti was Mahismati. Maharaja Pradyot was the honorable and foremost among the Northern kings. During his rule, the prosperity of Avanti was at its peak.

Matrimonial relationship of this Dynasty was with the Yadava royal family of Mathura, therefore the prince of Mathura was named Avantiputra. Pradyot King had strengthened his royal relationship by marrying his daughter Vasavadatta to Vatsa prince Udman.

In year 413, the powerful king of Pataliputra Magadha, Shishunag (413- 344 BC), defeated the last king of Pradyot Dynasty, Nandi Vardhana, and ended the Pradyot royal family. He merged the North and South Avanti into the kingdom of Magadha.

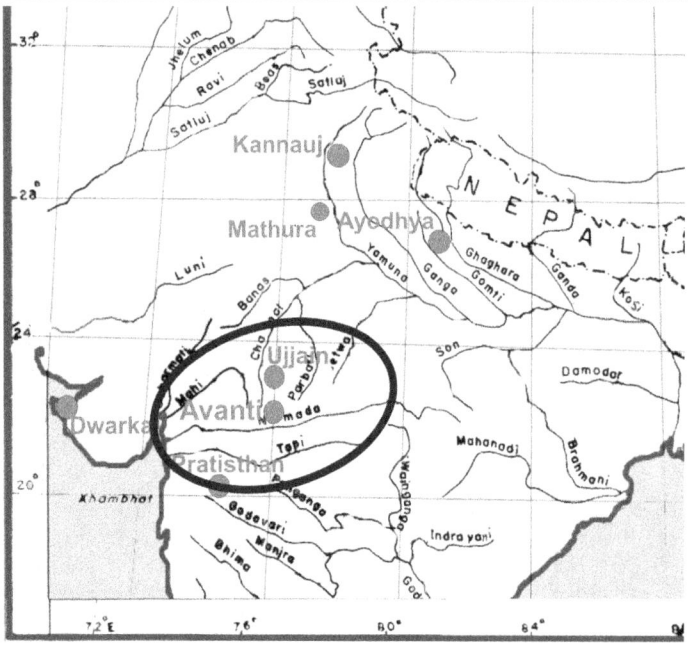

Hindu Rajtarangini

124. Pratapaditya Dynasty, Kashmir (167 BC-25 AD)

For the Earlier Dynasty, please see :
Gonaditya Dynasty, Kashmir (1182 BC–631 AD)

1. Pratapaditya-1　प्रतापादित्य-1　167–135 BC.
2. Jaluk　जलूक　135–103 BC
3. Tungajin　तुंगजीन　103–67 BC
4. Vijay　विजय　67–59 BC
5. Jayendra　जयेन्द्र　59–22 BC
6. Sandhimati　संधिमति　22BC–25 AD.

For the Next Dynasty, please see :
Gonaditya Dynasty, Kashmir (1182BC – 631AD)

Pratapaditya Dynasty
During the period of Gonaditya Dynasty of Shrinagar (1182-631 BC) Kashmir was ruled from year 212 to 167 by the Mauryas and then by the Sunga kings. from BC 167 to 25 AD, the power of the Pratapaditya Dynasty ruled over Kashmir (167 BC-25 AD) and then the Gonaditya Dynasty continued again to rule until year 631 AD.

125. Pravargupta Dynasty, Kashmir (949-1003)

For the Earlier Dynasty, please see :
Utpal Dynasty, Kashmir (855–949)

1. Pravaragupta　प्रवरगुप्त　949–950
2. Kshemagupta　क्षेमगुप्त　950–958
3. Abhimanyu　अभिमन्यु　958–972
4. Nandigupta　नन्दीगुप्त　972–973
5. Tribhuvangupta　त्रिभुवनगुप्त　973–975
6. Bhimagupta　भीमगुप्त　975–980
7. Queen Didda　रानी दिद्दा　980–1003

For the Next Dynasty, please see :
Lohar Dynasty, Kashmir (1003–1172)

Pravargupta Dynasty
Pravargupta, the secretary of the last king Sangramdev (948-949) of the Utpal Dynasty of Shrinagar (855-949), killed King Sangramdev and became the founder of the Pravargupta Dynasty and the ruler of Kashmir.

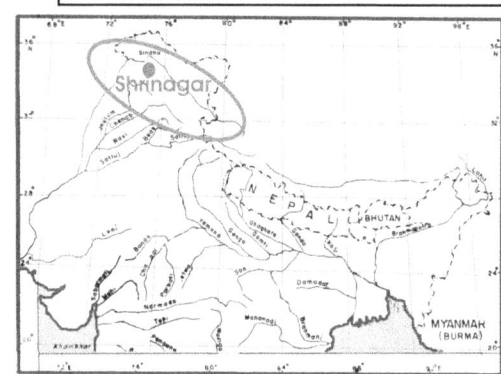

Hindu Rajtarangini

126. Pratihar-Gurjar Dynasty, Kannauj (725-1036)

For the Earlier Dynasty, please see :
Gurjar Dybasty (400–725)

1. Harishchandra हरिश्चंद्र –725
2. Nagbhatta-1 नागभट्ट–1 725–760
3. Devashakti देवशक्ति 760–783
4. Vatsaraj वत्सराज 783–815
5. Nagbhatta-2 नागभट्ट–2 815–833
6. Ramabhadra रामभद्र 833–843
7. Mihira Bhoja मिहिर भोज 843–893
8. Mahendrapal महेंद्रपाल 893–914
9. Mahipal महीपाल 914–948
10. Devpal देवपाल 948–960
11. Vijaypal विजयपाल 960–1018
12. Rajyapal राज्यपाल 1018–1019
13. Trilochanpal त्रिलोचनपाल 1019–1030
14. Yashpal यशपाल 1030–1036

For the Next Dynasty, please see :
Chauhan Dynasty, Sakambhari (684–1192)

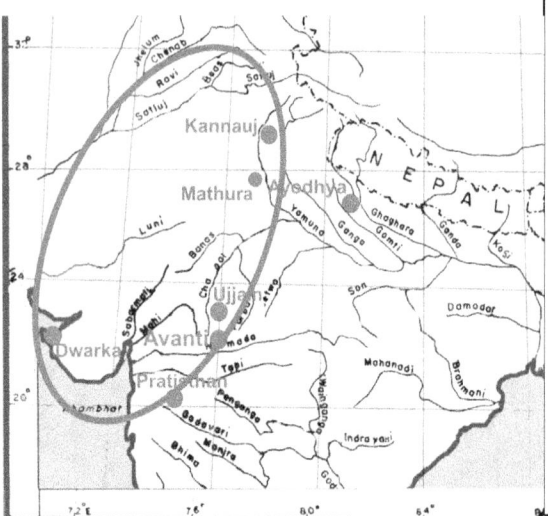

Pratihara-Gurjar Dynasty, Kannauj

The Gurjar-Pratihara Dynasty was founded by a king named Harishchandra in Bhinmal, Rajasthan, and he made Gujarat-Rajasthan became a dominant kingdom. King Nagabhatta-1 (725-760), a descendant of the same Dynasty established the Pratihara branch. The glorious Nagabhatta had stopped the Arab invaders and empowered Gujjar-Pratihar army to protect lands from Bharuch harbor to Gwalior, Mandore, Malwa. After this massive victory, the Pratiharas established their capital in Avanti (Ujjain).

During the time of Pratihara king Vatsaraja (783-815), when Rashtrakuta ruler Dhruvaraya (774-793) of Malkhed attacked Kannauj, Vatsaraja had to retreat to Bhinmal in Rajasthan. Some time later, King Vatsaraja, Nagabhatta-2 (815-833) conquered Kannauj from Rashtrakuta king Govindarai-3 (773-814) and established Kannauj, the capital of the Pratiharas. To commemoate this great victory, Nagabhatta-2 once again renovated the Shiva temple of Somnath. During the long reign of King Mihira Bhoja (843-893), the Pratihara Empire was at the height of prosperity. After Mihira Bhoja, King Mahendrapal (893-914), gave patronage to literature and arts. Image of Varaha (Boar) Avatar was inscribed on the coins of Pratiharas.

Hindu Rajtarangini

127. Pudukottai Dynasty, Tamil Nadu (1673-1948)

For the Earlier Dynasty, please see :
Chola Dynasty, Tanjavar (50–1279)

1. Raghunath Kilavan सेतुपति रघुनाथ   1673–1708
2. Vijay Raghunath   सेतुपति विजय रघुनाथ 1825–

Pudukottai Dynasty

The realm between Chola and Pandya,
is Pudukottai domain,
Its king Ramnad, was the actor main. 1
The kings of this House,
were known traitors,
Treachery was in their blood,
and patriotism haters. 2

Pudukottai Dynasty

The Pudukottai Royal House or the Setupati Dynasty is counted among the five major Dynasties of Tamil country. The history of the Pudukottai kingdom located between Tiruchirapalli and Tanjavar is well known. They had the Chola Empire (50-1279) in the North and Pandya Empire (50-1463) in the south.

In the seventeenth century, King Sethupathi Raghunath Keelavan of Ramnad (1673–1708) took possession of the Pudukottai region. The kingdom was modernized by King Vijay Raghunath Sethupathi in 1825.

Just as the traitor king of Kannauj, Jaichand Rathor (1170–1194) conspired with Ghori and Kachhwaha Kings Man Singh (1589–1614) and Mirza Jai Singh (1621–1666) of Jaipur became the slaves of the Mughals and played the role of scum, similarly the kings of the Setupati family intrigued with the foreigners and tarnished their faces in history of India with the sins of greed and treason.

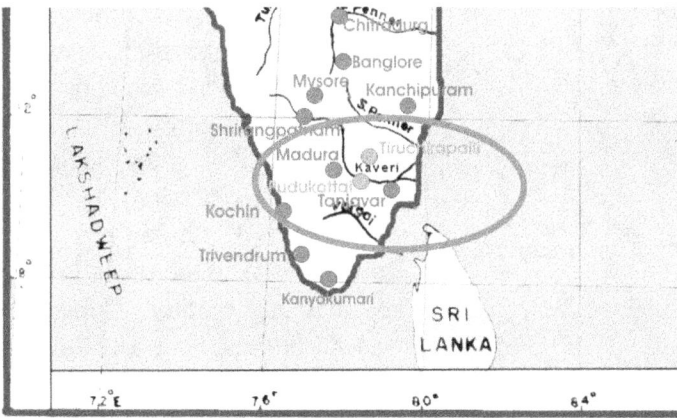

Hindu Rajtarangini

128. Pulastya Dynasty, Shri Lanka (Ancient Time)

1. Brahma — ब्रह्मा
2. Pulastya — पुलस्त्य
3. Vishrava — विश्रवा
4. Kuber — कुबेर
5. Ravan — रावण
6. Vibhishan — विभीषण

Vibhishana said to Ravan
Wise Vibhishana was, a brother of Ravan,
Vibhishana asked Ravan,
why do you do sins often. 1
You stole Sita, Shri Rama's holy wife,
You burnt Hanumana's tail,
you will repent for life. 2
Shri Rama is warrior, to him you are no match,
Hanumana got escaped, but you couldn't catch. 3
Go to Shri Rama, and his wife you give,
Shri Rama is kind, he will sure forgive. 4

Pulastya Dynasty

Prajapati Pulastya, the Vipriyogi was born from the ear of Brahma (Maha. Adi. 65). Pulastya's first wife Kaikashi had three sons : Ravan, Kumbhakarna and Vibhishana and a daughter Shurpanakha.

Pulastya's second wife Devavarnini or Ialabila's son was Kubera i.e. Vaishravan. Kubera had built his capital Lanka out of gold and he had a Pushpak aircraft which both were snatched by Ravan by force.

Ravan's wife Mandodari Devi had three sons: Indrajit i.e. Meghnad, Atikay and Akshkumar. Ravan's influence was wide spread from Shri Lanka to Dandakaranya. Kumbhakarna's wife Vajramala had two sons, Kumbh and Nikumbh. Vibhishan's wife Sarma Devi had seven sons.

Indrajit died before his father Ravan, therefore, after the death of Ravan, Vibhishan became the King of Lanka. Mayavi Ravan was as much unrighteous as much his brother Vibhishan was an ethical, and a religious man.

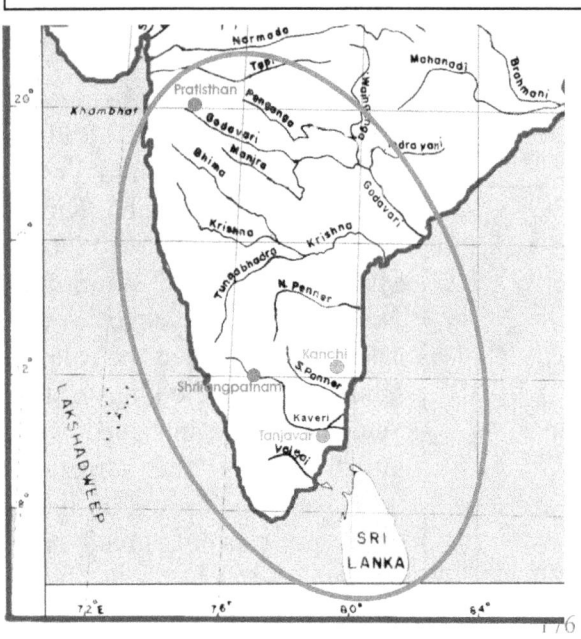

Ravan, King of Lanka

Ignorant and Wise Ravan

Ravan was well known,
Shiva's devotee great,
He did severe penance,
and got boons secret. 1
He got strength,
and wealth like a shower,
Immortality he received,
and magic power. 2
With these secret boons,
he became proud,
Womanizing cruel thug,
and became a maraud. 3
He snatched from Kubera,
Shri Lanka of Gold,
The Pushpak Airplane,
and he became bold. 4
He kidnapped Sita,
and killed Jatayu Bird,
Maricha got killed,
the demonic nerd. 5
He killed Anaranya,
with torture severe,
He molested Rambha,
wife of Nalkubar. 6
He abducted Devavati,
Kushadhvaja's daughter,
Ritusharma's wife,
Madanamanjiri fair. 7
He kidnapped Anasuya,
without acumen,
Svaha Devi and Pankaja,
and many other women. 8
He insulted Ashtavakra,
the great philosopher,
Vasishtha Mudgal Narad,
Datta Ashvinikumar. 9

Atrocities of Ignorant Ravan

Atrocious Ravan, was women abductor,
He killed ardent Jatayu, who was woman protector. 1
Ravan had taken,
King Anaranya's life,
He had also raped, Rambha,
Nalkubera's wife. 2
He also molested,
Madanamanjiri's honour,
And he abused Devavati,
Kushadhvaja's daughter. 3
Anasuya Sulekha Svaha, Pankaja abducted by coerce,
Ravan abducted women,
many other by force. 4

Wise Ravan on Death bed

When Rama shot him,
his ignorance vanished,
Ravan fell on the ground,
and wisdom flourished. 1
Ravan said to Rama,
O Lord! please forgive me,
Your Sita is pure,
untouched Yogini is she. 2
My ego has diminished,
it had made me proud,
Please crown Vibhishana,
now there is no feud. 3

129. Puru Dynasty (Ancient Time)

For the Earlier Dynasty, please see : Atri Dynasty (Ancient Time)

1. Yayati — ययाति
2. Puru — पुरु
3. Janmejaya — जन्मेजय
4. Prachinavan — प्राचिनवान
5. Pravir — प्रवीर
6. Namasyu — नमस्यु
7. Vitabhay — वीतभय
8. Sudymna — सुद्युम्न
9. Bahuvidh — बहुविध
10. Samyati — संयाति
11. Sahovadi — रहोवादी
12. Raudraksha — रौद्राक्ष
13. Riteyu — ऋतेयु
14. Ratinar — रंतिनार
15. Santurodh — संतुरोध
16. Dushyanta — दुष्यंत
17. Bharat — **भरत**

For the Next Dynasty, please see :
Bharat Dynasty (Ancient Time)

Puru Dynasty

*The Dynasty of Yayati,
was a heroic line,
Son of Shakuntala and Dushyant,
Bharat was ruler fine. 1*

*In this line of heroes,
Janamejaya had huge fame,
His grandson Bharat,
was a monarch gem. 2*

Puru Dynasty

Chandravanshi Maharaja Yayati had two wives Devayani and Sharmistha. Devayani's son was King Yadu and Sharmishtha's son was King Puru. King Janamejaya was born to King Puru's wife Kausalya (Maha. Adi. 1.94). King Janamejaya had a place in the court of Yamaraja (Maha. Adi. 1.95). Bharat, the meritorious son of Dushyanta and his wife Shakuntala, was the almighty king of the Puru Dynasty, the king whose sovereignty got the name Bharatvarsha (Maha. Adi. 2.96).

King Dushyant's empire had expanded from the South Sea to Himalayas (Maha. Adi. 68.3), and the public was prosperous from all sides (Maha. Adi. 68).

The name Bharata was given to the son of Dushyanta and Shakuntala by Bharadwaja Muni. Shakuntala was the daughter of Vishvamitra Maha muni and Apsara Maneka. His son used to play with a lion's cubs since childhood and had the courage to count lion's teeth, so Kashyap Muni had blessed him to be the Chakravarti Emperor.

130. Pushyabhuti-Vardhan Dynasty, Patliputra (505-647)

For the Earlier Dynasty, please see :
Gupta Dynasty, Patliputra-Ujjain (240–730)

1. Nara Vardhan — नरवर्धन — 505–525
2. Rajya Vardhan-1 — राज्यवर्धन-1 — 525–555
3. Aditya Vardhan — आदित्यवर्धन — 555–580
4. Prabhakar Vardhan — प्रभाकरवर्धन — 580–605
5. Rajya Vardhan-2 — राज्यवर्धन-2 — 605–606
6. Harsha Vardhan — हर्षवर्धन — 606–647

For the Next Dynasty, please see :
Maukhari Dynasty, Kannauj (540–725)

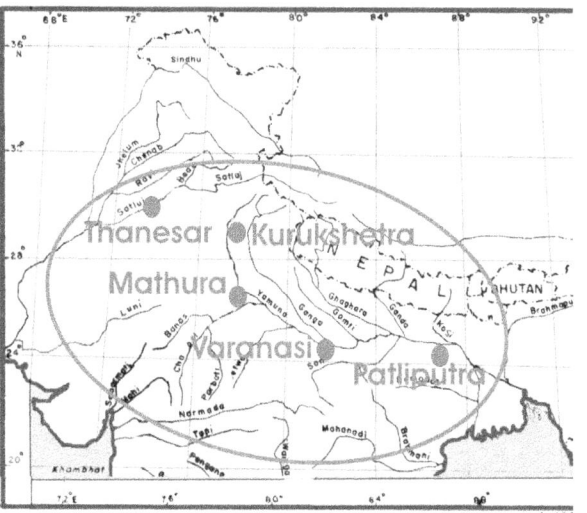

Pushyabhuti-Vardhan Dynasty

After the decline of Gupta Dynasty, Pushyabhuti Vardhan (505–647), Maukhari (540–725) and Maitraka (480–767) dynastie emerged emerger. The most prominent among them was the Royal House of Pushyabhuti.

The first ruler of the Pushyabhuti Dynasty was Narvardhan (505–525), after whom Prabhakar Vardhan (580–605) fixed his capital at Thanesar.

Under the Vardhan Empire, most of the North and northWest part of India was included in his kingdom. It extended as far as Assam in the East and Satpura mountains in the south.

King Harsha Vardhan Sheeladitya (606-647) shifted the capital from Thanesar to Kannauj. Emperor Harsha Vardhan was patron of art literature. In his court, Mahakavi Bana Bhatta had royal shelter. He wrote Harshacharitra and Kadambari, the best Sanskrit novels.

The princess Mahasena of the Gupta Dynasty was the mother of King Prabhakar Vardhan (580–605). Prabhakar Vardhan got married his daughter Rajashri to Maukhari King Graha Varma (600-612) of Kanyakubj (Kannauj).

Hindu Rajtarangini

131. Raghu Dynasty (Ancient Time)

For the Earlier Dynasty, please see :
Ikshavaky Dynasty (स्नातन काल)

1. Bhagirath — भगीरथ
2. Shritanath — श्रुतनाथ
3. Nabh — नाभ
4. Ambarish — अंबरीष
5. Sindhu Dwip — सिंधुद्वीप
6. Ayutashva — आयुताश्व
7. Rituparna — ऋतुपर्ण
8. Artaparni — आर्तपर्णी
9. Sudas — सुदास
10. Mitrasakha — मित्रसखा
11. Ashmak — अश्मक
12. Mulak — मूलक
13. Shatarath — शतरथ
14. Elavel — एलावेल
15. Vishvasaha — विश्वसह
16. Dilip — **दिलीप**
17. Dirghabahu — दीर्घबाहु
18. Raghu — रघु
19. Aja — अज
20. Dashrath — दशरथ
21. Shri Ram — श्रीराम
23. Lav and Kush — लव, कुश

For the Next Dynasty, please see :
Kush Dynasty (Ancient Time)

Raghu Dynasty

King Anshuman's son was King Bhagiratha's mentor Maharishi Tritul. King Bhagiratha had received the boon from Lord Shiva (Maha. One. 180.1). The rule of King Dilip was ideal and popular. The defeat and slaughter of the demon Viresen was the major event in the reign of King Dilip. King Dilip was one of the great sixteen kings of ancient India. King Dilip's wife Sudakshina was the daughter of the Emperor of Magadha. Vasistha Muni had explained the importance of the pilgrimage areas to King Dilip (Padma Parana 10). King Dilip's brave son was Emperor Raghu, whose Kshatriya clan is considered to be the best in the world and symbolizes truth, dignity, obedience, character, penance, sacrifice, valor, etc. Among the best kings of Solar Raghu Dynasty, the names of King Dasharatha and his son Shri Ram are forerunners. The eight ministers of King Dashrath's cabinet were : Sumantra, Jayant, Dhrishti, Vijay, Siddhartha, Arthasadhak, Ashok, and Mantrapala.

Kush Dynasty

Genealogy: (Ramayana period) Kush, Atithi, Nishadh, Nal, Pundarik, Kshemdhanwa, Devanik, Aheen, Paripatra, Dal, Bal, Aunk, Vajranath, Shankhan, Dhushitashtha, Vishwasah, Giranyanabha, Pushya, Dhruvandhi, Sudarshan, Agnivarna, Shighra, Maru, Prasushruta, Susandhi, Marsha, Sahaswan, Vishrutwan, Brihaddala **(Mahabharata period)**, Brihatakshaya, Jyaya, Vatsavuh, Diwakar, Sahadeva, Brihadeva, Bhanurath, Pratikashva, Supratik, Marudeva, Sunakshatra, Kinnar, Suparna, Anitrajita, Brihadraj, Dharmi, Kritanjaya, Rananjay, Sanjay, Shuddhodhan, Shakya, Rahul, Prasenjit, Khudrak, Ranak, Surath, Sumitra. King Mahapadma Dynasty (344–322 BC) of the Nanda Dynasty of Pataliputra (344–322 BCE) won the kingdom of Ayodhya after King Sumitra.

For the Next Dynasty, please see :
Nand Dynasty, Patliputra (344–322 BC)

Ayodhya of Raja Dashrath

Raja Dashrath's Ayodhya-1

Ayodhya, the Queen of cities, is Ikshavaku's capital,
Shri Rama and Sita's story, begins here monumental. 1
The spiritual and opulent, shining like gold,
The center of arts and learning, Ayodhya in the world. 2
The beautiful Ayodhya, on the Sarayu river,
Peaceful like heaven, and divine forever. 3
Solar Dynasty began, through Manu Vivasvata,
The Queen of the cities, glorified by Dashratha. 4

Raja Dashrath's Ayodhya-2

Irrigated with the water, of holy Sarayu river,
Home of Raghu Dynasty, the happiness giver. 5
The water of Sarayu, is clean and sweet,
It meets with Ganges, the confluence is neat. 6
The water of the river, is divine like nectar,
It grows fruits, sweet like sugar. 7

Raja Dashrath's Ayodhya-3

The gardens are nice, with colourful flowers,
Birds come to the flowers, the bees also hover. 8
Paths in the city, are clean and wide,
Lamps on the posts are, on the both side. 9
Houses in the city are, in the straight rows,
Like the plants in the field, every farmer grows. 10
People were happy, they had everything,
Their mother and the father, was the kind king. 11

Raja Dashrath's Ayodhya-4

Farmers grew fruits, and rice and wheat,
People had homes and, enough to eat. 12
Their hearts had joy, and peace of mind,
They took goodness, all they could find. 13
The markets were nice, filled with food,
Goods arranged properly, all looking good. 14
Trees in gardens had, flowers and birds,
The water of Sarayu, raised milch herds. 15
Every house had plants, that gave them food,
Fruits and vegetables, kept their health good. 16
They grew flowers with, scent and colour,
Rose Jasmine Lotus, and fruits with flavour. 17
Farmers raised animals, cows buffalos goats,
They grew cotton and, wheat maize oats. 18

Raja Dashrath's Ayodhya-5

With the holy water, of Sarayu river,
People were healthy, no sickness or fever. 19
Women and girls, all were noble,
Mothers like goddesses, loving adorable. 20
Everyone had good heart, soft and warm,
They followed scriptures, and caused no harm. 21
In Ayodhya of Dashrath, people were divine,
There were no thieves, there was no crime. 22

Raja Dashrath's Ayodhya-6

Dashrath was King, and kingdom was serene,
And like Mother Goddess, Kausalya was Queen. 23
It was a heaven, on the earth's face,
For the birth of Shri Rama, none other place. 24

गीत : राग रत्नाकर

अवध पुरी

स्थायी

अवध पुरी जग से न्यारी,
नर सुर ईश्वर की प्यारी ।

अंतरा-1

सरयू नद के तट पर नगरी,
अमृत जल की है गगरी ।

अंतरा-2

मातु प्रेम सम मंगलकारी,
जनपद की प्राण पियारी ।

अंतरा-3

राम-राज्य की नींव सुनहरी,
राम जनम की अधिकारी ।

अंतरा-4

भारत माँ की सुता दुलारी!
हम तेरे हैं बलिहारी ।

Raja Dashrath's Ayodhya

Song

Sthayi
*Ayodhya is unique city,
loved by men and Gods.*

Antara
*On the earth Ayodhya is,
Truly holy place. 1*

*Joy giver like the mother,
heaven on the earth. 2*

*Rama-Rajya is here,
Rama's birth place. 3*

*Daughter of India,
Ayodhya is great. 4*

Raja Dashrath of Ayodhya

King Dashrath

*Driving the chariot, in the sides ten,
King Nemi received, "Dashratha" name. 1
Dashratha was firm, and impartial judge,
once he says something, he would not budge. 2
Everyone was equal, always in his mind,
For wicked he was harsh, for good he was kind. 3
Truth and false he knew, never he went wrong,
His anger was short, blessings lasted long. 4
His aide was Sumantra, a very able man,
He helped the Dashratha, as much as he can. 5*

Raja Shri Ram of Ayodhya

Vasishtha Muni said

*Super human is Rama, among all men,
He is person divine, his aura is golden. 1*

*Rama is very prompt, an ocean of virtues,
He is loved by people, he unravels their issues. 2*

*Shri Rama is omniscient, protector of dharma,
He is benefactor of all, ever ready for karma. 3*

*Shri Rama removes sorrow, heart he captivates,
He is courageous, valor he motivates. 4*

*Knower of the Vedas, he is firm in resolves,
As a timely helper, difficulties he solves. 5*

*Raghava is intelligent, and wise he is utmost,
He should be our king, he is suitable most. 6*

Vishvamitra Muni said

Vishvamitra said, O King! let's do it right,
As per scriptures say, Rama we should anoint. 1

Sita's husband Rama, is image of peace,
Lotus eyed Rama, hasn't any vice. 2

Shri Rama is kind, he is truly wise,
He is charitable, he is person nice. 3

Shri Rama knows ethics, he always lives by rules,
He is auspicious, with justice he rules. 4

Shri Rama is truthful, and he is beautiful,
He is merciful, and he is dutiful. 5

He is Sun of wisdom, he is powerful,
Let us make him prince, he is wonderful. 6

Lakshmana Said

Brother Lakshmana said, my life breath and soul,
My brother Raghava, his service is my goal. 1

My every part of body, is occupied by Ram,
My day and night dreams, my worship is Shri Ram. 2

My each beat of heart, and each of my breath,
And my every thought, is Rama until death. 3

My life is for Shri Ram, Rama is my love,
Everything in my life, Shri Rama is above. 4

I am at his feet, I gave him everything,
Shri Rama is supreme, Rama should be King.

Prime Minister Sumantra said

Impossible in the world, Rama makes it possible,
With mercy of Shri Rama, improbable is probable. 1
Skillful is Shri Rama, his blessings we enjoy,
People follow his way, he is people's joy. 2
Rama reads your mind, he knows your thoughts,
With a simple glimpse, he can join the dots. 3
He is sea of knowledge, of science he is source,
He knows art of war, he knows every course. 4
Logic Rama knows, he has it understood,
His mind is always busy, for the people's good. 5

Ram is eloquent, he knows scriptures well,
He is the supreme archer, he is Yogi as well. 6
Shri Rama is pundit, enlightened is his soul,
Brilliant is his splendor, it enlightens world whole. 7
Shri Rama is humorous, his reasoning is sound,
He has no arrogance, by candor he is bound. 8
A brave warrior he is, infinite is his courage,
Also at adverse times, he does not have rage. 9
He is treasure of merits, from vices he is far,
He is pure like fire, invincible at war. 10

Rama's actions are sacred, like the Ganges water,
Rama's words are sweet, pleasant in every matter. 11
Rama's aura is bright, glowing and shiny,
Shri Rama is judicious, his self interest is tiny. 12
Joy is Sita-Ram, they fulfill your wish,
They grant your boons, heavenly and lavish. 13
Rama is the love, of mother and the father,
He is like a boat, to reach heaven and farther. 14
Rama is your body, he is your breath,
He is like your soul, Rama is your faith. 15

Rama gives you strength, he gives you brain,
Chanting Rama's name, does not go in vain. 16
Said Sumantra wise, Rama is our guide
He should be the king, his rule we all abide. 17

Deputy Minister said

Rama upholds Dharma, he knows everything,
He is ideal person, he should be the king. 1
Rama has no enemy, he respects all,
No one at Rama's court, is considered small. 2
Shri Rama is fair, like a flowering tree,
Guilty man is punished, not-guilty goes free. 3
He is equanimous, to the loss and gain,
For him both are equal, pleasure or the pain. 4
Shri Rama is focused, always at his aim,
He may win or lose, for him both are same. 5
Rama removes evil, and protects the right,
His arrows defend truth, and untruth they fight. 6
Rama praises the braves, of the warrior clan,
Selfless work he likes, and the honest man. 7
He has no addiction, Rama has no sin,
In front of Shri Rama, evil can not win. 8
The deputy Minister said, Shri Rama is supreme,
Shri Rama is our king, we are on his team. 9

Other Ministers said

The other Ministers said, our heart tells,
Shri Rama should be king, there is no one else. 1
Friend to everyone, he helps everyone,
Magnanimous like Rama, person there is none. 2
He is cardinal archer, can shoot eyes closed,
He can shower arrows, when danger is posed. 3
Shri Rama is hallowed, he is forgiver,
He is charitable, he is blessings giver. 4
He is Royal Person, a Jewel in the Crown,
He is like a lion, he earned that renown. 5
He forgives your mistakes, unknowingly done,
He punishes tyranny, you can not hide or run. 6
If you are at his feet, from sins you will be free,
Shri Rama is praised, by Gods of worlds three. 7

The Sages said
Saints and Sages said, Rama is venerable,
Rama should be worshipped, to make the life stable. 1
Rama is the Master, of our everything,
There is no one else, fit to be the king. 2

दादरा ताल
राम–राज्याभिषेक

स्थायी
गीत शारद ने मंजुल है गाया,
साज नारद मुनि ने बजाया ।
रत्नाकर से है मंगल रचाया,
रामायण को है सुंदर सजाया ।।

अंतरा–1
राम राजा अवध का महाना,
राम–का–राज जनपद ने माना ।
अभिषेचित भया रामराया,
आज अवधेश राघव कहाया ।।

अंतरा–2
दाँये सुग्रीऽव चँवरऽ डुलावे,
बाँये विभीषण जी चमरऽ हिलावे ।
हार मोती का सुंदर बनाया,
गले सीता के रामऽ पिन्हाया ।।

अंतरा–3
सिंहासन पर जब राघव बिराजे,
बजे मोदऽ के मंगऽल बाजे ।
हाथ दक्षिण गुरुऽ ने बढ़ाया,
शीश राघव के किरीट चढ़ाया ।।

Coronation of Shri Rama

Song

Sthayi
Sung lovely by Sarasvati,
Narad played the music,
Story written by Ratnakar,
Ramayan is a magic.

Antara
King of Ayodhya is Rama,
Ram-Rajya it is called,
Rama is being anointed,
Rama is the king. 1

On the left is Sugriva,
Vibhishana on the right,
They are fanning Shri Rama,
Rama put pearl necklace,
on his wife Sita. 2

Rama is sitting on throne,
Music is being played,
Vashshtha put the crown,
on Shri Rama's head. 3

Sung lovely by Sarasvati,
Narad played the music.

गीत : राग मिश्र, कहरवा ताल
जै श्री राम

स्थायी
जै श्री राम भजो मन मेरे,
नाम हरि के गारे ।
जनम-जनम के पाप उतारे,
तन के ताप उबारे ।।

अंतरा–1
घेरेंगे जब घोर अंधेरे,
मेघ घनेरे कारे ।
या छेड़ेंगे भय दुस्तारे,
मन वीणा की तारें ।
छोड़ेंगे यदि साथ पियारे,
भव सागर मझधारे ।। जै श्री राम ...

अंतरा–2
बोलेंगे जब शबद दुखारे,
निर्दय दुनियावारे ।
या काटेंगे साँप विषारे,
भूखे वदन पसारे ।
रोएँगे यदि गम के मारे,
तेरे प्राण बिचारे ।। जै श्री राम ...

अंतरा–3
झेलेंगे तब रामजी प्यारे,
दुख तन मन के सारे ।
खेलेंगे हरि खेल सुखारे,
हरने ताप तुम्हारे ।
लेलेंगे प्रभु परम कृपारे,
शरण में साँझ सकारे ।। जै श्री राम

Jai Shri Ram

Song

Sthayi
O My Mind! chant victory to Shri Rama, and sing Rama's names.
It will relieve all your pains and sins of past lives.

Antara
When the pitch darkness will surround you
and the dark clouds will come over you,
And the fears will twang the wires of the Veena of your mind,
If your dear ones will leave you stranded in the middle of the worldly ocean, ... 1

When the cruel people of the world will say painful words to you,
And when the poisonous snakes will bite you,
with their hungry fangs,
And if your poor soul will cry deep in sorrow, ... 2

Then Dear Shri Rama will take away the aches
from your body and mind,
And Hari will play
with you joyful games,
to lessen your troubles,
The supreme kind Lord
will take you in his shelter,
day and night, ... 3

132. Rai Dynasty, Alor, Sindh (489-631)

1. Devajna — देवाज्ञ — 489 ...
2. Meharsan — मेहरसन-1
3. Sahasi-1 — साहसी-1
4. Meharsan-2 — मेहरसन-2
5. Sahasi-2 — साहसी-2 ... 631

For the Next Dynasty, please see :
Chach Dynasty of Sindh (631–712)

Rai Dynasty of Sindh

Rai Dynasty of Sindh, is not much known,
But in the west,
it was very well grown. 1

From Saurashtra to Kashmir,
large was their sway,
They ruled Gandhar,
and beyond all the way. 2

They had built navy, on the Debal port,
They were brave fighters,
at Alor they had fort. 3

Rai Dynasty of Sindh

The vast empire of the Rai Dynasty of Alor Sindh was established on a vast territory from Gandhar in the West to the Kashmir border in the North and Sea Port of Surat in the south. The Rai kings had Surat and Debal as the main ports. A vast naval force stood ready for the protection of the kingdom from the Arab invaders.

The chronology of the kings of this Dynasty is not written well in the history.

Maharaja Chach, seizing power from the last king of this Dynasty, and ascended the throne of Alor with Empress Ladi.

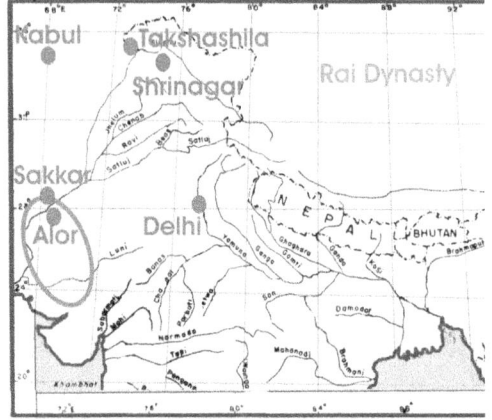

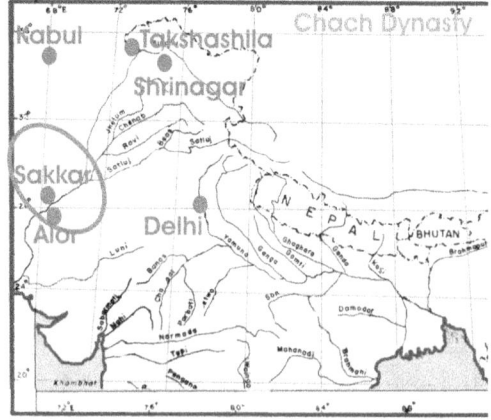

Hindu Rajtarangini

133. Rashtrakut Dynasty, Malkhed (620-973)

1.	Dantidurga-1	दंतीदुर्ग-1	620-630
2.	Indraraja-1	इंद्रराजा-1	630-650
3.	Govindraya-1	गोविंदराया-1	650-670
4.	Kakkaraya-1	कक्कराया-1	670-690
5.	Indraraya-2	इंद्रराया-2	690-713
6.	Dantidurg-2	दंतीदुर्ग-2	713-758
7.	Krishnaraya-1	कृष्णराया-1	758-773
8.	Govindraya-2	गोविंदराया-2	773-774
9.	Dhruvaraya-1	ध्रुवराया-1	774-793
10.	Govindraya-3	गोविंदराया-3	773-814
11.	Amoghvarsha-1	अमोघवर्ष-1	814-877
12.	Krishnaraya-2	कृष्णराया-2	877-911
13.	Jagattunga	जगतुंग	911-914
14.	Indraraya-3	इंद्रराया-3	914-916
15.	Amoghvarsha-2	अमोघवर्ष-2	916-918
16.	Govindraya-4	गोविंदराया-4	918-936
17.	Amoghvarsha-3	अमोघवर्ष-3	936-939
18.	Krishnaraya-3	कृष्णराया-3	939-968
19.	Khottiga	खोत्तिग	968-972
20.	Kakkaraya-2	कक्कराया-2	972-973

134. Rashtrakut Dynasty, Lat, Gujrat (806-888)

1.	Indraraja-3	इंद्रराजा-3	800-812
2.	Kakkaraja	कक्कराजा सौवर्णवर्ष	712-835
3.	Dhruvaraya-2	ध्रुवराया-2 धारावर्ष	835-850
4.	Govindraya-5	गोविंदराया-5 प्रभूतवर्ष	850-867
5.	Shubhatunga	शुभतुंग अकालवर्ष	867-867
6.	Dantivarma	दंतीवर्मा	867-888

Rashtrakuta Dynasty

The rulers of the oldest Rashtrakuta Dynasty were located in Maharashtra-Andhra-Karnataka from the time of Ashok Maurya (269-232 BC) or even before that. King Manank (350-375) was established in the valley of Krishna river in Kuntal country and he gave the title Kuntaleshwar to his Dynasty. It is well known in the history.

King Manank had built a capital named Manankpur or Manpur in the Satara region. It is said that Gupta Emperor Chandragupta-I (319-350) sent Court Poet Kalidasa as envoy to the court of King Devaraja, son of Manank. Therefore, Mahakavi Kalidasa composed Kuntaleshwaradautya poetry.

This second Royal House of Manpur was defeated by King Pulakeshi-2 (608-642) of Badami Chalukya and consequently the second branch of Rashtrakuta Dynasty emerged in Nandivardhana of Vidarbha and then later in Achalpur (Elichpur) as feudatory (611-642) of Badami Chalukya kings.

Rashtrakut Dynasty

Rashtrakutas were the kings,
famous in the South,
Three great families,
were praised by every mouth. 1
First family at Manpur, rulers were grand,
In the fifth century they ruled,
Karnataka was their land. 2
Achalpur was second, Rashtrakuta brand,
In the sixth century they ruled,
Vidarbha in their hand. 3
Their kingdom was rich,
they earned lot of fame,
They built many temples,
and earned glorious name. 4
Third House of Malkhed,
greatest in the three,
From Karnataka they ruled,
in the seventh century. 5
They were grand monarchs,
their rule was ethical,
Their sovereignty was long,
building work magical. 6
They built great temples,
divine their sculpture,
Well known in the world,
for the generations future. 7

Rashtrakuta Dynasty conntinued

The third and greatest Rashtrakuta Dynasty (620-973) settled at Malkhed making it the capital.

Dantidurga-2 (713-758), the first king of this Dynasty, threw Chalukya suzerainty and conquered the Lat of Gujarat, Vidarbha of Maharashtra, Malwa, Kalinga, etc. and extended the empire from Vindhya mountains in the North to Kanyakumari in the south.

Dantidurga was a great craftsman. From Rashtrakuta king Dantidurga-1 (620-630) to Indraraya-2 (690-713), five kings were feudatories of Kalyani Chalukya (696-1189) kings in Lattatur.

Rashtrakuta Dhruvaraya (774-793) had shifted the capital from Lattatur to Malkhed (Manyakhetra).

Indraraja-3 (800-812), brother of Rashtrakuta king Govindaraya (773-973), established a branch (800-888) of Rashtrakuta in Lat Gujarat by becoming the Malkhed Governor of the Rashtrakutas of Malkhed.

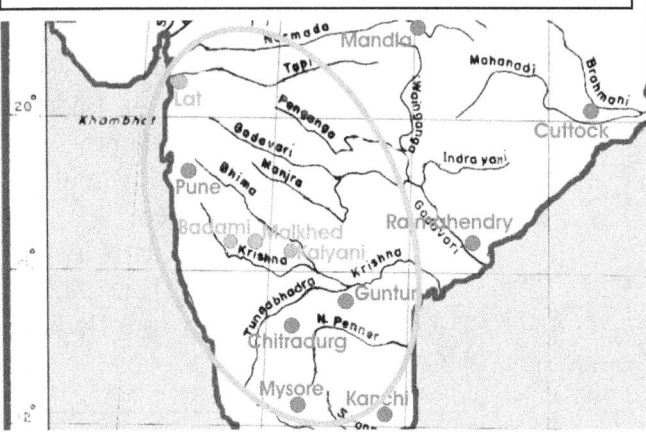

Hindu Rajtarangini

Rathor Dynasty, Jodhpur, Bikaner, Kishangadh (1250-1948)

1. Rathor Dynasty, Jodhpur (1250-1948)
2. Rathor Dynasty, Bikaner (1465-1948)
3. Rathor Dynasty, Kishangadh (1609-1948)

135. Rathor Dynasty, Jodhpur (1250-1948)

1.	Rao Siha	राव सीहा	1250–1273
2.	Rao Asthan	राव अस्थान	1273–1292
3.	Dhuhad Simha	धूहड़ सिंह	1292–1309
4.	Raipal Simha	रायपाल सिंह	1309–1313
5.	Kanpal Simha	कनपाल सिंह	1313–1323
6.	Jalanasi	जालाणसी	1323–1328
7.	Chhada Simha	छाड़ा सिंह	1328–1344
8.	Tida Simha	तीड़ा सिंह	1344–1357
9.	Salkha Simha	सलखा सिंह	1357–1374
10.	Viram Simha	विरम सिंह	1374–1394
11.	Rao Chunda Simha	राव चुण्डा सिंह	1394–1423
12.	Kanha Simha	कान्हा सिंह	1423–1427
13.	Ranmal Simha	रणमल सिंह	1427–1427
14.	Satta Simha	सता सिंह	1427–1438
15.	Rao Jodha Simha	राव जोधा सिंह	1438–1489
16.	Satal Simha	सातल सिंह	1489–1492
17.	Suja Simha	सुजा सिंह	1492–1515
18.	Ganga Simha	गंगा सिंह	1515–1532
19.	Maldev Simha	मालदेव सिंह	1532–1562
20.	Chandrasen	चंद्रसेन	1562–1582
21.	Rai Simha	राय सिंह	1582–1583
22.	Uday Simha	उदय सिंह	1583–1595
23.	Shur Simha	शूर सिंह	1595–1619
24.	Gaj Simha	गज सिंह	1619–1638

Rathor Dynasty

This majestic Solar Royal Dynasty who founded the city of Kannauj, was as much respectable as it was disgraced in the history by the treason and betrayal by the Gahadwal king Jaichand Rathor (1170-1194). In the lineage of Jaichand, King Chandradeva (1080–100), Madan Pal (1100–1114), Govindchandra Pal (1114–1155), Jaichand (1170–1194) and Harishchandra (1194–1200) were kings. This last king Harishchandra fled from Varanasi to Jodhpur (Rajasthan).

After the death of Maharana Prithviraj Chauhan (1177-1192) of Ajmer-Delhi, when Jaichand Rathor was also killed, Jaichand's son fled to Garhwal to hide his face and later he settled in Rajasthan.

Eventually three great monarchies at Jodhpur (1250–1948), Bikaner (1465–1948) and Kishangarh (1609–1948) emerged from this well known and able Rathor Dynasty.

25.	Jasvant Simha-1	जसवंत सिंह-1	1638-1678
26.	Durga Simha	दुर्गा सिंह	1678-1707
27.	Ajit Simha	अजित सिंह	1707-1724
28.	Abhay Simha	अभय सिंह	1724-1749
29.	Ram Simha	राम सिंह	1749-1751
30.	Bakhat Simha	बखत सिंह	1751-1752
31.	Vijay Simha	विजय सिंह	1752-1793
32.	Bhim Simha	भीम सिंह	1793-1803
33.	Man Simha	मान सिंह	1803-1843
34.	Takhta Simha	तख्त सिंह	1843-1873
35.	Jasvant Simha-2	जसवंत सिंह-2	1873-1895
36.	Sardar Simha	सरदार सिंह	1895-1911
37.	Sumer Simha	सुमेर सिंह	1911-1918
38.	Ummed Simha	उम्मेद सिंह	1918-1947
39.	Hanvant Simha	हनवंत सिंह	1947-1948

136. Rathor Dynasty, Bikaner (1465-1948)

1.	Rao Bika	राव बिका	1465-1504
2.	Narsi Simha	नरसी सिंह	1504-1505
3.	Lunkaran	लूणकरण	1505-1526
4.	Jaitsi Simha	जैतसी सिंह	1526-1542
5.	Kalyanmal	कल्याणमल	1542-1573
6.	Rai Simha	राय सिंह	1573-1612
7.	Dalpat Simha	दलपत सिंह	1612-1613
8.	Shur Simha	शूर सिंह	1613-1631
9.	Karna Simha	कर्ण सिंह	1631-1669
10.	Anup Simha	अनूप सिंह	1669-1698
11.	Scarup Simha	स्वरूप सिंह	1698-1700
12.	Sujan Simha	सुजान सिंह	1700-1736
13.	Zoravar Simha	जोरावर सिंह	1736-1746
14.	Gaj Simha	गज सिंह	1746-1787

Rathor Dynasty

1. Rathod Dynasty, Jodhpur

The founder of the Jodhpur family was Rao Siha (1250–1273) and his descendant Rao Chunda Singh (1394-1423). He was a great heroic warrior. He won the fort of Mandor (Mandu) and settled his capital there.

Rao Jodha (1438-1489), a descendant of Rao Chunda, established his Dynasty in Jodhpur. Rao Bicha (1465–1504), son of Rao Jodha, established his separate royal family (1465–1948) in Bikaner.

King Shursingh (1595–1619) of the Jodhpur branch accepted slavery of the Mughals. After this, his grandson Jaswant Singh (1638–1678) took the Mughal service and he fought bloody battles against the Maratha King Chhatrapati Shivaji (1630–1680).

2. Rathod Dynasty, Bikaner

Rao Bika (1465-1504), son of King Rao Jodha Singh (1438-1489) of the Jodhpur Rathor royal family (1250–1948), established Bikaner city in 1465 and made it his capital.

Continued

15.	Raj Simha	राज सिंह	1787–1787
16.	Pratap Simha	प्रताप सिंह	1787–1787
17.	Surat Simha	सूरत सिंह	1787–1828
18.	Ratan Simha	रतन सिंह	1828–1851
19.	Sardar Simha	सरदार सिंह	1851–1872
20.	Dungar Simha	डुंगर सिंह	1872–1887
21.	Ganga Simha	गंगा सिंह	1887–1943
22.	Shardul Simha	शार्दूल सिंह	1943–1948

137. Rathor Dynasty, Kishangadh (1609-1948)

1.	Hari Simha	हरि सिंह-1	1609–1611
2.	Kishan Simha	किशन सिंह	1611–1615
3.	Sahas Simha	साहस सिंह	1615–1618
4.	Jagmal Simha	जगमल सिंह	1618–1629
5.	Hari Simha	हरि सिंह-2	1629–1643
6.	Rup Simha	रूप सिंह	1643–1658
7.	Man Simha	मान सिंह	1658–1706
8.	Raj Simha	राज सिंह	1706–1748
9.	Bahadur Simha	बहादुर सिंह	1748–1748
10.	Samant Simha	सामंत सिंह	1748–1765
11.	Sardar Simha	सरदार सिंह	1765–1781
12.	Bidar Simha	बीदर सिंह	1781–1788
13.	Pratap Simha	प्रताप सिंह	1788–1798
14.	Kalyan Simha	कल्याण सिंह	1798–1839
15.	Mokham Simha	मोखम सिंह	1839–1841
16.	Prithvi Simha	पृथ्वी सिंह	1841–1879
17.	Shardul Simha	शार्दूल सिंह	1879–1900
18.	Madan Simha	मदन सिंह	1900–1926
19.	Yajnanarayan Simha	यज्ञनारायण	1926–1929
20.	Sumer Simha	सुमेर सिंह	1929–1948

Continued ...

Lunkaran Singh (1505–1526), grandson of Rao Bika Singh, received the "Karni" title. Uday Singh (1583-1595), son of King Maldev Singh (1532-1562) of Jodhpur family, settled in Ajmer in 1596. His grandson Kishan Singh (1611–1615) settled in Kishangarh in 1609 and started his new royal family (1609–1948).

3. Rathor Dynasty, Kishangadh

Maharaja Kishan Singh (1611–1615) was a very intelligent and efficient ruler. Maharaja Roop Singh (1643–1658) built the fort of Kishangarh in 1649, which was named Roopnath Garh in honor of the Maharaja.

Kishangarh kings gave great importance to art. Their Bani-Thani paintings are immortal.

138. Ratta Dynasty, Belgaon, Karnatak (850-1240)

For the Earlier Dynasty, please see :
Chalukya Dynasty, Kalyani (696–1189)

1.	Nanna	नन्न	950–980
2.	Kartvirya-1	कार्तवीर्य-1	980–
3.	Davari	दावरी	–1000
4.	Kanna-1	कन्न-1	1000–1040
5.	Erag	एरग	1040–1048
6.	Ak	अंक	1048–1060
7.	Kalasen-1	कालसेन-1	1060–1076
8.	Kanna-2	कन्न-2	1076–1087
9.	Kartvirya-2	कार्तवीर्य-2	1087–1102
10.	Kalasen-2	कालसेन-2	1102–1143
11.	Kartvirya-3	कार्तवीर्य-3	1143–1165
12.	Lakshmidev-1	लक्ष्मीदेव-1	1165–1190
13.	Kartvirya-4	कार्तवीर्य-4	1190–1204
14.	Mallikarjun	मल्लिकार्जुन	1204–1228
15.	Lakshmideva-2	लक्ष्मीदेव-2	1228–1240

For the Next Dynasty, please see :
Yadav Dynasty, Devgiri (850–1311)

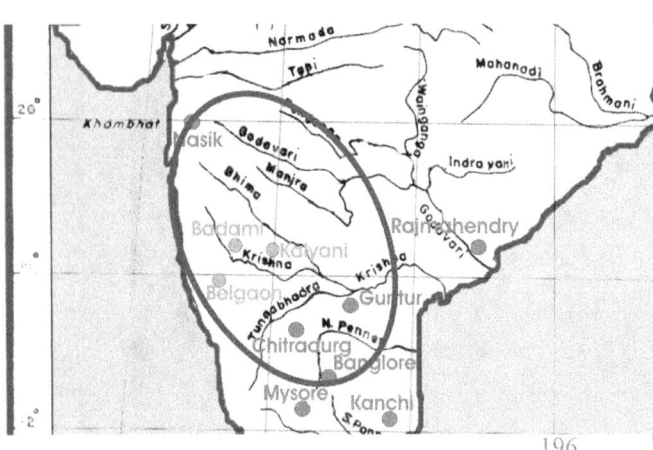

Ratta Dynasty

This ancient Royal House of Karnataka was known by the names Ratta, Rattagudi or Rattagudlu. This royal family was started by Prithviram, the son of Saundhati, the king of Merad, at a place called Saundati in about 850 AD. At this time it was a feudatory (875-973) of the Rashtrakuta Dynasty (620-973). After that, the Ratta Dynasty became the feudatories of Kalyani Chalukyas (696–1189). The capital of the Ratta kings was shifted to Belgaum (Belugram).

In the middle of the twelfth century, King Kartavirya-3 (1143–1165) declared the Ratta Dynasty to be independent of the Kalyani Chalukya Dynasty. Now Ratta Kings bore the titles such as Mahamandaleshwar, Rattalu Puravartheeswarar, Lattanur Poorvartheeshwar, Ratta Narayana, Ratta Martand, Chakravati, etc. And, the Ratta King bore Suvarnagarudadhvaja (Golden Eagle) on their chariot. Their kingdom was divided in political areas like Ratta kingdoms of Nesargi, Sugandhvratra, Hubli, Banihalli, Belgaum, Belvola, Banavasi etc. The last Ratta king Lakshmidev-2 (1128-1240) was defeated by the Yadava king Singhan-2 (1200- 1247) of Devgiri and the Ratta kingdom merged into the Yadava kingdom.

139. Ror Dynasty, Roruk-Sakkar (Ancient Time)

1. Dhach Kumar	धच	2. Kunak	कुनक
3. Rurak	रुरक	4. Harak	हरक
5. Devnik	देवनिक	6. Ahinak	अहिनक
7. Paripat	परिपत	8. Bhalasha	भालशा
9. Vijaybhanu	विजयभानु	10. Khengar	खेंगार
11. Brihadrath	बृहद्रथ	12. Haramsha	हरअंश
13. Brihaddatta	बृहदत्त	14. Ishman	ईशमान
15. Shridhar	श्रीधर	16. Mohari	मोहरि
17. Prasanna	प्रसन्न	18. Amritvan	अमृतवान
19. Mahasen	महासेन	20. Brihaddhaula	बृहद्धौल
21. Harikirt	हरिकीर्त	22. Somaraja	सोमराजा
23. Mitravan	मित्रवान	24. Pushyapat	पुष्यपत
25. Sudaiva	सुदैव	26. Vidrik	विद्रक
27. Nahakman	नहकमान	28. Mangala Mitra	मंगल मित्र
29. Suraj	सूरज	30. Pushkar	पुष्कर
31. Antar	अंतर	32. Sutanjay	सुतजय
33. Brihadhvaj	बृहध्वज	34. Bahuk	बाहुक
35. Kampajayi	कम्पजयी	36. Agnish	अग्नीश
37. Kapish	कपीश	38. Sumantra	सुमन्त्र
39. Linglav	लिंगलव	40. Saanasjit	मानसजित
41. Sundar	सुंदर	42. Dadrod	द्द्रोड़

Ror Dynasty

Ror Kshatriya Dynasty was founded by King Dhach in the Sindh. Dhach King was also known as Ror or Roruk Shankar, or Rai Diyach, therefore, the capital of Ror kingdom was called Roruk.

The names of forty-two kings of this Dynasty are written in different ways in many chronicles, yet more specific historical information of this Dynasty is not available.

King Ror Kumar had created a governance center called Ror Shankar, which later became famous by the name Roruk or Shankar or Sakkar or Sakkhar.

Ror Dynasty

The Ror House of Sindh,
founder was Ror Kumar,
Forty-two kings ruled,
the list we know so far. 1
Roruk was their center, of the rule as shown,
But unfortunately now,
not much more is known. 2

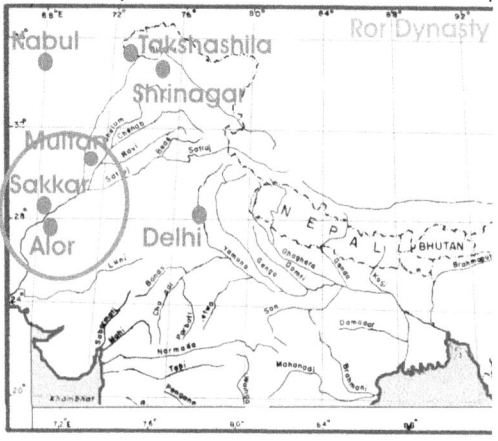

140. Saindhav Dynasty, Saurashtra (734-920)

For the Earlier Dynasty, please see : Sindhu Dynasty of Sindh (Ancient Time)

1. Ahi Varma-1 — अहिवर्मा-1
2. Pushyen — पुष्येन
3. Ahi Varma-2 — अहिवर्मा-2
4. Pushya Deva — पुष्यदेव — 734-754
5. Krishna Raj — कृष्णराज — 754-774
6. Aguka-1 — अगुक-1 — 774-794
7. Ranak-1 — राणक-1 — 794-814
8. Krishna Raj-2 — कृष्णराज-2 — 814-824
9. Jaika-1 — जैका-1 — 824-849
10. Aguk-2 — अगुक-2 — 849-870
11. Ranak-2 — राणक-2 — 870-880
12. Chamunda Raj — चामुण्डराज — 880-885
13. Aguk-3 — अगुक-3 — 885-900
14. Jaika-2 — जैका-2 — 900-920

For the Next Dynasty, please see :
Chudasma Dynasty, Junagadh (875-1505)

> **Saindhav Dynasty**
> *The descendents of Sindhu Dynasty,*
> *Saindhavas their name,*
> *They settled in Saurashtra, it became their home. 1*
> *Their ancestors were Maitrakas,*
> *they became Chudasama later,*
> *The navy of their kingdom, was larger and better. 2*

Saindhav Dynasty

The descendants of Jayadratha (Maha. 3.262), the son of Vriddhakshatra (see Sindh), were the kings of the Sanatan mythological Sindh. They were known as Saindhavas. They came to Sorath (Saurashtra) following the Maitraka (480-767) Dynasty of Vallabhi in the hills of Barda. Their area of power extended in Jamnagar, Dwarka, Rajkot, Morvi, Porbandar, etc. districts of Saurashtra. The chronology of this Dynasty is known to history from King Pushyadeva (734-754) after a long unknown lineage.

Saindhav king Pushyadeva was a contemporary of Maitraka king Sheeladitya-4 (722-760). As the Ghumali (Porbandar) region was on the West sea coast of Saurashtra, the naval army's emblem was Varuna Dev's fish.

Morvi state of North Saurashtra known after the Saindhav kings, came under the power of the Jadeja (1203-1948) Rajputs. The practical languages of the kingdom of the Saindhavas was Sanskrit and Prakrit. The rule of Chudasama (875-1505) Dynasty started in Saurashtra after Shaindhava Dynasty. The capital of the Chudasama Dynasty was Junagadh.

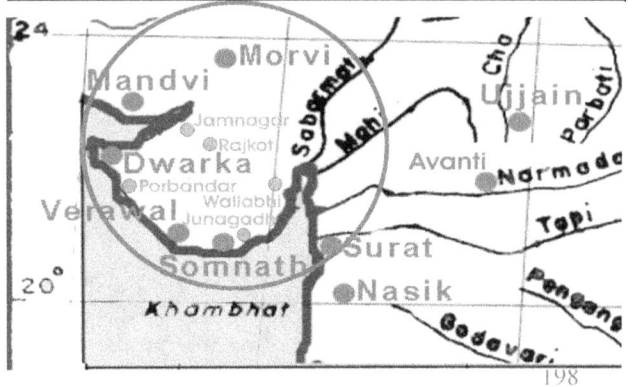

Hindu Rajtarangini

141. Satvahan Dynasty (271 BC-195 AD)

For the Earlier Dynasty, please see:
Kanva Dynasty (72–27 BC)

#	Name	Hindi	Period
1.	Simuk	सिमुक	271–248 BC
2.	Krishna	कृष्ण	248–230 BC
3.	Satkarni-1	सातकर्णी-1	230–220 BC
4.	Purnotsava	पूर्णोत्संग	220–202 BC
5.	Skandastambhi	स्कंदस्तंभी	202–184 BC
6.	Satkarni-2	सातकर्णी-2	184–128 BC
7.	Lambodar	लंबोदर	128–110 BC
8.	Apilak	अपिलक	110–98 BC
9.	Medhasvati	मेघस्वाति	98–80 BC
10.	Svati	स्वाति	80–62 BC
11.	Skandasvati	स्कन्दस्वाति	62–55 BC
12.	Mrigendra Svatikarna	मृगेंद्र	55–52 BC
13.	Kuntala Svatikarna	कुंतल	52–44 BC
14.	Svatikarna	स्वातिकर्ण	44–43 BC
15.	Pulumavi-1	पुलुमावी-1	43–07 BC
16.	Meghasvati	मेघवासित	07 BC–31 AD
17.	Gaurakrishna	गौरकृष्ण	31–56 AD
18.	Hal	हाल	56–61 AD
19.	Mahulak	मंडुलक	61–66 AD
20.	Purindrasen	पुरिंद्रसेन	66–71 AD
21.	Sundar Svatikarni	सुंदर	71–72 AD
22.	Rajadsvati	राजादस्वाति	72–72 AD
23.	Shivasvati	शिवस्वाति	72–100 AD
24.	Gautamiputra Satkarni	गौतमीपुत्र	100–121 AD
25.	Pulumavi-2	पुलुमावी-2	121–149 AD
26.	Shiva Shri Satkarni	शिव श्री	149–156 AD
27.	Shivaskanda Satkarni	शिवस्कंद	156–163 AD
28.	Yajna Shri Satkarni	यज्ञ श्री	163–178 AD
29.	Vijaya	विजय	178–188 AD
30.	Chandra Shri Satkarni	चंद्र श्री	188–195 AD
30.	Pulumavi-3	पुलुमावी-3	166–174 AD

Satavahana Dynasty

According to the Puranas, the first king of the Satavahana Dynasty of Andhra-Maharashtra region, Simuk (271-248 BC) ruled over the Dakkhan. Its capital was in Pratisthan (Paithan) on the banks of river Godavari in Maharashtra.

The official language of the Satavahanas was Prakrit written in the Brahmi script. In different Puranas, the names Shishuk (Matsya Purana), Vrishal (Bhagavata), Chishmak (Brahmand), Sindhuk (Vayu), Shiprak (Vishnu), etc. have been used for king Simuk. After King Simuk, his younger brother Krishna or Kanha came to power by assuming the title Satkarani.

Satkarni-1 (230–220 BC), son of King Simuk, became king after King Krishna (248–230 BC). He greatly expanded the kingdom. He was called the Dakshinapatha and the Aprahitchakra. He was the propagator of Yajnas. After the death of Chakravarti Ashok Maurya (232 BC), Satakarni-1 broke away from the Maurya kingdom and declared independence. After this, Satavahana king Pulumavi-1 (43-07 BC) had killed Susarma (37-27 BC), the last king of Kanva Dynasty of Pataliputra, and established Satavahana kingdom over

Satavahana Dynasty
(King Porus)

When the king Porus fought,
the most furious war, Sikandar turned back,
as he could not win so far. **1**
He waited for many days, on the Jhelum river,
He exhausted all arrows, from his mighty quiver. **2**
He could not move ahead, Porus held very strong,
Hindus fought on right side, Sikandar was wrong. **3**

(Satavahanas)

Nearly at that time, tells the history first hand,
There were kings in South, in the Dakkhan land. **4**
The Satavahana kings, sovereign ruler Lords,
Fought very well, with bows-arrows and swords. **5**

(At that time)

There were no missionaries, nor the Mughals brutal,
No religious conversions, it was freedom total. **6**
There were no pastors, nor any iconoclasts,
Everywhere ancient goodness,
there were no castes. **7**
Righteousness in the blood,
service was the Dharma,
As the Gita told, selfless acts was Karma. **8**
Simuk was the king, a brave hero first rank,
Ruled from Pratisthan, on Godavari river bank. **9**
Son of Satavahana, Simuk was king perfect,
There were thirty kings, in the Satavahana sect. **10**
Satavahana kings were brave, charitable and virtuous,
They were religious kings, they were all righteous. **11**

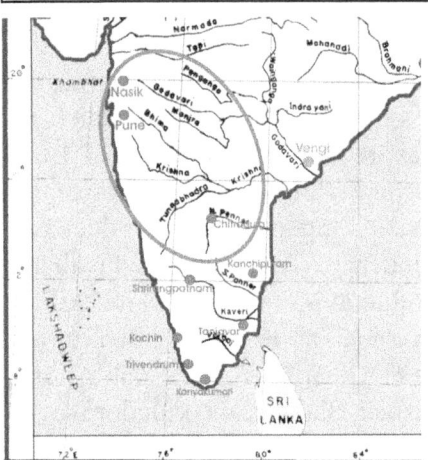

Emperor Gautamiputra Satakarni

Emperor Gautamiputra Satakarni (100-121) was considered the greatest king in the Satavahana Dynasty. He had the title of Trisamudratoyapaitvahana. Like Emperor Gautamiputra Satakarni, Maharaja Hal (56–61) proved to be an important ruler. As a pioneer peacekeeper, his tenure was only five years. King Hal was as much a political master as he was he was also a literary giant himself. In his kingship, Gunadhya Mahakavi wrote the famous collection of Brihat Katha Sangraha.

The reign of 72 years after the reign of king Hall is considered to be the Period of Victory for the Satavahana kingdom. In which they had lost not a single war.

The Satavahana kings had minted coins of lead metal. Famous Chaityas of Karli were built during the tenure of this kingdom and white marble stupas of Amravati were built.

We get the list of thirty kings of Satavahanas from Vishnu Purana, Vayu Purana, Matsya Purana, Brahmanda Purana and Bhagavata Purana. The present work gives a list based on the Matsya Purana, in which the names of 30 Satavahana kings have been directed, and here we have given the names of the kings as Devanagari words, based on the basis of the five Puranas.

142. Sauvir Dynasty, Sindh (Ancient Time)

For the Earlier Dynasty, please see :
  The Mahabharatiya family Tree
1. Rahugan   राहुगण
2. Sauvir   सौविर   Son of King Shibi

For the Next Dynasty, please see :
  Sindhu Dynasty of Sindh (Ancient Time)

Sauvir Dynasty

Sauvir was son of Shaibya,
the King of Shibi bold,
Sauvir kingdom was near,
the Sindhu Kingdom old. 1
Sindhu King Jayadrath,
was an aggressive man,
He occupied Sauvir and Shibi,
and as much land he can. 2

Sauvir Dynasty, Sindh

The capital of the Sauvir Dynasty that is mentioned in the Mahabharata and Vaidic era was Roruk Nagar in Sindh. King Ror Kumar of Roruk Nagar established the Ror Dynasty (see). It has been said in the ancient chronicles that the city of Roruk was not far from the city of Dwarka.

According to the Mahabharata, the great Indian villain of the Sindhu Dynasty was King Jayadrath, who was the brother-in-law of Durbuddhi Duryodhan (Gita 1.23). Sindhu King Jayadrath conquered the kingdoms of Sauvir and Shibi and merged them with his Sindhu kingdom. In the Mahabharata war, Jayadrath fought along with Duryodhan on the Kaurava side.

King Sauvir was a son of the Shibi king of Sindh. The other three sons of the Shibi king were: Madrak, Kekay and Vishadhar who were the rulers of Madra, Kekay and Sindhu kingdoms. The Shibi king is mentioned in the first chapter of the Shrimad Bhagavad Gita (Gita 1.5). Here he is gloriously called "Bull of Men."

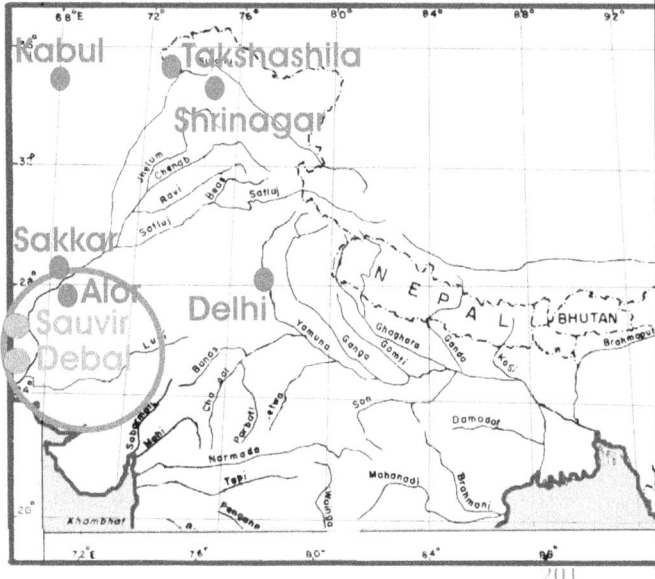

143. Sen Dynasty, Nadiya, Bengal (1074-1230)

For the Earlier Dynasty, please see :
Pal Dynasty of Mudagiri, Bengal (750–1174)

1. Samant Sen   सामंतसेन   1074–1095
2. Hemant Sen   हेमंतसेन   1095–1096
3. Vijay Sen   विजयसेन   1096–1159
4. Ballal Sen   बल्लालसेन   1159–1179
5. Lakshman Sen   लक्ष्मणसेन   1179–1205
6. Vishvarup Sen   विश्वरूपसेन   1205–1220
7. Keshav Sen   केशवसेन   1220–1250

Sen Dynasty
The Sena Kings of Bengal, were Shiva Devotees,
From the invaders, protected Hindu deities.

Their kings were authors,
who produced literature,
Originally they had in them, Karnataki nature.

Sen Dynasty

After the fall of Pal Dynasty of Bengal (750–1174), Ballal Sen (1159–1179) of Sen's Royal House declared independence at Lucknauti.

During the time of King Devpal (815-850) of the Pala Royal Family, many of the royal officials who came from Karnataka state were appointed in the Pala Kingdom. They themn became the Rulers of Bengal, as a result of the fall of the Pala Empire.

The first king among these Carnatic heroes was Samanta Sena (1074–1095), who decorated his lordship in Lucknauti district of Nadia. Nevertheless, King Vijay Sen (1096–1159) of the Sena Dynasty is considered to be the Founder of the Sena Royalty. Vimal Pradyumneshwar Temple of Devpada was built by King Vijayasena.

Raja Ballal Sen (1159–1179) was learned in litterateur. He composed the Dansagar Granth. And then, King Lakshmansen (1179–1205) completed a book Adbhutsagar began by king

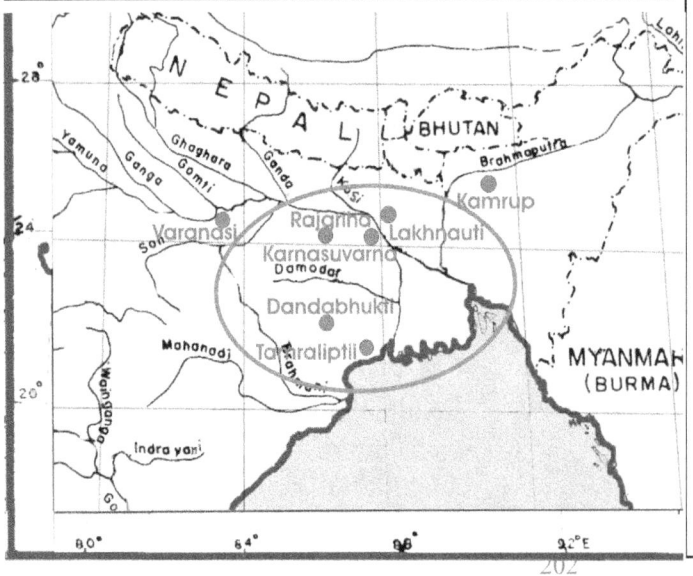

Hindu Rajtarangini

144. Shashank Dynasty, Gaur, Bengal (600-625)

For the Earlier Dynasty, please see :
Dupta Dynasty, Patliputra (240-730)

1. Shashank   शशांक   600-625
2. Manav   मानव   625-625

For the Next Dynasty, please see :
Pushyabhuti Dynasty, Patliputra (505-647)

Shashank Dynasty

The Gauda kingdom of Bengal,
is also called Shashank,
Shashank ruled from Karnasuvarna,
he was king of first rank. 1
He brought together,
all neighboring States,
He built a huge army,
and closed all the gates. 2
After the death of Shashank,
king became his son,
Manava was his name,
ground work he had not done. 3
Pushyabhuti king,
pretended to be his friend,
Attacked kingdom suddenly,
Manava could not defend. 4
Manava was defeated, he lost everything,
Shashank Dynasty ended,
Pushyabhuti became king. 5

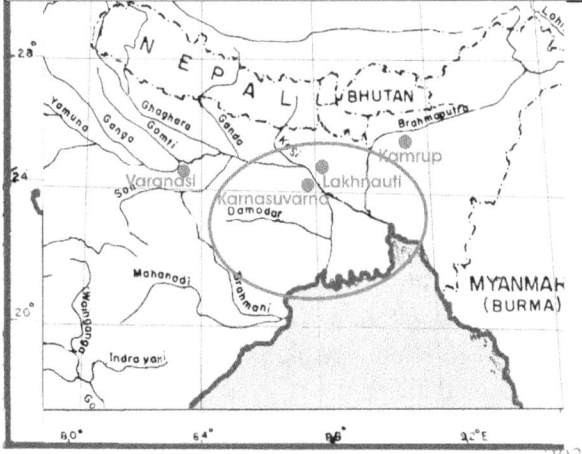

Shashank Dynasty

Shashank Dynasty is also called **Pundravardhana Dynasty**. During the fall of the Gupta Empire (240-730), many feudatory states of Bengal became independent. As a result, soon a new Pundravardhana kingdom was formed by the association of the Gaur State, Dandabhukti state, Bankura State, Karnasuvarna State, Varenda State, Rath State, Vanga State, Harikela State, Lakhnauti State of Bengal, etc. Karnasuvarna or the Paundra Nagar became the capital of this new kingdom.

Maharaja Shashank (600-625) of this Pundravardhana empire received the titles of Bengal King and Gaur Naresh. King Shashank was a native of Magadha country. King Shashank was contemporary of Pushyabhuti King Harshavardhana Shiladitya (606-647).

After the death of King Shashank, King Harshavardhana ended the Shashank kingdom by conquering Shashank's son King Manav (625-625). The Shashank Royal House ended after just two kings.

145. Shakya Gautam Dynasty (Ancient Time)

For the Earlier Dynasty, please see :
Raghu Dynasty (Ancient Time)

1. Okamukh Gautam — ओकामुख गौतम
2. Shivasanjaya Gautam — शिवसंजय गौतम
3. Shrihassar Gautam — श्रीहस्सर गौतम
4. Jayasen Gautam — जयसेन गौतम
5. Shrihahanu Gautam — श्रीहाहनु गौतम
6. Shuddhodhan Gautam — शुद्धोधन गौतम
7. Siddhartha Gautam — **सिद्धार्थ गौतम**
8. Rahul Gautam — राहुल गौतम
9. Angadev Gautam — अंगदेव गौतम
10. Balibhadra Gautam — बलिभद्र गौतम
11. Shriman Gautam — श्रीमान गौतम
12. Dhvajaman Gautam — ध्वजमान गौतम
13. Shivaman Gautam — शिवमान गौतम

For the Next Dynasty, please see :
Nand Dynasty (344–322 BC)

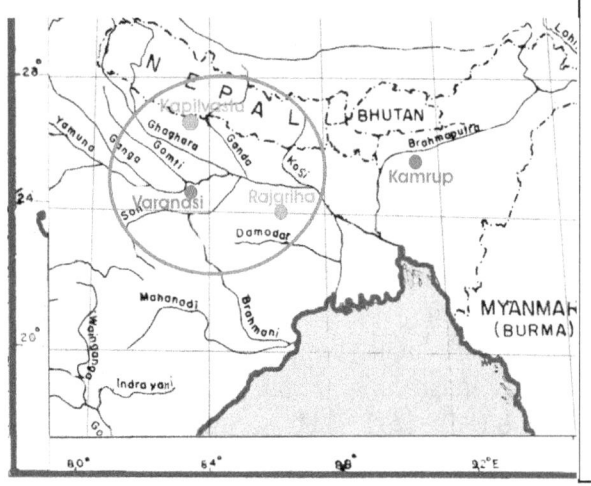

Shakya Dynasty of Kapilvastu

In Vishnu Purana, Brahma Purana and Bhagavata Purana it is said that, the Shakya Kshatriya Dynasty is the branch of the Solar Dynasty of King Ikshvaku. The Shakya Dynasty had its own independent kingdom with its capital at Kapilvastu.

During the Dynasty Yayati, Mandhata, Sagar, etc. had become great rulers. Okamukh was the first king of the Shakya clan in this Dynasty. The descendants of his son Shivsanjaya and grandson Shrihassar, are known to the Shakya people. Shrihassar's son Jayasen and his son was King Shrihahanu Gautama, whose son was the famous Maharaja Shuddhodhan.

In the kingdom of Maharaja Shuddhodhan, vast regions from Nepal to Magadha came. In this vast empire, there was a great ancient kingdom, Kashi, whose holy capital was Varanasi.

Angiras was the tribe of King Shuddhodhan. His great son Siddhartha (653–483 BC) who was the last great Hindu emperor of the Gautama Dynasty. Emperor Siddhartha Gautama retired and after the greatness of the Kshatriya Gautama kingdom came to an end. After the death of Siddhartha Gautama, his followers founded their own group by the side of Hindus, which later became known as Buddhism.

Hindu Monarch Siddhartha Gautam Buddha (653-483 BC)

Emperor Siddharth Gautam

Hindu Emperor Siddhartha Gautama was the only son of Shakya Maharaja Shuddhodhan Gautam and Queen Mayawati of the Kapilavastu in the Magadha country. Siddhartha's mother died within a few days after his birth, so he was brought up by Mahaprajapati Gautami, the maternal second queen. On his birth, the Royal Priest Kaundinya predicted that this child will either become a great Emperor or a great ascetic. As Siddhartha grew and started participating in battles, he witnessed torturing and killing of the subjects and he realized the transience of life. He discovered that nothing is eternal in the world. The living beings are trapped in a circle of life and death. He started pondering over the question of how to get salvation from all this. Finally, one night in search of a solution, he left his sleeping wife Yashodhara and the newborn son Rahul.

While doing austerities in the Urubilv forest for 35 years in search of Nirvana, one night Siddhartha came to know the fact of the "middle path." Around year 528, Siddhartha attained wisdom while meditating under a Banyan tree on a full moon night. He knew the four "Noble Truths" of life. 1. There is sorrow in life, 2. Grief arises from craving, 3. Prevention of craving is possible, 4. And there is an Eight Fold Path to make all this possible.

Analyzing this "Eight Fold Path," Siddhartha knew a series of twelve hierarchical links : 1. The first is ignorance, 2. the birth is a result of samskara, 3. Samskara gives beingness and form, 4. After that the knowledge of feeling arises, 5. Whereby the tactile knowledge, 6. Intellectual affliction of touch, 7. Craving from compassion, 8. Gratitude comes from craving, 9. Gratitude generates the desire for life, 10. Desire to have life gives rebirth, 11. which begins the cycle of birth and death, 12. which gives sorrow.

To get rid of this twelve-spoked cycle, Siddhartha discovered the Eight Fold Path of Nirvana : 1. Right vision, 2. Right thinking, 3. Right speech, 4. Right karma, 5. Right living, 6. Right memory, 7. Right wisdom, and 8. Right physique. By the practice of this eight-fold path, the being can get rid of the birth and death cycle. Siddhartha Gautama received such adjectives as the Buddha, the Arhant or the Siddha as a result of the attainment of the ultimate intelligence.

The first follower of Gautama Buddha was his nephew Anand and then the Magadha emperor Bimbisara (522–494 BC). After the death of Hindu Emperor Siddhartha Gautama Buddha in Kushinara in year 483 BC. Anand convened the first Buddhist assembly in Rajgriha in the same year and compiled "Five pillars" of Buddhism. After this council, the followers started giving the teachings of Buddha in the form of a religion. According to Hinduism, Lord Buddha is the ninth incarnation of Lord Vishnu.

146. Shalasthambha Dynasty, Kamrup, Assam (665-990)

For the Earlier Dynasty, please see :
Ahom Dynasty, Kamrup, Assam (355–1826)

#	Name	Devanagari	Years
1.	Shalastambha	शालस्तंभ	665–675
2.	–		675–725
3.	Shriharsha Deva	श्रीहर्षदेव	725–750
4.	Bal Varma-1	बालवर्मा-1	750–765
5.	Bal Varma-2	बालवर्मा-2	765–810
6.	Prolambha	प्रोलंभ	810–815
7.	Harjar Varma	हर्जरवर्मा	815–835
8.	Vanamal Varma	वनमाल्लवर्मा	835–865
9.	Jayamalla Varma	जयमलवर्मा	865–885
10.	Bal Varma-2	बालवर्मा-3	885–910
11.	–		910–970
12.	Tyaga Simha	त्यागसिंह	970–990

For the Next Dynasty, please see :
Ahom Dynasty, Kamruo, Assam (355–1826)

Shalastambha Dynasty

Shalastambha kings of Assam,
established their good name,
King Harshadeva of this line,
earned tremendous fame. 1
Their territory was wide, from Nepal to Bengal,
It also included, Wajji Magadh and Kosal. 2

Shalastambha Dynasty

After Ahom king Bhaskaravarma (594–650), The Shalastambha King (665–675) acquired the authority over Kamarup. After King Shalastambha's death, the great and best king of the Shalastambha Royal Dynasty (665-990) was Shri Harshadeva (725-750). Harshadeva's power extended from Assam to Bengal (Gaur) and Kosala.

King Harshadeva's sister was the wife of Thakur King Jayadeva-2 (705-729) of Nepal. The influence of Lichchhavi power now extended from Nepal to Magadha and Wajji Maha-Janapadas.

King Harjara Varma (815-835) bore the titles of Maha Rajadhiraj, Parameshwara, etc. Shalastambha kings were devotees of Shiva. The grand Mahabhairav temple of Sonitpur built by them is a proof of this devotion.

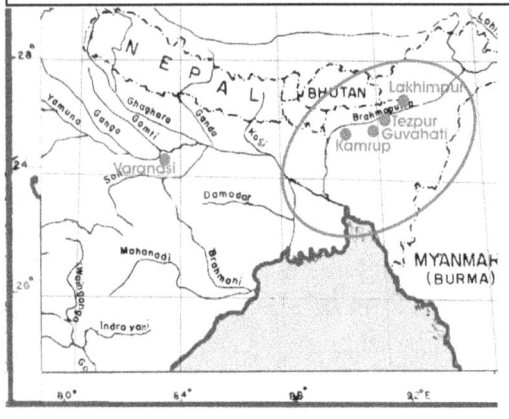

Shilahar Dynasty, Thana, Maharashtra (765-1265)

1. North Konkan (800-1265)
2. South Konkan (765-1024)
3. Kolhapur-Satara (940-1212)

147. Shilahar Dynasty, North Knokan (800-1265)

For the Earlier Dynasty, please see : Rashtrakut Dynasty, Malkhed (620–973)

#	Name	Devanagari	Period
1.	Vidyadhar	विद्याधर जिमूतवाहन ...	
2.	Kapardi-1	कपर्दी-1	800–825
3.	Pulashakti	पुलशक्ति	825–850
4.	Kapardi-2	कपर्दी-2	850–880
5.	Vappuvan	वप्पुवन	880–910
6.	Jhanjha	झंझ	910–930
7.	Goggiraj	गोग्गीराज	930–945
8.	Vajjad Deva-1	वज्जडदेव-1	945–965
9.	Chhadvi Deva	छद्वीदेव	965–975
10.	Aparajita	अपराजित	975–1010
11.	Vajjad Deva-2	वज्जडदेव-2	1010–1015
12.	Arikesari	अरिकेसरी	1015–1020
13.	Chhittaraj	छित्तराज	1020–1035
14.	Nagarjuna	नागार्जुन	1035–1045
15.	Mumminiraj	मुम्मिनीराज	1045–1070
16.	Anantpal	अनंतपाल-1	1070–1110
17.	Apararka	अपरार्क	1110–1139
18.	Haripal Deva	हरिपालदेव	1139–1155
19.	Mallikarjun	मल्लिकार्जुन	1155–1170
20.	Aparaditya	अपरादित्य	1170–1195
21.	Anant Deva-1	अनंतदेव-2	1195–1200
22.	Keshi Deva	केशीदेव	1200–1245
23.	Anant Deva-2	अनंतदेव-2	1245–1255
24.	Someshvar	सोमेश्वर	1255–1265

Shilahar Dynasty

Three branches of the Shilahar Dynasty existed in Maharashtra. 1. One was located in Thana-Kulaba region of North Konkan, 2. the second branch in Goa-Ratnagiri region of South Konkan and 3. the third branch was located in Kolhapur-Satara-Belgaum region of South Maharashtra. These three branches were established by Vidyadhar Jimutavahana of Nagarpur. The Shilahar kings were Kannada speakers, but became Marathi speakers as they lived in Maharashtra for five hundred years.

1. Shilahar of North Konkan :

The capital of this branch was in Sthanak (Thana). This branch was born as a feudatory of the Rashtrakuta Dynasty of Malkhed (620-973). The first king of this family was Kapardi-1 (800- 825) feudatory of Rashtrakuta emperor Govind-3 (773-814).

The contribution of the Shilahar kings of North Konkan is inscribed in the caves of Kanheri. King Chittaraja (1020–1035) was a patron of art and learning. He built many temples. King Apark (1110-1139) was adept at diverse arts and theology. He wrote a commentary on Yagyavalkyasamriti. Idols of Brahma, Vishnu, Mahesh, Mahishasura-mardini are worshipped in Shilahar temples.

148. Shilahar Dynasty, South Knokan (765-1024)

For the Earlier Dynasty, please see :
Rashtrakut Dynasty, Malkhed (620–973)

1.	Vidyadhar	विद्याधर जिमूतवाहन	...
2.	Sanafulla	सणफुल्ल	765–785
3.	Dhammiyar	धम्मियर	785–820
4.	Aiyapraj	ऐयपराज	820–845
5.	Avasar-1	अवसर–1	845–870
6.	Aditya Varma	आदित्यवर्मा	870–895
7.	Avasar-2	अवसर–2	895–920
8.	Indraraj	इन्द्रराज	920–945
9.	Bhima	भीम	945–970
10.	Avasar-3	अवसर–3	970–995
11.	Rattaraj	रट्टराज	995–1024

149. Shilahar, Kolhapur (940-1212)

For the Earlier Dynasty, please see :
Rashtrakut Dynasty, Malkhed (620–973)

1.	Jatig-1	जतिग–1	940–960
2.	Nyaya Deva	न्यायवर्मा	960–980
3.	Chandra	चंद्र	980–1000
4.	Jatig-2	जतिग–2	1000–1020
5.	Goka	गोक	1020–1050
6.	Mar Simha	मारसिंह	1050–1075
7.	Guhal	गुहल	1075–1085
8.	Bhojraj-1	भोजराज–1	1085–1100
9.	Ballal	बल्लाळ	1100–1110
10.	Gandraditya	गंडरादित्य	1110–1135
11.	Vijayaditya	विजयादित्य	1135–1175
12.	Bhojraj-2	भोजराज–2	1175–1212

Shilahar Dynasty

2. Shilahar of South Konkan :

This Shilahar Dynasty was also a feudatory of the Rashtrakuta kings. Their capital was in a village called Chandora in Goa. These people were descendants of the Ratta (850–1240) kings. Shilahar king Sanfulla (765-785) had established Ratnagiri city. King Bhima (945–970) had the title Ajatashatru. The Rashtrakuta power declined during their reign and thus the Shilahars became independent.

3. Shilahar of Kolhapur :

Like the Shilahar kings of North Konkan, the Shilahars of Kolhapur were also descendants of King Vidyadhar Jimutavahana and were also feudatories of the Rashtrakuta kingdom. The deity of the Kolhapur Shilahars was Shri Mahalakshmi. They believed that they got power from the grace of Mahalakshmi Devi.

The original founder of this branch Jatig-1 (940-960) was the care taker at the fortress of Gomant for the Rashtrakuta king Krishnaraya-3 (939-968) in Karnataka. Shilahar King Gandaraditya (1110-1135) had done public service by building many temples and ponds. The great Kopeshwar temple at Khidrapur, on the banks of the Krishna River, is the gift of this king. The descriptions of Shiva, Vishnu, Bhagwati, Digpal, Saraswati, Aditya etc. are found in the articles of Shilaharas as well as Shri Mahalakshmi. The temple of Ambernath built by King Marasingh (1050-1075) is the best temple of this period.

150. Shishunag Dynasty, Patliputra (413-344 BC)

For the Earlier Dynasty, please see :
Haryak Dynasty (544–413 BC)

1. Shishunag   शिशुनाग   413–394 BC
2. Kalashok   कालशोक   394–366 BC
3. Dashaputra   दशपुत्र   366–344 BC

For the Next Dynasty, please see :
Nand Dynasty (344–322 BC)

Shishunaga Dynasty

*King Shishunaga of Kashi,
defeated the Haryak ruler,
He became emperor,
and grew his kingdom bigger. 1*

*They ruled for hundred years,
and became very wealthy,
Ten brothers came together,
and made the kingship healthy. 2*

Shishunaga Dynasty

In year 413, King Shishunag (413-394 BC) of Shishunag Dynasty of Kashi killed King Nandivardhan of Pradyot Dynasty of Avanti (546-413 BC) and became the independent Governor of Pataliputra in Magadh country.

The great historical Pataliputra city of Magadha was founded by Emperor Ajatashatru (494–462 BC) of the Harayak Dynasty (544–413 BC). Later, the power of Shishunaga Dynasty grew to Avanti (Ujjain) and Malwa.

The Matsya Puran (272.6-17) says that King Shishunag had chosen Girivraj Nagar for his residence and appointed his son Kakavarna as the Governor of the kingdom of Varanasi (Kashi).

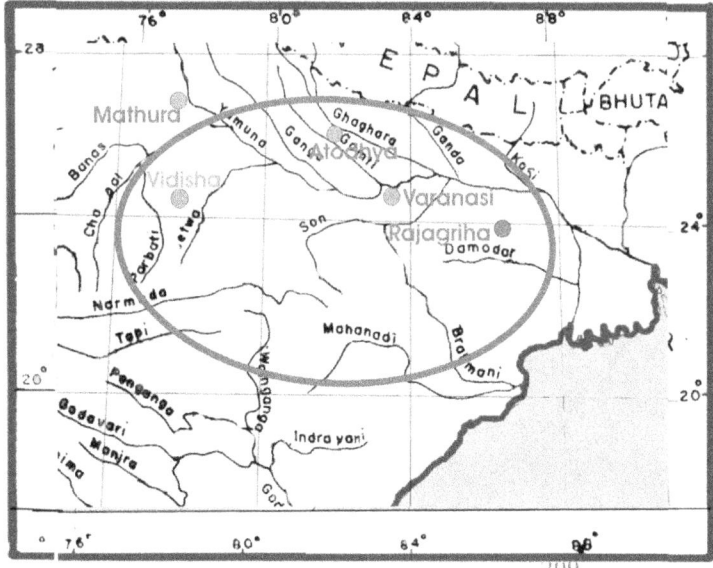

Hindu Rajtarangini

151. Simha Dynasty, Imphal, Manipur (1821-1948)

1.	Gambhir Simha-1	गंभीर सिंह–1	1821–1822
2.	Jai Simha	जय सिंह	1822–1823
3.	Jadu Simha	जादू सिंह	1823–1823
4.	Raghab Simha	रघब सिंह	1823–1824
5.	Bhagya Simha	भाग्य सिंह	1824–1825
6.	Gambhir Simha-2	गंभीर सिंह–2	1825–1834
7.	Chandra Kirti-1	चंद्रकीर्ति–1	1834–1844
8.	Nara Simha	नरसिंह	1844–1850
9.	Devendra Simha	देवेंद्र सिंह	1850–1850
10.	Chandra Kirti-2	चंद्रकीर्ति–2	1850–1886
11.	Suchandra Simha	सुचंद्र सिंह	1886–1890
12.	Kulachandra Simha	कुलचंद्र सिंह	1890–1891
13.	Chuda Simha	चूड़ा चंद्र सिंह	1891–1941
14.	Bodh Simha	बोध चंद्र	1941–1948

Simha Dynasty of Manipur

From 1129 BC to 44 AD, there was no known Royal Lineage on the land of Manipur. Imphal is the capital of the present kingdom of Manipur.

From King Nongda Pakhamba (33-154) to almost up to 1821 AD, the long but incomplete and vague non-Hindu history of present-day Manipur is written here and there.

King Garib Nivaz Singh accepted the Hindu religion in 1714 and named this kingdom Manipur (kingdom of diamonds) in 1724. The Kangla fort of Imphal became the capital of this Simha Dynasty. The border of Manipur at that time extended as far as Mandalay in Burma.

During the long reign of Maharaja Chuda Chandra Singh (1891–1941), the Indian cultural and diverse artistic skills of Manipur received a lot of encouragement and were promoted in other states. Today, the skillful work of art of Manipur is famous and popular all over India.

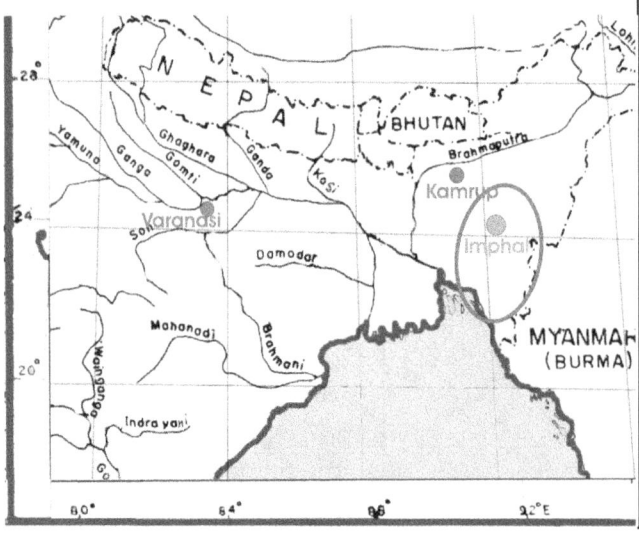

Shri lanka, Hindu Dynasties (429-1815)

1. Vijaya Dynasty (483 BC-352 AD)
2. Pandya Rula (429-455)
3. Chola Rule (1029-1055)
4. Arya Chakravarti Dynasty (1262-1619)
5. Nayak Rule (1739-1815)

The Royal House of Vijay, Anuradhapur

Shaivite Hinduism is the archaic culture of Shri Lanka, the history of which is generally in the Puranas. Buddhism came to Shri Lanka through the missionaries of Chakravarti Ashok Maurya (269–232 BC), when the seat of Hindu king of Vijayanagara in Shri Lanka, Devanampriya (247-207 BC), was in Tamrapani.

The available list of kings of Vijay Dynasty (based on The Mahavamsa) is as follows:

1. Vijay-1 (483–445 BC), **2.** Panduvasudeva (445–414 BC), **3.** Abhaya-1 (414–394 BC), **4.** Pandukabhaya (377–303) BC), **5.** Shiva-1 (307–247 BC), **6.** Devanampariya (247–207 BC), **7.** Uttiyan (207–197 BC), **8.** Shiva -2 (197–187 BC), **9.** Shura (187–177 BC), **10.** Sena-1 (177–155 BC), **11.** Asela (155–145 BC) .), **12.** Elara (145–101 BC), **13.** Dritagamani (101–77 BC), **14.** Shraddha (77–59 BC), **15.** Sthula (59–50 AD) BC), **16.** Vartagamani (44-17 BC), **17.** Mahakuli (17-3 BC), **18.** Naga-2 (3 BC-9 AD), **19.** Raj-1 (9-12 AD), **20.** Daru (12-16), **21.** Kutkan (16-38), **22.** Abhay-2 (38-66), **23.** Nag-3 (66-78), **24.** Amandanamani (78-88), **25.** Kani (88-91), **26.** Kulabhay (91-92), **27.** Shivali (92-95), **28.** Nag-4 (95-101), **29.** Shiva -3 (101–110), **30.** Yash (110–118), **31.** Raj – 2 (118–124), **32.** Vashbh (124–168), **33.** Nashik (168–171), **34.** Gajbahukmani (171-193), **35.** Nag-5 (193-199), **36.** Bhatik (199-223), **37.** Kanishtha (223-241), **38.** Nag-6 (241-243), **39.** Nag-7 (243-244), **40.** Nag-8 (244-263), **41.** Vahrak (263-285), **42.** Nag-9 (285-293), **43.** Nag-10 (293- 295), **44.** Vijay-2 (295-296), **45.** Sangh-1 (296-300), **46.** Sangh-2 (300-302), **47.** Abhay-3 (302-315), **48.** Raj -3 (315–325), **49.** Sena-2 (325–352).

152. Shri Lanka, Pandya Rule (429-455)

For the Earlier Dynasty, please see:
Pandya Dynasty, Madura (50–1310)

1. Pandu — पंडु — 429–434
2. Parindu — परिंदु — 434–437
3. Parindra — परिंद — 437–452
4. Dadhiya — दधिया — 452–455

153. Shri Lanka, Chola Rule (1029-1055)

For the Earlier Dynasty, please see:
Chola Dynasty, Tanjavar (50–1279)

1. Kashyap-1 — कश्यप-1 — 1029–1040
2. Mahalana — महालना — 1040–1042
3. Vikram — विक्रम — 1042–1043
4. Jagatpal — जगतपाल — 1043–1046
5. Parakram — पराक्रम — 1046–1048
6. Loka — लोक — 1048–1054
7. Kashyap-2 — कश्यप-2 — 1054–1055

154. Shri Lanka, Kendy Nayak Rule (1739-1815)

See No. 89, Kendy Nayak Dynasty, (1739–1815)

1. Vijay Rajsimha — विजय राजसिंह — 1739–1747
2. Kirti Shri Rajsimha — कीर्ति श्री राजसिंह — 1747–1782
3. Shri Rajsimha — श्री राजसिंह — 1782–1798
4. Vikram Rajsimha — विक्रम राजसिंह — 1798–1815

Tamil speaking Shiva of Telugu Nayak Dynasty of Madura Nayak Dynasty established the Nayak Dynasty in Kandy Shri Lanka (1739–1815). They were supported by the Nayak kings of Madura and Tanjavar.

The Royal Houses of Jaffna

1. Pandya Rule:

A large number of Sangam writings tell us about Tamil relations with the society of Jaffna. Ponappippu also states that Tamil was and is prevalent not only in Jaffna, but also in Puttalam, Anuradhapur and other interior parts of Shri Lanka.

Kulavamsa chronicle also mentions the existence of the Lambakarna Dynasty in the Pandya country. There is also evidence of a close relationship between Pandyas and the Lambarkarna clan in Shri Lanka. The northern part of Shri Lanka was the land of the Nagas. After a pause, Tamil kingdom continued in Jaffna.

2. Chola Rule:

The Chola princes ruled the entire Shri Lankan Tamil kingdom, during the reign of kings Elara, Sena and Katika (75 BC to 55 BC), after the invasion by Pandu and five other kings (43 AD to 62 AD) Madura dominated the rest of Shri Lanka Tamil. Came in

Shri Lanka was invaded by the Pandya king Shri Maru Shri Vallabh for the throne of Anuradhapur in the seventh century. Anuradhapur was seized by the Pandya armies. In an inscription by Rajadhiraja-1 (1044-1052), it is stated that the four kings of Shri Lanka lost the crown at the hands of the Chola Rajadhiraja.

3. Nayak Rule:

Tamil speaking Shiva devoted Telugu Nayak Dynasty of Madura Nayak Dynasty established the Nayak Dynasty in Kandy Shri Lanka (1739–1815). They were supported by

155. Shri Lanka, Arya Chakravarti Dynasty (1262-1619)

For the Earlier Dynasty, please see :
Pandya Dynasty, Madura (50-1422)

1. Kulashekhar — कुलशेखर प्रजाशेखरन — 1262–1284
2. Kulottunga — कुलोतुंग सागरशेखरन — 1284–1292
3. Vikram — विक्रम प्रजाशेखरन — 1292–1302
4. Varoday — वरोदय सागरशेखरन — 1302–1325
5. Martand — मार्तंड प्रजाशेखरन — 1325–1348
6. Guna Bhushan — गुणभूषण प्रजाशेखरन — 1348–1371
7. Viroday — वीरोदय प्रजाशेखरन — 1371–1380
8. Jayavira — जयवीर सागरशेखरन — 1308–1410
9. Gunavira — गुणवीर प्रजाशेखरन — 1410–1440
10. Kanak Surya — कनकसूर्य सागरशेखरन — 1440–1478
11. Singai — सिंगई प्रजाशेखरन-1 — 1478–1519
12. Singali-1 — सिंगली सागरशेखरन — 1519–1561
13. Purviraja-1 — पूर्वीराजा सागरशेखरन — 1561–1565
14. Kasi — कासी नायीनार — 1565–1570
15. Periya — पेरीया पिल्लाई सागरशेखरन — 1570–1582
16. Purviraja-2 — पूर्वीराजा सागरशेखरन — 1582–1591
17. Ethiriman — एथीरीमन प्रजाशेखरन — 1591–1617
18. Singali-2 — सिंगली प्रजाशेखरन-2 — 1617–1619

Arya Chakravarti Dynasty

Buddhism spread rapidly in Shri Lanka, only the Tamil people who came from Tamil Nadu in the Jaffna region of North Shri Lanka remained devoted to Hinduism. The Arya Chakravarti Dynasty of that Hindu society ruled from 1262 to 1619.

Shri Lankan Hindus mostly followed Shiva doctrine. Many people believe in the Shiva Siddhanta theory. Lord Shiva has five shrines in Shri Lanka. Shri Murugan is the most popular Hindu deity in Shri Lanka.

In the mythological accounts, mention of Nag people and Yaksha people in Sanatan period in Shri Lanka.

The Nag people were Shiva devotees and they worshiped snakes. No concrete evidence exists of whether the Nag people of Shri Lanka had any connection with the tribal Nag dynasties of Jharkhand (83–1948) or the Chhindak Nag Dynasty of Bastar (760–1324).

156. Sikh Dynasty, Punjab (1799-1849)

1. Ranjit Singh — रणजीत सिंह — 1799–1839
2. Kharak Singh — खड़क सिंह — 1839–1839
3. Naunihal Singh — नौनिहाल सिंह — 1839–1840
4. Rani Chand Kaur — चाँद कौर — 1841–1841
5. Sher Singh — शेर सिंह — 1841–1843
6. Dulip Singh — दुलीप सिंह — 1843–1849
7. Rani Jindan Kaur — जिंदन कौर — 1843–1849

Royal House of Sikhs

Maharaja Ranjit Singh (1780–1839) laid the foundation of the Sikh Empire in the northwestern region of India in 1799 in the city of Lahore, Punjab. Ranjit Singh united Sikh warrior groups (misls) to form a Sikh Khalsa state, which spread from the Khyber Valley in the West to the border of Tibet in the East and from Kashmir in the North to Mithan Kot in the south. But unfortunately, the Sikh empire could not last more than 50 years due to internal fighting and constant bloodshed.

Born a Hindu, Shri Guru Nanak Deva (1469-1539) is considered as the founder of Sikhism. He was followed by Guru Angad (1504–1552), Guru Amardas (1479–1574), Guru Ramdas (1534– 1581), Guru Arjun Deva (1563–1606), Guru Hargovind Singh (1595–1664), Guru Harai (1630–1661)), Guru Harkishan (1565–1664), Guru Tegh Bahadur (1621– 1675), and Guru Govind Singh (1666–1708).

गुरु नानक अमृत वाणी

अमृत वाणी, देन सबद की, आदिगुरु को, वाहेगुरु की
"दीपा मेरा एक नामु," सीख ले बंदे, बात शुरू की.
"ऐहु मेरा एक आधारु," पीयूष बानी, बाबेगुरु की.
"अंजन माही निरंजन रहिये, ऐहु जोगु," बोले गुरु जी.
"नानक दुखिया सब संसारु," सुनो भई साधो, बात गुरु की.

Guru Nanak
*The nectar words of the 'Shabad,'
Is the gift to Guru Nanak from God.
"Chanting the Name is the lamp of wisdom."
Learn it from Guru Nanak! 1
"This is my only Support,"
are the Nectar like words of Baaba Guru Nanak. 2
"The real Yoga is to remain sinless in the sinful world,"
says Guru Nanak. 3
"This whole world is filled with sorrow."
Listen O Disciple! says Guru Nanak. 4*

Hindu Rajtarangini

157. Sindhia Dynasty, Gwalior (1716-1948)

For the Earlier Dynasty, please see : Peshwa Dynasty (1713–1818)

1. Dattaji Shinde-1   दत्ताजी शिंदे
2. Jankoji   जनकोजी-1
3. Ranoji-1   राणोजी-1   1716-1745
4. Jayappa   जयप्पा   1745-1755
5. Dattaji-2   दत्ताजी   1755-1760
6. Jankoji-2   जनकोजी-2   1760-1763
7. Kadraji   कदराजी   1763-1763
8. Manaji   मानाजी   1764-1768
9. Mahadaji   **महादजी**   1768-1794
10. Daulatrao   दौलतराव   1794-1827
11. Jankoji-3   जनकोजी-3   1827-1843
12. Jayajirao   जयाजीराव   1843-1886
13. Madhavarao   माधवराव   1886-1925
14. Shivajirao   जिवाजीराव   1925-1948

Scindia Dynasty
*There were three great wars,
in the name of Panipat,
With long lasting consequences,
in the history of Bharat.* **1**
*The first battle was between, Lodi and Babar,
the second was between, Hemu and Akbar.* **2**
*The third war was between, Abdali and Peshwas,
Marathas got slaughtered, horrendous loss it was.*

Scindia Dynasty

Janakoji-1 Scindia (Shinde) was appointed in the army of Peshwa Balaji Vishwanathrao (1713-1720). His son Ranoji became a foot soldier in year 1716. Ranoji died in 1745 and after that Jayappa (1745–1755), Dattaji (1755–1760) and Janakoji-2 (1760–1763) earned name and fame in history with their heroism.

The most eminent king of the Scindia family was Mahadaji Scindia (1768–1794), a great warrior son of Ranoji and Chimabai. Mahadaji had done incredible valor in the reign of thirty years. He won many wars, like the battle og Talegav, Aurangabad, Sakharkheda, etc. and created fear in the minds of the Mughals of Delhi.

With Bhau Saheb Sadashivrao Peshwa (1730-1761), Mahadaji participated in the great Battle of Panipat-3 in 1761. After the death of Bhau Saheb Peshwa, Mahadaji Scindia (1727–1794) and Jaanakoji Scindia-2 (1760–1763) came out of the war, but Janakoji Sindhia, aged 16, got caught. He was put to death by Abdali (Durani) in 1763.

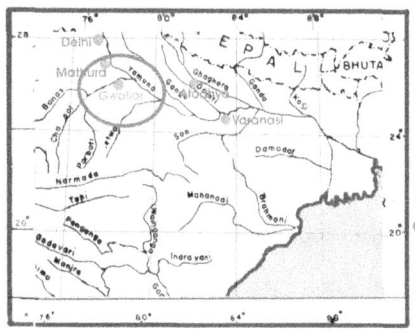

158. Sindhu Dynasty (Ancient Time)

For the Earlier Dynasty, please see :
The Mahabharatiya Great Family Tree

1. Shibi   शिबि (शिबीराज) ...
2. Vrishadarbha   वृषदर्भ ...
3. Vriddhakshetra   वृद्धक्षेत्र
4. Jayadrath   जयद्रथ (सिंधुराज)

For the Next Dynasty, please see :
Kaurav Dynasty (Ancient Time)

Sindhu Dynasty

Jayadratha was the king, of Sindhu Country,
He came from a good family,
but was power hungryy. 1
He overpowered all his neighbors,
foes and friends as well,
He got encouraged more,
to commit sins like hell. 2
He kidnapped Draupadi, with an evil mind,
And to kill unarmed Abhimanyu,
audacity he could find. 3
Arjun took revenge, with a severe vow,
In the Battle killed him,
with his Gandiva bow. 4

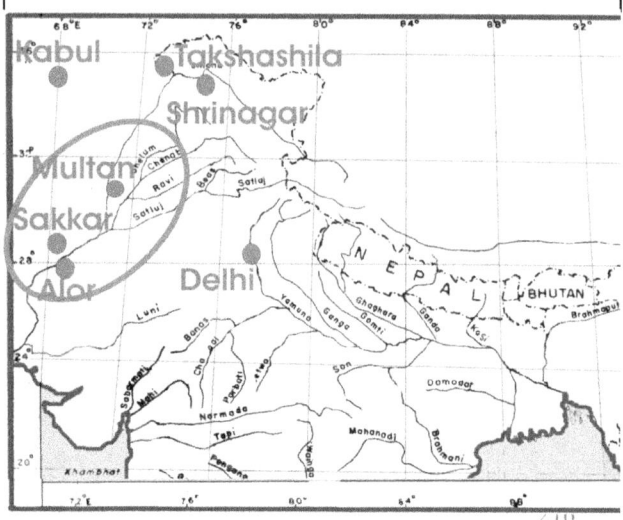

Sindhu Dynasty

Mentioned in the Mahabharata (Maha. Adi. 11.22) and Harivamsh Purana (2.56.26), the Sindhu Royal House of Sindh country was established in the Sanatan period by Vrishadarbha, son of Shibi Raja. Sindhu people were known as the Saindhavas. Five cities of the ancient period of this civilization, Mahenjodaro, Harapp, Chanhudango, Lothal and Kalibanga are well known at the present time.

The chief and eminent king of the Sindhu Dynasty was Jayadratha, son of Vriddhakshatra (Maha. 3.262). Jayadratha was the husband of Dusshila, the only daughter of the blind king Dhritarashtra. During the period of 12 year of exile of the Pandavas, Jayadratha tried to kidnap Draupadi with an evil mind. Therefore, Arjun trapped Jayadratha in the Chakravyuha during the Mahabharata War and killed him. It is known from the Mahabharata that after the death of Sindhu King Jayadratha in the Great War, his wife Dusshila returned back to the Sindhu country.

Hindu Rajtarangini

159. Sisodiya Dynasty, Chittor, Mewad (1303-1948)

For Earlier Dynasty, please see : Guhila Dynasty, Mewad (550–1303) #47

	Ratna Simha	रत्नसिंह (गुहिल)	1301-1303
1.	Lakshman Simha	लक्ष्मणसिंह	1303-1314
2.	Ari Simha-1	अरिसिंह–1	1314-1326
3.	Hammira-1	हम्मीर–1	1326-1364
4.	Kshetra Simha	क्षेत्रसिंह	1364-1382
5.	Lakha Simha	लाखासिंह	1382-1421
6.	Mokal	मोकल	1421-1433
7.	Kumbha	राणा कुंभा	1433-1468
8.	Udaykarn	उदयकर्ण	1468-1473
9.	Raymal	रायमल	1473-1506
10.	Sangram Simha-1	संग्रामसिंह–1, सांगा	1506-1528
11.	Ratan Simha	रतनसिंह	1527-1531
12.	Vikramjit Simha	विक्रमजीतसिंह	1531-1536
13.	Uday Simha	उदयसिंह	1537-1572
14.	Pratap Simha	प्रतापसिंह –1	1572-1597
15.	Amar Simha-1	अमरसिंह–1	1597-1620
16.	Karna Simha	कर्णसिंह	1620-1628
17.	Jagat Simha-1	जगतसिंह–1	1628-1652
18.	Raj Simha-1	राजसिंह–1	1652-1680
19.	Jai Simha	जयसिंह	1680-1699
20.	Amar Simha-2	अमरसिंह–2	1699-1716
21.	Sangram Simha-2	संग्रामसिंह–2	1716-1734
22.	Jagat Simha-2	जगतसिंह–2	1734-1752
23.	Pratap Simha-2	प्रतापसिंह–2	1752-1755
24.	Raj Simha-2	राजसिंह–2	1755-1762
25.	Ari Simha-2	अरिसिंह–2	1762-1773
26.	Hammira-2	हम्मीर–2	1773-1778
27.	Bhima Simha	भीमसिंह	1778-1828
28.	Jawan Simha	जवानसिंह	1828-1838

Sisodiya Maharana Dynasty

After the mass slaying of Guhilot Rajputs by the Mughals and then the self immolation by 16,000 Rajput ladies with Queen Padmini of Chittor in 1303, Rana Hammir Singh (1326-1364), the grandson of Maharana Lakshman Singh became the founder of the Sisodiya kingdom in 1326.

Maharana Hammir is considered to be the most powerful Rajput Rana of that time.

Rana Mokal (1421–1433) married the princess Saubhagya Devi of the Parmar Dynasty and formed relations in two Royal Houses. Maharana Kumbh or Kumbhakarna, son of Rana Mokal, was made Maharana in 1433. Kumbhakarna was born in 1423. He was offered the crown of Maharana after the death of his father at the age of ten (1433–1465).

Maharana Kumbha was a good ruler and politician. Maharana Kumbha had built the Kirti Stambha of Chittor to commemorate the Malwa victory. Maharana Sangram Singh (1506-1528) and Maharana Pratap Singh (1572–1597) are the two celestial stars of Indian history.

29. Sardar Simha	सरदारसिंह	1838–1842
30. Svarup Simha	स्वरूपसिंह	1842–1861
31. Shambhu Simha	शंभूसिंह	1861–1874
32. Sajjan Simha	सज्जनसिंह	1874–1884
33. Fateh Simha	फतहसिंह	1884–1930
34. Bhupal Simha	भूपालसिंह	1930–1948

Sisodiya Maharana Dynasty

(Background)
My dear fellow Indians,
I am writing the Rajput History,
As told by our forefathers,
presented here with glory. 1
Read it with patience,
each word is Amrit nectar,
You will know the truth,
brought to light hereafter. 2
Me, Ratnakar is writing,
as inspired by the Lord,
It is a precious subject,
therefore help me, God! 3

VICTORY TOWER, CHITTORGARH
1 Re INDIA

History of the Brave Rajpurs

Importance

Background gives us insight,
or else history is incomplete,
With love for my India,
here is account complete. 4
Background makes you aware,
who did what and when,
It teaches you lessons,
for each situation then. 5
Without having this experience,
one who acts with whim,
In the pit he falls, no one then can save him. 6
He walks in the dark,
without having a clue,
He runs in to stone wall,
his broken face turns blue. 7

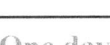

One day

One day long time ago, wonderful thing took place,
When the Lord was meditating, peace was on his face. 8
The storm had just calmed down, the dust had settled still,
Darkness was all gone, worldly ocean paused at will. 9
The sky had become all clear, ocean water was all blue,
Lakshmi ji was happy, Vishnu ji has imminent view. 10
Vishnu ji was resting, on the Shesh Nag bed,
Goddess Lakshmi with him, was sitting ahead. 11
Lakshmi said to Vishnu, hear the divine sound,
Shiva is playing Damru, and no evil is around. 12
Vishnu ji said, Yes! and he focused on Om!
The ambiance became sacred, divine every symptom. 13
When the moment was right, and favorable were the stars,
From the navel of Vishnu, arose a lotus stellar. 14
The stem of the lotus grew, up to sky from the ground,
on the thalamus there was, a throne shaped round. 15
Seated on the throne, was the Brahma Lord,
Four headed deity, reciting the celestial word. 16

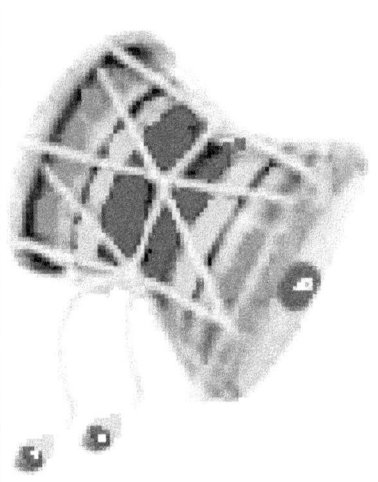

Miracle

Then the miracle occurred, in the early morn,
From the Brahma's body, Prajapatis were born. 17
From each Brahma's organ, hands legs and mind,
Prajapatis took birth, of Twenty-One kind. 18
The Prajapatis then made,
progenies in various herds,
Four classes of humans, plants animals birds. 19
Beings were put on earth, using the sixty-four arts,
Earth was happy to see, lives of different sorts. 20
Human race at the top, then animals birds and trees,
Humans of four classes, as per attributes three. 21

Kshatriyas

Kshatriyas were those, who could withstand wars,
They were fit to be kings, they were shining stars. 22
Best one among this class,
is Dashrath's son Shri Ram,
Righteous, and ethical, brave and always calm. 23
On that sacred land, known as Rajasthan,
Kshatriyas took birth, superior warrior clan. 24
Courageous faithful smart, fearless and charitable,
Powerful are those, Kshatriyas brave and able. 25

And

Putting their life on line, they do serve the land,
Rajasthan produced men,
they are Kshatriyas grand 26
Their seeds arose from Yajnas,
done by Vasishtha sage,
Thirty-Six primal branches,
who set warrior stage. 27
Names of those warrior clans, are written in Gold,
Rajasthan is that land, holy
Kshatriyas stronghold. 28
Kakutsa Mat Guhilot, Rajpal and Chauhan,
Lotpal and Dhanpal, Solanki Makwan. 29
Marud Saindhav Gaur, Chaulukya Chhand Parmar,
Chapotkat and Rathod, Nikumbhavar Pratihar. 30
Hehay Yautik Tank, Haritat Dadhishta Sihar,
Kavinis and Rosajut, Sadavar and Parihar . 31
Devar and Kalap, main thirty-six Rajput Parivar. 32

Maharani Padmini of Mewad (d. 1303)

Maharani Padmini of Mewad

Evil Sultan

Year thirteen-hundred and three,
witnessed the gruesome act,
Done by Delhi Sultan,
immoral as a fact, 1
The fourteenth Sultan of Delhi,
Ala-ud-din Khilji name,
Doing murders and molestation,
was his favorite game. 2
The moment he had heard,
about Queen Padmini's beauty,
He lost his complete head,
and forgot his moral duty. 3
His evil lust caught fire, to seize her by force,
Molesting other's wife,
Sultani mentality coarse. 4
Mean licentious cruel, that deceitful snake,
Body filled with poison, he was sinful and fake. 5
A mouse coveting lioness, evil desiring heaven,
A demon craving Goddess,
swan being desired by raven. 6

Thus

Khilji attacked Chittor,
with a tremendous horror,
Rajputs fought bravely, to protect their honor. 7
As the men got slaughtered,
the women would lose honor,
Knowing the habits of Sultans,
and history of their horror. 8
The ladies jumped in fire,
to avoid their molestation,
Sixteen-thousand attained heaven,
in a mass-immolation. 9

Then

When Khilji entered the fort,
all he got was their ashes,
The dead attained victory,
and the Sultan historic bashes. 10

Maharana Sangram Simha of Mewad (1509-1527)

Maharana Sangram Simha of Mewad

The Maharaja of Mewad, Rana Sanga the great,
Supreme freedom warrior, hero among the best. 1
A Sisodiya Rajput hero, super star on the battlefield,
Devoted to Lord Shiva, he would never yield. 2
Wounded in many battles, he had eighty scars,
From his head to toes, with weapons in different wars. 3
He had lost one eye, his one hand was broken,
His one leg was chopped, but courage was not shaken. 4
He won every battle, not one he ever lost,
He defeated Sultan Lodi, and won at heavy cost. 5
He won war of Gujrat, for the political cause,
Ahmadnagar Khatoli Idar, without rest or pause. 6
Even with terrible losses, he never had remorse,
He moved with electric speed, he had amazing horse. 7
A powerful warrior he was, had a very kind heart,
He was an ethical ruler, as well as he was smart. 8
King Rana Sanga had, trusted his army men,
He was brother to them, they were his brethren. 9
Safety of his kingdom, and his country men,
Was his foremost duty, his subjects loved him then. 10
He loved his motherland, with his humble heart,
His forefathers he adored, with respect on his part. 11

And

Steady like mountain, his hallow had a glow,
He had energy unending, like a river flow. 12
Praises of this lion, we can sing for ever,
From our heart, that would stop never. 13
Sanga was a fighter, like Bappa Raval,
Bappa was a hero, very high level. 14
The horse of Rana Sanga, spotless white stout,
With electric speed he ran, served Rana throughout. 15
Majestic looking horse, one in million creatures,
Big eyes and legs, all attractive features. 16

Also

Queen of Rana Sanga, Karunavati her name,
Beautiful like an angel, noble was her fame. 17
She was mother of Chittor, She was ruler able,
Goddess of the Mewad, she was valuable. 18

Rana was the Monarch, Rani was the Empress,
Enemies were afraid, Rana did them impress. 19

And then
In year Twenty-seven, grave danger came,
On the peaceful Rajasthan,
Mughals played their game. 20

Battle of Khanwa
Lodi was defeated, Mughals took the throne,
Babar became Sultan, with Sultani backbone. 21
Mughal turned their guns, to pulverize Rajastan,
Quickly Rana stood up, to oppose that Sultan. 22
Battlefield was Khanwa,
where the war took place,
Four kings joined Sanga,
in the battle with grace. 23

As
Ambar Chandi Bundi,
and Ajmer was the fourth,
Rajputs came to battle, crucial on the earth. 24
As the war ensued, Rajput men fought well,
But the Mughal guns,
hammered them like hell. 25
Mughals moved slowly, cannons throwing fire,
Rajputs were stunned, army startled entire. 26
Partners lost their courage,
and left the battlefield,
Rana's men stood firm,
as they refused to yield. 27
Rana's men got slaughtered,
few remained to defend,
Rana was wounded, and the war came to end. 28
Rana turned his horse, he went far away,
To assemble new force,
and to pave a new way. 29
Rana died soon then, with his dream in flame,
World will never forget,
Rana Sanga's good name. 30
Babar conquered Delhi, no one there to match,
No one was so brave,
to stop the Mughal march. 31

Hindu Rajtarangini

गीत – राग : यमन कल्याण

राणा संग

स्थायी

महावीर मेरा, महा संग राणा ।

अंतरा-1

किसी शस्त्र से ना, गिरा सूरमा ये ।
किसी दुःख से ना, दुखा आत्मा ये ।
खुशी से इसी के, स्तुति गीत गाना ।।

अंतरा-2

इसे देह पर घाव अस्सी हुए थे ।
यदि पाँव, कर, आँख आहत भए थे ।
तभी जंग में जीतता ये शहाणा ।।

अंतरा-3

इसे धर्मवीरों का है वीर माना ।
इसे कर्मवीरों का भी वीर माना ।
महा शूर योद्धा यही एक जाना ।।

Rana Sanga

Song

My Rana Sanga is very brave!

This hero will not fall with any weapon,
Nor does he becomes sad with any loss,
Let's sing his praises,
with our happy heart.

On his body he had, eighty war wounds,
His one eye was broken,
hand and foot was cut,
Still he fought and won,
many many wars.

He was the hero of freedom fighters,
He was the bravest of the brave men,
He was the hero of the brave men.

Maharana Pratap Simha of Mewad (1572-1597)

Maha Rana Pratap Simha

Rana Pratap Simha, was a great warrior,
The glory of his fame, was up to sky and higher. 1
This hero from Udaipur, was like Bajrang,
Sisodiya Rajput, his grandfather was Rana Sang. 2
Rana of the Mewar, on the battlefield,
Was so powerful, many evils he had killed. 3
He protected Hindu Dharma, with his heart and soul,
Protecting Motherland, was his supreme goal. 4
He fought with the Mughals, in many different wars,
He had many wounds, and received many scars. 5
His arms were strong, his stature very tall,
Firm was his faith, that would never fall. 6
He fought with a spear, of long heavy steel,
He had armor on his body, from his head to the heel. 7
Energy everlasting, he loved his motherland,
We should all sings his songs, raising right hand. 8

Battle of Haldighati

In Fifteen-seventy-six, the powerful Sultan,
Akbar was his name, attacked Rajastan. 1
His army very big, with guns cannons swords,
A Lakh evil men, breaking all records. 2
From Delhi they marched, on the way to Rajastan,
Winning many kings, destroying as much they can. 3
Demolished many temples, killed holy men,
Burnt many towns, molested Hindu women. 4
They reached Rajasthan, their final goal,
To capture golden land, to convert kingdom whole. 5
Mughals Hundred-thousand, with very evil mind,
Thirsty of the blood, and religious blind. 6

From this side

Rajputs also marched, to protect their land,
They trusted their king, Rana Pratap Grand. 7
Haldighati was the place, where two armies met,
The battle took place, to decide result net. 8
Rajputs Ten-thousand, ratio one-to-ten,
Rajputs in that ratio, killed the Mughal men. 9

Hindu Rajtarangini

Battle of Haldighati
continued

Akbar kept his elephant, in the middle of the army,
Protected from all sides, from the Rajput enemy. 10
Rana turned his horse, to fight with the Sultan,
And stood in the front, of the Mughal Satan. 11
And then
Looking at the Sultan, he poised the spear to kill,
Akbar looked at Rana, and shouted religious shrill. 12
Seeing the giant spear, and knowing Rajput skill,
He knew he will kill, but there is a moment still. 13
He bowed down in the fear, to miss the spear strike,
As if he was begging, for a mercy-like. 14
Rana accepted Akbar's, request to spare his life,
Rana turned back horse, and left the war strife. 15
Mughals had no ethics, nor they had any shame,
Killing looting conversion, is their real game. 16
Rana knew the rules, and ethics of a war,
As told by Shri Krishna, at Mahabharat prewar. 17

Lord Krishna had told
In an ethical war, you fight as a duty,
Not for taking revenge, nor to loot the booty. 18
It is same win or lose, same is also gain or loss,
The ethics for the Kshatriya, the net is your gross. 19
Other man's woman, is your sister daughter mother,
Other man is your, father son brother. 20
He who has surrendered, or put the weapon down,
Whose weapon is lost, or broken or thrown; 21
<u>He who is scared, and bowed his head</u>,
Or who has turned back, or who is dead; 22
Do not hit that man, or hurt him or kill,
This is war ethics, which you have to fulfill. 23
May you be the king, or may be a soldier,
For an ethical war, word of scriptures older. 24
Therefore
In front of Rana Pratap, Akbar bowed his head,
Rana thus forgave him, and horse he moved ahead. 25
O Rana! you are the one, who really won this war,
We will sing your songs, you are Shiva's avatar. 26

गीत – दादरा ताल

राणा प्रताप

स्थायी

तूने स्वातंत्र्य का बीज बोया,
और चलाई प्रणाली अमर है ।

अंतरा–1

तेरे पथ पर चला है शिवाजी,
उसने तुझको ही आदर्श माना ।
तूने सीनों में गौरव पिरोया,
तेरे कर्मों का अद्भुत असर है ।।

अंतरा–2

राजपूतों ने है तुझको पूजा,
तुमसे आदर्श ना कोई दूजा ।
तू ही अर्जुन यथा पांडवों का,
तेरी कीर्ति धरा पर अजर है ।।

अंतरा–3

शूर वीरों ने तुझको है माना,
तुझको वीरों का भी वीर जाना ।
तुझको भूलें कभी ना जमाना,
एहसानों की जिसको कदर है ।।

Rana Pratap

Song

*You have sown the seeds
of freedom fight,
And started the new trend.*

*On your path Shivaji walked,
You were his role model,
You put inspiration in his heart,
your deeds have marvelous effect.*

*The Rajputs have worshipped you,
There is none superior to you,
You are Arjun of the Pandavas,
Your fame is immortal*

*Braves consider you the Brave,
Gallants consider you the Gallant,
The world will never forget you,
They will value your gratitude.*

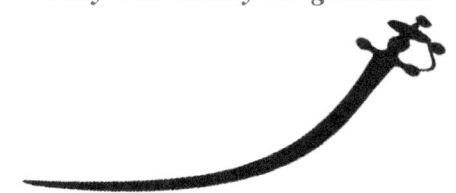

160. Shunga Dynasty, Vidisha (185-72 BC)

For the Earlier Dynasty, please see :
Maurya Dynasty, Paltiputra (322–184 BC)

1.	Pushyamitra	पुष्यमित्र	185–149 BC
2.	Agnimitra	अग्निमित्र	149–141 BC
3.	Vasujyeshtha	वसुज्येष्ठ	141–131 BC
4.	Vasumitra	वसुमित्र	131–124 BC
5.	Bhadra	भद्र	124–122 BC
6.	Pulindak	पुलिंदक	122–118 BC
7.	Ghoshavasu	घोषवसु	118–116 BC
8.	Vajramitra	वज्रमित्र	116–103 BC
9.	Bhagavat	भागवत	103–82 BC
10.	Devabhuti	देवभूति	82–72 BC

For the Next Dynasty, please see :
Kanva Dynasty, Patliputra (72–27 BC)

Sunga Dynasty

From the middle of the glorious Maurya Empire rule, due to the weakness of the rulers, their power gradually deteriorated and the last king Brihadratha (187-184 BC) was killed by his own commander Pushyamitra who took over the kingdom of Magadha. King Pushyamitra Sunga (185–149 BC) established the Sunga Dynasty in the capital city of Vidisha. This new state grew steadily from river Ganga to river Chambal in the West and to Wardha river in the south.

The Sanskrit Vyakarana-sutrakar Maharishi Patanjali was a contemporary of Pushyamitra. Patanjali had performed Ashwamedh Yajnas during Pushyamitra's coronation.

Pushyamitra, like the Maurya period, had to face the aggression of the Greeks. Sanskrit Mahakavi Kalidasa has mentioned this in his Malavikagnimitra play. Pushyamitra had also gained authority over the Vidarbha region.

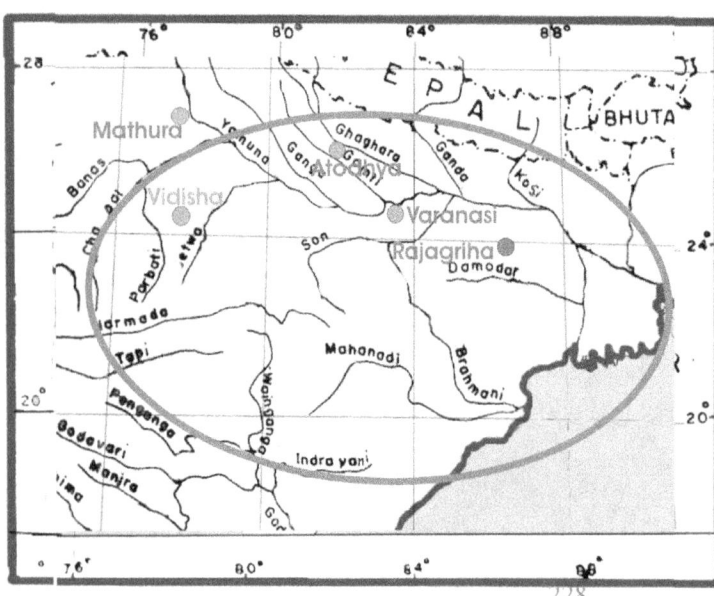

161. Shurasen Dynasty, Mathura (Ancient Time)

For the Earlier Dynasty, please see :
Vrishni Dynasty (Ancient Time)

1. Shurasen — शूरसेन
2. Ugrasen — उग्रसेन
3. Kamsa — कंस
4. Ugrasen — उग्रसेन   Second time

For the Next Dynasty, please see :
Brihadrath Dynasty (Ancient Time)

उग्रसेन की मथुरा

स्थायी
मथुरा नगरी भव में प्यारी,
स्नेह शाँति की फुलवारी ।
सुंदर मंगल जग में न्यारी,
स्वर्ग सेती सुखकारी है ।।

अंतरा-1
यहाँ न कोई चोरी लड़ाई, ना कुल द्रोही ना हरजाई ।
यहाँ सभी हैं भाई-भाई, सब मुख मीठी वाणी है ।।

अंतरा-2
सभी हैं दानी, सभी हैं ज्ञानी, सभी हैं स्नेही, सभी हैं प्रेमी
कोई न इनका कहीं है सानी, मथुरा जग की रानी है ।।

King Ugrsen's Mathura

Ugrasen's Mathura is a lovely city,
Peaceful and joy giving,
like Indra's heaven.
There is no thief, nor a traitor here,
Everyone is a brother,
speaking sweet to each other.
People are charitable, wise and loving,
Mathura is the Queen, on Yamuna river.

Shursen Dynasty

The ancient Yadava King Shursen was the ruler of Mathura. Shursen's son Vasudev and daughter Kunti were special in Mahabharatiya history. Vasudev's son Vaasudev was Shri Krishna. Kunti was the mother of Pandavas.

Shursen, the Lunar king of Mathura, was the son of King Devamidh (Maha. 147.29). Before this, Mathura kingdom was under the rule of Solar kings (Devi Bhagwat 4).

It is said in the Raghuvamsha of Kalidas that in Madhuban lived demon Lavan in the valley of Yamuna river, which was killed by Solar king Shatrughna of Raghu Dynasty and established power over Mathura. Shursen won the Mathura kingdom of from the Solar Dynasty and established Lunar power in Mathura.

After the death of Yadava king Shursen, his brother Vasudev continued to raise cows and Ugrasen became King of Mathura. King Ugrasen, the son of Ahuk, was a descendant of Yudhajit of the Vrishni clan.

Ugrasen's son Kamsa himself became king of Mathura after imprisoning his own father Ugrasen. Kamsa died at the hands of Shri Krishna with the permission from king Ugrasen. Ugrasen then again became the king of Mathura.

162. Simha Dynasty, Bharatpur, Rajastan (1722-1948)

1. Sua सुआ ...
2. Badan Simha बदन सिंह 1722–1756
3. Surajmal ब्रजेन्द्र सूरज मल 1756–1763
4. Jawahar Simha जवाहर सिंह 1763–1768
5. Ratan Simha रतन सिंह 1768–1769
6. Kesari Simha केशरी सिंह 1769–1771
7. Naval Simha नवल सिंह 1771–1776
8. Ranjit Simha रणजीत सिंह 1776–1805
9. Randhir Simha रणधीर सिंह 1805–1823
10. Baldev Simha बलदेव सिंह 1823–1825
11. Durjan Simha दुर्जन सिंह 1825–1826
12. Balvant Simha बलवंत सिंह 1826–1853
13. Jasvant Simha जसवंत सिंह 1853–1893
14. Ram Simha राम सिंह 1893–1900
15. Kishan Simha किशन सिंह 1900–1929
16. Brajendra Simha ब्रजेंद्र सिंह 1929–1947

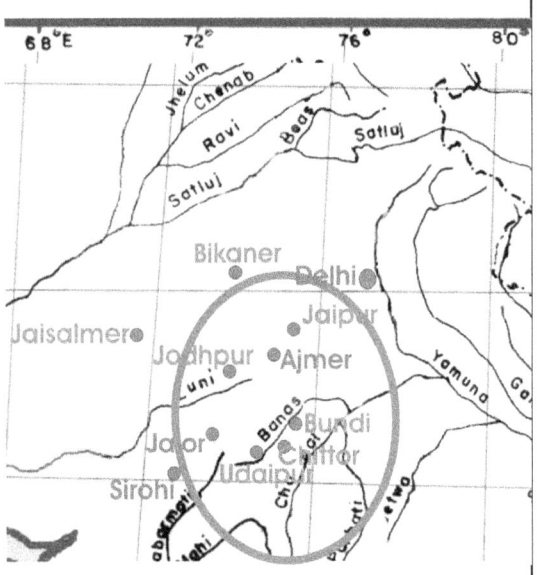

Simha Royal House, Bharatpur

In the fourteenth century, the great Jat Sardar Sua Simha of Rajasthan was a big landlord in the Bharatpur region. In the eighteenth century, his descendant Maharaja Badan Singh (1722–1756) founded the independent Bharatpur Dynasty.

Maharaja Brajendra Surajmal (1756-1763) took the fort of Agra from the Mughals in 1761 and that fort was in the hands of the Jats of Bharatpur till the death of Maharaja Surajmal (1774). Maharaja Surajmal is considered the most powerful and great ruler of Bharatpur. The rulers of Bharatpur from Maharaja Surajmal to Maharaja Ranjit Singh (1776–1805) were the partners in battles along with the Scindia regime of Gwalior (1776–1948).

Maharaja Badan Singh was conferred the title of Brajraj in 1722 by Kachhwaha Maharaja Sawai Jai Singh-2 (1853-1893) of Jaipur.

Maharaja Brijendra Suraj Mal had supported the Marathas in many battles, but Maharaja Jaswant Singh (1853–1893) accepted British slavery and fought in favor of the British against the Indians in the freedom struggle of 1857.

After that Bharatpur State became a feudatory of the British and ruled Bharatpur. In 1947, Maharaja Brajendra Singh (1929–1947) handed over the Bharatpur Institute to the Government of India and accepted retirement pay.

163. Solanki Dynasty, Patan, Gujrat (942-1244)

For the Earlier Dynasty, see : Chapotkat Dynasty, Anhilwad (690-942)

	Name	Devanagari	Years
	Bhuraj	भूराज	
	Karnaditya	कर्णादित्य	
	Chandraditya	चंद्रादित्य	
	Somaditya	सोमादित्य	
	Bhuvanaditya	भुवनादित्य	
1.	Moolraj-1	मूलराज-1	942-995
2.	Chamundraj	चामुंडराज	695-1010
3.	Vallabhraj	वल्लभराज	1010-1011
4.	Durlabhraj	दुर्लभराज	1011-1022
5.	Bhima Deva-1	भीमदेव-1	1022-1064
6.	Karna Deva	कर्णदेव	1064-1094
7.	Jaisimha-1	जयसिंह-1	1094-1143
8.	Kumarpal	कुमारपाल	1143-1172
9.	Ajaypal	अजयपाल	1171-1176
10.	Moolraj-2	मूलराज-2	1176-1178
11.	Bhima-2	भीम-2	1178-1223
12.	Jaisimha-2	जयसिंह-2	1223-1241
13.	Tribhuvanpal	त्रिभुवनपाल	1241-1244

Solanki Dynasty, Patan

The death of the last Chapotkat king Samanta Simha (935-942) created panic as he died without a successor.

Samant Simha's wife Queen Lilavati directed the power of Patan (Anhilwad) to their worthy son Moolraj. Moolraj took over the power of the Capattaka House tablished his Solanki Dynasty in Patan.

After two and a half years of rule, the Solanki power of Anhilwad fell into the hands of the Vaghela kings and the Solanki Rajput Dynasty of Patan came to an end.

For the Next Dynasty, please see : Waghela Dynasty, Anhilwad (1243-1304)

Solanki Dynasty

The last king Samant Simha,
of Chapotkat House,
Died Childless, and it created a Pause. 1
Sister of the king, was a smart woman,
She put forth her son,
to occupy the throne. 2
Prince Moolraj was, great warrior skilled,
He captured the throne,
and got his enemies killed. 3
He founded his House, by Solanki name,
They ruled two centuries,
then the Waghelas came. 4

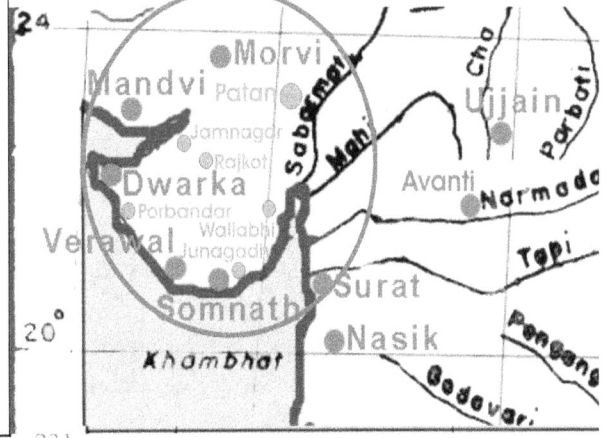

Hindu Rajtarangini

164. Sutiya Dynasty, Sadiya, Assam (1187-1524)

For the Earlier Dynasty, please see : Pal Dynasty of Bengal (750–1174)

#	Name	Devanagari	Period
1.	Bhishmak	भीष्मक	550–
2.	Virpal	वीरपाल	1187–1210
3.	Gauri Narayan	गौरी नारायण	1210–1250
4.	Shiv Narayan	शिव नारायण	1250–1270
5.	Jagat Narayan	जगत नारायण	1270–1585
6.	Prabho Narayan	प्रमो नारायण	1285–1305
7.	Hari Narayan	हरि नारायण	1305–1325
8.	Gokul Narayan	गोकुल नारायण	1325–1343
9.	Brij Narayan	ब्रिज नारायण	1343–1360
10.	Nandeshvar Narayan	नंदेश्वर	1360–1380
11.	Satya Narayan	सत्य नारायण	1380–1400
12.	Lakshmi Narayan	लक्ष्मी नारायण	1400–1420
13.	Dharma Narayan	धर्म नारायण	1420–1440
14.	Pratyaksha Narayan	प्रत्यक्ष नारायण	1440–1465
15.	Yash Narayan	यश नारायण	1465–1480
16.	Purnadhva Narayan	पूर्णध्व नारायण	1480–1500
17.	Dhir Narayan	धीर नारायण	1500–1522
18.	Chandra Narayan	चंद्र नारायण	1522–1524

For the Next Dynasty, please see :
Ahom Dynasty of Assam (355–1826)

Sutiya Dynasty

At the time of the decline of the Pala Empire (750–1174), Sutiya king Virpal (1187–1210) established his Sutiya kingdom on both sides of the Brahmaputra River in the Lakhimpur, Tinsukhia, Dibrugarh, Guwahati, etc. regions of Assam.

The Sutiya kings were devotees of Shiva and Vishnu. They had reverence for the Peacock, the vehicle of Sarasvati. Therefore, the names of their kings were based on Lord Shiva and Vishnu.

After the death of Mayuradhwaj Birpal, his son Gauri Narayan (1210-1250) became the king by assuming the title Ratnadvajpal. This king was powerful and always victorious. He gathered many Sutiya houses and built a huge army. As a result, the last king of Bengal, King Keshavsen (1220-1250), formed a matrimonial relationship with the Sutiya Dynasty. Sutiya rule was the largest kingdom of Assam during the time of Gauri Narayan (1210-1250). King Gauri Narayan displayed splendor by settling in the new capital at Sadiya.

During the time of King Chandra Narayan (1522–1524), Ahom king Swarga Narayana (1494–1539) annexed his kingdom after defeating the kingdom of Sutiya.

Thailand, Cambodia, Vietnam, Laos, Vietnam (50-1948)

1. Thailand   Vyadhpur   (50-627)
2.   Sukhdai   (1238-1438)
3.   Ayodhya   (1351-1782)
4.   Bangkok   (1782-1948)
4. Vietnam   Champa   (192-645)
5.   Chenla   (550-788)
6. Cambodia   Yashodpur   (802-1353)
7. Laos   Vyadhpur   (1353-1700)

Royal Houses of Thailand, Cambodia, Vietnam and Laos

Hindu culture had an astounding influence on the Sayam-Kampuchea region during the period of the Funan Kings (50–627), and it became so deep that at one time Hindu culture had become the national religion of the great Khmer Empire of Kampuchea (Cambodia).

In the twelfth century, as a result of this important work of emperor Suryavarma-2 (1113-1150) of Cambodia and sanctity enjoyed by the Khmer society, the public considered that king Suryavarma is blessed by God Vishnu. The world's greatest temple gave the eternal proof as the Angkor Wat (Vishnu-vishva) temple.

In Cambodia, Vietnam, Laos, along with Vishnu Lord Shiva was also worshiped in temple idols, of which amazing examples still exist in that eternal kingdom from place to place.

165. Thailand, Funan Dynasty, Vyadhpur (50-627)

For the Prior Dynasty, please see :
Chola Dynasty, Tanjavar (50–1279)

1. Kambu   कम्बू
2. Soma   सोम
3. Kaundinya-1   कौण्डिन्य-1
4. Kaundinya-2   कौण्डिन्य-2
5. Indra varma   इन्द्रवर्मा   434–
6. Jaya Varma   जयवर्मा   484–
7. Rudra Varma   रुद्रवर्मा   514–
8. Sarvabhauma Varma सार्वभौमवर्मा   550–627

166. Thailand, Indraditya Dynasty, Sukhdai (1238-1438)

For the Prior Dynasty, please see :
Funan Dynasty, Vyadhpur (50-627)

1. Indraditya   इन्द्रादित्य   1238–1275
2. Mahadharmaraj-1   महाधर्मराज–1   1275–1279
3. Rama   राम   1279–1317
4. Mahadharmaraj-2   महाधर्मराज–2   1317–1354
5. Mahadharmaraj-3   महाधर्मराज–3   1354–1376
6. Mahadharmaraj-4   महाधर्मराज–4   1376–1406
7. Mahadharmaraj-5   महाधर्मराज–5   1406–1419
8. Mahadharmaraj-6   महाधर्मराज–6   1419–1438

167. Thailand, Ram Dynasty, Ayodhya (Ayuthia) (1351-1782)

For the Prior Dynasty, please see :
Indraditya Dynasty, Sukhdai Thailand (1238-1438)

1. Ram-1 Tribodhi — राम–1 त्रिबोधी — 1351–1369
2. Ram-2 — राम–2 — 1369–1370
3. Bharma Raj-1 — ब्रह्मराज–1 — 1370–1388
4. Ram-3 — राम–3 — 1388–1395
5. Ram-4 — राम–4 — 1395–1408
6. Indra Raj — इन्द्रराज — 1408–1424
7. Brahma Raj-2 — ब्रह्मराज–2 — 1424–1448
8. Bharmaraj — ब्रह्मराज त्रैलोकनाथ — 1448–1488
9. Brahma Raj-3 — ब्रह्मराज–3 — 1488–1491
10. Ram-5 — राम–5 — 1491–1529
11. Brahma Raj-4 — ब्रह्मराज–4 — 1529–1534
12. Brahma Raj-5 — ब्रह्मराज–5 — 1758–1767
13. Dakshin — दक्षिण — 1767–1782

For the Next Dynasty, please see :
Ram Dynasty, Bangkok (1782-1948)

168. Thailand, Ram Dynasty, Bangkok (1782-1948)

For the Prior Dynasty, please see :
Funan Dynasty, Vyadhpur (50-627)

1. Ram-1, the Great — राम–1, महान — 1782–1809
2. Ram-2 — राम–2 — 1809–1824
3. Ram-3 — राम–3 — 1824–1851
4. Ram-4 — राम–4 — 1851–1868
5. Ram-5 — राम–5 — 1868–1910
6. Ram-6 — राम–6 — 1910–1925
7. Ram-7 — राम–7 — 1925–1935
8. Ram-8 — राम–8 — 1935–1946
9. Ram-9 — राम–9 — 1946–1948 (2016)

Royal Houses of Thailand, Cambodia, Vietnam and Laos

The sanctity of Laosi Ramayana *(Phra Lak Phra Lam)* had evoked deep interest in the nation towards the Hindu wisdom such as moral ethics, protection of women, affection, humility, humanity, selfless service, world is a family, etc.

Maharishi Markandeya brought Hindu culture to the island of Bali. In Cambodia, Ramayana became popular with the name of Rama-kirti and became a means of cultural progress. The Hindu kings of the Vietnam Islands had established their empire in to a chain by establishing the Champa Municipal Kingdoms.

Hindu culture was accepted as Rajdharma in Cambodia, Laos, Thailand, Vietnam, Java, Sumatra, Bali, etc. On the basis of this divine culture the Funan Empire (50-627) was based.

By the 15th century, before the advent of other religions, Cambodia and other southEast island societies had become a form of non-violent, peace loving, law abiding, well-to-do land like heaven, with the holy influence of Hinduism.

169. Vietnam, Shrimar Dynasty, Champa (192-645)

For the Prior Dynasty, please see :
Funan Dynasty, Vyadhpur (50-627)

1. Shrimar — श्रीमार — 192–
2. Bhadra Varma — भद्रवर्मा
3. Gang Raj — गंगराज
4. Manorath Varma — मनोरथवर्मा
5. Deva Varma — देववर्मा — 510–526
6. Vijay Varma — विजयवर्मा — 526–529
7. Rudra Varma — रुद्रवर्मा — 529–572
8. Shambhu Varma — शंभुवर्मा — 572–629
9. Prabhasa Varma — प्रभासवर्मा — 629–645

For the Next Dynasty, please see : Bhavavarma (550-802)

170. Vietnam, Bhava varma Dynasty, Chenla (550-788)

For the Prior Dynasty, please see :
Shrimar Dynasty Champa (192-645)

1. Bhava Varma-1 — भववर्मा–1 — 550–600
2. Mahendra Varma — महेंद्रवर्मा — 600–616
3. Ishanya Varma — ईशान्यवर्मा — 616–635
4. Bhava Varma-2 — भववर्मा–2 — 635–657
5. Jaya Varma-1 — जयवर्मा–1 — 657–690
6. Queen Jaya Devi — रानी जयदेवी — 690–713
7. Shambhu Varma-1 — शंभुवर्मा–1 — 713–716
8. Pushkaraksha — पुष्कराक्ष — 716–730
9. Shambhu Varma-2 — शंभुवर्मा–2 — 730–760
10. Rajendra Varma-2 — राजेन्द्रवर्मा — 760–780
11. Mahipati Varma — महीपतिवर्मा — 780–788

171. Cambodia, Varma Dynasty, Yashodapur (802-1353)

For the Prior Dynasty, please see :
Funan Dynasty, Vyadhpur (50-627)

1. Jaya Varma-1 — जयवर्मा–1 — 802–850
2. Jaya Varma-2 — जयवर्मा–2 — 850–876

Royal Houses of Thailand, Cambodia, Vietnam and Laos

Ramayana, popular in Thailand, is called Ramkin (Rama-kirti), which did a great work of public awakening.

This Ramkin Ramayana was written by the great King Ram-1 (1782–1809) of the Ram Dynasty (1782–1948) of Bangkok Thailand.

The plays and dances of this Ramayana were decorated with color on the stages and colorful pictures of the beautiful scenes of the plays were put in the palaces of Bangkok.

3.	Indra Varma-1	इन्द्रवर्मा-1	876–889
4.	Yasho Varma-1	यशोवर्मा-1	889–900
5.	Harsha Varma-1	हर्षवर्मा-1	900–921
6.	Ishanya Varma	ईशान्यवर्मा	921–928
7.	Jaya Varma-3	जयवर्मा-3	928–942
8.	Harsha Varma-2	हर्षवर्मा-2	968–944
9.	Rajendra Varma	राजन्द्रवर्मा	944–968
10.	Jaya Varma-4	जयवर्मा-4	968–1001
11.	Udayaditya Varma-1	उदयादित्यवर्मा-1	1001–1002
12.	Jaya Varma-4	जयवर्मा-5	1002–1003
13.	Surya Varma-1	सूर्यवर्मा-1	1003–1050
14.	Udayaditya Varma-2	उदयादित्यवर्मा-2	1050–1066
15.	Harsha-3	हर्षवर्मा-3	1066–1080
16.	Jaya Varma-6	जयवर्मा-6	1080–1107
17.	Dharnidhar Varma-1	धरणीधरवर्मा-1	1107–1113
18.	Surya Varma-2	सूर्यवर्मा-2	1113–1150
19.	Dharnidhar Varma-2	धरणीधरवर्मा-2	1150–1160
20.	Yasho Varma-2	यशोवर्मा-2	1160–1166
21.	Tribhuvanaditya Varma-2	त्रिभुवनवर्मा	1166–1181
22.	Jaya Varma-7	जयवर्मा-7	1181–1219
23.	Indra Varma-2	इन्द्रवर्मा-2	1219–1243
24.	Jaya Varma-8	जयवर्मा-8	1243–1295
25.	Indra Varma-3	इन्द्रवर्मा-3	1295–1308
26.	Indra Varma-4	इन्द्रवर्मा-4	1308–1327
27.	Jaya Varma-9	जयवर्मा-9	1327–1353

172. Laos, Lain Zang Dynasty, Vyadhpur (1353-1706)

For the Prior Dynasty, please see :
Varma Dynasty, Cambodia, Yashodapur (802-1353)

1.	Shri Shuddha Nagar	श्री शुद्ध नगर	1353–1372
2.	Shri Bhuvananathdeva	श्री भुवननाथ देव	1372–1417
3.	Shri Lakshman Simha	श्री लक्ष्मण सिंह	1417–1428

Royal Houses of Thailand, Cambodia, Vietnam and Laos

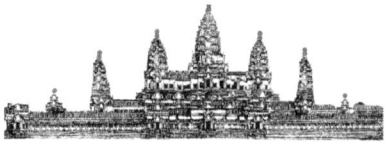

Like Thialand, in Cambodia also the plays, songs and dances from the stories of Ramayana were staged on a big scale. It spread the Hindu culture in the kingdoms of Vietnam, Laos, Malaya, Java, Sumatra and all other minor islands of this region.

#	Name	Devanagari	Years
4.	Shri Brahma Kumar	श्री ब्रह्म कुमार	1428–1429
5.	Shri Yugadhar	श्री युगाधर	1429–1430
6.	Shri Kunikam	श्री कुणिकाम	1430–1432
7.	Shri Kama Dharmasar	श्री काम धर्मसार	1432–1433
8.	Shri Bhuvana Ban	श्री भुवन बाण	1433–1436
9.	Shri Kama Kirti	श्री काम कीर्ति	1436–1438
10.	Shri Bhima Mahadevi	श्री भीम महादेवी	1438–1441
11.	Shri Shankha Chakrapati	श्री शंख चक्रपति	1441–1479
12.	Shri Suvarma	श्री सुवर्मा	1479–1486
13.	Shri Dayabhuvannath	दया भुवन नाथ	1486–1495
14.	Shri Jambuya Rajashri	जंबूय राजश्री	1495–1500
15.	Shri Vishnu	श्री विष्णु	1500–1520
16.	Shri Narendra	भूमि नरेन्द्र	1520–1548
17.	Shri Bhuvanadipati	भुवनादि आदिपति	1548–1572
18.	Shri Buddhisen	बुद्धिसेन	1572–1575
19.	Vira Varma	वीर वर्मा	1575–1580
20.	Shri Sumangal	श्री सुमंगल	1580–1583
21.	Navi Raja	नवी राजा	1583–1591
22.	Raja Bhupati	राजा भूपति	1591–1596
23.	Vira Vaman	वीर वामन	1596–1622
24.	Buddhisha	बुद्धीश	1622–1627
25.	Manikya	माणिक्य	1627–1633
26.	Dharma Karma	धर्म कर्म	1633–1637
27.	Vijaya Raj	विजय राज	1637–1638
28.	Surya Varma	सूर्यवर्मा	1638–1690
29.	Chandralaya	चंद्रालय	1690–1695
30.	Nandraj	नंदराज	1695–1698
31.	Dharmik Chandrapuri	धार्मिक चंद्रपुरी	1698–1706

Royal Houses of Thailand, Cambodia, Vietnam and Laos

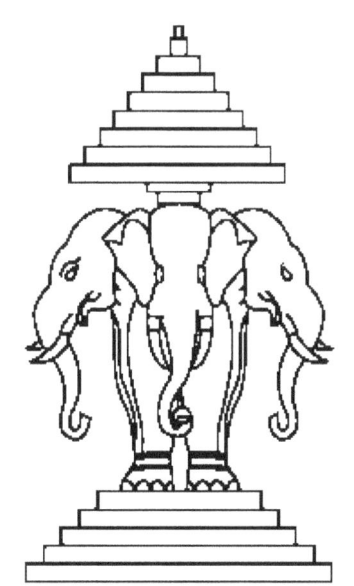

Hindu Dynasties of Laos

The holy souls of Laos, were soaked in Hindu Culture,
With devotion to Shiva and Vishnu, their sins were washed pure. 1
As long Hindu Dharma was, all over the kingdom,
So long impurity was at bay, world was filled with wisdom. 2

173. Tomar Dynasty, Delhi (736-1192), Gwalior (1375-1523)

For the Prior Dynasty, please see : Gurjar-Pratihar Dynasty (400–725)

1. Anangpal-1 अनंगपाल-1 736-754
2. Vishal विशाल 754-773
3. Gangeyadev गांगेय देव 773-794
4. Prithvimal पृथ्वीमल 794-814
5. Jagdev जगदेव 814-834
6. Narpal नरपाल 834-849
7. Udaypal उदयपाल 849-875
8. Apricchhadev आपृच्छदेव 875-897
9. Pipalraidev पीपलरायदेव 897-919
10. Raghupal रघुपाल 919-940
11. Tilhanpal तीव्हनपाल 940-944
12. Tolpal तोलपाल 944-961
13. Gopal गोपाल 961-979
14. Sulakshanpal सुलक्षणपाल 979-1005
15. Yashpal यशपाल 1005-1021
16. Kunvarpal कुंवरपाल 1021-1051
17. Anangpal-2 अनंगपाल-2 1051-1081
18. Tezpal तेजपाल 1081-1105
19. Mahipal महीपाल 1105-1130
20. Vijaypal विजयपाल 1130-1151
21. Madanpal मदनपाल 1151-1167
22. Prithviraj पृथ्वीराज 1167-1189
23. Govindraj गोविंदराज 1189-1192

Son of Prithvi Raj Chauhan

For the Next Dynasty, please see : Chauhan, Ranthambhor (1194–1301)

Tomar Dynasty

The Tomar Rajputs established their authority over Delhi and the surrounding areas while power of the royal family of the Gurjar-Pratihara (400-725) was eroding in the Delhi region. The founder of the Tomar Dynasty is believed to be King Anangpal (736-754), the creator of Lalkot fort in Delhi.

King Anangpal-2 (1051-1081) was the maternal grandfather of Samyogita, the wife of King Rai Pithora Prithviraj Chauhan (1177-1192) of Ajayameru (Ajmer). The infamous King Jaiachand Rathor (1170-1194) of Kannauj was her father. Thousands of years after the Pandavas ruled Indraprastha, the Tomar Dynasty had the auspicious opportunity to re-establish the Delhi as Rajdhani. Apart from Delhi, the states of Punjab, Haryana, Gwalior Uttar Pradesh were also under the Tomar rulers of Delhi. The names of the Tomar Kings **Anangpal-1, Bealdev, Jauldev,** etc. are also known in the history.

At the time of Tomar King Madanpal (1151-1167), the mighty ruler of Ajayameru, Vigraharaj-4 Chauhan (1153-1166), had established authority over Delhi. Madanpal Tomar, impressed by the bravery of Vigraharaj, gave him his daughter Desaladevi in marriage.

174. Tomar Dynasty of Gwalior

1. Virsingh 1375-1400
2. Uddharan 1400-1402
3. Viramdev 1402-1423
4. Ganpati 1423-1425
5. Dungar 1425-1459
6. Kirtisingh 1459-1480
7. Kalyan 1480-1486
8. Mansingh 1486-1516
9. Vikram 1516-1523

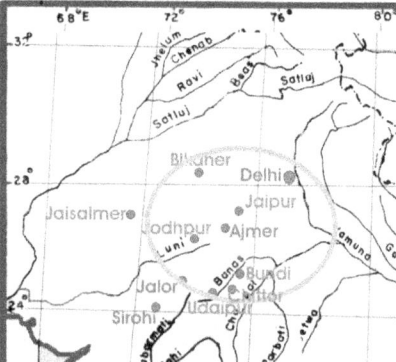

Hindu Rajtarangini

175. Traikutak Dynasty, Junnar, Maharashtra (388-492)

For the Prior Dynasty, please see :
Vakatak Dynasty of Nandivardhan (250–510)

1. Shiva Datta   शिवदत्त   –
2. Indra Sen   इन्द्रसेन   388–445
3. Dhrha Sen   दहसेन   445–475
4. Vyaghra Sen   व्याघ्रसेन   475–492

For the Next Dynasty also, please see :
Vakatak Dynasty of Nandivardhan (250–510)

Traikutak Dynasty

The Traikutaks of Maharashtra,
were a line of Hehays,
Descendents of Indradatta,
ruled Konkan in those days. 1

King Indradatta was,
Shivadatta's son,
Vishnu's devotee he was,
he was religious person. 2

Traikutak Dynasty

The Traikutaks, as stated in the epic Raghuvamsha of Mahakavi Kalidasa, were natives of North Konkan in West Maharashtra and South Gujarat. The capital of the Traikutak Dynasty was in the city of Junnar in Maharashtra. The Traikutak Dynasty was originally an older branch of the Yadava or Ahir or Aabhir Dynasty of Devgiri, which is considered a as descendant of the Vakataka clan (250-510).

The Traikutak people are also considered as descendants of the Hehaya clan of Gujarat. The noble Vrishni Yadavas or Ahirs of Gujarat are relatives of the Yadavas of Devgiri in Maharashtra. The mother of Shivadatt's son King Indrasen (388-445) was of Modhar Gotra. The invasion of the Vakataka king Harishen (490–510) of Nandivardhana in year 492 led to the end of the Traikutak Dynasty. The Traikutak kings were devoted to Lord Vishnu. They minted their own silver coins. King Dahrasen performed Ashwamedha yajna.

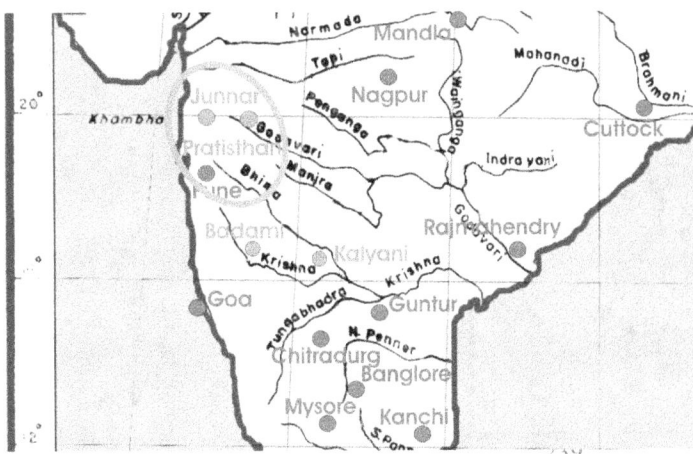

Hindu Rajtarangini

176. Uchchhakalpa Dynasty, Baghelkhand (400-533)

For the Prior Dynasty, please see :
Gupta Dynasty (240–730)

1. Ogha Deva   ओघदेव   400–
2. Kumar Deva   कुमारदेव
3. Jaya Swami   जयस्वामी
4. Vyaghra Deva   व्याघ्रदेव
5. Jaya Nath   जयनाथ   493–508
6. Sarva Nath   सर्वनाथ   508–533

For the Next Dynasty, please see :
Pushyabhuti Dynasty (505–647)

The Dohas tell us :
Uchchhakalpa Dynasty

This Royal House great, grew in Panna land,
Under Gupta Monarchs, holding their hand. 1

Brave Oghadeva, was their first king,
The following rulers bore, Maharaja ranking. 2

The Uchcchakalpa kings, were feudatory,
Of the Gupta Monarchs, who gave them glory. 3

Panna was their region, and the Capital City,
Six kings were great, known in this dynasty. 4

When Guptas were defeated,
by Pushyabhuti masters,
Uchchhakalpas also ended,
and Pushyabhutis became rulers. 5

Royal House of Uchchhakalpa

This royal family of central India was a neighbor of Parivrajak Royal House of Baghelkhand in the east. Like the Parivrajak kings, the kings of the Ucchhakalpa Dynasty were feudal kings under the Gupta emperors. Their capital was the city of Uchchhakalpa (Panna).

Maharaja Oghadeva of this Dynasty flourished in the fifth century. The names of five kings after King Oghadeva are known in the history.

The history of this Royal Family is known to Indian history only through the copper plates and rock edicts.

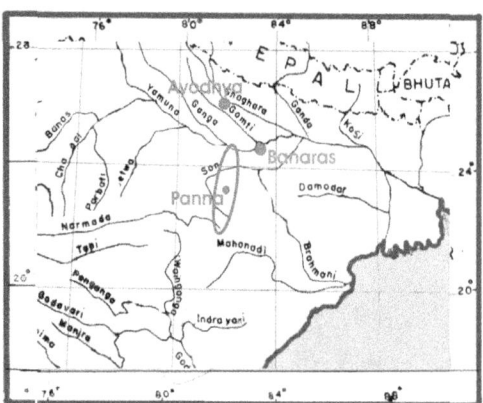

177. Utpal Dynasty, Kashmir (855-949)

For the Next Dynasty, please see :
Karkot Dynasty (631–855)

#	Name	(Devanagari)	Years
1.	Avanti Varma	अवंतिवर्मा	855–883
2.	Shankar Varma	शंकरवर्मा	883–902
3.	Gopal Varma	गोपालवर्मा	920–904
4.	Sankat Varma	संकटवर्मा	904–904
5.	Queen Sugandha	रानी सुगंधा	904–906
6.	Partha Varma-1	पार्थवर्मा (1)	906–920
7.	Nirjit Varma Pangu	निर्जितवर्मा पंगु	920–922
8.	Chakra Varma-1	चक्रवर्मा (1)	922–933
9.	Shura Varma-1	शूरवर्मा 1	933–934
10.	Partha Varma-2	पार्थवर्मा (2)	934–935
11.	Chakra Varma-2	चक्रवर्मा (2)	935–935
12.	Shambhu Vardhan	शंभुवर्धन	935–935
13.	Chakra Varma-3	चक्रवर्मा (3)	935–935
14.	Unmarravanti	उन्मत्तवन्ती	937–939
15.	Shura Varma-2	शूरवर्मा 2	939–939
16.	Yashaskar Deva	यशस्करदेव	939–948
17.	Sangrama Deva	संग्रामदेव	948–949

For the Next Dynasty, please see :
Pravargupta Dynasty (949–1003)

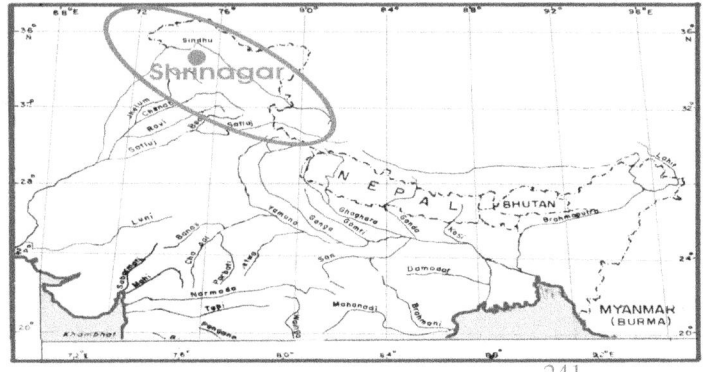

Utpal Dynasty

Avantivarma, the founder of Avantipur established the Utpal Dynasty by seizing power from Utpalpid (851-855), the last king of the Karkota Royal House of Kashmir (631-855).

The first two kings of this Dynasty, King Avanti Varma (855-883) and King Shankar varma (883-902), were most well known.

King Shura Varma-2 (939-939) was the illegitimate son of King Unmattavanti, therefore, his shrewd minister Prabhakar Deva placed his own son Yashaskaradeva (939-948) on the throne of Kashmir.

Many historians count the clan following King Yashskara Deva as an independent Yashaskar Dynasty (939-949) of Kashmir.

Hindu Rajtarangini

178. Wadiyar Dynasty, Mysore (1399-1947)

For the Earlier Dynasty, please see :
Tuluv Nayak Dynasty, ivajayanagar (1503–1565)

#	Name	Devanagari	Years
1.	Yadu Dev Ray	यदु देवराय	1399-1423
2.	Hariya Bettad Chamraj-1	चामराज–1	1423-1459
3.	Timma Raj-1	तिम्मराज–1	1479-1479
4.	Hariya Bettad Chamraj-2	चामराज–2	1479-1513
5.	Hariya Bettad Chamraj-3	चामराज–3	1513-1533
6.	Timma Raj-2	तिम्मराज–2	1553-1572
7.	Bol Chamraj-4	बोल चामराज–4	1572-1576
8.	Bettad Chamraj Mummadi	चामराज–5	1576-1578
9.	Raj-1	राज–1	1578-1617
10.	Chamraj-6	चामराज–6	1617-1637
11.	Immadi Raj	इम्मडि राज	1637-1638
12.	Kanthirav Narasraj-1	नरसराज–1	1638-1659
13.	Kamp Devraj	कम्प देवराज	1659-1673
14.	Chikka Devraj	चिक्क देवराज	1673-1704
15.	Kanthirav Narasraj-2	नरसराज–2	1704-1714
16.	Krishnaraj-1	दोड्ड कृष्णराज	1714-1732
17.	Chamraj-7	चामराज–7	1732-1734
18.	Krishnaraj-2	इम्मडि कृष्णराज–2	1734-1766
19.	Chamraj-8	खासा चामराज–8	1766-1770
20.	Chamraj-9	बेट्टद चामराज–9	1770-1776
21.	Chamraj-10	खासा चामराज–10	1776-1796
22.	–	1796-1799 Tipu Sultan's usurpation	
23.	Krishnaraj-3	मुम्मडि कृष्णराज–3	1799-1868
24.	Chamraj-11	मुम्मडि चामराज–11	1868-1895
25.	Krishnaraj-4	नाल्वडि कृष्णराज–4	1895-1940
26.	Chamraj-12	जय चामराज–12	1940-1947

Wadiyar Dynasty

After the fall of the Vijayanagar Empire (1565), the Mysore King Timmaraja-2 (1553–1572) declared the Kingdom of Mysore independent. The kingdom of Mysore was the feudatory of Vijayanagar from the time of King Yadu Devaraj (1399-1423).

The Wadiyar king was the patron of Karnatak culture, arts and music. In 1399, Queen Mother Chikkadevi, of the Yadavas, married her daughter Dovajammanni to Devarai Wadiyar and anointed Yadu Devaraj at the throne of Mysore. In this way, King Devrat became the first Lunar Dynasty of Mysore (1399-1423).

In 1610, Raj-1 (1578–1617) shifted the capital from Mysore to Shrirangapatnam, but in 1799 Mummadi Krishnaraja-3 (1799–1868) restored the capital back to Mysore. Since then, the heaven like garden and grandeur of Mysore is not built anywhere else in India.

Maharaja Krishnaraj Wadiyar, Mysore (1895-1940)

The Vrindavan Garden of Mysore

The Garden of Vrindavan,
has beautiful flowers,
Irrigated with divine, Kaveri river waters. 1
The ground covered with grass,
nowhere there is dust,
The water in the ponds,
ripples with every gust. 2
Bees on the flowers, and the butterflies,
The fish in the ponds,
heart touching and nice. 3
The colourful gold fish,
and turtles in the water,
Are very playful, the beauty that is super. 4
The frogs make sounds, in their playful mood,
They won't let you touch,
but you may give them food. 5
Gentle breeze of wind, tickles your face,
Vines on the trees, swing with the grace. 6
Paths are decorated, with the stone tiles,
Rows of flowering trees,
long miles and miles. 7
The water sprinklers musical,
throw mist in the air,
Rainbow in the sky, appears very dear. 8
Hundred types of Roses, each in separate bed,
Lovely fragrant flowers, pink yellow red. 9
In this charming Garden, it's like a paradise,
Singing parrots peacocks,
flying butterflies. 10
Several waterfalls, fall in dancing fashion,
In sync with the music, it is live attraction. 11
this Vrindavan Garden,
is wonder of the nature,
In the Mysore kingdom,
like Wadiyar signature. 12

Maharaja Nalvadi Krishnaraja.

After the fall of the Vijayanagar Empire (1565), the Mysore King Timmaraja-2 (1553–1572) declared the Kingdom of Mysore independent. The kingdom of Mysore was the feudatory of Vijayanagar from the time of King Yadu Devaraj (1399-1423).

The Wadiyar king was the patron of Karnatak culture, arts and music. In 1399, Queen Mother Chikkadevi, of the Yadavas, married her daughter Dovajammanni to Devarai Wadiyar and anointed Yadu Devaraj at the throne of Mysore. In this way, King Devrat became the first Lunar Dynasty of Mysore (1399-1423).

In 1610, Raj-1 (1578– 1617) shifted the capital from Mysore to Shrirangapatnam, but in 1799 Mummadi Krishnaraja-3 (1799–1868) restored the capital to Mysore. Since then, the heaven like garden and beauty of Mysore is not built anywhere else in India.

179. Waghela Dynasty, Anhilwad Gujrat (1243-1304)

For the Earlier Dynasty, please see :
Solanki Dynasty (942–1244)

1. Vyaghra Deva — व्याघ्रदेव
2. Vira Dhaval — वीरधवल — ...
3. Bisal Deva — बीसलदेव — 1243–1261
4. Arjun Deva — अर्जुनदेव — 1261–1274
5. Ram Deva — रामदेव — 1274–1275
6. Sarang Deva — सारंगदेव — 1275–1280
7. Karna Deva — कर्णदेव — 1280–1304
8. ...

For the Next Dynasty, please see :
Waghela Dynasty, Riva (1618–1948)

Waghela Dynasty, Gujrat

Waghela or Baghel is a Gujarati branch of the Rajput Chaulukya Solanki Dynasty.

The ancestors of Vyaghradeva were feudatories of Bhimdev-2 Solanki (1178-1223) of Anhilwad. Among those feudatories, Veeradhaval was a heroic chieftain who took the power of King Bhimdev's power into his own hands.

Later on king of Veeradhaval's son Bisaldev became the king of Anhilwad (1243-1261).

A long lasting branch of the same Dynasty was established in Baghelkhand, Madhya Pradesh, in Riwa region (1648–1948).

Waghela Dynasty, Gujrat

The Waghelas of Gujrat,
were the Solakis,
They were the Chaulukyas,
as the history sees. 1
The Waghela Rajputs,
and Baghela are same,
Vyaghradeva's descendents,
Waghela their name. 2
Virdhaval was king,
a hero very staunch,
In the central India,
founded Riva branch. 3
Vyghra is the tiger Vagh,
Vaagh is a Bagh,
From Bagh became Baghel,
and Baghelkhand Vibhag. 4
Kingdom was their large,
wide and was far,
The king of Riva became,
Baghel Rajkumar. 5

244
Hindu Rajtarangini

180. Waghela Dynasty, Riwa, Bagelkhand (1648-1948)

For the Earlier Dynasty, please see:
Solanki Dynasty (942-1244)

1. Vikramaditya — विक्रमादित्य — 1618–1630
2. Amar Simha — अमरसिंह — 1630–1643
3. Anup Simha — अनूपसिंह — 1643–1660
4. Bhava Simha — भावसिंह — 1660–1704
5. Aniruddha Simha — अनिरुद्धसिंह — 1704–1709
6. Avadhut Simha — अवधूतसिंह — 1709–1758
7. Ajit Simha — अजीतसिंह — 1758–1808
8. Jai Simha — जयसिंह — 1808–1835
9. Vishva Nath Simha — विश्वनाथसिंह — 1835–1854
10. Riddha Raj Simha — ऋद्धराजसिंह — 1854–1880
11. Vyankat Raman — व्यंकटरमण — 1880–1918
12. Gulab Simha — गुलाबसिंह — 1918–1946
13. Martand Simha — मार्तंडसिंह — 1946–1948
14. Pushpa Raj Simha — पुष्पराजसिंह — 1948.

Waghela Dynasty, Riwa

*Baghels are Solankis,
in Riva different name,
Ruled in Baghelkhand,
and earned lots of fame. 1
Lakshman is their deity,
Rama's younger brother,
In Lakshman's name runs,
their kingdom further. 2
Largest branch of Waghelas,
is the Riva line,
It ruled till last day,
until it was fine. 3*

Waghela Dynasty, Riwa

The Waghela or Baghela Dynasty is a branch of the Solanki Dynasty of Gujrat settled in central India. Their ancestors were Chalukya Solanki Rajputs of Anhilwad. This Solanki Dynasty of Vyaghradeva ruled around Riwa, therefore, that region got the name Baghelkhand. 35 generations of this Baghel Dynasty ruled in Riwa. The names of 14 kings are given in the listing of Riwa Dynasty.

Shri Lakshman, the brother of Shri Rama, the king of Ayodhya, is considered as the deity by the ruler of the Baghel Dynasty and they rule in his name. From the seventeenth century till 1948, the Waghela Dynasty of Riwa was recognized as a Royal House, by the Government of India.

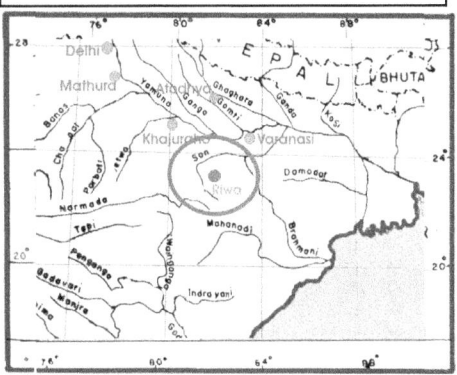

181. Vakatak Dynasty, Nandivardhan, Vidarbha (250-510)

For the Earlier Dynasty, please see :
Satvahan Dynasty (271 BC–195 AD.)

1.	Vindhya Shakti	विंध्यशक्ति	250–270
2.	Pravar Sen	प्रवरसेन	270–330
3.	Rudra Sen-2	रुद्रसेन–1	330–350
4.	Prithvi Sen	पृथ्वीसेन–1	350–400
5.	Rudra Sen-2	रुद्रसेन–2	400–405
6.	Diwakar Sen	दिवाकरसेन	405–420
7.	Damodar Sen	दामोदरसेन	420–450
8.	Narendra Sen	नरेंद्रसेन	450–470
9.	Prithvi Sen-2	पृथ्वीसेन–2	470–490
10.	Hari Sen	हरिषेण	490–510

For the Next Dynasty, please see :
Kalchuri Dynasty (550–1745)

Vakataka Dynasty

Vindhyashakti (250-270), the first ruler of the Vakataka Dynasty, was adorned with the title of Vindhyashakti because he was well-known on the Vindhya region. His son Pravarsen (270–330) had extended the power of the Vakataka Dynasty from central India to Andhra Pradesh. The capital of this branch was in Pravarpur or Nandivardhan (Nanded) in Vidarbha.

After the death of King Pravarsen (270-330) of the main branch of Vakataka (250-510), his son Rudrasen-1 (330-350), held the title of Dharmaraja. He founded his lineage in Vatsagulma.

The last king of this Vatsagulma branch, Harishen (490-510), is called the conqueror of Kuntal, Avanti (Ujjain), Lat, Kosala, Kalinga and Andhra Pradesh in the epigraphs of Ajanta caves. During the era of Vakataka, the art of mural painting of Ajanta was greatly encouraged. The period of Maharaja Harishen has been called the period of exaltation flourishing for the Royal House of Vakataka. After this, the kings of the Kalachuri Dynasty (550–1745) ended the Vakataka Dynasty.

Vakataka Dynasty

*Vakatakas were main,
rulers of the legion,
Second ancient House,
of the Vidarbha region. 1*

*Names of the rulers,
and their icons,
Great deeds of wonder,
are carved on the stones. 2*

*Vindhyakirti king, was the ruler first,
Vidarbha was his land,
he was king august. 3*

*Vindhyashakti title,
he received for his worth,
He ruled up to Vindhya,
the mountain in the north. 4*

*Vakatakas were brave,
charitable and wise,
People were happy,
their progress was on rise. 5*

*It was the golden age,
of the Vidarbha land,
For two-hundred years,
on the scale grand. 6*

*Sanskrit and the Prakrit,
poetic works great,
Were written many,
popular at that date. 7*

*Kalidasa made, reference to this style,
In his epic works, going extra mile. 8*

*The renowned wall paintings,
of the Vakataka days,
In the Ajanta caves,
will inspire us always. 9*

182. Varma Kulashekhar Dynasty, Venad Kerla (1102-1729)

For the Earlier Dynasty, please see : चेर राजवंश, कोचीन (800–1102)

1. Martand Varma-1 कोठ मार्तंड वर्मा-1 1102-1125
2. Vir Keral Varma-1 वीर केरळ वर्मा-1 1125-1145
3. Keral Varma-2 कोडै केरळ वर्मा-2 1145-1161
4. Ravi Varma-1 वीर रवि वर्मा-1 1161-1164
5. Keral Varma-3 वीर केरळ व6र्मा-3 1164-1167
6. Aditya Varma-1 वीर आदित्य वर्मा-1 1167-1173
7. Martand Varma-2 उदत मार्तंड वर्मा-2 1173-1192
8. Keral Varma-4 देवेंद्र केरळ वर्मा-4 1192-1195
9. **Ravi Keral Varma-2** रवि केरळ वर्मा-2 1195-1209
10. Keral Varma-5 केरळ वर्मा तिरुवदी-5 1209-1214
11. Keral Varma-6 केरळ वर्मा तिरुवदी-6 1214-1240
12. Martand Varma-3 पद्मनाभ तिरुवदी-3 1240-1252
13. Jaya Simha Varma जयसिंह देव वर्मा 1252-1299
14. Ravi Varma-2 वीर रवि वर्मा-2 1299-1313
15. Martand Varma-4 उदय मार्तंड वर्मा-4 1313-1333
16. Aditya Varma-2 आदित्य तिरुवदी-2 1333-1335
17. Martand Varma-5 मार्तंड तरुवदी-5 1335-1342
18. Keral Varma-7 केरळ तिरुवदी-7 1342-1363
19. Martand Varma-6 वीर मार्तंड वर्मा-6 1363-1366
20. Martand Varma-7 राम मार्तंड वर्मा-7 1366-1382
21. Ravi Varma-3 वीर रवि वर्मा-3 1382-1416
22. Ravi Varma-4 वीर रवि वर्मा-4 1416-1417
23. Martand Varma-8 केरळ मार्तंड वर्मा-8 1417-1433
24. Martand Varma-9 उदय मार्तंड वर्मा-9 1433-1444
25. Ravi Varma-5 वीर रवि वर्मा-5 1444-1458
26. Martand Varma-10 मार्तंड वर्मा-10 1458-1468
27. Aditya Varma-3 आदित्य वर्मा-3 1468-1484

Varma Dynasty of Venad

Venad rule was one of the five government departments of Venad, Shripadam, Shrivalamkondai and Devingnad etc. of Perumal Cher State.

Towards the end of the eleventh century, the Pandya (50–1463) kings of Madurai conquered the southern part of Travankor (Travancore). Travankor was made feudatory by the Tuluva Brave Emperors Achyutaray (1530–1542) and Sadashivaray (1543–1565) of Vijayanagar.

After the fall of the Tuluva Nayak power at the Battle of Talikot (1565), Venad's King Brave Udai Varma declared Venad an independent kingdom.

In Kerala until the ninth century, Perumal was the power of the Cher Dynasty. King Shekhar Varma (820-844) of this Cher Dynasty was a great Pundit in Sanskrit and Tamil languages.

28. Ravi Varma-6	वीर रवि वर्मा-6	1484-1503
29. Martand Varma-11	कुलशेखर वर्मा-11	1503-1504
30. Ravi Varma-7	रवि केरल वर्मा-7	1504-1514
31. Jayasimha Varma-	जयसिंह वर्मा	1514-1516
32. Martand Varma-12	उदय मार्तंड वर्मा-12	1516-1535
33. Ravi Varma-8	भूतल वीर रवि वर्मा-8	1535-
34. Keral Varma-8	राम केरल वर्मा-8	-
35. Aditya Varma-4	आदित्य वर्मा-4	
36. Keral Varma-9	वीर केरल वर्मा-9	1544-1545
37. Rama Varma-1	राम वर्मा-1	1545-1556
38. Keral Varma-9	उन्नी केरल वर्मा-9	1556-
39. Uday Varma	वीर उदय वर्मा	-
40. Ravi Varma-7	वीर रवि वर्मा-7	1595-1609
41. Aditya Varma-5	आदित्य वर्मा-5	1609-1610
42. Rama Varma-2	राम वर्मा-2	1610-1610
43. Rama Varma-3	राम वर्मा-3	1610-1611
44. Ravi Varma-8	रवि वर्मा-8	1611-1663
45. Ravi Varma-9	रवि वर्मा-9	1663-1672
46. Aditya Varma-6	आदित्य वर्मा-6	1672-1677
47. Rani Unmanaarayan	रानी उम्मन्नारायण	1677-1684
48. Ravi Varma-01	रवि वर्मा-10	1684-1714
49. Aditya Varma-7	आदित्य वर्मा-7	1714-1721
50. Rama Varma-4	राम वर्मा-4	1721-1729
51. Martand Varma-13	मार्तंड वर्मा-13	1729-1757

For the Next Dynasty, please see :
Varma Dynasty, Travankor (1729–1947)

Varma Dynasty of Venad continued

King Rajasekhara Varma (820-844) of the Perumal Chera Dynasty of Kerala called Kollam Gathering in year 825 and decided to give royal shelter to the Vedanta teachings of Shankaracharya (788-820). They started the Kollam Shaka era in celebration of this assembly. From the ninth century, the Cher Dynasty (800–1102) came to power in Kerala and after them the Varma Royal House (1102–1729) of Venad came to power. After that King Martand Varma-12 (1729-1757) of Venad started a separate Royal House in Travankor.

In this way Martand Varma-12, the last king of Venad, became the first king of Travankor and he started counting the Kollam period from the time of his coronation.

King Ravivarma-6 of Venad (1484–1503) was also called the king of Kollam and his descendants are considered as the **Kulasekhara Dynasty**. King Cheraman Perumal (742-800) was the great ruler of the Cher Perumal royal family of Kerala.

183. Varma Dynasty, Kochin, Kerla (1500-1947)

For the Earlier Dynasty, please see:
Varma Dynasty, Venad (1102–1729)

1.	Unni Raman-1	उन्नी रामन–1	1500–1503
2.	Unni Raman-2	उन्नी रामन–2	1503–1537
3.	Keral Varma-1	केरळ वर्मा–1	1537–1565
4.	Ram Varma-1	राम वर्मा–1	1565–1601
5.	Keral Varma-2	केरळ वर्मा–2	1601–1615
6.	Ravi Varma-1	रवि वर्मा–1	1615–1624
7.	Keral Varma-3	केरळ वर्मा–3	1624–1637
8.	Godai Varma-1	गोडै वर्मा–1	1637–1645
9.	Rayir Varma	वीर रायिर वर्मा	1645–1646
10.	Keral Varma-4	वीर केरळ वर्मा–4	1646–1650
11.	Ram Varma-2	राम वर्मा–2	1650–1656
12.	Queen Lakshmi	रानी लक्ष्मी	1656–1658
13.	Ram Varma-3	राम वर्मा–3	1658–1662
14.	Goda Varma-2	गोडै वर्मा–2	1662–1663
15.	Keral Varma-5	वीर केरळ वर्मा–5	1663–1687
16.	Ram Varma-4	राम वर्मा–4	1687–1693
17.	Ravi Varma-2	रवि वर्मा–2	1663–1697
18.	Ram Varma-5	राम वर्मा–5	1697–1701
19.	Ram Varma-6	राम वर्मा–6	1701–1721
20.	Ravi Varma-3	रवि वर्मा–3	1721–1731
21.	Ram Varma-7	राम वर्मा–7	1731–1746
22.	Keral Varma-6	केरळ वर्मा–6	1746–1749
23.	Ram Varma-8	राम वर्मा–8	1749–1760
24.	Keral Varma-7	केरळ वर्मा–7	1760–1775
25.	Ram Varma-9	राम वर्मा–9	1775–1790
26.	Ram Varma-10	राम वर्मा–10	1790–1805
27.	Ram Varma-11	राम वर्मा–11	1805–1809

Varma Dynasty of Kochin

Rama Varma-16 (1895–1914) of the Great Varma Dynasty of Cochin (Kochin) Kerala, was the patron of arts. At their court, Sanskrit and Malayalam Mahakavi Keralavarma Koittumpuran (1845–1914) was the court poet of this Dynasty. Keralavarma wrote many poetry, drama, akhayika, attakatha, sphutya kavya, alankar literature as well as he wrote literature on grammar, logic, epistemology.

Pandit Keralvarma's epic Mayurusandesh written in Sanskrit and Malayalam languages is an immortal composition of Kerala poetry.

Situated between the Western mountain range and the West Sea on the South coast of India, this land of Kerala can be considered the queen of nature or the image of Tirupalkadal Shrikrishnaswamy, the deity of the royal family of Varma is worshiped in the temples. All the royal families of Kerala are considered descendants of the 1st to 4th century Ay Dynasty of South India.

28. Keral Varma-8	केरळ वर्मा-8	1809–1828
29. Ram Varma-12	राम वर्मा-12	1828–1837
30. Ram Varma-13	राम वर्मा-13	1837–1844
31. Ram Varma-14	राम वर्मा-14	1844–1851
32. Keral Varma-9	केरळ वर्मा-9	1851–1853
33. Ravi Varma-8	रवि वर्मा-8	1853–1864
34. Ram Varma-15	राम वर्मा-15	1864–1888
35. Keral Varma-10	केरळ वर्मा-10	1888–1895
36. Ram Varma-16	राम वर्मा-16	1895–1914
37. Ram Varma-17	राम वर्मा-17	1914–1932
38. Ram Varma-18	राम वर्मा-18	1932–1941
39. Keral Varma-11	केरळ वर्मा-11	1941–1943
40. Ravi Varma-9	रवि वर्मा-9	1943–946
41. Keral Varma-12	केरळ वर्मा-12	1946–1947

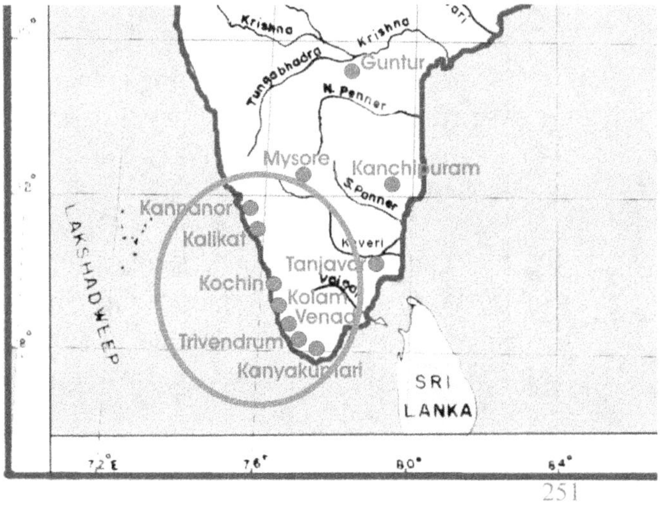

Varma Dynasty of Kochin

*The beautiful land of Kerala,
comprises aspects three,
Ocean shore, Mountain ranges,
and forest grass and tree. 1*

*At the sea shore very long,
aquatic life is great,
Fish and pearls are plenty,
main sea ports are eight. 2*

*Pleasing natural splendor,
of this beautiful kind,
That makes Kerala unique,
no where one can find. 3*

*Western mountain ranges,
grow vegetation gracious,
Tea spices rubber,
and medicines precious. 4*

*Perumal were the rulers,
Vaidic their past,
Did not bother writing,
their history vast. 5*

*Then came the Cheras,
unique were their deeds,
Cheral was their culture,
Kerala grew those seeds. 6*

*Portuguese Dutch British,
Arabs took their lands,
Hindu rulers lost,
and they washed their hands. 7*

*Foreigners became Masters,
Hindus became slaves,
As it happened elsewhere,
situation grave. 8*

184. Varma Dynasty, Travankor, kerla (1729-1948)

For the Earlier Dynasty, please see :
Varma Dynasty of Venad (1102–1729)

1. Martand Varma-1 मार्तंड (वेनाड) 1729–1757
2. Ram Varma-1 राम वर्मा-1 1757–1798
3. Balram Varma-1 बलराम वर्मा-1 1798–1810
4. Queen Lakshmi-1 रानी लक्ष्मी 1810–1815
5. Queen Gauri रानी गौरी बाई 1815–1829
6. Tirumal-1 स्वाति तिरुमल 1829–1847
7. Martand Varma-2 मार्तंड वर्मा-2 1847–1860
8. Tirumal-2 तिरुमल-2 1860–1880
9. Tirumal-3 तिरुमल-3 1880–1885
10. Ram Varma-2 राम वर्मा-2 1885–1924
11. Queen Lakshmi-2 रानी लक्ष्मी-2 1924–1931
12. Balram Varma बलराम वर्मा-2 1931–1948

Varma Dynasty of Travankor
*The last king of Venad,
was Varma Martand,
Travankor he ruled, he was ruler grand. 1
Travankor was ruled, by the kings wise,
Temples were built, of the grand size. 2*

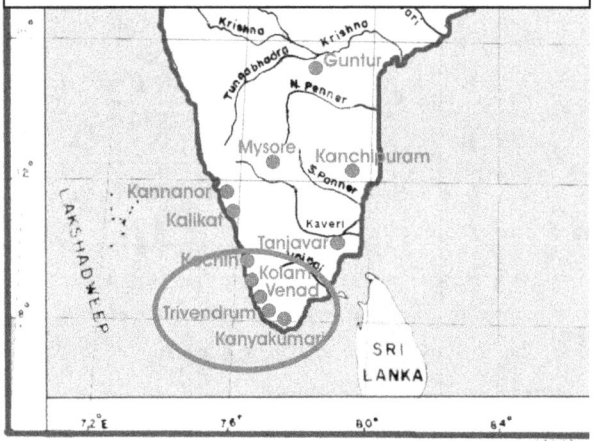

Varma Dynasty of Travankor
Martand Varma-12 (1729–1757), the last king of the Venad State of Kerala (1102–1729), established the Travankor (Thiruvitankur) kingdom and became the Maharaja of the Travankor kingdom himself. Therefore, he is considered as the architect of the Travankor kingdom.

King Martand Varma, having equipped his forces in modern way, had established several palaces and grand temples in the city and he installed an embankment around the city. Martand Varma ruled with religious instinct, becoming the devotee of Padmanabha Devi.

After Martand Varma, his son Kartik Varma (1757-1798), having shown friendship with the Cochin Institute, gave shelter in his kingdom to many people of Cochin. King Ram Varma (1880–1885) received the title of Dharmaraja. King Mulam Tirumal Ramavarma (1885– 1924) supported the social work of Shri Narayanaguru Alwar (1856– 1924) of Thiruvanantapuram. Dewan Chepat Pattabhiraman Ramaswamy Athyar (1879–1947) of King Shri Chitra Tirumal Balarama Varma (1931–1948) agitated in favour of temple entry for all people of Travankor.

185. Varma Dynasty, Kamrup, Assam (350-650)

For the Earlier Dynasty, please see :
Ahom Dynasty, Assam (355–1826)

1. Pushya Varma — पुष्यवर्मा — 350–374
2. Samudra Varma — समुद्रवर्मा — 374–398
3. Bal Varma — बालवर्मा — 398–422
4. Kalyan Varma — कल्याणवर्मा — 422–446
5. Ganapati Varma — गणपतिवर्मा — 446–470
6. Mahendra Varma — महेंद्रवर्मा — 470–494
7. Narayan Varma — नारायणवर्मा — 494–518
8. Bhuti Varma — भूतिवर्मा — 518–542
9. Chandramukh Varma — चंद्रमुखवर्मा — 542–566
10. Sthita Varma — स्थितवर्मा — 566–590
11. Susthita Varma — सुस्थितवर्मा — 590–595
12. Suprasthita Varma — सुप्रस्थितवर्मा — 595–600
13. Bhaskar Varma — भास्करवर्मा — 600–650

For the Next Dynasty, please see :
Ahom Dynasty, Assam (355–1826)

Varma Dynasty of Kamrup

King Samudravarma (374-398) of Kamarup (Pragjyotishpur) conquered all the inner and outer enemies of the kingdom and established his own independent Varma Dynasty (350-650). Samudra Varma received the title of Samudravarma for being a contemporary and same personality as the Gupta Emperor Samudragupta (350-375), the king of Magadh.

King Bhutivarma (518–542) had extended the state's boundary to Silhut in the south. The greatest king of this family was Bhaskaravarma (600–650) with whom Pushyabhuti Emperor Harshavardhana-2 Sheeladitya (606–647) partnered to dominate the Maukhari kingdom (540–725) of Thanesar (Kannauj). And on the other hand, King Bhaskaravarma of Kamarup conquered the last Shashank King Manav (625-625) of Karnasuvarna and extended the boundary of the Kamarup kingdom of Assam to Karnasuvarna in the south.

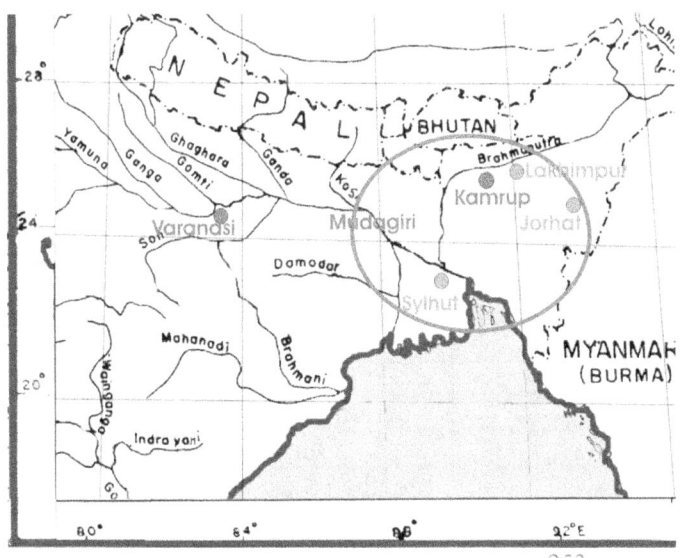

Hindu Rajtarangini

186. Velu Nachchiyar, Queen of Ramand (1730-1790)

1. Chellamuttu   चेल्लमुत्तु सेतुपति   –1780
2. Queen Velu Nacchiyar रानी वेलु नाच्चियार 1780–1790

Queen Velu Nacchiyar
*The brave Tamil warrior Queen,
Velu Nacchiyar,
Rejected the British rule, and declared a war. 1
She fought against them,
with courage and bravery,
She laid her life down,
and rejected the slavery. 2*

Queen Velu Nacchiyar
The Brave Queen Velu Nacchiyar (1703-1790) of Tamil Nadu was daughter of Chellamuthu Vijayaragunt Setupathi, the king of Ramnad and she was wife of King Madhuvasugandha Pettiyadu Nachiyar of Sivagangai. In 1772, King Madhuvsugandha was killed while fighting the British foreigners. After the death of the king, the queen Velu took power in her own hands and started daring attacks against the British foreigners.

In 1780, for taking revenge against the British, she sent a suicide attack on the gunpowder warehouses of the British and caused great damage.

The British surrounded Shivgangai. They took over the kingdom of Queen Velu Nachiyar. But the queen could not be caught by them.

Velu Nachiyar continued her fight till her last breath. People came to know her by the name Veeramangai. Finally, in year 1790, Queen Velu Nachiyar breathed her last and attained heaven.

187. Vivasvan Dynasty (Ancient Time)

1. Brahma — ब्रह्मा
2. Marichi Prajapati — मरीचि प्रजापति
3. Kashyap Prajapati — कश्यप प्रजापति
4. Vivasvan Manu — विवस्वान मनु
5. Vaivasvat Manu — वैवस्वत मनु
6. Ikshavaku — इक्ष्वाकु

For the Next Dynasty, please see :
Ikshavaku Dynasty (Ancient Time)

Vivaswan Dynasty

Prajapatis came from Brahma,
twenty-one in number,
From His body parts,
arose primal member. 1
Kashyap Kardam Yama Stanu, Atri Angiras Heti,
Vashshtha Marichi Pracheta,
Narad Pulaha Pracheti; 2
Bhrigu Sthanu Samsraya Nemi,
Manu Sanatkumars two,
Daksha Kratu Vikrit Dharma,
gave life to nature's zoo. 3
The twelve sons of Aditi, Adityas they were called,
One of them was Vivaswan,
from whom Sun is evolved. 4
He was preacher of Yoga,
from Krishna he had learned,
He taught Yajna also,
the knowledge he had earned. 5
Vaisvat spread Dharma, in that ancient age,
Son of Vivasvan he was,
found the Solar lineage. 6
Krishna gave the yoga, to Aditya Vivasvan,
Vivasvan gave it to Manu,
Manu gave to his clan. 7
Thank you Lord Krishna! now we understood,
You sent eternal Yoga to us, for our own good. 8

Vivaswan Dynasty

Brahma's son Marichi was one of the Prajapatis. The son of Marichi, was Kashyap. He is considered to be the beginning of all humans and creatures.

Prajapati Kashyap and his wife Aditi had a son named Vivaswan, to whom Lord Krishna gave yoga first (Gita 4.1). In the Puranas, Vivaswan is known as the Sun. Vivasvan was one of the twelve Aditya (Surya) sons of Kashyap and his wife Aditi. The capital of Vivaswan was Kosala (Ayodhya). Vaivasvat, the son of Vivaswan and his wife Sanjna, was one of the fourteen Manus. Vivasvan's son Manu Vaivasvat is the beginning of the Solar Dynasty.

Vivaswan's second son was Vikukshi, from whom the Janak Dynasty of Mithila started. Yama was the brother of Vaivasvat Manu. Vaivasvat Manu is considered to be the seventh Manu. For the list of the fourteen Manus, please see the Swayambhuva Dynasty. The historic Great Flood took place during the time of Vaivaswat Manu. The elder son of Vaivasvata Manu was Ikshvaku. The capital of King Ikshvaku was Ayodhya. See the Ikshvaku Dynasty.

188. Vrishni Dynasty (Ancient Time)

(For the Earlier Dynasty, please see :
Yadu Dynasty (Ancient Time)

1. Vrishni — वृष्णि ...
2. Sudhajit — सुधाजित
3. Shini — शिनि
4. Satyak — सत्यक
5. Satyaki — सात्यकी
6. Jaya — जय
7. Kuni — कुणी
8. Anamitra — अनामित्र
9. Prashni — प्रश्नि
10. Chitrarath — चित्ररथ
11. Vidurth — विदुरथ
12. Shura — शूर
13. Sini — सिनि
14. Bhoja — भोज
15. Hridik — हृदिक
16. Shursen — शूरसेन
17. Vasudev — वसुदेव
18. Vaasudeva Shri Krishna — वासुदेव श्रीकृष्ण

Vrishni Dynasty
*In the family of Vrishni,
Lord Krishna was born,
Shri Krishna was the eighth,
Vasudeva-Devaki's son. 1
Devaki's father was Devak,
who was Ugrasen's brother,
Devaki was Kamsa's sister,
Ugrasen Kamsa's father. 2*

Vrishni Dynasty

The great Yadava king of Yayati's Dynasty was Vrishni, in whose clan Lord Krishna was born. The people of Vrishni clan are also called Yadavas or Ahirs. The Capital City of Kartviryarjun, a descendant of King Yadu, was Mahishmati. Kartviryarjun established the Bhadardeep Pratishtha on the bank of the river Narmada. Kartviryarjun considered Dattatreya as Guru (Brahmanda Purana 1.44). All the neighboring kings of Mahishmati considered Kartviryarjun as Chakravarti Maharaja (Brahmanda Puran 1.16).

Shri Krishna has stolen the historic Syamantak Mani was the confusion in his mind and thus Kartviryarjun had enmity with Shri Krishna (Brahmanda. 3.71.1).

King Vrishni had two wives, Madri and Gandhari (Vayu Purana 1.94). Queen Madri's son was King Devmidh, in whose family Shri Krishna's father Vasudev was born. The son of Devmeedh was Shursen. The son of Shursen was Vasudev. The daughter of Ugrasen's brother Devak was Shri Krishna's mother Devaki.

Vrishni Yaduvar Dwarkadhish Shri Krishna

श्रीकृष्ण की द्वारिका नगरी

हरि चरणन की अमृत गगरी ।
धाम द्वारिका पावन नगरी,
मथुरा कांची अवध पुरी ।। 1

राज महल माधव का सुनहरा,
यादव का भगवा ध्वज फहरा ।
सागर तट पर लावण्य खड़ी,
स्वागत करती जल की परी ।। 2

पँच धाम पावन जग जाने,
हरि दरशन के जो हैं दीवाने ।
भगत जनन की भीड़ बड़ी,
पावन नगरी जादू भरी ।। 3

मथुरा से हरि गोकुल आयो,
राधा मिलन वृंदावन लायो ।
मधुबन से द्वारिका नगरी,
आयो सुदामा मिलन हरि ।। 4

Dwarka of Shri Krishna

*Sanctified by the feet of Lord Krishna,
Dwarka is a holy city,
Like the Mathura, Ayodhya and
Kanchipuram.*

*The Gold Palace of
Shri Krishna is here,
On which flies Bhagva Flag,
Dwarka is on the sea shore,
The water-maid welcomes you there.*

*Five places are known most divine,
Dwarka is one of them, for sure.
The devotees come here,
in this magical city,
Lord Krishna went
from Gokul to Vrindavan
and then he came here.*

*One day Shri Krishna's old friend,
Sudama came to meet
his old friend Kanha.*

Shri Krishna, the King of Dwarka

Freeing his mother and father, from Kamsa's prison,
He became king of Dwarka,
Krishna the blessed son. 1
Krishna is going to Dwarka, with his wife Rukmini,
But not going with him, is Shri Radhe Rani. 2
Union and separation are, two facts of life,
Friend is a friend, and wife is the wife. 3
Krishna went to Dwarka, Radha became sad,
Radha returned to Barsana,
to make her mother glad. 4
Bravo! Bravo! Radhe! holy is your grace,
Wherever Krishna is worshipped,
you have a pious place. 5

गीत : राग मालकंस, कहरवा ताल

नरा-नारायण कृष्ण-सुदामा

स्थायी

जग अलग-अलग कहता दोनों,
जो अलग कहत उसे रहने दो ।

बचपन के हैं दोनों साथी,
भव सागर में, बिछुड़े हैं ।
कृष्ण सुदामा रूप अलग हैं,
नर नारायण, एक हि हैं ।। 1

आर है गोकुल पार मथुरा,
दोनों जमुना तीर पे हैं ।
राधा सखी है सखा सुदामा,
सखी सखा सब, एक हि हैं ।। 2

रंक सुदामा राजा हरि हैं,
केवल मौखिक, अंतर है ।
अंतर तन का, नहीं है मन का,
दो तन दो मन, एक ही हैं ।। 3

Krishna-Sudama
Song

The world says Krishna and Sudama are
two different persons.
Let them say whatever they want.
Leave him alone who thinks of them
differently.

They are childhood friends,
got separated in this worldly ocean.
Krishna and Sudama are two forms,
But Nar and Narayan, both are one. 1
On this side is Gokul,
on the other side is Mathura.
Both are on the banks of one Jamuna.
Radha is friend and Sudama is friend,
friends all are one. 2
Sudama is poor, Krishna is a king,
the difference is only verbal.
The difference is of the bodies only,
but not of mind.
Two bodies and two minds are one. 3

189. Vuppadeva Dynasty, Kashmir (1172-1301)

For the Earlier Dynasty, please see :
Lohar Dynasty, Kashmir (1003–1172)

1. Vuppa Deva — वुप्पदेव — 1172-1181
2. Jashshaka Deva — जश्शकदेव — 1181-1199
3. Jag Drva — जगदेव — 1199-1212
4. Raj Deva — राजदेव — 1212-1235
5. Sangrama Deva — संग्रामदेव — 1235-1252
6. Ramj Deva — रामदेव — 1252-1273
7. Lakshman Deva — लक्ष्मणदेव — 1273-1286
8. Simha Deva — सिंहदेव — 1286-1301
9. Saha Deva — सहदेव — 1301-1339
10. Queen Kota — कोटा रानी — 1339-1389

For the Next Dynasty, please see :
Dogra Dynasty (1812–1947)

Vuppadeva Dynasty

Vantideva (1165–1172), the last king of the Lohar Dynasty of Shrinagar was overthrown by his minister Vuppadeva, who then came to power in Kashmir. He established his new Vuppadeva Dynasty of Shrinagar (1172- 1301). After Vuppadeva, his brother Jashshakadev (1181–1199) came to power but due to his bizarre behavior, the ministers expelled him from the kingdom and gave power to Jashkadev's grandson Rajdev (1212–1235). After that his grandson Sangram Deva became king (1235–1252) but he was also expelled from the kingdom. The last ruler, Kota Rani, ruled for 50 years (1339–1389) in Kashmir.

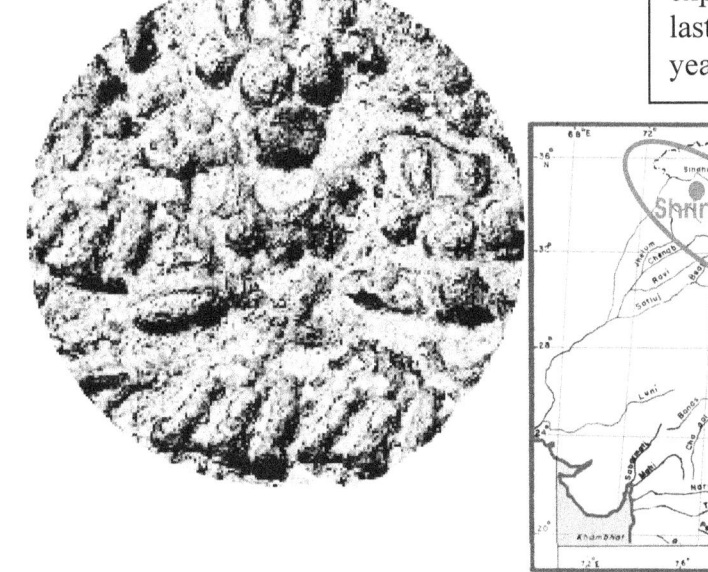

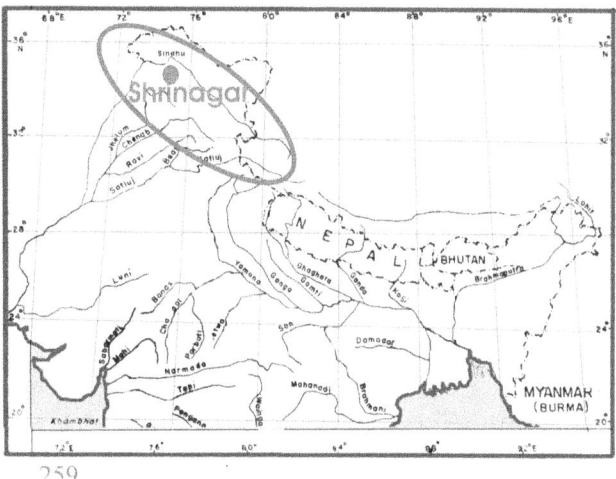

Hindu Rajtarangini

190. Yadav Dynasty, Devgiri (850-1311)

For the Earlier Dynasty, please see : 1. Chalukyas of Kalyani (696–1189);
2. Rashtrakuts of Malkhed (620–973)

#	Name	Devanagari	Period
1.	Dvidha Prahar	द्विधाप्रहार	...
2.	Sayunchandra-1	सयूनचंद्र	850–874
3.	Dhadhiyappa-1	धदियप्पा-1	874–900
4.	Amar Ganga	अमरगंगा	900–925
5.	Bhillam	भिल्लम-1	925–950
6.	Vadugi-1	वदुगी-1	950–974
7.	Dhadiyappa-2	धदियप्पा-2	974–975
8.	Bhillam-2	भिल्लम-2	975–1005
9.	Vadugi-2	वदुगी-2	1005–1020
10.	Bhillam-3	भिल्लम-3	1020–1055
11.	Vadugi-3	वदुगी-3	1055–1068
12.	Seyunchandra-2	सेयूनचंद्र-2	1068–1085
13.	Airamdeva	ऐरमदेव	1085–1115
14.	Singhan-1	सिंघण-1	1115–1145
15.	Mallugi-1	मल्लुगी-1	1145–1150
16.	Amar Ganga-2	अमरगंगा	1150–1160
17.	Govindaraja	गोविंदराजा	1160–1160
18.	Amar Mallugi-1	मल्लुगी-1	1160–1165
19.	Kaliya Ballal	कालीया	1165–1173
20.	Bhillam-4	भिल्लम-4	1173–1192
21.	Jaitugi-1	जैतुगी-1	1192–1200
22.	Singhan-2	सिंघण-2	1200–1247
23.	Kannar	कन्नर	1247–1261
24.	Mahadev	महादेव	1261–1271
25.	Amman	अम्मन	1271–1271
26.	Ramachandrdev	रामचंद्रदेव	1271–1311
27.	Shankardev	शंकरदेव	1311–1317

Yadava Dynasty

The former head of the Lunar Kshatriya Yadava Dynasty, ruled as feudal lords of the Rashtrakutas (620-973) of Malkhed and the Chalukyas of Kalyani (696-1189), the king. Later, when the great king Veer Balal-2 (1173-1220) of the Hoysala Dynasty (1026-1348) weakened the Chalukyas by invading the Kalyani Chalukya king Someshwar-4 (1183-1189). Now, the Yadava kings became liberated from Chalukyas of Kalyani. Yadava King Ballala-2 acquired and established the great fort of Devgiri in 1203 and established a thriving capital there.

The first great king of the Yadavas, Sayunchandra (850-874), considered his clan to be originated from Shri Krishna's Yadu Dynasty of Mathura and Dwarka. Sayunchandra's father Dwidhaprahar and his father Subahu were under the Chalukya kings of Kalyani.

In 1187, the Yadava king Bhillam-4 (1173–1192) conquered Kalyani by defeating the Chalukya king Someshwar (1183–1189). Yadava King Singhan-2 (1200-1247) greatly expanded the kingdom. The king of the Yadavas, Ramachandradeva (1271–1311), had extended the extent of the Yadava kingdom from the Tungabhadra river in the South to the Narmada river in north.

Yadava Dynasty

The kings of Lunar Dynasty,
kept peace in the country,
They were descendents of Yadu,
the Yadava Dynasty. 1

The big Yadava family, had many branches,
The House of Hehaya, had growth chances. 2

King Seunchandra was, great in Yadava line,
His Devgiri became, Yadava city fine. 3

King Singhana had, many gems at his court,
They discusses subjects, of many sort. 4

House of Yadava produced, many kings prime,
It was the golden age, of that time. 5

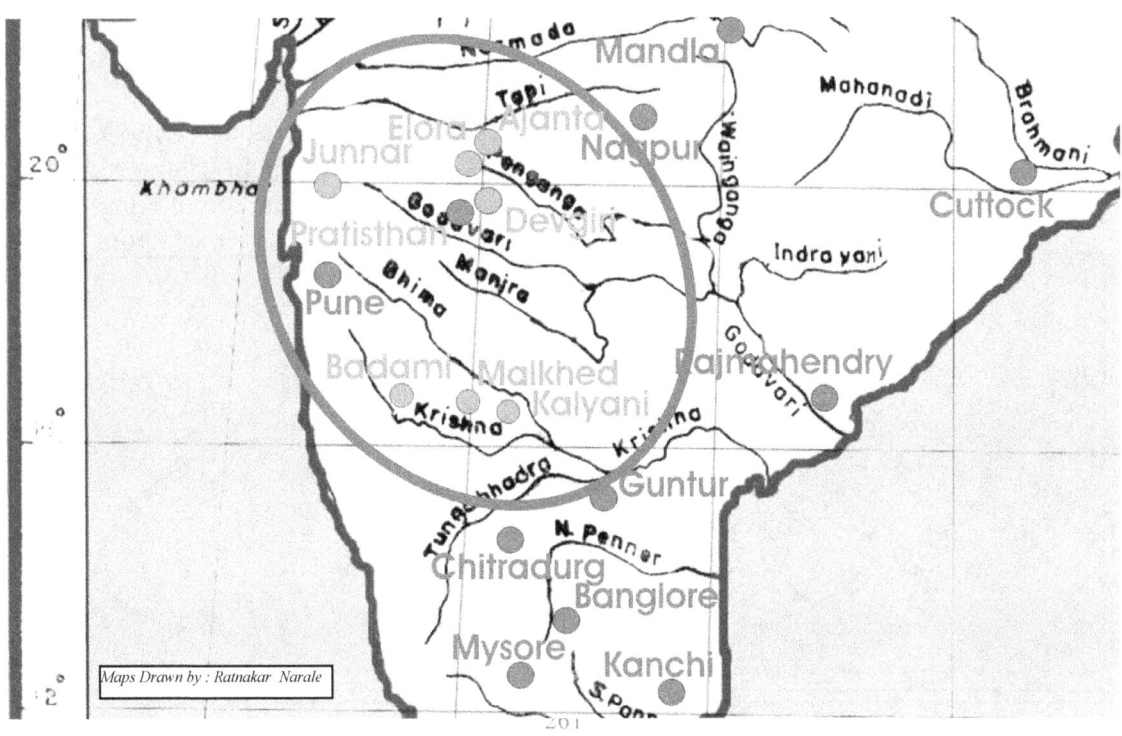

Maps Drawn by : Ratnakar Narale

Hindu Rajtarangini

191. Yadu Dynasty (Ancient Time)

For the Earlier Dynasty, please see :
Yayati Dynasty (Ancient Time)

1. Yayati — ययाति
2. Yadu — यदु
3. Sahasrajit — सहस्रजीत
4. Satjit — सतजीत
5. Hehaya — हेहय
6. Dharma — धर्म
7. Kunti — कुंति
8. Bhadrasen — भद्रसेन
9. Dhanak — धनक
10. Kartavirya — कार्तवीर्य
11. Kartaviryarjun — कार्तवीर्यार्जुन
12. Madhu — मधु
13. Vrishni — वृष्णि

For the Next Dynasty, please see :
Vrishni Dynasty (Ancient Time)

Yadu Dynasty

The Royal House of Maharaja Yadu is known by the name of Yadava or Ahir. Prajapati Kardam's daughter Anasuya was the wife of Maharishi Atri whose sons Dattatreya and Chandra became very famous in history. Dynasty of King Chandra was succeeded by Yayati Dynasty, Yadu Dynasty, Puru Dynasty and Kuru Dynasty.

Tara Devi, wife of King Chandra, was the daughter of King Brihaspati. Brihaspati's son was Budha, which led to the creation of the entire Soma Dynasty. It ruled from Prayagraj.

King Nahusha's great son Yayati from whom many eminent Dynasties were originated.

King Yadu was the son of King Yayati's wife Devayani. Vrishni clan originated from king Koshtra, the son of King Yadu. Lord Krishna was born in Mathura in the

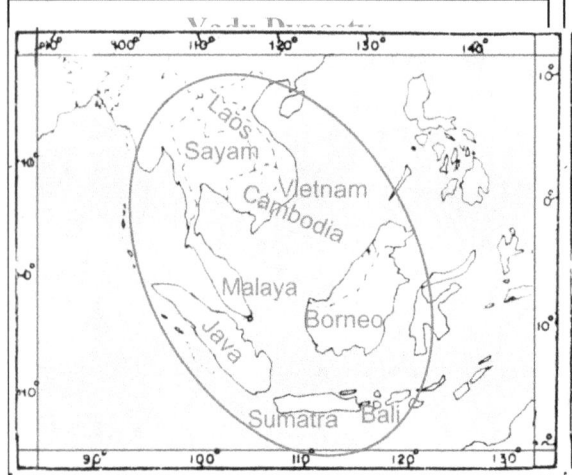

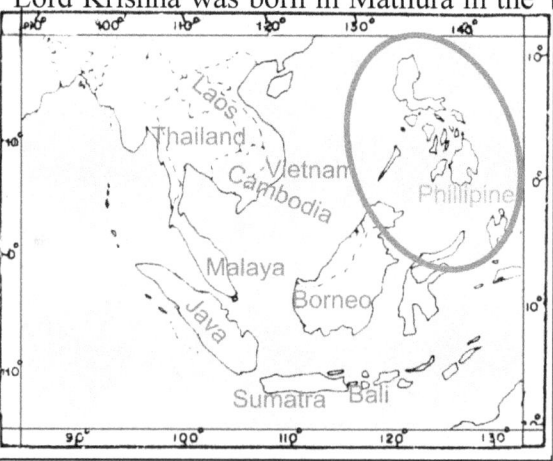

192. Yayati Dynasty (Ancient Time)

For the Earlier Dynasty, please see :
Atri Dynasty (Ancient Time)

1. Nahush — नहुष
2. Tayati — ययाति
3. Yadu and Puru — यदु और पुरु

For the Next Dynasty, please see :
Yadu Dynasty (Ancient Time)

Yayati Dynasty

In Yayati's Lunar Dynasty,
great kings were born,
Yadu Puru Kuru were,
like the Solar kings stubborn. 1

In the Solar Dynasty,
Ikshavaku was benefactor,
In the Lunar Dynasty,
King Yayati had honor. 2

In the Lunar Dynasty,
was born Bharat Emperor,
Just as Harischandra was,
Solar Dynasty's mentor. 3

As Shri Krishna was,
splendor of Lunar Dynasty,
So was Shri Rama,
grandeur of Solar Dynasty. 4

As the Pandavas were,
stars of Lunar Dynasty,
So king Janak was,
the Sun of Solar Dynasty. 5

Yayati Dynasty

King Nahusha had five sons: Puru, Yadu, Turvasu, Anu and Druhu, who are called Panchanandas in the Vedas. Even before his retirement Maharaja Yayati divided his kingdom in five parts. 1. King Puru received Central India, 2. King Yadu got the South-West, 3. King Turvasu got the South-East, 4. King Anu got the North, and 5. King Druhu got the West.

There were many majestic and famous kings in the Dynasty of King Puru. The kingdom of Yayati earned the name of Bhaarat Varsha after the name of Emperor Bharat. In the clan of King Puru, there was King Shantanu, whose son Pitamaha Bhishma was the best Acharya. In the Puru Dynasty, there were kings Yudhishthir, Arjun, Bhima, Abhimanyu, Parikshit, Janamejaya, all of whom were known as Pauravas.

The Bharat Dynasty consisted of King Kuru, in whose clan there was King Hasti, laid the foundation of Hastinapur. In this Puru Dynasty was born King Kuru whose descendents were the Kaurava clans.

The blind king Dhritarashtra was born to Ambika, wife of King Vichitravirya, King Pandu and Vidura from Ambalaika.

193. Yudhishthir Dynasty (Ancient Time)

For the Earlier Dynasty, please see :
Pandava Dynasty (Ancient Time)

1. Yudhishthir, 2. Parikshit, 3. Janmejay, 4. Ashwamedha, 5. Rama, 6. Chhatrasala, 7. Chitrarath, 8. Dushtashailya, 9. Ugrasen, 10. Shursen-1, 11. Bhuvanapati, 12. Ranjit, 13. Rakshak, 14. Sukhdev, 15. Narhari, 16. Shuchirath, 17. Shursen-2, 18. Parvatasena, 19. Medhavi, 20. Shonchir, 21. Bhima-1, 22. Nrihari, 23. Purna, 24. Karadavi, 25. Alamik, 26. Udaypal, 27. Sangharaj, 28. Duvan, 29. Damat, 30. Kshmak, 31. Vishrava, 32. Purasaini, 33. Veerashrayani, 34. Andagashai, 35. Harijit, 36. Paramshrayani, 37. Sukhpatal, 38. Kadru, 39. Sajj, 40. Amarachud, 41. Avanipal, 42. Dasaratha, 43. Veerasal-1, 44. Veerasal-2, 45. Mahaveer, 46. Ajitsimha, 47. Sarvadatta, 48. Bhuvanapati, 49. Veerasen-1, 50. Mahipal-1, 51. Shatarshal, 52. Sangharaj, 53. Tejahpal, 54. Manikchandra, 55. Kamshreni, 56. Shatru Mardan, 57. Jeevalok, 58. Harirao, 59. Veerasen-2, 60. Adityaketu, 61. Dhandhar, 62. Maharishi, 63. Sunrachi, 64. Mahayuddha, 65. Doornath, 66. Jeevanaraja, 67. Rudrasen, 68. Aarolok, 69. Rajpal, 70. Mahanpal, 71. Vikramaditya, 72. Samudra Pal, 73. Chandrapal, 74. Sahayapal, 75. Devpal, 76. Narasimhapal, 77. Rampal, 78. Amritpal, 79. Balipal, 80. Mahipal-2, 81. Haripal, 82. Shishpal, 83. Madanpal, 84. Karmapala, 85. Vikrampal, 86. Mulakhchandra, 87. Vikramchandra, 88. Amichandra, 89. Ramachandra, 90. Harichandra, 91. Kalyanchandra, 92. Bhimchandra, 93. Lovachandra, 94. Govindchandra, 95. Padmavati, 96. Hariprem, 97. Govindprame, 98. Gopalprem, 99. Mahabahu, 100. Adhisen, 101. Bilavalsen 102. Keshavsen, 103. Madyasen, 104. Mayursen, 105. Kalyansen, 106. Harisen, 107. Kshemasen. 108. Narayansen, 109. Lakshmisen, 110. Damodarsen, 111. Do Simha, 112. Raj Simha, 113. Narasimha, 114. Harisimha, 115. Jeevan Simha, 116. Anangpal, 117. Prithviraj Chauhan.

For the Next Dynasty, please see :
Chauhan Dynasty (684–1192)

Yudhishthir Dynasty

After the Great War of Mahabharata, King Yudhishthir retired and started pilgrimage to the Himalayas for retirement and he handed over the kingdom to Abhimanyu's son Parikshit. King Parikshit was the son of Abhimanyu and Uttara. Arjun and Subhadra's son Brave Abhimanyu was trapped in the Chakravyuha and was killed at the hands of Duhshasan. King Parikshit ruled Hastinapur almost 60 years with virtue (Maha. Adi. 49). After Parikshit, his son Janmejaya became king. Janmajeya's mother's name was Madravati. Janamejaya's wife's name was Vapushtama, who was the daughter of Suvarnavarma, the king of Kashi.

Alphabetical Index of the Hindu Kings/Queens and their Dynasties

NOTE : For the details of each Hindu King/Queen, please see the **Dynasty Number** in the pages above.

King/Queenr	राजा /रानी	Dynasty	Ruling Period	Dynasty No.
Queen Ahilyabai Holkar	अहल्या बाई	Holkar Dynasty	1725–1795	54.
Queen Didda	रानी दिद्दा	Pravargupta Dynasty, Kashmir	980–1003	125.
Queen Durgavati	रानी दुर्गावती	Chandela Dynasty	1524–1565	23.
Queen Durgavati	रानी दुर्गावती	Gond Dynasty, Mandla	1550–1564	45.
Queen Hira Bai	हीराबाई	Gond Dynasty, Vidarbha	1521–1550	46.
Queen Lakshmi Bai	लक्ष्मी बाई	Nevalkar Dynasty, Jhansi	1853–1858	113.
Queen Sugandha	रानी सुगंधा	Utpal Dynasty, Kashmir	904–906	177.
Queen, Chand Kaur	चाँद कौर	Sikh Dynasty, Punjab	1841–1841	156.
Queen, Channamma	रानी चन्नम्मा	Channamma Dynasty, Kittur	778–1829	24.
Queen, Gauri	रानी गौरी बाई	Varma Dynasty, Travankor	1815–1829	184.
Queen, Jaya Devi	रानी जयदेवी	Vietnam, Bhava varma Dynasty, Vietnam	690–713	170.
Queen, Jindan Kaur	जिंदन कौर	Sikh Dynasty, Punjab	1843–1849	156.
Queen, Kota	कोटा रानी	Vuppadeva Dynasty, Kashmir	1339–1389	189.
Queen, Lakshmi	रानी लक्ष्मी	Varma Dynasty, Kochin	1656–1658	183.
Queen, Lakshmi-1	रानी लक्ष्मी	Varma Dynasty, Travankor	1810–1815	184.
Queen, Lakshmi-2	रानी लक्ष्मी-2	Varma Dynasty, Travankor	1924–1931	184.
Queen Meera Bai	मीरा बाई	Meera Bai Dynasty, Mewar	1498–1573	82.
Queen, Velu Nacchiyar	रानी वेलु नाच्चियार	Nachchiyar Dynasty, Ramand	1780–1790	186.
Abhay Malla Deva	अभय मल्ल	Malla Dynasty, Nepal	1216–1235	111.
Abhay Simha	अभय सिंह	Rathor Dynasty, Jodhpur	1724–1749	135.
Abhimanyu	अभिमन्यु	Pravargupta Dynasty, Kashmir	958–972	125.
Achyutappa	अच्युतप्पा	Tanjavar Nayak Dynasty	1580–1600	97.
Acyutadevaraya	अच्युतदेवराया	Tuluv Nayak Dynasty	1530–1542	89.
Adhipati	अधिपति	Nal Dynasty		84.
Adhirajendra	अधिराजेंद्र परोकेसरी वर्मा	Chola Dynasty	1067–1070	36.
Aditya Narayan Simha		Narayan Dynasty	1931–1939	86.

265
Hindu Rajtarangini

Name	Devanagari	Dynasty	Period	Page
Aditya Rajkesari	आदित्य राजकेसरी वर्मा	Chola Dynasty	881–907	36.
Aditya Vardhan	आदित्यवर्धन	Pushyabhuti-Vardhan Dynasty	555–580	130.
Aditya Varma	आदित्यवर्मा	Shilahar Dynasty, Konkan	870–895	148.
Aditya Varma-1	वीर आदित्य वर्मा -1	Varma Dynasty, Venad	1167–1173	182.
Aditya Varma-2	आदित्य तिरुवदी-2	Varma Dynasty, Venad	1333–1335	182.
Aditya Varma-3	आदित्य वर्मा-3	Varma Dynasty, Venad	1468–1484	182.
Aditya Varma-4	आदित्य वर्मा-4	Varma Dynasty, Venad		182.
Aditya Varma-5	आदित्य वर्मा-5	Varma Dynasty, Venad	1609–1610	182.
Aditya Varma-6	आदित्य वर्मा-6	Varma Dynasty, Venad	1672–1677	182.
Aditya Varma-7	आदित्य वर्मा-7	Varma Dynasty, Venad	1714–1721	182.
Adityasen	आदित्यसेन	Gupta Dynasty, Patliputra	655–680	48.
Agnimitra	अग्निमित्र	Shunga Dynasty	149–141 BC	160.
Aguk-2	अगुक-2	Saindhav Dynasty	849–870	140.
Aguk-3	अगुक-3	Saindhav Dynasty	885–900	140.
Aguka-1	अगुक-1	Saindhav Dynasty	774–794	140.
Ahalya Bai	अहल्याबाई	Holkar Dynasty	1767–1795	54.
Ahavamalla	आहवमल्ल	Kalchuri Dynasty, Kalyani	1180–1183	68.
Ahil	अहिल	Chaunah Dynasty, Nadol	1019–1024	27.
Ahuk	आहुक	Kukkur Dynasty	Ancient	72.
Ainyankbhima-1	ऐन्यंकभीम-1	Ganga Dynasty, Kalinga	1189–1197	41.
Ainyankbhima-2	ऐन्यंकभीम-2	Ganga Dynasty, Kalinga	1200–1238	41.
Airamdeva	ऐरमदेव	Yadav Dynasty, Devgiri	1085–1115	190.
Aiyapraj	ऐयपराज	Shilahar Dynasty, Konkan	820–845	148.
Aja Varma	अजवर्मा	Kadamb Dynasty	565–566	62.
Aja	अज	Raghu Dynasty	Ancient	131.
Ajatshatru	अजातशत्रु	Haryak Dynasty	494–462 BC.	51.
Ajay Varma	अजयवर्मा	Parmar Dynasty	1138–1143	120.
Ajaydev	अजयदेव	Chauhan Dynasty, Sakambhari	1110–1130	26.
Ajaypal	अजयपाल	Solanki Dynasty	1171–1176	163.
Ajit Simha	अजित सिंह	Rathor Dynasty, Jodhpur	1707–1724	135.
Ajit Simha	अजीतसिंह	Waghela Dynasty, Riwa	1758–1808	180.
Ajitpid	अजीतपीड़	Karkota Dynasty, Kashmir	840–850	69.
Ajitsingh	अजीत सिंह	Chauhan Dynasty, Kota	(1756–1758)	33.
Ajmidh	अजमीढ़	Ajamidh Dynasty	Ancient	3.
Ajnipal	अहनिपाल	Chaunah Dynasty, Nadol	1024–1055	27.
Ak	अंक	Ratta Dynasty	1048–1060	138.
Akhairaj	अखैराज	Chauhan Dynasty, Sirohi	1527 …	30.

Name	Devanagari	Dynasty	Period	Page
Aksha Simha	अक्ष सिंह	Bhati Raval Dynasty	1722-1762	8.
Aksha	अक्ष	Gonaditya Dynasty, Kashmir	460-400	44.
Alhandev	आल्हणदेव	Chaunah Dynasty, Nadol	1153-1161	27.
Allat	अल्लट	Guhil Dynasty, Mewad	951-972	47.
Amana Devi	अमना देवी	Brihadrith Dynasty, Magadh	Ancient	15.
Amar Ganga	अमरगंगा	Yadav Dynasty, Devgiri	900-925	190.
Amar Ganga-2	अमरगंगा	Yadav Dynasty, Devgiri	1150-1160	190.
Amar Malla Deva	अमर मल्ल देव	Malla Dynasty, Nepal	1530-1538	111.
Amar Mallugi-1	मल्लुगी-1	Yadav Dynasty, Devgiri	1160-1165	190.
Amar Manikya	अमर माणिक्य	Manikya Dynasty, Tripura	1577-1585	79.
Amar Simha	अमर सिंह	Bhati Raval Dynasty	1661-1702	8.
Amar Simha	अमर सिंह	Bhosle Dynasty, Tanjavar	1787-1798	11.
Amar Simha	अमरसिंह	Waghela Dynasty, Riwa	1630-1643	180.
Amar Simha-1	अमरसिंह-1	Sisodiya Dynasty	1597-1620	159.
Amar Simha-2	अमरसिंह-2	Sisodiya Dynasty	1699-1716	159.
Amarji	जाम अमरजी	Jadeja Dynasty	1490-1510	60.
Ambaprasad	अम्बाप्रसाद	Guhil Dynasty, Mewad	993-1007	47.
Ambarish	अंबरीष	Raghu Dynasty	Ancient	131.
Amman	अम्मन	Yadav Dynasty, Devgiri	1271-1271	190.
Ammaraja-1	अम्मराजा-1	Chalukya Dynasty, Vengi	918-925	22.
Ammaraja-2	अम्मराजा-2	Chalukya Dynasty, Vengi	945-973	22.
Amoghvarsha-1	अमोघवर्ष-1	Rashtrakut Dynasty, Malkhed	814-877	133.
Amoghvarsha-2	अमोघवर्ष-2	Rashtrakut Dynasty, Malkhed	916-918	133.
Amoghvarsha-3	अमोघवर्ष-3	Rashtrakut Dynasty, Malkhed	936-939	133.
Anamitra	अनामित्र	Vrishni Dynasty	Ancient	188.
Anand Rao	आनंदराव	Gaikwad Dynasty	1800-1818	39.
Anandpal	आनंदपाल	Hindu Shahi Dynasty	1002-1021	53.
Anangpal-1	अनंगपाल-1	Tomar Dynasty, Delhi	736-754	173.
Anangpal-2	अनंगपाल-2	Tomar Dynasty, Delhi	1051-1081	173.
Anangpid	अनंगपीड़	Karkota Dynasty, Kashmir	850-851	69.
Anant Deva-1	अनंतदेव-2	Shilahar Dynasty, Konkan	1195-1200	147.
Anant Deva-2	अनंतदेव-2	Shilahar Dynasty, Konkan	1245-1255	147.
Anant Manikya	अनंत माणिक्य	Manikya Dynasty, Tripura	1563-1567	79.
Anant Varma	अनंतवर्मा	Ganga Dynasty, Kalinga	1078-1100	41.
Anantpal	अनंतपाल-1	Shilahar Dynasty, Konkan	1070-1110	147.
Anantraja	अनंतराजा	Lohar Dynasty, Kashmir	1028-1063	75.
Anaranya	अनारण्य	Ikshavaku Dynasty	Ancient	56.

Name	Devanagari	Dynasty	Dates	Page
Anant Malla Deva	अनंत मल्ल देव	Malla Dynasty, Nepal	1274–1310	111.
Andiya	अंदिया	Gond Dynasty, Vidarbha		46.
Andund Rai	अंदुंदराय	Nag Dynasty	932–969	83.
Anena	अनेन	Ikshavaku Dynasty	Ancient	56.
Angadev Gautam	अंगदेव गौतम	Shakya Gautam Dynasty		145.
Aniruddha Simha	अनिरुद्धसिंह	Waghela Dynasty, Riwa	1704–1709	180.
Anirudh	राव अनिरुध	Chauhan Dynasty, Bundi	(1658–1695)	32.
Ankbhupal	अंकभूपाल	Chennai Nayak Dynasty		99.
Anna Vema Reddi	अन्ना	Kondavidu Reddi Dynasty	1364–1386	102.
Anna Vota Reddi	अन्ना	Kondavidu Reddi Dynasty	1353–1364	102.
Anshuman	अंशुमान	Ikshavaku Dynasty	Ancient	56.
Anup Simha	अनूप सिंह	Rathor Dynasty, Bikaner	1669–1698	136.
Anup Simha	अनूपसिंह	Waghela Dynasty, Riwa	1643–1660	180.
Anushyati	अनुष्यति	Simha Shri Dynasty, Java	1227–1248	58.
Aparaditya	अपरादित्य	Shilahar Dynasty, Konkan	1170–1195	147.
Aparajita	अपराजित	Pallav Dynasty	893–897	116.
Aparajita	अपराजित	Shilahar Dynasty, Konkan	975–1010	147.
Apararka	अपरार्क	Shilahar Dynasty, Konkan	1110–1139	147.
Apilak	अपिलक	Satvahan Dynasty	110–98 BC	141.
Appa Saheb	आप्पा साहेब, मुधोजी-3	Bhosle Dynasty, Nagpur	1817–1818	12.
Apparaja	अप्पाराजा	Haleri Nayak Dynasty		103.
Apricchhadev	आपृच्छदेव	Tomar Dynasty, Delhi	875–897	173.
Ari Malla Deva	अरि मल्ल	Malla Dynasty, Nepal	1200–1216	111.
Ari Simha-1	अरिसिंह-1	Sisodiya Dynasty	1314–1326	159.
Ari Simha-2	अरिसिंह-2	Sisodiya Dynasty	1762–1773	159.
Arikesari	अरिकेसरी	Shilahar Dynasty, Konkan	1015–1020	147.
Arinjay	अरिंजय	Chola Dynasty	956–956	36.
Arisimha	अरिसिंह	Guhil Dynasty, Mewad	1127–1138	47.
Arju Raj	अर्जुन राज	Ahom Dynasty	1675–1677	2.
Arjun Deva	अर्जुनदेव	Waghela Dynasty, Gujrat	1261–1274	179.
Arjun Singh	अर्जुन सिंह	Chauhan Dynasty, Kota	(1727–1756)	33.
Arjun Varma	अर्जुनवर्मा-1	Parmar Dynasty	1200–1218	120.
Arjun Varma-2	अर्जुनवर्मा-2	Parmar Dynasty	1270–1285	120.
Arjun	अर्जुन	Gond Dynasty, Mandla		45.
Arka	अर्क	Ajmidh-Dynasty	Ancient	3.
Arnoraj	अर्णोराज	Chauhan Dynasty, Sakambhari	1130–1153	26.
Artaparni	आर्तपर्णी	Raghu Dynasty	Ancient	131.

Name	Devanagari	Dynasty	Period	Page
Aryak	आर्यक	Pradyot Dynasty		123
Asamanjas	असमंजस	Ikshavaku Dynasty	Ancient	56
Ashmak	अश्मक	Raghu Dynasty	Ancient	131
Ashok	अशोक	Maurya Dynasty	269–232 BC	81
Ashvapal	अश्वपाल	Chaunah Dynasty, Nadol	1015–1019	27
Ashvaraj	अश्वराज	Chaunah Dynasty, Nadol	110–1119	27
Ashwamedha	अश्वमेध	Yudhishthir Dynasty	Ancient	193
Athoji	जाम आठोजी	Jadeja Dynasty	1385–1405	60
Atri	अत्रि प्रजापति	Atri Dynasty	Ancient	1
Avadhut Simha	अवधूतसिंह	Waghela Dynasty, Riwa	1709–1758	180
Avani Varma-1	अवनिवर्मा-1	Chalukya Dynasty, Saurashtra		21
Avani Varma-2	अवनिवर्मा-2, योग	Chalukya Dynasty, Saurashtra	900	21
Avanti Bai	अवंती बाई	Avanti Bai. Dynasty	1857–1858	5
Avanti Varma	अवंतिवर्मा	Maukhari Dynasty	580–600	80
Avanti Varma	अवंतिवर्मा	Utpal Dynasty, Kashmir	855–883	177
Avasar-1	अवसर-1	Shilahar Dynasty, Konkan	845–870	148
Avasar-2	अवसर-2	Shilahar Dynasty, Konkan	895–920	148
Avasar-3	अवसर-3	Shilahar Dynasty, Konkan	970–995	148
Avinit	अविनीत	Ganga Dynasty, Talkad	500–540	42
Ayu	आयु	Atri Dynasty	Ancient	1
Ayutashva	आयुताश्व	Raghu Dynasty	Ancient	131
Ayyakarai Vayyappa	अय्याकरै	Madura Nayak Dynasty	1531–1535	95
Ayyanna-1	अय्यन्ना-1	Chalukya Dynasty, Kalyani		19
Ayyanna-2	अय्यन्ना-2	Chalukya Dynasty, Kalyani	1014–1018	19
Ayyappa	अय्यप्पा	Chennai Nayak Dynasty		99
Baba Saheb	बाबा साहेब	Bhosle Dynasty, Tanjavar	1735–1736	11
Babarao	बाबाराव	Angre Dynasty	1799–1813	4
Babuji Naik	बाबूजी नाईक जोशी	Peshva Dynasty	1740–1740	121
Badan Simha	बदन सिंह	Simha Dynasty, Bharatpur	1722–1756	162
Bahadur Simha	बहादुर सिंह	Rathor Dynasty, Kishangadh	1748–1748	137
Bahadur Singh	बहादुर सिंह	Chauhan Dynasty, Bundi	(1945–1948)	32
Baharendra Say	बाहरेंद्र साय	Kalchuri Dynasty, Ratnapuri	1480–1535	67
Bahirji	बहिरजीपंत मोरेश्वर पिंगळे	Peshva Dynasty	1707–1713	121
Bahuk	बाहुक	Ikshavaku Dynasty	Ancient	56
Bahuvidh	बहुविध	Puru Dynasty	Ancient	129
Bairisal	बैरीसाल	Bhati Raval Dynasty	1864–1890	8
Bairisal	बैरीसाल	Nag Dynasty	1599–1614	83

Name	Devanagari	Dynasty	Period	Page
Bajirao-1	बाजीराव-1, विश्वास बल्लाळ	Peshva Dynasty	1720–1740	121.
Bajirao-2	बाजीराव रघुनाथ बल्लाळ	Peshva Dynasty	1795–1818	121.
Bak	बक	Gonaditya Dynasty, Kashmir	665–602	44.
Bakhat Simha	बखत सिंह	Rathor Dynasty, Jodhpur	1751–1752	135.
Bal Varma	बालवर्मा	Varma Dynasty, Kamrup	398–422	185.
Bal Varma-1	बालवर्मा-1	Shalasthambha Dynasty, Assam	750–765	146.
Bal Varma-2	बालवर्मा-2	Shalasthambha Dynasty, Assam	765–810	146.
Bal Varma-2	बालवर्मा-3	Shalasthambha Dynasty, Assam	885–910	146.
Bala krishnappa	बाल कृष्णप्पा	Jinji Nayak Dynasty	1509–1521	93.
Bala Varma-1	बालवर्मा-1	Ahom Dynasty	405–420	2.
Baladitya	बालादित्य	Gonaditya Dynasty, Kashmir	631 AD	44.
Balaharsha Deva	बालहर्षदेव	Kalchuris, Dynasty, Tripuri	910–925	66.
Balaji Vishvanath	बाळाजी विश्वनाथ	Peshva Dynasty	1713–1720	121.
Balaputra	बालपुत्र	Shri Vijaya Dynasty, Sumatra	835	59.
Balavarma	बालवर्मा	Chalukya Dynasty, Saurashtra	.	21.
Baldev Simha	बलदेव सिंह	Simha Dynasty, Bharatpur	1823–1825	162.
Baldev	बलदेव	Bhati Raval Dynasty	1189–1189	8.
Baldeva	बलदेव	Thakur Dynasty, Nepal	(1059–1064)	110.
Balibhadra Gautam	बलिभद्र गौतम	Shakya Gautam Dynasty		145.
Baliraj	बलिराज	Chaunah Dynasty, Nadol	986–990	27.
Balitung	बालितुंग	Shailendra Dynasty, Java	898–910	57.
Ballal Sen	बल्लालसेन	Sen Dynasty, Bengal	1159–1179	143.
Ballal	बल्लाळ	Shilahar Dynasty, Kolhapur	1100–1110	149.
Balprasad	बालप्रसाद	Chaunah Dynasty, Nadol	1055–1070	27.
Balram Varma	बलराम वर्मा-2	Varma Dynasty, Travankor	1931–1948	184.
Balram Varma-1	बलराम वर्मा-1	Varma Dynasty, Travankor	1798–1810	184.
Balramnathshah	बलरामनाथशाह	Nag Dynasty		83.
Balvant Narayan Simha		Narayan Dynasty	1739–1770	86.
Balvant Simha	बलवंत सिंह	Simha Dynasty, Bharatpur	1826–1853	162.
Banbir Singh	बनबीरसिंह	Kachhavaha Dynasty	1413–1424	61.
Bangaru Timma Nayak	बंगरु	Pemmasani Nayak Dynasty	1540–1565	92.
Bappa Raval	बप्पा रावल	Guhil Dynasty, Mewad	730–753	47.
Basavappa-1	बासवप्पा-1	Keladi Nayak Dynasty	1697–1714	94.
Basavappa-2	बासवप्पा-2	Keladi Nayak Dynasty	1739–1754	94.
Baudshal	बौदाशाल	Nag Dynasty	1512–1530	83.
Ber Simha	बेर सिंह	Bhati Raval Dynasty	1439–1449	8.
Bettad Chamraj Mummadi	चामराज-5	Wadiyar Dynasty	1576–1578	178.

Name	Devanagari	Dynasty	Period	Page
Bhadra	भद्र	Shunga Dynasty	124-122 BC	160.
Bhadrasen	भद्रसेन	Yadu Dynasty	Ancient	191.
Bhag Raj	भाग राज	Ahom Dynasty	1641-1644	2.
Bhag Varma	भागवर्मा	Kadamb Dynasty	385-410	62.
Bhagan Rai	भगनराय	Nag Dynasty	772-811	83.
Bhagavan Das	भगवानदास	Kachhavaha Dynasty	1573-1589	61.
Bhagavat	भागवत	Shunga Dynasty	103-82 BC	160.
Bhagirath	भगीरथ	Ikshavaku Dynasty	Ancient	56.
Bhagya Simha	भाग्य सिंह	Simha Dynasty, Manipur	1824-1825	151.
Bhanudeva-1	भानुदेव-1	Ganga Dynasty, Kalinga	1264-1279	41.
Bhanudeva-2	भानुदेव-2	Ganga Dynasty, Kalinga	1306-1328	41.
Bhanudeva-3	भानुदेव-3	Ganga Dynasty, Kalinga	1352-1378	41.
Bhanudeva-4	भानुदेव-4	Ganga Dynasty, Kalinga	1414-1434	41.
Bhao Singh	भाओसिंह	Kachhavaha Dynasty	1614-1621	61.
Bharamanna	भरमन्ना	Chitradurg Nayak Dynasty	1689-1721	100.
Bharat	भरत	Bharat Dynasty	Ancient	7.
Bharat	भरत	Puru Dynasty	Ancient	129.
Bharma Raj-1	ब्रह्मराज-1	Ram Dynasty, Thailand	1370-1388	167.
Bharmal	भारमल	Kachhavaha Dynasty	1537-1573	61.
Bharmal-1	राव भरमल-1	Jadeja Dynasty	1585-1631	60.
Bharmal-2	राव भरमल-2	Jadeja Dynasty	1814-1819	60.
Bharmaraj	ब्रह्मराज त्रैलोकनाथ	Ram Dynasty, Thailand	1448-1488	167.
Bharmyashva	भर्म्याश्व	Ajmidh-Dynasty	Ancient	3.
Bhartridaman	भर्तृदामन	Kshatrap Dynasty	282-332	71.
Bharuk	भरुक	Ikshavaku Dynasty	Ancient	56.
Bhaskar Varma	भास्करवर्मा	Ahom Dynasty	594-650	2.
Bhaskar Varma	भास्करवर्मा	Varma Dynasty, Kamrup	600-650	185.
Bhaskara Deva	भास्करदेव	Thakur Dynasty, Nepal	(1046-1059)	110.
Bhaskararavi Varma-1	भास्कररविवर्मा-1	Cher Dynasty	962-979	34.
Bhaskararavi Varma-2	भास्कररविवर्मा-2	Cher Dynasty	979-1021	34.
Bhaskararavi Varma-3	भास्कररविवर्मा-3	Cher Dynasty	1043-1082	34.
Bhattarak	भट्टारक	Maitrak Dynasty	480-492	77.
Bhava Simha	भावसिंह	Waghela Dynasty, Riwa	1660-1704	180.
Bhava Varma-2	भववर्मा-2	Vietnam, Bhava varma Dynasty, Vietnam	635-657	170.
Bhavadatta	भवदत्त वर्मा	Nal Dynasty		84.
Bhavsingh	भवसिंह	Chauhan Dynasty, Bundi	(1658–1681)	32.
Bhavuk	भावुक	Kuru Dynasty	Ancient	73.

Name	Devanagari	Dynasty	Period	Ref
Bhhaskar Malla Deva	भास्कर	Malla Dynasty, Nepal	1700–1714	111.
Bhillam	भिल्लम-1	Yadav Dynasty, Devgiri	925–950	190.
Bhillam-2	भिल्लम-2	Yadav Dynasty, Devgiri	975–1005	190.
Bhillam-3	भिल्लम-3	Yadav Dynasty, Devgiri	1020–1055	190.
Bhillam-4	भिल्लम-4	Yadav Dynasty, Devgiri	1173–1192	190.
Bhilraja	भिल राजा	Gond Dynasty, Vidarbha		46.
Bhim Simha	भीम सिंह	Rathor Dynasty, Jodhpur	1793–1803	135.
Bhim Singh	भीमसिंह	Kachhavaha Dynasty	1527–1534	61.
Bhim Singh-2	भीम सिंह-2	Chauhan Dynasty, Kota	(1940–1948)	33.
Bhima Deva-1	भीमदेव-1	Solanki Dynasty	1022–1064	163.
Bhima Jetripal	भीम जेतृपाल	Hindu Shahi Dynasty	921–960	53.
Bhima Simha	भीम सिंह	Bhati Raval Dynasty	1577–1613	8.
Bhima Simha	भीमसिंह	Sisodiya Dynasty	1778–1828	159.
Bhima	भीम	Gond Dynasty, Vidarbha		46.
Bhima	भीम	Shilahar Dynasty, Konkan	945–970	148.
Bhima-1	भीम-1	Chalukya Dynasty, Kalyani		19.
Bhima-2	भीम-2	Chalukya Dynasty, Kalyani		19.
Bhima-2	भीम-2	Solanki Dynasty	1178–1223	163.
Bhimagupta	भीमगुप्त	Pravargupta Dynasty, Kashmir	975–980	125.
Bhimaji	जाम भीमजी	Jadeja Dynasty	1510–1525	60.
Bhimakarna	भीमकर्ण	Nag Dynasty	1098–1132	83.
Bhimsen	भीमसेन	Kuru Dynasty	Ancient	73.
Bhimsingh-1	भीम सिंह-1	Chauhan Dynasty, Kota	(1707–1727)	33.
Bhiratkarna	भिरातकर्ण	Nag Dynasty	1496–1501	83.
Bhirtribhatta	भर्तृभट्ट	Guhil Dynasty, Mewad	903–951	47.
Bhog Varma	भोगवर्मा	Maukhari Dynasty		80.
Bhogi Varma	भोगीवर्मा	Kadamb Dynasty	566–610	62.
Bhoja Deva-1	भोजदेव-1, राजा भोज	Parmar Dynasty	1010–1055	120.
Bhoja Deva-2	भोज देव-2	Parmar Dynasty	1285–1300	120.
Bhoja Varma	भोजवर्मा	Chandela Dynasty	1286–1288	23.
Bhoja	भोज	Vrishni Dynasty	Ancient	188.
Bhojdev	भोजदेव	Raghav Dynasty, Nepal	(1015-1015)	109.
Bhojdeva	भोजदेव	Bhati Raval Dynasty	1123–1155	8.
Bhojraj	राव भोजराज	Jadeja Dynasty	1631–1645	60.
Bhojraj-1	भोजराज-1	Shilahar Dynasty, Kolhapur	1085–1100	149.
Bhojraj-2	भोजराज-2	Shilahar Dynasty, Kolhapur	1175–1212	149.
Bhritakshetra	भृतक्षेत्र	Bharat Dynasty	Ancient	7.

Name	Devanagari	Dynasty	Period	Ref
Bhumi Mitra	भूमिमित्र	Kanva Dynasty	63–51 BC	63.
Bhupal Simha	भूपालसिंह	Sisodiya Dynasty	1930–1948	159.
Bhupatsimha	भुपतसिंह	Chudasama Dynasty	1472–1505	37.
Bhupendra Malla Deva	भूपेंद्र	Malla Dynasty, Nepal	1687–1700	111.
Bhutapal	भूतपाल	Nand Dynasty		85.
Bhuti Varma	भूतिवर्मा	Ahom Dynasty	510–555	2.
Bhuti Varma	भूतिवर्मा	Varma Dynasty, Kamrup	518–542	185.
Bhuyad	भूयाद	Chapotkat Dynasty	866–895	25.
Bidar Simha	बीदर सिंह	Rathor Dynasty, Kishangadh	1781–1788	137.
Bijjal	बिज्जल	Kalchuri Dynasty, Kalyani	1156–1167	68.
Bimbisar	बिंबिसार (श्रोणिक)	Haryak Dynasty	546–494 BC.	51.
Bimbisar	बिंबिसार	Brihadrith Dynasty, Magadh	554BC–492 BC	15.
Bindusar	बिंदुसार	Maurya Dynasty	298–271 BC	81.
Bisal Deva	बीसलदेव	Waghela Dynasty, Gujrat	1243–1261	179.
Bishna Singh	बिशनसिंह	Kachhavaha Dynasty	1688–1700	61.
Bodh Simha	बोध चंद्र	Simha Dynasty, Manipur	1941–1948	151.
Bol Chamraj-4	बोळ चामराज-4	Wadiyar Dynasty	1572–1576	178.
Brahma Raj-2	ब्रह्मराज-2	Ram Dynasty, Thailand	1424–1448	167.
Brahma Raj-3	ब्रह्मराज-3	Ram Dynasty, Thailand	1488–1491	167.
Brahma Raj-4	ब्रह्मराज-4	Ram Dynasty, Thailand	1529–1534	167.
Brahma Raj-5	ब्रह्मराज-5	Ram Dynasty, Thailand	1758–1767	167.
Brahma	ब्रह्म	Atri Dynasty	Ancient	1.
Brahma	ब्रह्मा	Atri Dynasty	Ancient	1.
Brahma	ब्रह्मा	Vivasvan Dynasty	Ancient	187.
Brajendra Simha	ब्रजेंद्र सिंह	Simha Dynasty, Bharatpur	1929–1947	162.
Brihadrath	बृहद्रथ	Brihadrith Dynasty, Magadh	Ancient	15.
Brihadrath	बृहद्रथ	Maurya Dynasty	187–184 BC	81..
Brihadrath	बृहद्रथ	Nimi Janak Dynasty	Ancient	114.
Brihaspati	बृहस्पति	Karkota Dynasty, Kashmir	825–840	69.
Brij Narayan	ब्रिज नारायण	Sutiya Dynasty, Assam	1343–1360	164.
Buddha Raj	बुद्धराज	Kalchuris Dynasty, Mahismati	600–620	65.
Buddha Singh	बुद्धसिंह	Chauhan Dynasty, Bundi	(1695–1739)	32.
Buddha Varma	बुद्धवर्मा	Pallav Dynasty	530–540	116.
Buddhavarma Raja	बुद्धवर्मा राजा	Chalukya Dynasty, Lat	610–643	20.
Buddhi Svargnarayan	बुद्धि स्वर्गनारायण	Ahom Dynasty	1494–1539	2.
Buddhisha	बुद्धीश	Lain Zang Dynasty, Laos	1622–1627	172.
Budh Simha	बुध सिंह	Bhati Raval Dynasty	1708–1720	8.

Name	Hindi	Dynasty	Period	Ref
Budha	बुध	Atri Dynasty	Ancient	1.
Bukka-1	बुक्क-1	Sangam Nayak Dynasty	1356-1377	87.
Bukka-2	बुक्क-2	Sangam Nayak Dynasty	1405-1406	87.
Butuga	बूतुग	Ganga Dynasty, Talkad	937-955	42.
Chach Maharaja	महाराजा चाच	Chach Dynasty, Sindh	643-671	17.
Chachan Simha	चाचन सिंह	Chauhan Dynasty, Jalor	1257-1282	29.
Chador Namgyal	चदोर नामग्याल	Namgyal Dynasty, Sikkim	1700-1717	14.
Chait Narayan Simha		Narayan Dynasty	1770-1780	86.
Chakchakdeva-1	चकचकदेव-1	Bhati Raval Dynasty	1218-1242	8.
Chakchakdeva-2	चकचकदेव-2	Bhati Raval Dynasty	1449-1455	8.
Chakra Dhvaja Simha	चक्रध्वज सिंह	Ahom Dynasty	1664-1670	2.
Chakra Varma-1	चक्रवर्मा (1)	Utpal Dynasty, Kashmir	922-933	177.
Chakra Varma-2	चक्रवर्मा (2)	Utpal Dynasty, Kashmir	935-935	177.
Chakra Varma-3	चक्रवर्मा (3)	Utpal Dynasty, Kashmir	935-935	177.
Chalukya Bhima-1	चालुक्य भीम-1	Chalukya Dynasty, Vengi	892-918	22.
Chalukya Bhima-1	चालुक्य भीम-1	Chalukya Dynasty, Vengi	926-934	22.
Chalukya Bhima-2	चालुक्य भीम-2	Chalukya Dynasty, Vengi	934-945	22.
Chamraj-10	खासा चामराज-10	Wadiyar Dynasty	1776-1796	178.
Chamraj-11	मुम्मडि चामराज-11	Wadiyar Dynasty	1868-1895	178.
Chamraj-12	जय चामराज-12	Wadiyar Dynasty	1940-1947	178.
Chamraj-6	चामराज-6	Wadiyar Dynasty	1617-1637	178.
Chamraj-7	चामराज-7	Wadiyar Dynasty	1732-1734	178.
Chamraj-8	खासा चामराज-8	Wadiyar Dynasty	1766-1770	178.
Chamraj-9	बेट्टद चामराज-9	Wadiyar Dynasty	1770-1776	178.
Chamunda Raj	चामुण्डराज	Saindhav Dynasty	880-885	140.
Chamundraj	चामुंडराज	Chauhan Dynasty, Sakambhari	1040-1065	26.
Chamundraj	चामुंडराज	Solanki Dynasty	695-1010	163.
Chanchu	चंचु	Ikshavaku Dynasty	Ancient	56.
Chandra Kirti-1	चंद्रकीर्ति-1	Simha Dynasty, Manipur	1834-1844	151.
Chandra Kirti-2	चंद्रकीर्ति-2	Simha Dynasty, Manipur	1850-1886	151.
Chandra Narayan	चंद्र नारायण	Sutiya Dynasty, Assam	1522-1524	164.
Chandra Rai	चंद्रराय	Nag Dynasty	905-932	83.
Chandra Sen	चंद्रसेन	Kachhavaha Dynasty	1453-1502	61.
Chandra Shri Satkarni	चंद्र श्री	Satvahan Dynasty	188-195 AD	141.
Chandra	चंद्र	Atri Dynasty	Ancient	1.
Chandra	चंद्र	Chach Dynasty, Sindh	671-679	17.
Chandra	चंद्र	Gond Dynasty, Mandla		45.

Name	Devanagari	Dynasty	Period	Page
Chandra	चंद्र	Shilahar Dynasty, Kolhapur	980–1000	149.
Chandragupta	चंद्रगुप्त	Maurya Dynasty	322–298 BC	81.
Chandragupta-1	चंद्रगुप्त-1	Gupta Dynasty, Patliputra	319–350	48.
Chandragupta-2	चंद्रगुप्त-2 (विक्रमादित्य-1)	Gupta Dynasty, Patliputra	375–415	48.
Chandrakant Simha-1	चंद्रकांत सिंह	Ahom Dynasty	1811–1818	2.
Chandrakant Simha-2	चंद्रकांत सिंह	Ahom Dynasty	1819–1821	2.
Chandralaya	चंद्रालय	Lain Zang Dynasty, Laos	1690–1695	172.
Chandra-mukh Varma	चंद्रमुखवर्मा	Ahom Dynasty	555–565	2.
Chandramukh Varma	चंद्रमुखवर्मा	Varma Dynasty, Kamrup	542–566	185.
Chandraraj-1	चंद्रराज-1	Chauhan Dynasty, Sakambhari	759–771	26.
Chandraraj-2	चंद्रराज-2	Chauhan Dynasty, Sakambhari	636–863	26.
Chandraraj-3	चंद्रराज-3	Chauhan Dynasty, Sakambhari	890–917	26.
Chandrasen	चंद्रसेन	Rathor Dynasty, Jodhpur	1562–1582	135.
Channamma	रानी चन्नम्मा	Keladi Nayak Dynasty	1672–1697	94.
Chaolung Sukpha	शौलंग सुखफा	Ahom Dynasty	1228–1262	2.
Chaudappa Nayak	चौदप्पा नायक	Keladi Nayak Dynasty	1499–1530	94.
Chaudsimha	चौड़सिंह	Guhil Dynasty, Mewad	1138–1148	47.
Chellamuttu	चेल्लमुत्तु सेतुपति	Nachchiyar Dynasty, Ramand	1780	186.
Chenna Basavappa	चेन्नबासवप्पा	Keladi Nayak Dynasty	1754–1757	94.
Chenna Venkat	चेन्न वेंकट	Chennai Nayak Dynasty		99.
Chenna Vibhudu	चेन्न विभुदु	Pemmasani Nayak Dynasty	1505–1540	92.
Chennappa Nayak	चेन्नप्पा नायक	Chennai Nayak Dynasty		99.
Cheraman	चेरमान् पेरुमल	Cher Dynasty	742–800	34.
Chetansimha	चेतनसिंह	Guhil Dynasty, Mewad	793–813	47.
Chhada Simha	छाड़ा सिंह	Rathor Dynasty, Jodhpur	1328–1344	135.
Chhadvideva	छत्रीदेव	Shilahar Dynasty, Konkan	965–975	147.
Chhatra Manikya	छत्र माणिक्य	Manikya Dynasty, Tripura	1661–1667	79.
Chhatrakarna	छत्रकर्ण	Nag Dynasty	1469–1496	83.
Chhittaraj	छित्तराज	Shilahar Dynasty, Konkan	1020–1035	147.
Chikanna	चिकन्ना	Chitradurg Nayak Dynasty	1676–1686	100.
Chikka Devraj	चिक्क देवराज	Wadiyar Dynasty	1673–1704	178.
Chikka Virappa	चिक्क वीरप्पा	Haleri Nayak Dynasty	1736–1766	103.
Chikka	चिक्का	Keladi Nayak Dynasty	1570–1580	94.
Chinna Timma Nayak	चिन्न तिम्म	Pemmasani Nayak Dynasty	1623–1652	92.
Chinnabhumi Nayak	चिन्नभूमि नायक	Vellor Nayak Dynasty	1526	96.
Chinnappa	चिन्नप्पा	Madura Nayak Dynasty	1526–1531	95.
Chitrarath	चित्ररथ	Kukkur Dynasty	Ancient	72.

Name	Devanagari	Dynasty	Period	Page
Chitrarath	चित्ररथ	Vrishni Dynasty	Ancient	188.
Chokannath	चोकन्नाथ	Madura Nayak Dynasty	1670–1685	95.
Chuda Simha	चूड़ा चंद्र सिंह	Simha Dynasty, Manipur	1891–1941	151.
Chudachandra	चुडाचंद्र	Chudasama Dynasty	875–907	37.
Chudamani	चुडामणि	Shri Vijaya Dynasty, Sumatra	988	59.
Dadda-1	दद्दा-1	Gurjar Dynasty	400	49.
Dadda-2	दद्दा-2 (प्रशान्तराग)	Gurjar Dynasty	478	49.
Dadda-3	दद्दा-3	Gurjar Dynasty		49.
Dadda-4	दद्दा-4 (प्रशान्तराग)	Gurjar Dynasty	580	49.
Dadda-5	दद्दा-5 (सुसहाय)	Gurjar Dynasty	628–640	49.
Dadda-6	दद्दा-6	Gurjar Dynasty		49.
Dahir Maharaja	महाराजा दाहिर	Chach Dynasty, Sindh	679–712	17.
Daksha	दक्ष	Shailendra Dynasty, Java	910–919	57.
Dakshin	दक्षिण	Ram Dynasty, Thailand	1767–1782	167.
Dalpat Simha	दलपत सिंह	Rathor Dynasty, Bikaner	1612–1613	136.
Dalpat	दलपत	Gond Dynasty, Mandla		45.
Damadaksha-1	दामक्षद-1	Kshatrap Dynasty	150–178	71.
Damaji Rao-1	दमाजीराव-1	Gaikwad Dynasty	1720–1721	39.
Damaji Rao-2	दमाजीराव-2	Gaikwad Dynasty	1732–1767	39.
Damasen-1	दामसेन-1	Kshatrap Dynasty	223–236	71.
Damasen-2	दामसेन-2	Kshatrap Dynasty	250–265	71.
Damodar Sen	दामोदरसेन	Vakatak Dynasty	420–450	181.
Damodar	दामोदर	Parivrajak Dynasty		119.
Damodargupta	दामोदरगुप्त	Gupta Dynasty, Patliputra	560–562	48.
Danarnava	दानार्णव	Chalukya Dynasty, Vengi	973	22.
Danarnava	दानार्णव	Ganga Dynasty, Kalinga		41.
Danti Varma	दंतीवर्मा	Pallav Dynasty	796–847	116.
Dantidurg-2	दंतीदुर्ग-2	Rashtrakut Dynasty, Malkhed	713–758	133.
Dantidurga-1	दंतीदुर्ग-1	Rashtrakut Dynasty, Malkhed	620–630	133.
Dantivarma	दंतीवर्मा	Rashtrakut Dynasty, Lat, Gujrat	867–888	134.
Daridra	दरिद्र	Kukkur Dynasty	Ancient	72.
Dashaputra	दशपुत्र	Shishunag Dynasty	366–344 BC	150.
Dashrath	दशरथ	Maurya Dynasty	228–224 BC	81.
Dashrath	दशरथ	Raghu Dynasty	Ancient	131.
Dattaji-2	दत्ताजी	Sindhia Dynasty	1755–1760	157.
Daulatrao	दौलतराव	Sindhia Dynasty	1794–1827	157.
Davari	दावरी	Ratta Dynasty	1000	138.

Name		Dynasty	Period	Page
Dayit Vushnu	दयितविष्णु	Pal Dynasty, Bengal		115.
Desal-1	राव देसल-1	Jadeja Dynasty	1718-1741	60.
Desal-2	राव देसल-2	Jadeja Dynasty	1819-1860	60.
Dev Manikya	देव माणिक्य	Manikya Dynasty, Tripura	1520-1530	79.
Deva Varma	देववर्मा	Maurya Dynasty	202-195 BC	81.
Deva Varma	देववर्मा	Shrimar Dynasty, Vietnam	510-526	169.
Devabhuti	देवभूति	Shunga Dynasty	82-72 BC	160.
Devadhya	देवाढ्य	Parivrajak Dynasty		119.
Devagupta	देवगुप्त	Gupta Dynasty, Patliputra	680-700	48.
Devajna	देवज्ञ	Rai Dynasty, Sindh	489	132.
Devamidh	देवमीढ़	Nimi Janak Dynasty	Ancient	114.
Devanand	दैवानंद	Nand Dynasty		85.
Devapal	देवपाल	Parmar Dynasty	1218-1236	120.
Devapparaja	देवप्पाराजा	Haleri Nayak Dynasty	1770-1774	103.
Devaraya	देवराया-2	Sangam Nayak Dynasty	1425-1446	87.
Devaraya-1	देवराया-1	Sangam Nayak Dynasty	1406-1413	87.
Devashakti	देवशक्ति	Pratihar-Gurjar Dynasty	760-783	126.
Devatithi	देवातिथि	Kuru Dynasty	Ancient	73.
Devendra Simha	देवेंद्र सिंह	Simha Dynasty, Manipur	1850-1850	151.
Devendra Varma	देवेंद्रवर्मा	Chandela Dynasty	1051-1098	23.
Devidas	देवीदास	Bhati Raval Dynasty	1455-1496	8.
Devnathshah	देवनाथशाह	Nag Dynasty		83.
Devpal	देवपाल	Pal Dynasty, Bengal	815-850	115.
Devpal	देवपाल	Pratihar-Gurjar Dynasty	948-960	126.
Devraj	देवराज	Bhati Raval Dynasty	853-908	8.
Devrat	देवरात	Nimi Janak Dynasty	Ancient	114.
Dhadhiyappa-1	धदियप्पा-1	Yadav Dynasty, Devgiri	874-900	190.
Dhadiyappa-2	धदियप्पा-2	Yadav Dynasty, Devgiri	974-975	190.
Dhammiyar	धम्मियर	Shilahar Dynasty, Konkan	785-820	148.
Dhanak	धनक	Yadu Dynasty	Ancient	191.
Dhananand	धनानंद	Nand Dynasty	329 -322 BC	85.
Dhanga	धंग	Chandela Dynasty	954-1000	23.
Dhanush	धनुष	Brihadrith Dynasty, Magadh	Ancient	15.
Dhanya Manikya	धन्य माणिक्य	Manikya Dynasty, Tripura	1489-1515	79.
Dharapatta	धारपट्ट	Maitrak Dynasty	540-559	77.
Dharavarsha	धारावर्ष	Chindak Nag Dynasty		35.
Dharma Karma	धर्म कर्म	Lain Zang Dynasty, Laos	1633-1637	172.

Name	Devanagari	Dynasty	Period	Page
Dharma Manikya-1	धर्म माणिक्य -1	Manikya Dynasty, Tripura	1431–1462	79.
Dharma Manikya-2	धर्म माणिक्य-2	Manikya Dynasty, Tripura	1714–1725	79.
Dharma Narayan	धर्म नारायण	Sutiya Dynasty, Assam	1420–1440	164.
Dharma	धर्म	Yadu Dynasty	Ancient	191.
Dharmapal	धर्मपाल	Pal Dynasty, Bengal	769–815	115.
Dharmasen-1	धर्मसेन-1	Maitrak Dynasty	492–500	77.
Dharmasen-2	धर्मसेन-2	Maitrak Dynasty	571–605	77.
Dharmasen-3	धर्मसेन-3	Maitrak Dynasty	623–629	77.
Dharmasen-4	धर्मसेन-4	Maitrak Dynasty	645–653	77.
Dharmasetu	धर्मसेतु	Shri Vijaya Dynasty, Sumatra	725	59.
Dharmik Chandrapuri	धार्मिक चंद्रपुरी	Lain Zang Dynasty, Laos	1698–1706	172.
Dharnidhar Varma-1	धरणीधरवर्मा-1	Varma Dynasty, Cambodia	1107–1113	171.
Dharnidhar Varma-2	धरणीधरवर्मा-2	Varma Dynasty, Cambodia	1150–1160	171.
Dhat Rai	धटराय	Nag Dynasty	232–273	83.
Dhir Narayan	धीर नारायण	Sutiya Dynasty, Assam	1500–1522	164.
Dhrha Sen	दहसेन	Traikutak Dynasty	445–475	175.
Dhripanathshah	धृपनाथशाह	Nag Dynasty		83.
Dhrishtaketu	धृष्टकेतु	Nimi Janak Dynasty	Ancient	114.
Dhritarashtra	धृतराष्ट्र	Kaurava Dynasty		70.
Dhruvaraya-1	ध्रुवराया-1	Rashtrakut Dynasty, Malkhed	774–793	133.
Dhruvaraya-2	ध्रुवराया—2 धारावर्ष	Rashtrakut Dynasty, Lat, Gujrat	835–850	134.
Dhruvasen-1	ध्रुवसेन-1	Maitrak Dynasty	526–540	77.
Dhruvasen-2	ध्रुवसेन-2	Maitrak Dynasty	629–645	77.
Dhruvasen-3	ध्रुवसेन-3	Maitrak Dynasty	653–656	77.
Dhuhad Simha	धूहड़ सिंह	Rathor Dynasty, Jodhpur	1292–1309	135.
Dhvaj Manikya	ध्वज माणिक्य	Manikya Dynasty, Tripura	1515–1520	79.
Dhvajaman Gautam	ध्वजमान गौतम	Shakya Gautam Dynasty		145.
Dilip	दिलीप	Raghu Dynasty	Ancient	131.
Dinkar	दिनकर	Gond Dynasty, Vidarbha		46.
Dirghabahu	दीर्घबाहु	Raghu Dynasty	Ancient	131.
Divodas	दिवोदास	Ajmidh-Dynasty	Ancient	3.
Diwakar Sen	दिवाकरसेन	Vakatak Dynasty	405–420	181.
Doddaraja	दोद्दा वीरप्पा	Haleri Nayak Dynasty	1687–1736	103.
Drona Simha	द्रोणसिंह	Maitrak Dynasty	500–526	77.
Drupad	द्रुपद	Ajmidh-Dynasty	Ancient	3.
Dudar	दुदर	Bhati Raval Dynasty	1295–1311	8.
Dulhe Rai	दूल्हेराय	Kachhavaha Dynasty	1036–1037	61.

Name	Devanagari	Dynasty	Period	Page
Dulip Singh	दुलीप सिंह	Sikh Dynasty, Punjab	1843-1849	156.
Dundhubhi	दुंदुभी	Kukkur Dynasty	Ancient	72.
Dungar Simha	डुंगर सिंह	Rathor Dynasty, Bikaner	1872-1887	136.
Dungar Simha	डुंगर सिंह	Tomar Dynasty, Gwalior	1425-1459	174.
Durga Prasad Manikya	दुर्गाप्रसाद माणिक्य	Manikya Dynasty, Tripura	1809-1813	79.
Durga Simha	दुर्गा सिंह	Rathor Dynasty, Jodhpur	1678-1707	135.
Durjan Simha	दुर्जन सिंह	Simha Dynasty, Bharatpur	1825-1826	162.
Durjansal	दुर्जनसाल	Nag Dynasty	1614-1640	83.
Durlabh Vardhan	दुर्लभवर्धन	Karkota Dynasty, Kashmir	631-680	69.
Durlabhraj	दुर्लभराज	Solanki Dynasty	1011-1022	163.
Durlabhraj-1	दुर्लभराज-1	Chauhan Dynasty, Sakambhari	784-809	26.
Durlabhraj-2	दुर्लभराज-2	Chauhan Dynasty, Sakambhari	998-1012	26.
Durlabhraj-3	दुर्लभराज-3	Chauhan Dynasty, Sakambhari	1065-1070	26.
Duryodhan	दुर्योधन	Kaurava Dynasty		70.
Dusaj	दुसज	Bhati Raval Dynasty	1044-1123	8.
Dushyant	दुष्यंत	Bharat Dynasty	Ancient	7.
Dushyant	दुष्यंत	Gandhar Dynasty		43.
Dushyanta	दुष्यंत	Puru Dynasty	Ancient	129.
Dvidha Prahar	द्विधाप्रहार	Yadav Dynasty, Devgiri		190.
Ekoji	एकोजी राजे	Bhosle Dynasty, Tanjavar	1675-1684	11.
Elavel	एलावेल	Raghu Dynasty	Ancient	131.
Erag	एरग	Ratta Dynasty	1040-1048	138.
Ereyang	एरेयंग	Hoysal Dynasty	1063-1100	55.
Ethiriman	एथीरीमन प्रजाशेखरन	Arya Chakravarti Dynasty, Shri Lanka	1591-1617	155.
Fani Mukut Rai	फणी मुकुटराय	Nag Dynasty	83-177	83.
Fateh Simha	फतहसिंह	Sisodiya Dynasty	1884-1930	159.
Fula	जाम फूला	Jadeja Dynasty	1300-1320	60.
Futsog Namgyal-1	फुंटसोग नामग्याल-1	Namgyal Dynasty, Sikkim	1642-1670	14.
Futsog Namgyal-2	फुंटसोग नामग्याल-2	Namgyal Dynasty, Sikkim	1733-1780	14.
Gadadhar Simha	गदाधर सिंह	Ahom Dynasty	1681-1696	2.
Gaj Simha	गज सिंह	Rathor Dynasty, Bikaner	1746-1787	136.
Gaj Simha	गज सिंह	Rathor Dynasty, Jodhpur	1619-1638	135.
Gaja Simha	गजसिंह	Bhati Raval Dynasty	1819-1846	8.
Gajraj Rai	गजराजराय	Nag Dynasty	601-627	83.
Gambhir Simha-1	गंभीर सिंह-1	Simha Dynasty, Manipur	1821-1822	151.
Gambhir Simha-2	गंभीर सिंह-2	Simha Dynasty, Manipur	1825-1834	151.
Ganapati Varma	गणपतिवर्मा	Ahom Dynasty	440-450	2.

Name	Devanagari	Dynasty	Years	Page
Ganapati Varma	गणपतिवर्मा	Varma Dynasty, Kamrup	446-470	185.
Ganapati	गणपति	Kakatiya Dynasty	1199-1262	64.
Ganda	गंड	Chandela Dynasty	1000-1019	23.
Gandaraditya	गण्डरादित्य	Chola Dynasty	949-956	36.
Gandhar	गांधार	Gandhar Dynasty		43.
Gandharva Rai	गंधर्वराय	Nag Dynasty	1047-1098	83.
Gandir	गाण्डीर	Gandhar Dynasty		43.
Gandraditya	गंडरादित्य	Shilahar Dynasty, Kolhapur	1110-1135	149.
Ganga Simha	गंगा सिंह	Rathor Dynasty, Bikaner	1887-1943	136.
Ganga Simha	गंगा सिंह	Rathor Dynasty, Jodhpur	1515-1532	135.
Gangeyadev	गांगेय देव	Tomar Dynasty, Delhi	773-794	173.
Gangryadeva	गंगेयदेव विक्रमादित्य	Kalchuris, Dynasty, Tripuri	1037-1042	66.
Ganpat Rao	गणपतराव	Gaikwad Dynasty	1847-1856	39.
Ganpati	गणपति	Tomar Dynasty, Gwalior	1423-1425	174.
Gargeya Raj	गार्गेयान राज	Ahom Dynasty	1539-1525	2.
Garung	गरुंग	Shailendra Dynasty, Java	819-838	57.
Gaurakrishna	गौरकृष्ण	Satvahan Dynasty	31-56 AD	141.
Gauri Narayan	गौरी नारायण	Sutiya Dynasty, Assam	1210-1250	164.
Gaurinath Simha	गौरीनाथ सिंह	Ahom Dynasty	1780-1795	2.
Gautamiputra Satkarni	गौतमीपुत्र	Satvahan Dynasty	100-121 AD	141.
Gayakarna Deva	गयाकर्णदेव	Kalchuris, Dynasty, Tripuri	1151-1155	66.
Ghar Simha	घरसिंह	Bhati Raval Dynasty	1316-1334	8.
Ghatotkacha	घटोत्कच	Gupta Dynasty, Patliputra	280-319	48.
Ghoshavasu	घोषवसु	Shunga Dynasty	118-116 BC	160.
Giridhar Simha	गिरिधर सिंह	Bhati Raval Dynasty	1949-1950	8.
Girvan Shuddha Vikram Shah	विक्रम	Shah Dynasty, Nepal	1799-1816	112.
Givindpal	गोविंदपाल	1161-1174 Pal Dynasty, Bengal		115.
Gobhar Simha	गोभर सिंह	Ahom Dynasty	1674-1675	2.
Goda Varma-2	गोडै वर्मा-2	Varma Dynasty, Kochin	1662-1663	183.
Godai Varma-1	गोडै वर्मा-1	Varma Dynasty, Kochin	1637-1645	183.
Godaji	जाम गोदाजी-1	Jadeja Dynasty	1405-1430	60.
Godaji-2	राव गोदाजी-2	Jadeja Dynasty	1715-1718	60.
Godaji-3	राव गोदाजी-3	Jadeja Dynasty	1760-1778	60.
Goggiraj	गोग्गीराज	Shilahar Dynasty, Konkan	930-945	147.
Goka	गोंक	Shilahar Dynasty, Kolhapur	1020-1050	149.
Gokarna	गोकर्ण	Gonaditya Dynasty, Kashmir	340-282	44.
Gokarna	गोकर्ण	Nag Dynasty	1218-1236	83.

Name	Devanagari	Dynasty	Period	Page
Gokul Narayan	गोकुल नारायण	Sutiya Dynasty, Assam	1325–1343	164.
Gonand	गोनन्द -2	Gonaditya Dynasty, Kashmir	1182–1147 BC	44.
Gondu Rai	गोंडुराय I	Nag Dynasty	548–563	83.
Gopaditya	गोपादित्य	Gonaditya Dynasty, Kashmir	400–340	44.
Gopal Varma	गोपालवर्मा	Utpal Dynasty, Kashmir	920–904	177.
Gopal	गोपाल	Tomar Dynasty, Delhi	961–979	173.
Gopal-1	गोपाल-1	Pal Dynasty, Bengal	750–769	115.
Gopal-2	गोपाल-2	Pal Dynasty, Bengal	935–952	115.
Gopendraraji1	गोपेंद्रराज	Chauhan Dynasty, Sakambhari	771–784	26.
Govind Bajirao	गोविंद बाजीराव	Peshva Dynasty	1851–1857	121.
Govind Manikya-1	गोविंद माणिक्य-1	Manikya Dynasty, Tripura	1660–1661	79.
Govind Manikya-2	गोविंद माणिक्य-2	Manikya Dynasty, Tripura	1667–1673	79.
Govind Rao-1	गोविंदराव-1	Gaikwad Dynasty	1768–1771	39.
Govind Rao-2	गोविंदराव-1	Gaikwad Dynasty	1793–1800	39.
Govind Varma	गोविंदवर्मा	Chalukya Dynasty, Vengi	535–555	22.
Govindaraja	गोविंदराजा	Yadav Dynasty, Devgiri	1160–1160	190.
Govindnath	गोविंदनाथशाहदेव	Nag Dynasty	1806–1822	83.
Govindraj	गोविंदराज	Tomar Dynasty, Delhi	1189–1192	173.
Govindraj	गोविंदराज	Chauhan Dynasty, Ranthambhor	1194	28.
Govindraj	गोविंदराज	Chauhan Dynasty, Sakambhari	1012–1026	26.
Govindraj-2	गोविंदराज-2	Chauhan Dynasty, Sakambhari	1192–1193	26.
Govindraya-1	गोविंदराया-1	Rashtrakut Dynasty, Malkhed	650–670	133.
Govindraya-2	गोविंदराया-2	Rashtrakut Dynasty, Malkhed	773–774	133.
Govindraya-3	गोविंदराया-3	Rashtrakut Dynasty, Malkhed	773–814	133.
Govindraya-4	गोविंदराया-4	Rashtrakut Dynasty, Malkhed	918–936	133.
Govindraya-5	गोविंदराया-5 प्रभूतवर्ष	Rashtrakut Dynasty, Lat, Gujrat	850–867	134.
Gpoal	गोपाल	Pradyot Dynasty		123.
Graha Varma	ग्रहवर्मा	Maukhari Dynasty	600–612	80.
Guhadatta	गुहदत्त (गुहिल)	Guhil Dynasty, Mewad	550	47.
Guhal	गुहल	Shilahar Dynasty, Kolhapur	1075–1085	149.
Guhalla	गुहल्ल	Kadamb Dynasty, Goa	980–1007	64.
Guhasen	गुहसेन	Maitrak Dynasty	559–571	77.
Gulab Simha	गुलाबसिंह	Waghela Dynasty, Riwa	1918–1946	180.
Gulab Singh	गुलाब सिंह	Dogra Dynasty	1822–1856	38.
Guman Singh	गुमन सिंह	Chauhan Dynasty, Kota	(1764–1771)	33.
Guna Bhushan	गुणभूषण प्रजाशेखरन	Arya Chakravarti Dynasty, Shri Lanka	1348–1371	155.
Gunakamadev	गुणकामदेव	Thakur Dynasty, Nepal	(1187–1193)	110.

Name	Devanagari	Dynasty	Period	Page
Gunamaharnava	गुणमहार्णव	Ganga Dynasty, Kalinga	871–898	41.
Gunavira	गुणवीर प्रजाशेखरन	Arya Chakravarti Dynasty, Shri Lanka	1410–1440	155.
Gundamma-1	गुण्डम्मा-1	Ganga Dynasty, Kalinga	942–945	41.
Gundamma-2	गुण्डम्मा-2	Ganga Dynasty, Kalinga	1016–1019	41.
Gurmed Namgyal	गुरमेद नामग्याल	Namgyal Dynasty, Sikkim	1717–1733	14.
Gutta-1	गुत्त-1	Gutta Dynasty		50.
Gutta-2	गुत्त-2	Gutta Dynasty	1181–1187	50.
Gutta-3	गुत्त-3	Gutta Dynasty	1262	50.
Guvak-2	गुवक-2	Chauhan Dynasty, Sakambhari	809–836	26.
Guvak-3	गुवक-3	Chauhan Dynasty, Sakambhari	863–890	26.
Hada Chauhan	हाड़ा चौहान	Chauhan Dynasty, Hadauti	1342	31.
Hal	हाल	Satvahan Dynasty	56–61 AD	141.
Hama	राव सिंह	Chauhan Dynasty, Bundi	(1370–1403)	32.
Hamirji	जाम हमीरजी	Jadeja Dynasty	1525–1537	60.
Hammir Dev	हम्मीरदेव	Chauhan Dynasty, Ranthambhor	1283–1301	28.
Hammira Varma	हम्मीरवर्मा	Chandela Dynasty	1288–1311	23.
Hammira-1	हम्मीर-1	Sisodiya Dynasty	1326–1364	159.
Hammira-2	हम्मीर-2	Sisodiya Dynasty	1773–1778	159.
Hanvant Simha	हनवंत सिंह	Rathor Dynasty, Jodhpur	1947–1948	135.
Hari Narayan	हरि नारायण	Sutiya Dynasty, Assam	1305–1325	164.
Hari Rai	हरिराय	Nag Dynasty	563–601	83.
Hari Sen	हरिषेण	Vakatak Dynasty	490–510	181.
Hari Simha	हरि सिंह-1	Rathor Dynasty, Kishangadh	1609–1611	137.
Hari Simha	हरि सिंह-2	Rathor Dynasty, Kishangadh	1629–1643	137.
Hari Singh	हरि सिंह	Dogra Dynasty	1925–1947	38.
Hari Varma	हरिवर्मा	Ganga Dynasty, Talkad	450–460	42.
Hari Varma	हरिवर्मा	Kadamb Dynasty	537–547	62.
Hari Varma	हरिवर्मा	Maukhari Dynasty	500	80.
Harihar-1	हरिहर-1	Sangam Nayak Dynasty	1336–1356	87.
Harihar-2	हरिहर-2	Sangam Nayak Dynasty	1377–1404	87.
Haripal Deva	हरिपालदेव	Shilahar Dynasty, Konkan	1139–1155	147.
Hariraj	हरिराज	Chauhan Dynasty, Sakambhari	1193–1194	26.
Hariraja	हरिराजा	Lohar Dynasty, Kashmir	1028–1028	75.
Harirao	हरिराव	Holkar Dynasty	1834–1843	54.
Harishchandra	हरिश्चंद्र	Thakur Dynasty, Nepal	(1090–1099)	110.
Harishchandra Deva	हदिश्चंद्र देव	Chindak Nag Dynasty	1324	35.
Harishchandra	हरिश्चंद्र	Pratihar-Gurjar Dynasty	725	126.

Name	Devanagari	Dynasty	Period	Page
Harishchandra	राजा हरिश्चंद्र	Ikshavaku Dynasty	Ancient	56.
Hariya Bettad Chamraj-1	चामराज-1	Wadiyar Dynasty	1423–1459	178.
Hariya Bettad Chamraj-2	चामराज-2	Wadiyar Dynasty	1479–1513	178.
Hariya Bettad Chamraj-3	चामराज-3	Wadiyar Dynasty	1513–1533	178.
Hariya Deva	हरीयदेव	Gutta Dynasty		50.
Harjar Varma	हर्जरवर्मा	Shalasthambha Dynasty, Assam	815–835	146.
Harraj	हरराज	Bhati Raval Dynasty	1561–1577	8.
Harsha Vardhan	हर्षवर्धन	Pushyabhuti-Vardhan Dynasty	606–647	130.
Harsha Varma-1	हर्षवर्मा-1	Varma Dynasty, Cambodia	900–921	171.
Harsha Varma-2	हर्षवर्मा-2	Varma Dynasty, Cambodia	968–944	171.
Harsha-3	हर्षवर्मा-3	Varma Dynasty, Cambodia	1066–1080	171.
Harshadeva	हर्षदेव	Chandela Dynasty	914–948	23.
Harsharaja	हर्षराजा	Lohar Dynasty, Kashmir	1089–1101	75.
Haryashva	हर्यश्व	Ikshavaku Dynasty	Ancient	56.
Haryashva	हर्यश्व	Nimi Janak Dynasty	Ancient	114.
Hasti	हस्ति	Bharat Dynasty	Ancient	7.
Hasti	हस्ती	Parivrajak Dynasty	475–518	119.
Hehaya	हेहय	Yadu Dynasty	Ancient	191.
Hemachandra Vikramaditya,		Delhi	1555–1556	52.
Hemant Sen	हेमंतसेन	Sen Dynasty, Bengal	1095–1096	143.
Hillu	हिल्लु	Chach Dynasty, Sindh	712–712	17.
Hir-1	हीर-1	Gond Dynasty, Vidarbha		46.
Hir-2	हीर-2	Gond Dynasty, Vidarbha	1495–1521	46.
Hiranya	हिरण्य	Gonaditya Dynasty, Kashmir	89–120	44.
Hiranyaksha	हिरण्याक्ष	Gonaditya Dynasty, Kashmir	983–855	44.
Hiranyakula	हिरण्यकुल	Gonaditya Dynasty, Kashmir	855–795	44.
Hrasvaroma	ह्स्वरोम	Nimi Janak Dynasty	Ancient	114.
Hridik	ह्रदिक	Vrishni Dynasty	Ancient	188.
Huna Deva	हूण देव	Kachhavaha Dynasty	1038–1053	61.
Huvishka-1	हुविष्क-1	Kushan Dynasty	130–143	74.
Huvishka-2	हुविष्क-2	Kushan Dynasty	150–166	74.
Ikshavaku	इक्ष्वाकु	Vivasvan Dynasty	Ancient	187.
Ikshvaku	इक्ष्वाकु	Ikshavaku Dynasty	Ancient	56.
Immadi	इम्माडी नरसिंहराय	Saluv Nayak Dynasty	1492–1505	88.
Immadi Raj	इम्मडि राज	Wadiyar Dynasty	1637–1638	178.
Indra Bhattarak	इंद्र भट्टारक	Chalukya Dynasty, Vengi	663–663	22.
Indra Manikya	इन्द्र माणिक्य	Manikya Dynasty, Tripura	1530–1532	79.

Name	Devanagari	Dynasty	Dates	Page
Indra Manikya-2	इन्द्र माणिक्य-2	Manikya Dynasty, Tripura	1744–1746	79.
Indra Raj	इन्द्रराज	Ram Dynasty, Thailand	1408–1424	167.
Indra Sen	इन्द्रसेन	Traikutak Dynasty	388–445	175.
Indra Varma	इन्द्रवर्मा	Chalukya Dynasty, Vengi	480–515	22.
Indra varma	इन्द्रवर्मा	Funan Dynasty, Thailand	434	165.
Indra Varma-1	इन्द्रवर्मा-1	Varma Dynasty, Cambodia	876–889	171.
Indra Varma-2	इन्द्रवर्मा-2	Varma Dynasty, Cambodia	1219–1243	171.
Indra Varma-4	इन्द्रवर्मा-4	Varma Dynasty, Cambodia	1308–1327	171.
Indraditya	इन्द्रादित्य	Indraditya Dynasty, Thailand	1238–1275	166.
Indrajit	इंद्रजीत	Gonaditya Dynasty, Kashmir	1094–1059	44.
Indraraj	इन्द्रराज	Shilahar Dynasty, Konkan	920–945	148.
Indraraja-1	इंद्रराजा-1	Rashtrakut Dynasty, Malkhed	630–650	133.
Indraraja-3	इंद्रराजा-3	Rashtrakut Dynasty, Lat, Gujrat	800–812	134.
Indraraya-2	इंद्रराया-2	Rashtrakut Dynasty, Malkhed	690–713	133.
Indraraya-3	इंद्रराया-3	Rashtrakut Dynasty, Malkhed	914–916	133.
Ishan Chandra Manikya	ईशानचंद्र माणिक्य	Manikya Dynasty, Tripura	1849–1862	79.
Ishanya Varma	ईशान्यवर्मा	Maukhari Dynasty		80.
Ishanya Varma	ईशान्यवर्मा	Varma Dynasty, Cambodia	921–928	171.
Ishanya Varma	ईशान्यवर्मा	Vietnam, Bhava varma Dynasty, Vietnam	616–635	170.
Ishvar Manikya	ईश्वर माणिक्य	Manikya Dynasty, Tripura	1600–1600	79.
Ishvar Singh	ईश्वरीसिंह	Kachhavaha Dynasty	1743–1750	61.
Ishvar Varma	ईश्वरवर्मा	Maukhari Dynasty	540–550	80.
Ishvardatta	ईश्वरदत्त	Kshatrap Dynasty	236–239	71.
Ishvari Narayan Simha		Narayan Dynasty	1835–1889	86.
Ishwar Singh	ईश्वर सिंह	Chauhan Dynasty, Bundi	(1927–1945)	32.
Jadu Simha	जादू सिंह	Simha Dynasty, Manipur	1823–1823	151.
Jag Drva	जगदेव	Vuppadeva Dynasty, Kashmir	1199–1212	189.
Jagadekmalla-2	जगदेकमल्ल-2	Chalukya Dynasty, Kalyani	1138–1150	19.
Jagan Rai	जगनराय	Nag Dynasty	756–772	83.
Jagannath	जगन्नाथ	Gond Dynasty, Mandla		45.
Jagat Jai Malla Deva	जगत जय	Malla Dynasty, Nepal	1722–1736	111.
Jagat Manikya	जगत माणिक्य	Manikya Dynasty, Tripura	1725–1729	79.
Jagat Narayan	जगत नारायण	Sutiya Dynasty, Assam	1270–1585	164.
Jagat Simha-1	जगतसिंह-1	Sisodiya Dynasty	1628–1652	159.
Jagat Simha-2	जगतसिंह-2	Sisodiya Dynasty	1734–1752	159.
Jagat Singh-1	जगतसिंह-1	Kachhavaha Dynasty	1614–1614	61.
Jagat Singh-2	जगतसिंह-2	Kachhavaha Dynasty	1803–1818	61.

Name	Devanagari	Dynasty	Period	Page
Jagatsingh	जगत सिंह	Chauhan Dynasty, Kota	(1658–1683)	33.
Jagattunga	जगतुंग	Rashtrakut Dynasty, Malkhed	911–914	133.
Jagdev	जगदेव	Tomar Dynasty, Delhi	814–834	173.
Jagdhat Rai	जगधटराय	Nag Dynasty	869–905	83.
Jagmal Simha	जगमल सिंह	Rathor Dynasty, Kishangadh	1618–1629	137.
Jai Ari Malla Deva	जय अरि	Malla Dynasty, Nepal	1326–1347	111.
Jai Arjun Malla Deva	जय अर्जुन	Malla Dynasty, Nepal	1361–1382	111.
Jai Bhima Malla Deva	जय भीम	Malla Dynasty, Nepal	1258–1271	111.
Jai Dharma Malla Deva	जय धर्म	Malla Dynasty, Nepal	1395–1408	111.
Jai Dhvaja Raj	जयध्वज सिंह	Ahom Dynasty	1650–1664	2.
Jai Jyoti Malla Deva	जय ज्योति	Malla Dynasty, Nepal	1408–1428	111.
Jai Malla Deva	जय मल्ल देव	Malla Dynasty, Nepal	1235–1258	111.
Jai Manikya	जय माणिक्य	Manikya Dynasty, Tripura	1573–1577	79.
Jai Nand Malla Deva	जय नंद	Malla Dynasty, Nepal	1310–1320	111.
Jai Nripendra Malla Deva	जय	Malla Dynasty, Nepal	1674–1680	111.
Jai Prakash Malla Dev	जय प्रकाश	Malla Dynasty, Nepal	1736–1768	111.
Jai Raj Malla Deva	जय राज	Malla Dynasty, Nepal	1347–1361	111.
Jai Rudra Malla Deva	जय रुद्र	Malla Dynasty, Nepal	1320–1326	111.
Jai Simha Malla Deva	जय सिंह	Malla Dynasty, Nepal	1271–1274	111.
Jai Simha	जय सिंह	Simha Dynasty, Manipur	1822–1823	151.
Jai Simha	जयसिंह	Sisodiya Dynasty	1680–1699	159.
Jai Simha	जयसिंह	Waghela Dynasty, Riwa	1808–1835	180.
Jai Simha-1	जयसिंह-1	Parmar Dynasty	1055–1059	120.
Jai Simha-2	जयसिंह-2	Parmar Dynasty	1265–1270	120.
Jai Singh-1	जयसिंह-1	Kachhavaha Dynasty	1621–1666	61.
Jai Singh-3	जयसिंह-3	Kachhavaha Dynasty	1818–1835	61.
Jai Sthiti Malla Deva	जय स्थिति	Malla Dynasty, Nepal	1382–1395	111.
Jai Varma-1	जयवर्मा-1	Parmar Dynasty	1135–1138	120.
Jai Varma-2	जयवर्मा-2	Parmar Dynasty	1255–1265	120.
Jai Yaksha Malla Deva	जय यक्ष	Malla Dynasty, Nepal	1428–1482	111.
Jaika-1	जैका-1	Saindhav Dynasty	824–849	140.
Jaika-2	जैका-2	Saindhav Dynasty	900–920	140.
Jaipal	जयपाल	Hindu Shahi Dynasty	960–1002	53.
Jairaj	जयराज	Chauhan Dynasty, Sakambhari	721–734	26.
Jaisal	जैसाल	Bhati Raval Dynasty	1155–1167	8.
Jaisimha Deva	जयसिंह देव	Chindak Nag Dynasty		35.
Jaisimha-1	जयसिंह-1	Solanki Dynasty	1094–1143	163.

Name	Devanagari	Dynasty	Period	Ref
Jaisimha-2	जयसिंह-2	Solanki Dynasty	1223-1241	163.
Jait Simha	जैतसिंह	Chaunah Dynasty, Nadol	1193-1197	27.
Jait Simha-2	जैतसिंह-2	Bhati Raval Dynasty	1496-1528	8.
Jaital Deva	जैतल देव	Kachhavaha Dynasty	1146-1179	61.
Jaitrasimha	जैत्रसिंह	Chauhan Dynasty, Ranthambhor	1248-1283	28.
Jaitrasimha	जैत्रसिंह	Guhil Dynasty, Mewad	1213-1256	47.
Jaitsi Simha	जैतसी सिंह	Rathor Dynasty, Bikaner	1526-1542	136.
Jaitsimha	जैतसिंह-1	Bhati Raval Dynasty	1276-1293	8.
Jaitug Deva	जैतुगदेव	Parmar Dynasty	1236-1255	120.
Jaitugi-1	जैतुगी-1	Yadav Dynasty, Devgiri	1192-1200	190.
Jajjala Deva-1	जाजल्लदेव-1	Kalchuri Dynasty, Ratnapuri	1114-1141	67.
Jajjala Deva-2	जाजल्लदेव-2	Kalchuri Dynasty, Ratnapuri	1167-1181	67.
Jalakarna	जलकर्ण	Nag Dynasty	1180-1218	83.
Jalanasi	जालाणसी	Rathor Dynasty, Jodhpur	1323-1328	135.
Jaluk	जलूक	Pratapaditya Dynasty, Kashmir	135-103 BC	124.
Janak (Shiradhvaja)	जनक (शीरध्वज)	Nimi Janak Dynasty	Ancient	114.
Janha Deva	जान्ह देव	Kachhavaha Dynasty	1053-1070	61.
Janhu	जन्हू	Kuru Dynasty	Ancient	73.
Jankoji-2	जनकोजी-2	Sindhia Dynasty	1760-1763	157.
Jankoji-3	जनकोजी-3	Sindhia Dynasty	1827-1843	157.
Janmejay	जनमेजय	Yudhishthir Dynasty	Ancient	193.
Janmejaya	जन्मेजय	Puru Dynasty	Ancient	129.
Janoji-1	जानोजी-1	Bhosle Dynasty, Nagpur	1755-1772	12.
Janoji-2	जानोजी-2, यशवंतराव	Bhosle Dynasty, Nagpur	1853-1854	12.
Jarasandha	जरासंध	Brihadrith Dynasty, Magadh	Ancient	15.
Jashkarna	जाशकर्ण	Nag Dynasty	1132-1180	83.
Jashshaka Deva	जश्शकदेव	Vuppadeva Dynasty, Kashmir	1181-1199	189.
Jasvant Simha	जसवंत सिंह	Simha Dynasty, Bharatpur	1853-1893	162.
Jasvant Simha-1	जसवंत सिंह-1	Rathor Dynasty, Jodhpur	1638-1678	135.
Jasvant Simha-2	जसवंत सिंह-2	Rathor Dynasty, Jodhpur	1873-1895	135.
Jatavarma-1	जटावर्मा कुलशेखर	Pandya Dynasty	1190-1216	118.
Jatavarma-2	जटावर्मा सुंदर	Pandya Dynasty	1251-1253	118.
Jatavarma-3	जटावर्मा वीर पांड्या	Pandya Dynasty	1253-1275	118.
Jatavarma-4	जटावर्मा पराक्रम	Pandya Dynasty	1422-1429	118.
Jatavarma-5	जटावर्मा कुलशेखर	Pandya Dynasty	1429-1473	118.
Jatavarma-6	जटावर्मा श्रीवल्लभ	Pandya Dynasty	1534-1543	118.
Jatavarma-7	जटावर्मा अतिवीरराम	Pandya Dynasty	1564-1604	118.

Name	Devanagari	Dynasty	Period	Page
Jatig-1	जतिग-1	Shilahar Dynasty, Kolhapur	940-960	149.
Jatig-2	जतिग-2	Shilahar Dynasty, Kolhapur	1000-1020	149.
Jatsimha-3	जतसिंह-3	Chudasama Dynasty	1415-1440	37.
Jawahar Simha	जवाहर सिंह	Simha Dynasty, Bharatpur	1763-1768	162.
Jawahar Simha	जवाहर सिंह	Bhati Raval Dynasty	1914-1949	8.
Jawan Simha	जवानसिंह	Sisodiya Dynasty	1828-1838	159.
Jaya Deva-1	जयदेव-1	Gutta Dynasty		50.
Jaya Deva-2	जयदेव-2	Gutta Dynasty	1238	50.
Jaya Deva-4	जयदेव-4	Gutta Dynasty		50.
Jaya Manikya-2	जय माणिक्य-2	Manikya Dynasty, Tripura	1739-1744	79.
Jaya Nandi Varma	जयनंदीवर्मा	Bana Dynasty		6.
Jaya Nath	जयनाथ 493-508	Uchchhakalpa Dynasty		176.
Jaya Simha Varma	जयसिंह देव वर्मा	Varma Dynasty, Venad	1252-1299	182.
Jaya Simha	जयसिंह	Chalukya Dynasty, Badami	500-525	18.
Jaya Simha-1	जयसिंह-1	Chalukya Dynasty, Vengi	632-663	22.
Jaya Simha-2	जयसिंह-2	Chalukya Dynasty, Vengi	696-709	22.
Jaya Swami	जयस्वामी	Uchchhakalpa Dynasty		176.
Jaya Varma	जयवर्मा	Chandela Dynasty	1117-1125	23.
Jaya Varma	जयवर्मा	Funan Dynasty, Thailand	484	165.
Jaya Varma-1	जयवर्मा-1	Varma Dynasty, Cambodia	802-850	171.
Jaya Varma-1	जयवर्मा-1	Vietnam, Bhava varma Dynasty, Vietnam	657-690	170.
Jaya Varma-2	जयवर्मा-2	Varma Dynasty, Cambodia	850-876	171.
Jaya Varma-3	जयवर्मा-3	Varma Dynasty, Cambodia	928-942	171.
Jaya Varma-4	जयवर्मा-4	Varma Dynasty, Cambodia	968-1001	171.
Jaya Varma-4	जयवर्मा-5	Varma Dynasty, Cambodia	1002-1003	171.
Jaya Varma-6	जयवर्मा-6	Varma Dynasty, Cambodia	1080-1107	171.
Jaya Varma-7	जयवर्मा-7	Varma Dynasty, Cambodia	1181-1219	171.
Jaya Varma-8	जयवर्मा-8	Varma Dynasty, Cambodia	1243-1295	171.
Jaya Varma-9	जयवर्मा-9	Varma Dynasty, Cambodia	1327-1353	171.
Jaya	जय	Vrishni Dynasty Ancient		188.
Jayabhatta-1	जयभट्ट-1	Gurjar Dynasty		49.
Jayabhatta-2	जयभट्ट-2 (वीतराग)	Gurjar Dynasty		49.
Jayabhatta-3	जयभट्ट-3	Gurjar Dynasty	640	49.
Jayabhatta-4	जयभट्ट-4	Gurjar Dynasty	706-725	49.
Jayadaman	जयदामन	Kshatrap Dynasty	126-145	71.
Jayadrath	जयद्रथ (सिंधुराज)	Sindhu Dynasty Ancient		158.
Jayajirao	जयाजीराव	Sindhia Dynasty	1843-1886	157.

Name	Devanagari	Dynasty	Period	Page
Jayakatvang	जयकत्वंग	Simha Shri Dynasty, Java	1292-1293	58.
Jayamalla Varma	जयमलवर्मा	Shalasthambha Dynasty, Assam	865-885	146.
Jayamalla	जयमल्ल	Chudasama Dynasty	1201-1230	37.
Jayanagar	जयनगर	Simha Shri Dynasty, Java	1309-1329	58.
Jayanti Varma	जयंतीवर्मा	Pandya Dynasty	645-670	118.
Jayapid, Jajja	जयपीड़, जज्जा	Karkota Dynasty, Kashmir	780-810	69.
Jayappa	जयप्पा	Sindhia Dynasty	1745-1755	157.
Jayasen Gautam	जयसेन गौतम	Shakya Gautam Dynasty		145.
Jayashakti	जयशक्ति	Chandela Dynasty	865-885	23.
Jayasimha Deva	जयसिंहदेव	Kalchuris, Dynasty, Tripuri	1175-1180	66.
Jayasimha Raja	जयसिंह राजा	Chalukya Dynasty, Lat	590-610	20.
Jayasimha Varma-	जयसिंह वर्मा	Varma Dynasty, Venad	1514-1516	182.
Jayasimha	जयसिंह	Chalukya Dynasty, Kalyani	1018-1040	19.
Jayasimha	जयसिंह	Lohar Dynasty, Kashmir	1128-1155	75.
Jayasimha-1	जयसिंह-1	Chudasama Dynasty	1152-1180	37.
Jayasimha-2	जयसिंह-2	Chudasama Dynasty	1351-1373	37.
Jayasimhavarma	धाराश्रय जयसिंहवर्मा	Chalukya Dynasty, Lat	655-669	20.
Jayatsen	जयत्सेन	Kuru Dynasty	Ancient	73.
Jayavardhan	जयवर्धन	Simha Shri Dynasty, Java	1293-1309	58.
Jayavarma	जयवर्मा	Shri Vijaya Dynasty, Sumatra	825	59.
Jayavira	जयवीर सागरशेखरन	Arya Chakravarti Dynasty, Shri Lanka	1308-1410	155.
Jayendra	जयेन्द्र	Pratapaditya Dynasty, Kashmir	59-22 BC	124.
Jayendraraj	जयेंद्रराज	Chaunah Dynasty, Nadol	1070-1080	27.
Jaykeshi-1	जयकेशी-1	Kadamb Dynasty, Goa	1052-1080	64.
Jaykeshi-2	जयकेशी-2	Kadamb Dynasty, Goa	1110-1147	64.
Jaykeshi-3	जयकेशी-3	Kadamb Dynasty, Goa	1187-1220	64.
Jhanjha	झंझ	Shilahar Dynasty, Konkan	910-930	147.
Jigme Dorgi Wangchuk	जिग्मे दोरजी वांगचुक	Wangchuk Dynasty, Bhutan	1926-1948	13.
Jivitagupta	जीवितगुप्त	Gupta Dynasty, Patliputra	730	48.
Junsi Deva	जुणसी देव	Kachhavaha Dynasty	1317-1366	61.
Kadraji	कदराजी	Sindhia Dynasty	1763-1763	157.
Kadungona	कदुंगोन	Pandya Dynasty	590-620	118.
Kailan	कैलन	Bhati Raval Dynasty	1189-1218	8.
Kakharua Deva	कखरुआ देव	Gajapati Dynasty	1541-1541	40.
Kakkaraja	कक्कराजा सौवर्णवर्ष	Rashtrakut Dynasty, Lat, Gujrat	712-835	134.
Kakkaraya-1	कक्कराया-1	Rashtrakut Dynasty, Malkhed	670-690	133.
Kakkaraya-2	कक्कराया-2	Rashtrakut Dynasty, Malkhed	972-973	133.

Name	Devanagari	Dynasty	Dates	Page
Kakustha Varma	काकुस्थवर्मा	Kadamb Dynasty	425–450	62.
Kakutsa	ककुत्स्थ	Ikshavaku Dynasty	Ancient	56.
Kalasen-1	कालसेन-1	Ratta Dynasty	1060–1076	138.
Kalasen-2	कालसेन-2	Ratta Dynasty	1102–1143	138.
Kalasharaja	कलशराजा	Lohar Dynasty, Kashmir	1063–1089	75.
Kalashok	कालशोक	Shishunag Dynasty	394–366 BC	150.
Kalhar Deva	कन्हार देव-1	Chindak Nag Dynasty	1111–1122	35.
Kalhar	कहार	Hindu Shahi Dynasty	867–870	53.
Kalinga Raj	कलिंगराज	Kalchuri Dynasty, Ratnapuri	1000–1020	67.
Kaliya Ballal	कालीया	Yadav Dynasty, Devgiri	1165–1173	190.
Kalla	कल्ल राजा	Chalukya Dynasty, Saurashtra	750	21.
Kalua Deva	कालुआ देव	Gajapati Dynasty	1540–1541	40.
Kalyan Dimha	कल्याण सिंह	Bhati Raval Dynasty	1613–1627	8.
Kalyan Manikya	कल्याण माणिक्य	Manikya Dynasty, Tripura	1618–1660	79.
Kalyan Simha	कल्याण सिंह	Rathor Dynasty, Kishangadh	1798–1839	137.
Kalyan Varma	कल्याणवर्मा	Ahom Dynasty	420–440	2.
Kalyan Varma	कल्याणवर्मा	Varma Dynasty, Kamrup	422–446	185.
Kalyan	कल्याणसिंह	Tomar Dynasty, Gwalior	1480–1486	174.
Kalyanmal	कल्याणमल	Rathor Dynasty, Bikaner	1542–1573	136.
Kamaiya	कामय्या	Madura Nayak Dynasty	1524–1526	95.
Kamal Raj	कमलराज	Kalchuri Dynasty, Ratnapuri	1020–1045	67.
Kamal Varma	कमलवर्मा	Hindu Shahi Dynasty	895–921	53.
Kamarnava-1	कामार्णव-1	Ganga Dynasty, Kalinga		41.
Kamarnava-2	कामार्णव-2	Ganga Dynasty, Kalinga		41.
Kamarnava-3	कामार्णव-3	Ganga Dynasty, Kalinga		41.
Kamarnava-4	कामार्णव-4	Ganga Dynasty, Kalinga	945–977	41.
Kamarnava-5	कामार्णव-5	Ganga Dynasty, Kalinga	1015–1016	41.
Kamarnava-6	कामार्णव-6	Ganga Dynasty, Kalinga	1100–1151	41.
Kambu	कम्बू	Funan Dynasty, Thailand		165.
Kamleshvar Simha	कमलेश्वर सिंह	Ahom Dynasty	1795–1811	2.
Kamp Devraj	कम्प देवराज	Wadiyar Dynasty	1659–1673	178.
Kamsa	कंस	Shurasen Dynasty, Mathura	Ancient	161.
Kamsa	कंस, मथुराधिपति	Kukkur Dynasty	Ancient	72.
Kanak Surya	कनकसूर्य सागरशेखरन	Arya Chakravarti Dynasty, Shri Lanka	1440–1478	155.
Kang Varma	कंगवर्मा	Kadamb Dynasty	360–385	62.
Kanha Simha	कान्हा सिंह	Rathor Dynasty, Jodhpur	1423–1427	135.
Kanhaddev Simha	कान्हड़देव सिंह	Chauhan Dynasty, Jalor	1305–1311	29.

Name	Devanagari	Dynasty	Years	Page
Kanhar deva	कन्हार देव-2	Chindak Nag Dynasty		35.
Kanhoji Angre-1	कान्होजी आंग्रे-1	Angre Dynasty	1690-1729	4.
Kanhoji	जाम कान्होजी	Jadeja Dynasty	1470-1490	60.
Kanhoji	कान्होजी	Bhosle Dynasty, Nagpur	1709-1731	12.
Kanhoji-2	कान्होजी-2	Angre Dynasty	1838-1839	4.
Kanhoji-3	कान्होजी-3	Angre Dynasty	1839-1844	4.
Kanishka-1	कनिष्क-1	Kushan Dynasty	103-126	74.
Kanishka-2	कनिष्क-2	Kushan Dynasty	143-150	74.
Kanishka-3	कनिष्क-3	Kushan Dynasty	200-222	74.
Kankil Deva	कांकिल देव	Kachhavaha Dynasty	1037-1038	61.
Kanna-1	कन्न-1	Ratta Dynasty	1000-1040	138.
Kanna-2	कन्न-2	Ratta Dynasty	1076-1087	138.
Kannar	कन्नर	Yadav Dynasty, Devgiri	1247-1261	190.
Kanpal Simha	कनपाल सिंह	Rathor Dynasty, Jodhpur	1313-1323	135.
Kanta	कांता	Chitradurg Nayak Dynasty	1675-1676	100.
Kanthirav Narasraj-1	नरसराज-1	Wadiyar Dynasty	1638-1659	178.
Kanthirav Narasraj-2	नरसराज-2	Wadiyar Dynasty	1704-1714	178.
Kapardi-1	कपर्दी-1	Shilahar Dynasty, Konkan	800-825	147.
Kapardi-2	कपर्दी-2	Shilahar Dynasty, Konkan	850-880	147.
Kapay Nayak	कापय नायक	Musunuri Nayak Dynasty	1333-1368	91.
Kapilendra Deva	कपिलेन्द्र देव	Gajapati Dynasty	1434-1466	40.
Kapotrom	कपोतरोम	Kukkur Dynasty	Ancient	72.
Karan Simha	करन सिंह	Bhati Raval Dynasty	1242-1270	8.
Karan Simha	करन सिंह	Bhati Raval Dynasty	1528-1528	8.
Karna Deva	कर्णदेव	Kalchuris, Dynasty, Tripuri	1042-1120	66.
Karna Deva	कर्णदेव	Solanki Dynasty	1064-1094	163.
Karna Deva	कर्णदेव	Waghela Dynasty, Gujrat	1280-1304	179.
Karna Simha	कर्ण सिंह	Rathor Dynasty, Bikaner	1631-1669	136.
Karna Simha	कर्णसिंह	Sisodiya Dynasty	1620-1628	159.
Kartavijay	कार्तविजय	Simha Shri Dynasty, Java	1447-1451	58.
Kartavirya	कार्तवीर्य	Yadu Dynasty	Ancient	191.
Kartaviryarjun	कार्तवीर्यार्जुन	Yadu Dynasty	Ancient	191.
Kartvirya-1	कार्तवीर्य-1	Ratta Dynasty	980	138.
Kartvirya-2	कार्तवीर्य-2	Ratta Dynasty	1087-1102	138.
Kartvirya-3	कार्तवीर्य-3	Ratta Dynasty	1143-1165	138.
Kartvirya-4	कार्तवीर्य-4	Ratta Dynasty	1190-1204	138.
Kashi Chandra Manikya	काशी चंद्र माणिक्य	Manikya Dynasty, Tripura	1826-1829	79.

Name	Devanagari	Dynasty	Period	Page
Kashirao	काशीराव	Holkar Dynasty	1797-1798	54.
Kashyap Prajapati	कश्यप प्रजापति	Vivasvan Dynasty	Ancient	187.
Kasi	कासी नायीनार	Arya Chakravarti Dynasty, Shri Lanka	1565-1570	155.
Katukraj	कटुकराज	Chaunah Dynasty, Nadol	1145-1153	27.
Kaundinya-1	कौण्डिण्य-1	Funan Dynasty, Thailand		165.
kaundinya-2	कौण्डिण्य-2	Funan Dynasty, Thailand		165.
Kavant	कवांट	Chudasama Dynasty	1140-1152	37.
Kehar Simha	केहर सिंह	Bhati Raval Dynasty	1334-1394	8.
Kehar Simha	केहर सिंह	Bhati Raval Dynasty	731-806	8.
Kelhandev	केल्हणदेव	Chaunah Dynasty, Nadol	1161-1165	27.
Keral Varma-1	केरळ वर्मा-1	Varma Dynasty, Kochin	1537-1565	183.
Keral Varma-10	केरळ वर्मा-10	Varma Dynasty, Kochin	1888-1895	183.
Keral Varma-11	केरळ वर्मा-11	Varma Dynasty, Kochin	1941-1943	183.
Keral Varma-12	केरळ वर्मा-12	Varma Dynasty, Kochin	1946-1947	183.
Keral Varma-2	केरळ वर्मा-2	Varma Dynasty, Kochin	1601-1615	183.
Keral Varma-2	कोडै केरळ वर्मा-2	Varma Dynasty, Venad	1145-1161	182.
Keral Varma-3	केरळ वर्मा-3	Varma Dynasty, Kochin	1624-1637	183.
Keral Varma-3	वीर केरळ व6र्मा-3	Varma Dynasty, Venad	1164-1167	182.
Keral Varma-4	देवेंद्र केरळ वर्मा-4	Varma Dynasty, Venad	1192-1195	182.
Keral Varma-4	वीर केरळ वर्मा-4	Varma Dynasty, Kochin	1646-1650	183.
Keral Varma-5	केरळ वर्मा तिरुवदी-5	Varma Dynasty, Venad	1209-1214	182.
Keral Varma-5	वीर केरळ वर्मा-5	Varma Dynasty, Kochin	1663-1687	183.
Keral Varma-6	केरळ वर्मा तिरुवदी-6	Varma Dynasty, Venad	1214-1240	182.
Keral Varma-6	केरळ वर्मा-6	Varma Dynasty, Kochin	1746-1749	183.
Keral Varma-7	केरळ तिरुवदी-7	Varma Dynasty, Venad	1342-1363	182.
Keral Varma-7	केरळ वर्मा-7	Varma Dynasty, Kochin	1760-1775	183.
Keral Varma-8	केरळ वर्मा-8	Varma Dynasty, Kochin	1809-1828	183.
Keral Varma-8	राम केरळ वर्मा-8	Varma Dynasty, Venad		182.
Keral Varma-9	केरळ वर्मा-9	Varma Dynasty, Kochin	1851-1853	183.
Keral Varma-9	उन्नी केरळ वर्मा-9	Varma Dynasty, Venad	1556	182.
Keral Varma-9	वीर केरळ वर्मा-9	Varma Dynasty, Venad	1544-1545	182.
Kesar	केसर	Gond Dynasty, Vidarbha		46.
Kesari Simha	केशरी सिंह	Simha Dynasty, Bharatpur	1769-1771	162.
Keshav Sen	केशवसेन	Sen Dynasty, Bengal	1220-1250	143.
Keshi Deva	केशीदेव	Shilahar Dynasty, Konkan	1200-1245	147.
Khadgagraha-2	खड्गग्रह-2	Maitrak Dynasty	656-669	77.
Khande Rao	खंडेराव	Gaikwad Dynasty	1856-1870	39.

Name	Devanagari	Dynasty	Period	Page
Khanderao	खंडेराव	Holkar Dynasty	1843–1844	54.
Khando	खंडो	Gond Dynasty, Vidarbha	1470–1495	46.
Kharak Singh	खड़क सिंह	Sikh Dynasty, Punjab	1839–1839	156.
Kharja	खरजा	Gond Dynasty, Vidarbha		46.
Khdagagraha-1	खड्गग्रह-1	Maitrak Dynasty	609–623	77.
Khengar-1	रा खेंगार -1	Chudasama Dynasty	1098–1114	37.
Khengar-1	राव खेंगार-1	Jadeja Dynasty	1548–1585	60.
Khengar-2	खेंगार-2	Chudasama Dynasty	1253–1260	37.
Khengar-2	राव खेंगार-2	Jadeja Dynasty	1645–1654	60.
Khengar-3	खेंगार-3	Chudasama Dynasty	1325–1351	37.
Khengar-3	राव खेंगार-3	Jadeja Dynasty	1876–1942	60.
Khottiga	खोत्तिग	Rashtrakut Dynasty, Malkhed	968–972	133.
Khummanasimha-1	खुम्मणसिंह-1	Guhil Dynasty, Mewad	828–853	47.
Khummanasimha-2	खुम्मणसिंह-2	Guhil Dynasty, Mewad	878–903	47.
Khura Raj	खुरा राज	Ahom Dynasty	1552–1603	2.
Kilhan Deva	किल्हण देव	Kachhavaha Dynasty	1216–1276	61.
Kiratrao	कीरतराव	Chandela Dynasty	1520–1524	23.
Kirit Manikya	किरीट माणिक्य	Manikya Dynasty, Tripura	1947–1948	79.
Kirti Shri Rajsimha	कीर्ति	Kendy Nayak Dynasty	1747–1782	101.
Kirti Varma	कीर्तिवर्मा	Chandela Dynasty	1098–1100	23.
Kirtipal	कीर्तिपाल	Chaunah Dynasty, Nadol	1165–1193	27.
Kirtirat	कीर्तिरात	Nimi Janak Dynasty	Ancient	114.
Kirtirath	कीर्तिरथ	Nimi Janak Dynasty	Ancient	114.
Kirtisingh	कीर्तिसिंह	Tomar Dynasty, Gwalior	1459–1480	174.
Kirtivarma	कीर्तिवर्मा	Guhil Dynasty, Mewad	1035–1051	47.
Kirtivarma-1	कीर्तिवर्मा-1	Chalukya Dynasty, Badami	566–597	18.
Kirtivarma-2	कीर्तिवर्मा-2	Chalukya Dynasty, Badami	746–753	18.
Kirtivarma-3	कीर्तिवर्मा-3	Chalukya Dynasty, Kalyani		19.
Kirtnagar	कीर्तनगर	Simha Shri Dynasty, Java	1268–1292	58.
Kishan Simha	किशन सिंह	Simha Dynasty, Bharatpur	1900–1929	162.
Kishan Simha	किशन सिंह	Rathor Dynasty, Kishangadh	1611–1615	137.
Kishor Singh–1	किशोर सिंह-1	Chauhan Dynasty, Kota	(1684–1696)	33.
Kishor Singh-2	किशोर सिंह-2	Chauhan Dynasty, Kota	(1819-1827)	33.
Kochchhalaiyan	कोच्छलैयन रणधीर	Pandya Dynasty	700–730	118.
Kokkal Deva-1	कोक्कलदेव-1	Kalchuris, Dynasty, Tripuri	850–890	66.
Kokkal Deva-2	कोक्कलदेव-2	Kalchuris, Dynasty, Tripuri	1000–1037	66.
Kokkoli	कोक्किलि	Chalukya Dynasty, Vengi	709–709	22.

Name	Devanagari	Dynasty	Period	Page
Komaragiri Reddi	रेड्डी	Kondavidu Reddi Dynasty	1385-1402	102.
Konguni Varma	कोंगुनिवर्मा	Ganga Dynasty, Talkad	350-400	42.
Kotha Varma	कोठवर्मा	Cher Dynasty	944-962	34.
Krishna Manikya	कृष्ण माणिक्य-1	Manikya Dynasty, Tripura	1760-1783	79.
Krishna Manikya-2	कृष्ण माणिक्य-2	Manikya Dynasty, Tripura	1829-1849	79.
Krishna Raj	कृष्णराज	Kalchuris Dynasty, Mahismati	550-575	65.
Krishna Raj	कृष्णराज	Saindhav Dynasty	754-774	140.
Krishna Raj-2	कृष्णराज-2	Saindhav Dynasty	814-824	140.
Krishna Varma	कृष्णवर्मा	Kadamb Dynasty	547-565	62.
Krishna	कृष्ण	Gond Dynasty, Mandla		45.
Krishna	कृष्ण	Satvahan Dynasty	248-230 BC	141.
Krishnadeva Raya	कृष्णदेवराया	Tuluv Nayak Dynasty	1509-1530	89.
Krishnagupta	कृष्णगुप्त	Gupta Dynasty, Patliputra	530-540	48.
Krishnaraj-1	दोड्ड कृष्णराज	Wadiyar Dynasty	1714-1732	178.
Krishnaraj-2	इम्मडि कृष्णराज-2	Wadiyar Dynasty	1734-1766	178.
Krishnaraj-3	मुम्मडि कृष्णराज-3	Wadiyar Dynasty	1799-1868	178.
Krishnaraj-4	नाल्वडि कृष्णराज-4	Wadiyar Dynasty	1895-1940	178.
Krishnaraya-1	कृष्णराया-1	Rashtrakut Dynasty, Malkhed	758-773	133.
Krishnaraya-2	कृष्णराया-2	Rashtrakut Dynasty, Malkhed	877-911	133.
Krishnaraya-3	कृष्णराया-3	Rashtrakut Dynasty, Malkhed	939-968	133.
Kshemagupta	क्षेमगुप्त	Pravargupta Dynasty, Kashmir	950-958	125.
Kshemaraj	क्षेमराज	Chapotkat Dynasty	841-866	25.
Kshemsimha	क्षेमसिंह	Guhil Dynasty, Mewad	1168-1171	47.
Kshetra Simha	क्षेत्रसिंह	Sisodiya Dynasty	1364-1382	159.
Kshitinand	क्षितिनंद	Gonaditya Dynasty, Kashmir	602-572	44.
Kuber	कुबेर	Pulastya Dynasty	Ancient	128.
Kuduki Iranjeral	कुडुकी इरंजेराळ इरुंपोडई	Cher Dynasty	190-210	34.
Kujula Kadphises	कुजूला कडफिसेस	Kushan Dynasty	30-80	74.
Kukkur	कुक्कुर	Kukkur Dynasty	Ancient	72.
Kulachandra Simha	कुलचंद्र सिंह	Simha Dynasty, Manipur	1890-1891	151.
Kulashekhar	कुलशेखर अलवार	Cher Dynasty	800-820	34.
Kulashekhar	कुलशेखर प्रजाशेखरन	Arya Chakravarti Dynasty, Shri Lanka	1262-1284	155.
Kulashekhardeva	कुलशेखरदेव	Pandya Dynasty	1479-1534	118.
Kulottunga	कुलोत्तुंग सागरशेखरन	Arya Chakravarti Dynasty, Shri Lanka	1284-1292	155.
Kulottunga	कुलोत्तुंग-2	Chola Dynasty	1133-1146	36.
Kulottunga-3	कुलोत्तुंग-3	Chola Dynasty	1178-1216	36.
Kumar Deva	कुमारदेव	Uchchhakalpa Dynasty		176.

Name	Devanagari	Dynasty	Period	Page
Kumar Timma Nayak-1	तम्म-1	Pemmasani Nayak Dynasty	1423–1462	92.
Kumar Timma Nayak-2	तिम्म-2	Pemmasani Nayak Dynasty	1652–1685	92.
Kumar Vishnu	कुमारविष्णु-1	Pallav Dynasty	355–370	116.
Kumar Vishnu-2	कुमारविष्णु-2	Pallav Dynasty	510–530	116.
Kumar Vishnu-3	कुमारविष्णु-3	Pallav Dynasty	540–560	116.
Kumaragupta-1	कुमारगुप्त-1	Gupta Dynasty, Patliputra	415–455	48.
Kumaragupta-2	कुमारगुप्त-2	Gupta Dynasty, Patliputra	473–477	48.
Kumaragupta-3	कुमारगुप्त-3	Gupta Dynasty, Patliputra	550–560	48.
Kumarpal	कुमारपाल	Pal Dynasty, Bengal	1120–1125	115.
Kumarpal	कुमारपाल	Solanki Dynasty	1143–1172	163.
Kumarsimha	कुमारसिंह	Guhil Dynasty, Mewad	1179–1191	47.
Kumbha	कुंभा	Sisodiya Dynasty	1433–1468	159.
Kunal	कुणाल	Maurya Dynasty	232–228 BC	81.
Kundan Rai	कुन्दनराय	Nag Dynasty	710–756	83.
Kuni	कुणी	Vrishni Dynasty	Ancient	188.
Kuntal Deva	कुन्तल देव	Kachhavaha Dynasty	1276–1317	61.
Kuntala Svatikarna	कुंतल	Satvahan Dynasty	52–44 BC	141.
Kunti	कुंति	Yadu Dynasty	Ancient	191.
Kunvarpal	कुंवरपाल	Tomar Dynasty, Delhi	1021–1051	173.
Kuru Timmappa	कुरु तिम्मप्पा	Madura Nayak Dynasty	1519–1524	95.
Kuru	कुरु	Ajamidh Dynasty	Ancient Time	3.
Kuru	कुरु	Kuru Dynasty	Ancient	73.
Kushagra	कुशाग्र	Brihadrith Dynasty, Magadh	Ancient	15.
Kuvalayapid	कुवलयापीड़	Karkota Dynasty, Kashmir	767–768	69.
Lakha Ghurara-1	लाखा घुरारा-1	Jadeja Dynasty	1231–1270	60.
Lakha Simha	लाखासिंह	Sisodiya Dynasty	1382–1421	159.
Lakha-1	जाम लाखा-2	Jadeja Dynasty	1320–1350	60.
Lakha-3	राव लाखा-3	Jadeja Dynasty	1741–1760	60.
Lakhaji-1	लाखोजी-1	Jadeja Dynasty	1203–1231	60.
Lakshman Deva	लक्ष्मणदेव	Parmar Dynasty	1087–1097	120.
Lakshman Deva	लक्ष्मणदेव	Vuppadeva Dynasty, Kashmir	1273–1286	189.
Lakshman Manikya	लक्ष्मण माणिक्य	Manikya Dynasty, Tripura	1748–1760	79.
Lakshman Rai-1	लक्ष्मणराय-1	Kalchuris, Dynasty, Tripuri	825–850	66.
Lakshman Rai-2	लक्ष्मणराय-2	Kalchuris, Dynasty, Tripuri	950–970	66.
Lakshman Sen	लक्ष्मणन सेन	Bhati Raval Dynasty	1270–1274	8.
Lakshman Sen	लक्ष्मणसेन	Sen Dynasty, Bengal	1179–1205	143.
Lakshman Simha	लक्ष्मणसिंह	Sisodiya Dynasty	1303–1314	159.

Name	Devanagari	Dynasty	Years	Ref
Lakshman	लक्ष्मण	Bhati Raval Dynasty	1394–1439	8.
Lakshmanraj	लक्ष्मणराज	Chaunah Dynasty, Nadol	950–962	27.
Lakshmi Narayan Malla Deva		Malla Dynasty, Nepal	1620–1641	111.
Lakshmi Narayan	लक्ष्मी नारायण	Sutiya Dynasty, Assam	1400–1420	164.
Lakshmi Simha	लक्ष्मी सिंह	Ahom Dynasty	1769–1780	2.
Lakshmidev-1	लक्ष्मीदेव-1	Ratta Dynasty	1165–1190	138.
Lakshmideva-2	लक्ष्मीदेव-2	Ratta Dynasty	1228–1240	138.
Lakshmikamadev	लक्ष्मीकामदेव	Thakur Dynasty, Nepal	(1193–1196)	110.
Lakshmikarmadeva	लक्ष्मीकर्मदेव	Raghav Dynasty, Nepal	(1015–1039)	109.
Lalitaditya Muktipid	ललितादित्य मुक्तिपीड़	Karkota Dynasty, Kashmir	725–767	69.
Lalitpid	ललितपीड़	Karkota Dynasty, Kashmir	810–820	69.
Lambodar	लंबोदर	Satvahan Dynasty	128–110 BC	141.
Lav and Kush	लव, कुश	Raghu Dynasty	Ancient	131.
Lingaraja-1	लिंगराजा-1	Haleri Nayak Dynasty	1774–1780	103.
Lingraja-2	लिंगराजा-2	Haleri Nayak Dynasty	1809–1820	103.
Lokpal	लोकपाल	Shailendra Dynasty, Java	850–898	57.
Lumba	लुम्बा	Chauhan Dynasty, Sirohi	1311	30.
Lunkaran	लूनकरन	Bhati Raval Dynasty	1528–1550	8.
Lunkaran	लूणकरण	Rathor Dynasty, Bikaner	1505–1526	136.
Madakari-1	मदकरी-1	Chitradurg Nayak Dynasty	1652–1674	100.
Madakari-2	मदकरी-2	Chitradurg Nayak Dynasty	1686–1688	100.
Madakari-3	मदकरी-3	Chitradurg Nayak Dynasty	1721–1748	100.
Madakari-4	मदकरी-4	Chitradurg Nayak Dynasty	1754–1779	100.
Madan Rai	मदनराय	Nag Dynasty	273–326	83.
Madan Simha	मदन सिंह	Rathor Dynasty, Kishangadh	1900–1926	137.
Madan Varma	मदनवर्मा	Chandela Dynasty	1129–1165	23.
Madanpal	मदनपाल	Tomar Dynasty, Delhi	1151–1167	173.
Madanpal	मदनपाल	Pal Dynasty, Bengal	1144–1161	115.
Madansimha	मदन सिंह	Gond Dynasty, Mandla	1116	45.
Madhava Varma-1	माधववर्मा-1	Chalukya Dynasty, Vengi	440–460	22.
Madhava Varma-2	माधववर्मा-2	Chalukya Dynasty, Vengi	555–615	22.
Madhava-1	माधव-1	Ganga Dynasty, Talkad	400–450	42.
Madhava-2	माधव-2	Ganga Dynasty, Talkad	460–500	42.
Madhavagupta	माधवगुप्त	Gupta Dynasty, Patliputra	601–655	48.
Madhavarao	माधवराव बल्लाल	Peshva Dynasty	1761–1772	121.
Madhavarao	माधवराव	Sindhia Dynasty	1886–1925	157.
Madho Simha	माधो सिंह	Chauhan Dynasty, Hadauti	1631 …	31.

Name	Devanagari	Dynasty	Period	Page
Madho Singh-1	मधोसिंह-1	Kachhavaha Dynasty	1750–1768	61.
Madhosingh	मधो सिंह	Chauhan Dynasty, Kota	(1631–1649)	33.
Madhu	मधु	Yadu Dynasty	Ancient	191.
Madhukamarnava	मधुकामार्णव	Ganga Dynasty, Kalinga	1019–1038	41.
Madhukar	मधुकर	Gond Dynasty, Mandla		45.
Madhurantak	मधुरांतक देव	Chindak Nag Dynasty		35.
Madhurantak	मधुरांतक	Chola Dynasty	969–985	36.
Madhusimha	मधुसिंह	Nag Dynasty	1530–1599	83.
Madraji	जाम मदराजी	Jadeja Dynasty	1450–1470	60.
Mahadaji	महादजी	Sindhia Dynasty	1768–1794	157.
Mahadev	महादेव	Yadav Dynasty, Devgiri	1261–1271	190.
Mahadeva-1	महादेव-1	Kakatiya Dynasty	1196–1199	64.
Mahadharmaraj-1	महाधर्मराज-1	Indraditya Dynasty, Thailand	1275–1279	166.
Mahadharmaraj-2	महाधर्मराज-2	Indraditya Dynasty, Thailand	1317–1354	166.
Mahadharmaraj-3	महाधर्मराज-3	Indraditya Dynasty, Thailand	1354–1376	166.
Mahadharmaraj-4	महाधर्मराज-4	Indraditya Dynasty, Thailand	1376–1406	166.
Mahadharmaraj-5	महाधर्मराज-5	Indraditya Dynasty, Thailand	1406–1419	166.
Mahadharmaraj-6	महाधर्मराज-6	Indraditya Dynasty, Thailand	1419–1438	166.
Mahaguttal	महागुत्तल	Gutta Dynasty	1080	50.
Mahajagannath	महाजगन्नाथशाह	Nag Dynasty	1822–1872	83.
Mahalak Deva	महलकदेव	Parmar Dynasty	1300–1305	120.
Mahalla Raja	महल्ल राजा	Chalukya Dynasty, Saurashtra	.	21.
Mahalla	महल्ल	Chalukya Dynasty, Saurashtra	.	21.
Mahamanikya	महामाणिक्य	Manikya Dynasty, Tripura	1400–1431	79.
Mahapadma	महापद्म	Nand Dynasty	362 BC.	85.
Maharana Sanga	महाराणा संग	Meera Bai Dynasty	1473–1527	82.
Maharoma	महारोम	Nimi Janak Dynasty	Ancient	114.
Mahaudaynath	महाउदयनाथशाह	Nag Dynasty	1872–1950	83.
Mahavir	महावीर	Nimi Janak Dynasty	Ancient	114.
Mahendra Malla Deva-1	महेंद्र-1	Malla Dynasty, Nepal	1560–1574	111.
Mahendra Malla Deva-2	महेंद्र-2	Malla Dynasty, Nepal	1714–1722	111.
Mahendra Manikya	महेन्द्र माणिक्य	Manikya Dynasty, Tripura	1712–1714	79.
Mahendra Varma	महेंद्रवर्मा	Ahom Dynasty	450–480	2.
Mahendra Varma	महेंद्रवर्मा	Varma Dynasty, Kamrup	470–494	185.
Mahendra Varma	महेंद्रवर्मा	Vietnam, Bhava varma Dynasty, Vietnam	600–616	170.
Mahendra Varma-1	महेंद्रवर्मा-1	Pallav Dynasty	580–630	116.
Mahendra Varma-2	महेंद्रवर्मा-2	Pallav Dynasty	668–674	116.

Name	Devanagari	Dynasty	Years	Page
Mahendra Varma-3	महेंद्रवर्मा-3	Pallav Dynasty	728-731	116.
Mahendra	महेंद्र	Chola Dynasty	1052-1062	36.
Mahendrapal	महेंद्रपाल	1125-1144 Pal Dynasty, Bengal		115.
Mahendrapal	महेंद्रपाल	Chaunah Dynasty, Nadol	994-1015	27.
Mahendrapal	महेंद्रपाल	Pratihar-Gurjar Dynasty	893-914	126.
Maheshagupta	महेशगुप्त	Gupta Dynasty, Patliputra	562-601	48.
Mahidhrak	महीध्रक	Nimi Janak Dynasty	Ancient	114.
Mahinathshah	महीनाथशाह	Nag Dynasty		83.
Mahip Narayan Simha		Narayan Dynasty	1780-1794	86.
Mahipal	महीपाल	Tomar Dynasty, Delhi	1105-1130	173.
Mahipal	महीपाल	Pratihar-Gurjar Dynasty	914-948	126.
Mahipal-1	महीपाल-1	Chudasama Dynasty	1184-1201	37.
Mahipal-1	महीपाल-1	995-1048 Pal Dynasty, Bengal		115.
Mahipal-2	महीपाल-2	Chudasama Dynasty	1230-1253	37.
Mahipal-2	महीपाल-3	Chudasama Dynasty	1308-1325	37.
Mahipal-2	महीपाल-2	1071-1075 Pal Dynasty, Bengal		115.
Mahipal-4	महीपाल-4	Chudasama Dynasty	1373-1373	37.
Mahipal-5	महीपाल-5	Chudasama Dynasty	1440-1451	37.
Mahipati Varma	महीपतिवर्मा	Vietnam, Bhava varma Dynasty, Vietnam	780-788	170.
Mahulak	मंडुलक	Satvahan Dynasty	61-66 AD	141.
Maitreyu	मैत्रेयु	Ajmidh-Dynasty	Ancient	3.
Maldev Simha	मालदेव सिंह	Rathor Dynasty, Jodhpur	1532-1562	135.
Maldev	मालदेव	Bhati Raval Dynasty	1550-1561	8.
Malerao	मालेराव	Holkar Dynasty	1767-1767	54.
Malhar Rao	मल्हाराव	Gaikwad Dynasty	1870-1875	39.
Malharrao-1	मल्हाराव-1	Holkar Dynasty	1731-1766	54.
Malharrao-2	मल्हाराव-2	Holkar Dynasty	1797-1797	54.
Malharrao-3	मल्हाराव-3	Holkar Dynasty	1807-1833	54.
Malla Deva	मल्लदेव	Bana Dynasty		6.
Malladeva	मरुलदेव	Ganga Dynasty, Talkad	955-960	42.
Mallideva	मल्लीदेव	Gutta Dynasty	1115	50.
Mallikarjun	मल्लिकार्जुन	Ratta Dynasty	1204-1228	138.
Mallikarjun	मल्लिकार्जुन	Sangam Nayak Dynasty	1446-1465	87.
Mallikarjun	मल्लिकार्जुन	Shilahar Dynasty, Konkan	1155-1170	147.
Mallugi-1	मल्लुगी-1	Yadav Dynasty, Devgiri	1145-1150	190.
Malsi Deva	मलसी देव	Kachhavaha Dynasty	1084-1146	61.
Man Simha	मान सिंह	Rathor Dynasty, Jodhpur	1803-1843	135.

Name	Devanagari	Dynasty	Period	Page
Man Simha	मान सिंह	Rathor Dynasty, Kishangadh	1658-1706	137.
Man Singh-1	मानसिंह-1	Kachhavaha Dynasty	1589-1614	61.
Manaji Rao	मानाजीराव	Gaikwad Dynasty	1789-1793	39.
Manaji	मानाजी	Sindhia Dynasty	1764-1768	157.
Manaji-1	मानाजी-1	Angre Dynasty,	1735-1758	4.
Manaji-2	मानाजी-2	Angre Dynasty,	1793-1799	4.
Manaji-3	मानाजी-3	Angre Dynasty,	1813-1817	4.
Manav	मानव	Shashank Dynasty, Bengal	625-625	144.
Mandhata	मांधाता	Ikshavaku Dynasty	Ancient	56.
Mandhatri Varma	मंधातृवर्मा	Kadamb Dynasty	490-497	62.
Mandlik-1	मांडलिक-1	Chudasama Dynasty	1260-1306	37.
Mandlik-2	मांडलिक-2	Chudasama Dynasty	1397-1400	37.
Mandlik-3	मांडलिक-3	Chudasama Dynasty	1451-1472	37.
Mangaldeva	मंगलदेव	Chudasama Dynasty	1400-1415	37.
Mangammal	रानी मंगम्मल	Madura Nayak Dynasty	1689-1704	95.
Mangi Yuvaraja	मंगी युवराजा	Chalukya Dynasty, Vengi	672-696	22.
Manglesha	मंगलेश	Chalukya Dynasty, Badami	597-608	18.
Manikya	माणिक्य	Lain Zang Dynasty, Laos	1627-1633	172.
Manohar Das	मनोहर दास	Bhati Raval Dynasty	1627-1648	8.
Mansaram		Narayan Dynasty	1737-1739	86.
Mansingh	मानसिंह	Tomar Dynasty, Gwalior	1486-1516	174.
Manthanasimha	मंथनसिंह	Guhil Dynasty, Mewad	1191-1211	47.
Mar Simha	मारसिंह	Shilahar Dynasty, Kolhapur	1050-1075	149.
Mara Varma-1	मारवर्माअवनिशूलमणि	Pandya Dynasty	620-645	118.
Marasimha	मारसिंह	Ganga Dynasty, Talkad	960-974	42.
Maravarma-2	मारवर्मा अरिकेसरी	Pandya Dynasty	670-700	118.
Maravarma-3	मारवर्मा राजसिंह-1	Pandya Dynasty	730-775	118.
Maravarma-4	मारवर्मा राजसिंह-2	Pandya Dynasty	900-920	118.
Maravarma-5	मारवर्मा सुंदर-1	Pandya Dynasty	1216-1238	118.
Maravarma-6	मारवर्मा सुंदर-2	Pandya Dynasty	1238-1251	118.
Maravarma-7	मारवर्मा कुलशेखर	Pandya Dynasty	1275-1310	118.
Marichi Prajapati	मरीचि प्रजापति	Vivasvan Dynasty	Ancient	187.
Martand Simha	मार्तंडसिंह	Waghela Dynasty, Riwa	1946-1948	180.
Martand Varma-1	कोठ मार्तंड वर्मा-1	Varma Dynasty, Venad	1102-1125	182.
Martand Varma-1	मार्तंड (वेनाड)	Varma Dynasty, Travankor	1729-1757	184.
Martand Varma-10	मार्तंड वर्मा -10	Varma Dynasty, Venad	1458-1468	182.
Martand Varma-11	कुलशेखर वर्मा -11	Varma Dynasty, Venad	1503-1504	182.

Martand Varma-12	उदय मार्तंड वर्मा-12	Varma Dynasty, Venad	1516-1535	182.
Martand Varma-13	मार्तंड वर्मा-13	Varma Dynasty, Venad	1729-1757	182.
Martand Varma-2	मार्तंड वर्मा-2	Varma Dynasty, Travankor	1847-1860	184.
Martand Varma-2	उदत मार्तंड वर्मा-2	Varma Dynasty, Venad	1173-1192	182.
Martand Varma-3	पद्मनाभ तिरुवदी-3	Varma Dynasty, Venad	1240-1252	182.
Martand Varma-4	उदय मार्तंड वर्मा-4	Varma Dynasty, Venad	1313-1333	182.
Martand Varma-5	मार्तंड तरुवदी-5	Varma Dynasty, Venad	1335-1342	182.
Martand Varma-6	वीर मार्तंड वर्मा-6	Varma Dynasty, Venad	1363-1366	182.
Martand Varma-7	राम मार्तंड वर्मा-7	Varma Dynasty, Venad	1366-1382	182.
Martand Varma-8	केरळ मार्तंड वर्मा-8	Varma Dynasty, Venad	1417-1433	182.
Martand Varma-9	उदय मार्तंड वर्मा-9	Varma Dynasty, Venad	1433-1444	182.
Martand	मार्तंड प्रजाशेखरन	Arya Chakravarti Dynasty, Shri Lanka	1325-1348	155.
Martandrao	मार्तण्डराव	Holkar Dynasty	1834-1834	54.
Maru	मरु	Nimi Janak Dynasty	Ancient	114.
Mauryanand	मौर्यानंद	Nand Dynasty		85.
Mayur Sharma	मयूरशर्मा	Kadamb Dynasty	340-360	62.
Medhasvati	मेघस्वाति	Satvahan Dynasty	98-80 BC	141.
Meghasvati	मेघवास्ति	Satvahan Dynasty	07 BC-31AD	141.
Meghavarna	मेघवर्ण	Gonaditya Dynasty, Kashmir	25-59 AD	44.
Meharsan	मेहरसन-1	Rai Dynasty, Sindh		132.
Meharsan-2	मेहरसन-2	Rai Dynasty, Sindh		132.
Mihira Bhoja	मिहिर भोज	Pratihar-Gurjar Dynasty	843-893	126.
Mihirakul	मिहिरकुल	Gonaditya Dynasty, Kashmir	735-665	44.
Minakshi	मीनाक्षी अम्मल	Madura Nayak Dynasty	1734-1736	95.
Mithi	मिथि	Nimi Janak Dynasty	Ancient	114.
Mitragupta	मित्रगुप्त	Gonaditya Dynasty, Kashmir	120-125	44.
Mitrasakha	मित्रसखा	Raghu Dynasty	Ancient	131.
Mohan Rai	मोहनराय	Nag Dynasty	811-869	83.
Mohan Simha	मोहनसिंह	Kalchuri Dynasty, Ratnapuri	1741-1745	67.
Mohansimha	मोहनसिंह	Chandela Dynasty	1470...	23.
Mokal	मोकल	Sisodiya Dynasty	1421-1433	159.
Mokham Simha	मोखम सिंह	Rathor Dynasty, Kishangadh	1839-1841	137.
Moodha	जाम मूड़ा	Jadeja Dynasty	1270-1295	60.
Moolraj-1	मूलराज-1	Bhati Raval Dynasty	1293-1295	8.
Moolraj-1	मूलराज-1	Solanki Dynasty	942-995	163.
Moolraj-2	मूलराज-2	Bhati Raval Dynasty	1762-1819	8.
Moolraj-2	मूलराज-2	Solanki Dynasty	1176-1178	163.

Name	Devanagari	Dynasty	Period	Page
Moropant	मोरोपंत त्र्यंबक पिंगळे	Peshva Dynasty	1662–1681	121.
Mrigendra Svatikarna	मृगेंद्र	Satvahan Dynasty	55–52 BC	141.
Mrigendra Varma	मृगेंद्रवर्मा	Kadamb Dynasty	475–490	62.
Mudduraja	मुद्दूराजा-1	Haleri Nayak Dynasty	1633–1687	103.
Mudduraja-2	मुद्दूराजा-2	Haleri Nayak Dynasty	1766–1770	103.
Mudgal	मुद्गल	Ajmidh-Dynasty	Ancient	3.
Mudhoji-2	मुधोजी-2	Bhosle Dynasty, Nagpur	1775–1778	12.
Muktasimha	मुक्तसिंह	Chudasama Dynasty	1373–1397	37.
Mukul	मुकुल	Gonaditya Dynasty, Kashmir	795–735	44.
Mukund Manikya	मुकुन्द माणिक्य	Manikya Dynasty, Tripura	1733–1739	79.
Mukund Rai	मुकुन्दराय	Nag Dynasty	635–653	83.
Mukund Singh	मुकुंद सिंह	Chauhan Dynasty, Kota	(1649–1658)	33.
Mukut Manikya	मुकुट माणिक्य	Manikya Dynasty, Tripura	1488–1489	79.
Mukut Rai	मुकुटराय	Nag Dynasty	177–232	83.
Mulak	मूलक	Raghu Dynasty	Ancient	131.
Mumminiraj	मुम्मिनीराज	Shilahar Dynasty, Konkan	1045–1070	147.
Mundha	मुंध	Bhati Raval Dynasty	908–979	8.
Mutailu	मुतैलु	Jinji Nayak Dynasty	1540–1550	93.
Muttu Krishnappa	मुत्तु कृष्णप्पा	Madura Nayak Dynasty	1602–1609	95.
Muttu Virappa	मुत्तु वीरप्पा	Madura Nayak Dynasty	1609–1623	95.
Nabh	नाभ	Raghu Dynasty	Ancient	131.
Nagam Nayak	नागम नायक	Madura Nayak Dynasty	1544–1558	95.
Nagarjuna	नागार्जुन	Shilahar Dynasty, Konkan	1035–1045	147.
Nagbhatta-1	नागभट्ट-1	Pratihar-Gurjar Dynasty	725–760	126.
Nagbhatta-2	नागभट्ट-2	Pratihar-Gurjar Dynasty	815–833	126.
Nagdarshak	नागदर्शक	Haryak Dynasty	437–413 BC	51.
Nahapana	नहपान	Kshatrap Dynasty	78–126	71.
Nahuk	नाहुक	Kukkur Dynasty	Ancient	72.
Nahush	नहुष	Yayati Dynasty	Ancient	192.
Nahusha	नहुष	Atri Dynasty	Ancient	1.
Namasyu	नमस्यु	Puru Dynasty	Ancient	129.
Nanasaheb	बाळाजी बाजीराव, नानासाहेब	Peshva Dynasty	1740–1761	121.
Nandan Varma	नंदन वर्मा	Nal Dynasty		84.
Nandeshvar Narayan	नंदेश्वर	Sutiya Dynasty, Assam	1360–1380	164.
Nandi vardhan	नंदिवर्धन	Pradyot Dynasty	413 BC	123.
Nandi Varma-1	नन्दीवर्मा-1	Pallav Dynasty	480–510	116.
Nandi Varma-2	नन्दीवर्मा-2	Pallav Dynasty	731–796	116.

Name	Devanagari	Dynasty	Period	Page
Nandigupta	नन्दीगुप्त	Pravargupta Dynasty, Kashmir	972-973	125.
Nandivardhan	नंदिवर्धन	Nimi Janak Dynasty	Ancient	114.
Nandraj	नंदराज	Lain Zang Dynasty, Laos	1695-1698	172.
Nanna	नन्न	Ratta Dynasty	950-980	138.
Nannuka Chandravarma	नब्बुक चंद्रवर्मा	Chandela Dynasty	831-845	23.
Nar Raj	नर राज	Ahom Dynasty	1644-1650	2.
Nar-1	नर-1	Gonaditya Dynasty, Kashmir	1023-983	44.
Nara Simha	नरसिंह	Simha Dynasty, Manipur	1844-1850	151.
Nara Vardhan	नरवर्धन	Pushyabhuti-Vardhan Dynasty	505-525	130.
Nara Varma	नरवर्मा	Parmar Dynasty	1097-1134	120.
Nara-2	नर-2	Gonaditya Dynasty, Kashmir	520-460	44.
Narahar	नरहर	Gond Dynasty, Mandla	1742-1781	35.
Narasa Pillai	नरसा पिल्लई	Madura Nayak Dynasty	1509-1519	95.
Narasimha Varma-2	नरसिंहवर्मा-2	Pallav Dynasty	700-728	116.
Narasimha	नरसिंह	Ganga Dynasty, Talkad	935-936	42.
Narasimha	नरसिंह	Gond Dynasty, Mandla	900	45.
Narasimha-1	नरसिंह-1	Ganga Dynasty, Kalinga	1238-1264	41.
Narasimha-1	नरसिंह-1	Hoysal Dynasty	1152-1173	55.
Narasimha-2	नरसिंह-2	Ganga Dynasty, Kalinga	1279-1306	41.
Narasimha-2	नरसिंह-2	Hoysal Dynasty	1220-1233	55.
Narasimha-3	नरसिंह-3	Ganga Dynasty, Kalinga	1328-1352	41.
Narasimha-3	नरसिंह-3	Hoysal Dynasty	1254-1291	55.
Narasimha-4	नरसिंह-3	Ganga Dynasty, Kalinga	1378-1414	41.
Narasimhagupta	नरसिंहगुप्त (बालादित्य)	Gupta Dynasty, Patliputra	467-473	48.
Narasimhagupta	नरसिंहगुप्त (बालादित्य)	Gupta Dynasty, Patliputra	495-530	48.
Narasimharay	नरसिंहराय	Saluv Nayak Dynasty	1485-1490	88.
Naravahan	नरवाहन	Guhil Dynasty, Mewad	972-973	47.
Naravarma	नरवर्मा	Guhil Dynasty, Mewad	1021-1035	47.
Narayan Varma	नारायणवर्मा	Ahom Dynasty	480-510	2.
Narayan Varma	नारायणवर्मा	Varma Dynasty, Kamrup	494-518	185.
Narayan	नारायण	Kanva Dynasty	51-37 BC	63.
Narayanpal	नारायणपाल	Pal Dynasty, Bengal	875-908	115.
Narayanrao	नारायणराव बल्लाळ	Peshva Dynasty	1772-1773	121.
Narendra Dhaval	नरेंद्र धवल	Nal Dynasty	935-960	84.
Narendra Malla Deva	नरेंद्र मल्ल	Malla Dynasty, Nepal	1538-1560	111.
Narendra Manikya	नरेंद्र माणिक्य	Manikya Dynasty, Tripura	1693-1695	79.
Narendra Rajaraj	नरेंद्र राजाराज	Chalukya Dynasty, Vengi	1022-1062	22.

Name	Devanagari	Dynasty	Years	Page
Narendra Sen	नरेंद्रसेन	Vakatak Dynasty	450–470	181.
Narendraditya-1	नरेंद्रादित्य-1	Gonaditya Dynasty, Kashmir	282–246	44.
Narendraditya-2	नरेंद्रादित्य-2	Gonaditya Dynasty, Kashmir	206–219	44.
Narhari	नरहरी आनंदराव	Peshva Dynasty	1661–1662	121.
Naro Singh	नारोसिंह	Kachhavaha Dynasty	1388–1413	61.
Narpal Singh	नरपाल सिंह	Chauhan Dynasty, Bundi	(1346–1370)	32.
Narpal	नरपाल	Tomar Dynasty, Delhi	834–849	173.
Narsa Nayak	नरसा नायक	Tuluv Nayak Dynasty	1491–1505	89.
Narsi Simha	नरसी सिंह	Rathor Dynasty, Bikaner	1504–1505	136.
Narsima Nayak	नरसिंह नायक	Pemmasani Nayak Dynasty	1565–1598	92.
Narsimha Deva	नरसिंह देव	Chindak Nag Dynasty		35.
Narsimha Deva	नरसिंहदेव	Kalchuris, Dynasty, Tripuri	1155–1175	66.
Narsimha Varma-1	नरसिंहवर्मा-1	Pallav Dynasty	630–668	116.
Naunihal Singh	नौनिहाल सिंह	Sikh Dynasty, Punjab	1839–1840	156.
Navaghan-1	रा नवघण-1	Chudasama Dynasty	1125–1140	37.
Naval Simha	नवल सिंह	Simha Dynasty, Bharatpur	1771–1776	162.
Navghan-2	नवघण-2	Chudasama Dynasty	1306–1308	37.
Navi Raja	नवी राजा	Lain Zang Dynasty, Laos	1583–1591	172.
Nayapal	नयपाल	1048–1055 Pal Dynasty, Bengal		115.
Nedunjalaiyan-1	नेडुंजलैयन-1	Pandya Dynasty		118.
Nedunjalaiyan-2	नेडुंजलैयन-2	Pandya Dynasty		118.
Nedunjalaiyan-2	नेडुंजलैयन-2	Pandya Dynasty	775–815	118.
Nelvelli Maran	नेल्वेली मारन्	Pandya Dynasty	1552–1564	118.
Nil	नील	Ajmidh-Dynasty	Ancient	3.
Nilopant	निलोपंत मोरेश्वर पिंगळे	Peshva Dynasty	1681–1707	121.
Nimi	निमि	Nimi Janak Dynasty	Ancient	114.
Nirjit Varma Pangu	निर्जितवर्मा पंगु	Utpal Dynasty, Kashmir	920–922	177.
Nitimarga-1	नीतिमार्ग-1	Ganga Dynasty, Talkad	853–870	42.
Nitimarga-2	नीतिमार्ग-2	Ganga Dynasty, Talkad	907–935	42.
Nripakam	नृपकाम	Hoysal Dynasty	1022–1047	55.
Nripatibhushan	नृपति भूषण	Chindak Nag Dynasty	945–1023	35.
Nripendra Rai	नृपेंद्रराय	Nag Dynasty	1004–1047	83.
Nripottunga Varma	नृपोतुंगवर्मा	Pallav Dynasty	847–872	116.
Nyaya Deva	न्यायवर्मा	Shilahar Dynasty, Kolhapur	960–980	149.
Obanna-1	ओबन्ना-1	Chitradurg Nayak Dynasty	1588–1602	100.
Obanna-2	ओबन्ना-2	Chitradurg Nayak Dynasty	1674–1675	100.
Ogha Deva	ओघदेव	Uchchhakalpa Dynasty	400	176.

Name	Devanagari	Dynasty	Period	Page
Okamukh Gautam	ओकामुख गौतम	Shakya Gautam Dynasty		145.
Padmasimha	पद्मसिंह	Guhil Dynasty, Mewad	1211-1213	47.
Palak	पालक	Pradyot Dynasty		123.
Panchal	पांचाल	Ajmidh-Dynasty	Ancient	3.
pandan	पंदन	Simha Shri Dynasty, Java	1466-1478	58.
Pandu	पांडु	Pandava Dynasty		117.
Pandugati	पांडुगति	Nand Dynasty		85.
Panduka	पांडुक	Nand Dynasty		85.
Panetu Rai	पानेतुराय	Nag Dynasty	1501-1512	83.
Pangkaran	पंगकरन	Shailendra Dynasty, Java	760-780	57.
Panungalan	पनुंगलन	Shailendra Dynasty, Java	780-800	57.
Parakram Kulashekhar	पराक्रम	Pandya Dynasty	1543-1552	118.
Parameshvara Varma-1	परमेश्वरवर्मा-1	Pallav Dynasty	674-700	116.
Parameshvara Varma-2	परमेश्वरवर्मा-2	Pallav Dynasty	731-731	116.
Parankaka-1	परांतक-2	Chola Dynasty	956-970	36.
Parantak Viranarayan	वीरनारायण	Pandya Dynasty	880-900	118.
Parantaka-1	परांतक-1	Chola Dynasty	907-948	36.
Parikshit	परिक्षित	Yudhishthir Dynasty	Ancient	193.
Parmanuk	परमाणुक	Lohar Dynasty, Kashmir	1155-1165	75.
Parmardi Deva	परमारदीदेव	Chandela Dynasty	1165-1203	23.
Parsoji-1	परसोजी-1 नागपुरकर	Bhosle Dynasty, Nagpur	1699-1707	12.
Parsoji-2	परसोजी-2	Bhosle Dynasty, Nagpur	1816-1817	12.
Partha Varma-1	पार्थवर्मा (1)	Utpal Dynasty, Kashmir	906-920	177.
Partha Varma-2	पार्थवर्मा (2)	Utpal Dynasty, Kashmir	934-935	177.
Parthivendra Malla Deva	पार्श्विंद्र	Malla Dynasty, Nepal	1680-1687	111.
Parvatiya Simha	पर्वतीय सिंह	Ahom Dynasty	1677-1679	2.
Peda Komargiri Reddi	पेडा	Kondavidu Reddi Dynasty	1402-1420	102.
Periya Krishnappa	कृष्णप्पा	Madura Nayak Dynasty	1563-1573	95.
Periya Virappa	वीरप्पा	Madura Nayak Dynasty	1573-1602	95.
Periya	पेरीया पिल्लाई सागरशेखरन	Arya Chakravarti Dynasty, Shri Lanka	1570-1582	155.
Perumal Parakram	पेरुमाल पराक्रम	Pandya Dynasty	1473-1479	118.
Piktan	पिकतन	Shailendra Dynasty, Java	838-850	57.
Pilaji Rao	पिलाजीराव	Gaikwad Dynasty	1721-1732	39.
Pipalraidev	पीपलरायदेव	Tomar Dynasty, Delhi	897-919	173.
Poojan Deva	पूजन देव	Kachhavaha Dynasty	1070-1084	61.
Prabhakar Vardhan	प्रभाकरवर्धन	Pushyabhuti-Vardhan Dynasty	580-605	130.
Prabhanjan	प्रभंजन	Parivrajak Dynasty		119.

Name	Devanagari	Dynasty	Period	Ref
Prabhasa Varma	प्रभासवर्मा	Shrimar Dynasty, Vietnam	629–645	169.
Bhava Varma-1	भववर्मा-1	Vietnam, Bhava varma Dynasty, Vietnam	550–600	170.
Prabho Narayan	प्रभो नारायण	Sutiya Dynasty, Assam	1285–1305	164.
Prabhu Meru Deva	प्रभुमेरुदेव	Bana Dynasty		6.
Prabhu Narayan Simha		Narayan Dynasty	1889–1931	86.
Prachinavan	प्राचिनवान	Puru Dynasty	Ancient	129.
Pradyot	प्रद्योत	Pradyot Dynasty	546 BC.	123.
Pradyumna	राव प्रद्युम्न	Jadeja Dynasty	1947–1948	60.
Pragmal-1	राव प्रागमल-1	Jadeja Dynasty	1697–1715	60.
Pragmal-2	राव प्रागमल-2	Jadeja Dynasty	1860–1876	60.
Pramatt Simha	प्रमत्त सिंह	Ahom Dynasty	1744–1751	2.
Prashnajit	प्रश्नजीत	Ikshavaku Dynasty	Ancient	56.
Prashni	प्रश्नि	Vrishni Dynasty	Ancient	188.
Pratap Malla Deva	प्रताप मल्ल	Malla Dynasty, Nepal	1641–1674	111.
Pratap Manikya	प्रताप माणिक्य	Manikya Dynasty, Tripura	1487–1487	79.
Pratap Rai	प्रताप राय	Nag Dynasty	326–353	83.
Pratap Simha Shah	प्रताप सिंह शाह	Shah Dynasty, Nepal	1775–1778	112.
Pratap Simha	प्रताप सिंह	Ahom Dynasty	1603–1641	2.
Pratap Simha	प्रताप सिंह	Bhosle Dynasty, Satara	1808–1839	9.
Pratap Simha	प्रताप सिंह	Bhosle Dynasty, Tanjavar	1739–1763	11.
Pratap Simha	प्रताप सिंह	Rathor Dynasty, Bikaner	1787–1787	136.
Pratap Simha	प्रताप सिंह	Rathor Dynasty, Kishangadh	1788–1798	137.
Pratap Simha	प्रतापसिंह-1	Sisodiya Dynasty	1572–1597	159.
Pratap Simha	प्रतापसिंह	Gaikwad Dynasty	1939–1951	39.
Pratap Simha-2	प्रतापसिंह-2	Sisodiya Dynasty	1752–1755	159.
Pratap Singh	प्रताप सिंह	Dogra Dynasty	1885–1925	38.
Pratap Singh	प्रताप सिंह	Kachhavaha Dynasty	1778–1803	61.
Pratapaditya	प्रतापादित्य	Karkota Dynasty, Kashmir	680–712	69.
Pratapaditya-1	प्रतापादित्य-1	Pratapaditya Dynasty, Kashmir	167–135 BC.	124.
Pratapkarna	प्रतापकर्ण	Nag Dynasty	1451–1469	83.
Pratapmalla	प्रतापमल्ल	Kalchuri Dynasty, Ratnapuri	1220–1222	67.
Prataprudra Deva	प्रतापरुद्र देव	Gajapati Dynasty	1497–1540	40.
Prataprudra Deva-1	प्रतापरुद्रदेव-1	Kakatiya Dynasty	1163–1196	64.
Prataprurda Deva-2	प्रतापरुद्रदेव-2	Kakatiya Dynasty	1295–1323	64.
Pratip	प्रतीप	Kuru Dynasty	Ancient	73.
Pratyaksha Narayan	प्रत्यक्ष नारायण	Sutiya Dynasty, Assam	1440–1465	164.
Pravar Sen	प्रवरसेन	Vakatak Dynasty	270–330	181.

Name	Devanagari	Dynasty	Period	Page
Pravaragupta	प्रवरगुप्त	Pravargupta Dynasty, Kashmir	949–950	125.
Pravarasen	प्रवरसेन	Gonaditya Dynasty, Kashmir	125–185	44.
Pravartak	प्रवंतक	Nimi Janak Dynasty	Ancient	114.
Pravir	प्रवीर	Puru Dynasty	Ancient	129.
Prem Narayan	प्रेम नारायण	Gond Dynasty, Mandla		45.
Prem Singh	प्रेम सिंह	Chauhan Dynasty, Kota	(1683–1684)	33.
Prithulashva	पृथुलाश्व	Ikshavaku Dynasty	Ancient	56.
Prithvi Deva-1	पृथ्वीदेव-1	Kalchuri Dynasty, Ratnapuri	1065–1114	67.
Prithvi Deva-2	पृथ्वीदेव-2	Kalchuri Dynasty, Ratnapuri	1145–1167	67.
Prithvi Deva-3	पृथ्वीदेव-3	Kalchuri Dynasty, Ratnapuri	1190–1220	67.
Prithvi Narayan Shah	पृथ्वी नारायण	Shah Dynasty, Nepal	1768–1775	112.
Prithvi Raj Singh-1	पृवीराजसिंह-1	Kachhavaha Dynasty	1502–1527	61.
Prithvi Sen	पृथ्वीसेन-1	Vakatak Dynasty	350–400	181.
Prithvi Sen-2	पृथ्वीसेन-2	Vakatak Dynasty	470–490	181.
Prithvi Simha	पृथ्वी सिंह	Rathor Dynasty, Kishangadh	1841–1879	137.
Prithvi Singh-2	पृथ्वीसिंह-2	Kachhavaha Dynasty	1768–1778	61.
Prithvi Varma	पृथ्वीवर्मा	Chandela Dynasty	1125–1129	23.
Prithvi Vir Vikram Shah	पृथ्वी	Shah Dynasty, Nepal	1881–1911	112.
Prithvimal	पृथ्वीमल	Tomar Dynasty, Delhi	794–814	173.
Prithvipal	पृथ्वीपाल	Chaunah Dynasty, Nadol	1080–1091	27.
Prithvipid	पृथ्वीपीड़	Karkota Dynasty, Kashmir	775–780	69.
Prithviraj	पृथ्वीराज	Tomar Dynasty, Delhi	1167–1189	173.
Prithviraj	पृथ्वीराज	Nal Dynasty	600–630	84.
Prithviraj-2	पृथ्वीराज-2	Chauhan Dynasty, Sakambhari	1166–1169	26.
Prithviraj-3	पृथ्वीराज-1	Chauhan Dynasty, Sakambhari	1090–1110	26.
Prithviraj-3	पृथ्वीराज-3	Chauhan Dynasty, Sakambhari	1177–1192	26.
Prithvivyaghra	पृथ्वीव्याघ्र	Nal Dynasty		84.
Prodaraj-1	प्रोदराज-1	Kakatiya Dynasty	1030–1075	64.
Prodraj-2	प्रोदराज-2	Kakatiya Dynasty	1110–1163	64.
Prolambha	प्रोलंभ	Shalasthambha Dynasty, Assam	810–815	146.
Prolay Nayak	प्रोलय नायक	Musunuri Nayak Dynasty	1325–1333	91.
Prolaya Vema Reddi	वेमा	Kondavidu Reddi Dynasty	1325–1353	102.
Pukakeshi	पुलकेशी	Chalukya Dynasty, Lat	738–750	20.
Pulakeshi-1	पुलकेशी-1	Chalukya Dynasty, Badami	543–566	18.
Pulakeshi-2	पुलकेशी-2	Chalukya Dynasty, Badami	608–642	18.
Pulashakti	पुलशक्ति	Shilahar Dynasty, Konkan	825–850	147.
Pulastya	पुलस्त्य	Pulastya Dynasty	Ancient	128.

Name	Devanagari	Dynasty	Period	Ref
Pulindak	पुलिंदक	Shunga Dynasty	122–118 BC	160.
Pulumavi-1	पुलुमावी-1	Satvahan Dynasty	43–07 BC	141.
Pulumavi-2	पुलुमावी-2	Satvahan Dynasty	121–149 AD	141.
Pulumavi-3	पुलुमावी-3	Satvahan Dynasty	166–174 AD	141.
Punyapal	पुण्यपाल	Bhati Raval Dynasty	1274–176	8.
Pura	जाम पूरा	Jadeja Dynasty	1350–1365	60.
Purandra Simha	पुरंदर सिंह	Ahom Dynasty	1818–1819	2.
Purindrasen	पुरिंद्रसेन	Satvahan Dynasty	66–71 AD	141.
Purnadhva Narayan	पूर्णध्व नारायण	Sutiya Dynasty, Assam	1480–1500	164.
Purnatalla	पूर्णतल्ल	Chauhan Dynasty, Sakambhari	709–721	26.
Purnotsava	पूर्णोत्संग	Satvahan Dynasty	220–202 BC	141.
Puru	पुरु	Puru Dynasty	Ancient	129.
Puru	पुरु	Yayati Dynasty	Ancient	192.
Puruj	पुरुज	Ajmidh-Dynasty	Ancient	3.
Purukutsa	पुरुकुत्स	Ikshavaku Dynasty	Ancient	56.
Pururava	पुरुरव	Atri Dynasty	Ancient	1.
Purushottam Deva	पुरुषोत्तम देव	Gajapati Dynasty	1466–1497	40.
Purvavishesh	पूर्वविशेष	Simha Shri Dynasty, Java	1456–1466	58.
Purviraja-1	पूर्वीराजा सागरशेखरन	Arya Chakravarti Dynasty, Shri Lanka	1561–1565	155.
Purviraja-2	पूर्वीराजा सागरशेखरन	Arya Chakravarti Dynasty, Shri Lanka	1582–1591	155.
Pushkaraksha	पुष्कराक्ष	Vietnam, Bhava varma Dynasty, Vietnam	716–730	170.
Pushpa Raj Simha	पुष्पराजसिंह	Waghela Dynasty, Riwa	1948	180.
Pushya Deva	पुष्यदेव	Saindhav Dynasty	734–754	140.
Pushya Varma	पुष्यवर्मा	Ahom Dynasty	355–380	2.
Pushya Varma	पुष्यवर्मा	Varma Dynasty, Kamrup	350–374	185.
Pushyamitra	पुष्यमित्र	Shunga Dynasty	185–149 BC	160.
Pushyant	पुष्यवंत	Brihadrith Dynasty, Magadh	Ancient	15.
Radha Kishor Manikya	राधाकिशोर माणिक्य	Manikya Dynasty, Tripura	1896–1909	79.
Radhashankar	राधाशंकर	Lohar Dynasty, Kashmir	1111–1112	75.
Raghab Simha	रघब सिंह	Simha Dynasty, Manipur	1823–1824	151.
Raghav	राघव	Ganga Dynasty, Kalinga	1151–1165	41.
Raghoba	राघोबादादा बाजीराव बल्लाळ	Peshva Dynasty	1773–1774	121.
Raghu Nath Simha	रघुनाथसिंह	Kalchuri Dynasty, Ratnapuri	1732–1741	67.
Raghu Nath Varma	रघुनाथवर्मा	Kadamb Dynasty	410–425	62.
Raghu	रघु	Raghu Dynasty	Ancient	131.
Raghuji-1	रघुजी-1	Angre Dynasty	1759–1793	4.
Raghuji-1	रघुजी-1	Bhosle Dynasty, Nagpur	1731–1755	12.

Name	Devanagari	Dynasty	Period	Page
Raghuji-2	रघुजी-2	Angre Dynasty	1817–1838	4.
Raghuji-2	रघुजी-2	Bhosle Dynasty, Nagpur	1772–1775	12.
Raghuji-3	रघुजी-3	Bhosle Dynasty, Nagpur	1788–1816	12.
Raghuji-4	रघुजी-4, बाजीबा	Bhosle Dynasty, Nagpur	1818–1853	12.
Raghunath Hari	रघुनाथ हरि	Nevalkar Dynasty, Jhansi		113.
Raghunath Kilavan	सेतुपति रघुनाथ	Pudukottai Dynasty	1673–1708	127.
Raghunathshah	रघुनाथशाह	Nag Dynasty	1665–1706	83.
Raghunathy Nayak	रघुनाथ	Tanjavar Nayak Dynasty	1600–1634	97.
Raghupal	रघुपाल	Tomar Dynasty, Delhi	919–940	173.
Raghuvir Singh	रघुवीर सिंह	Chauhan Dynasty, Bundi	(1889–1927)	32.
Rahila	राहिला	Chandela Dynasty	885–914	23.
Rahugan	रहुगण	Sauvir Dynasty, Sindh	Ancient	142.
Rahul Gautam	राहुल गौतम	Shakya Gautam Dynasty		145.
Rai Simha	राय सिंह	Rathor Dynasty, Bikaner	1573–1612	136.
Rai Simha	राय सिंह	Rathor Dynasty, Jodhpur	1582–1583	135.
Raipal Simha	रायपाल सिंह	Rathor Dynasty, Jodhpur	1309–1313	135.
Raj Deva	राज देव	Kachhavaha Dynasty	1179–1216	61.
Raj Deva	राजदेव	Vuppadeva Dynasty, Kashmir	1212–1235	189.
Raj Simha	राज सिंह	Rathor Dynasty, Bikaner	1787–1787	136.
Raj Simha	राज सिंह	Rathor Dynasty, Kishangadh	1706–1748	137.
Raj Simha-1	राजसिंह-1	Sisodiya Dynasty	1652–1680	159.
Raj Simha-2	राजसिंह-2	Sisodiya Dynasty	1755–1762	159.
Raj-1	राज-1	Wadiyar Dynasty	1578–1617	178.
Raja Bhupati	राजा भूपति	Lain Zang Dynasty, Laos	1591–1596	172.
Raja Gangadhar Rao	गंगाधरराव	Nevalkar Dynasty, Jhansi	1838–1853	113.
Raja Mallasaraja	राजा मल्लसराजा	Channamma Dynasty, Kittur		24.
Raja Vema Reddi	राजा	Kondavidu Reddi Dynasty	1420–1423	102.
Rajadhiraj-1	राजाधिराज-1	Chola Dynasty	1044–1052	36.
Rajadhiraj-2	राजाधिराज-2	Chola Dynasty	1163–1178	36.
Rajaditya	राजादित्य	Chola Dynasty	948–949	36.
Rajadsvati	राजदस्वाति	Satvahan Dynasty	72–72 AD	141.
Rajara-1, the Great	राजाराज-1 (महान)	Chola Dynasty	985–1014	36.
Rajaraj-1	राजाराज-1	Ganga Dynasty, Kalinga	1050–1078	41.
Rajaraj-2	राजाराज-2	Chola Dynasty	1146–1163	36.
Rajaraj-2	राजाराज-2	Ganga Dynasty, Kalinga	1165–1189	41.
Rajaraj-3	राजाराज-3	Chola Dynasty	1216–1246	36.
Rajaraj-3	राजाराज-3	Ganga Dynasty, Kalinga	1197–1200	41.

Name		Dynasty	Period	Page
Rajaram	राजाराम	Bhosle Dynasty, Kolhapur	1689–1700	10.
Rajaram	राजाराम	Bhosle Dynasty, Satara	1689–1700	9.
Rajaram-1	राजाराम-1	Bhosle Dynasty, Kolhapur	1866–1870	10.
Rajaram-2	राजाराम-2	Bhosle Dynasty, Kolhapur	1922–1940	10.
Rajas	राजस	Simha Shri Dynasty, Java	1222–1227	58.
Rajasbai	राजसबाई	Bhosle Dynasty, Kolhapur	1940–1942	10.
Rajasvardhan	राजसवर्धन	Simha Shri Dynasty, Java	1451–1456	58.
Rajatsimha	रजतसिंह	Guhil Dynasty, Mewad	773–793	47.
Rajdhar Manikya	राजधर माणिक्य-1	Manikya Dynasty, Tripura	1585–1600	79.
Rajdhar Manikya	राजधर माणिक्य-2	Manikya Dynasty, Tripura	1783–1804	79.
Rajendra Varma	राजन्द्रवर्मा	Varma Dynasty, Cambodia	944–968	171.
Rajendra Varma-2	राजेन्द्रवर्मा	Vietnam, Bhava varma Dynasty, Vietnam	760–780	170.
Rajendra Vir Vikram Shah	राजेंद्र	Shah Dynasty, Nepal	1816–1847	112.
Rajendra	राजेन्द्र	Chalukya Dynasty, Vengi	1062–1062	22.
Rajendra-1	राजेंद्र-1 पराकेसरी वर्मा	Chola Dynasty	1014–1044	36.
Rajendra-2	राजेंद्र-2 कुलोतुंग	Chola Dynasty	1070–1118	36.
Rajendra-3	राजेंद्र-3	Chola Dynasty	1246–1279	36.
Rajeshvar Simha	राजेश्वर सिंह	Ahom Dynasty	1751–1769	2.
Rajmalla-1	राजमल्ल-1	Ganga Dynasty, Talkad	817–853	42.
Rajmalla-2	राजमल्ल-2	Ganga Dynasty, Talkad	870—907	42.
Rajmalla-3	राजमल्ल-3	Ganga Dynasty, Talkad	936–937	42.
Rajmalla-4	राजमल्ल-4	Ganga Dynasty, Talkad	974–985	42.
Rajsangar	राजसंगर	Simha Shri Dynasty, Java	1350–1389	58.
Rajshekhar Varma	राजशेखरवर्मा	Cher Dynasty	820–844	34.
Rajsimha	राजसिंह	Cher Dynasty	1028–1043	34.
Rajya Vardhan-1	राज्यवर्धन-1	Pushyabhuti-Vardhan Dynasty	525–555	130.
Rajya Vardhan-2	राज्यवर्धन-2	Pushyabhuti-Vardhan Dynasty	605–606	130.
Rajyapal	राज्यपाल	Pal Dynasty, Bengal	908–935	115.
Rajyapal	राज्यपाल	Chaunah Dynasty, Nadol	1132–1145	27.
Rajyapal	राज्यपाल	Pratihar-Gurjar Dynasty	1018–1019	126.
Rakkas	रक्कस	Ganga Dynasty, Talkad	985–1024	42.
Raksh	रक्ष	Ajamidh Dynasty	Ancient Time	3.
Ram Chandra	रामचंद्र	Bhati Raval Dynasty	1648–1651	8.
Ram Deva	रामदेव	Waghela Dynasty, Gujrat	1274–1275	179.
Ram Ganga Manikya-1	राम गंगा माणिक्य-1	Manikya Dynasty, Tripura	1804–1809	79.
Ram Ganga Manikya-2	राम गंगा माणिक्य-2	Manikya Dynasty, Tripura	1813–1826	79.
Ram Manikya	राम माणिक्य	Manikya Dynasty, Tripura	1673–1684	79.

Ram Simha	राम सिंह	Rathor Dynasty, Jodhpur	1749–1751	135.
Ram Simha	राम सिंह	Simha Dynasty, Bharatpur	1893–1900	162.
Ram Singh	राम सिंह	Chauhan Dynasty, Bundi	(1821–1889)	32.
Ram Singh-1	रामसिंह-1	Kachhavaha Dynasty	1666–1688	61.
Ram Singh-2	रामसिंह-2	Kachhavaha Dynasty	1835–1881	61.
Ram Varma-1	राम वर्मा-1	Varma Dynasty, Travankor	1757–1798	184.
Ram Varma-10	राम वर्मा-10	Varma Dynasty, Kochin	1790–1805	183.
Ram Varma-11	राम वर्मा-11	Varma Dynasty, Kochin	1805–1809	183.
Ram Varma-12	राम वर्मा-12	Varma Dynasty, Kochin	1828–1837	183.
Ram Varma-13	राम वर्मा-13	Varma Dynasty, Kochin	1837–1844	183.
Ram Varma-14	राम वर्मा-14	Varma Dynasty, Kochin	1844–1851	183.
Ram Varma-15	राम वर्मा-15	Varma Dynasty, Kochin	1864–1888	183.
Ram Varma-16	राम वर्मा-16	Varma Dynasty, Kochin	1895–1914	183.
Ram Varma-17	राम वर्मा-17	Varma Dynasty, Kochin	1914–1932	183.
Ram Varma-18	राम वर्मा-18	Varma Dynasty, Kochin	1932–1941	183.
Ram Varma-2	राम वर्मा-2	Varma Dynasty, Travankor	1885–1924	184.
Ram Varma-2	राम वर्मा-2	Varma Dynasty, Kochin	1650–1656	183.
Ram Varma-3	राम वर्मा-3	Varma Dynasty, Kochin	1658–1662	183.
Ram Varma-4	राम वर्मा-4	Varma Dynasty, Kochin	1687–1693	183.
Ram Varma-5	राम वर्मा-5	Varma Dynasty, Kochin	1697–1701	183.
Ram Varma-6	राम वर्मा-6	Varma Dynasty, Kochin	1701–1721	183.
Ram Varma-7	राम वर्मा-7	Varma Dynasty, Kochin	1731–1746	183.
Ram Varma-8	राम वर्मा-8	Varma Dynasty, Kochin	1749–1760	183.
Ram Varma-9	राम वर्मा-9	Varma Dynasty, Kochin	1775–1790	183.
Ram Varma-	राम वर्मा-1	Varma Dynasty, Kochin	1565–1601	183.
Ram-1 Tribodhi	राम-1 त्रिबोधी	Ram Dynasty, Thailand	1351–1369	167.
Ram-1, the Great	राम-1, महान	Ram Dynasty, Thailand	1782–1809	168.
Ram-2	राम-2	Ram Dynasty, Thailand	1369–1370	167.
Ram-2	राम-2	Ram Dynasty, Thailand	1809–1824	168.
Ram-3	राम-3	Ram Dynasty, Thailand	1388–1395	167.
Ram-3	राम-3	Ram Dynasty, Thailand	1824–1851	168.
Ram-4	राम-4	Ram Dynasty, Thailand	1395–1408	167.
Ram-4	राम-4	Ram Dynasty, Thailand	1851–1868	168.
Ram-5	राम-5	Ram Dynasty, Thailand	1491–1529	167.
Ram-5	राम-5	Ram Dynasty, Thailand	1868–1910	168.
Ram-6	राम-6	Ram Dynasty, Thailand	1910–1925	168.
Ram-7	राम-7	Ram Dynasty, Thailand	1925–1935	168.

Name	Devanagari	Dynasty	Period	Page
Ram-8	राम-8	Ram Dynasty, Thailand	1935–1946	168.
Ram-9	राम-9	Ram Dynasty, Thailand	1946–1948	168.
Rama	राम	Yudhishthir Dynasty	Ancient	193.
Rama Dhvaja Simha	रामध्वज सिंह	Ahom Dynasty	1672–1674	2.
Rama Varma-1	राम वर्मा -1	Varma Dynasty, Venad	1545–1556	182.
Rama Varma-1	रामवर्मा-1	Cher Dynasty	885–917	34.
Rama Varma-2	राम वर्मा-2	Varma Dynasty, Venad	1610–1610	182.
Rama Varma-2	रामवर्मा-2	Cher Dynasty	1082–1090	34.
Rama Varma-3	राम वर्मा-3	Varma Dynasty, Venad	1610–1611	182.
Rama Varma-4	राम वर्मा-4	Varma Dynasty, Venad	1721–1729	182.
Rama	राम	Indraditya Dynasty, Thailand	1279–1317	166.
Ramabhadra	रामभद्र	Pratihar-Gurjar Dynasty	833–843	126.
Ramachandra	रामचंद्र	Gond Dynasty, Mandla		45.
Ramachandrdev	रामचंद्रदेव	Yadav Dynasty, Devgiri	1271–1311	190.
Ramagupta	रामगुप्त	Gupta Dynasty, Patliputra	375–375	48.
Ramakrishnappa	रामकृष्णप्पा	Jinji Nayak Dynasty	1620–1649	93.
Ramaraja	रामराजा	Keladi Nayak Dynasty	1580–1586	94.
Ramaraya	रामराया	Tuluv Nayak Dynasty	1543–1565	89.
Ramchandrray	रामचंद्र राय	Sangam Nayak Dynasty	1422–1425	87.
Ramdevaraya	रामदेवराय	Aravidu Nayak Dynasty	1618–1630	90.
Ramj Deva	रामदेव	Vuppadeva Dynasty, Kashmir	1252–1273	189.
Rampal	रामपाल	Pal Dynasty, Bengal	1080–1120	115.
Ramraja	रामराजा	Bhosle Dynasty, Satara	1749–1777	9.
Ramshah	रामशाह	Nag Dynasty	1640–1665	83.
Ramsimha	राम सिंह	Gond Dynasty, Vidarbha		46.
Ramsingh–1	राम सिंह-1	Chauhan Dynasty, Kota	(1696–1707)	33.
Ramsingh-2	राम सिंह-2	Chauhan Dynasty, Kota	(1827–1865)	33.
Rana Bahadur Shah	राणा बहादुर	Shah Dynasty, Nepal	1778–1799	112.
Rana Bhoj Raj	राणा भोजराज	Meera Bai Dynasty	1495–1530	82.
Ranaditya	रणादित्य	Gonaditya Dynasty, Kashmir	219–261	44.
Ranak-1	राणक-1	Saindhav Dynasty	794–814	140.
Ranak-2	राणक-2	Saindhav Dynasty	870–880	140.
Ranaraga	रणरंगा	Chalukya Dynasty, Badami	525–543	18.
Ranarnava	राणार्णव	Ganga Dynasty, Kalinga		41.
Ranasimha	रणसिंह	Guhil Dynasty, Mewad	1158–1168	47.
Ranbir Singh	रणबीर सिंह	Dogra Dynasty	1856–1885	38.
Randhir Simha	रणधीर सिंह	Simha Dynasty, Bharatpur	1805–1823	162.

Name	Devanagari	Dynasty	Years	Page
Rang Krishna	रंग कृष्ण	Madura Nayak Dynasty	1685–1689	95.
Rang Krishna	रंग कृष्ण	Madura Nayak Dynasty	1731–1734	95.
Rangappa-1	रंगप्पा-1	Chitradurg Nayak Dynasty	1602–1652	100.
Rangappa-2	रंगप्पा-2	Chitradurg Nayak Dynasty	1688–1689	100.
Rangappa-2	रंगप्पा-3	Chitradurg Nayak Dynasty	1748–1754	100.
Rani Unmanaarayan	रानी उम्मन्नारायण	Varma Dynasty, Venad	1677–1684	182.
Ranjit Simha	रणजीत सिंह	Simha Dynasty, Bharatpur	1776–1805	162.
Ranjit Simha	रणजीत सिंह	Bhati Raval Dynasty	1846–1864	8.
Ranjit Singh	रणजीत सिंह	Sikh Dynasty, Punjab	1799–1839	156.
Ranmal Simha	रणमल सिंह	Rathor Dynasty, Jodhpur	1427–1427	135.
Ranoji-1	राणोजी-1	Sindhia Dynasty	1716–1745	157.
Ranya	रण्य	Kuru Dynasty	Ancient	73.
Rao Asthan	राव अस्थान	Rathor Dynasty, Jodhpur	1273–1292	135.
Rao Beshilal	राव बेशीलाल	Chauhan Dynasty, Bundi	(1413–1459)	32.
Rao Bhanda	राव भांडा	Chauhan Dynasty, Bundi	(1459–1503)	32.
Rao Bhoja	राव भोज	Chauhan Dynasty, Bundi	(1585–1607)	32.
Rao Bika	राव बिका	Rathor Dynasty, Bikaner	1465–1504	136.
Rao Chunda Simha	राव चुण्डा सिंह	Rathor Dynasty, Jodhpur	1394–1423	135.
Rao Jodha Simha	राव जोधा सिंह	Rathor Dynasty, Jodhpur	1438–1489	135.
Rao Narayan	राव नारायण	Chauhan Dynasty, Bundi	(1503–1527)	32.
Rao Siha	राव सीहा	Rathor Dynasty, Jodhpur	1250–1273	135.
Rashtrapal	राष्ट्रपाल	Nand Dynasty		85.
Ratan Simha	रतन सिंह	Rathor Dynasty, Bikaner	1828–1851	136.
Ratan Simha	रतन सिंह	Simha Dynasty, Bharatpur	1768–1769	162.
Ratan Simha-2	रतनसिंह	Sisodiya Dynasty	1527–1531	159.
Ratan Singh	रतन सिंह	Chauhan Dynasty, Bundi	(1607–1631)	32.
Ratinar	रंतिनार	Puru Dynasty	Ancient	129.
Ratna Deva-1	रत्नदेव-1	Kalchuri Dynasty, Ratnapuri	1045–1065	67.
Ratna Deva-2	रत्नदेव-2	Kalchuri Dynasty, Ratnapuri	1141–1145	67.
Ratna Deva-3	रत्नदेव-3	Kalchuri Dynasty, Ratnapuri	1181–1190	67.
Ratna Dhvaja Simha	रत्नध्वज सिंह	Ahom Dynasty	1679–1681	2.
Ratna Malla Deva	रत्न मल्ल देव	Malla Dynasty, Nepal	1482–1520	111.
Ratna Manikya-1	रत्न माणिक्य-1	Manikya Dynasty, Tripura	1462–1487	79.
Ratna Manikya-2	रत्न माणिक्य-2	Manikya Dynasty, Tripura	1684–1693	79.
Ratna Manikya-2	रत्न माणिक्य-3	Manikya Dynasty, Tripura	1695–1712	79.
Ratna Simha-1	रत्नसिंह (गुहिल)	Sisodiya Dynasty	1301–1303	159.
Ratna Singh	रतनसिंह	Kachhavaha Dynasty	1534–1537	61.

Name	Devanagari	Dynasty	Period	Page
Ratnaditya	रत्नादित्य	Chapotkat Dynasty	920-935	25.
Ratnapal	रत्नपाल	Chaunah Dynasty, Nadol	1119-1132	27.
Ratnasimha	रत्नसिंह	Guhil Dynasty, Mewad	1301-1303	47.
Rattaraj	रट्टराज	Shilahar Dynasty, Konkan	995-1024	148.
Raudraksha	रौद्राक्ष	Puru Dynasty	Ancient	129.
Ravalji	जाम रावलजी	Jadeja Dynasty	1537-1548	60.
Ravalsimha	रावलसिंह	Guhil Dynasty, Mewad	813-828	47.
Ravan	रावण	Gonaditya Dynasty, Kashmir	1059-1058	44.
Ravan	रावण	Pulastya Dynasty	Ancient	128.
Ravi Keral Varma-2	रवि केरळ वर्मा-2	Varma Dynasty, Venad	1195-1209	182.
Ravi Varma	रविवर्मा	Kadamb Dynasty	497-537	62.
Ravi Varma-01	रवि वर्मा-10	Varma Dynasty, Venad	1684-1714	182.
Ravi Varma--1	रवि वर्मा-1	Varma Dynasty, Kochin	1615-1624	183.
Ravi Varma-1	वीर रवि वर्मा-1	Varma Dynasty, Venad	1161-1164	182.
Ravi Varma-2	रवि वर्मा-2	Varma Dynasty, Kochin	1663-1697	183.
Ravi Varma-2	रविवर्मा	Cher Dynasty	917-944	34.
Ravi Varma-2	वीर रवि वर्मा-2	Varma Dynasty, Venad	1299-1313	182.
Ravi Varma-3	रवि वर्मा-3	Varma Dynasty, Kochin	1721-1731	183.
Ravi Varma-3	वीर रवि वर्मा-3	Varma Dynasty, Venad	1382-1416	182.
Ravi Varma-4	वीर रवि वर्मा-4	Varma Dynasty, Venad	1416-1417	182.
Ravi Varma-5	वीर रवि वर्मा-5	Varma Dynasty, Venad	1444-1458	182.
Ravi Varma-6	वीर रवि वर्मा-6	Varma Dynasty, Venad	1484-1503	182.
Ravi Varma-7	रवि केरळ वर्मा-7	Varma Dynasty, Venad	1504-1514	182.
Ravi Varma-7	वीर रवि वर्मा-7	Varma Dynasty, Venad	1595-1609	182.
Ravi Varma-8	भूतल वीर रवि वर्मा-8	Varma Dynasty, Venad	1535	182.
Ravi Varma-8	रवि वर्मा-8	Varma Dynasty, Kochin	1853-1864	183.
Ravi Varma-8	रवि वर्मा-8	Varma Dynasty, Venad	1611-1663	182.
Ravi Varma-9	रवि वर्मा-9	Varma Dynasty, Kochin	1943-946	183.
Ravi Varma-9	रवि वर्मा-9	Varma Dynasty, Venad	1663-1672	182.
Ravivarma Kulashekhar	रविवर्मा कुलशेखर	Cher Dynasty	1090-1102	34.
Raydhan-1	जाम रायधन-1	Jadeja Dynasty	1365-1385	60.
Raydhan-2	राव रायधन-2	Jadeja Dynasty	1662-1697	60.
Raydhan-3	राव रायधन-3	Jadeja Dynasty	1778-1814	60.
Rayir Varma	वीर रायिर वर्मा	Varma Dynasty, Kochin	1645-1646	183.
Raymal	रायमल	Sisodiya Dynasty	1468-1473	159.
Riddha Raj Simha	ऋद्धराजसिंह	Waghela Dynasty, Riwa	1854-1880	180.
Riksha	ऋक्ष	Kuru Dynasty	Ancient	73.

Name	Devanagari	Dynasty	Period	Page
Ripunjaya	रिपुंजय	Brihadrith Dynasty, Magadh	Ancient	15.
Riteyu	ऋतेयु	Puru Dynasty	Ancient	129.
Rituparna	ऋतुपर्ण	Raghu Dynasty	Ancient	131.
Rohit	रोहित	Ikshavaku Dynasty	Ancient	56.
Rudra Sen-2	रुद्रसेन-1	Vakatak Dynasty	330-350	181.
Rudra Sen-2	रुद्रसेन-2	Vakatak Dynasty	400-405	181.
Rudra Simha Svargadev	रुद्रसिंह स्वर्गदेव	Ahom Dynasty	1696-1714	2.
Rudra Varma	रुद्रवर्मा	Funan Dynasty, Thailand	514	165.
Rudra Varma	रुद्रवर्मा	Shrimar Dynasty, Vietnam	529-572	169.
Rudra	रुद्र	Gond Dynasty, Mandla		45.
Rudradaman-1	रुद्रदामन-1	Kshatrap Dynasty	145-150	71.
Rudradaman-2	रुद्रदामन-2	Kshatrap Dynasty	332-348	71.
Rudradeva	रुद्रदेव	Raghav Dynasty, Nepal	(1008-1015)	109.
Rudramma Devi	रानी रुद्रम्मा देवी	Kakatiya Dynasty	1262-1295	64.
Rudrasen-1	रुद्रसेन-1	Kshatrap Dynasty	199-222	71.
Rudrasen-2	रुद्रसेन-2	Kshatrap Dynasty	256-279	71.
Rudrasen-3	रुद्रसेन-3	Kshatrap Dynasty	348-378	71.
Rudrasimha-1	रुद्रसिंह-1	Kshatrap Dynasty	188-199	71.
Rudrasimha-2	रुद्रसिंह-2	Kshatrap Dynasty	388-395	71.
Rup Simha	रूप सिंह	Rathor Dynasty, Kishangadh	1643-1658	137.
Sabal Simha	सबल सिंह	Bhati Raval Dynasty	1651-1661	8.
Sadashiv Nayak	सदाशिव	Keladi Nayak Dynasty	1530-1566	94.
Sadashiva Malla Deva	सदाशिव	Malla Dynasty, Nepal	1574-1578	111.
Sadashivaraya	सदाशिवराया	Tuluv Nayak Dynasty	1543-1565	89.
Sadashivray	सदाशिवराय	Penukonda Nayak Dynasty	1565-1585	98.
Sagar	सगर	Ikshavaku Dynasty	Ancient	56.
Saha Deva	सहदेव	Vuppadeva Dynasty, Kashmir	1301-1339	189.
Sahadeva	सहदेव	Ajmidh-Dynasty	Ancient	3.
Sahadeva	सहदेव	Brihadrith Dynasty, Magadh	Ancient	15.
Sahas Simha	साहस सिंह	Rathor Dynasty, Kishangadh	1615-1618	137.
Sahasi-1	साहसी-1	Rai Dynasty, Sindh		132.
Sahasi-2	साहसी-2	Rai Dynasty, Sindh	631	132.
Sahasmal	साहसमल	Chauhan Dynasty, Sirohi	1425	30.
Sahasrajit	सहस्रजीत	Yadu Dynasty	Ancient	191.
Sahayaksimha	महायक	Guhil Dynasty, Mewad	853-878	47.
Sahovadi	रहोवादी	Puru Dynasty	Ancient	129.
Sahu-1 (Shivaji)	साहू-1	Bhosle Dynasty, Satara	1708-1749	9.

Name	Devanagari	Dynasty	Period	Page
Sahu-2	साहू-2	Bhosle Dynasty, Satara	1777–1808	9.
Sajjan Simha	सज्जनसिंह	Sisodiya Dynasty	1874–1884	159.
Sal	सळ	Hoysal Dynasty	1006–1022	55.
Salhan	सलहण	Lohar Dynasty, Kashmir	1112–1112	75.
Salkha Simha	सलखा सिंह	Rathor Dynasty, Jodhpur	1357–1374	135.
Samant Sen	सामंतसेन	Sen Dynasty, Bengal	1074–1095	143.
Samant Simha	सामंत सिंह	Chauhan Dynasty, Jalor	1282–1305	29.
Samant Simha	सामंत सिंह	Rathor Dynasty, Kishangadh	1748–1765	137.
Samant Simha	सामंतसिंह	Chapotkat Dynasty	935–942	25.
Samant	सामंत	Hindu Shahi Dynasty	870–895	53.
Samantraj	सामंतराज	Chauhan Dynasty, Sakambhari	684–709	26.
Samantsimha	सामंतसिंह	Chaunah Dynasty, Nadol	1197–1200	27.
Samantsimha	सामंतसिंह	Guhil Dynasty, Mewad	1171–1179	47.
Samar Gravir	समर ग्रवीर	Shailendra Dynasty, Java	800–819	57.
Samar Simha	समर सिंह	Chauhan Dynasty, Jalor	1182–1205	29.
Samar Singh	संग्राम सिंह	Chauhan Dynasty, Bundi	(1343–1346)	32.
Samarsimha	समरसिंह	Guhil Dynasty, Mewad	1273–1301	47.
Samartung	समरतुंग	Shri Vijaya Dynasty, Sumatra	792	59.
Sambhaji Raje	संभाजी राजे	Bhosle Dynasty, Satara	1680–1689	9.
Sambhaji	संभाजी	Angre Dynasty,	1734–1735	4.
Sambhava	संभव	Brihadrith Dynasty, Magadh	Ancient	15.
Samprati	संप्रति	Maurya Dynasty	224–215 BC	81.
Samudra Varma	समुद्रवर्मा	Varma Dynasty, Kamrup	374–398	185.
Samudra Varma	समुद्रवर्मा	Ahom Dynasty	380–405	2.
Samudragupta	समुद्रगुप्त (पराक्रमांक)	Gupta Dynasty, Patliputra	350–375	48.
Samvarna	संवर्ण	Ajamidh Dynasty	Ancient Time	3.
Samyati	संयाति	Puru Dynasty	Ancient	129.
Sanafulla	सणफुल्ल	Shilahar Dynasty, Konkan	765–785	148.
Sandhimati	संधिमति	Pratapaditya Dynasty, Kashmir	22BC–25 AD.	124.
Sangam-1	संगम-1	Sangam Nayak Dynasty		87.
Sanghadaman	संघदामन	Kshatrap Dynasty	222–223	71.
Sangram Simha-1	संग्रामसिंह-1 (संगा)	Sisodiya Dynasty	1473–1527	159.
Sangram Simha-2	संग्रामसिंह-2	Sisodiya Dynasty	1716–1734	159.
Sangram	संग्राम	Gond Dynasty, Mandla		45.
Sangrama Deva	संग्रामदेव	Utpal Dynasty, Kashmir	948–949	177.
Sangrama Deva	संग्रामदेव	Vuppadeva Dynasty, Kashmir	1235–1252	189.
Sangramapid	संग्रामपीड़-1	Karkota Dynasty, Kashmir	780–780	69.

Name	Devanagari	Dynasty	Period	Page
Sangramaraja	संग्रामराजा	Lohar Dynasty, Kashmir	1003–1028	75.
Sangrampid-2	संग्रामपीड़-2	Karkota Dynasty, Kashmir	820–825	69.
Sankat Varma	संकटवर्मा	Utpal Dynasty, Kashmir	904–904	177.
Sankshobha	संक्षोभ	Parivrajak Dynasty	518–528	119.
Santurodh	संतुरोध	Puru Dynasty	Ancient	129.
Sara	जाम सारा	Jadeja Dynasty	1295–1300	60.
Sarang Deva	सारंगदेव	Waghela Dynasty, Gujrat	1275–1280	179.
Sardar Simha	सरदार सिंह	Rathor Dynasty, Bikaner	1851–1872	136.
Sardar Simha	सरदार सिंह	Rathor Dynasty, Jodhpur	1895–1911	135.
Sardar Simha	सरदार सिंह	Rathor Dynasty, Kishangadh	1765–1781	137.
Sardar Simha	सरदारसिंह	Kalchuri Dynasty, Ratnapuri	1712–1732	67.
Sardar Simha	सरदारसिंह	Sisodiya Dynasty	1838–1842	159.
Sarfoji-1	सरफ़ोजी-1	Bhosle Dynasty, Tanjavar	1712–1728	11.
Sarfoji-2	सरफ़ोजी-2	Bhosle Dynasty, Tanjavar	1798–1824	11.
Sarva Nath	सर्वनाथ	Uchchhakalpa Dynasty	508–533	176.
Sarvabhaum	सार्वभौम	Kuru Dynasty	Ancient	73.
Sarvabhauma Varma	सार्वभौमवर्मा	Funan Dynasty, Thailand	550–627	165.
Satal Simha	सातल सिंह	Rathor Dynasty, Jodhpur	1489–1492	135.
Satjit	सतजीत	Yadu Dynasty	Ancient	191.
Satkarni-1	सातकर्णी-1	Satvahan Dynasty	230–220 BC	141.
Satkarni-2	सातकर्णी-2	Satvahan Dynasty	184–128 BC	141.
Satta Simha	सता सिंह	Rathor Dynasty, Jodhpur	1427–1438	135.
Satya Narayan	सत्य नारायण	Sutiya Dynasty, Assam	1380–1400	164.
Satyadaman	सत्यदामन	Kshatrap Dynasty	178–188	71.
Satyadhrita	सत्यधृत	Brihadrith Dynasty, Magadh	Ancient	15.
Satyak	सत्यक	Vrishni Dynasty	Ancient	188.
Satyaki	सात्यकी	Vrishni Dynasty	Ancient	188.
Satyashraya	सत्याश्रय शीलादित्य	Chalukya Dynasty, Lat	669–738	20.
Satyashraya Irivabedanga	सत्याश्रय इरिवाबेडंगा	Chalukya Dynasty, Kalyani	997–1009	19.
Satyavrat	सत्यव्रत	Ikshavaku Dynasty	Ancient	56.
Sauvir	सौविर	Sauvir Dynasty, Sindh	Ancient	142.
Savai Jai Singh-2	सवाई जयसिंह-2	Kachhavaha Dynasty	1700–1743	61.
Savai Madhavrao	सवाई माधवराव	Peshva Dynasty	1774–1795	121.
Savai Madho Singh-2	सवाई मधोसिंह-2	Kachhavaha Dynasty	1881–1922	61.
Savai Man Singh-2	सवाई मानसिंह-2	Kachhavaha Dynasty	1922–1948	61.
Savai Shahaji	सवाई शहाजी	Bhosle Dynasty, Tanjavar	1738–1738	11.
Sawai Simha	सवाई सिंह	Bhati Raval Dynasty	1722–1722	8.

Name	Devanagari	Dynasty	Period	Page
Sayaji Rao-1	सयाजीराव-1	Gaikwad Dynasty	1771–1789	39.
Sayaji Rao-2	सयाजीराव-2	Gaikwad Dynasty	1818–1847	39.
Sayaji Rao-3	सयाजीराव-3	Gaikwad Dynasty	1875–1939	39.
Sayaji	सयाजी	Bhosle Dynasty, Tanjavar	1738–1739	11.
Sayunchandra-1	सयूनचंद्र	Yadav Dynasty, Devgiri	850–874	190.
Scarup Simha	स्वरूप सिंह	Rathor Dynasty, Bikaner	1698–1700	136.
Seyunchandra-2	सेयूनचंद्र-2	Yadav Dynasty, Devgiri	1068–1085	190.
Shahaji	शाहाजी	Bhosle Dynasty, Tanjavar	1684–1712	11.
Shahaji-1	शाहाजी-1	Bhosle Dynasty, Kolhapur	1821–1837	10.
Shahaji-2	शाहाजी	Bhosle Dynasty, Satara	1839–1848	9.
Shahaji-2	शाहाजी-2	Bhosle Dynasty, Kolhapur	1947–1949	10.
Shahu	शाहू	Bhosle Dynasty, Kolhapur	1883–1922	10.
Shailendra	शैलेन्द्र	Shailendra Dynasty, Java	674–717	57.
Shakanna	शंकन्ना	Keladi Nayak Dynasty	1566–1570	94.
Shakriddhava	शक्रोद्धत	Kuru Dynasty	Ancient	73.
Shaktikumar	शक्तिकुमार	Guhil Dynasty, Mewad	977–993	47.
Shakuni	शकुनि	Gandhar Dynasty		43.
Shalastambha	शालस्तंभ	Shalasthambha Dynasty, Assam	665–675	146.
Shalishuk	शालिशुक	Maurya Dynasty	215–202 BC	81.
Shalivahan	शालिवाहन	Bhati Raval Dynasty	1167–1189	8.
Shalivahan	शालिवाहन	Bhati Raval Dynasty	1890–1914	8.
Shalivahan	शालिवाहन	Guhil Dynasty, Mewad	973–977	47.
Shalti Varma-1	शक्तिवर्मा-1	Chalukya Dynasty, Vengi	1000–1010	22.
Shalya	शल्य	Madra Dynasty	Ancient Time	76.
Shambhu Simha	शंभूसिंह	Sisodiya Dynasty	1861–1874	159.
Shambhu Vardhan	शंभुवर्धन	Utpal Dynasty, Kashmir	935–935	177.
Shambhu Varma	शंभुवर्मा	Shrimar Dynasty, Vietnam	572–629	169.
Shambhu Varma-1	शंभुवर्मा-1	Vietnam, Bhava varma Dynasty, Vietnam	713–716	170.
Shambhu Varma-2	शंभुवर्मा-2	Vietnam, Bhava varma Dynasty, Vietnam	730–760	170.
Shambhuji-1	शंभुजी-1	Bhosle Dynasty, Kolhapur	1712–1760	10.
Shambhuji-2	शंभुजी-2	Bhosle Dynasty, Kolhapur	1813–1821	10.
Shanit Varma	शांतिवर्मा	Kadamb Dynasty	450–475	62.
Shankam	शंकम	Kalchuri Dynasty, Kalyani	1177–1180	68.
Shankar Deva	शंकरदेव	Thakur Dynasty, Nepal	(1067–1080)	110.
Shankar Varma	शंकरवर्मा	Utpal Dynasty, Kashmir	883–902	177.
Shankardev	शंकरदेव	Yadav Dynasty, Devgiri	1311–1317	190.
Shankargan Deva-1	शंकरगणदेव-1	Kalchuris, Dynasty, Tripuri	750–775	66.

Name	Devanagari	Dynasty	Period	Page
Shankargan Deva-2	शंकरगणदेव-2	Kalchuris Dynasty, Tripuri	890-910	66.
Shankargan Deva-3	शंकरगणदेव-3	Kalchuris Dynasty, Tripuri	970-974	66.
Shankargan	शंकरगण	Kalchuris Dynasty, Mahismati	575-600	65.
Shantanu	शान्तनु	Kuru Dynasty	Ancient	73.
Shantanu	शान्तनु	Shailendra Dynasty, Java		57.
Shanti	शांति	Ajmidh-Dynasty	Ancient	3.
Shardul Simha	शार्दूल सिंह	Rathor Dynasty, Bikaner	1943-1948	136.
Shardul Simha	शार्दूल सिंह	Rathor Dynasty, Kishangadh	1879-1900	137.
Shashad	शशाद	Ikshavaku Dynasty	Ancient	56.
Shashank	शशांक	Shashank Dynasty, Bengal	600-625	144.
Shata Dhanva	शतधन्वा	Maurya Dynasty	195-187 BC	81.
Shatarath	शतरथ	Raghu Dynasty	Ancient	131.
Shatarshal-1	राव शत्रसाल	Chauhan Dynasty, Bundi	(1631-1658)	32.
Shatarshal-2	शत्रशाल-1	Chauhan Dynasty, Kota	(1758-1764)	33.
Shatarshal-3	शत्रशाल-2	Chauhan Dynasty, Kota	(1865-1888)	33.
Shatdev-1	षटदेव-1	Kadamb Dynasty, Goa	1007-1052	64.
Shatdev-2	षटदेव-2	Kadamb Dynasty, Goa	1246-1250	64.
Shekhoji	शेखोजी	Angre Dynasty	1729-1733	4.
Sher Singh	शेर सिंह	Sikh Dynasty, Punjab	1841-1843	156.
Shibi	शिबि (शिबीराज)	Sindhu Dynasty	Ancient	158.
Shiladitya-1	शीलादित्य-1	Maitrak Dynasty	605-609	77.
Shiladitya-2	शीलादित्य-2	Maitrak Dynasty	669-691	77.
Shiladitya-3	शीलादित्य-3	Maitrak Dynasty	691-722	77.
Shiladitya-4	शीलादित्य-4	Maitrak Dynasty	722-760	77.
Shiladitya-5	शीलादित्य-5	Maitrak Dynasty	760-766	77.
Shiladitya-6	शीलादित्य-6	Maitrak Dynasty	766-767	77.
Shini	शिनि	Vrishni Dynasty	Ancient	188.
Shisha	शीश	Chach Dynasty, Sindh	712-724	17.
Shishuk	शिशुक	Nal Dynasty	290-330	84.
Shishunag	शिशुनाग	Shishunag Dynasty	413-394 BC	150.
Shiv Narayan	शिव नारायण	Sutiya Dynasty, Assam	1250-1270	164.
Shiva Datta	शिवदत्त	Traikutak Dynasty		175.
Shiva Deva	शिवदेव	Thakur Dynasty, Nepal	(1099-1126)	110.
Shiva Shri Satkarni	शिव श्री	Satvahan Dynasty	149-156 AD	141.
Shiva Simha Malla Deva	शिव	Malla Dynasty, Nepal	1578-1620	111.
Shiva Simha	शिवसिंह	Ahom Dynasty	1714-1744	2.
Shiva Varma-1	शिववर्मा-1	Pallav Dynasty	315-345	116.

Shivachitta	शिवचित्त	Kadamb Dynasty, Goa	1147-1174	64.
Shivadaskarna	शिवदासकर्ण	Nag Dynasty	1367-1389	83.
Shivaji Chhatrapati	शिवाजी छत्रपति	Bhosle Dynasty, Satara	1674-1680	9.
Shivaji	शिवाजी	Bhosle Dynasty, Tanjavar	1824-1855	11.
Shivaji-1	शिवाजी-1	Bhosle Dynasty, Kolhapur	1700-1712	10.
Shivaji-2	शिवाजी-2	Bhosle Dynasty, Kolhapur	1760-1813	10.
Shivaji-2	शिवाजी-2	Bhosle Dynasty, Kolhapur	1821-1822	10.
Shivaji-3	शिवाजी-3	Bhosle Dynasty, Kolhapur	1837-1866	10.
Shivaji-4	शिवाजी-4	Bhosle Dynasty, Kolhapur	1870-1883	10.
Shivaji-5	शिवाजी-5	Bhosle Dynasty, Kolhapur	1942-1947	10.
Shivajirao	जिवाजीराव	Sindhia Dynasty	1925-1948	157.
Shivajirao	शिवाजीराव	Holkar Dynasty	1886-1903	54.
Shivaman Gautam	शिवमान गौतम	Shakya Gautam Dynasty		145.
Shivamara-1	शिवमार-1	Ganga Dynasty, Talkad	750-760	42.
Shivamara-2	शिवमार-2	Ganga Dynasty, Talkad	788-817	42.
Shivanathshah	शिवनाथशाह	Nag Dynasty	1724-1733	83.
Shivappa Nayak	शिवप्पा	Tanjavar Nayak Dynasty	1532-1580	97.
Shivappa	शिवप्पा	Keladi Nayak Dynasty	1645-1660	94.
Shivaram Bhau	शिवराम भाऊ	Nevalkar Dynasty, Jhansi	1838	113.
Shivasanjaya Gautam	शिवसंजय गौतम	Shakya Gautam Dynasty		145.
Shivaskanda Satkarni	शिवस्कंद	Satvahan Dynasty	156-163 AD	141.
Shivasvati	शिवस्वाति	Satvahan Dynasty	72-100 AD	141.
Shobhitraj	शोभित	Chaunah Dynasty, Nadol	962-986	27.
Shreshthasen	श्रेष्ठसेन	Gonaditya Dynasty, Kashmir	59-89	44.
Shri Bhima Mahadevi	श्री भीम महादेवी	Lain Zang Dynasty, Laos	1438-1441	172.
Shri Bhuvana Ban	श्री भुवन बाण	Lain Zang Dynasty, Laos	1433-1436	172.
Shri Bhuvanadipati	भुवनादि आदिपति	Lain Zang Dynasty, Laos	1548-1572	172.
Shri Bhuvananathdeva	श्री भुवननाथ देव	Lain Zang Dynasty, Laos	1372-1417	172.
Shri Brahma Kumar	श्री ब्रह्म कुमार	Lain Zang Dynasty, Laos	1428-1429	172.
Shri Buddhisen	बुद्धिसेन	Lain Zang Dynasty, Laos	1572-1575	172.
Shri Dayabhuvannath	दया भुवन नाथ	Lain Zang Dynasty, Laos	1486-1495	172.
Shri Jambuya Rajashri	जंबूय राजश्री	Lain Zang Dynasty, Laos	1495-1500	172.
Shri Kama Dharmasar	श्री काम धर्मसार	Lain Zang Dynasty, Laos	1432-1433	172.
Shri Kama Kirti	श्री काम कीर्ति	Lain Zang Dynasty, Laos	1436-1438	172.
Shri Kunikam	श्री कुणिकाम	Lain Zang Dynasty, Laos	1430-1432	172.
Shri Lakshman Simha	श्री लक्ष्मण सिंह	Lain Zang Dynasty, Laos	1417-1428	172.
Shri Narendra	भूमि नरेन्द्र	Lain Zang Dynasty, Laos	1520-1548	172.

Name	Devanagari	Dynasty	Dates	Page
Shri Paduka	श्री पादुका	Majapihit Dynasty, Malaya	1375–1388	78.
Shri Parameshwar	श्री परमेश्वर	Majapihit Dynasty, Malaya	1388–1391	78.
Shri Purusha	श्रीपुरुष	Ganga Dynasty, Talkad	760–788	42.
Shri Rajsimha	राजसिंह	Kendy Nayak Dynasty	1782–1798	101.
Shri Ram	श्रीराम	Raghu Dynasty	Ancient	131.
Shri Rana Vir Vikram	श्री राणा वीर विक्रम	Majapihit Dynasty, Malaya	1362–1375	78.
Shri Shankha Chakrapati	श्री शंख चक्रपति	Lain Zang Dynasty, Laos	1441–1479	172.
Shri Shuddha Nagar	श्री शुद्ध नगर	Lain Zang Dynasty, Laos	1353–1372	172.
Shri Sumangal	श्री सुमंगल	Lain Zang Dynasty, Laos	1580–1583	172.
Shri Suvarma	श्री सुवर्मा	Lain Zang Dynasty, Laos	1479–1486	172.
Shri Tribhuvan	श्री त्रिभुवन	Majapihit Dynasty, Malaya	1299–1347	78.
Shri Vikram Besar	श्री विक्रम बेसर	Majapihit Dynasty, Malaya	1347–1362	78.
Shri Vishnu	श्री विष्णु	Lain Zang Dynasty, Laos	1500–1520	172.
Shri Yugadhar	श्री युगाधर	Lain Zang Dynasty, Laos	1429–1430	172.
Shrigupta	श्रीगुप्त	Gupta Dynasty, Patliputra	240–280	48.
Shrihahanu Gautam	श्रीहाहनु गौतम	Shakya Gautam Dynasty		145.
Shriharsha Deva	श्रीहर्षदेव	Shalasthambha Dynasty, Assam	725–750	146.
Shrihassar Gautam	श्रीहस्सर गौतम	Shakya Gautam Dynasty		145.
Shriman Gautam	श्रीमान गौतम	Shakya Gautam Dynasty		145.
Shrimar Shrivallabh	श्रीमार श्रीवल्लभ	Pandya Dynasty	815–862	118.
Shrimar	श्रीमार	Shrimar Dynasty, Vietnam		192
Shripati Rai	श्रीपतिराय	Nag Dynasty	969–997	83.
Shrirang-1	श्रीरंग-1	Aravidu Nayak Dynasty	1572–1585	90.
Shrirang-2	श्रीरंग-2	Aravidu Nayak Dynasty	1614–1618	90.
Shrirang-3	श्रीरंग-3	Aravidu Nayak Dynasty	1642–1649	90.
Shritanath	श्रुतनाथ	Raghu Dynasty	Ancient	131.
Shrivajay	श्रीविजय	Shri Vijaya Dynasty, Sumatra	683	59.
Shubhatunga	शुभतुंग अकालवर्ष	Rashtrakut Dynasty, Lat, Gujrat	867–867	134.
Shuddhodhan Gautam	शुद्धोधन गौतम	Shakya Gautam Dynasty		145.
Shur Simha	शूर सिंह	Rathor Dynasty, Bikaner	1613–1631	136.
Shur Simha	शूर सिंह	Rathor Dynasty, Jodhpur	1595–1619	135.
Shura Varma-1	शूरवर्मा 1	Utpal Dynasty, Kashmir	933–934	177.
Shura Varma-2	शूरवर्मा 2	Utpal Dynasty, Kashmir	939–939	177.
Shura	शूर	Vrishni Dynasty	Ancient	188.
Shurasen	शूरसेन	Shurasen Dynasty, Mathura	Ancient	161.
Shurpal	शूरपाल	1075–1080 Pal Dynasty, Bengal		115.
Shursen	शूरसेन	Vrishni Dynasty	Ancient	188.

Name	Devanagari	Dynasty	Period	Page
Shyamrao	शामराव निळकंठ रांझेकर	Peshva Dynasty	1640–1661	121.
Shyamsundarnathshah	श्यामसुंदरनाथशाह	Nag Dynasty		83.
Siddha	सिद्ध	Gonaditya Dynasty, Kashmir	983–923	44.
Siddhartha Gautam	सिद्धार्थ गौतम	Shakya Gautam Dynasty		145.
Sidkang Namgyal-1	सिदकंग नामग्याल-1	Namgyal Dynasty, Sikkim	1863–1874	14.
Sidkang Namgyal-2	सिदकंग नामग्याल-2	Namgyal Dynasty, Sikkim	1914–1914	14.
Simha Deva	सिंहदेव	Vuppadeva Dynasty, Kashmir	1286–1301	189.
Simha Varma-1	सिंहवर्मा-1	Pallav Dynasty	435–460	116.
Simha Vishnu	सिंहविष्णु	Pallav Dynasty	560–580	116.
Simharaj	सिंहराज	Chauhan Dynasty, Sakambhari	944–971	26.
Simhasen	सिंहसेन	Kshatrap Dynasty	382–388	71.
Simuk	सिमुक	Satvahan Dynasty	271–248 BC	141.
Sindhu Dwip	सिंधुद्वीप	Raghu Dynasty	Ancient	131.
Sindhuraj	सिंधुराज	Parmar Dynasty	995–1010	120.
Sindok	सिंडोक	Shailendra Dynasty, Java	929–947	57.
Singai	सिंगई प्रजाशेखरन-1	Arya Chakravarti Dynasty, Shri Lanka	1478–1519	155.
Singali-1	सिंगली सागरशेखरन	Arya Chakravarti Dynasty, Shri Lanka	1519–1561	155.
Singali-2	सिंगली प्रजाशेखरन-2	Arya Chakravarti Dynasty, Shri Lanka	1617–1619	155.
Singhan	सिंघण	Kalchuri Dynasty, Kalyani	1183–1184	68.
Singhan-1	सिंघण-1	Yadav Dynasty, Devgiri	1115–1145	190.
Singhan-2	सिंघण-2	Yadav Dynasty, Devgiri	1200–1247	190.
Sini	सिनि	Vrishni Dynasty	Ancient	188.
Sisthiti Varma	सुस्थितिवर्मा	Ahom Dynasty	585–593	2.
Siyak-1	सीयक-1	Parmar Dynasty	843–893	120.
Siyak-2, Harsha	सीयक-2 हर्ष	Parmar Dynasty	948–972	120.
Skand Varma	स्कन्दवर्मा	Nal Dynasty		84.
Skand Varma-1	स्कन्दवर्मा-1	Pallav Dynasty	345–350	116.
Skand Varma-2	स्कन्दवर्मा-2	Pallav Dynasty	370–385	116.
Skand Varma-3	स्कन्दवर्मा-3	Pallav Dynasty	400–435	116.
Skand Varma-4	स्कन्दवर्मा-4	Pallav Dynasty	460–480	116.
Skandagupta	स्कन्दगुप्त	Gupta Dynasty, Patliputra	455–467	48.
Skandastambhi	स्कंदस्तंभी	Satvahan Dynasty	202–184 BC	141.
Skandasvati	स्कन्दस्वाति	Satvahan Dynasty	62–55 BC	141.
Soma	सोम	Funan Dynasty, Thailand		165.
Somak	सोमक	Ajmidh-Dynasty	Ancient	3.
Someshvar	सोमेश्वर देव	Chindak Nag Dynasty	1069–1111	35.
Someshvar	सोमेश्वर	Chauhan Dynasty, Sakambhari	1169–1177	26.

Name	Devanagari	Dynasty	Period	Ref
Someshvar	सोमेश्वर	Hoysal Dynasty	1233–1254	55.
Someshvar	सोमेश्वर	Kalchuri Dynasty, Kalyani	1167–1177	68.
Someshvar	सोमेश्वर	Shilahar Dynasty, Konkan	1255–1265	147.
Someshvar-1	सोमेश्वर-1 त्रैलोक्यमल्ल	Chalukya Dynasty, Kalyani	1040–1069	19.
Someshvar-1	सोमेश्वर-1	Keladi Nayak Dynasty	1662–1697	94.
Someshvar-2	सोमेश्वर-2 भुवनैकमल्ल	Chalukya Dynasty, Kalyani	1069–1076	19.
Someshvar-2	सोमेश्वर-2	Keladi Nayak Dynasty	1714–1739	94.
Someshvar-3	सोमेश्वर-3 भूलोकमल्ल	Chalukya Dynasty, Kalyani	1127–1138	19.
Someshvar-4	सोमेश्वर-4 त्रिभुवनमल्ल	Chalukya Dynasty, Kalyani	1184–1189	19.
Sonopant	सोनोपंत विश्वनाथ बहुलकर	Peshva Dynasty	1638–1640	121.
Sthanuravi Varma	स्थाणुरविवर्मा	Cher Dynasty	844–885	34.
Sthita Varma	स्थितवर्मा	Varma Dynasty, Kamrup	566–590	185.
Sthiti Varma	स्थितिवर्मा	Ahom Dynasty	555–585	2.
Sua	सुआ	Simha Dynasty, Bharatpur		162.
Subal	सुबल	Gandhar Dynasty		43.
Subhatavarma	सुभटवर्मा	Parmar Dynasty	1178–1200	120.
Suchandra Simha	सुचंद्र सिंह	Simha Dynasty, Manipur	1886–1890	151.
Suchivarma	सुचिवर्मा	Guhil Dynasty, Mewad	1007–1021	47.
Sudas	सुदास	Ajmidh-Dynasty	Ancient	3.
Sudas	सुदास	Raghu Dynasty	Ancient	131.
Sudeva	सुदेव	Ikshavaku Dynasty	Ancient	56.
Sudhajit	सुधाजित	Vrishni Dynasty	Ancient	188.
Sudharma	सुधर्म	Brihadrith Dynasty, Magadh	Ancient	15.
Sudhriti	सुधृति	Nimi Janak Dynasty	Ancient	114.
Sudymna	सुद्युम्न	Puru Dynasty	Ancient	129.
Sugfud Namgyal	सुगफुद नामग्याल	Namgyal Dynasty, Sikkim	1793–1863	14.
Suhit	सुहित	Simha Shri Dynasty, Java	1429–1447	58.
Suhotra	सुहोत्र	Bharat Dynasty	Ancient	7.
Suja Simha	सुजा सिंह	Rathor Dynasty, Jodhpur	1492–1515	135.
Sujaba Bai	सुजनाबाई	Bhosle Dynasty, Tanjavar	1736–1738	11.
Sujan Simha	सुजान सिंह	Rathor Dynasty, Bikaner	1700–1736	136.
Sujan Simha	सुरजन सिंह	Chauhan Dynasty, Hadauti	1569 ...	31.
Suketu	सुकेतु	Nimi Janak Dynasty	Ancient	114.
Sulakshan Varma	सुलक्षणवर्मा	Chandela Dynasty	1100–1117	23.
Sulakshanpal	सुलक्षणपाल	Tomar Dynasty, Delhi	979–1005	173.
Sumer Simha	सुमेर सिंह	Rathor Dynasty, Jodhpur	1911–1918	135.
Sumer Simha	सुमेर सिंह	Rathor Dynasty, Kishangadh	1929–1948	137.

Name	Devanagari	Dynasty	Period	Page
Sumitsimha	सुमितसिंह	Guhil Dynasty, Mewad	753-773	47.
Sundar Rai	सुंदरराय	Nag Dynasty	627-635	83.
Sundar Svatikarni	सुंदर	Satvahan Dynasty	71-72 AD	141.
Suprasthita Varma	सुप्रस्थितवर्मा	Varma Dynasty, Kamrup	595-600	185.
Supratik Varma	सुप्रतिवर्मा	Ahom Dynasty	593-594	2.
Suraj	सूरज	Gond Dynasty, Vidarbha	1445-1470	46.
Surajmal	सूरजलल	Chauhan Dynasty, Bundi	(1527–1531)	32.
Surajmal	ब्रजेन्द्र सूरज मल	Simha Dynasty, Bharatpur	1756-1763	162.
Surat Simha	सूरत सिंह	Rathor Dynasty, Bikaner	1787-1828	136.
Surath	सुरथ	Kuru Dynasty	Ancient	73.
Surendra Vir Vikram Shah	सुरेन्द्र	Shah Dynasty, Nepal	1847-1881	112.
Surjan Singh	सुरजन सिंह	Chauhan Dynasty, Bundi	(1554–1585)	32.
Surtana	राव सुरतन	Chauhan Dynasty, Bundi	(1531–1554)	32.
Surya Malla Deva	सूर्य मल्ल देव	Malla Dynasty, Nepal	1520-1530	111.
Surya Varma	सूर्यवर्मा	Lain Zang Dynasty, Laos	1638-1690	172.
Surya Varma-1	सूर्यवर्मा-1	Varma Dynasty, Cambodia	1003-1050	171.
Surya Varma-2	सूर्यवर्मा-2	Varma Dynasty, Cambodia	1113-1150	171.
Sushanti	सुशांति	Ajmidh-Dynasty	Ancient	3.
Susharma	सुशर्मा	Kanva Dynasty	37-27 BC	63.
Susharma	सुशर्मा	Parivrajak Dynasty	400	119.
Sussaharaja	सुश्शलराजा	Lohar Dynasty, Kashmir	1112-1123	75.
Susthita Varma	सुस्थितवर्मा	Maukhari Dynasty		80.
Susthita Varma	सुस्थितवर्मा	Varma Dynasty, Kamrup	590-595	185.
Sutanva	सुतन्व	Ikshavaku Dynasty	Ancient	56.
Svarup Simha	स्वरूपसिंह	Sisodiya Dynasty	1842-1861	159.
Svati	स्वाति	Satvahan Dynasty	80-62 BC	141.
Svatikarna	स्वातिकर्ण	Satvahan Dynasty	44-43 BC	141.
Swarnaroma	स्वर्णरोम	Nimi Janak Dynasty	Ancient	114.
Tailap-1	तैलप-1	Chalukya Dynasty, Kalyani		19.
Tailap-2	तैलप-2 आहवमल्ल नुरमाडी	Chalukya Dynasty, Kalyani	973-997	19.
Tailap-3	तैलप-3 त्रैलोक्यमल्ल	Chalukya Dynasty, Kalyani	1150-1156	19.
Takhta Simha	तख्त सिंह	Rathor Dynasty, Jodhpur	1843-1873	135.
Talvar	तलवार	Gond Dynasty, Vidarbha		46.
Tamachi	राव तमाची	Jadeja Dynasty	1654-1662	60.
Tano Simha	तानो सिंह	Bhati Raval Dynasty	806-821	8.
Tarabai	ताराबाई	Bhosle Dynasty, Satara	1700-1708	9.
Tashi Namgyal	ताशी नामग्याल	Namgyal Dynasty, Sikkim	1914-1948	14.

Name	Devanagari	Dynasty	Period	Page
Tayati	ययाति	Yayati Dynasty	Ancient	192
Tejsimha	तेजसिंह	Guhil Dynasty, Mewad	1256–1273	47
Tensing Namgyal	तेनसिंह नामग्याल	Namgyal Dynasty, Sikkim	1780–1793	14
Tensung Namgyal	तेनसुंग नामग्याल	Namgyal Dynasty, Sikkim	1670–1700	14
Tez Simha	तेज सिंह	Bhati Raval Dynasty	1720–1722	8
Tezpal	तेजपाल	Tomar Dynasty, Delhi	1081–1105	173
Thutob Namgyal	थुतोब नामग्याल	Namgyal Dynasty, Sikkim	1874–1914	14
Tida Simha	तीड़ा सिंह	Rathor Dynasty, Jodhpur	1344–1357	135
Tilhanpal	तील्हणपाल	Tomar Dynasty, Delhi	940–944	173
Timma Bhupal	तिम्म भूपाल	Saluv Nayak Dynasty	1490–1492	88
Timma Nayak	तिम्म नायक	Pemmasani Nayak Dynasty	1598–1623	92
Timma Raj-1	तिम्मराज-1	Wadiyar Dynasty	1479–1479	178
Timma Raj-2	तिम्मराज-2	Wadiyar Dynasty	1553–1572	178
Timmanna	तिम्मन्ना	Chitradurg Nayak Dynasty	1588	100
Timmappa Nayak	तिम्मप्पा नायक	Tanjavar Nayak Dynasty		97
Timmappa	तिम्मप्पा	Chennai Nayak Dynasty		99
Tirumal Nayak	तिरुमल नायक	Aravidu Nayak Dynasty	1565–1572	90
Tirumal Nayak	तिरुमल नायक	Madura Nayak Dynasty	1623–1659	95
Tirumal-1	स्वाति तिरुमल	Varma Dynasty, Travankor	1829–1847	184
Tirumal-2	तिरुमल-2	Varma Dynasty, Travankor	1860–1880	184
Tirumal-3	तिरुमल-3	Varma Dynasty, Travankor	1880–1885	184
Tolpal	तोलपाल	Tomar Dynasty, Delhi	944–961	173
Trailokya Varma	त्रैलोक्यवर्मा	Chandela Dynasty	1203–1245	23
Trailokyamal Deva	त्रैलोक्यमलदेव	Kalchuris Dynasty, Tripuri	1210–1212	66
Trasadasyu	त्रसदस्यु	Ikshavaku Dynasty	Ancient	56
Trayyarunya	त्र्य्यरुण्य	Ikshavaku Dynasty		56
Tribhuvan Vir Vikram Shah	त्रिभुवन	Shah Dynasty, Nepal	1911–1948	112
Tribhuvan	त्रिभुवन	Kadamb Dynasty, Goa	1220–1146	64
Tribhuvan	त्रिभुवन	Simha Shri Dynasty, Java	1329–1350	58
Tribhuvanaditya Varma-2	त्रिभुवनवर्मा	Varma Dynasty, Cambodia	1166–1181	171
Tribhuvangupta	त्रिभुवनगुप्त	Pravargupta Dynasty, Kashmir	973–975	125
Tribhuvanpal	त्रिभुवनपाल	Solanki Dynasty	1241–1244	163
Trilochalpal	त्रिलोचनपाल	Hindu Shahi Dynasty	1021–1026	53
Trilochanpal	त्रिलोचनपाल	Pratihar-Gurjar Dynasty	1019–1030	126
Tryambak Krishnappa	त्र्यंबक	Jinji Nayak Dynasty	1570–1600	93
Tukoji	तुकोजी	Bhosle Dynasty, Tanjavar	1728–1735	11
Tukojirao-1	तुकोजीराव-1	Holkar Dynasty	1766–1767	54

Name	Devanagari	Dynasty	Dates	Page
Tukojirao-2	तुकोजीराव-2	Holkar Dynasty	1795-1797	54.
Tukojirao-3	तुकोजीराव-3	Holkar Dynasty	1844-1886	54.
Tukojirao-4	तुकोजीराव-4	Holkar Dynasty	1903-1926	54.
Tuljaji	तुलजाजी	Bhosle Dynasty, Tanjavar	1763-1787	11.
Tulodang	तुलोदंग	Shailendra Dynasty, Java	919-924	57.
Tumbru	तुंबरु	Kukkur Dynasty	Ancient	72.
Tungajin	तुंगजीन	Pratapaditya Dynasty, Kashmir	103-67 BC	124.
Tyaga Simha	त्यागसिंह	Shalasthambha Dynasty, Assam	970-990	146.
Ubhaya Karan	उदयकरण	Kachhavaha Dynasty	1366-1388	61.
Ucchharaja	उच्छराजा	Lohar Dynasty, Kashmir	1011-1111	75.
Udavasu	उदावसु	Nimi Janak Dynasty	Ancient	114.
Uday Manikya	उदय माणिक्य	Manikya Dynasty, Tripura	1567-1573	79.
Uday Simha	उदय सिंह	Chauhan Dynasty, Jalor	1205-1257	29.
Uday Simha	उदय सिंह	Rathor Dynasty, Jodhpur	1583-1595	135.
Uday Simha	उदयसिंह	Sisodiya Dynasty	1537-1572	159.
Uday Varma	वीर उदय वर्मा	Varma Dynasty, Venad		182.
Udaya Rai	उदायराय	Nag Dynasty	653-710	83.
Udayaditya Simha	उदयादित्य सिंह	Ahom Dynasty	1670-1672	2.
Udayaditya Tarapid	उदयादित्य तारपीड़	Karkota Dynasty, Kashmir	720-725	69.
Udayaditya Varma-1	उदयादित्यवर्मा-1	Varma Dynasty, Cambodia	1001-1002	171.
Udayaditya Varma-2	उदयादित्यवर्मा-2	Varma Dynasty, Cambodia	1050-1066	171.
Udayaditya	उदयादित्य	Parmar Dynasty	1059-1087	120.
Udayibhadra	उदायीभद्र	Haryak Dynasty	462-442 BC	51.
Udaykarna	उदयकर्ण	Nag Dynasty	1389-1451	83.
Udaynathshah	उदयनाथशाह	Nag Dynasty	1733-1740	83.
Udaypal	उदयपाल	Tomar Dynasty, Delhi	849-875	173.
Uddharan	उद्धरण	Tomar Dynasty, Gwalior	1400-1402	174.
Udha Rao	उधाराव	Kachhavaha Dynasty	1424-1453	61.
Udit Narayan Simha		Narayan Dynasty	1794-1835	86.
Ugraperu Veladi	उग्रपेरु वेलाडी	Pandya Dynasty	150	118.
Ugrasen	उग्रसेन	Kukkur Dynasty	Ancient	72.
Ugrasen	उग्रसेन	Shurasen Dynasty, Mathura	Ancient	161.
Umed Singh	उमेद सिंह	Chauhan Dynasty, Bundi	(1739–1771)	32.
Umed Singh-1	उमेद सिंह-1	Chauhan Dynasty, Kota	(1771-1819)	33.
Umed Singh-2	उमेद सिंह -1	Chauhan Dynasty, Kota	(1888–1940)	33.
Ummed Simha	उम्मेद सिंह	Rathor Dynasty, Jodhpur	1918-1947	135.
Unmarravanti	उन्मत्तवन्ती	Utpal Dynasty, Kashmir	937-939	177.

Name	Devanagari	Dynasty	Period	Page
Unni Raman-1	उन्नी रामन-1	Varma Dynasty, Kochin	1500–1503	183.
Unni Raman-2	उन्नी रामन-2	Varma Dynasty, Kochin	1503–1537	183.
Upendraraj	उपेंद्रराज (कृष्णराज)	Parmar Dynasty	800–818	120.
Urja	उर्ज	Brihadrith Dynasty, Magadh	Ancient	15.
Utkarsharaja	उत्कर्षराजा	Lohar Dynasty, Kashmir	1089–1089	75.
Utpalaksha	उत्पलक्ष	Gonaditya Dynasty, Kashmir	923–893	44.
Utpalpid	उत्पलपीड़	Karkota Dynasty, Kashmir	851–855	69.
Uttam	उत्तम	Chola Dynasty	970–969	36.
Vaasudeva Shri Krishna	वासुदेव श्रीकृष्ण	Vrishni Dynasty	Ancient	188.
Vadugi-1	वदुगी-1	Yadav Dynasty, Devgiri	950–974	190.
Vadugi-2	वदुगी-2	Yadav Dynasty, Devgiri	1005–1020	190.
Vadugi-3	वदुगी-3	Yadav Dynasty, Devgiri	1055–1068	190.
Vahuk Dhaval	वाहुकधवल	Chalukya Dynasty, Saurashtra	.	21.
Vaiappa Nayak	वैयप्पा नायक	Jinji Nayak Dynasty	1491–1509	93.
Vairat	वैरट	Guhil Dynasty, Mewad	1068–1088	47.
Vairi Simha	वैरीसिंह	Chapotkat Dynasty	895–920	25.
Vairi Simha-1	वैरीसिंह-1	Parmar Dynasty	818–843	120.
Vairi Simha-2	वैरीसिंह-2	Parmar Dynasty	918–948	120.
Vairisimha	वैरीसिंह	Guhil Dynasty, Mewad	1103–1108	47.
Vaisvat Manu	वैवस्वत मनु	Ikshavaku Dynasty	Ancient	56.
Vaivasvat Manu	वैवस्वत मनु	Vivasvan Dynasty	Ancient	187.
Vajayaditya-1	विजयदित्य-1	Chalukya Dynasty, Vengi	746–764	22.
Vajjad Deva-1	वज्जडदेव-1	Shilahar Dynasty, Konkan	945–965	147.
Vajjad Deva-2	वज्जडदेव-2	Shilahar Dynasty, Konkan	1010–1015	147.
Vajraditya Chandrapid	वज्रादित्य चंद्रपीड़	Karkota Dynasty, Kashmir	712–720	69.
Vajrahast-2	वज्रहस्त-2	Ganga Dynasty, Kalinga	898–942	41.
Vajrahasta-1	वज्रहस्त-1	Ganga Dynasty, Kalinga		41.
Vajrahasta-3	वज्रहस्त-3	Ganga Dynasty, Kalinga	980–1015	41.
Vajrahasta-4	वज्रहस्त-4	Ganga Dynasty, Kalinga	1038–1050	41.
Vajramitra	वज्रमित्र	Shunga Dynasty	116–103 BC	160.
Vakpati	वाक्पति	Chandela Dynasty	845–865	23.
Vakpatiraj	वाक्पतिराज	Parmar Dynasty	893–918	120.
Vakpatiraj-1	वाक्पतिराज-1	Chauhan Dynasty, Sakambhari	917–944	26.
Vakpatiraj-2	वाक्पतिराज-2	Chauhan Dynasty, Sakambhari	1026–1040	26.
Vakpatiraj-2, Munja	वाक्पतिराज-2 मुंज	Parmar Dynasty	972–995	120.
Vallabhraj	वल्लभराज	Solanki Dynasty	1010–1011	163.
Vamadeva	वामदेव	Thakur Dynasty, Nepal	(1080–1090)	110.

Vamdev Rai	वामदेवराय	Kalchuris, Dynasty, Tripuri	675–700	66.
Vamraj	वनराज	Chapotkat Dynasty	746–806	25.
Vamshapal	वंशपाल	Guhil Dynasty, Mewad	1088–1103	47.
Vanamal Varma	वनमालवर्मा	Shalasthambha Dynasty, Assam	835–865	146.
Vanhi	वन्हि	Kukkur Dynasty	Ancient	72.
Vantideva	वंतीदेव	Lohar Dynasty, Kashmir	1165–1172	75.
Vappuvan	वप्पुवन	Shilahar Dynasty, Konkan	880–910	147.
Varadappa	वरदप्पा	Jinji Nayak Dynasty	1600–1620	93.
Varaguna-1	वरगुण-1	Pandya Dynasty		118.
Varaguna-2	वरगुण-2	Pandya Dynasty	862–880	118.
Varagunaram	वरगुणराम	Pandya Dynasty	1612–1618	118.
Varaharaj	वराहराज	Nal Dynasty	330–370	84.
Varattunga	वरतुंग	Pandya Dynasty	1604–1612	118.
Varjaditya Bappiyak	वज्रादित्य बप्पीयक	Karkota Dynasty, Kashmir	768–775	69.
Varma-3	इन्द्रवर्मा-3	Varma Dynasty, Cambodia	1295–1308	171.
Varoday	वरोदय सागरशेखरन	Arya Chakravarti Dynasty, Shri Lanka	1302–1325	155.
Varudha	वरूढ	Gandhar Dynasty		43.
Vashishka	वशिष्क	Kushan Dynasty	126–130	74.
Vasu	वसु	Brihadrith Dynasty, Magadh	Ancient	15.
Vasu	वसु	Kukkur Dynasty	Ancient	72.
Vasudev	वसुदेव	Kanva Dynasty	72–63 BC	63.
Vasudev	वसुदेव	Vrishni Dynasty	Ancient	188.
Vasudeva	वसुदेव	Gond Dynasty, Mandla		45.
Vasudeva-1	वसुदेव-1	Kushan Dynasty	166–200	74.
Vasudeva-2	वसुदेव-2	Kushan Dynasty	222–244	74.
Vasujyeshtha	वसुज्येष्ठ	Shunga Dynasty	141–131 BC	160.
Vasuman	वसुमन	Ikshavaku Dynasty	Ancient	56.
Vasumitra	वसुमित्र	Shunga Dynasty	131–124 BC	160.
Vasunand	वसुनंद	Gonaditya Dynasty, Kashmir	572–520	44.
Vatsaraj	वत्सराज	Pratihar-Gurjar Dynasty	783–815	126.
Vava	वावा	Shailendra Dynasty, Java	924–929	57.
Veer Singh	वीर सिंह	Chauhan Dynasty, Bundi	(1403–1413)	32.
Vehanji	जाम वेहांजी	Jadeja Dynasty	1430–1450	60.
Vema Kadphises	वेमा कडफिसेस	Kushan Dynasty	80–103	74.
Venkat-1	वेंकट-1	Aravidu Nayak Dynasty	1585–1614	90.
Venkat-2	वेंकट-2	Aravidu Nayak Dynasty	1630–1642	90.
Venkatapati	वेंकटपति	Penukonda Nayak Dynasty	1585–1614	98.

Name	Devanagari	Dynasty	Period	Page
Venkatappa	वेंकटप्पा	Chennai Nayak Dynasty		99.
Venkatappa	वेंकटप्पा	Jinji Nayak Dynasty	1550-1570	93.
Venkatappa-1	वेंकटप्पा-1	Keladi Nayak Dynasty	1586-1629	94.
Venkatappa-2	वेंकटप्पा-2	Keladi Nayak Dynasty	1660-1662	94.
Venkataraya	वेंकटराया	Tuluv Nayak Dynasty	1542-1543	89.
Verivarshelaiyan	वेरीवरशेलैयन	Pandya Dynasty	75	118.
Vetraj Tribhuvanmalla	वेतराज त्रिभुवन	Kakatiya Dynasty	1075-1110	64.
Vibhishan	विभीषण	Pulastya Dynasty	Ancient	128.
Vibhishan-1	विभीषण-1	Gonaditya Dynasty, Kashmir	1147-1094	44.
Vibhishan-2	विभीषण-2	Gonaditya Dynasty, Kashmir	1058-1023	44.
Vibhuti Narayan Simha	नारायण	Narayan Dynasty	1939-1948	86.
Vibudh	विबुध	Nimi Janak Dynasty	Ancient	114.
Vichitravirya	विचित्रवीर्य	Pandava Dynasty		117.
Vichitravirya	विचित्रवीर्य	Kaurava Dynasty		70.
Vichitravirya	विचित्रवीर्य	Kuru Dynasty	Ancient	73.
Vidurth	विदूरथ	Kuru Dynasty	Ancient	73.
Vidurth	विदूरथ	Vrishni Dynasty	Ancient	188.
Vidyadhar	विद्याधर जिमूतवाहन	Shilahar Dynasty		147.
Vidyadhara	विद्याधर	Chandela Dynasty	1019-1037	23.
Vidyadhara-2	विद्याधर-1	Bana Dynasty		6.
Vidyadhara-2	विद्याधर-2	Bana Dynasty		6.
Vidyadhara-3	विद्याधर-3	Bana Dynasty		6.
Vigrahapal	विग्रहपाल	Chaunah Dynasty, Nadol	990-994	27.
Vigrahapal-1	विग्रहपाल-1	850-875 Pal Dynasty, Bengal		115.
Vigrahapal-2	विग्रहपाल-2	952-995 Pal Dynasty, Bengal		115.
Vigrahapal-3	विग्रहपाल-3	1055-1070 Pal Dynasty, Bengal		115.
Vigraharaj-1	विग्रहराज-1	Chauhan Dynasty, Sakambhari	734-759	26.
Vigraharaj-2	विग्रहराज-2	Chauhan Dynasty, Sakambhari	971-998	26.
Vigraharaj-3	विग्रहराज-3	Chauhan Dynasty, Sakambhari	1070-1090	26.
Vigraharaj-4	विग्रहराज-4	Chauhan Dynasty, Sakambhari	1153-1166	26.
Vijay Manikya-1	विजय माणिक्य-1	Manikya Dynasty, Tripura	1487-1488	79.
Vijay Manikya-2	विजय माणिक्य-2	Manikya Dynasty, Tripura	1532-1563	79.
Vijay Manikya-3	विजय माणिक्य-3	Manikya Dynasty, Tripura	1746-1748	79.
Vijay Raghav	विजय राघव	Tanjavar Nayak Dynasty	1634-1673	97.
Vijay Raghunath	सेतुपति विजय रघुनाथ	Pudukottai Dynasty	1825	127.
Vijay Rang	विजय रंग चोकन्नाथ	Madura Nayak Dynasty	1704-1731	95.
Vijay Sen	विजयसेन	Sen Dynasty, Bengal	1096-1159	143.

Name	Devanagari	Dynasty	Period	Page
Vijay Simha	विजय सिंह	Rathor Dynasty, Jodhpur	1752–1793	135.
Vijay Varma	विजयवर्मा	Shrimar Dynasty, Vietnam	526–529	169.
Vijay	विजय	Pratapaditya Dynasty, Kashmir	67–59 BC	124.
Vijay-1	विजय-1	Bhati Raval Dynasty	821–853	8.
Vijay-2	विजय-2	Bhati Raval Dynasty	979–1044	8.
Vijaya Raj	विजय राज	Lain Zang Dynasty, Laos	1637–1638	172.
Vijaya Raja	विजय राजा	Chalukya Dynasty, Lat	643–655	20.
Vijaya Rajsimha	विजय राजसिंह	Kendy Nayak Dynasty	1739–1747	101.
Vijaya Ramchandra	विजय रामचंद्र	Jinji Nayak Dynasty	1521–1540	93.
Vijaya	विजय	Satvahan Dynasty	178–188 AD	141.
Vijayaditya Parakesari	विजयादित्य पराकेसरी वर्मा	Chola Dynasty	846–881	36.
Vijayaditya	विजयादित्य	Chalukya Dynasty, Badami	696–733	18.
Vijayaditya	विजयादित्य	Chalukya Dynasty, Kalyani	696–733	19.
Vijayaditya	विजयादित्य	Shilahar Dynasty, Kolhapur	1135–1175	149.
Vijayaditya-1	विजयादित्य-1	Bana Dynasty		6.
Vijayaditya-2	विजयादित्य-2	Bana Dynasty		6.
Vijayaditya-2	विजयादित्य-2	Chalukya Dynasty, Vengi	799–843	22.
Vijayaditya-3	विजयादित्य-3	Bana Dynasty		6.
Vijayaditya-3	विजयादित्य-3, गुणक	Chalukya Dynasty, Vengi	844–892	22.
Vijayaditya-4	विजयादित्य-4	Chalukya Dynasty, Vengi	1062–1070	22.
Vijayaditya-4	विजयादित्य-4	Chalukya Dynasty, Vengi	918–918	22.
Vijayaditya-5	विजयादित्य-5, कण्ठिका	Chalukya Dynasty, Vengi	925–926	22.
Vijayakamadev	विजयकामदेव	Thakur Dynasty, Nepal	(1196–1200)	110.
Vijayakamdev	विजयकर्मदेव	Raghav Dynasty, Nepal	(1039–1046)	109.
Vijayapaldeva	विजयपालदेव	Chandela Dynasty	1037–1051	23.
Vijayashakti	विजयशक्ति	Chandela Dynasty	865–885	23.
Vijayasimah Deva	विजयसिंहदेव	Kalchuris, Dynasty, Tripuri	1180–1210	66.
Vijayditya-1	विजयादित्य-1	Kadamb Dynasty, Goa	1080–1110	64.
Vijayditya-2	विजयादित्य-2	Kadamb Dynasty, Goa	1174–1187	64.
Vijaypal	विजयपाल	Tomar Dynasty, Delhi	1130–1151	173.
Vijaypal	विजयपाल	Pratihar-Gurjar Dynasty	960–1018	126.
Vijayraj	राव विजयराज	Jadeja Dynasty	1942–1947	60.
Vijaysen	विजयसेन	Kshatrap Dynasty	240–250	71.
Vijaysimha	विजयसिंह	Guhil Dynasty, Mewad	1108–1127	47.
Vikram Manikya	विक्रम माणिक्य	Manikya Dynasty, Tripura	1923–1947	79.
Vikram Rajsimha	विक्रम	Kendy Nayak Dynasty	1798–1815	101.
Vikram	विक्रम प्रजाशेखरन	Arya Chakravarti Dynasty, Shri Lanka	1292–1302	155.

Name	Devanagari	Dynasty	Years	Page
Vikram	विक्रम	Tomar Dynasty, Gwalior	1516–1523	174
Vikrama Parakesari	विक्रम पराकेसरी वर्मा	Chola Dynasty	1118–1133	36
Vikramaditya	विक्रमादित्य	Chalukya Dynasty, Vengi	926–934	22
Vikramaditya	विक्रमादित्य	Gonaditya Dynasty, Kashmir	261–297	44
Vikramaditya	विक्रमादित्य	Waghela Dynasty, Riwa	1618–1630	180
Vikramaditya-1	विक्रमादित्य-1	Chalukya Dynasty, Badami	642–680	18
Vikramaditya-2	विक्रमादित्य-2	Chalukya Dynasty, Badami	733–746	18
Vikramaditya-3	विक्रमादित्य-3	Chalukya Dynasty, Kalyani		19
Vikramaditya-4	विक्रमादित्य-4	Chalukya Dynasty, Kalyani		19
Vikramaditya-5	विक्रमादित्य-5 जगदेकमल्ल	Chalukya Dynasty, Kalyani	1009–1014	19
Vikramaditya-6	विक्रमादित्य-6 त्रिभुवनमल्ल	Chalukya Dynasty, Kalyani	1076–1127	19
Vikramavardhan	विक्रमवर्धन	Simha Shri Dynasty, Java	1389–1429	58
Vikramendra Varma-1	विक्रमेंद्रवर्मा-1	Chalukya Dynasty, Vengi	460–480	22
Vikramendra Varma-2	विक्रमेंद्रवर्मा-2	Chalukya Dynasty, Vengi	515–535	22
Vikramjit Simha	बिक्रमजीतसिंह	Sisodiya Dynasty	1531–1536	159
Vikramjit Singh	विक्रमजीत सिंह	Avanti Bai, Dynasty	1851–1857	5
Vikramsimha	विक्रमसिंह	Guhil Dynasty, Mewad	1148–1158	47
Vilastung	विलासतुंग	Nal Dynasty	630–642	84
Vilom	विलोम	Kukkur Dynasty	Ancient	72
Vimaladitya	विमलादित्य	Chalukya Dynasty, Vengi	1010–1022	22
Vinayaditya	विनयादित्य	Chalukya Dynasty, Badami	680–696	18
Vinayaditya	विनयादित्य	Ganga Dynasty, Kalinga	977–980	41
Vinayaditya	विनयादित्य	Hoysal Dynasty	1047–1063	55
Vindhya Shakti	विंध्यशक्ति	Vakatak Dynasty	250–270	181
Vindhya Varma	विंध्यवर्मा	Parmar Dynasty	1143–1178	120
Vira Ballal-1	वीर बल्लाळ-1	Hoysal Dynasty	1100–1110	55
Vira Ballal-2	वीर बल्लाळ-2	Hoysal Dynasty	1173–1220	55
Vira Ballal-3	वीर बल्लाळ-3	Hoysal Dynasty	1291–1342	55
Vira Ballal-4	वीर बल्लाळ-4 (वीरुपक्ष)	Hoysal Dynasty	1342–1348	55
Vira Chandra Manikya	वीरचंद्र माणिक्य	Manikya Dynasty, Tripura	1862–1896	79
Vira Dhaval	वीरधवल	Waghela Dynasty, Gujrat		179
Vira Keral Varma-1	वीर केरळ वर्मा-1	Varma Dynasty, Venad	1125–1145	182
Vira Keralvarma	वीर केरलवर्मा	Cher Dynasty	1021–1028	34
Vira Narasimha	वीर नरसिंह	Tuluv Nayak Dynasty	1505–1509	89
Vira Narayan	वीर नारायण	Gond Dynasty, Mandla		45
Vira Rajendra-1	वीरराजेन्द्र-1	Haleri Nayak Dynasty	1780–1809	103
Vira Rajendra-2	वीरराजेंद्र-2	Haleri Nayak Dynasty	1820–1834	103

Name	Devanagari	Dynasty	Years	Page
Vira Vaman	वीर वामन	Lain Zang Dynasty, Laos	1596–1622	172.
Vira Varma	वीर वर्मा	Lain Zang Dynasty, Laos	1575–1580	172.
Vira Varma	वीरवर्मा	Pallav Dynasty	385–400	116.
Vira Varma-1	वीरवर्मा-1	Chandela Dynasty	1245–1286	23.
Vira Varma-2	वीरवर्मा-2	Chandela Dynasty	1315...	23.
Vira Vikramaditya-1	वीर विक्रमादित्य-1	Gutta Dynasty		50.
Vira Vikramaditya-2	वीर विक्रमादित्य-2	Gutta Dynasty	1187–1238	50.
Vira Vikramaditya-3	वीर विक्रमादित्य-3	Gutta Dynasty		50.
Virabhadra Reddi	वीर	Kondavidu Reddi Dynasty	1423–1448	102.
Virabharda-1	वीरभद्र-1	Keladi Nayak Dynasty	1629–1645	94.
Viram Simha	विरम सिंह	Rathor Dynasty, Jodhpur	1374–1394	135.
Viramdev	विरमदेव	Tomar Dynasty, Gwalior	1402–1423	174.
Viramma	रानी वीरम्मा	Keladi Nayak Dynasty	1757–1763	94.
Virappa Nayak	वीरप्पा नायक	Madura Nayak Dynasty	1659–1670	95.
Viraraja	वीरराजा	Haleri Nayak Dynasty		103.
Virarajendra	वीरराजेंद्र राजकेसरी वर्मा	Chola Dynasty	1062–1067	36.
Virasimha	वीरसिंह	Ganga Dynasty, Kalinga		41.
Virendra Manikya	वीरेन्द्र माणिक्य	Manikya Dynasty, Tripura	1909–1923	79.
Viroday	वीरोदय प्रजाशेखरन	Arya Chakravarti Dynasty, Shri Lanka	1371–1380	155.
Virpal	वीरपाल	Sutiya Dynasty, Assam	1187–1210	164.
Virsimha	वीरसिंह	Chauhan Dynasty, Sakambhari	1070–1070	26.
Virsingh	वीरसिंह	Tomar Dynasty, Gwalior	1375–1400	174.
Virupaksha	विरूपाक्ष	Nal Dynasty	630–630	84.
Virupaksha	विरूपक्ष-2	Sangam Nayak Dynasty	1465–1485	87.
Virvijay-1	वीरविजय-1	Sangam Nayak Dynasty	1413–1422	87.
Viryaram	वीर्यराम	Chauhan Dynasty, Sakambhari	1040–1040	26.
Vishal Deva	विशालदेव	Bhati Raval Dynasty	1311–1316	8.
Vishal	विशाल	Tomar Dynasty, Delhi	754–773	173.
Vishnu Vardhan-1	विष्णुवर्धन-1, कुब्ज	Chalukya Dynasty, Vengi	615–632	22.
Vishnu Vardhan-2	विष्णुवर्धन-2	Chalukya Dynasty, Vengi	663–672	22.
Vishnu Vardhan-3	विष्णुवर्धन-3	Chalukya Dynasty, Vengi	709–746	22.
Vishnu Vardhan-4	विष्णुवर्धन-4	Chalukya Dynasty, Vengi	764–799	22.
Vishnu Vardhan-5	विष्णुवर्धन-5, काली	Chalukya Dynasty, Vengi	843–844	22.
Vishnuvardhan	विष्णुवर्धन त्रिभुवनमल्ल	Hoysal Dynasty	1110–1152	55.
Vishnuvardhan	विष्णुवर्धन	Simha Shri Dynasty, Java	1248–1268	58.
Vishnugupta	विष्णुगुप्त	Gupta Dynasty, Patliputra	700	48.
Vishnusingh	विष्णु सिंह	Chauhan Dynasty, Bundi	(1771–1821)	32.

Name	Devanagari	Dynasty	Dates	Page
Vishrava	विश्रवा	Pulastya Dynasty	Ancient	128.
Vishva Nath Simha	विश्वनाथसिंह	Waghela Dynasty, Riwa	1835–1854	180.
Vishvanath Ayyar	अय्यर	Madura Nayak Dynasty	1535–1544	95.
Vishvanath Nayak	विश्वनाथ	Madura Nayak Dynasty	1558–1563	95.
Vishvarup Sen	विश्वरूपसेन	Sen Dynasty, Bengal	1205–1220	143.
Vishvasaha	विश्वसह	Raghu Dynasty	Ancient	131.
Vishvasen	विश्वसिंह	Kshatrap Dynasty	279–282	71.
Visnho Gopa	विष्णुगोप	Pallav Dynasty	350–355	116.
Vitabhay	वीतभय	Puru Dynasty	Ancient	129.
Vivasvan Manu	विवस्वान	Vivasvan Dynasty	Ancient	187.
Vriddhakshetra	वृद्धक्षेत्र	Sindhu Dynasty	Ancient	158.
Vriksha	वृश्व	Brihadrith Dynasty, Magadh	Ancient	15.
Vrishadarbha	वृषदर्भ	Sindhu Dynasty	Ancient	158.
Vrishni	वृष्णि	Vrishni Dynasty	Ancient	188.
Vrishni	वृष्णि	Yadu Dynasty	Ancient	191.
Vrupaksh-1	विरूपक्ष-1	Sangam Nayak Dynasty	1404–1405	87.
Vuppa Deva	वुप्पदेव	Lohar Dynasty, Kashmir	1172	75.
Vuppa Deva	वुप्पदेव	Vuppadeva Dynasty, Kashmir	1172–1181	189.
Vyaghra Deva	व्याघ्रदेव	Uchchhakalpa Dynasty		176.
Vyaghra Deva	व्याघ्रदेव	Waghela Dynasty, Gujrat		179.
Vyaghra Sen	व्याघ्रसेन	Traikutak Dynasty	475–492	175.
Vyankat Raman	व्यंकटरमण	Waghela Dynasty, Riwa	1880–1918	180.
Yadu	यदु	Yayati Dynasty	Ancient	192.
Yadu Dev Ray	यदु देवराय	Wadiyar Dynasty	1399–1423	178.
Yadu	यदु	Yadu Dynasty	Ancient	191.
Yadunathshah	यदुनाथशाह	Nag Dynasty	1706–1724	83.
Yajna Shri Satkarni	यज्ञ श्री	Satvahan Dynasty	163–178 AD	141.
Yajnabhag	यज्ञभंग	Nand Dynasty		85.
Yajnanarayan Simha	यज्ञनारायण	Rathor Dynasty, Kishangadh	1926–1929	137.
Yarraya Vetaraj	यर्रया वेतराज	Kakatiya Dynasty	1000–1030	64.
Yash Narayan	यश नारायण	Sutiya Dynasty, Assam	1465–1480	164.
Yasha Varma	यशवर्मा	Chandela Dynasty	948–954	23.
Yashakarna Deva	यशकर्णदेव	Kalchuris, Dynasty, Tripuri	1120–1151	66.
Yashaskar Deva	यशस्करदेव	Utpal Dynasty, Kashmir	939–948	177.
Yasho Varma	यशोवर्मा	Maukhari Dynasty	725	80.
Yasho Varma-1	यशोवर्मा-1	Varma Dynasty, Cambodia	889–900	171.
Yasho Varma-2	यशोवर्मा-2	Varma Dynasty, Cambodia	1160–1166	171.

Name		Dynasty	Years	Page
Yashodaman	यशोदामन	Kshatrap Dynasty	239–240	71.
Yashodhar Manikya	यशोधर माणिक्य	Manikya Dynasty, Tripura	1600–1618	79.
Yashovarma	यशोवर्मा	Parmar Dynasty	1134–1135	120.
Yashpal	यशपाल	Tomar Dynasty, Delhi	1005–1021	173.
Yashpal	यशपाल	Pratihar-Gurjar Dynasty	1030–1036	126.
Yashvant Simha	यशवंत सिंह	Bhati Raval Dynasty	1702–1708	8.
Yashvantrao-1	यशवंतराव-1	Holkar Dynasty	1798–1807	54.
Yashvantrao-2	यशवंतराव-2	Holkar Dynasty	1926–1948	54.
yasimha	यसिंह	Chudasama Dynasty	1180–1184	37.
Yayati	ययाति	Atri Dynasty	Ancient	1.
Yogaraj	योगराज	Chapotkat Dynasty	806–841	25.
Yogendra Rai	योगेंद्रराय	Nag Dynasty	997–1004	83.
Yogeshvar Simha	योगेश्वर सिंह	Ahom Dynasty	1821–1826	2.
Yogivarma	योगीवर्मा	Guhil Dynasty, Mewad	1051–1068	47.
Yojaldev	योजलदेव	Chaunah Dynasty, Nadol	1091–1110	27.
Yudhishthir	युधिष्ठिर	Pandava Dynasty		117.
Yudhishthir-1	युधिष्ठिर-1	Gonaditya Dynasty, Kashmir	246–212 BC	44.
Yudhishthir-2	युधिष्ठिर-2	Gonaditya Dynasty, Kashmir	185–206	44.
Yugen Wangchuk	युगेन वांगचुक	Wangchuk Dynasty, Bhutan	1907–1926	13.
Yuvanashva	युवनाश्व	Ikshavaku Dynasty	Ancient	56.
Yuvaraj Deva-1	युवराजदेव-1	Kalchuris, Dynasty, Tripuri	925–950	66.
Yuvaraj Deva-2	युवराजदेव-2	Kalchuris, Dynasty, Tripuri	974–1000	66.
Zoravar Simha	जोरावर सिंह	Rathor Dynasty, Bikaner	1736–1746	136.

www.ingramcontent.com/pod-product-compliance
Lightning Source LLC
Chambersburg PA
CBHW081343070526
44578CB00005B/704